Public Health
What It Is and How It Works
Fifth Edition

Bernard J. Turnock, MD, MPH
Clinical Professor and Director
Division of Community Health Sciences
School of Public Health
University of Illinois at Chicago
Chicago, Illinois

JONES & BARTLETT
LEARNING

World Headquarters
Jones & Bartlett Learning
5 Wall Street
Burlington, MA 01803
978-443-5000
info@jblearning.com
www.jblearning.com

Jones & Bartlett Learning
Canada
6339 Ormindale Way
Mississauga, Ontario L5V 1J2
Canada

Jones & Bartlett Learning
International
Barb House, Barb Mews
London W6 7PA
United Kingdom

Jones & Bartlett Learning books and products are available through most bookstores and online booksellers. To contact Jones & Bartlett Learning directly, call 800-832-0034, fax 978-443-8000, or visit our website www.jblearning.com.

Substantial discounts on bulk quantities of Jones & Bartlett Learning publications are available to corporations, professional associations, and other qualified organizations. For details and specific discount information, contact the special sales department at Jones & Bartlett Learning via the above contact information or send an e-mail to specialsales@jblearning.com.

This publication is designed to provide accurate and authoritative information in regard to the Subject Matter covered. It is sold with the understanding that the publisher is not engaged in rendering legal, accounting, or other professional service. If legal advice or other expert assistance is required, the service of a competent professional person should be sought.

Production Credits
Publisher: Michael Brown
Associate Editor: Maro Gartside
Editorial Assistant: Teresa Reilly
Senior Marketing Manager: Sophie Fleck
Production Director: Amy Rose
Production Manager: Tracey McCrea
Senior Production Editor: Renée Sekerak
Production Assistant: Sean Coombs
Manufacturing and Inventory Control Supervisor: Amy Bacus
Cover Design: Kate Ternullo
Cover Image: © Christian Lagerek/ShutterStock, Inc.
Composition: Cape Cod Compositors, Inc.
Printing and Binding: Malloy, Inc.
Cover Printing: Malloy, Inc.

Library of Congress Cataloging-in-Publication Data
Turnock, Bernard J.
    Public health : what it is and how it works / Bernard J. Turnock. — 5th ed.
        p. ; cm.
    Includes bibliographical references and index.
    ISBN-13: 978-1-4496-0024-2 (pbk. : alk. paper)
    ISBN-10: 1-4496-0024-7 (pbk. : alk. paper)
    1. Public health—United States.   2. Public health administration—United States.   I. Title.
    [DNLM: 1. Public Health Administration—United States.   2. Public Health Practice—United States.
WA 540 AA1]
    RA445.T86 2012
    362.10973—dc22

                                                                            2011006264

6048
Printed in the United States of America
15 14 13 12 11   10 9 8 7 6 5 4 3 2

Dedication

To Colleen

Contents

Preface

The early decades of a new century provide a unique opportunity to reflect on where we have been and what we have accomplished as a nation and as a society. For public health, it is truly an opportunity to examine what we might call, for lack of a better phrase, a century of progress. What a spectacular century it has been!

My grandparents were children at the turn of the previous century. At that time, they lived in a young and rapidly developing nation whose 75 million people held not unreasonable hopes of a long and healthy life. They also faced an alarmingly large number of health hazards and risks that, when taken together, offered them the prospect of an average life expectancy of only approximately 47 years. Smallpox, tuberculosis, pneumonia, diphtheria, and a variety of diarrheal diseases were frequent, although unwelcome, visitors. It was not uncommon for families to bury several of their children before they reached adulthood.

By the time my parents were children in the 1920s and 1930s, a variety of economic, social, and scientific advances offered more than one additional decade of average life expectancy, despite even the massive social and economic disruption of the Great Depression. Still, tuberculosis, scarlet fever, whooping cough, measles, and other diseases were common. Fewer childhood deaths occurred, but many families still experienced one or more deaths among their children.

Members of the post World War II Baby Boom Generation, like me and my four siblings, enjoyed the prospect of living to and even beyond the age of 65 years and the so-called Golden Years. When I was a child, polio was one of the few remaining childhood infectious disease threats. Some of my most vivid childhood memories are of the mass immunization programs that took place in my hometown. Childhood deaths were an uncommon experience and more likely the result of causes other than infectious diseases.

As the 21st century unfolds, more than 310 million Americans, my children and yours, now look forward to an average life expectancy of about 80 years. Today there are no fewer than two dozen different conditions for which immunizations are available—more than a dozen of which are recommended for use in all children—to prevent virtually all of the conditions that threatened their parents, grandparents, and great-grandparents during the 20th century. Today, our children are even being immunized against cervical and liver cancer! Overall, childhood deaths have declined more than 95% from their levels a century earlier. That means that 19 of the 20 deaths that used to occur to children in this country no longer take place!

To many of us, a century seems like a long time. In the grand scheme of things, however, it is not, and it seems even shorter when we consider how lifetimes and generations are so interconnected. Just look at the connections linking each of us with our grandparents and our children and even our children's children, each of whom held, hold, or will hold quite different expectations for their lives and health. These links and connections play critical roles when it comes to understanding the value and the benefits of the work of public health. At the turn of the next century, an estimated 570 million Americans will be enjoying the fruits of public health's labors over the preceding centuries. The vast majority of the people who will benefit from what public health does are yet to be born!

As someone who has spent 15 years in public health practice and another 20 years in teaching and researching the field, I have been concerned about why those who work in the field and those who benefit from its work do not better understand something so important and useful. Throughout my career as a public health professional, I have developed a profound respect for the field, the work, and the workers. I must admit, however, that even while serving as director of a large state health department, I lacked a full understanding and appreciation of this unique enterprise.

What has become clear to me is that the story of public health is not simple to tell. There is no one official at the helm, guiding it through the turbulence that is constantly encountered. There is no clear view of its intended destination and of what work needs to be done, and by whom, to get there. We cannot turn to our family physicians, elected officials, or even to distinguished public health officials, such as our Surgeon General, for vision and direction. Surely, these people play important roles, but public health is so broadly involved with the biologic, environmental, social, cultural, behavioral, and service utilization factors associated with health that no one is accountable for addressing everything. Still, we all share in the successes and failures of our collective decisions and actions, making us all accountable to each other for the results of these efforts. My hope is that this book presents a broad view of the public health system and deters current and future public health workers from narrowly defining public health in terms of only what they do. At its core, the purpose of this book is to describe public health simply and clearly in terms of what it is, what it does, how it works, and why it is important to all of us.

Although there is no dearth of fine books in this field, there is most certainly a shortage of understanding, appreciation, and support for public health and its various manifestations. Many of the current texts on public health attempt to be comprehensive in covering the field without the benefit of a conceptual framework understandable to insiders and outsiders alike. The dynamism and complexity of the field suggest that public health texts are likely to become even larger and more comprehensive as the field advances.

In contrast, this book aims to present the essentials of public health, with an emphasis on comprehensibility, rather than comprehensiveness. It presents fundamental concepts but links those concepts to practice in the real world.

These are essential topics for public health students early in their academic careers, and they are increasingly important for students in the social and political sciences and other health professions as well. This book is intended as much for public health practitioners as it is for students. It represents the belief that public health cannot be adequately taught through a text and that it is best learned through exploration and practice of its concepts and methods. In that light, this book should be viewed as a framework for learning and understanding public health rather than the definitive catalog of its principles and practices. Its real value will be its ability to encourage thinking "outside the book."

The first four chapters cover topics of interest to general audiences. Basic concepts underlying public health are presented in Chapter 1, including definitions, historical highlights, and unique features of public health. This and subsequent chapters focus largely on public health in the United States, although information on global public health and comparisons among nations appear in Chapters 2 and 3. Health and illness and the various factors that influence health and quality of life are presented from an ecological perspective in Chapter 2. This chapter also presents data and information on health status and risk factors in the United States and introduces a method for analyzing health problems to identify their precursors. Chapter 3 addresses the overall health system and its intervention strategies, with a special emphasis on trends and developments that are important to public health. It highlights interfaces between public health and a rapidly changing health system. Chapter 4 examines the organization of public health responsibilities in the United States by reviewing its legal basis and the current structure of public health agencies at the federal, state, and local levels. Together, these first four chapters serve as a primer on what public health is and how it relates to health interests in modern America.

The final five chapters flesh out the skeleton of public health introduced in the first half of the book. They examine how public health does what it does, addressing issues of the inner workings of public health that are critical for the more serious students of the field. Chapter 5 reviews the core functions and essential services of public health and both how and how well these are currently being addressed. This chapter identifies key processes or practices that operationalize public health's core functions and tools that have been developed to improve public health practice. Chapter 6 builds on the governmental structure of American public health (from Chapter 4) and examines the basic building blocks of the public health system, including human, informational, and fiscal resources. Outputs of the public health system and intervention strategies in the form of programs and services are the subjects of Chapter 7. Evidence-based public health practice is examined in terms of its population-based community prevention services and clinical preventive services, and an approach to program planning and evaluation for public health interventions is presented. Chapter 8 describes the emergency preparedness and response roles of public health, including the opportunities afforded by increased public health expectations and a substantial influx of federal funding. The final chapter looks to the future of public health in the second decade of a new century and beyond, building on the lessons learned from the preceding century. Emerging problems, opportunities afforded by the expansion of collaborations and partnerships, and obstacles impeding public health responses are also examined in the concluding chapter.

Each chapter uses a variety of figures and tables to illustrate the concepts and provide useful resources for public health practitioners. A glossary of public health terminology is provided for the benefit of those unfamiliar with some of the commonly used terms, as well as to convey the intended meaning for terms that may have several different connotations in practice. Eight of the chapters include Public Health Spotlights that provide a focused examination, case study, or problem-solving exercise for issues or topics germane to that chapter. At the end of each chapter are discussion questions and exercises, many of which involve Internet-based resources that complement the topics presented and provide a framework for thought and discussion. These allow the text to be used more flexibly in public health courses at various levels, using different formats for learners at different levels of their training and careers.

Together, the book's content offers a systems approach to public health, grounded in a conceptual model that characterizes public health by its mission, functions, capacity, processes, and outcomes. This model is the unifying construct for this text. It provides a framework for examining and questioning the wisdom of our current investment strategy that directs 100 times more resources toward medical services than it spends for population-based prevention strategies—even though treatment strategies contributed only 5 of the 30 years of increased life expectancy at birth that have been achieved in the United States since 1900.

Many of the core competencies established by the Association of Schools of Public Health for graduates of master's in public health degree programs are addressed in this book, especially those in the professionalism, leadership, systems thinking, health policy and management, and program planning categories. A partial list of those competencies includes proficiency in the following:

1. Embracing a definition of public health that captures the unique characteristics of the field (e.g., population-focused, community-oriented, prevention-motivated, and rooted in social justice) and how these contribute to professional practice
2. Articulating an achievable mission, set of core values and vision for public health
3. Discussing sentinel events in the history and development of the public health profession and their relevance for practice in the field
4. Applying basic principles of ethical analysis (e.g., Public Health Code of Ethics, human rights framework, other oral theories) to issues of public health practice and policy
5. Promoting high standards of personal and organizational integrity, compassion, honesty, and respect for all people

6. Describing how social, behavioral, environmental, and biologic factors contribute to specific individual and community health outcomes

7. Analyzing determinants of health and disease using an ecological framework

8. Prioritizing individual, organizational, and community concerns and resources for public health programs in collaboration with others

9. Distinguishing between population and individual ethical consideration in relationship to the benefits, costs, and burdens of public health programs

10. Appreciating the importance of a working collaborative with diverse communities and constituencies (e.g., practitioners, agencies, organizations, and researchers)

11. Identifying the main components and issues of the organization, financing, and delivery of health services and public health systems in the United States

12. Describing the legal and ethical basis for public health and health services

13. Analyzing the potential impacts of legal and regulatory environments on the conduct of ethical public health practice

14. Applying the core functions of assessment, policy development, and assurance in the analysis of public health problems and their solutions

15. Analyzing the effects of political, social, and economic policies on public health systems at the local, state, national, and international levels

16. Describing the attributes of leadership in public health

17. Describing alternative strategies for collaboration and partnership among organizations, focused on public health goals

18. Using collaborative methods for achieving organizational and community health goals

19. Identifying key characteristics of public health systems

20. Identifying unintended consequences produced by changes made to a public health system

21. Illustrating how changes in public health systems (including input, processes, and outputs) can be measured

22. Applying evidence-based principles and the scientific knowledge base to critical evaluation and decision making in public health

23. Applying principles of program planning, development, budgeting, management, and evaluation in organizational and community initiatives

24. Describing the tasks necessary to ensure that program implementation occurs as intended

25. Preparing a program budget with justification

26. Explaining the contribution of logic models in program development, implementation, and evaluation

27. Differentiating among goals, measurable objectives, related activities, and expected outcomes for a public health program

28. Differentiating the purposes of process and outcome evaluation
29. Explaining how the findings of a program evaluation can be used
30. Explaining methods of ensuring community health safety and preparedness

Whatever wisdom might be found in this book has filtered through to me from my mentors, colleagues, co-workers, students, and friends. For those about to toil in this vineyard of challenge and opportunity, this is meant to be a primer on public health in the United States. It is a book that seeks to reduce the vast scope, endless complexities, and ever-expanding agenda to a format simple enough to be understood by first-year students and state health commissioners alike.

Internet-based resources for courses based on this text are available at http://go.jblearning.com/phturnock5e.

Acknowledgments

Many people have shaped the concepts and insights provided in this text. This book evolved from an introductory course on public health concepts and practice that I have been teaching at the University of Illinois at Chicago School of Public Health since 1991. During that time, more than 4,000 current and aspiring public health professionals have influenced the material included in this book. Their enthusiasm and expectations have challenged me to find ways to make this subject interesting and valuable to learners at all levels of their careers.

Many parts of this book rely heavily on the work of public health practitioners and public health practice organizations. Over the years, I have had the opportunity to work with public health practice leaders at the Centers for Disease Control and Prevention, several of whom deserve special acknowledgment for their encouragement and contributions, especially Ed Baker, Paul Halverson, and Bill Dyal. Other valuable contributions came from public health colleagues, including John Lumpkin, Chris Atchison, Laura Landrum, Judith Munson, and Patrick Lenihan. Arden Handler has long been my colleague and collaborator on many public health capacity-building projects. In several chapters, I have drawn on the work of two public health agencies at which I have worked during my career, the Illinois Department of Public Health and the Chicago Department of Public Health. The influence of some outstanding public health figures who have served as mentors and role models—Jean Pakter, Paul Peterson, Quentin Young, George Pickett, and C. Arden Miller—is also apparent in this book.

Lloyd Novick provided early encouragement and support for this undertaking, as well as useful suggestions on the scope and focus of this text. Mike Brown at Jones & Bartlett Learning has consistently provided valuable suggestions and guidance. I am grateful for the many and varied contributions from all of these sources.

About the Author

Bernard J. (Barney) Turnock, MD, MPH, is currently Clinical Professor and Director of the Division of Community Health Sciences and Director of the Center for Public Health Practice and Illinois Public Health Preparedness Center at the School of Public Health, University of Illinois at Chicago (UIC). Since he joined UIC School of Public Health in 1990, he has also served as Acting Dean and Associate Dean for Public Health Practice. His major areas of interest involve performance measurement, capacity building, and workforce development within the public health system. He is board certified in Preventive Medicine and Public Health and has extensive practice experience, having served as Director of the Illinois Department of Public Health from 1985 through 1990, Deputy Commissioner and Acting Commissioner of the Chicago Department of Health, and state program director for Maternal and Child Health and Emergency Medical Services during his distinguished career. He has played major roles in a wide variety of public policy and public health issues in Illinois since 1978. He frequently consults on a variety of public health and healthcare issues and has served as a member of the Illinois State Board of Health and as President of the Illinois Public Health Association. He is also the author of two other recently published works: *Public Health: Career Choices That Make a Difference* and *Essentials of Public Health, Second Edition*. He has received two prestigious awards from the American Public Health Association: one for Excellence in Health Planning and Practice and another for Excellence in Health Administration. He is also a recipient of the UIC School of Public Health's "Golden Apple" award for excellence in teaching, and he was the developer and instructor for UIC's first completely online course: Public Health Concepts and Practice (CHSC 400).

Chapter 1

What Is Public Health?

OBJECTIVES

After completing Chapter 1, learners will be proficient in describing what public health is, including its unique and important features, to general audiences. Key aspects of this competency expectation include the following:

- Articulating several different definitions of public health
- Describing the origins and content of public health responses over history
- Tracing the development of the public health system in the United States
- Broadly characterizing the contributions and value of public health
- Identifying three or more distinguishing features of public health
- Describing public health as a system with inputs, processes, outputs, and results, including the role of core functions and essential public health services
- Identifying five or more Internet websites that provide useful information on the U.S. public health system

The passing of one century and the early decades of another afford a rare opportunity to look back at where public health has been and forward to the challenges that lie ahead. Imagine a world 100 years from now where life expectancy is 30 years longer and infant mortality rates are 95% lower than they are today. The average human life span would be more than 107 years, and less than 1 of every 2,000 infants would die before their first birthday. These seem like unrealistic expectations and unlikely achievements; nevertheless, they are no greater than the gains realized during the 20th century in the United States. In 1900, few envisioned the century of progress in public health that lay ahead; yet by 1925, public health leaders such as C.E.A. Winslow were noting a nearly 50% increase in life expectancy (from 36 years to 53 years) for residents of New York City between the years 1880 and 1920.[1] Accomplishments such as these caused Winslow to speculate what might be possible through widespread application of scientific knowledge. With the even more spectacular achievements over the rest of the 20th century, we all should wonder what is possible in the century that has just begun.

This year will be remembered for many things, but it is unlikely that many people will remember it as a spectacular year for public health in the United States. No major discoveries, innovations, or triumphs are likely to set the year apart from other years in recent memory. Nevertheless, on closer examination, maybe there are! Like the story of the wise man who invented the game of chess for his king and asked for payment by having the king place one grain of wheat on the first square of the chessboard, two on the second, four on the third, eight on the fourth, and so on, the small victories of public health over the past century have resulted in cumulative gains so vast in scope that they are difficult to comprehend.

This year there will be nearly 900,000 fewer cases of measles reported than in 1941, 200,000 fewer cases of diphtheria than in 1921, more than 250,000 fewer cases of whooping cough than in 1934, and 21,000 fewer cases of polio than in 1951.[2] The early years of the new century are witnessing 50 million fewer smokers than would have been expected, given trends in tobacco use through 1965. More than 2 million Americans are alive today who otherwise would have died from heart disease and stroke, and nearly 100,000 Americans are alive as a result of automobile seatbelt use. Protection of the U.S. blood supply has prevented more than 1.5 million hepatitis B and hepatitis C infections and more than 50,000 human immunodeficiency virus (HIV) infections, as well as more than $5 billion in medical costs associated with these three diseases.[3] Today, the average blood lead levels in children are less than one third of what they were a quarter century ago. This catalog of accomplishments could be expanded many times over. Figure 1-1 summarizes this progress, including two of the most widely followed measures of a population's health status: life expectancy and infant mortality.

These results did not occur by themselves. They came about through decisions and actions that represent the essence of what is public health. It is the story of public health and its immense value and importance in our lives that is the focus of this text. With this impressive litany of accomplishments, it would seem that public health's story would be easily told. For many reasons, however, it is not. As a result, public health remains poorly understood by its prime beneficiary—the public—as well as many of its dedicated practitioners. Although public health's results, as measured in terms of improved health status, diseases prevented, scarce resources saved, and improved quality of life, are more apparent today than ever before, society seldom links the activities of public health with its results. This suggests that the public health community must more effectively communicate what public health is and what it does so that its results can be readily traced to their source.

This chapter is an introduction to public health that links basic concepts to practice. It considers three questions:

- What is public health?
- Where did it come from?
- Why is it important in the United States today?

To address these questions, this chapter begins with a sketch of the historical development of public health activities in the United States. It then exam-

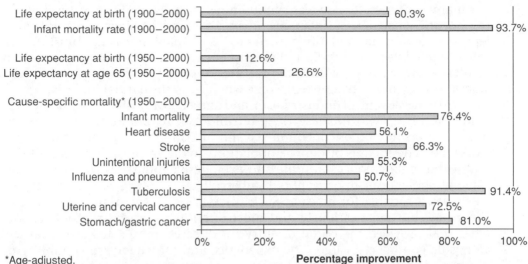

*Age-adjusted.

Figure 1-1 Percentage improvement in selected measures of life expectancy and age-adjusted, cause-specific mortality for the time periods 1900–2000 and 1950–2000, United States. *Source:* Data from Centers for Disease Control and Prevention, National Center for Health Statistics. *Health, United States 2009.* Hyattsville, MD: NCHS; 2009 and Rust G, Satcher D, Fryer GE, Levine RS, Blumenthal DS. Triangulating on success: innovation, public health, medical care, and cause-specific U.S. mortality over a half century (1950–2000). *Am J Public Health.* 2010; 100:S95–S104.

ines several definitions and characterizations of what public health is and explores some of its unique features. Finally, it offers insights into the value of public health in biologic, economic, and human terms.

Taken together, the topics in this chapter provide a foundation for understanding what public health is and why it is important. A conceptual framework that approaches public health from a systems perspective is introduced to identify the dimensions of the public health system and facilitate an understanding of the various images of public health that coexist in the United States today. We see that, as in the story of the blind men examining the elephant, with each blind person describing the animal in terms of the part that they encountered, various sectors of our society have mistaken separate components of public health for the entire system. Later chapters more thoroughly examine and discuss the various components and dimensions of the public health system.

A BRIEF HISTORY OF PUBLIC HEALTH IN THE UNITED STATES

Early Influences on American Public Health

Although the complete history of public health is a fascinating saga in its own right, this section presents only selected highlights. When ancient cultures perceived illness as the manifestation of supernatural forces, they also felt that little in the way of either personal or collective action was possible.

For many centuries, disease was synonymous with epidemic. Diseases, including horrific epidemics of infectious diseases such as the Black Death (plague), leprosy, and cholera, were phenomena to be accepted. It was not until the so-called Age of Reason and the Enlightenment that scholarly inquiry began to challenge the "givens" or accepted realities of society. Eventually, the expansion of the science and knowledge base would reap substantial rewards.

With the advent of industrialism and imperialism, the stage was set for epidemic diseases to increase their terrible toll. As populations shifted to urban centers for purpose of commerce and industry, public health conditions worsened. The mixing of dense populations living in unsanitary conditions and working long hours in unsafe and exploitative industries with wave after wave of cholera, smallpox, typhoid, tuberculosis, yellow fever, and other diseases was a formula for disaster. Such disaster struck again and again across the globe, but most seriously and most often at the industrialized seaport cities that provided the portal of entry for diseases transported as stowaways alongside commercial cargo. The experience and subsequent susceptibility of different cultures to these diseases partly explain how relatively small bands of Europeans were able to overcome and subjugate vast Native American cultures. Seeing the Europeans unaffected by scourges such as smallpox served to reinforce beliefs that these light-skinned visitors were supernatural figures, unaffected by natural forces.[4]

The British colonies in North America and the fledgling United States certainly bore their share of the burden. American diaries of the 17th and 18th centuries chronicle one infectious disease onslaught after another. These epidemics left their mark on families, communities, and even history. For example, the national capital had to be moved out of Philadelphia because of a devastating yellow fever epidemic in 1793. This epidemic also prompted the city to develop its first board of health in that same year.

The formation of local boards of distinguished citizens, the first boards of health, was one of the earliest organized responses to epidemics. This response was revealing in that it represented an attempt to confront disease collectively. Because science had not yet determined that specific microorganisms were the causes of epidemics, avoidance had long been the primary tactic used. Avoidance meant evacuating the general location of the epidemic until it subsided or isolating diseased individuals or those recently exposed to diseases on the basis of a mix of fear, tradition, and scientific speculation. Several developments, however, were swinging the pendulum ever closer to more effective counteractions.

The work of public health pioneers such as Edward Jenner, John Snow, and Edwin Chadwick illustrates the value of public health, even when its methods are applied amid scientific uncertainty. Long before Koch's postulates established scientific methods for linking bacteria with specific diseases and before Pasteur's experiments helped to establish the germ theory, both Jenner and Snow used deductive logic and common sense to do battle with smallpox and cholera, respectively. In 1796, Jenner successfully used vaccination for a disease that ran rampant through communities across the globe. This was the initial shot in a long and arduous campaign that by the year 1977 had totally eradicated smallpox from all of its human hiding places in every country in the world. The potential for its reemergence through the actions of terrorists is a topic left to Chapter 8.

Snow's accomplishments even further advanced the art and science of public health. In 1854, Snow traced an outbreak of cholera to the well water drawn from the pump at Broad Street and helped to prevent hundreds, perhaps thousands, of cholera cases. In that same year, he demonstrated that another large outbreak could be traced to one particular water company that drew its water from the Thames River, downstream from London, and that another company that drew its water upstream from London was not linked with cholera cases. In both efforts, Snow's ability to collect and analyze data allowed him to determine causation, which in turn allowed him to implement corrective actions that prevented additional cases. All of this occurred without the benefit of the knowledge that there was an odd-shaped little bacterium that was carried in water and spread from person to person by hand-to-mouth contact!

England's General Board of Health conducted its own investigations of these outbreaks and concluded that air, rather than contaminated water, was the cause.[5] Its approach, however, was one of collecting a vast amount of information and accepting only that which supported its view of disease causation. Snow, on the other hand, systematically tested his hypothesis by exploring evidence that ran in contrast to his initial expectations.

Chadwick was a more official leader of what has become known as the sanitary movement of the latter half of the 19th century. In a variety of official capacities, he played a major part in structuring government's role and responsibilities for protecting the public's health. Because of the growing concern over the social and sanitary conditions in England, the National Vaccination Board was established in 1837. Shortly thereafter, Chadwick's "Report on an Inquiry into the Sanitary Conditions of the Laboring Population of Great Britain" articulated a framework for broad public actions that served as a blueprint for the growing sanitary movement. One result was the establishment in 1848 of the General Board of Health. Interestingly, Chadwick's interest in public health had its roots in Jeremy Bentham's utilitarian movement. For Chadwick, disease was viewed as causing poverty, and poverty was responsible for the great social ills of the time, including societal disorder and high taxation to provide for the general welfare.[6] Public health efforts were necessary to reduce poverty and its wider social effects. This view recognizes a link between poverty and health that differs somewhat from current views. Today, it is more common to consider poor health as a result of poverty, rather than as its cause.

Chadwick was also a key participant in the partly scientific, partly political debate that took place in British government as to whether deaths should be attributed to clinical conditions or to their underlying factors, such as hunger and poverty. It was Chadwick's view that pathologic, as opposed to less proximal social and behavioral, factors should be the basis for classifying deaths.[6] Chadwick's arguments prevailed, although aspects of this debate continue to this day. William Farr, sometimes called the father of modern vital statistics, championed the opposing view.

In the latter half of the 19th century, as sanitation and environmental engineering methods evolved, more effective interventions became available against epidemic diseases. Furthermore, the scientific advances of this period paved the way for modern disease control efforts targeting specific microorganisms.

Growth of Local and State Public Health Activities in the United States

In the United States, Lemuel Shattuck's "Report of the Sanitary Commission of Massachusetts" in 1850 outlined existing and future public health needs for that state and became America's blueprint for development of a public health system. Shattuck called for the establishment of state and local health departments to organize public efforts aimed at sanitary inspections, communicable disease control, food sanitation, vital statistics, and services for infants and children. Although Shattuck's report closely paralleled Chadwick's efforts in Great Britain, acceptance of his recommendations did not occur for several decades. In the latter part of the century, his farsighted and far-reaching recommendations came to be widely implemented. With greater understanding of the value of environmental controls for water and sewage and of the role of specific control measures for specific diseases (including quarantine, isolation, and vaccination), the creation of local health agencies to carry out these activities supplemented—and, in some cases, supplanted—local boards of health. These local health departments developed rapidly in the seaports and other industrial urban centers, beginning with a health department in Baltimore in 1798, because these were the settings where the problems were reaching unacceptable levels. An illustration of such local public health efforts is presented at the end of this chapter in a Public Health Spotlight, which traces public health activities in Chicago from 1834 to 2003. The history summarized in this case study parallels that of other American cities through the 19th and 20th centuries.

Because infectious and environmental hazards are no respecters of local jurisdictional boundaries, states began to develop their own boards and agencies after 1870. These agencies often had very broad powers to protect the health and lives of state residents, although the clear intent at the time was that these powers be used to battle epidemics of infectious diseases. In later chapters, we revisit these powers and duties because they serve as both a stimulus and a limitation for what can be done to address many contemporary public health issues and problems.

Federal Public Health Activities in the United States

This sketch of the development of public health in the United States would be incomplete without a brief introduction to the roles and powers of the federal government. Federal health powers, at least as enumerated in the U.S. Constitution, are minimal. It is surprising to some to learn that the word health does not even appear in the Constitution. As a result of not being a power granted to the federal government (such as defense, foreign diplomacy, international and interstate commerce, or printing money), health became a power to be exercised by states or reserved to the people themselves.

Two sections of the Constitution have been interpreted over time to allow for federal roles in health, in concert with the concept of the so-called implied powers necessary to carry out explicit powers. These are the ability to tax in order to provide for the "general welfare" (a phrase appearing in both the preamble and body of the Constitution) and the specific power to regulate commerce, both international and interstate. These opportunities allowed the federal government to establish a beachhead in health, initially through the Marine Hospital Service (eventually to become the Public Health Service). After the ratification of the 16th Amendment in 1916, authorizing a national income tax, the federal government acquired the ability to raise vast sums of money, which could then be directed toward promoting the general welfare. The specific means to this end were a variety of grants in aid to state and local governments. Beginning in the 1960s, federal grant-in-aid programs designed to fill gaps in the medical care system nudged state and local governments further and further into the business of medical service provision. Federal grant programs for other social, substance abuse, mental health, and community prevention services soon followed. The expansion of federal involvement into these areas, however, was not accomplished by these means alone.

Before 1900, and perhaps not until the Great Depression, Americans did not believe that the federal government should intervene in their social circumstances. Social values shifted dramatically during the Depression, a period of such great social insecurity and need that the federal government was now permitted—indeed, expected—to intervene. Chapters 4, 5, and 8 expand on the growth of the federal government's influence on public health activities and its impact on the activities of state and local governments.

To explain more easily the broad trends of public health in the United States, it is useful to delineate distinct eras in its history. One simple scheme, illustrated in Table 1-1, uses the years 1850, 1950, and 2000 as approximate dividers. Prior to 1850, the system was characterized by recurrent epidemics of infectious diseases, with little in the way of collective response possible. During the sanitary movement in the second half of the 19th and first half of the 20th century, science-based control measures were organized and deployed through a public health infrastructure that was developing in the form of local and state health departments. After 1950, gaps in the medical care system and federal grant dollars acted together to increase public provision of a wide range of health services. That increase set the stage for the current reexamination of the links between medical and public health practice. Some retrenchment from the direct service provision role has occurred since about 1990. As we will examine in subsequent chapters, a new era for public health that seeks to balance community-driven public health practice with preparedness and response for public health emergencies lies ahead.

Table 1-1 Major Eras in Public Health History in the United States

Before 1850	Battling epidemics
1850–1949	Building state and local infrastructure
1950–1999	Filling gaps in medical care delivery
After 1999	Preparing for and responding to community health threats

IMAGES AND DEFINITIONS OF PUBLIC HEALTH

The historical development of public health activities in the United States provides a basis for understanding what public health is today. Nonetheless, the term public health evokes several different images among the general public and those dedicated to its improvement. To some, the term describes a broad social enterprise or system.

To others, the term describes the professionals and workforce whose job it is to solve certain important health problems. At a meeting in the early 1980s to plan a community-wide education and outreach campaign to encourage early prenatal care in order to reduce infant mortality, a community relations director of a large television station made some comments that reflected this view. When asked whether his station had been involved in infant mortality reduction efforts in the past, he responded, "Yes, but that's not our job. If you people in public health had been doing your job properly, we wouldn't be called on to bail you out!" Obviously, this man viewed public health as an effort of which he was not a part.

Still another image of public health is that of a body of knowledge and techniques that can be applied to health-related problems. Here, public health is seen as what public health does. Snow's investigations exemplify this perspective.

Similarly, many people perceive public health primarily as the activities ascribed to governmental public health agencies. For the majority of the public, this latter image represents public health in the United States, resulting in the common view that public health primarily involves the provision of medical care to indigent populations. Since 2001, however, public health has also emerged as a front-line defense against bioterrorism and other threats to personal security and safety.

A final image of public health is that of the intended results of these endeavors. In this image, public health is literally the health of the public, as measured in terms of health and illness in a population. The term population health, often defined as health outcomes and their distribution in a population, is increasingly used for this image of public health.[7]

This chapter focuses primarily on the first of these images, public health as a social enterprise or system. It is important to understand what people mean when they speak of public health. As presented in Table 1-2, the profession, the methods, the governmental services, the ultimate outcomes, and even the broad social enterprise itself are all commonly encountered images of what public health is today.

With varying images of what public health is, we would expect no shortage of definitions. There have been many, and it serves little purpose to try to catalog all of them here. Three definitions, each separated by a generation, provide important insights into what public health is; these are summarized in Table 1-3.

In 1988, the prestigious Institute of Medicine (IOM) provided a useful definition in its landmark study of public health in the United States, "The Future of Public Health." The IOM report characterized public health's mis-

Table 1-2   Images of Public Health

- Public health: the system and social enterprise
- Public health: the profession
- Public health: the methods (knowledge and techniques)
- Public health: governmental services (especially medical care for the poor)
- Public health: the health of the public

Table 1-3   Selected Definitions of Public Health

- "The science and art of preventing disease, prolonging life, and promoting health and efficiency through organized community effort . . ."[9] (Winslow, 1920)
- ". . . successive re-definings of the unacceptable"[10] (Vickers, 1958)
- "fulfilling society's interest in assuring conditions in which people can be healthy"[8] (IOM, 1988)

Source: Data from Institute of Medicine, National Academy of Sciences. *The Future of Public Health*, Washington, DC: National Academy Press; 1988; Winslow CEA. The untilled field of public health. *Mod Med*. 1920;2;183–191; and Vickers G. What sets the goals of public health? *Lancet*. 1958;1: 599–604.

sion as "fulfilling society's interest in assuring conditions in which people can be healthy."[8] This definition directs our attention to the many conditions that influence health and wellness, underscoring the broad scope of public health and legitimizing its interest in social, economic, political, and medical care factors that affect health and illness. The definition's premise that society has an interest in the health of its members implies that improving conditions and health status for others is acting in our own self-interest. The assertion that improving the health status of others provides benefits to all is a core value of public health.

Another core value of public health is reflected in the IOM definition's use of the term *assuring*. Assuring conditions in which people can be healthy means vigilantly promoting and protecting everyone's interests in health and well-being. This value echoes the wisdom in the often-quoted African aphorism that "it takes a village to raise a child." Former Surgeon General David Satcher, the first African American to head this country's most respected federal public health agency, the Centers for Disease Control and Prevention (CDC), once described a visit to Africa in which he met with African teenagers to learn firsthand of their personal health attitudes and behaviors. Satcher was struck by their concerns over the rapid urbanization of the various African nations and the changes that were affecting their culture and sense of community. These young people felt lost and abandoned; they questioned Satcher as to what the CDC, the U.S. government, and the world community would be willing to do to help them survive these changes. As one young man put it, "Where will we find our village?" Public health's role is one of serving us all as our village, whether we are teens in

Africa or adults in the United States. The IOM report's characterization of public health advocated for just such a social enterprise and stands as a bold philosophical statement of mission and purpose.

The IOM report also sought to define the boundaries of public health by identifying three core functions of public health: assessment, policy development, and assurance. In one sense, these functions are comparable to those generally ascribed to the medical care system involving diagnosis and treatment. Assessment is the analogue of diagnosis, except that the diagnosis, or problem identification, is made for a group or population of individuals. Similarly, assurance is analogous to treatment and implies that the necessary remedies or interventions are put into place. Finally, policy development is an intermediate role of collectively deciding which remedies or interventions are most appropriate for the problems identified (the formulation of a treatment plan is the medical system's analogue). These core functions broadly describe what public health does (as opposed to what it is) and are examined more thoroughly in Chapters 5 and 6.

The concepts embedded in the IOM definition are also reflected in Winslow's definition, developed nearly a century ago. His definition describes both what public health does and how this gets done. It is a comprehensive definition that has stood the test of time in characterizing public health as

> The science and art of preventing disease, prolonging life, and promoting health and efficiency through organized community effort for the sanitation of the environment, the control of communicable infections, the education of the individual in personal hygiene, the organization of medical and nursing services for the early diagnosis and preventive treatment of disease, and for the development of the social machinery to insure everyone a standard of living adequate for the maintenance of health, so organizing these benefits as to enable every citizen to realize his birthright of health and longevity.[9]

There is much to consider in Winslow's definition. The phrases "science and art," "organized community effort," and "birthright of health and longevity" capture the substance and aims of public health. Winslow's catalog of methods illuminates the scope of the endeavor, embracing public health's initial targeting of infectious and environmental risks, as well as current activities related to the organization, financing, and accountability of medical care services. His allusion to the "social machinery to insure everyone a standard of living adequate for the maintenance of health" speaks to the relationship between social conditions and health in all societies.

There have been many other attempts to define public health, although these have received less attention than either the Winslow or IOM definitions. Several build on the observation that, over time, public health activities reflect the interaction of disease with two other phenomena that can be roughly characterized as science and social values: what do we know and what do we choose to do with that knowledge?

A prominent British industrialist, Geoffrey Vickers, provided an interesting addition to this mix a half century ago while serving as secretary of the

Medical Research Council. In identifying the forces that set the agenda for public health, Vickers noted, "The landmarks of political, economic, and social history are the moments when some condition passed from the category of the given into the category of the intolerable. I believe that the history of public health might well be written as a record of successive re-definings of the unacceptable."[10]

The usefulness of Vickers' formulation lies in its focus on the delicate and shifting interface between science and social values. Through this lens, we can view a tracing of public health over history, facilitating an understanding of why and how different societies have reacted to health risks differently at various points in time and space. In this light, the history of public health is one of blending knowledge with social values to shape responses to problems that require collective action after they have crossed the boundary from the acceptable to the unacceptable.

Each of these definitions offers important insights into what public health is and what it does. Individually and collectively, they describe a social enterprise that is both important and unique, as we see in the sections that follow.

PUBLIC HEALTH AS A SYSTEM

So what is public health? Maybe no single answer will satisfy everyone. There are, in fact, several views of public health that must be considered. One or more of them may be apparent to the inquirer. The public health described in this chapter is a broad social enterprise, more akin to a movement, that seeks to extend the benefits of current knowledge in ways that will have the maximum impact on the health status of a population. It does so by identifying problems that call for collective action to protect, promote, and improve health, primarily through preventive strategies. This public health is unique in its interdisciplinary approach and methods, its emphasis on preventive strategies, its linkage with government and political decision making, and its dynamic adaptation to new problems placed on its agenda. Above all else, it is a collective effort to identify and address the unacceptable realities that result in preventable and avoidable health and quality of life outcomes, and it is the composite of efforts and activities that are carried out by people and organizations committed to these ends.

With this broad view of public health as a social enterprise, the question shifts from what public health is to what these other images of public health represent and how they relate to each other. To understand these separate images of public health, a conceptual model would be useful. Surprisingly, an understandable and useful framework to tie these pieces together has been lacking. Other enterprises have found ways to describe their complex systems, and from what appears to be an industrial production model, we can begin to look at the various components of our public health system.

This framework brings together the mission and functions of public health in relationship to the inputs, processes, outputs, and outcomes of the system. Table 1-4 provides general descriptions for the terms used in this framework. It is sometimes easier to appreciate this model when a more familiar industry, such as the automobile industry, is used as an example.

Table 1-4   Dimensions of the Public Health System

Capacity (Inputs):
- The resources and relationships necessary to carry out the core functions and essential services of public health (e.g., human resources, information resources, fiscal and physical resources, and appropriate relationships among the system components)

Process (Practices and Outputs):
- Those collective practices or processes that are necessary and sufficient to assure that the core functions and essential services of public health are being carried out effectively, including the key processes that identify and address health problems and their causative factors and the interventions intended to prevent death, disease, and disability and to promote quality of life

Outcomes (Results):
- Indicators of health status, risk reduction, and quality-of-life enhancement outcomes are long-term objectives that define optimal, measurable future levels of health status; maximum acceptable levels of disease, injury, or dysfunction; or prevalence of risk factors

Source: Adapted from Centers for Disease Control and Prevention, Public Health Program Office, 1990.

The mission or purpose might be expressed as meeting the personal transportation needs of the population. This industry carries out its mission by providing passenger cars to its customers; this characterizes its function. In this light, we can now examine the inputs, processes, outputs, and outcomes of the system set up to carry out this function. Inputs would include steel, rubber, plastic, and so forth, as well as the workers, know-how, technology, facilities, machinery, and support services necessary to allow the raw materials to become automobiles. The key processes necessary to carry out the primary function might be characterized as designing cars, making or acquiring parts, assembling parts into automobiles, moving cars to dealers, and selling and servicing cars after purchase. No doubt this is an incomplete listing of this industry's processes; it is oversimplified here to make the point. In any event, these processes translate the abstract concept of getting cars to people into the operational steps necessary to carry out this basic function. The outputs of these processes are cars located where people can purchase them. The outcomes include satisfied customers and company profits.

Applying this same general framework to the public health system is also possible but may not be so obvious to the general public. The mission and functions of public health are well described in the IOM report's framework. The core functions of assessment, policy development, and assurance are considerably more abstract functions than making cars but can still be made operational through descriptions of their key steps or practices.[11,12] The inputs of the public health system include its human, organizational, informational, fiscal, and other resources. These resources and relationships are structured to carry out public health's core functions through a variety of processes that can also be termed essential public health practices or services. These processes include a variety of interventions that result from some of the more basic processes of assessing health needs and planning effective strategies.[13] These outputs or interventions are intended to produce the desired results, which, with public health, might well be characterized as health or quality-of-life outcomes. Figure 1-2 illustrates these relationships.

In this model, not all components are as readily understandable and measurable as others. Several of the inputs are easily counted or measured, including human, fiscal, and organizational resources. Outputs are also generally easy to recognize and count (e.g., prenatal care programs, number of immunizations provided, health messages on the dangers of tobacco). Health outcomes are also readily understood in terms of mortality, morbidity, functional disability, time lost from work or school, and even more sophisticated measures, such as years of potential life lost and quality-of-life years lost. At an aggregate level, outcomes reflect how effective the system is (improved population health status), how equitable it is (eliminating or reducing disparities among segments of the population), and how efficiently (or cost beneficially) the system performs. The elements that are most difficult to understand and visualize are the processes or essential services of the public health system. Although this is an evolving field, there have been efforts to characterize these operational aspects of public health. By such efforts, we are better able to understand public health practice, to measure it, and to relate it to its outputs and outcomes. A national work group was assembled by the U.S. Public Health Service in 1994 in an attempt to develop a consensus statement of what public health is and does in language understandable to those both

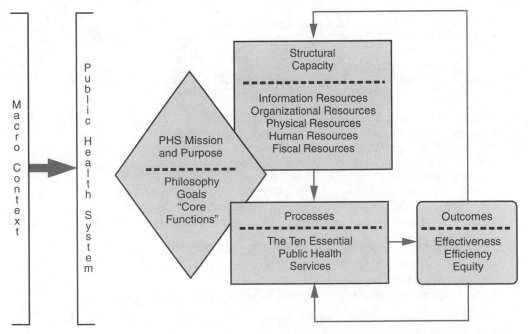

Figure 1-2 Conceptual framework of the public health system as a basis for measuring system performance. *Source:* From Handler A, Issel LM, Turnock BJ. A conceptual framework to measure performance of the public health system. *Am J Public Health.* 2001;91(8): 1235–1239. © 2001, American Public Health Association.

inside and outside the field of public health. Table 1-5 presents the result of that process in a statement entitled "Public Health in America."[14] The conceptual framework identified in Figure 1-2 and the narrative representation in the "Public Health in America" statement are useful models for understanding the public health system and how it works, as we see throughout this text.

This framework attempts to bridge the gap between what public health is, what it does (purpose/mission and functions, Figure 1-2), and how it does what it does (through its capacity, processes, and outcomes). It also allows us to examine the various components of the system so that we can better appreciate how the pieces fit together. Subsequent chapters refer back to this model as the capacity, processes, and outcomes of the public health system are examined in greater depth.

Table 1-5   Public Health in America

Vision:
Healthy People in Healthy Communities
Mission:
*Promote Physical and Mental Health
and Prevent Disease, Injury, and Disability*

Public Health
- Prevents epidemics and the spread of disease
- Protects against environmental hazards
- Prevents injuries
- Promotes and encourages healthy behaviors
- Responds to disasters and assists communities in recovery
- Assures the quality and accessibility of health services

Essential Public Health Services
- Monitor health status to identify community health problems
- Diagnose and investigate health problems and health hazards in the community
- Inform, educate, and empower people about health issues
- Mobilize community partnerships to identify and solve health problems
- Develop policies and plans that support individual and community health efforts
- Enforce laws and regulations that protect health and ensure safety
- Link people with needed personal health services and assure the provision of health care when otherwise unavailable
- Assure a competent public health and personal healthcare workforce
- Evaluate effectiveness, accessibility, and quality of personal and population-based health services
- Research for new insights and innovative solutions to health problems

Source: From Essential Public Health Services Working Group of the Core Public Health Functions Steering Committee, U.S. Public Health Service, 1994.

Table 1-6   Selected Unique Features of Public Health

- Basis in social justice philosophy
- Inherently political nature
- Dynamic, ever-expanding agenda
- Link with government
- Grounding in the sciences
- Use of prevention as a prime strategy
- Uncommon culture and bond

UNIQUE FEATURES OF PUBLIC HEALTH

Several unique features of public health individually and collectively serve to make understanding and appreciation of this enterprise difficult (Table 1-6). These include the underlying social justice philosophy of public health; its inherently political nature; its ever-expanding agenda, with new problems and issues being assigned over time; its link with government; its grounding in a broad base of biologic, physical, quantitative, social, and behavioral sciences; its focus on prevention as a prime intervention strategy; and the unique bond and sense of mission that links its proponents.

Social Justice Philosophy

It is vital to recognize the social justice orientation of public health and even more critical to understand the potential for conflict and confrontation that it generates. Social justice is the foundation of public health. The concept first emerged around 1848, a time that might be considered the birth of modern public health. Social justice argues that public health is properly a public matter and that its results in terms of death, disease, health, and well-being reflect the decisions and actions that a society makes, for good or for ill.[15] Justice is an abstract concept that determines how each member of a society is allocated his or her fair share of collective burdens and benefits. Societal benefits to be distributed may include happiness, income, or social status. Burdens include restrictions of individual action and taxation. Justice dictates that there is fairness in the distribution of benefits and burdens; injustices occur when persons are denied some benefit to which they are entitled or when some burden is imposed unduly. If access to health services, or even health itself, is considered to be a societal benefit (or if poor health is considered to be a burden), the links between the concepts of justice and public health become clear. Market justice and social justice represent two forms of modern justice.

Market justice emphasizes personal responsibility as the basis for distributing burdens and benefits. Other than respecting the basic rights of others, individuals are responsible primarily for their own actions and are free from collective obligations. Individual rights are highly valued, whereas collective responsibilities are minimized. In terms of health, individuals assume primary responsibility for their own health. There is little expectation that society should act to protect or promote the health of its members beyond addressing risks that cannot be controlled through individual action.

Social justice argues that significant factors within the society impede the fair distribution of benefits and burdens.[16] Examples of such impediments include social class distinctions, heredity, racism, and ethnism. Collective action, often leading to the assumption of additional burdens, is necessary to neutralize or overcome those impediments. In the case of public health, the goal of extending the potential benefits of the physical and behavioral sciences to all groups in the society, especially when the burden of disease and ill health within that society is unequally distributed, is largely based on principles of social justice. It is clear that many modern public health (and other public policy) problems disproportionately affect some groups, usually a minority of the population, more than others. As a result, their resolution requires collective actions in which those less affected take on greater burdens, while not commensurately benefiting from those actions. When the necessary collective actions are not taken, even the most important public policy problems remain unsolved, despite periodically becoming highly visible.[16] This scenario reflects responses to such intractable American problems as inadequate housing, poor public education systems, unemployment, racial discrimination, and poverty; however, it is also true for public health problems such as tobacco-related illnesses, infant mortality, substance abuse, mental health services, long-term care, and environmental pollution. The failure to effect comprehensive national health reform in 1994 is an example of this phenomenon. At that time, middle-class Americans deemed the modest price tag of health reform to be excessive, refusing to pay more out of their own pockets when they perceived that their own access and services were not likely to improve. The bitter political conflict accompanying the enactment of national health reform legislation in 2010 further illustrated these sentiments.

These and similar examples suggest that a critical challenge for public health as a social enterprise lies in overcoming the social and ethical barriers that prevent us from doing more with the tools already available to us.[16] Extending the frontiers of science and knowledge may not be as useful for improving public health as shifting the collective values of our society to act on what we already know. Recent public health successes, such as public attitudes toward smoking in both public and private locations and operating motor vehicles after alcohol consumption, provide evidence in support of this assertion. These advances came through changes in social norms, rather than through bigger and better science.

Inherently Political Nature

The social justice underpinnings of public health serve to stimulate political conflict. Public health is both public and political in nature. It serves populations, which are composites of many different communities, cultures, and values. Politics allows for issues to be considered, negotiated, and finally determined for populations. At the core of political processes are differing values and perspectives as to both the ends to be achieved and the means for achieving those ends. Advocating causes and agitating various segments of society to identify and address unacceptable conditions that adversely affect health status often lead to increased expectations and demands on society, generally through government. As a result, public health advocates appear at times as antigovernment and anti-institutional. Governmental public health agencies seeking to serve the interests of both government and public health are frequently caught in the middle. This creates tensions and conflict that can put these agencies at odds with governmental leaders on the one hand and external public health advocates on the other.

Expanding Agenda

A third unique feature of public health is its broad and ever-increasing scope. Traditional domains of public health interest include biology, environment, lifestyle, and health service organization. Within each of these domains are many factors that affect health status; in recent decades, many new public policy problems have been moved onto the public health agenda as their predisposing factors have been identified and found to fall into one or more of these domains. A multilevel, multidimensional view of health, often termed an ecological model of health (Figure 1-3), has emerged to guide public health practice. Chapter 2 examines this model in some depth.

The assignment of new problems to the public health agenda is an interesting phenomenon. For example, before 1900, the primary problems addressed by public health were infectious diseases and related environmental risks. After 1900, the focus expanded to include problems and needs of children and mothers to be addressed through health education and maternal and child health services as public sentiment over the health and safety of children increased. In the middle of the century, chronic disease prevention and medical care fell into public health's realm as an epidemiologic revolution began to identify causative agents for chronic diseases and links between use of health services and health outcomes. Later, substance abuse, mental illness, teen pregnancy, long-term care, and other issues fell to public health, as did several emerging problems, most notably the epidemics of violence and HIV infections, including acquired immune deficiency syndrome (AIDS). The public health agenda expanded even further as a result of the recent national dialogue over health reform and how health services will be organized and managed. Bioterrorism preparedness is an even more recent addition to this agenda amid heightened concerns and expectations after the events of September 11, 2001, and the anthrax attacks the following month.

Link with Government

A fourth unique facet of public health is its link with government. Although public health is far more than the activities of federal, state, and local health departments, many people think only of governmental public health agencies when they think of public health. Government does play a unique role in seeing that the key elements are in place and that public

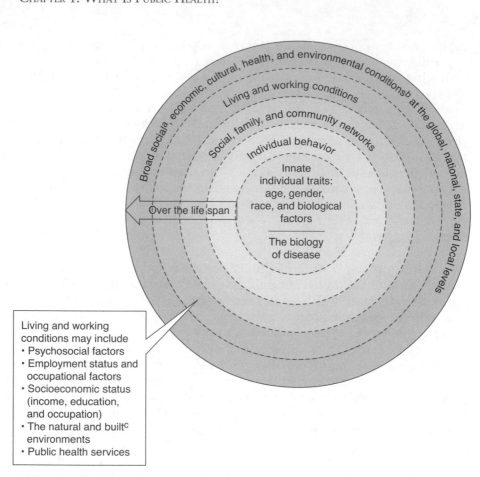

Figure 1-3   A guide to thinking about the determinants of population health.

Notes: Adapted from Dahlgren and Whitehead, 1991. The dashed lines between levels of the model denote interaction effects between and among the various levels of health determinants (Worthman, 1999).

a. Social conditions include, but are not limited to: economic inequality, urbanization, mobility, cultural values, attitudes, and policies related to discrimination and intolerance on the basis of race, gender, and other differences.

b. Other conditions at the national level might include major sociopolitical shifts, such as recession, war, and governmental collapse.

c. The built environment includes transportation, water and sanitation, housing, and other dimensions of urban planning.

Source: From The Committee on Assuring the Health of the Public in the 21st Century, Institute of Medicine. *The Future of the Public's Health in the 21st Century.* Washington, DC: National Academy Press; 2003. Reprinted with permission, copyright 2003, National Academy of Sciences.

health's mission gets addressed. Only government can exercise the enforcement provisions of our public policies that limit the personal and property rights of individuals and corporations in areas such as retail food establishments, sewage and water systems, occupational health and safety, consumer product safety, infectious disease control, and drug efficacy and safety. Government also can play the convener and facilitator role for identifying and prioritizing health problems that might be addressed through public resources and actions. These roles derive from the underlying principle of beneficence, in that government exists to improve the well-being of its members. Beneficence often involves a balance between maximizing benefits and minimizing harms on the one hand and doing no harm on the other.

Two general strategies are available for governmental efforts to influence public health. At the broadest level, governments can modify public policies that influence health through social and environmental conditions, such as policies for education, employment, housing, public safety, child welfare, pollution control, workplace safety, and family support. In line with the IOM report's definition of public health, these actions seek to ensure conditions in which people can be healthy. Another strategy of government is to provide directly the programs and services that are designed to meet the health needs of the population. It is often easier to garner support for relatively small-scale programs directed toward a specific problem (such as tuberculosis or HIV infections) than to achieve consensus around broader health and social issues. This strategy is basically a "command-and-control" approach, in which government attempts to increase access to and use of services largely through deployment of its own resources rather than through working with others. A variation of this strategy for government is to ensure access to healthcare services through public financing approaches (Medicare and Medicaid are prime examples) or through specialized delivery systems (such as the Veterans Administration facilities, the Indian Health Service, and federally funded community health centers).

Whereas the United States has generally opted for the latter of these strategies, other countries have acted to place greater emphasis on broader social policies. Both the overall level of investment for and relative emphasis between these strategies contribute to the widely varying results achieved in terms of health status indicators among different nations (discussed in Chapter 2).

Many factors dictate the approaches used by a specific government at any point in time. These factors include history, culture, the structure of the government in question, and current social circumstances. There are also several underlying motivations that support government intervention. For paternalistic reasons, governments may act to control or restrict the liberties of individuals to benefit a group, whether or not that group seeks these benefits. For utilitarian reasons, governments intervene because of the perception that the state as a whole will benefit in some important way. For equality considerations, governments act to ensure that benefits and burdens are equally distributed among individuals. For equity considerations, governments justify interventions in order to distribute the benefits of society in proportion to need. These motivations reflect the views of each society as to whether health itself or merely access to health services is to be considered a right of individuals and populations within that society. Many societies, including the United States, act through government to ensure equal access to a broad array of preventive and treatment services. Equity in health status for all groups within the society may not be an explicit aspiration, however, even where efforts are in place to ensure equality in access. Even more important for achieving equity in health status are concerted efforts to improve health status in population groups with the greatest disadvantage, mechanisms to monitor health status and contributing factors across all population groups, and participation of disadvantaged population groups in the key political decision-making processes within the society.[17] To the extent that equity in health status among all population groups does not guide actions of a society's government, these other elements will be only marginally effective.

As noted previously, the link between government and public health makes for a particularly precarious situation for governmental public health agencies. The conflicting value systems of public health and the wider community generally translate into public health agencies having to document their failure in order to make progress. It is said that only the squeaky wheel gets the grease; in public health, it often takes an outbreak, disaster, or other tragedy to demonstrate public health's value. Since 1985, increased funding for basic public health protection programs quickly followed outbreaks related to bacteria-contaminated milk in Illinois, tainted hamburgers in Washington State, and contaminated public water supplies in Milwaukee. Following concerns over preparedness of public health agencies to deal with bioterrorism and other public health threats, a massive infusion of federal funding occurred.

The assumption and delegation of public health responsibilities are quite complex in the United States, with different patterns in each of the 50 states (described in Chapter 4). Over recent decades, the concept of a governmental presence in health has emerged and gained widespread acceptance within the public health community. This concept characterizes the role of local government, often, but not necessarily always, operating through its official health agencies, which serve as the residual guarantors that needed services will actually be there when needed. In practice it means that, no matter how duties are assigned locally, there is a presence that ensures that health needs are identified and considered for collective action. We return to this concept and how it is operationalized in Chapters 4, 5, and 6.

Grounded in Science

One of the most unique aspects of public health—and one that continues to separate public health from many other social movements—is its grounding in science.[18] This relationship is clear for the medical and physical sciences that govern our understanding of the biologic aspects of humans, microorganisms, and vectors, as well as the risks present in our physical environments; however, it is also true for the social sciences of anthropology, sociology, and psychology that affect our understanding of human culture and behaviors influencing health and illness. The quantitative sciences of epidemiology and biostatistics remain essential tools and methods of public health practice. Often five basic sciences of public health are identified: epidemiology, biostatistics, environmental science, management sciences, and behavioral sciences. These constitute the core education of public health professionals.

The importance of a solid and diverse scientific base is both a strength and weakness of public health. Surely there is no substitute for science in the modern world. The public remains curiously attracted to scientific advances, at least in the physical and biologic sciences, and this base is important to market and promote public health interventions. For many years, epidemiology has been touted as the basic science of public health practice, suggesting that public health itself is applied epidemiology. Modern public health thinking views epidemiology less as the basic science of public health than as one of many contributors to a complex undertaking. In recent decades, knowledge from the social sciences has greatly enriched and supplemented the physical and biologic sciences. Yet these are areas less familiar to and perhaps less well appreciated by the public, making it difficult to garner public support for newer, more behaviorally mediated public health interventions. The old image of public health based on the scientific principles of environmental sanitation and communicable disease control is being superseded by a new image of public health approaches more grounded in what the public perceives to be "softer" science. This transition, at least temporarily, threatens public understanding and confidence in public health and its methods.

Focus on Prevention

If public health professionals were pressed to provide a one-word synonym for public health, the most frequent response would probably be prevention. In general, prevention characterizes actions that are taken to reduce the possibility that something will happen or in hopes of minimizing the damage that may occur if it does happen. Prevention is a widely appreciated and valued concept that is best understood when its object is identified. Although prevention is considered by many to be the purpose of public health, the specific intentions of prevention can vary greatly. Prevention can be aimed at deaths, hospital admissions, days lost from school, consumption of human and fiscal resources, and many other ends. There are as many targets for prevention as there are various health outcomes and effects to be avoided.

Prevention efforts often lack a clear constituency because success results in unseen consequences. Because these consequences are unseen, people are less likely to develop an attachment for or support of the efforts preventing them. Advocates for such causes as mental health services, care for individuals with developmental disabilities, and organ transplants often make their presence felt; however, few state capitols have seen candlelight demonstrations by thousands of people who did not get diphtheria. This invisible constituency for prevention is partly a result of the interdisciplinary nature of public health. With no predominant discipline, it is even more difficult for people to understand and appreciate the work of public health. From one perspective, the undervaluation of public health is understandable; the majority of the beneficiaries of recent and current public health prevention efforts have not yet been born! Despite its lack of recognition, prevention as a strategy has been remarkably successful and appears to offer great potential for future success, as well. Chapter 3 in particular explores this potential in greater depth.

Uncommon Culture

The final unique feature of public health to be discussed here appears to be both a strength and weakness. The tie that binds public health professionals is neither a common preparation through education and training nor a common set of work experiences and work settings. Public health is unique in that the common link is a set of intended outcomes toward which many different sciences, strategies, and methods can contribute. As a result, public health professionals include anthropologists, sociologists, psychologists, physicians, nurses, nutritionists, lawyers, economists, political scientists, social workers, laboratorians, managers, sanitarians, engineers, epidemiologists, biostatisticians, gerontologists, disability specialists, and dozens of other professions and disciplines. All are bound to common ends, and all employ somewhat different perspectives from their diverse education, training, and work experiences. "Whatever it takes to get the job done" is the theme, suggesting that the basic task is one of problem solving around health issues. This aspect of public health is the foundation for strategies and methods that rely heavily on collaborations and partnerships.

This multidisciplinary and interdisciplinary approach is unique among professions, calling into question whether public health is really a profession at all. There are several strong arguments that public health is not a profession. There is no minimum credential or training that distinguishes public health professionals from either other professionals or nonprofessionals. Only a tiny proportion of those who work in organizations dedicated to improving the health of the public possess one of the academic public health degrees (the master's of public health degree and several other master's and doctoral degrees granted by schools of public health and other institutions). With the vast majority of public health workers not formally trained in public health, it is difficult to characterize its workforce as a profession. In many respects, it is more reasonable to view public health as a movement than as a profession.

VALUE OF PUBLIC HEALTH

How can we measure the value of public health efforts? This question is addressed both directly and indirectly throughout this text. Chapters 2 and 3 examine the dimensions of public health's value in terms of lives saved and diseases prevented, as well as in dollars and cents. Nonetheless, some initial information will set the stage for greater detail later.

Public opinion polls conducted in recent years suggest that public health is highly valued in the United States.[19] The overwhelming majority of the public rated a variety of key public health services as "very important."

- Ninety-one percent of all adults believe that prevention of the spread of infectious diseases such as tuberculosis, measles, flu, and AIDS is very important.
- Eighty-eight percent also believe that conducting research into the causes and prevention of disease is very important.
- Eighty-seven percent believe that immunization to prevent diseases is very important.
- Eighty-six percent believe that ensuring that people are not exposed to unsafe water, air pollution, or toxic waste is very important.
- Eighty-five percent believe that it is very important to work to reduce death and injuries from violence.

- Sixty-eight percent believe that it is important to encourage people to live healthier lifestyles, to eat well, and not to smoke.
- Sixty-six percent believe that it is important to work to reduce death and injuries from accidents at work, in the home, and on the streets.

In a related poll conducted in 1999, the Pew Charitable Trusts found that 46% of all Americans thought that "public health/protecting populations from disease" was more important than "medicine/treating people who are sick." Almost 30% thought medicine was more important than public health; 22% said both were equally important, and 3% had no opinion. Public opinion surveys suggest that public health's contributions to health and quality of life have not gone unnoticed. Other assessments of the value of public health support this contention.

In 1965, McKeown concluded, "Health has advanced significantly only since the late 18th century and until recently owed little to medical advances."[20] This conclusion is bolstered by more recent studies finding that public health's prevention efforts are responsible for 25 years of the nearly 30-year improvement in life expectancy at birth in the United States since 1900. This bold claim is based on evidence that only 5.2 years of the 30-year improvement are the result of medical care.[21] Of these 5.2 years, medical treatment accounts for 3.7 years, and clinical preventive services (such as immunizations and screening tests) account for 1.5 years. The remaining 25 years have resulted largely from prevention efforts in the form of social policies, community actions, and personal decisions. Many of these decisions and actions targeted infectious diseases affecting infants and children early in the 20th century. Later in that century, gains in life expectancy have also been achieved through reductions in chronic diseases affecting adults, including cardiovascular disease. A study of life years gained from modern coronary heart disease treatments and changes in population risk factors in England and Wales from 1981 to 2000 concluded that 79% of the increase in life years gained was attributed to reductions in major risk factors. Only 21% of the life years gained could be attributed to medical and surgical treatments of coronary heart disease.[22]

Many notable public health achievements occurred during the 20th century (Table 1-7). This text spotlights many of these achievements to illustrate the value of public health to American society in the 21st century by telling the story of its accomplishments in the preceding century. The first of these chronicles the prevention and control of infectious diseases in 20th-century America (see the Public Health Spotlight on the Control of Infectious Diseases, which appears at the end of this chapter).

The value of public health in our society can be described in human terms as well as by public opinion, statistics of infections prevented, and values in dollars and cents. A poignant example dates from the 1950s, when the United States was in the midst of a terrorizing polio epidemic (Table 1-8). Few communities were spared during the periodic onslaughts of this serious disease during the first half of the 20th century in America. Public fear was so great that public libraries, community swimming pools, and other group activities were closed during the summers when the disease was most feared.

Table 1-7   Ten Great Public Health Achievements—United States, 1900–1999

  1. Vaccination
  2. Motor-vehicle safety
  3. Safer workplaces
  4. Control of infectious diseases
  5. Decline in deaths from coronary heart disease and stroke
  6. Safer and healthier foods
  7. Healthier mothers and babies
  8. Family planning
  9. Fluoridation of drinking water
  10. Recognition of tobacco use as a health hazard

Source: Data from Centers for Disease Control and Prevention. Ten great public health achievements—United States, 1900–1999. *MMWR.* 1999;48:241–243.

Table 1-8   The Value of Public Health: Fear of Polio, United States, 1950s

"I can remember no experience more horrifying than watching by the bedside of my five-year-old stricken with polio. The disease attacked his right leg, and we watched helplessly as his limb steadily weakened. On the third day, the doctor told us that he would survive and that paralysis was the worst he would suffer. I was grateful, although I continued to agonize about whether my wife and unborn child would be affected. What a blessing that no other parent will have to endure the terror that my wife and I and thousands of others shared that August."

—Morton Chapman, Sarasota, Florida

Source: From U.S. Public Health Service. *For a Healthy Nation: Returns on Investment in Public Health.* Washington, DC: Public Health Service; 1994.

Biomedical research had discovered a possible weapon against epidemic polio in the form of the Salk vaccine, however, which was developed in 1954 and licensed for use 1 year later. A massive and unprecedented campaign to immunize the public was quickly undertaken, setting the stage for a triumph of public health. The real triumph came in a way that might not have been expected, however, because soon into the campaign, isolated reports of vaccine-induced polio were identified in Chicago and California. Within 2 days of the initial case reports, action by governmental public health organizations at all levels resulted in the determination that these cases could be traced to one particular manufacturer. This determination was made only a few hours before the same vaccine was to be provided to hundreds of thousands of California children. The result was prevention of a disaster and rescue of the credibility of an immunization campaign that has virtually cut this disease off at its knees. The campaign proceeded on schedule, and 5 decades later, wild poliovirus has been eradicated from the Western hemisphere.

Similar examples have occurred throughout history. The battle against diphtheria is a case in point. A major cause of death in 1900, diphtheria infections are virtually unheard of today. This achievement cannot be traced solely to advances in bacteriology and the antitoxins and immunizations that were deployed against this disease. Neither was it defeated by brilliant political and programmatic initiatives led by public health experts. It was the confluence of scientific advances and public perception of the disease itself that resulted in diphtheria's demise as a threat to entire populations. These forces shaped public health policies and the effectiveness of intervention strategies. In the end, diphtheria made some practices and politics possible, whereas it constrained others.[23] The story is one of science, social values, and public health.

CONCLUSION

Public health evokes different images for different people, and even to the same people, it can mean different things in different contexts. The intent of this chapter has been to describe some of the common perceptions of public health in the United States. Is it a complex, dynamic, social enterprise, akin to a movement? Or is it best characterized as a goal of the improved health outcomes and health status that can be achieved by the work of all of us, individually and collectively? Or is public health some collection of activities that move us ever closer toward our aspirations? Or is it the profession that includes all of those dedicated to its cause? Or is public health merely what we see coming out of our official governmental health agencies—a strange mix of safety-net medical services for the poor and a variety of often-invisible community prevention services?

Although it is tempting to consider expunging the term public health from our vocabularies because of the baggage associated with these various images, this would do little to address the obstacles to accomplishing our central task because public health encompasses all of these images and perhaps more!

Based on principles of social justice, inherently political in its processes, addressing a constantly expanding agenda of problems, inextricably linked with government, grounded in science, emphasizing preventive strategies, and with a workforce bound by common aspirations, public health is unique in many ways. Its value, however, transcends its uniqueness. Public health efforts have been major contributors to recent improvements in health status and can contribute even more as we approach a new century with new challenges.

By carefully examining the various dimensions of the public health system in terms of its inputs, practices, outputs, and outcomes, we can gain insights into what it does, how it works, and how it can be improved. Better results do not come from setting new goals; they come from understanding and improving the processes that will then produce better outputs, in turn leading to better outcomes. This theme of understanding the public health system and public health practice as a necessary step toward its improvement recurs throughout this text.

DISCUSSION QUESTIONS AND EXERCISES

1. What definition of public health best describes public health in the 21st century?
2. To what extent has public health contributed to improvement in health status and quality of life over history?
3. What historical phenomena are most responsible for the development of public health responses?
4. Which features of public health make it different from other fields? Which features are most unique and distinctive? Which are most important?
5. Because of your interest in a public health career, a producer working at a local television station has asked you to provide input into the development of a video explaining public health to the general public. What themes or messages would you suggest for this video? How would you propose presenting or packaging these messages?
6. There is little written in history books about public health problems and responses, suggesting that these issues have had little impact on history. Consider the European colonization of the Americas, beginning in the 16th century. How was it possible for Cortez and other European figures to overcome immense Native American cultures with millions of people? What role, if any, did public health themes and issues play?
7. Choose a relatively recent (within the last 3 years) occurrence/ event that has drawn significant media attention to a public health issue or problem (e.g., bioterrorism, contaminated meat products, tobacco settlement, hurricane, and flooding). Have different understandings of what public health is influenced public, as well as governmental responses, to this event? If so, in what ways?
8. Review the history of public health activities in your state or community, and describe how public health strategies and interventions have changed over time in the United States. What influences were most responsible for these changes? Does this suggest that public health functions have changed over time, as well? (If no such history or time line is available, review the Public Health Spotlight on the History of Public Health in Chicago, which appears later in this chapter.)
9. Access the website of Delta Omega, the national honorary society for public health (at www.deltaomega.org) and select one of the public health classics that are available there. Then describe the significance of this classic in terms of the history of modern public health practice.
10. Examine each of the websites listed later here, and become familiar with their general contents. Which ones are most useful for providing information and insights related to the question "what is

public health?" Why? Are there other websites you would suggest adding to this list?
- American Public Health Association: http://www.apha.org
- Association of State and Territorial Health Officials: http://www.astho.org
- National Association of County and City Health Officials: http://www.naccho.org
- Public Health Foundation: http://www.phf.org
- U.S. Department of Health and Human Services: http://www.dhhs.gov and its various Public Health Service Agencies (e.g., Centers for Disease Control and Prevention, http://www.cdc.gov; Food and Drug Administration, http://www.fda.gov; Health Resources and Services Administration, http://www.hrsa.dhhs.gov; National Institutes of Health, http://www. nih.gov; and Agency for Healthcare Research and Quality, http://www.ahrq.gov)
- U.S. Environmental Protection Agency: http://www.epa.gov
- State health departments, available through the Association of State and Territorial Health Officials website at www.astho.org
- Local health departments, available through the websites of state health departments, the National Association of County and City Health Officials, and other national public health organizations
- Association of Schools of Public Health (ASPH): http://www.asph.org and individual schools, available through the ASPH website

REFERENCES

1. Winslow CEA. Public health at the crossroads. *Am J Public Health*. 1926;16:1075–1085.
2. Hinman A. Eradication of vaccine-preventable diseases. *Annu Rev Public Health*. 1999;20:211–229.
3. U.S. Public Health Service. *For a Healthy Nation: Returns on Investment in Public Health*. Washington, DC: PHS; 1994.
4. McNeil WH. *Plagues and Peoples*. New York: Doubleday; 1977.
5. Paneth N, Vinten-Johansen P, Brody H. A rivalry of foulness: official and unofficial investigations of the London cholera epidemic of 1854. *Am J Public Health*. 1998;88:1545–1553.
6. Hamlin C. Could you starve to death in England in 1839? The Chadwick-Farr controversy and the loss of the "social" in public health. *Am J Public Health*. 1995;85:856–866.
7. Kindig DA. Understanding population health terminology. *Milbank Q*. 2007;85:139–161.
8. Institute of Medicine, National Academy of Sciences. *The Future of Public Health*. Washington, DC: National Academy Press; 1988.
9. Winslow CEA. The untilled field of public health. *Mod Med*. 1920;2:183–191.
10. Vickers G. What sets the goals of public health? *Lancet*. 1958;1:599–604.
11. Baker EL, Melton RJ, Stange PV, et al. Health reform and the health of the public. *JAMA*. 1994;272:1276–1282.
12. Harrell JA, Baker EL. The essential services of public health. *Leadership Public Health*. 1994;3: 27–30.

13. Handler A, Issel LM, Turnock BJ. A conceptual framework to measure performance of the public health system. *Am J Public Health*. 2001;91:1235–1239.

14. Public Health Functions Steering Committee. *Public Health in America*. Washington, DC: U.S. Public Health Service; 1995.

15. Krieger N, Brin AE. A vision of social justice as the foundation of public health: commemorating 150 years of the spirit of 1848. *Am J Public Health*. 1998;88:1603–1606.

16. Beauchamp DE. Public health as social justice. *Inquiry*. 1976;13:3–14.

17. Susser M. Health as a human right: an epidemiologist's perspective on public health. *Am J Public Health*. 1993;83:418–426.

18. Afifi AA, Breslow L. The maturing paradigm of public health. *Annu Rev Public Health*. 1994;15: 223–235.

19. Centers for Disease Control and Prevention. Public opinion about public health, United States. *MMWR*. 2000;49(12):258–260.

20. McKeown T. *Medicine in Modern Society*. London: Allen & Unwin; 1965.

21. Bunker JP, Frazier HS, Mosteller F. Improving health: measuring effects of medical care. *Milbank Q*. 1994;72:225–258.

22. Unal B, Critchley JA, Fidan D, Capewell S. Life-years gained from modern cardiological treatments and population risk factor changes in England and Wales, 1981–2000. *Am J Public Health*. 2005;95:103–108.

23. Hammonds EM. *Childhood's Deadly Scourge: The Campaign to Control Diphtheria in New York City, 1880–1930*. Baltimore, MD: Johns Hopkins University Press; 1999.

Public Health Spotlight on the History of Public Health in Chicago

The history of public health events in Chicago tells the story of how public health responses and activities have changed over the past 175 years in the United States. What influences have been most responsible for these changes? Does this history suggest that public health functions have changed over time, as well? Consider these questions as you review this history.

SELECTED HISTORY OF PUBLIC HEALTH EVENTS IN CHICAGO, 1834–2003

1834   A temporary board of health was formed to fight the threat of cholera.

1835   Chicago Board of Health was established by the state legislature to secure the general health of the inhabitants because of the threat of cholera epidemic. Chicago, then a town, had an estimated 3,265 residents.

1837   Chicago was incorporated as a city of 4,170 residents. Three health commissioners and a health officer were named to inspect marketplaces, prepare death certificates, construct a pest house, visit persons suffering from infectious diseases in their homes, and board vessels in the harbor to check on the health of crews.

1841   Vital statistics started in a limited way with collection of data (age, gender, disease) related to deaths; an ordinance requiring reports of death was passed but not enforced for several years.

1846   A committee of the Chicago Medical Society reported the mortality rates through 1850.

1848   The first cooperative effort of the medical profession and city officials was begun to prevent the spread of smallpox as physicians volunteered to vaccinate the poor without charge.

1849   Cholera was brought to Chicago by the emigrant boat John Drew from New Orleans, killing 1 in 36 of the entire population. A district health officer was appointed for each city block.

1851   A new city charter provided greater powers in health matters to the City Council. In the mid 1850s, with the city free from smallpox and cholera, the powers of the Board of Health were reduced accordingly.

1855   Sewerage became an issue; the Board of Sewerage Commissioners was appointed, and the first sewers were constructed the following year. The quarantine placard was introduced with signs reading "Smallpox Here" after 30 died of the disease.

1857   The financial depression of 1857 caused the Board of Health to be viewed as a luxury; it was abolished, and its duties were transferred to the Police Department. A new permanent city hospital was completed at a cost of $75,000 (later taken over by Cook County Hospital as one of its earlier buildings).

1862   A smallpox outbreak caused the city council to appoint a health officer to work with the police department, but severely circumscribed tenure and duties rendered the position meaningless.

1867   A new Board of Health was established in response to the 1866 cholera outbreak with authority independent of the city council and police department.

1868   A meat inspection was initiated at Union Stock Yards.

1869   The Board of Health required vaccination of all children.

1870   The first milk ordinance was instituted, making it illegal to sell skim milk unless so labeled.

1871   Help was given to refugees of Chicago fire; camps of homeless were inspected, and controls were initiated for food supply and epidemic prevention. Birth and death records were lost in the fire.

1872   In aftermath of the Great Fire, the death rate increased 32.6% to 27.6 deaths per 1,000 persons. Smallpox attacked 2,382 and killed 655. Fatalities among children under 5 years old were the highest ever recorded. (For the period 1843 to 1872, children under 5 years old accounted for half of all deaths occurring in the city.)

1876   The health functions of city government were reorganized under a department of health, and the Commissioner of Health position was established.

1877   The Commissioner of Health required the reporting of contagious diseases by physicians, a move opposed by many physicians.

1885   A cholera and typhoid epidemic killed 90,000 Chicagoans when a heavy storm washed sewage into Lake Michigan, the city's source of drinking water.

1888   The Chicago Visiting Nurse Association was founded.

1889   Drainage and plumbing regulations were issued, and five women inspectors of tenements were appointed.

1890   Garbage disposal was placed under the direction of a general sanitary officer in the health department.

1892   Full milk inspection started. Laws requiring reporting of communicable diseases existed; however, doctors argued that they should receive payments for reporting as they received under state law for reporting births. Without this reimbursement, many physicians refused to comply and were prosecuted.

1893   Bacteriological laboratory opened to conduct microscopic examinations of milk samples and examine throat cultures for diphtheria. A "Boil the Water" crusade against typhoid was conducted.

1893/94 The last smallpox epidemic to cause great loss of life occurred (1,033 died in its second year). Vigorous vaccination efforts (1,084,500 given) resulted in a reduction of cases to seven in 1897. During this period, the department was the first to proclaim the superiority of hermetically sealed glycerinated vaccine. Circulars distributed on hot weather care of babies were one of the first public education efforts. The health department began publishing a monthly statement of mortality.

1895   The first diphtheria antitoxin was issued, and a corps of antitoxin administrators was appointed. Daily analysis of the water supply was inaugurated.

1896   Medical school inspections were inaugurated—the second city in the United States to do so. Rules regulating the practice of midwifery were promulgated.

1899   A campaign against infant mortality enlisted support of a voluntary corps of 73 physicians.

1900   Sanitary engineers reversed the flow of the Chicago River to prevent a recurrence of epidemics, giving the city the world's only river that runs backward. Department published a study reporting that the average span of life in Chicago more than doubled in a generation.

1901   An ordinance was passed prohibiting spitting in public places. The health department began publishing the state of the city's health every week in the newspapers; the monthly statement of mortality was discontinued.

1902   The Milk Commission of Chicago was established to ensure that pasteurized milk was made available for needy children; dairy inspections were started with the salaries of two dairy inspectors initially paid for by the Chicago Civic Federation. Fourth of July "Don'ts" were first promulgated to prevent accidents.

1903   A tuberculosis committee of the Visiting Nurse Association was established; it reorganized in 1906 as the Chicago Tuberculosis Institute.

1905   The 39th Street intercepting sewer opened, resulting in a marked decrease in typhoid deaths.

1906   The city council passed an ordinance providing for the licensing and control of restaurants.

1907   The Chicago Tuberculosis Institute opened dispensaries for the diagnosis and treatment of tuberculosis cases.

1908   A full communicable disease program was inaugurated, and 100 physicians were sent to congested districts during July and August to instruct mothers in baby care. Forty nurses were loaned to the department by the Visiting Nurses Association of Chicago to help in a scarlet fever epidemic. They were so effective that the city council appropriated funds to hire the department's first nurses to work in maternal and child welfare and communicable and venereal diseases.

1909   Chicago became the first city in the United States to adopt a compulsory milk pasteurization ordinance. Public health nurses from the Board of Health, Visiting Nurse Association, and United Charities collaborated to become "finders of sick infants" and referred these babies and their mothers to tent camps where treatment was provided and hygiene classes were held.

1910   The Municipal Social Hygiene Clinic was established, and dispensaries were required to report venereal diseases. New milk standards were applied to ice cream. Health Department nurses were assigned to conduct intensive follow-up on babies in hospital wards where infant death rates were high; the Infant Welfare Society was organized as the successor to the Milk Commission.

1911   Common drinking cups and common roller towels were prohibited by ordinance.

1912   Sterilization of Chicago's water began, and within 4 years, the entire supply was being treated, causing a dramatic decline in the city's typhoid fever rate—from second highest among the 20 largest U.S. cities in 1881 to the lowest by 1917.

1915   The Eastland, a lake excursion boat docked at the Clark Street bridge, rolled over while loaded with passengers; 812 died, 300 more than the Titanic. Dental services were provided in Chicago public schools after a 3-year introductory pilot program was funded by a local philanthropist. The Municipal Tuberculosis Sanitarium opened.

1916   A policy was initiated to hospitalize all cases of infantile paralysis (polio) after 34 of 254 afflicted patients died.

1917   The Municipal Contagious Disease Hospital was established. New health ordinances ranged from requiring the reporting

	and treatment of venereal diseases to requiring the screening of residence, stables, and barns against fleas. Immunization against diphtheria with von Behring's toxin-antitoxin started in public schools and institutions.
1918	Influenza became a reportable disease with the pandemic of influenza reaching Chicago, to cause 381 deaths on one day (October 17) alone.
1919	The department won its first case in the prosecution of landlords for failure to provide sufficient heat to tenants.
1920	The right of the department to quarantine carriers of contagion was upheld in the Superior Court of Cook County.
1922	A new health commissioner began a campaign against venereal disease, proposing education and distribution of prophylactic outfits in brothels; opposition from the medical profession was based more on moral than medical grounds.
1923	A committee was appointed on prenatal care in the first concerted effort to coordinate the activities of all agencies doing prenatal work in the city. Inspection of summer camps for children was inaugurated. Venereal disease clinics were established at the Cook County Jail and House of Correction.
1924	Venereal disease prevention literature was distributed to 500,000 homes in Chicago.
1925	The department instituted a regular schedule of home visits by nurses during the first 6 months of an infant's life. Conferences were inaugurated for care of preschool children. Installation of sanitary types of drinking fountains was ordered.
1927	The health commissioner was forced to resign when the mayor directed that the health department include political literature with information about baby care being distributed to all Chicago mothers.
1930	An intensive campaign against diphtheria resulted in 400,219 injections being given in 3 months.
1932	The staff of 300 nurses were carried throughout the city on buses to give diphtheria inoculations. Physicians were sent to the homes of mothers unable to take children to welfare stations for shots. After the campaign, cases dropped to 154 with nine deaths compared with 1,266 cases with 68 deaths the previous year.
1933	There is an outbreak of amebic dysentery among out-of-town guests who came to the Century of Progress (1,409 cases and 98 deaths scattered in 43 states, the Territory of Hawaii, and three Canadian provinces) in the first recognized waterborne epidemic of the disease in a civilian population. The cause was traced to water contamination through faulty plumbing.
1934	A plumbing survey for cross-connections in hotels and mercantile buildings was begun to prevent future amebic dysentery outbreaks. As a result of drinking from contaminated water supply at the Union Stock Yards fire on May 19, 69 persons contracted typhoid fever, 11 of whom died.

1935   An ordinance was passed requiring that only grade A milk and milk products could be sold in Chicago. A premature-infant welfare program was initiated. A mother's milk station started operating to supply breast milk to premature, sick, or debilitated infants whose parents could not afford this expense.

1936   Summer brought 210 deaths from sunstroke and exhaustion compared with 11 from the same cause in 1935. With 1,000 premature infants under supervision, two additional premature stations opened, making 31 conferences available each week.

1937   Chicago public schools opened 3 weeks late because of a polio scare. The Chicago Syphilis Control Project was established, with the emphasis on breaking the chain of infection.

1942   The Chicago Intensive Treatment Center for venereal disease launched an effort so successful that it won a War Department commendation in 1943 and recorded a declining venereal disease rate after World War II demobilization, in contrast to soaring rates in other large cities.

1946   The Chicago-Cook County health survey was undertaken by the U.S. Public Health Service, including an audit of all city and county facilities conducted by outside experts. Various recommendations were made, including more food inspection staff, establishment of district health centers, restructuring of the Board of Health with an executive director and deputies in charge of engineering, preventive medicine, and district health services.

1947   The mental health section for the health department was approved.

1948   A federal grant of $46,270 was made available through the state to subsidize a psychiatric program. A comprehensive food ordinance was adopted by the city council.

1952   Chicago counted 1,203 cases of polio, including 82 deaths and hundreds of persons with paralysis. Frightened parents kept their youngsters out of movies and swimming pools. Beaches closed. An insect and rodent control program started.

1955   Chicago was one of the first cities in the United States to introduce the Salk vaccine after it was pronounced safe and effective against the polio virus on April 12.

1956   With warning signs of an approaching polio epidemic, mass inoculations of Salk vaccine were given in all parts of the city, with department staff working in vacant stores, garages, and street corners, from the backs of trucks, and in park field houses. Chicago took the lead among major American cities in introducing a water fluoridation program, which reduced tooth decay among children.

1957   The Nursing Home Section and Hospital Inspection Unit was initiated.

1958   A section for chronic illness was activated, with mental health as one of its activities.

1959   The First Community Mental Health Center started on the south side.

1960   The Bureau of Institutional Care consolidated nursing home and hospital inspection services.

1961   The Division of Adult Health and Aging began consolidating activities of chronic diseases, cardiovascular diseases, diabetes, cervical cancer, rheumatic heart fever, and nutrition. A lead poison survey began on Chicago's West Side.

1962   The mental health division, with more than 15 community-based mental health centers, was established in the health department.

1965   Family planning was initiated in limited number of clinics.

1966   Testing for sickle cell was initiated; citywide lead poisoning screening and treatment began.

1968   Planning for Comprehensive Neighborhood Health Centers in four areas began in cooperation with the Chicago Model Cities program.

1970   First Model Cities Neighborhood Health Center opened in Uptown. A record 1.2 million inoculations were provided for Chicago children in immunization drive.

1973   Englewood Neighborhood Health Center opened. Forty hospitals were approved as trauma centers in accordance with state statute on emergency medical services.

1974   The Women, Infant, and Children supplemental nutrition program was initiated. Senior citizen clinic and new hypertension center opened while plans were unveiled to phase out the Tuberculosis Sanitarium.

1975   The city council revised the municipal code to delineate the duties of the nine-member board of health as a policy making body and the department of health as the agency administering health programs and enforcing regulations. Outpatient tuberculosis services were decentralized to five health centers.

1976   The health department formed interdisciplinary committee on child abuse with representatives from health, law enforcement, and welfare agencies.

1979   The first Hispanic health commissioner was appointed.

1981   The Chicago Alcohol Treatment Center came under the jurisdiction of the health department, only to be closed several years later with its funding used to support community-based providers of substance abuse treatment services. The refugee health program was initiated.

1983   The Chicago Area AIDS Task Force was established, and the health department created the AIDS Activity Office.

1984   The first African American health commissioner was appointed.

1984   The Partnerships in Health program was initiated with hospitals to ensure continuity of care for health department patients.

1985   The health department sponsored the city's first major pastoral conference on religion and health.

1986	An infant mortality reduction strategic plan was developed.

1986   An infant mortality reduction strategic plan was developed.

1987   The first child lead poisoning death in nearly a decade led to the establishment of the Mayor's Task Force on Lead Poisoning.

1989   The health department coordinated development of the Chicago AIDS Strategic Plan through a multidisciplinary advisory council of 125 individuals.

1990   The Chicago/Cook County Health Care Summit produced a plan to improve local delivery of health services, calling for ambulatory care reforms, restructuring of inpatient care, and changes in system financing. As a result, the Chicago and Cook County Ambulatory Care Council was established to assess health needs and undertake initiatives.

1991   The Epidemiology Office was established in the health department.

1993   The first woman and nonphysician health commissioner was appointed.

1995   Extreme heat conditions in Chicago during July resulted in 514 heat-related deaths. The Violence Prevention Office was established.

1997   The city council passed the Managed Care Consumer Protection ordinance, calling for the health department to create the Office of Managed Care—the nation's first municipal effort to monitor the managed care industry.

1998   The health department coordinated the development of the Chicago Violence Prevention Strategic Plan, developed by more than 150 participants.

1999   The Chicago Turning Point Partnership convened to develop a plan to strengthen the public health infrastructure in Chicago.

2001   The Bioterrorism Preparedness unit was established.

2002   The health department received its first federal grant for bioterrorism preparedness and response.

2003   Chicago participated in national bioterrorism response exercise involving top officials of city, state, and federal government.

Sources: Data from Chicago Department of Health. *150 Years of Municipal Health Care in the City of Chicago: Board of Health, Department of Health 1835–1985*. Chicago, IL: Chicago Department of Health; 1985. Bonner TN. Medicine in Chicago: 1850–1950. In: *The Social and Scientific Development of a City*. Urbana, IL: University of Illinois Press; 1991. Rawlings ID. *The Rise and Fall of Disease in Illinois*. Springfield, IL: Illinois Department of Public Health; 1927.

Public Health Spotlight on the Control of Infectious Diseases

Prior to 1900, infectious diseases represented the most serious threat to the health of populations in the United States and across the globe. The 20th century witnessed a dramatic shift in the balance of power in the centuries-long battle between humans and microorganisms. Advances in both science and social values contributed to the assault on microbes, setting into motion the forces of organized community efforts to improve the health of the public. This approach served as a model for later public health initiatives targeting other major threats to health and well-being. This Public Health Spotlight examines this achievement as well as the unfinished agenda that lies ahead in the early decades of the 21st century.

PUBLIC HEALTH ACHIEVEMENTS IN 20TH CENTURY AMERICA[1,2]

Before 1900, infectious diseases represented the most serious threat to the health of populations across the globe. The 20th century witnessed a dramatic shift in the balance of power in the centuries-long battle between humans and microorganisms. Changes in both science and social values contributed to the assault on microbes, setting into motion the forces of organized community efforts to improve the health of the public. This approach served as a model for later public health initiatives targeting other major threats to health and well-being.

Deaths from infectious diseases declined markedly in the United States during the 20th century (Figure 1-4). This decline contributed to a sharp drop in infant and child mortality[3,4] and to the 29.2-year increase in life expectancy.[4] In 1900, 30.4% of all deaths occurred among children less than 5 years old; in 1997, that percentage was only 1.4%. In 1900, the three leading causes of death were pneumonia, tuberculosis, and diarrhea and enteritis, which (together with diphtheria) caused one third of all deaths. Of these deaths, 40% were among children less than 5 years old.[3] In 1997, heart disease and cancers accounted for 54.7% of all deaths, with 4.5% attributable to pneumonia, influenza, and HIV infection.[4] Despite this overall progress, one of the most devastating epidemics in human history occurred during the 20th century—the 1918 influenza pandemic that resulted in 20 million deaths, including 500,000 in the United States, in less than 1 year. These total more than have died in as short a time during any war or famine in the world.[5] HIV infection, first recognized in 1981, has caused a pandemic that is still in progress, affecting 33 million people

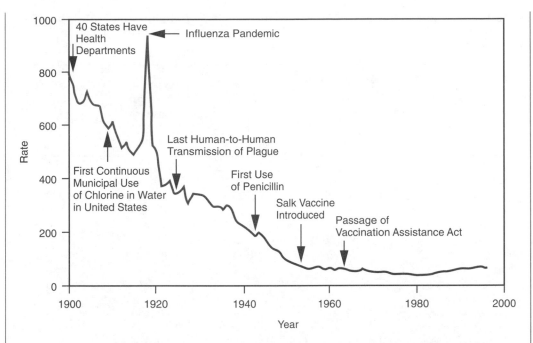

Figure 1-4 Crude death rate (per 100,000) for infectious diseases, United States, 1900–1996. *Source:* From Centers for Disease Control and Prevention. Public health achievements, United States, 1900–1999: control of infectious diseases. *MMWR.* 1999;48:621–629.

and causing an estimated 13.9 million deaths.[6] These episodes illustrate the volatility of infectious disease death rates and the unpredictability of disease emergence.

Public health action to control infectious diseases is based on the 19th century discovery of microorganisms as the cause of many serious diseases (e.g., cholera and tuberculosis). Disease control resulted from improvements in sanitation and hygiene, the discovery of antibiotics, and the implementation of universal childhood vaccination programs. Scientific and technologic advances played a major role in each of these areas and are the foundation for today's disease surveillance and control systems. Scientific findings also have contributed to a new understanding of the evolving relation between humans and microbes.[7]

At the beginning of the 20th century, infectious diseases were widely prevalent in the United States and exacted an enormous toll on the population (Table 1-9). In 1900, for example, 21,064 smallpox cases were reported, and 894 patients died.[8] In 1920, there were 469,924 measles cases reported, and 7,575 patients died; 147,991 diphtheria cases were reported, and 13,170 patients died. In 1922, the total number of pertussis cases reported was 107,473, and 5,099 patients died.[9,10]

The 19th century shift in population from country to city that accompanied industrialization and immigration led to overcrowding in

Table 1-9   Baseline 20th Century Annual Morbidity, 2005 Morbidity, and 2010 Targets for Nine Diseases with Vaccines Recommended Before 1990 for Universal Use for Children, United States

	Baseline 20th Century Annual Morbidity	2007 Morbidity	Percentage Decrease Baseline 20th Century to 2007	2010 Target
Smallpox	48,164	0	100%	0
Diphtheria	175,885	0	100%	0
Pertussis	147,271	10,454	92.9%	2,000
Tetanus	1,314	28	97.9%	0
Poliomyelitis (paralytic)	16,316	0	100%	0
Measles	503,282	43	100%	0
Mumps	152,209	800	99.5%	0
Rubella	47,745	12	100%	0
Congenital rubella syndrome	823	0	99.9%	0
Haemophilus influenzae type b infection (children <5 yrs)	20,000	226	98.9%	0

Sources: Data from Centers for Disease Control and Prevention. Public health achievements, United States, 1900–1999: impact of vaccines universally recommended for children. *MMWR*. 1999;48: 243–248; Centers for Disease Control and Prevention. Summary of notifiable diseases, United States, 2009. *MMWR*. 2009;56(53):1–94; and U.S. Department of Health and Human Services, Office of Disease Prevention and Health Promotion. *Healthy People 2010: Understanding and Improving Health*. Rockville, MD: ODPHP; 2000.

poor housing served by inadequate or nonexistent public water supplies and waste-disposal systems. These conditions resulted in repeated outbreaks of cholera, dysentery, tuberculosis, typhoid fever, influenza, yellow fever, and malaria.

By 1900, however, the incidence of many of these diseases had begun to decline because of public health improvements, implementation of which continued into the 20th century. Local, state, and federal efforts to improve sanitation and hygiene reinforced the concept of collective "public health" action (e.g., to prevent infection by providing clean drinking water). By 1900, of the 45 states, 40 had established health departments. The first county health departments were established in 1908.[11] From the 1930s through the 1950s, state and local health departments made substantial progress in disease prevention activities, including sewage disposal, water treatment, food safety, organized solid waste disposal, and public education about hygienic practices (e.g., food handling and hand washing). Chlorination and other treatments of drinking water began in the early 1900s and became widespread public health practices, further decreasing the incidence of water-borne diseases. The incidence of tuberculosis also declined as improvements in housing reduced crowding and tuberculosis control programs were initiated. In 1900, of every 100,000 U.S. residents, 194 died from tuberculosis; most were residents of urban areas. In 1940 (before the introduction of antibiotic therapy), tuberculosis remained a leading cause of death, but the crude death rate had decreased to 46 per 100,000 persons.[12]

Animal and pest control also contributed to disease reduction. Nationally sponsored, state-coordinated vaccination and animal-control programs eliminated dog-to-dog transmission of rabies. Malaria, once endemic throughout the southeastern United States, was reduced to negligible levels by the late 1940s; regional mosquito-control programs played an important role in these efforts. Plague also diminished; the U.S. Marine Hospital Service (which later became the Public Health Service) led quarantine and ship inspection activities and rodent- and vector-control operations. The last major rat-associated outbreak of plague in the United States occurred during 1924 to 1925 in Los Angeles. This outbreak included the last identified instance of human-to-human transmission of plague (through inhalation of infectious respiratory droplets from coughing patients) in this country.

In 1900, few effective treatment and preventive measures existed to prevent infectious diseases. Although the first vaccine against smallpox was developed in 1796, more than 100 years later, its use had not been widespread enough to control the disease fully.[13] Four other vaccines—against rabies, typhoid, cholera, and plague—had been developed late in the 19th century but were not used widely by 1900.

Between 1900 and 2000, vaccines were developed or licensed against 21 other diseases.[14] Ten of these vaccines have been recommended for use only in selected populations at high risk because of area of residence, age, medical condition, or risk behaviors. The other 11 have been recommended for use in all U.S. children.[15]

During the 20th century, substantial achievements have been made in the control of many vaccine-preventable diseases. Smallpox has been eradicated. Poliomyelitis caused by wild-type viruses has been eliminated, and measles and *Haemophilus influenzae* type b invasive disease among children aged less than 5 years old have been reduced to record low numbers of cases.

National efforts to promote vaccine use among all children began with the appropriation of federal funds for polio vaccination after introduction of the vaccine in 1955.[14] Since then, federal, state, and local governments and public and private healthcare providers have collaborated to develop and maintain the vaccine-delivery system in the United States. Dramatic declines in morbidity have been reported for the nine vaccine-preventable diseases for which vaccination was universally recommended for use in children before 1990 (excluding hepatitis B, rotavirus, and varicella). Morbidity associated with smallpox and polio caused by wild-type viruses has declined 100% and nearly 100% for each of the other seven diseases.

Penicillin was developed into a widely available medical product that provided quick and complete treatment of previously incurable bacterial illnesses, with a wider range of targets and fewer side effects than sulfa drugs. Discovered fortuitously in 1928, penicillin was not developed for medical use until the 1940s, when it was produced in substantial quantities and used by the U.S. military to treat sick and wounded soldiers.

Technologic changes that increased capacity for detecting, diagnosing, and monitoring infectious diseases included development early in the century of serologic testing and, more recently, the development of molecular assays based on nucleic acid and antibody probes. The use of computers and electronic forms of communication enhanced the ability to gather, analyze, and disseminate disease surveillance data.

During the last quarter of the 20th century, molecular biology has provided powerful new tools to detect and characterize infectious pathogens. The use of nucleic acid hybridization and sequencing techniques has made it possible to characterize the causative agents of previously unknown diseases (e.g., hepatitis C, human ehrlichiosis, hantavirus pulmonary syndrome, AIDS, and Nipah virus disease). Molecular tools have enhanced capacity to track the transmission of new threats and find new ways to prevent and treat them. Had AIDS emerged 100 years ago, when laboratory-based diagnostic methods were in their infancy, the disease might have remained a mysterious syndrome for many decades. Moreover, the drugs used to treat HIV-infected persons and prevent perinatal transmission (e.g., replication analogues and protease inhibitors) were developed based on a modern understanding of retroviral replication at the molecular level.

21ST CENTURY PUBLIC HEALTH CHALLENGES

Success in reducing morbidity and mortality from infectious diseases during the first three quarters of the 20th century placed infectious disease control low on the public agenda in the 1980s and 1990s, but then the HIV/AIDS epidemic appeared and tuberculosis reemerged with multidrug-resistant strains resulting in an overall increase in infectious disease mortality. It soon became clear that new diseases will appear because microbes can evolve. This underscores the importance of disease prevention through continual monitoring of underlying factors that may encourage the emergence or reemergence of diseases. With advances in molecular genetics came a new appreciation of the remarkable ability of microbes to evolve, adapt, and develop drug resistance in an unpredictable and dynamic fashion.

Reemergence of infectious diseases, however, has not been limited only to uncommon microorganisms. This phenomenon also occurs with common childhood infections for which immunizations have been remarkably effective in reducing infections to such levels that the occurrence of a few thousand cases of mumps in 2006 was regarded as a significant public health event (Figure 1-5).

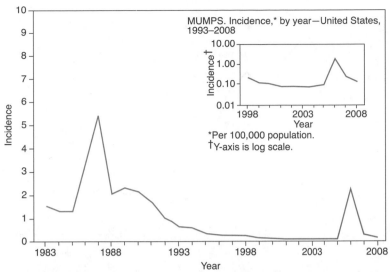

Figure 1-5 Mumps incidence (per 100,000 population), by year, United States, 1983–2008. *Source:* From Centers for Disease Control and Prevention. Summary of notifiable diseases, United States, 2008. *MMWR.* 2010;57(54):1–94. http://www.cdc.gov/mmwr/preview/mmwrhtml/mm5754a1.htm. Accessed July 6, 2010.

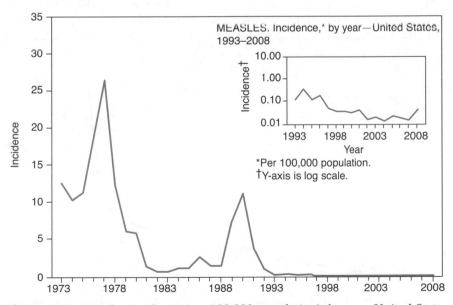

Figure 1-6 Measles incidence (per 100,000 population), by year, United States, 1973–2008. *Source:* From Centers for Disease Control and Prevention. Summary of notifiable diseases, United States, 2008. *MMWR.* 2010;57(54):1–94. http://www.cdc.gov/mmwr/preview/mmwrhtml/mm5754a1.htm. Accessed July 6, 2010.

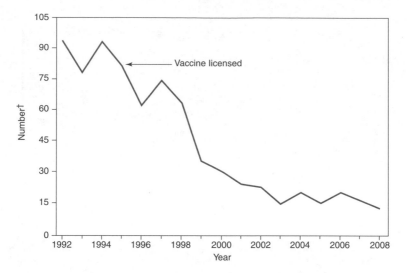

Figure 1-7 Varicella (chickenpox). Number of reported cases, Illinois, Michigan, Texas, and West Virginia*, 1992–2008.

*These four states maintained consistent and adequate surveillance by reporting cases constituting ≥5% of their birth cohort during 1990–1995 (*Source*: CDC. National Immunization Program 1994–2005).

† in thousands

Source: From Centers for Disease Control and Prevention. Summary of notifiable diseases, United States, 2008. *MMWR*. 2010;57(54):1–94. http://www.cdc.gov/mmwr/preview/mmwrhtml/mm5754a1.htm. Accessed July 6, 2010. Data from National Center for Immunization and Respiratory Diseases.

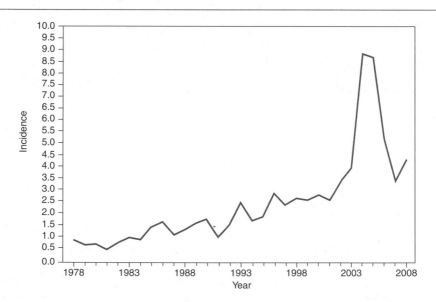

Figure 1-8 Pertussis incidence (per 100,000 population) by year, United States, 1978–2008. *Source:* From Centers for Disease Control and Prevention. Summary of notifiable diseases, United States, 2008. *MMWR*. 2010;57(54):1–94. http://www.cdc.gov/mmwr/preview/mmwrhtml/mm5754a1.htm. Accessed July 6, 2010.

Vigilance remains a critical component of today's arsenal to combat infectious disease threats, including the emergence of new infectious diseases, the reemergence of old diseases (sometimes in drug-resistant forms), large food-borne outbreaks, and acts of bioterrorism. Continuous surveillance and outbreak response capacity at all levels, combined with ongoing research into causes and countermeasures, comprise our 21st century challenges for controlling infectious diseases.

Vaccines and immunizations have been potent weapons in the war against infectious diseases. Figures 1-6 and 1-7 demonstrate reductions in the incidence of measles and chickenpox in recent decades. Figure 1-8 highlights recent trends for pertussis, a persistent infectious disease, to say the least.

The Task Force on Community Preventive Services' systematic reviews of the effectiveness of selected population-based interventions (see Chapter 7) focused on strategies aimed at improving coverage of universally recommended vaccines in children, adolescents, and adults and targeted vaccines for high-risk populations. The task force found strong evidence of the effectiveness of several population-based interventions, while other interventions lacked sufficient evidence or reviews were pending as of June 2010.[16]

Strategies examined included increasing access to vaccination services, increasing community demand for vaccinations, and expanded provider- or system-based interventions. For universally recommended vaccines for all individuals in a specified age range, the Task Force on Community Preventive Services rated the following community-oriented interventions as effective and evidence based:

- Home visits to increase vaccination coverage
- Multicomponent interventions for expanding access in healthcare settings
- Reducing client out-of-pocket costs
- Vaccination programs in schools
- Vaccination programs in Women, Infants, and Children settings
- Client reminder and recall systems
- Multicomponent interventions that include education
- Vaccination requirements for child-care, school, and college attendance
- Provider assessment and feedback when used alone
- Provider reminder systems when used alone
- Standing orders when used alone

For targeted vaccine coverage for individuals at higher risk of contracting a specific disease, the Task Force on Community Preventive Services classified the following community-oriented interventions as effective and evidence based:

- Multiple interventions implemented in combination
- Provider reminder systems when used alone
- Vaccination programs in schools and organized child-care settings

The U.S. agenda for disease prevention and health promotion included in the Healthy People 2020 effort (see Chapter 2) identifies immunizations

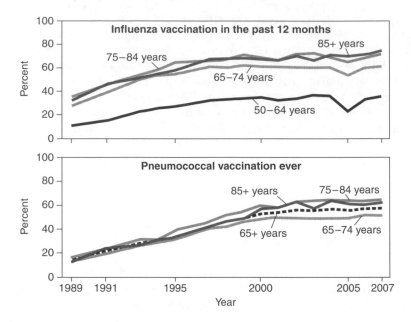

Figure 1-9 Influenza and pneumococcal vaccinations among adults. *Source:* From Centers for Disease Control and Prevention, National Center for Health Statistics. *Health, United States 2009*, Figure 9. Hyattsville, MD: NCHS; 2009. Data from the National Health Interview Survey.

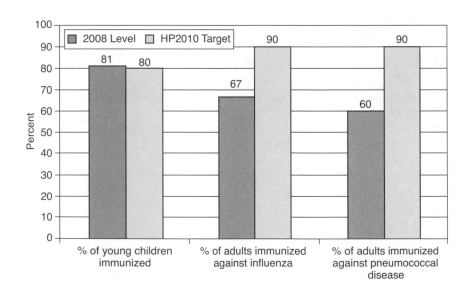

Figure 1-10 Scorecard for selected Healthy People 2010 leading indicators for immunizations comparing 2008 levels with 2010 targets. *Source:* Data from Data 2010, Healthy People 2010 database. http://wonder.cdc.gov/data2010/ftpselec .htm. Accessed May 31, 2010.

and infectious disease control as a continuing national health priority. Leading indicators for this priority focus on both childhood and adult immunizations. Figure 1-9 traces progress toward the year 2010 adult immunization targets, which were set at 90% for the 65 and older population for both influenza and pneumococcal vaccinations. Figure 1-10 demonstrates the gap between achieved levels and the year 2010 targets for adult immunizations and the achievement of the target for childhood immunizations. Together these figures suggest the war against infectious disease threats continues into the second decade of the 21st century.

REFERENCES

1. Reprinted in part and adapted from Centers for Disease Control and Prevention. Achievements in public health, 1900–1999: control of infectious diseases. *MMWR.* 1999;48:621–629.

2. Reprinted in part and adapted from Centers for Disease Control and Prevention. Achievements in public health, 1900–1999; impact of vaccines universally recommended for children. *MMWR.* 1999;48:243–248.

3. Department of Commerce and Labor, Bureau of the Census. *Mortality Statistics, 1900 to 1904.* Washington, DC: U.S. Department of Commerce and Labor; 1906.

4. Hoyert DL, Kochanek KD, Murphy SL. *Deaths: Final Data for 1997.* Hyattsville, MD: U.S. Department of Health and Human Services, Public Health Service, Centers for Disease Control, National Center for Health Statistics, 1999. (National vital statistics reports, vol 47, no 19).

5. Crosby AW Jr. *Epidemic and Peace, 1918.* Westport, CT: Greenwood Press; 1976:311.

6. United Nations Program on HIV/AIDS and World Health Organization. *AIDS Epidemic Update: December 1998.* Geneva, Switzerland: World Health Organization; 1999.

7. Lederberg J, Shope RE, Oaks SC Jr, eds. *Microbial Threats to Health in the United States.* Washington, DC: National Academy Press; 1992.

8. Fenner F, Henderson DA, Arita I, et al. *Smallpox and Its Eradication.* Geneva, Switzerland: World Health Organization; 1988.

9. U.S. Department of Health, Education, and Welfare. *Vital Statistics—Special Report, National Summaries: Reported Incidence of Selected Notifiable Diseases, United States, Each Division and State, 1920–50.* Washington, DC: U.S. Department of Health, Education, and Welfare, Public Health Service, National Office of Vital Statistics; 1953:37.

10. U.S. Department of Health, Education, and Welfare. *Vital Statistics Rates in the United States, 1940–1960.* Washington, DC: U.S. Department of Health, Education, and Welfare, Public Health Service, National Center for Health Statistics; 1968.

11. Hinman A. 1889 to 1989: a century of health and disease. *Public Health Rep.* 1990;105:374–380.

12. National Office of Vital Statistics. *Vital Statistics—Special Reports, Death Rates by Age, Race, and Sex, United States, 1900–1953: Tuberculosis, All Forms* (vol 43, no 2). Washington, DC: U.S. Department of Health, Education, and Welfare; 1956.

13. Centers for Disease Control and Prevention. Reported morbidity and mortality in the United States, 1970. *MMWR.* 1971;19:1–74.

14. Centers for Disease Control and Prevention. Provisional cases of selected notifiable diseases, United States, cumulative, week ending January 2, 1999 (52nd week). *MMWR.* 1999;47:1125.

15. Centers for Disease Control and Prevention. Provisional cases of selected notifiable diseases preventable by vaccination, United States, weeks ending January 2, 1999, and December 27, 1997 (52nd week). *MMWR.* 1999;47:1128–1129.

16. Task Force on Community Preventive Services. *The Community Guide.* http://www.thecommunityguide.org. Accessed May 31, 2010.

Health from an Ecological Perspective

The 21st century began much as its predecessor did, with immense opportunities to advance the public's health through actions to ensure conditions favorable for health and quality of life. All systems direct their efforts toward certain outcomes; they track progress by ensuring that these outcomes are clearly defined and measurable. In public health, this calls for clear definitions and measures of health and quality of life in populations. That task is the focus of this chapter. Key questions to be addressed are as follows:

- What is health?
- What factors influence health and illness?

- How can health status and quality of life be measured?
- What do current measures tell us about the health status and quality of life of Americans in the early decades of the 21st century?
- How can this information be used to develop effective public health interventions and public policy?

The relevance of these questions resides in their focus on factors that cause or influence particular health outcomes. Efforts to identify and measure key aspects of health and factors influencing health have relied on traditional approaches over the past century, although there are signs that this pattern may be changing. The key questions listed above are addressed slightly out of order, for reasons that should become apparent as we proceed.

HEALTH IN THE UNITED STATES

Many important indicators of health status in the United States have improved considerably over the past century, although there is evidence that health status could be even better than it is. At the turn of the 20th century, nearly 2% of the U.S. population died each year. The crude mortality rate in 1900 was about 1,700 deaths per 100,000 population. Life expectancy at birth was 47 years. Additional life expectancy at the age of 65 years was another 12 years. Medicine and health care were largely proprietary in 1900 and of questionable benefit to health. More extensive information on the health status of the population at that time would be useful, but very little exists.

Indicators of health status improved in the United States throughout the 20th century.[1] Between 1900 and 2000, the crude mortality rate was cut nearly in half to 854 per 100,000. By the year 2000, life expectancy at birth was nearly 77 years, and life expectancy at 65 years old was another 18 years.

The leading causes of death also changed dramatically over the 20th century, as demonstrated in Figure 2-1. In 1900, the leading causes of death were influenza and pneumonia, tuberculosis, diarrhea and related diseases, heart disease, liver disease, stroke, chronic nephritis, accidents, cancer, perinatal conditions, and diphtheria. By the year 2000, tuberculosis, gastroenteritis, and diphtheria dropped off the list of the top 10 killers, and deaths from influenza and pneumonia fell from first to seventh position on the list. Diseases of aging and other chronic conditions superseded these infectious disease processes, as changes in the age structure of the population, especially the increase in persons over age 65 years, resulted in higher overall crude rates for heart disease and cancer and the appearance of diabetes, Alzheimer's disease, chronic kidney conditions, and septicemia on the modern list of the top 10 killers.

Changes in crude death rates, however, only partly explain the gains in life expectancy realized for all age groups over the 20th century. On an age-adjusted basis, improvements were even more impressive. Age-adjusted mortality rates fell about 75% between 1900 and 2000. Over the course of the entire 20th century, infant and child mortality rates fell 95%. Adolescent and young adult mortality rates dropped 80%. Rates for adults aged 25 to 64 years fell 60%, and rates for older adults (older than 65 years) declined 35%.

During the second half of the 20th century, overall age-adjusted mortality rates fell about 50% (see Figure 2-2), whereas infant mortality rates declined

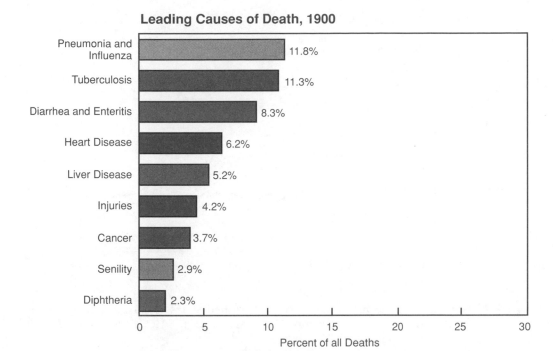

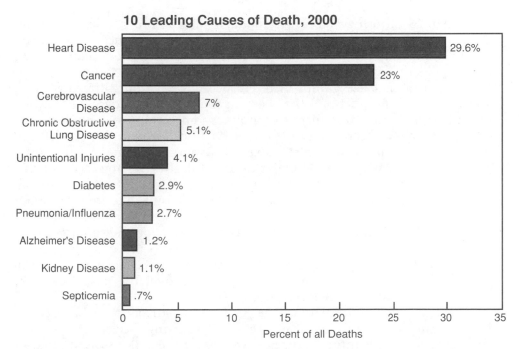

Figure 2-1 The 10 leading causes of death as a percentage of all deaths in the United States, 1900 and 2000. *Sources:* From U.S. Dept. of Health and Human Services, Office of Disease Prevention and Health Promotion. *Healthy People 2010: Understanding and Improving Health.* Rockville, MD: ODPHP; 2000 and Centers for Disease Control and Prevention, National Center for Health Statistics. *Health, United States, 2002.* Hyattsville, MD: NCHS; 2002.

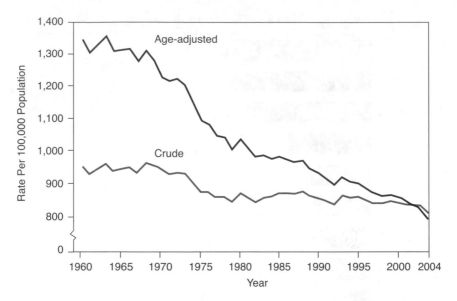

Figure 2-2   Crude and age-adjusted mortality rates, United States, 1960–2004. *Source:* From Centers for Disease Control and Prevention, National Center for Health Statistics, *Health, United States, 2006*. Hyattsville MD: NCHS; 2006.

more than 75%. During that period, mortality rates among children and young adults (ages 1 to 24 years) and adults 45 to 64 years were reduced by more than one half. Mortality rates among adults 25 to 44 years fell more than 40%, and rates for older persons (65 years old and older) fell about one third.

Gains for adult age groups in recent decades have outstripped those for younger age groups, a trend that began about 1960 as progress accelerated toward reduction of mortality from injuries and certain major chronic diseases that largely affected adults (earlier reductions for children also left little room for further improvements). Table 2-1 demonstrates changes in the age-adjusted frequency of selected major causes of death over the second half of the 20th century. Dramatic reductions in the death rates for heart disease, stroke, unintentional injuries, influenza and pneumonia, and infant mortality have been joined by more recent reductions in rates for human immunodeficiency virus (HIV) infections, liver diseases, and suicide. Age-adjusted death rates have increased for diabetes, Alzheimer's disease, and chronic lung and kidney conditions, signaling the new morbidities associated with longer life spans. Homicide rates have improved somewhat over the past decade, but they reflect a substantial increase since 1950.

Table 2-1 also demonstrates the considerable disparities that exist for many of the major causes of death. Differences among races are notable, but there are also significant differences by gender for the various causes of death. These differences are often dramatic and run from top to bottom through the chain of causation. Disparities are found not only in indicators of poor health outcomes, such as mortality, but also in the levels of risk factors in the population groups most severely affected. A poignant example of these disparities

Table 2-1   Year 2000 Age-Adjusted Death Rates (Per 100,000 Population) for Selected
Leading Causes of Death, Percentage of All 2000 Deaths, Percentage Rate Change from 1950
to 2000, and 2000 Ratio by Gender and Race, United States

Cause of Death	Percentage of 2000 Deaths	Year 2000 Rate*	Percentage Change in Rates* 1950 to 2000	Male to Female 2000 Rate* Ratio	Black to White 2000 Rate* Ratio
Diseases of the heart	29.6	257.9	−56.0	1.5	1.3
Malignant neoplasms	23.0	201.0	−3.7	1.5	1.3
Cerebrovascular disease	7.0	60.8	−66.4	1.0	1.4
Chronic lung disease	5.1	44.3	x	1.4	0.7
Accidents and adverse effects	4.1	35.5	−54.5	2.3	1.1
Diabetes	2.9	25.2	−9.1	1.2	2.2
Influenza and pneumonia	2.7	23.7	−50.7	1.3	1.1
Suicide	1.2	10.6	−19.7	4.5	0.5
Chronic liver disease and cirrhosis	1.1	9.6	−15.0	2.2	1.0
Homicide	0.7	6.1	−19.6	3.3	5.7

*Rates age-adjusted to the 2000 U.S. population.

x = 1950 comparison rate not available, although believed to be much lower than 2000 rate.

Source: From National Center for Health Statistics. *Health, United States, 2002*. Hyattsville, MD:
NCHS; 2002.

is reflected in the 12-year difference in life expectancy between white females
and African American males.

There is also evidence that health is improving and that disability levels
are declining in the population over time. Disability levels among individuals
aged 55 to 70 years who were offspring of the famous Framingham Heart
Study cohort were substantially lower in comparison with their parents' experience at the same age.[2] In addition, fewer offspring had chronic diseases or
perceived their health as fair or poor. Self-reported health status and activity
limitations caused by chronic conditions changed little during the 1990s, and
injuries with lost workdays steadily declined during the 1990s.

In summary, U.S. health indicators tell two very different tales. By many
measures, the American population has never been healthier. By others, much
more needs to be done for specific racial, ethnic, and gender groups. The gains
in health status over the past century have not been shared equally by all subgroups of the population. In fact, relative differences have been increasing.
This widening gap in health status creates both a challenge and a dilemma for
future health improvement efforts. The greatest gains can be made through
closing these gaps and equalizing health status within the population. Nevertheless, the burden of greater risk and poorer health status resides in a relatively small part of the total population, calling for efforts that target those
minorities with increased resources. An alternative approach is to continue

current strategies and resource deployment levels. Although this may continue the steady overall improvement among all groups in the population, it is likely to continue or worsen existing gaps. In the early years of the new century, the major health challenge facing the United States appears to be less related to the need to improve population-wide health outcomes than the need to eliminate or reduce disparities. This challenges the nation's commitment to its principles of equality and social justice; however, addressing inequalities in measures of health and quality of life requires a greater understanding of health and the measures used to describe it than afforded by death rates and life expectancies.

HEALTH, ILLNESS, AND DISEASE

The relationship between health outcomes and the factors that influence them is complex, often confounded by different understandings of the concepts in question and how they are measured. Health is difficult to define and more difficult yet to measure. For much of history, the notion of health has been negative. This was due in part to the continuous onslaught of epidemic diseases. With disease a frequent visitor, health became the disease-free state. One was healthy by exclusion.

As knowledge of disease increased and methods of prevention and control improved, however, health was more commonly considered from a positive perspective. The World Health Organization (WHO) seized this opportunity in its 1946 constitution, defining health as not merely the absence of disease but a state of complete physical, mental, and social well-being.[3] This definition of health emphasizes that there are different, complexly related forms of wellness and illness, and suggests that a wide range of factors can influence the health of individuals and groups. It also suggests that health is not an absolute.

Although health and well-being may be synonyms, health and disease are not necessarily opposites. Most people view health and illness as existing along a continuum and as opposite and mutually exclusive states; however, this simplistic, one-dimensional model of health and illness does not comport very well with the real world. A person can have a disease or injury and still be healthy or at least feel well. There are many examples, but certainly Olympic wheelchair racers would fit into this category. It is also possible for someone without a specific disease or injury to feel ill or not well. If health and illness are not mutually exclusive, then they exist in separate dimensions, with wellness and illness in one dimension and the presence or absence of disease or injury in another.

These distinctions are important because disease is a relatively objective, pathologic phenomenon, whereas wellness and illness represent subjective experiences. This allows for several different states to exist: wellness without disease or injury, wellness with disease or injury, illness with disease or injury, and illness without physical disease or injury. This multidimensional view of health states is consistent with the WHO delineation of physical, mental, and social dimensions of health or well-being. Health or wellness is more than the absence of disease alone. Furthermore, one can be physically but not mentally and socially well.

With health measurable in several different dimensions, the question arises as to whether there is some maximum or optimal end point of health or well-being, or perhaps health is a state that can always be improved through changes in its physical, mental, and social facets. Should the goal of health policies be a minimal acceptable level of health, rather than a state of complete and absolute health? In part because of these considerations, WHO revised its definition in 1978, calling for a level of health that permits people to lead socially and economically productive lives.[4] This shifts the focus of health from an end in itself to a resource for everyday life, linking physical to personal and social capacities. It also suggests that it will be easier to identify measures of illness than of health.

Disease and injury are often viewed as phenomena that may lead to significant loss or disability in social functioning, making one unable to carry out one's main personal or social functions in life, such as parenting, schooling, or employment. In this perspective, health is equivalent to the absence of disability; individuals able to carry out their basic functions in life are healthy. This characterization of health as the absence of significant functional disabilities is perhaps the most common one for this highly sought state. Still, this definition is negative in that it defines health as the absence of some undesirable state.

In attempting to measure health, both quantity and quality become important considerations. It is not always easy to answer the questions, however: How much? Compared with what? For example, physical health for a 10-year-old child carries a much different expectation than physical health for an 80-year-old. It is reasonable to conclude that the natural processes of aging lead to gradual diminution of functional reserve capacity and that this is normal and not easily prevented. Thus, our perceptions of normal functioning are influenced by social and cultural factors.

The concept of well-being advanced in the WHO definition goes beyond the physical aspects of health that are the usual focus of measurements and comparisons. Including the mental and social aspects of well-being or health legitimizes the examination of factors that affect mental and social health. Together, these themes suggest that we need to consider carefully what we are measuring in order to understand what these measures are telling us about health, illness, and disease states in a population and the factors that influence these outcomes.

MEASURING HEALTH

The availability of information on health outcomes suggests that measuring the health status of populations is a simple task; however, although often interesting and sometimes even dramatic, the commonly used measures of health status fail to paint a complete picture of health. Many of the reasons are obvious. The commonly used measures actually reflect disease and mortality, rather than health itself. The long-standing misperception that health is the absence of disease is reinforced by the relative ease of measuring disease states, in comparison with states of health. Actually, the most commonly used indicators focus on a state that is neither health nor disease—namely, death.

Despite the many problems with using mortality as a proxy for health, mortality data are generally available and widely used to describe the health status of populations. This is ironic because such data only indirectly describe the health status of living populations. Unfortunately, data on morbidity (illnesses, injuries, and functional limitations of the population) are neither as available nor as readily understood as are mortality data. This situation is improving, however, as new forms and sources of information on health conditions become more readily available. Sources for information on morbidities and disabilities now include medical records from hospitals, managed care organizations, and other providers, as well as information derived from surveys, businesses, schools, and other sources. Assessments of the health status of populations are increasingly using measures from these sources. Chapter 6 identifies a variety of useful data and information sources for public health practice. An excellent compilation of data and information on both health status and health services, *Health, United States*,[1] is published annually by the Centers for Disease Control and Prevention (CDC), National Center for Health Statistics. Many of the data used in this chapter are derived from this source.

Mortality-Based Measures

Although mortality-based indicators of health status are both widely used and useful, there are some important differences in their use and interpretation. The most commonly used are crude mortality, age-specific and age-adjusted mortality, life expectancy, and years of potential life lost (YPLL). Although all are based on the same events, each provides somewhat different insights as to the health status of a population.

Crude mortality rates count deaths within the entire population and are not sensitive to differences in the age distribution of different populations. The mortality comparisons presented in Figure 2-2 illustrate the limitations of using crude death rates to compare the mortality experience of the U.S. population late in the 20th century with that of the year 1950. On the basis of these data, we might conclude that mortality rates in the United States had declined about 20% since 1950; however, because there was a greater proportion of the late 20th century population in the higher age categories, these are not truly comparable populations. The 20% reduction actually understates the differences in mortality experience over the 20th century. Because differences in the age characteristics of the two populations are a primary concern, we look for methods to correct or adjust for the age factor. Age-specific and age-adjusted rates do just that.

Age-specific mortality rates relate the number of deaths to the number of persons in a specific age group. The infant mortality rate is probably the best known example, describing the number of deaths of live-born infants occurring in the first year of life per 1,000 live births. Public health studies often use age-adjusted mortality rates to compensate for different mixes of age groups within a population (e.g., a high proportion of children or older persons). Age-adjusted rates are calculated by applying age-specific rates to a standard population (we now use the 2000 U.S. population). This adjustment permits more meaningful comparisons of mortality experience between populations with different age distribution patterns. Differences between crude and age-adjusted mortality rates can be substantial, such as those in Figure 2-2. The explanation is simply that the population at the end of the 20th century had a greater proportion of persons in older age groups than the 1900 or 1950 populations. Using crude rates, the improvement between 1950 and 2000 was about 20%; age-adjusted rates showed a 40% improvement. This 50-year period witnessed decreases of 50% or more for age-adjusted mortality rates for stroke, heart disease, infant deaths, tuberculosis, influenza and pneumonia, syphilis, unintentional injuries, HIV infections, gastric cancer, and uterine and cervical cancer. Figure 2-3 demonstrates that improvements in age-adjusted mortality rates for five leading causes of death are continuing in the early years of the new century.

Life expectancy, also based on the mortality experience of a population, is a computation of the number of years between any given age (e.g., birth or age of 65 years) and the average age of death for that population. Figure 2-4 provides recent data on life expectancy at birth and age 65 in the United States. Together with infant mortality rates, life expectancies are commonly used in comparisons of health status among nations. These two mortality-based indicators are often perceived as general indicators of the overall health status of a population. Infant mortality and life expectancy measures for the United States are mediocre in comparison with those of other developed nations. Figure 2-5 presents international comparisons of life expectancy by gender for the United States and selected other countries for 2004.

YPLL is a mortality-based indicator that places greater weight on deaths that occur at younger ages. Years of life lost before some arbitrary age (often

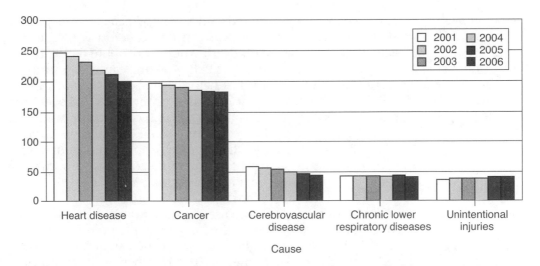

Figure 2-3 Age-adjusted death rates (per 1,000,000 standard population) for the five leading causes of death, United States, 2001–2006. *Source:* From Centers for Disease Control and Prevention. Age-adjusted death rates for the five leading causes of death, United States, 2001–2006. *MMWR.* 2008;57(24):666. Data from Heron M, Hoyert DL, Xu J, Scott C, Tejada B. Deaths: preliminary data for 2006. *Natl Vital Stat Rep.* 2008;56(16). http://www.cdc.gov/nchs/data/nvsr/nvsr56/nvsr56_16.pdf

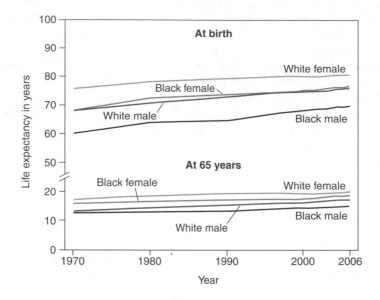

Figure 2-4 Life expectancy at birth and at age 65 years by race and gender, United States, 1970–2006. *Source:* From Centers for Disease Control and Prevention, National Center for Health Statistics. *Health, United States, 2009*, Figure 16. Hyattsville, MD: NCHS; 2009. Data from the National Vital Statistics System.

the age of 65 or 75 years) are computed and used to measure the relative impact on society of different causes of death. If 65 years old is used as the threshold for calculating YPLL, an infant death would contribute 65 YPLL, and a homicide at age 25 would contribute 40 YPLL. A death caused by stroke at age 70 would contribute no years of life lost before age 65 and so on. Until relatively recently, the age of 65 years was widely used as the threshold age. With life expectancies now exceeding 75 years at birth, YPLL calculations using age 75 as the threshold have become more common. Table 2-2 presents data on YPLL before age 75, illustrating the usefulness of this approach in providing a somewhat different perspective as to which problems are most important in terms of their magnitude and impact. The use of YPLL ranks cancer, HIV/acquired immune deficiency syndrome (AIDS), and various forms of injury-related deaths higher than does the use of crude numbers or rates. Conversely, the use of crude rates ranks heart disease, stroke, pneumonia, diabetes, and chronic lung and liver diseases higher than does the use of YPLL. Four of the top 10 causes of death, as determined by the number of deaths, do not appear in the list of the top 10 causes of YPLL.

Each of these different mortality indicators can be examined for various racial and ethnic subpopulations to identify disparities among these groups. For example, age-adjusted rates of YPLL before age 75 for 2000 ranged from 6,284 per 100,000 population for Hispanics to 7,029 for whites and 13,177 for African Americans. The rate for all groups was 7,694 per 100,000. The large disparity for African Americans is attributable primarily to differences in infant mortality, homicide, and HIV infection deaths.

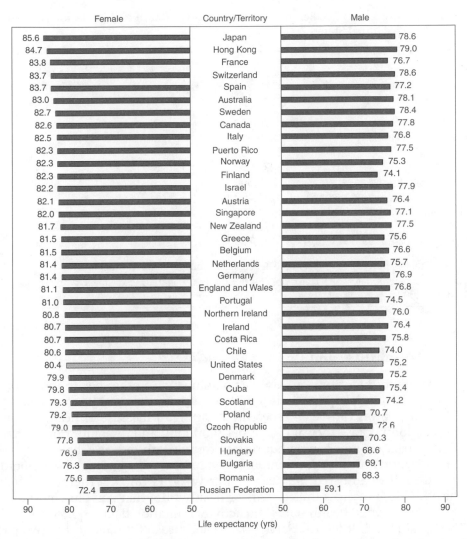

Female	Country/Territory	Male
85.6	Japan	78.6
84.7	Hong Kong	79.0
83.8	France	76.7
83.7	Switzerland	78.6
83.7	Spain	77.2
83.0	Australia	78.1
82.7	Sweden	78.4
82.6	Canada	77.8
82.5	Italy	76.8
82.3	Puerto Rico	77.5
82.3	Norway	75.3
82.3	Finland	74.1
82.2	Israel	77.9
82.1	Austria	76.4
82.0	Singapore	77.1
81.7	New Zealand	77.5
81.5	Greece	75.6
81.5	Belgium	76.6
81.4	Netherlands	75.7
81.4	Germany	76.9
81.1	England and Wales	76.8
81.0	Portugal	74.5
80.8	Northern Ireland	76.0
80.7	Ireland	76.4
80.7	Costa Rica	75.8
80.6	Chile	74.0
80.4	United States	75.2
79.9	Denmark	75.2
79.8	Cuba	75.4
79.3	Scotland	74.2
79.2	Poland	70.7
79.0	Czech Republic	72.6
77.8	Slovakia	70.3
76.9	Hungary	68.6
76.3	Bulgaria	69.1
75.6	Romania	68.3
72.4	Russian Federation	59.1

Life expectancy (yrs)

Figure 2-5   Life expectancy ranking at birth, by sex, selected countries and territories, 2004.

Notes:

• Rankings are from the highest to lowest female life expectancy at birth.

• Life expectancy at birth represents the average number of years that a group of infants would live if the infants were to experience throughout life the age-specific death rates present at birth.

• Countries and territories were selected based on quality of data, high life expectancy, and a population of at least 1 million population. Differences in life expectancy reflect differences in reporting methods, which can vary by country, and actual differences in mortality rates.

• 2004 data except for Ireland and Italy (2003 data).

Source: From Centers for Disease Control and Prevention. Life expectancy ranking at birth, by sex, selected countries and territories, 2004. *MMWR.* 2008; 57(13):346. Data from Organisation for Economic Co-operation and Development. OECD health data 2007: statistics and indicators for 30 countries. Paris, France: Organisation for Economic Co-operation and Development; 2008. http://www.oecd.org/health/healthdata. CDC. *Health, United States, 2007. With chartbook on trends in the health of Americans.* Hyattsville, MD: U.S. Department of Health and Human Services, CDC, National Center for Health Statistics; 2007. http://www.cdc.gov/nchs/data/hus/hus07.pdf. Accessed May 31, 2010.

Table 2-2   Age-Adjusted YPLL Before Age 75 by Cause of Death and Ranks for YPLL and Number of Deaths, United States, 2000

Causes of Death	YPLL	Rank by YPLL	Rank by Number of Deaths
Cancer	1,698,500	1	2
Heart disease	1,270,700	2	1
Unintentional injuries	1,052,500	3	5
Suicide	343,300	4	11
Homicide	274,200	5	14
Cerebrovascular diseases	226,500	6	3
Chronic obstructive lung disease	190,700	7	4
Diabetes mellitus	181,200	8	6
HIV infections	178,900	9	18
Chronic liver disease and cirrhosis	141,700	10	12

Note: Years lost before age 75 per 100,000 population younger than 75 years of age.

Source: Adapted from National Center for Health Statistics. *Health, United States, 2002*. Hyattsville, MD: NCHS; 2002.

Morbidity, Disability, and Quality Measures

Mortality indicators can also be combined with other health indicators that describe quality considerations to provide a measure of the span of healthy life. These indicators can be an especially meaningful measure of health status in a population because they also consider morbidity and disability from conditions that impact on functioning but do not cause death (e.g., cerebral palsy, schizophrenia, and arthritis). A commonly used measure of aggregate disease burden is the disability-adjusted life year. Other variants on this theme are span-of-healthy-life indicators (called years of healthy life) that combine mortality data with self-reported health status and activity limitation data acquired through the National Health Interview Survey. This concept is illustrated in the two components of Figure 2-6, which shows life expectancy at birth and at age 65 by race and gender as well as several views of the expectancy of healthy life within the overall life expectancy. Years associated with self-reported good or better health, years free of activity limitation, and years free of selected chronic diseases are also presented. Depending on the healthy life expectancy measure, Figure 2-6 demonstrates that Americans average about 10 years of poor health, 15 years of activity limitation, and 30 years of living with a chronic disease. Women have better health status than men, and whites do better than blacks on virtually all of these measures. For healthy life expectancies at age 65, a similar picture appears. The implication is that extending healthy life expectancy can be achieved through several pathways. One would be to extend life expectancy without increasing the measures of poor health, activity limitation, and chronic disease burden. Another would be to reduce the measures of poor health, activity limitation, and chronic disease burden within a constant life expectancy. The optimal approach would accomplish both by extending life expectancy and reducing the burden of poor health, activity limitation, and chronic disease.

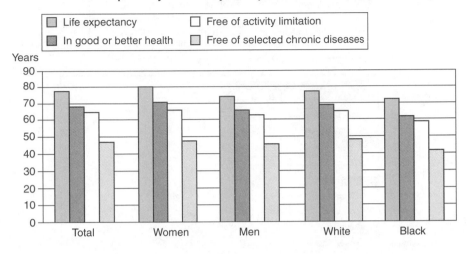

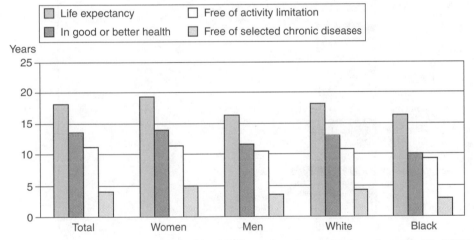

Figure 2-6   Life expectancy and healthy life expectancies at birth and at age 65, 2000–2001. *Source:* From National Health Interview Survey (NHIS), NCHS, CDC; National Vital Statistics System (NVSS), NCHS, CDC.

Although less frequently encountered, indicators of morbidity and disability are also quite useful in measuring health status. Figure 2-7 presents information on both morbidity and disability for children in terms of the prevalence of specific childhood diseases (here, the percentage of children 0 to 17 years old who have ever had these conditions) and the relationship between these conditions and self-reported health and activity status (a measure of disability). Similarly, few people appreciate that arthritis is now the leading cause of disability in the United States. Its burden is expected to grow as a result of the aging of the population and increases in obesity along with decreased physical activity.

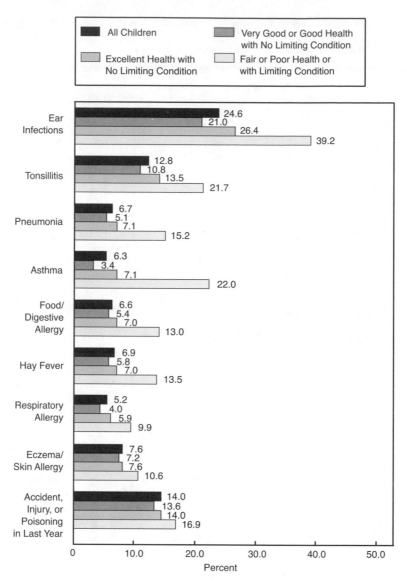

Figure 2-7 Percentage of children 0 to 17 years old who have had selected childhood diseases by child's health and limitations status, United States, 1998. *Source:* From Coiro MJ, Zill N, and Bloom B, Health of our nation's children. *Vital Health Stat.* 1994;10(191):1–64.

Both the prevalence (the number or rate of cases at a specific point or period in time) and incidence (the number or rate of new cases occurring during a specific period) are widely used measures of morbidity. One of the earliest systems for reporting on diseases of public health significance is the national notifiable disease-reporting system for specific diseases. This system operates through the collaboration of local, state, and federal health agencies. Although initially developed to track the incidence of communicable diseases, this system has steadily moved toward collecting information on noninfectious conditions, as well as important risk factors.

Increasingly, information on self-reported health status and on days lost from work or school caused by acute or chronic conditions is available through surveys of the general population. The National Center for Health Statistics also conducts ongoing surveys of health providers on complaints and conditions requiring medical care in outpatient settings. These surveys provide direct information on self-reported health status and illuminate some of the factors, such as race, ethnicity, and household income levels, depicted in Figures 2-8 through 2-10, that are associated with health status.

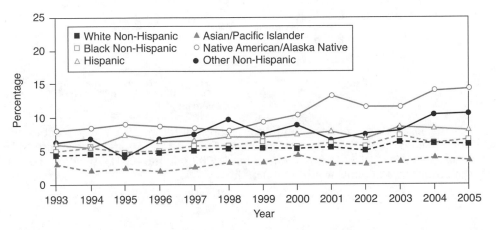

Figure 2-8 Percentage of individuals with 14 or more activity limitation days by race and ethnicity, United States, 1993–2005. *Source:* From Centers for Disease Control and Prevention, National Center for Health Statistics, National Household Interview Survey Data.

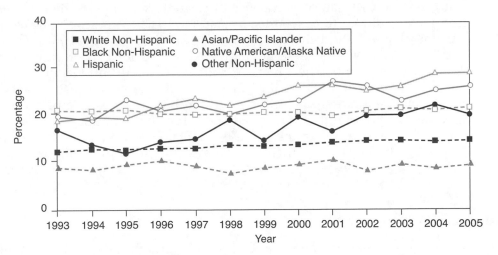

Figure 2-9 Percentage of individuals with fair or poor self-rated health by race and ethnicity, United States, 1993–2005. *Source:* From Centers for Disease Control and Prevention, National Center for Health Statistics, National Household Interview Survey Data.

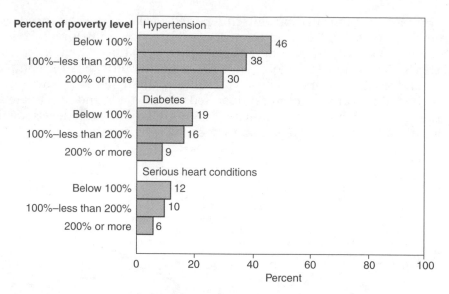

Figure 2-10   Respondent-reported conditions among adults age 45–64 by percent of poverty level, United States, 2007. *Source:* From Centers for Disease Control and Prevention, National Center for Health Statistics, *Health, United States 2009*, Figure 10. Hyattsville, MD: NCHS; 2009. Data from the National Health Interview Survey.

INFLUENCES ON HEALTH

In 1996, public health surveillance in the United States took a historic step, reflecting changes in national morbidity and mortality patterns as well as in the ability to identify specific factors that result in disease and injury. At that time, the CDC added prevalence of cigarette smoking to the list of diseases and conditions to be reported by states to CDC.[5] This action marked the first time that a health behavior, rather than an illness or disease, was considered nationally reportable—a groundbreaking step for surveillance efforts. How the focus of public health efforts shifted from conventional disease outcomes to reporting on underlying causes amenable to public health intervention is an important story. That story is closely linked to one of the most important and most bitterly contested public health achievements of the 20th century, the recognition of tobacco use as a major health hazard. One of this chapter's Public Health Spotlights chronicles this story, providing important lessons for public health efforts in the 21st century seeking to improve measures of health status and quality of life.

Risk Factors

The recognition of tobacco use as a major health hazard was no simple achievement, partly because many factors directly or indirectly influence the level of a health outcome in a given population. For example, greater per capita tobacco use in a population is associated with higher rates of heart disease and lung cancer, and lower rates of early prenatal care are associated with higher infant mortality rates. Because these factors are part of the chain of causation for health outcomes, tracking their levels provides an early indication as to the direction in which the health outcome is likely to change. These factors increase the likelihood or risk of particular health outcomes occurring and can be characterized broadly as risk factors.

The types and number of risk factors are as varied as the influences themselves. Depending on how these factors are lumped or split, traditional categories include biologic factors (from genetic endowment to aging), environmental factors (from food, air, and water to communicable diseases), lifestyle factors (from diet to injury avoidance and sexual behaviors), psychosocial factors (from poverty to stress, personality, and cultural factors), and the use of and access to health-related services. Refinements of this framework differentiate several outcomes of interest, including disease, functional capacity, prosperity, and well-being, that can be influenced by various risk factors (Figure 2-11). These various components are often interrelated (e.g., stress, a social environmental factor, may stimulate individual responses, such as tobacco or illicit drug use, which, in turn, influences the likelihood of disease, functional capacity, and well-being). In addition, variations in one outcome, such as disease, may influence changes in others, such as well-being, depending on the mix of other factors present. This complex set of interactions, consistent with the ecological model introduced in Chapter 1, draws attention to general factors that

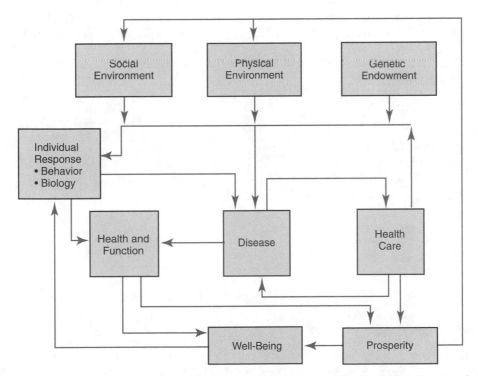

Figure 2-11 Determinants of health. *Source:* From Evans RG, Stoddard GL. Producing health, consuming health care. *Soc Sci Med.* 1990;31:1359. Reprinted with permission, copyright 1990, from Elsevier Science.

can result in many diseases, rather than focusing on specific factors that contribute little to population-wide health outcomes.

Although many factors are causally related to health outcomes, some are more direct and proximal causes than others. Specific risk factors have been clearly linked to specific adverse health states through epidemiologic studies. For example, numerous studies have linked unintentional injuries with a variety of risk factors, including the accessibility to firearms and the use of alcohol, tobacco, and seat belts. Tobacco, hypertension, overnutrition, and diabetes are well-known risk factors for heart disease. Epidemiologic research and studies over the past 50 years have identified behavioral risk factors for many common diseases and conditions,[6] as shown in Table 2-3. In recent decades, for example, the prevalence of obesity has doubled in virtually all gender, age, racial, and ethnic groups. Ongoing behavioral risk factor surveys (often through telephone interviews) are conducted by governmental public health agencies to track trends in the prevalence of many important risk behaviors within the population. These surveys document that the health-related behaviors of tens of millions of Americans place them at risk for developing chronic disease and injuries.

Despite the recent emphasis on behavioral factors, risk factors in the physical environment remain important influences on health. Air pollution, for example, is directly related to a wide range of diseases, including lung cancer, pulmonary emphysema, chronic bronchitis, and bronchial asthma. National standards exist for many of the most important air pollutants and are tracked to determine the extent of these risks in the general population. The proportion of the U.S. population residing in counties that have exceeded national standards for these pollutants suggests that air pollution risks, like behavioral

Table 2-3 Selected Behavioral Risk Factors Related to Leading Causes of Deaths in the United States, 2000

Cause of Death and Percentage of All Deaths	Smoking	High Fat/ Low Fiber	Sedentary Lifestyle	High Blood Pressure	Elevated Cholesterol	Obesity	Alcohol Use
Heart disease (30%)	X	X	X	X	X	X	X
Cancer (23%)	X	X	X			X	X
Stroke (7%)	X	X		X	X	X	
Chronic lung disease (5%)	X						
Unintentional injuries (4%)	X						X
Pneumonia and influenza (3%)	X						
Diabetes (3%)		X	X			X	
HIV infection (1%)							
Suicide (1%)							X
Chronic liver disease (1%)							X
Atherosclerosis (1%)	X	X	X		X		

Sources: Data for causes and percent deaths from National Center for Health Statistics. *Health, United States 2002.* Hyattsville, MD: NCHS; 2002. Data for risk factors related to causes from Brownson RC, Remington PL, Davis JR, et al. *Chronic Disease Epidemiology and Control.* 2nd ed. Washington, DC; American Public Health Association; 1998; and U.S. Public Health Service. *The Surgeon General's Report on Nutrition and Health.* Washington, DC: Public Health Service; 1988.

risks, affect tens of millions of Americans.[7] Environmental risks are ubiquitous and growing in the United States. Estimates from the CDC are that 22 to 30 million people drink water from private wells; 40 to 45 million people are exposed to extreme heat; 150 million people are exposed to environmental tobacco smoke; and 65 million people reside in homes built before 1950, when lead paint was banned for residential use.

The physical environment influences health through several pathways, including facilitating risk-taking behaviors, influencing social relationships, and even exposing residents to visual cues that can arouse fear, anxiety, and depression. The "broken windows" theory suggests that a neighborhood in disrepair sends out messages that no one cares and that otherwise unacceptable behaviors will be tolerated in the area.[7]

Behavioral and environmental risk factors are clearly germane to public health interest and efforts. Focusing on these factors provides a different perspective of the enemies of personal and public health than that conveyed by disease-specific incidence or mortality data. Such a focus also promotes rational policy development and interventions. Unfortunately, determining which underlying factors are most important is more difficult than it appears because of differences in the outcomes under study and measures used. For example, a study using 1980 data found tobacco, hypertension, and overnutrition responsible for about three fourths of deaths before the age of 65 years and injury risks, alcohol, tobacco, and gaps in primary prevention accountable for about three fourths of all YPLL before the age of 65 years.[8] Further complicating these analyses is the finding that individual risk factors may result in several different health outcomes. For example, alcohol use is linked with motor vehicle injuries, other injuries, cancer, and cirrhosis; tobacco use can result in heart disease, stroke, ulcers, fire and burn injuries, and low birth weight, as well as cancer.[6,8]

Despite problems with their measurement, the identification of antecedent causes is important for public health policy and interventions. Table 2-4 provides a comparison of 2000 deaths by their listed causes of death and their actual causes (major risk factors).[9] The two lists provide contrasting views as to the major health problems and needs of the U.S. population. Although this debate has continued since the days of Chadwick and Farr (see Chapter 1), it is by no means settled.

Coroners and medical examiners view immediate and underlying causes of death somewhat differently from the perspective offered in Table 2-4. Death certificates have two parts, one for entering the immediate and underlying conditions that caused the death and a second for identifying conditions or injuries that contributed to that death. For example, a death attributed to cardiovascular disease might list cardiac tamponade as the immediate cause or as a consequence of a ruptured myocardial infarction, which itself was a consequence of coronary arteriosclerosis. For this death, hypertensive cardiovascular disease might be listed as a significant condition contributing to, but not causing, the immediate and underlying causes. Thus, where do smoking, obesity, diet, and physical inactivity get identified as the real causes of such deaths? Perhaps the Chadwick-Farr debate continues into the 21st century in terms of whether deaths in the year 2000 should be attributed to tobacco use and dietary excesses, just as many of those in England in 1839 should have been attributed to starvation.

Table 2-4 Listed and Actual Causes of Death, United States, 2000

10 Leading Causes of Death	Number	Actual Causes of Death	Number
Heart disease	710,760	Tobacco	435,000
Malignant neoplasm	553,091	Poor diet and physical inactivity	400,000
Cerebrovascular disease	167,661	Alcohol consumption	85,000
Chronic lower respiratory tract diseases	122,009	Microbial agents	75,000
		Toxic agents	55,000
Unintentional injuries	97,900	Motor vehicle	43,000
Diabetes mellitus	69,301	Firearms	29,000
Influenza and pneumonia	65,313	Sexual behavior	20,000
Alzheimer disease	49,558	Illicit drug use	17,000
Nephritis, nephrotic syndrome, and nephrosis	37,251		
Septicemia	31,224		
Other	499,283		
Total	2,403,351	Total	1,159,000

Source: Data from Mokdad AH, Marks JS, Stroup DF, et al. Actual causes of death in the United States, 2000. *JAMA.* 2004;291:1238–1245.

Social and Cultural Influences

Understanding the health effects of biologic, behavioral, and environmental risk factors is straightforward in comparison with understanding the effects of social, economic, and cultural factors on the health of populations. This is due in part to a lack of agreement as to what is being measured. Socioeconomic status and poverty are two factors that generally reflect position in society. There is considerable evidence that social position is an overarching determinant of health status, even though the indicators used to measure social standing are imprecise, at best.

Social class affects lifestyle, environment, and the use of services; it remains an important predictor of good and poor health in our society. Social class differences in mortality have long been recognized around the world. In 1842, Chadwick reported that the average ages at death for occupationally stratified groups in England were as follows: "gentlemen and persons engaged in the professions, 45 years; tradesmen and their families, 26 years; mechanics, servants and laborers, and their families, 16 years."[10] Life expectancies and other health indicators have improved considerably in England and elsewhere since 1842, but differences in mortality rates among the various social classes persist to this day.

Some countries (such as Great Britain and the United States) have identifiable social strata that permit comparisons of health status by social class. Britain conducts ongoing analyses of socioeconomic differences according to official categorizations based on general social standing within the community. For the United States, educational status, race, and family income are often used as indirect or proxy measures of social class. Despite the differences in approaches and indicators, there is little evidence of any real difference between Britain and the United States in terms of what is being measured. In both countries, explanations for the differences in mortality appear to relate primarily to inequalities in social position and material resources.[11,12] This effect operates all up and down the hierarchy of social standing; at each step, improvements in social status are linked with improvements in measures of health status. For example, a study based on 1971 British census follow-up data found that a relatively affluent, home-owning group with two cars had a lower mortality risk than did a similar relatively privileged group with only one car.[11]

In the United States, epidemiologists have studied socioeconomic differences in mortality risk since the early 1900s. Infant mortality has been the subject of many studies that have consistently documented the effects of poverty. Findings from the National Maternal and Infant Health Survey, for example, demonstrated that the effects of poverty were greater for infants born to mothers with no other risk factors than for infants born to high-risk mothers.[13] Poverty status was associated with a 60% higher rate of neonatal mortality and a 200% higher rate for postneonatal mortality than for those infants of higher-income mothers.

Poverty affects many health outcomes, as illustrated in Figure 2-10 and Table 2-5. Low-income families in the United States have an increased likelihood (or relative risk) of a variety of adverse health outcomes, often two to five times greater than that of higher income families. The percentage of persons reporting fair or poor health is about four times as high for persons living below the poverty level as for those with family income at least twice the poverty level.[1]

The implications of the consistent relationship between measures of social status and health outcomes suggest that studies need to consider how and how well social class is categorized and measured. Imprecise measures may understate the actual differences that are the result of socioeconomic position in society. Importantly, if racial or ethnic differences are simply the result of social class differences, factors that operate through race and ethnicity, such as racism or ethnism, will be overlooked. These additional factors also affect the difference

Table 2-5 Selected Outcomes and Relative Risk for Low-Income Families, as Compared with High-Income Families

Outcome	Relative Risk
Child neglect	9
Child abuse	4.5
Iron-deficiency anemia	3 to 4
Childhood mortality	.3
Fair or poor health	3
Fatal injuries	2–3
Growth retardation	2.5
Severe asthma	2
Pneumonia	1.6
Infant mortality	1.3 to 1.5
Low birth weight	1.2 to 2.2
Extreme behavioral problems	1.3

Source: Data from Geltman PL, Meyers AF, Greenberg J, et al. Welfare reform and children's health. *Health Policy Child Health*. 1996;3:1–5.

between the social position one has and the position one would have attained, were it not for one's race or ethnicity. It is clear that race in the United States, independent of socioeconomic status, is linked to mortality, although these effects vary across age and disease categories.[14] Nevertheless, anthropologists concluded long ago that race is not an appropriate generic category for comparing health outcomes. Its usefulness does not derive from any biologic or genetic differences but rather from its social, cultural, political, and historical meanings.

Studies of the effect of social factors on health status across nations add some interesting insights. In general, health appears to be closely associated with income differentials within countries, but there is only a weak link between national mortality rates and average income among the developed countries.[15] This pattern suggests that health is affected less by changes in absolute material standards across affluent populations than by relative income differences and the resulting disadvantage in each country. It is not the richest countries that have the greatest life expectancy. Rather, it is those developed nations with the narrowest income differentials between rich and poor, as suggested by Figure 2-5. This finding argues that health in the developed world is less a matter of a population's absolute material wealth than of how the population's circumstances compare with those of other members of their society. A similar perspective views income to be related to health through two pathways: a direct effect on the material conditions necessary for survival and an effect on social participation and the opportunity to control one's own life circumstances.[16] In settings or societies that provide little in the way of material conditions (e.g., clean water, sanitation services, ample food, and adequate housing), income is more important for health. Where material conditions are conducive to good health, income acts through social participation.

The effects of culture on health and illness are also becoming better understood. To medical anthropologists, diseases are not purely independent phenomena. Rather, they are to be viewed and understood in relation to ecology and culture. Certainly, the type and severity of disease vary by age, gender, social class, and ethnic group. For example, as documented in Figure 2-12, Puerto Rican children overall have a higher prevalence of asthma than Mexican American, non-Hispanic white, and African American children. Differences in poverty status do not explain the disparities for Puerto Rican and African American children, two populations that have higher asthma rates than non-Hispanic white and Mexican American children regardless of poverty status. The reason for the higher rate among Puerto Rican children overall is unknown, but the different distributions and social patterns suggest differences in culture-mediated behaviors.

Such insights are essential to developing successful prevention and control programs. Culture serves to shape health-related behaviors, as well as human responses to diseases, including changes in the environment, which in turn affect health. As a mechanism of adapting to the environment, culture has great potential for both positively and negatively affecting health.

There is evidence that different societies shape the ways in which diseases are experienced and that social patterns of disease persist, even after risk factors are identified and effective interventions become available.[17-19] For example, the link between poverty and various outcomes has been well established; nevertheless, even after advances in medicine and public health and significant

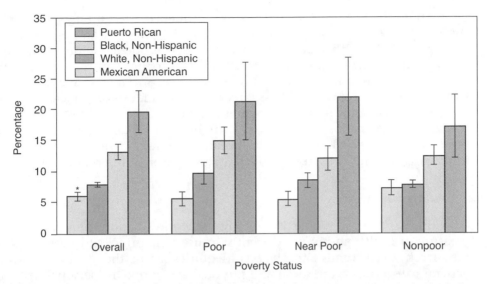

Figure 2-12 Percentage of children younger than age 18 who currently have asthma, by race/ethnicity[†] and poverty status[§], United States, 2003–2005.

Notes:

* 95% confidence interval.

[†] Data are shown for two Hispanic subpopulations (Puerto Rican and Mexican American) because these groups have adequate sample sizes to provide stable estimates. Estimates for other Hispanic subpopulations are not reliable.

[§] Poor is defined as annual household income <100% of the poverty threshold, near poor as 100%–199%, and nonpoor as >200%, based on U.S. Bureau of the Census thresholds. For example, in 2004, for a family of four (two adults and two children aged <18 years), the poverty threshold was $19,157, and poverty status levels were as follows: poor: <$19,157; near poor: $19,157–$38,314; nonpoor: >$38,315.

Source: From Centers for Disease Control and Prevention. Percentage of children aged <18 years who currently have asthma, by race/ethnicity and poverty status, United States, 2003–2005. *MMWR.* 2007;56(05):99.

improvement in general living and working conditions, the association persists. One explanation is that as some risks were addressed, others developed, such as health-related behaviors, including violent behavior and alcohol, tobacco, and drug use. In this way, societies create and shape the diseases that they experience. This makes sense, especially if we view the social context in which health and disease reside—the setting and social networks. For problems such as HIV/AIDS, sexually transmitted diseases, and illicit drug use, spread is heavily influenced by the links between those at risk.[20] This also helps to explain why people in disorganized social structures are more likely to report their own health as poor than are similar persons with more social capital.[21,22]

Societal responses to diseases are also socially constructed. Efforts to prevent the spread of typhoid fever by limiting the rights of carriers (such as Typhoid Mary) differed greatly from those to reduce transmission risks from diphtheria carriers. Because many otherwise normal citizens would have been subjected to extreme measures in order to avoid the risk of transmission, it was not socially acceptable to invoke similar measures for these similar risks.

If these themes of social and cultural influences are on target, they place the study of health disparities at the top of the public health agenda. They also argue that health should be viewed as a social phenomenon. Rather than attempting to identify each and every risk factor that contributes only marginally to disparate health outcomes of the lower social classes, a more effective approach would be to address directly the broader social policies (distribution of wealth, education, employment, and the like) that foster the social disparities that cause the observed differences in health outcomes.[19] This broad view of health and its determinants is critical to understanding and improving health status in the United States, as well as internationally.

Global Health Influences

Considerable variation exists among the world's nations on virtually every measure of health and illness currently in use. The principal factors responsible for observed trends and obvious inequities across the globe fall into the general categories of the social and physical environment, personal behavior, and health services. Given the considerable variation in social, economic, and health status among the developed, developing, and underdeveloped nations, it is naive to make broad generalizations. Countries with favorable health status indicators, however, generally have a well-developed health infrastructure, ample opportunities for education and training, relatively high status for women, and economic development that counterbalances population growth. Nonetheless, countries at all levels of development share some problems, including the escalating costs involved in providing a broad range of health, social, and economic development services to disadvantaged subgroups within the population. Social and cultural upheaval associated with urbanization is another problem common to countries at all levels of development. Over the course of the 20th century, the proportion of the world's population living in urban areas tripled—to about 40%; that trend is expected to continue throughout the new century.

The principal environmental hazards in the world today appear to be those associated with poverty. This is true for developed as well as developing and underdeveloped countries. Some international epidemiologists predict that in the 21st century the effects of overpopulation and production of greenhouse gases will join poverty as major threats to global health. These factors represent human effects on the world's climate and resources and are easily remembered as the "3 Ps" of global health (pollution, population, and poverty):

- Pollution of the atmosphere by greenhouse gases, which will result in significant global warming, affecting both climate and the occurrence of disease
- Worldwide population growth, which will result in a population of 10 to 12 billion people within the next century
- Poverty, which is always associated with ill health and disease[23,24]

It surprises many Americans that population is a major global health concern. Birth rates vary inversely with the level of economic development and the status of women among the nations of the world. Continuing high birth rates and declining death rates will mean even more rapid growth in population in developing countries. It has taken all of history to reach the world's current population level, but it will take less than half a century to double that. Many factors have influenced this growth, including public health, which has increased the chances of conception by improving the health status of adults, increasing infant and child survival, preventing premature deaths of adults in the most fertile age groups, and reducing the number of marriages dissolved by one partner's death.

Global warming represents yet another phenomenon with considerable potential for health effects. Climate change has direct temperature effects on humans and increases the likelihood of extreme weather events. A number of infectious diseases are also climate sensitive, some because of effects on mosquitoes, ticks, and other vectors in terms of their population size and density and changes in population movement, forest clearance and land use practices, surface water configurations, and human population density.[25] Global warming will also contribute to air quality-related health conditions and concerns.

In general, public health approaches to dealing with world health problems must overcome formidable obstacles, including the unequal and inefficient distribution of health services, a lack of appropriate technology, poor management, poverty, and inadequate or inappropriate government programs to finance needed services. Much of the preventable disease in the world is concentrated in the developing and underdeveloped countries, where the most profound differences exist in terms of social and economic influences. Table 2-6 provides estimates of the preventable toll caused by water-related diseases worldwide.

Although many of these factors appear to stem from low levels of national wealth, the link between national health status and national wealth is not firm, and comparisons across nations are seldom straightforward. Improved health status correlates more closely with changes in standards of living, advances in the politics of human relations, and a nation's literacy, education, and welfare policies than with specific preventive interventions. The complexities involved in identifying and understanding these forces and their interrelationships often confound comparisons of health status between the United States and other nations.

ANALYZING HEALTH PROBLEMS FOR CAUSATIVE FACTORS

The ability to identify risk factors and pathways for causation is essential for rational public health decisions and actions to address important health problems in a population. First, however, it is necessary to define what is meant by health problem. Here, health problem means a condition of humans that can be represented in terms of measurable health status or quality-of-life indicators. In later chapters, additional dimensions will be added to this basic definition for the purposes of community problem solving and the development of interventions. This characterization of a health problem as something measured only in terms of outcomes is difficult for some to accept. They point to important factors, such as access to care or poverty itself, and feel that these should rightfully be considered as health problems. Important problems they may be, but if they are truly important in the causation of some unacceptable

Table 2-6   WHO Estimates of Morbidity and Mortality of Water-Related Diseases, Worldwide, 1995

Disease	Morbidity (Episodes Per Year)	Mortality (Deaths Per Year)	Relationship to Water Supply Sanitation
Diarrhea (drinking)	1 billion	3.3 million	Unsanitary excreta disposal, poor personal and domestic hygiene, unsafe water
Infection with intestinal helminths	1.5 billion*	100,000	Unsanitary excreta disposal, poor personal, and domestic hygiene
Schistosomiasis	200 million*	200,000	Unsanitary excreta disposal and absence of nearby sources of safe water
Dracunculiasis	100,000*†	—	Unsafe drinking water
Trachoma	150 million‡	—	Lack of face washing, often because of absence of nearby sources of safe water
Malaria	400 million	1.5 million	Poor water management and storage, poor operation of water points and drainage
Dengue fever	1.75 million	20,000	Poor solid wastes management, water storage, and operation of water points and drainage
Poliomyelitis (drinking)	114,000	—	Unsanitary excreta disposal, poor personal and domestic hygiene, unsafe water
Trypanosomiasis	275,000	130,000	Absence of nearby sources of safe water
Bancroftian filariasis	72.8 million*	—	Poor water management and storage, poor operation of water points and drainage
Onchocerciasis	17.7 million*§	40,000	Poor water management and large-scale projects

* People currently infected.
† Excluding Sudan.
‡ Case of active disease. Approximately 5.9 million cases of blindness or severe complications of trachoma occur annually.
§ Includes an estimated 270,000 blind.

Source: From WHO Wams of Inadequate Communicable Disease Prevention, U.S. Public Health Service. *Prevent Health Rep.* 1996;111:296–297.

health outcome, they can be dealt with as related factors rather than health problems.

The factors linked with specific health problems are often generically termed risk factors and can exist at one of three levels. Those risk factors most closely associated with the health outcome in question are often termed determinants. Risk factors that play a role further back in the chain of causation are called direct and indirect contributing factors. Risk factors can be described at either an individual or a population level. For example, tobacco use for an individual increases the chances of developing heart disease or lung cancer, and an increased prevalence of tobacco use in a population increases that population's incidence of (and mortality rates from) these conditions.

Determinants are scientifically established factors that relate directly to the level of a health problem. As the level of the determinant changes, the level of the health outcome changes. Determinants are the most proximal risk factors through which other levels of risk factors act. The link between the determinant and the health outcome should be well established through scientific or epidemiologic studies. For example, for neonatal mortality rates, two well-established determinants are the low-birth-weight rate (the number of infants born weighing less than 2,500 g, or about 5.5 lb, per 100 live births) and weight-specific mortality rates. Improvement in the neonatal mortality rate cannot occur unless one of these determinants improves. Health outcomes can have one or many determinants.

Direct contributing factors are scientifically established factors that directly affect the level of a determinant. Again, there should be solid evidence that the level of the direct contributing factor affects the level of the determinant. For the neonatal mortality rate example, the prevalence of tobacco use among pregnant women has been associated with the risk of low birth weight. A determinant can have many direct contributing factors. For low birth weight, other direct contributing factors include low maternal weight gain and inadequate prenatal care.

Indirect contributing factors affect the level of the direct contributing factors. Although several steps distant from the health outcome in question, these factors are often proximal enough to be modified. The indirect contributing factor affects the level of the direct contributing factor, which in turn affects the level of the determinant. The level of the determinant then affects the level of the health outcome. Many indirect contributing factors can exist for each direct contributing factor. For prevalence of tobacco use among pregnant women, indirect contributing factors might include easy access to tobacco products for young women, a lack of health education, and a lack of smoking cessation programs.

The health problem analysis framework begins with the identification of a health problem (defined in terms of health status indicators) and proceeds to establish one or more determinants; for each determinant, one or more direct contributing factors; and for each direct contributing factor, one or more indirect contributing factors. Intervention strategies at the community level generally involve addressing these indirect contributing factors. When completed, an analysis identifies as many of the causal pathways as possible to determine which contributing factors exist in the setting in which an intervention strategy is planned. The framework for this approach is presented in Table 2-7 and Figure 2-13. This framework forms the basis for developing

Table 2-7   Risk Factors

Determinant	Scientifically established factor that relates directly to the level of the health problem. A health problem may have any number of determinants identified for it.	Example: Low birth weight is a prime determinant for the health problem of neonatal mortality.
Direct contributing factor	Scientifically established factor that directly affects the level of the determinant.	Example: Use of prenatal care is one factor that affects the low-birth-weight rate.
Indirect contributing factor	Community-specific factor that affects the level of a direct contributing factor. Such factors can vary considerably from one community to another.	Example: Availability of day care or transportation services within the community may affect the use of prenatal care services.

Source: Data from Centers for Disease Control and Prevention, Public Health Practice Program Office, 1991.

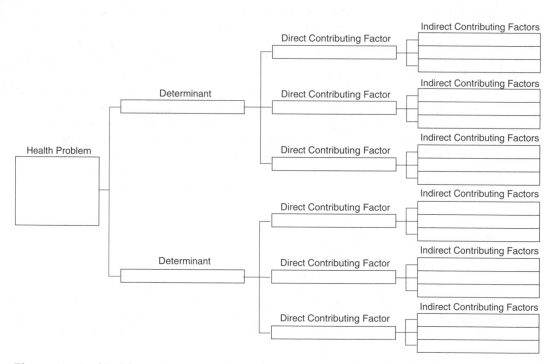

Figure 2-13   Health problem analysis worksheet. *Source:* From Centers for Disease Control and Prevention, Public Health Practice Program Office, 1991.

meaningful interventions; it is used in several of the processes and instruments to assess community health needs that are currently in wide use at the local level. Community health improvement processes and tools comprise a major focus of Chapter 5.

Although this framework is useful, it does not fully account for the relationships among the various levels of risk factors. Some direct contributing factors may affect more than one determinant, and some indirect contributing factors may influence more than one direct contributing factor. For example, illicit drug use during pregnancy influences both the likelihood of low birth weight and birth weight-specific survival rates. To account fully for these interactions, some direct and indirect contributing factors may need to be included in several different locations on the worksheet. Despite the advancement of epidemiologic methods, many studies ignore the contributing factors that affect the level of these major risk factors, leading to simplistic formulations of multiple risk factors for health problems that exist at the community level.[26]

ECONOMIC DIMENSIONS OF HEALTH OUTCOMES

The ability to measure and quantify outcomes and risks is essential for rational decisions and actions. Specific indicators, as well as methods of economic analysis, are available to provide both objective and subjective valuations. Several health indicators attempt to value differentially health status, outcomes, including age-adjusted rates, span of healthy life, and YPLL. For example, YPLL represents a method of weighting or valuing health outcomes by placing a higher value on deaths that occur at earlier ages. Years of life lost thus become a common denominator or, in one sense, a common currency. Health outcomes can be translated into this currency or into an actual currency, such as dollars. This translation allows for comparisons to be made among outcomes in terms of which costs more per person, per episode, or per another reference point. Cost comparisons of health outcomes and health events have become common in public health. Approaches include cost-benefit, cost-effectiveness, and cost-utility studies.

Cost-benefit analyses provide comprehensive information on both the costs and the benefits of an intervention. All health outcomes and other relevant impacts are included in the determination of benefits. The results are expressed in terms of net costs, net benefits, and time required to recoup an initial investment. If the benefits are expressed in health outcome terms, years of life gained or quality-adjusted life years may be calculated. This provides a framework for comparing disparate interventions. Quality-adjusted life years are calculated from a particular perspective that determines which costs and consequences are included in the analysis. For public health analyses, societal perspectives are necessary. When comprehensively performed, cost-benefit analyses are considered the gold standard of economic evaluations.

Cost-effectiveness analyses focus on one outcome to determine the most cost-effective intervention when several options are possible. Cost-effectiveness examines a specific option's costs to achieve a particular outcome. Results are often specified as the cost per case prevented or cost per life saved. For example, screening an entire town for a specific disease might identify cases at a cost of $150 per new case, whereas a screening program directed only at high-risk groups within that town might identify cases at a cost of $50 per new case. Although useful for evaluating different strategies for achieving the same result, cost-effectiveness approaches are not very helpful in evaluating interventions intended for different health conditions.

Cost-utility analyses are similar to cost-effectiveness studies, except that the results are characterized as cost per quality-adjusted life years. These are most useful when the intervention affects both morbidity and mortality, and there are a variety of possible outcomes that include quality of life.

These approaches are especially important for interventions based on preventive strategies. The argument is frequently made that "an ounce of prevention is worth a pound of cure." If this wisdom is true, preventive interventions should result in savings equal to 16 times their actual cost. Not all preventive interventions measure up to this standard, but even crude information on the costs of many health outcomes suggests that prevention has economic as well as human savings. Table 2-8 presents information from Healthy People 2000[27] (HP2000) regarding the economics of prevention for a number of common diseases and conditions; for each, the potential savings represents an enormous sum. Figure 2-14 illustrates that the impacts of disease and injuries can be many in terms of medical care costs for treatment in outpatient, emergency department, and hospital settings.[28] The U.S. Public Health Service has estimated that as much as 11% of projected health expenditures for the year 2000 could have been averted through investments in public health for six conditions: motor vehicle injuries, occupationally related injuries, stroke, coronary heart disease, firearms-related injuries, and low-birth-weight infants.[29] Beyond the direct medical effects, there are often nonmedical costs related to lost wages, taxes, and productivity.

Economists assert that the future costs for care and services that result from prevention of mortality must be considered a negative benefit of prevention. For example, the costs of preventing a death caused by motor vehicle injuries should include all subsequent medical care costs for that individual over his or her lifetime because these costs would not have occurred otherwise. They also argue that it is unfair to compare future savings to the costs of current prevention programs and that those savings must be discounted to their current value. If a preventive program will save $10 million 20 years from now, that $10 million must be translated into its current value in computing cost benefits, cost-effectiveness, or cost utility. It may be that the value of $10 million 20 years from now is only $4 million now. If the program costs $1 million, its benefit/cost ratio would be 4:1 instead of 10:1 before we even added any additional costs associated with medical care for the lives that were saved. These economic considerations contribute to the difficulty of marketing preventive interventions.

Two additional economic considerations are important for public health policy and practice. The first of these is what economists term opportunity costs. These represent the costs involved in choosing one course of action over another. Resources spent for one purpose are not available to be spent for

Table 2-8   The Economics of Prevention

Condition	Overall Magnitude	Avoidable Intervention*	Cost/Patient†
Heart disease	7 million with coronary artery disease 500,000 deaths/year 284,000 bypass procedures/year	Coronary bypass surgery	$30,000
Cancer	1 million new cases/year 510,000 deaths/year	Lung cancer treatment Cervical cancer treatment	$29,000 $28,000
Stroke	600,000 strokes/year 150,000 deaths/year	Hemiplegia treatment and rehabilitation	$22,000
Injuries	2.3 million hospitalizations per year 142,500 deaths/year 177,000 persons with spinal cord injuries in the United States	Quadriplegia treatment and rehabilitation Hip fracture treatment and rehabilitation	$570,000 (lifetime) $40,000
HIV infection	1–1.5 million infected 118,000 AIDS cases (as of January 1990)	Severe head injury treatment and rehabilitation AIDS treatment	$310,000 $75,000 (lifetime)
Alcoholism	18.5 million abuse alcohol 105,000 alcohol-related deaths/year	Liver transplant	$250,000
Drug abuse	Regular users: 1 to 3 million, cocaine 900,000, IV drugs 500,000, heroin	Treatment of cocaine-exposed infant	$66,000 (5 years)
LBW infants	Drug-exposed infants: 375,000 260,000 low birth weight infants/year	Neonatal intensive care for low birth weight infant	$10,000
Inadequate immunization	23,000 deaths/year Lacking basic immunization series: 20% to 30% aged 2 and younger 3% aged 6 and older	Congenital rubella syndrome treatment	$354,000 (lifetime)

* Interventions represent examples (other interventions may apply).

† Representative first-year costs, except as noted. Not indicated are nonmedical costs, such as lost productivity to society.

Source: From Healthy People 2000. Washington, DC: U.S. Public Health Service; 1990.

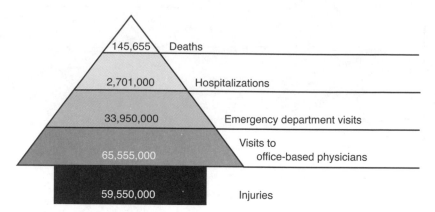

Figure 2-14   Health impacts of injuries. *Source:* From Burt CW. Injury-related visits to hospital emergency departments: United States, 1992. *Adv Data.* 1995:1–20.

another. As a result, there is a need to consider the costs of not realizing the benefits or gains from paths not chosen. A second economic consideration important for public health is related to the heavy emphasis of public health on preventive strategies. The savings or gains from successful prevention efforts are generally not reinvested in public health or even other health purposes. These savings or gains from investments in prevention are lost. Maybe this is proper because the overall benefits accrue more broadly to society and public health remains, above all else, a social enterprise; however, imagine the situation for American industry and businesses if they could not reinvest their gains to grow their businesses. This is often the situation faced by public health, further exacerbating the difficulty of arguing for and securing needed resources.

HEALTHY PEOPLE 2020

The data and discussion in this chapter only broadly describe health status measures in the United States in the early decades of the new century. Several common themes emerge, however, that form the basis for national health objectives focusing on the year 2020.[30] Figure 2-15 (similar to the model presented in Figure 2-11) depicts a national Healthy People process grounded in a broad view of the many factors influencing health. The year 2020 objectives build on the nation's experience with three previous panels of health objectives established for the years 1990, 2000, and 2010. The Healthy People 1990 effort was initiated in the late 1970s through the efforts of Surgeon General Julius Richmond and coordinated by the Office of Disease Prevention and Health Promotion within the Office of the Assistant Secretary for Health.

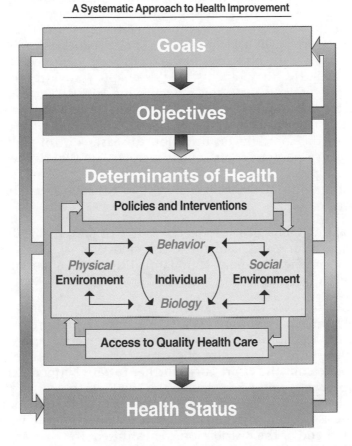

Figure 2-15 The Healthy People 2010 model. *Source:* From U.S. Dept. of Health and Human Services, Office of Disease Prevention and Health Promotion. *Healthy People 2010: Understanding and Improving Health.* Rockville, MD: ODPHP; 2000.

Assessments of the HP2000 and Healthy People 2010 (HP2010) efforts yielded similar findings. In general, progress was apparent for many of the broader goals, especially the age-adjusted mortality targets for age groups under age 70. Nonetheless, a substantial proportion of the objectives targeting special populations, especially African Americans and Native Americans, were found to be moving in the wrong direction. These findings fueled concerns that health inequities and disparities were persisting, if not increasing, in the United States. In addition, with nearly 500 objectives established in both the 2000 and 2010 efforts, tracking became a complex undertaking. Many objectives could not be tracked because of the unavailability of or lack of consensus for the tracking measures.

The HP2010 process, for the first time, highlighted a panel of leading health indicators for 10 categories that would summarize and synthesize overall population health status and trends (Table 2-9). The Healthy People 2020 (HP2020) process will likely establish a similar panel of leading health indicators drawn from the objectives in the focus areas identified in Table 2-10. One of the Public Health Spotlights for this chapter provides additional information on the progress made toward achieving HP2010's overarching goals and objectives. A second Public Health Spotlight for this chapter reviews progress and problems related to achieving HP2020 objectives related to tobacco use, similar to the spotlight on infectious disease control and immunizations included in Chapter 1. Subsequent chapters spotlight other leading health indicator topics.

Central to the HP2020 effort are two of the four overarching goals, which focus on:

1. Attaining high-quality, longer lives free of preventable disease, disability, injury, and premature death; and
2. Achieving health equity, eliminating disparities, and improving the health of all groups.

Although these two overarching goals appear appropriate, they are only arguably linked. From one perspective, they represent two very different approaches to improving outcomes for the population as a whole. If we view the health status of the entire population as a Gaussian curve, one approach would be to shift the entire curve further toward better outcomes, and a second approach would be to change the shape of the curve, reducing the difference between the extremes. These represent quite different strategies that would be associated with quite different policies and interventions. Focusing on the tail end of the distribution of health requires investment in questionably effective attempts that benefit relatively few and fail to promote the health of the majority. On the other hand, even small improvements in overall society-wide health measures have provided greater gains for society than very perceptible improvements in the health of a few.[31] The choice is one that can be viewed as focusing on "epiphenomena," such as risk factors or on the larger context and social environment. HP2010 ambitiously seeks to do both.

Monitoring all national health objectives is especially cumbersome at the state and local level. Instead, priorities linked to the national health objectives will likely be tracked. An Institute of Medicine committee in 1997 identified a basic set of indicators for use in community health improvement processes (Table 2-11). This panel is notably more comprehensive than one promoted for use with the HP2000 activities of the 1990s. Together with the catalog of leading health indicators from the current Healthy People process, these measures offer a useful starting point for population-based health improvement initiatives.

Table 2-9   Healthy People 2010 Leading Indicators

Physical Activity
- Proportion of adolescents who engage in vigorous physical activity that promotes cardio-respiratory fitness 3 or more days per week for 20 or more minutes per occasion
- Proportion of adults who engage regularly, preferably daily, in moderate physical activity for at least 30 minutes a day

Overweight and Obesity
- Proportion of children and adolescents who are overweight or obese
- Proportion of adults who are obese

Tobacco Use
- Proportion of adolescents who smoke
- Proportion of adults who smoke

Substance Abuse
- Proportion of adolescents not using alcohol or any illicit drugs during the past 30 days
- Proportion of adults using any illicit drug during the past 30 days
- Proportion of adults engaging in binge drinking of alcoholic beverages during the past month

Responsible Sexual Behavior
- Proportion of adolescents who abstain from sexual intercourse or use condoms if sexually active
- Proportion of sexually active persons who use condoms

Mental Health
- Proportion of adults with recognized depression who receive treatment

Injury and Violence
- Death rates caused by motor vehicle crashes
- Death rates caused by homicides

Environmental Quality
- Proportion of persons exposed to air that does not meet the U.S. Environmental Protection Agency's health-based standards for ozone
- Proportion of nonsmokers exposed to environmental tobacco smoke

Immunization
- Proportion of young children who receive all vaccines that have been recommended for universal administration for at least 5 years
- Proportion of noninstitutionalized adults who are vaccinated annually against influenza and ever vaccinated against pneumococcal disease

Access to Health Care
- Proportion of persons with health insurance
- Proportion of persons who have a specific source of ongoing care
- Proportion of pregnant women who begin prenatal care in the first trimester of pregnancy

Source: From the Office of Disease Prevention and Health Promotion. *Healthy People 2010: Understanding and Improving Health.* Rockville, MD: Office of Disease Prevention and Health Promotion; 2000.

Table 2-10   Healthy People 2020 Vision, Mission, Goals, and Focus Areas

Vision
A society in which all people live long, healthy lives.

Mission
Healthy People 2020 strives to:
* Identify nationwide health improvement priorities;
* Increase public awareness and understanding of the determinants of health, disease, and disability and the opportunities for progress;
* Provide measurable objectives and goals that are applicable at the national, state, and local levels;
* Engage multiple sectors to take action to strengthen policies and improve practices that are driven by the best available evidence and knowledge;
* Identify critical research, evaluation, and data collection needs.

Overarching Goals
* Attain high quality, longer lives free of preventable disease, disability, injury, and premature death.
* Achieve health equity, eliminate disparities, and improve the health of all groups.
* Create social and physical environments that promote good health for all.
* Promote quality of life, healthy development, and healthy behaviors across all life stages.

Focus Areas
1. Access to health services
2. Adolescent health
3. Arthritis, osteoporosis, and chronic back conditions
4. Blood disorders and blood safety
5. Cancer
6. Chronic kidney diseases
7. Diabetes
8. Disability and secondary conditions
9. Early and middle childhood
10. Educational and community-based programs
11. Environmental health
12. Family planning
13. Food safety
14. Genomics
15. Global health
16. Health communication and health IT
17. Healthcare-associated infections
18. Hearing and other sensory or communication disorders (ear, nose, throat—voice, speech, and language)
19. Heart disease and stroke
20. HIV
21. Immunization and infectious diseases
22. Injury and violence prevention
23. Maternal, infant, and child health
24. Medical product safety
25. Mental health and mental disorders
26. Nutrition and weight status
27. Occupational safety and health

Table 2-10   Healthy People 2020 Vision, Mission, Goals, and Focus Areas (continued)

28. Older adults
29. Oral health
30. Physical activity and fitness
31. Public health infrastructure
32. Quality of life and well-being
33. Respiratory diseases
34. Sexually transmitted diseases
35. Social determinants of health
36. Substance abuse
37. Tobacco use
38. Vision

Source: Data from U.S. Department of Health and Human Services. Healthy People 2020 website. www.healthypeople.gov. Accessed May 2010.

CONCLUSION

From an ecological perspective, the health status of a population is influenced by many factors drawn from biology, behavior, the environment, and the use of health services. Social and cultural factors also play an important role in the disease patterns experienced by different populations, as well as in the responses of these populations to disease and illness. Globally, risks associated with population growth, pollution, and poverty result in mortality and morbidity that are still associated with infectious disease processes. In the United States, behaviorally mediated risks, including tobacco, diet, alcohol, and injury risks, rather than infectious disease processes, remain major contributors to health status, and the considerable gap between low-income minority populations and other Americans continues to widen. Public health activities strive to improve population health status (effectiveness) through cost-beneficial strategies and interventions (efficiency) and with equal benefits for all segments of the population (equity). Elimination and reduction of the disparities in health status among population groups have emerged as perhaps the most critical national health goal for the year 2020. With the increasing availability of data on health status, as well as on determinants and contributing factors, the potential for more rational policies and interventions has increased. Over the long term, public policies that narrow income disparities and increase access to education, jobs, and housing will be more likely to improve the health status of populations than efforts to provide more health-care services. Health improvement efforts in the new century will require more than data on health problems and contributing factors, although these view health from a negative perspective. Also needed is information from a positive perspective, in terms of community capacities, assets, and willingness. More important still, there must be recognition and acceptance that the right to health is a basic human right and one inextricably linked to all other

Table 2-11   Proposed Indicators for a Community Health Profile

Sociodemographic Characteristics
 1. Distribution of the population by age and race/ethnicity
 2. Number and proportion of persons in groups such as migrants, homeless, or the non-English speaking for whom access to community services and resources may be a concern
 3. Number and proportion of persons aged 25 and older with less than a high school education
 4. Ratio of the number of students graduating from high school to the number of students who entered ninth grade 3 years previously
 5. Median household income
 6. Proportion of children less than 15 years of age living in families at or below the poverty level
 7. Unemployment rate
 8. Number and proportion of single-parent families
 9. Number and proportion of persons without health insurance

Health Status
 10. Infant mortality rate by race/ethnicity
 11. Numbers of deaths or age-adjusted death rates for motor vehicle crashes, work-related injuries, suicide, homicide, lung cancer, breast cancer, cardiovascular diseases, and all causes by age, race, and gender, as appropriate
 12. Reported incidence of AIDS, measles, tuberculosis, and primary and secondary syphilis by age, race, and gender, as appropriate
 13. Births to adolescents (ages 10 to 17) as the proportion of total live births
 14. Number and rate of confirmed abuse and neglect cases among children

Health Risk Factors
 15. Proportion of 2-year-old children who have received all age-appropriate vaccines, as recommended by the Advisory Committee on Immunization Practices
 16. Proportion of adults 65 years old and older who have ever been immunized for pneumococcal pneumonia; proportion who have been immunized in the past 12 months for influenza
 17. Proportion of the population who smoke, by age, race, and gender, as appropriate
 18. Proportion of the population aged 18 or older who are obese
 19. Number and type of U.S. Environmental Protection Agency air quality standards not met
 20. Proportion of assessed rivers, lakes, and estuaries that support beneficial uses (e.g., fishing and swimming approved)

Healthcare Resource Consumption
 21. Per-capita healthcare spending for Medicare beneficiaries (the Medicaid-adjusted average per capita cost)

Functional Status
 22. Proportion of adults reporting that their general health is good to excellent
 23. During the past 30 days, the average number of days for which adults report that their physical or mental health was not good

Quality of Life
 24. Proportion of adults satisfied with the healthcare system in the community
 25. Proportion of persons satisfied with the quality of life in the community

Source: Data from the Institute of Medicine. *Using Performance Monitoring to Improve Community Health: A Role for Performance Monitoring.* Washington, DC: National Academy Press; 1997.

human rights, lest quality of life be seriously compromised.[32] It is this right to health that enables the practice of public health and challenges public health workers to measure health and quality of life in ways that promote its improvement.

DISCUSSION QUESTIONS AND EXERCISES

1. Is poverty a cause of poor health in a community, or is poor health a cause of poverty? How would different views of this question influence public health policy?
2. You have been asked to review and improve the consensus list of important health status indicators (see Table 2-11). Identify and justify five indicators you would add to this list.
3. Visit the Internet website of one of the national print media and use the search features to identify articles on public health for a recent month. Catalog the health problems (both conditions and risks) from that search and compare this with the listing of health problems and issues on Table 2-4. Are the types of conditions and risks you encountered in the print media similar to those on Table 2-4? Were some conditions and risks either overrepresented or underrepresented in the media, in comparison with their relative importance as suggested by Table 2-4? What are the implications for the role of the media in informing and educating the public regarding public health issues?
4. Examine each of these websites. Which ones are most useful for the major topics examined in this part of the course? Why?
   - Healthfinder: http://www.healthfinder.gov, a Department of Health and Human Services-sponsored gateway site that provides links to more than 550 websites (including more than 200 federal sites and 350 state, local, not-for-profit, university, and other consumer health sources), nearly 500 selected online documents, frequently asked questions on health issues, and databases and Web search engines by topic and agency
   - Fedstats: http://www.fedstats.gov, a gateway to a variety of federal agency data and information, including health statistics
   - National Center for Health Statistics: http://www.cdc.gov/nchswww, an invaluable resource for data and information, especially "Health, United States," which can be downloaded from this site
   - CDC Mortality and Morbidity Weekly Report: http://www2.cdc.gov/mmwr, and MMWR morbidity and mortality data by time and place: http://www2.cdc.gov/mmwr/distrnds.html
   - U.S. Census data: http://www.census.gov, the best general denominator data anywhere

5. Compare the two 20th century public health achievements presented in the Public Health Spotlights for Chapter 1 (control of infectious diseases) and Chapter 2 (tobacco use). Which of these accomplishments, in your opinion, has had the greatest impact on the health status and quality of life of Americans living in the early 21st century? Justify your selection.

6. After reviewing the Chapter 2 Public Health Spotlight on Tobacco Use, select a health outcome related to tobacco use and analyze that problem for its determinants and contributing factors, using the method described in the text. Identify at least two major determinants for the problem that you select. For each determinant, identify at least two direct contributing factors, and for each direct contributing factor, identify at least two indirect contributing factors. At what level of your analysis does tobacco use appear as a risk factor?

7. The Public Health Spotlight on Tobacco Use presents data on several HP2020 objectives related to tobacco use. What are some important factors that must be addressed to achieve these targets in view of trends since 1990?

8. Population, poverty, and pollution are sometimes cited as the three most important factors influencing global health status today. After examining the WHO website (http://www.who.ch), cite reasons for agreeing or disagreeing with this assertion.

9. Great Debate: There are three propositions to be considered. Proposition A: Disease entities should be listed as official causes of death. Proposition B: Underlying factors that result in these diseases should be listed as official causes of death. Proposition C: No causes of death should be listed on death certificates. Select one of these positions and develop a position statement with your rationale.

10. Projections call for a continuing increase in life expectancy through the first half of the 21st century. What effect will increased life expectancy have on the major goals of HP2020—increasing the quality and years of healthy life and eliminating health disparities?

REFERENCES

1. Centers for Disease Control and Prevention, National Center for Health Statistics. *Health, United States, 2006.* Hyattsville, MD: NCHS; 2006.

2. Allaire SH, LaValley MP, Evans SR, et al. Evidence for decline in disability and improved health among persons aged 55 to 70 years: the Framingham heart study. *Am J Public Health.* 1999;89:1678–1683.

3. Constitution of World Health Organization. In: *World Health Organization. Chronicle of World Health Organization.* Geneva, Switzerland: World Health Organization; 1947;1:29–43.

4. Whaley RF, Hashim TJ. *A Textbook of World Health.* New York: Parthenon; 1995.

5. Centers for Disease Control and Prevention. First reportable underlying cause of death. *MMWR.* 1996;45:537.

6. Brownson RC, Remington PL, Davis JR, eds. *Chronic Disease Epidemiology and Control*. 2nd ed. Washington, DC: American Public Health Association; 1998.

7. Cohen D, Mason K, Bedimo A, et al. Neighborhood physical conditions and health. *Am J Public Health*. 2003;93:467–471.

8. Amler RW, Eddins DL. Cross-sectional analysis: precursors of premature death in the U.S. In: Amler RW, Dull DL, eds. *Closing the Gap*. Atlanta, GA: Carter Center; 1985:181–187.

9. Mokdad AH, Marks JS, Stroup DF, et al. Actual causes of death in the United States, 2000. *JAMA*. 2004;291:1238–1245.

10. Chadwick E. *Report on the Sanitary Conditions of the Labouring Population of Great Britain 1842*. Edinburgh, Scotland: Edinburgh University Press; 1965.

11. Smith GD, Egger M. Socioeconomic differences in mortality in Britain and the United States. *Am J Public Health*. 1992;82:1079–1081.

12. Schrijvers CTM, Stronks K, van de Mheen HD, et al. Explaining educational differences in mortality: the role of behavioral and material factors. *Am J Public Health*. 1999;89:535–540.

13. Centers for Disease Control and Prevention. Poverty and infant mortality: United States, 1988. *MMWR*. 1996;44:922–927.

14. Ng-Mak DS, Dohrenwend BP, Abraido-Lanza AF, et al. A further analysis of race differences in the national longitudinal mortality study. *Am J Public Health*. 1999;89:1748–1751.

15. Wilkenson RG. National mortality rates: the impact of inequality. *Am J Public Health*. 1992;82:1082–1084.

16. Marmot M. The influence of income on health: views of an epidemiologist. *Health Aff*. 2002; 21:31–46.

17. Sargent CF, Johnson TM, eds. *Medical Anthropology: Contemporary Theory and Method*. Rev ed. Westport, CT: Praeger Publishers; 1996.

18. Susser M, Watson W, Hopper K. *Sociology in Medicine*. New York: Oxford University Press; 1985.

19. Link BG, Phelan JC. Understanding sociodemographic differences in health: the role of fundamental social causes. *Am J Public Health*. 1996;86:471–473.

20. Friedman SR, Curtis R, Neaigus A, et al. *Social Networks, Drug Injectors' Lives and HIV/AIDS*. New York: Kluwer Academic Publishers; 1999.

21. Kawachi I, Kennedy BP, Glass R. Social capital and self-rated health: a contextual analysis. *Am J Public Health*. 1999;89:1187–1193.

22. Malmstom M, Sundquist J, Johansson SE. Neighborhood environment and self-reported health status: a multilevel analysis. *Am J Public Health*. 1999;89:1181–1186.

23. Doll R. Health and the environment in the 1990s. *Am J Public Health*. 1992;82:933–941.

24. Winkelstein W. Determinants of worldwide health. *Am J Public Health*. 1992;82:931–932.

25. Intergovernmental Panel on Climate Change. Impacts, Adaptation, and Vulnerability. Contribution of Working Group II to the Third Assessment Report of the Intergovernmental Panel on Climate Change. In: McCarthy JJ, Canziani OF, Leary NA, Dokken DJ, White KS, eds. *Climate Change 2001*. Cambridge UK; Cambridge University Press, 2001.

26. Fielding JE. Public health in the twentieth century: advances and challenges. *Annu Rev Public Health*. 1999;20:xiii–xxx.

27. Centers for Disease Control and Prevention, National Center for Health Statistics. *Healthy People 2000*. Hyattsville, MD: NCHS; 1990.

28. Burt CW. Injury-related visits to hospital emergency departments: United States, 1992. *Adv Data*. 1995:261:1–20.

29. U.S. Public Health Service. *For a Healthy Nation: Return on Investments in Public Health*. Washington, DC: PHS; 1994.

30. Centers for Disease Control and Prevention, National Center for Health Statistics. *Healthy People 2000 Final Review*. Hyattsville, MD: NCHS; 2001.

31. McKinlay JB, Marceau LD. A tale of 3 tails. *Am J Public Health*. 1999;89:295–298.

32. Universal Declaration of Human Rights. GA res 217 A(iii), UN Doc A/810, art 25(1);1948.

Public Health Spotlight on Healthy People 2010 Progress[1]

The Healthy People 2020 process provides a comprehensive, national health promotion and disease prevention agenda and serves as a road map for improving the health of all people in the United States during the second decade of the 21st century. Table 2-10 summarizes the vision, mission, and overarching goals that provide structure and guidance for achieving the HP2020 objectives. While general in nature, they offer specific, important areas of emphasis where action must be taken if the United States is to achieve better health by the year 2020. Developed under the leadership of the Federal Interagency Workgroup, the HP2020 framework is the product of an exhaustive collaborative process among the U.S. Department of Health and Human Services (see Chapter 4) and other federal agencies, public stakeholders, and the Secretary's Advisory Committee on Health Promotion and Disease Prevention Objectives for 2020. In order to better appreciate where the Healthy People process is going, it is useful to see where it has been. This Public Health Spotlight traces the nation's progress toward achieving the objectives established for the year 2010. The midcourse review in 2005 provided an opportunity to assess the progress made during the first half of the decade. This assessment focused on 467 objectives and 2 over-arching goals: increasing quality and years of healthy life and eliminating health disparities.

GOALS

The first HP2010 goal highlighted the importance of increasing and maximizing both years and quality of healthy life. Progress toward this goal was assessed by measuring life expectancy and healthy life expectancies. These assessments resulted in several conclusions, including:

- Life expectancy continues to improve for the populations that could be assessed in the midcourse review.
- Women continue to have a longer life expectancy than men, and the white population has a longer life expectancy than the African American population.
- Three different measures of healthy life expectancy demonstrate gender and racial differences: expected years in good or better health, expected years free of activity limitations, and expected years free of selected chronic diseases.
- Expected years in good or better health and expected years free of activity limitations increased slightly, and expected years free of selected chronic conditions decreased.

The second goal of HP2010 sought to address the substantial dispar-ities among populations in specific measures of health, life expectancy, and quality of life. That goal was to eliminate health disparities that occur by race and ethnicity, gender, education, income, geographic location, disability status, or sexual orientation. There has been widespread improvement in objectives for nearly all of the populations associated with these characteristics; however, progress toward the target for individual populations and progress toward the goal to eliminate disparities are independent of each other. Improvements for individual populations—even improvements for all of the populations for a characteristic—do not necessarily ensure the elimination of disparities. This section focuses specifically on relative disparities between populations and changes in these relative disparities over time, regardless of whether the rates for specific populations are moving toward or away from the targets for each objective.

Disparities between populations and the persistence of disparities over time have been well documented. Unlike previous Healthy People initiatives, HP2010 called for monitoring objectives for an extensive array of specific population characteristics. All population-based objectives and subobjectives were monitored by race and ethnicity, by income or education, and by gender (if applicable). Monitoring for other characteristics (i.e., geographic location and disability status) was optional. HP2010, therefore, provided the basis for a broad examination of disparities among populations and changes in disparities over time. The findings concerning disparities among populations are summarized here.

- Substantial disparities between populations were evident for many HP2010 objectives.
- Both increases and decreases in relative disparities were evident for individual populations for specific objectives and subobjectives; however, there was no change in disparity for most of the objectives and subobjectives with data for any group.
- Among 195 objectives and subobjectives with trend data for racial and ethnic groups, disparities decreased for 24 and increased for 14.
- Among 238 objectives and subobjectives with trend data for males and females, disparities decreased for 25 and increased for 15. Females more often had the best group rate, and reductions in disparity were more frequent among males.
- Among education groups, disparities decreased for 3 objectives and subobjectives and increased for 14.
- Among income groups, among geographic groups, and between persons with disabilities and persons without disabilities, there were few changes in disparities.

OBJECTIVES

Through the midcourse review, the status of 467 specific objectives in 28 focus areas was assessed. One hundred forty-two of these objectives consisted of two or more subobjectives that identified specific aspects of an objective (such as types of vaccines and types of air pollutants). Altogether, there were 955 objectives and subobjectives. Baseline values were established for each objective and subobjective with data at the beginning of the decade, and specific targets were set to be achieved by the year 2010. Progress was assessed for objectives and subobjectives with tracking data (i.e., with baseline data and data more recent than the baseline) as of January 2005. More recent data are monitored as they become available. The DATA2010 database is updated regularly.

The status of the 467 objectives as of January 2005 is shown in Table 2-12. Based on an evaluation of each objective and comments received from the public as part of the midcourse review process, 28 objectives were deleted because data were not available or because of a change in science. As of January 2005, tracking data were not available to assess progress for 158 objectives (34% of the total). Baseline data were not available but are anticipated by the end of the decade for 87 of these objectives. Timely availability of data continues to be an issue in monitoring the health of the nation.

Progress was assessed for the 281 objectives with tracking data available:

- Twenty-nine objectives (10%) met the target.
- One hundred thirty-eight objectives (49%) moved toward the target.
- Forty objectives (14%) demonstrated mixed progress because they included subobjectives that moved both toward and away from the target.
- Seventeen objectives (6%) demonstrated no change from the baseline.
- Fifty-seven objectives (20%) moved away from the target.

In Table 2-13, similar assessments are shown for each of the 28 focus areas. In all focus areas, there are some objectives that met, exceeded, or

Table 2-12 Healthy People 2010 Objectives: Status at the Midcourse and Summary of Progress Toward Target Attainment

467 Total Objectives in Healthy People 2010

	Percentage	Number of Objectives
Dropped at midcourse	6%	28
Could not be assessed	34%	158
Tracking data available (see following section of table)	60%	281

281 Objectives with Tracking Data

	Percentage	Number of Objectives
Met or exceeded target	10%	29
Moved toward target	49%	138
Demonstrated no change	6%	17
Mixed (toward and away)	14%	40
Moved away from target	20%	57

Source: From U.S. Department of Health and Human Services, Office of Disease Prevention and Health Promotion. *Healthy People 2010 Mid Course Review*. Rockville, MD: Office of Disease Prevention and Health Promotion; 2006.

Table 2-13 Healthy People 2010 Objectives: Summary of Progress for Each Focus Area

Focus Area	Met or Exceeded Target	Moved Toward Target	Demonstrated No Change	Demonstrated Mixed Progress	Moved Away From Target	Could Not Be Assessed	Dropped at Midcourse	Total
1. Access to quality health services	1	4	1	2	1	6	1	16
2. Arthritis, osteoporosis, and chronic back conditions	0	4	2	1	2	2	0	11
3. Cancer	2	7	2	2	0	2	0	15
4. Chronic kidney disease	0	1	0	0	5	2	0	8
5. Diabetes	3	6	1	0	4	1	2	17
6. Disability and secondary conditions	0	4	0	1	2	6	0	13
7. Educational- and community-based programs	1	1	0	1	1	4	4	12
8. Environmental health	1	7	0	2	1	17	2	30
9. Family planning	0	4	0	0	4	5	0	13
10. Food safety	0	1	0	3	0	2	1	7
11. Health communication	0	1	0	0	1	4	0	6
12. Heart disease and stroke	1	6	1	1	1	6	0	16
13. HIV	1	7	1	1	1	3	4	18
14. Immunization and infectious diseases	8	15	0	2	1	4	1	31
15. Injury and violence prevention	2	15	0	2	11	9	0	39
16. Maternal, infant, and child health	1	4	0	5	3	10	0	23
17. Medical product safety	1	1	0	1	0	1	2	6
18. Mental health and mental disorders	0	3	2	0	3	6	0	14
19. Nutrition and overweight	0	1	1	1	5	9	1	18
20. Occupational safety and health	1	2	1	0	0	7	0	11
21. Oral health	0	6	1	2	1	7	0	17
22. Physical activity and fitness	0	7	0	0	3	5	0	15
23. Public health infrastructure	0	1	1	0	0	12	3	17
24. Respiratory diseases	0	6	1	3	0	2	0	12
25. Sexually transmitted diseases	2	4	0	2	0	3	7	18
26. Substance abuse	2	4	1	6	6	6	0	25
27. Tobacco use	1	3	0	1	1	9	0	21
28. Vision and hearing	0	3	0	1	0	13	1	18
Total	29	138	17	40	57	158	28	467

Source: From U.S. Dept. of Health and Human Services, Office of Disease Prevention and Health Promotion. *Healthy People 2010 Mid Course Review.* Rockville, MD: Office of Disease Prevention and Health Promotion; 2006.

moved toward the target. In Cancer (Focus Area 3), Diabetes (Focus Area 5), Immunization and Infectious Diseases (Focus Area 14), and Occupational Safety and Health (Focus Area 20), more than half of the objectives met or moved toward their targets. The proportion of objectives that could not be assessed is relatively large in Environmental Health (Focus Area 8), Health Communication (Focus Area 11), Public Health Infrastructure (Focus Area 23), and Vision and Hearing (Focus Area 28).

Of the 955 objectives and subobjectives, a total of 67 objectives and subobjectives were dropped at the midcourse, and 381 objectives and subobjectives lacked tracking data. Progress was assessed for the 507 objectives and subobjectives with data at the baseline and data for the most recent data point available in the Healthy People data system as of January 2005:

- Seventy objectives and subobjectives (14%) met the target.
- Two hundred eighty-six objectives and subobjectives (56%) moved toward the target.
- Thirty-eight objectives and subobjectives (8%) demonstrated no change.
- One hundred thirteen objectives and subobjectives (22%) moved away from the target.

POPULATIONS

Progress was also assessed for specific populations. For each population, the number of objectives and subobjectives is shown for each of the following: moved away from the target, demonstrated no change, moved toward the target, and met or exceeded the target. Because a single target was set for all populations, there are some instances where a population met the HP2010 target at the baseline. The numbers of these objectives and subobjectives are shown separately in Table 2-14.

In general, the number of population-based objectives and subobjectives that moved toward the target or for which the target was met at baseline exceeds the number that moved away from the target. For the American Indian or Alaska Native population, for example, 87 objectives and subobjectives moved toward their respective targets, whereas 41 moved away. This population demonstrated no change between the baseline and the most recent data point for 10 objectives and subobjectives. The number of objectives and subobjectives that moved toward the target or met the target at baseline exceeds the number that moved away from the target by a ratio of at least 2:1 for all but the following: the Asian or Pacific Islander population, the Asian population, the Native Hawaiian or other Pacific Islander population, persons identifying with two or more races, persons with less than a high school education, high school graduates, and persons in both the poor and near-poor income groups. For the Native Hawaiian or other Pacific Islander population, there were more objectives and subobjectives that moved away from the target (19) than moved toward the target (15).

Table 2-14 Number of Objectives and Subobjectives with Tracking Data According to the Progress Quotient for Population Groups

Characteristics and Groups	Moved Away from Target					Demonstrated No Change	Moved Toward Target				
			Percent of Targeted Change Achieved								
	Total	Target Met at Baseline*	100+	50 to 99	1 to 49	0	1 to 49	50 to 99	100+	Target Met at Baseline	Total
						(Number of Objectives)					
Race and Ethnicity											
American Indian or Alaska Native	41	1	5	3	32	10	54	17	7	9	87
Asian or Pacific Islander	26	1	12	3	10	3	15	10	11	10	46
Asian	28	0	12	4	12	7	23	8	15	5	51
Native Hawaiian or other Pacific Islander	19	3	2	5	9	5	9	3	2	1	15
Two or more races	21	2	4	4	11	6	18	2	7	3	30
Hispanic	77	0	10	8	59	19	104	38	19	13	174
Black non-Hispanic[†]	86	2	18	17	49	24	126	38	33	2	199
White non-Hispanic[†]	94	3	26	22	43	29	90	43	50	12	195
Gender											
Female	81	5	16	16	44	27	103	44	31	22	200
Male	78	7	13	5	53	18	116	40	21	10	187
Education											
Less than high school	27	0	2	2	23	10	44	6	1	0	51
High school graduate	32	0	3	8	21	14	34	7	1	1	43
At least some college	22	2	5	2	13	9	28	10	9	11	58

(continues)

Table 2-14 Number of Objectives and Subobjectives with Tracking Data According to the Progress Quotient for Population Groups (continued)

Income											
Poor	27	2	1	3	21	5	31	9	5	3	48
Near poor	25	0	3	4	18	8	22	8	3	6	39
Middle/high	21	3	5	4	9	9	20	6	11	8	45
Location											
Urban/metropolitan	11	0	0	2	9	7	13	6	3	2	24
Rural/nonmetropolitan	10	0	5	3	2	7	14	7	1	3	25
Disability status											
Persons with disabilities	15	0	1	1	13	4	23	5	5	2	35
Persons without disabilities	14	0	2	5	7	7	21	7	5	1	34

* Among population groups, the target for some objectives and subobjectives was met at the baseline, but more recent data indicate that the target was no longer achieved. The percentage of target achieved could not be calculated.

† For some objectives and subobjectives, data include persons of Hispanic origin.

Source: From the U.S. Department of Health and Human Services, Office of Disease Prevention and Health Promotion. *Healthy People 2010 Mid Course Review.* Rockville, MD: Office of Disease Prevention and Health Promotion; 2006.

In Table 2-14, a progress quotient is used to quantify the degree of progress toward or away from the target for those population-based objectives and subobjectives with tracking data. The progress quotient measures the percent of targeted change that has been achieved. The baseline value, the most recent value, and the target are used to compute the progress quotient. A progress quotient of 50%, for example, indicates that the difference between the baseline and the target has been reduced by 50% or by one half. A progress quotient greater than 100% indicates that the target has been exceeded. Negative progress quotients indicate that the change from the baseline is away from the target.

LEADING HEALTH INDICATORS

The national agenda for disease prevention and health promotion also identified 10 leading indicators of population health and measures that would assist communities and the nation in tracking progress toward improved health status. Table 2-15 provides a composite look at the 10 leading indicators and 22 measures related to those indicators in terms of progress being made toward achieving national targets estab-

Table 2-15   Healthy People 2010 Leading Health Indicators

Immunization
- Objective 14-24: Increase the proportion of young children and adolescents who receive all vaccines that have been recommended for universal administration for at least 5 years.
- Objective 14-29a: Increase the proportion of noninstitutionalized adults who are vaccinated annually against influenza.
- Objective 14-29b: Increase the proportion of noninstitutionalized adults who are ever vaccinated against pneumococcal disease.

Tobacco Use
- Objective 27-1a: Reduce tobacco use by adults—cigarette smoking.
- Objective 27-2b: Reduce tobacco use by adolescents—cigarettes.

Access to Health Care
- Objective 1-1: Increase the proportion of persons with health insurance.
- Objective 1-4a: Increase the proportion of persons of all ages who have a specific source of ongoing care.
- Objective 16-6a: Increase the proportion of pregnant women who receive early and adequate prenatal care beginning in the first trimester of pregnancy.

Environmental Quality
- Objective 8-1a: Reduce the proportion of persons exposed to air that does not meet the U.S. Environmental Protection Agency's health-based standards for harmful air pollutants—ozone.
- Objective 27-10: Reduce the proportion of nonsmokers exposed to environmental tobacco smoke.

Physical Activity
- Objective 22-2: Increase the proportion of adults who engage in moderate physical activity for at least 30 minutes per day 5 or more days per week or vigorous physical activity for at least 20 minutes per day 3 or more days per week.
- Objective 22-7: Increase the proportion of adolescents who engage in vigorous physical activity that promotes cardiorespiratory fitness 3 or more days per week for 20 or more minutes per occasion.

Overweight and Obesity
- Objective 19-2: Reduce the proportion of adults who are obese.
- Objective 19-3c: Reduce the proportion of children and adolescents aged 6 to 19 who are overweight or obese.

Injury and Violence
- Objective 15-5: Reduce deaths caused by motor vehicle crashes.
- Objective 15-32: Reduce homicides.

Mental Health
- Objective 18-9b: Increase the proportion of adults aged 18 years and older with recognized depression who receive treatment.

Substance Abuse
- Objective 26-10a: Increase the proportion of adolescents not using alcohol or any illicit drugs during the past 30 days.

(continues)

Table 2-15   Healthy People 2010 Leading Health Indicators (continued)

- Objective 26-10c: Reduce the proportion of adults using any illicit drug during the past 30 days.
- Objective 26-11c: Reduce the proportion of persons aged 18 years and older engaging in binge drinking of alcoholic beverages.

Responsible Sexual Behavior
- Objective 13-6: Increase the proportion of sexually active persons who use condoms.
- Objective 25-11: Increase the proportion of adolescents who abstain from sexual intercourse or use condoms if currently sexually active.

Source: Data from the U.S. Department of Health and Human Services, Office of Disease Prevention and Health Promotion. *Healthy People 2010 Mid Course Review.* Rockville, MD: Office of Disease Prevention and Health Promotion; 2006.

lished for the year 2010. Baseline data for these measures come from a variety of sources and generally describe levels in the late 1990s when the HP2010 planning process was taking place. Figure 2-16 is a virtual scorecard of progress made from the baseline years through about the year 2005, delineating the percent of the targeted change that had been achieved at that time. Arguably, to be on track to achieve the year 2010 targets, about half of the targeted change should have been achieved by 2005.

Figure 2-16 summarizes the progress and problems the nation faced in achieving its public health aspirations for the year 2010. Progress was substantial for some leading indicators and their associated measures but not all. Some have actually experienced negative trends, moving further away from the year 2010 targets than we were in the late 1990s. The stories behind these developments and obstacles are included in the various chapters of this text. Chapter 1, for example, examined the leading indicator that focuses on immunizations and infectious diseases. Another Public Health Spotlight in this chapter looks at tobacco use in greater detail.

Although the list of leading indicators offers focus and consistency to state and local health improvement initiatives, some believe that 10 indicators and two dozen measures are too cumbersome and that a single public health index would be better. An index of leading health indicators (similar to the widely respected index of leading economic indicators) may be an element added to the national planning process for future iterations of the Healthy People Process. What that may look like challenges us all.

REFERENCE

1. U.S. Department of Health and Human Services. *Healthy People 2010: Mid Course Review.* Washington, DC; DHHS-PHS: 2006.

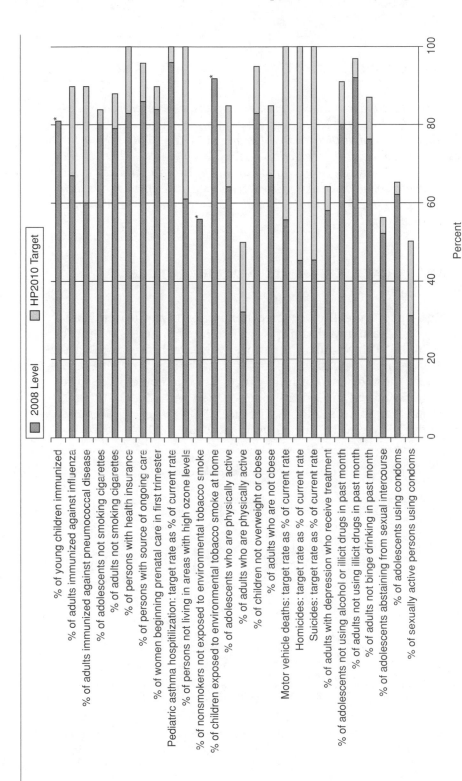

Figure 2-16 Scorecard for Healthy People 2010 leading indicators comparing 2008 levels with 2010 targets. *Source:* Data from Data 2010, Healthy People 2010 database. http://wonder.cdc.gov/data2010/ftpselec.htm. Accessed May 31, 2010.
*Indicates that 2010 targets had been reached and exceeded by 2008.

Public Health Spotlight on Tobacco Use

Initial suspicions that tobacco was harmful to humans were confirmed by epidemiologic studies in the mid 20th century, stimulating new interest in measures of health, illness, and their related factors. Since the 1990s, when the prevalence of tobacco use, a risk behavior, became a reportable condition, the deployment of a wide array of behavioral, social, legislative, and economic strategies to reduce tobacco use has become commonplace in public health practice. Highlights of these developments and today's challenges are captured in this Public Health Spotlight.

PUBLIC HEALTH ACHIEVEMENTS IN 20TH CENTURY AMERICA[1]

Smoking—once a socially accepted behavior—is the leading preventable cause of death and disability in the United States. During the first decades of the 20th century, lung cancer was rare; however, as cigarette smoking became increasingly popular, first among men and later among women, the incidence of lung cancer became epidemic (Figure 2-17). In 1930, the lung cancer death rate for men was 4.9 per 100,000; in 1990, the rate had increased to 75.6 per 100,000.[2] Other diseases and conditions now known to be caused by tobacco use include heart dis-

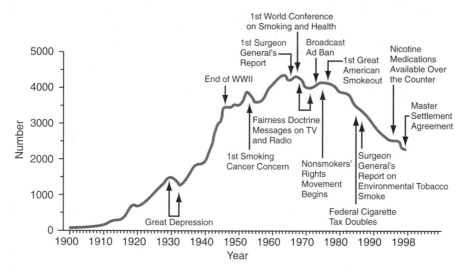

Figure 2-17 Annual adult per capita cigarette consumption and major smoking and health events, United States, 1900–1998. *Source:* From Centers for Disease Control and Prevention. Public health achievements, United States, 1900–1999: tobacco use. *MMWR.* 1999;48(43):986–993.

ease, atherosclerotic peripheral vascular disease, laryngeal cancer, oral cancer, esophageal cancer, chronic obstructive pulmonary disease, intrauterine growth retardation, and low birth weight. During the latter part of the 20th century, the adverse health effects from exposure to environmental tobacco smoke also were documented. These include lung cancer, asthma, respiratory infections, and decreased pulmonary function.[3]

Large epidemiologic studies conducted in the 1940s and 1950s linked cigarette smoking and lung cancer. In 1964, on the basis of approximately 7,000 articles relating to smoking and disease, the Advisory Committee to the U.S. Surgeon General concluded that cigarette smoking is a cause of lung and laryngeal cancer in men, a probable cause of lung cancer in women, and the most important cause of chronic bronchitis in both sexes.[4] The committee stated that "cigarette smoking is a health hazard of sufficient importance in the United States to warrant appropriate remedial action." Substantial public health efforts to reduce the prevalence of tobacco use began shortly after the risk was described in 1964. With the subsequent decline in smoking, the incidence of smoking-related cancers (including cancers of the lung, oral cavity, and pharynx) has also declined (with the exception of lung cancer among women).[5] In addition, age-adjusted death rates per 100,000 persons (standardized to the 1940 population) for heart conditions (i.e., coronary heart disease) have decreased from 307.4 in 1950 to 134.6 in 1996.[5] During 1964 to 1992, approximately 1.6 million deaths caused by smoking were prevented.[6]

Early in the 20th century, several events coincided that contributed to increases in annual per capita consumption, including the introduction of blends and curing processes that allowed the inhalation of tobacco, the invention of the safety match, improvements in mass production, transportation that permitted widespread distribution of cigarettes, and the use of mass media advertising to promote cigarettes.[7,8] Cigarette smoking among women began to increase in the 1920s, when targeted industry marketing and social changes reflecting the liberalization of women's roles and behavior led to the increasing acceptability of smoking among women.[9,10] Annual per capita cigarette consumption increased from 54 cigarettes in 1900 to 4,345 cigarettes in 1963 and then decreased to 2,261 in 1998.[11,12] Some decreases correlate with events, such as the first research suggesting a link between smoking and cancer in the 1950s, the 1964 Surgeon General's report, the 1968 Fairness Doctrine, and increased tobacco taxation and industry price increases during the 1980s (Figure 2-17).

An important accomplishment of the second half of the 20th century has been the reduction of smoking prevalence among persons aged greater than or equal to 18 years from 42.4% in 1965 to 24.7% in 1997, with the rate for men (27.6%) higher than for women (22.1%) (Figure 2-18). The percentage of adults who never smoked increased from 44% in the mid-1960s to 55% in 1997. In 1998, tobacco use varied within

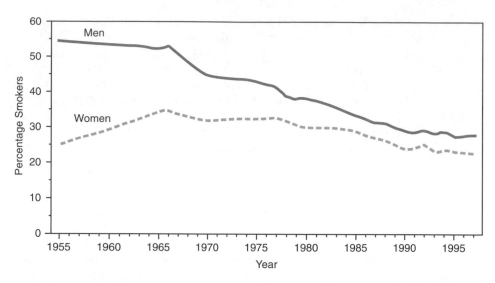

Figure 2-18   Trends in cigarette smoking among persons over 18 years by gender, United States, 1955–1997. *Source:* From Centers for Disease Control and Prevention. Public health achievements, United States, 1900–1999: tobacco use. *MMWR.* 1999;48(43):986–993.

and among racial/ethnic groups. The prevalence of smoking was highest among American Indians/Alaska Natives and second highest among black and Southeast Asian men. The prevalence was lowest among Asian American and Hispanic women.[13] Smokeless tobacco use has changed little since 1970, with a 5% prevalence in 1970 and a 6% prevalence in 1991 among men and 2% and 1%, respectively, for women. The prevalence of smokeless tobacco use is highest among high school males, with prevalence being 20% among white males, 6% among Hispanic males, and 4% among African American males. The prevalence of use tends to be lower in the northeastern region and higher in the southern region of the United States. Total consumption of cigars decreased from 8 million in 1970 to 2 million in 1993 but increased 68% to 3.6 million in 1997.[14]

Reductions in smoking result from many factors, including scientific evidence of the relationship among disease, tobacco use, and environmental exposure to tobacco; dissemination of this information to the public; surveillance and evaluation of prevention and cessation programs; campaigns by advocates for nonsmokers' rights; restrictions on cigarette advertising; counter advertising; policy changes (i.e., enforcement of minors' access laws, legislation restricting smoking in public places, and increased taxation); improvements in treatment and prevention programs; and an increased understanding of the economic costs of tobacco.

The cigarette itself has changed. When cigarettes were first associated with lung cancer in the early 1950s, most U.S. smokers smoked unfiltered cigarettes. With a growing awareness of the danger of smoking came the first filter, which was designed to reduce the tar inhaled in the smoke. Later, low-tar cigarettes were marketed; however, many smokers compensated by smoking more intensely and by blocking the filter's ventilation holes.[14] Adenocarcinoma has replaced squamous cell carcinoma as the leading cause of lung cancer-related death in the United States. This increase in adenocarcinoma parallels the changes in cigarette design and smoking behavior.[14]

Changes in the social norms surrounding smoking can be documented by examining changes in public policy, including availability of Fairness Doctrine counter advertising messages on television and radio and increased restrictions on tobacco advertising, beginning with the ban on broadcast advertising in 1971. Cigarette advertising no longer appears on television or billboards, and efforts to restrict sales and marketing to adolescents have increased. Indoor air policies switched from favoring smokers to favoring nonsmokers. Smoking is no longer permitted on airplanes, and many people, including 12.5% of adult smokers with children, do not smoke at home.[15] By 1999, 42 states had restrictions on smoking at government work sites, and 20 states had restrictions at private work sites.

One of the most effective means of reducing the prevalence of tobacco use is by increasing federal and state excise tax rates. A 10% increase in the price of cigarettes can lead to a 4% reduction in the demand for cigarettes. This reduction is the result of people smoking fewer cigarettes or quitting altogether.[16] Studies show that low income, adolescent, Hispanic, and African American smokers are more likely than others to stop smoking in response to a price increase.[16]

The November 1998 Master Settlement Agreement marked the end of the 20th century with an unprecedented event. Although admitting no wrongdoing, the tobacco companies signed an agreement with the attorneys general of 46 states. This agreement settled lawsuits totaling $206 billion; however, the agreement did not require that any of the state money be spent for tobacco use prevention and control.

21ST CENTURY PUBLIC HEALTH CHALLENGES

By the end of the 20th century, the tide had clearly turned in the war against tobacco, the nation's public health enemy number 1. Nevertheless, the United States still had nearly 50 million smokers and more than 400,000 tobacco-related deaths each year. Too many adolescents were initiating the tobacco habit, and the rate of adult smokers was no longer steadily falling. Tobacco use rates were substantially higher for African American and Native American males, and the harmful effects of environmental exposure to tobacco products, often known as second-hand smoke, for children and coworkers of smokers increased. Perhaps even more alarming, a dramatic increase in tobacco use was occurring worldwide. These and other trends are highlighted in the series of figures that follow.

Figure 2-19 highlights one of the reasons why tobacco consumption represents an imminent threat to developing countries where health warnings on tobacco packaging are much less frequent and effective. Figure 2-20 traces increases in federal and state excise taxes on tobacco products in the United States since 1995. Recent increases in federal excise taxes, coupled with the steady rise in state excise taxes, resulted in the combined federal and state excise tax rates achieving the $2-per-pack target established for the year 2010.

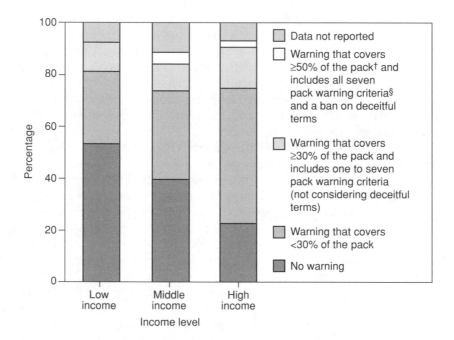

Figure 2-19   Percentage of countries that require health warnings on tobacco packaging, by extent of warning required and country income level*, World Health Organization, 2008.

* Countries are classified according to their 2007 gross national income per capita, calculated using the World Bank Atlas method, as low income (≤$935), middle income ($936–$11,455), and high income (≥ $11,456). Additional information is available at http://www.worldbank.org under Data and Research. Accessed May 31, 2010.

† http://www.who.int/tobacco/mpower/mpower_report_full_2008.pdf. Accessed May 31, 2010.

§ Data specific to health warnings were collected for seven criteria: (1) mandate of specific tobacco use health warnings; (2) inclusion of health warnings on tobacco packs and outside packaging; (3) use of large, clear, and visible health warnings; (4) rotation of health warnings; (5) use of the principal languages of the country; (6) inclusion of pictorial warnings; and (7) descriptions of specific harmful effects of tobacco use in health.

Source: From Centers for Disease Control and Prevention. Health warnings on tobacco products, worldwide, 2007. *MMWR.* 2009;58(19):528–529.

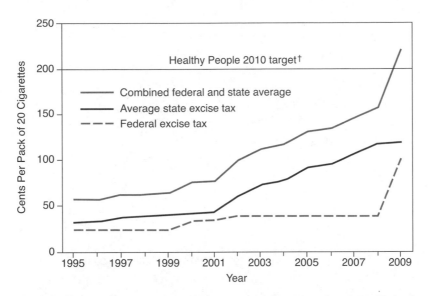

Figure 2-20 State and federal cigarette excise taxes, by year, United States,* 1995–2009.

* District of Columbia is included among results for states.

† Objective 27-21a: to increase the combined federal and average state cigarette excise tax to at least $2 per pack.

Source: From Centers for Disease Control and Prevention. Federal and state cigarette excise taxes, United States, 1995–2009. *MMWR.* 2009; 58(19):524–527.

Figures 2-21 and 2-22 illustrate current tobacco use rates among various segments of the population and document that the problem persists with about 438,000 deaths each year attributed to tobacco use.

Many different strategies and interventions appeared over recent decades to battle the huge tobacco threat. The Task Force on Community Preventive Services[17] systematically reviewed the effectiveness of a variety of strategies, including:

- Reducing tobacco use initiation
- Increasing tobacco use cessation
- Reducing exposure to environmental tobacco smoke
- Reducing minors' access to tobacco products
- Decreasing tobacco use in worksite settings, and
- Incentives and competitions to increase tobacco cessation

The task force found strong evidence of the effectiveness of several population-based interventions as of June 2010, including:

- Increasing the unit price for tobacco products
- Mass media campaigns when combined with additional interventions
- Provider reminder systems when used alone
- Provider reminder systems with provider education

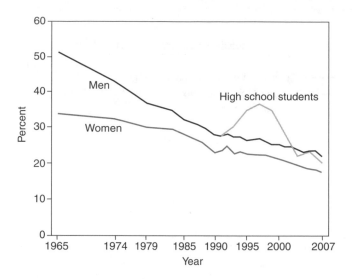

Figure 2-21   Cigarette smoking, selected populations, United States, 1965–2007. *Source:* From Centers for Disease Control and Prevention, National Center for Health Statistics, *Health, United States 2009*, Figure 6. Hyattsville, MD: NCHS; 2009.

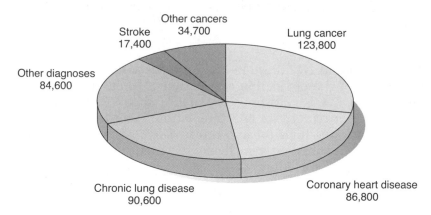

Figure 2-22   The tobacco problem persists: 438,000 deaths per year (average annual number of deaths 1997–2001). *Source:* From Centers for Disease Control and Prevention. *MMWR.* 2005;54(25):625–628.

- Reducing client out-of-pocket costs for cessation therapies
- Multicomponent interventions that include telephone support
- Smoking bans and restrictions
- Community mobilization with additional interventions
- Smoke-free policies to reduce tobacco use among workers
- Incentives and competitions when combined with additional interventions

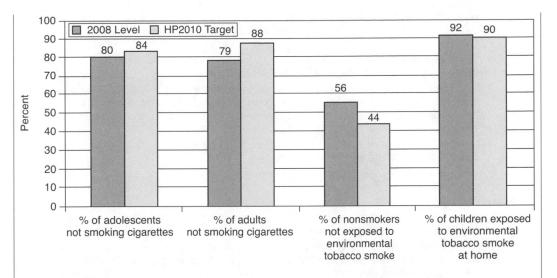

Figure 2-23 Scorecard for selected Healthy People 2010 leading indicators related to tobacco use comparing 2008 levels with 2010 targets. *Source:* Data from Data 2010, Healthy People 2010 database. http://wonder.cdc.gov/data2010/ftpselec.htm. Accessed May 31, 2010.

Figure 2-23 demonstrates progress toward measures for two HP2010 leading indicators related to tobacco use and environmental tobacco smoke exposure. Notably the year 2010 targets for environmental tobacco smoke exposure were achieved, but the targets for adolescent and adult smoking rates were not.

In the second decade of the 21st century, tobacco remains the leading cause of preventable death in the United States and continues to take an immense toll in terms of quality of life and impact on society. Expanding the use of interventions known to be effective will be necessary but will not likely be sufficient to make the elimination of the tobacco threat one of the crowning achievements of 21st century public health in America.

REFERENCES

1. Reprinted in part and adapted from Centers for Disease Control and Prevention. Achievements in public health, 1990–1999: tobacco use. *MMWR.* 1999;48:986–993.

2. American Cancer Society. *Cancer Facts and Figures—1999.* Atlanta: American Cancer Society; 1999.

3. Environmental Protection Agency. *Respiratory Health Effects of Passive Smoking: Lung Cancer and Other Disorders.* Washington, DC: Environmental Protection Agency, Office on Air and Radiation; 1992. Environmental Protection Agency publication EPA/600/6-90/006F.

4. U.S. Public Health Service. Smoking and health. *Report of the Advisory Committee to the Surgeon General of the Public Health Service.* Atlanta: U.S. Department of Health, Education, and Welfare, Public Health Service, Centers for Disease Control; 1964 (PHS publication no. 1103).

5. Wingo PA, Ries LA, Giovino GA, et al. Annual report to the nation on the status of cancer, 1973–1996, with a special section on lung cancer and tobacco smoking. *J Natl Cancer Inst.* 1999;91:675–690.

6. Centers for Disease Control and Prevention. Decline in deaths from heart disease and stroke—United States, 1900–1999. *MMWR.* 1999;48:649–656.

7. U.S. Department of Health and Human Services. *For a Healthy Nation: Returns on Investment in Public Health.* Atlanta: U.S. Department of Health and Human Services, Public Health Service, Office of Disease Prevention and Health Promotion and CDC; 1995.

8. Giovino GA, Henningfield JE, Tomar SL, et al. Epidemiology of tobacco use and dependence. *Epidemiol Rev.* 1995;17:48–65.

9. Waldron I. Patterns and causes of gender differences in smoking. *Soc Sci Med.* 1991;32: 989–1005.

10. U.S. Department of Health and Human Services. *The Health Consequences of Smoking for Women: A Report of the Surgeon General.* Washington, DC: U.S. Department of Health and Human Services, Public Health Service, Office of Smoking and Health; 1980.

11. Centers for Disease Control and Prevention. Surveillance for selected tobacco-use behaviors—United States, 1900–1994. In: CDC surveillance summaries, November 18, 1994. *MMWR.* 1994;43(no. SS-3).

12. U.S. Department of Agriculture, Economic Research Service. *Tobacco Situation & Outlook.* TBS-241/April 1999.

13. U.S. Department of Health and Human Services. *Tobacco Use Among U.S. Racial/Ethnic Minority Groups—African Americans, American Indians and Alaska Natives, Asian Americans and Pacific Islanders, and Hispanics: Report of the Surgeon General.* Atlanta: U.S. Department of Health and Human Services, Centers for Disease Control; 1998.

14. Fielding JF, Husten CG, Eriksen MP. Tobacco: health effects and control. In: Wallace RB, Doebbeling BN, Last JM, eds. *Public Health and Preventive Medicine.* 14th ed. Stamford, CT: Appleton & Lange; 1998.

15. Centers for Disease Control and Prevention. State-specific prevalence of cigarette smoking among adults, and children's and adolescents' exposure to environmental tobacco smoke—United States, 1996. *MMWR.* 1997;46:1038–1043.

16. Chaloupka FJ, Warner KE. The economics of smoking. In: Newhouse J, Culyer A, eds. *The Handbook of Health Economics.* Amsterdam, The Netherlands: Elsevier Science; 1999.

17. Task Force on Community Preventive Services. *The Community Guide.* http://www.thecommunityguide.org. Accessed May 31, 2010.

Public Health and the Health System

This chapter picks up where Chapter 2 left off—with influences on health. The influences to be examined in Chapter 3, however, are the interventions and services available through the health system.

The relationship between public health and other health-related activities has never been clear, but in recent years, it has become even less well defined. Some of the lack of clarity may be the result of the several different images of public health described in Chapter 1, but certainly not all. In addition to the U.S. health system remaining poorly understood by the public, there are different views among health professionals and policy makers as to whether public health is part of the health system or the health system is part of the public health enterprise. Most agree that these components serve the same ends but disagree as to the balance between the two and the locus for strategic decisions and actions. The issue of ownership—which component's leadership and strategies will predominate—underlies these different perspectives. In this text, the term health system refers to all aspects of the organization, financing, and provision of programs and services for the prevention and treatment of illness and injury. The public health system is a component of this larger health system. This view conflicts with the image that most people have of our health system; the public commonly perceives the health system to include only the medical care and treatment aspects of the overall system. Public health and the overall health sector will be referred to as systems, however, with the understanding that public health activities are part of a larger set of activities that focus on health, well-being, disease, and illness.

Although the relationships may not be clear, there is ample cause for public health interest in the health system. Perhaps most compelling is the sheer size and scope of the U.S. health system, characteristics that have made the health system an ethical issue. More than 15 million workers and nearly $3.0 trillion in resources are now devoted to health-related purposes[1]; however, this huge investment in fiscal and human resources may not be accomplishing all it can and should in terms of health outcomes. Lack of access to needed health services for an alarming number of Americans and inconsistent quality contribute to less than optimal health outcomes. Although access and quality have long been public health concerns, the excess capacity of the health system is a relatively new issue for public health.

This chapter examines the U.S. health system from several perspectives that consider the public health implications of costs and affordability, as well as several other important public policy and public health questions:

- Does the United States have a rational strategy for investing its resources to maintain and improve people's health?
- Is the current strategy excessive in ways that inequitably limit access to and benefit from needed services?
- Is the health system accountable to its end-users and ultimate payers for the quality and results of its services?

These issues of health, excess, access, accountability, and quality make the health system a public health concern.

Complementary, even synergistic, efforts within the overall health system involving medicine and public health are apparent in many of the important gains in health outcomes achieved during the 20th century. These tell this story from one perspective. Another perspective is drawn from a framework for linking various health strategies and activities to their strategic intent, level of prevention, relationship to medical and public health practice, and community or individual focus. Key economic, demographic, and resource trends are then briefly presented as a prelude to understanding important themes and emerging paradigm shifts. New opportunities afforded by sweeping changes in the health system, many of which relate to managed care strategies, are apparent in the review of these issues.

PREVENTION AND HEALTH SERVICES

The improvements in health status described in Chapters 1 and 2 are the result of a health system that influences health status through a variety of intervention strategies and services.[2] Key relationships among health, illness, and various interventions intended to maintain or restore health are summarily presented in Table 3-1. As discussed in Chapter 2, health and illness are dynamic states that are influenced by a wide variety of biologic, environmental, behavioral, social, and health service factors acting through an ecological model. The complex interaction of these factors results in the occurrence or absence of disease or injury, which in turn contributes to the health status of individuals and populations. Several different intervention points are possible, including two general strategies that seek to maintain health by intervening before the development of disease or injury.[2] These are health promotion and specific protection strategies. Both involve activities that alter the interaction of the various health-influencing factors in ways that contribute to either averting or altering the likelihood of occurrence of disease or injury.

Health Promotion and Specific Protection

Health promotion activities attempt to modify human behaviors by increasing the ability to resist disease or injury-inducing factors, thereby reducing or neutralizing risks to health. Examples of health promotion activities include interventions such as nutrition counseling, genetic counseling, family counseling, and the myriad activities that constitute health education; however, health promotion also properly includes the provision of adequate housing, employment, and recreational conditions, as well as other forms of community development activities. What is clear from these examples is that many fall outside the common public understanding of what constitutes

Table 3-1   Health Strategies, Prevention Levels, Practice Domains, and Targets

Strategy	State Addressed	Prevention Level	Practice Domain	Target
Health promotion	Health	Primary	Public health	Community
Specific protection	Health	Primary	Public health	Community or risk group
Early case finding and prompt treatment	Illness	Secondary	Public health and primary medical care	Individual
Disability limitation	Illness	Tertiary	Secondary/tertiary medical care	Individual
Rehabilitation	Illness	Tertiary	Long-term care	Individual and group

Source: Data from Leavell HR, Clark EG. *Preventive Medicine for the Doctor in His Community.* 3rd ed. New York: McGraw-Hill; 1965.

health care. Several of these are viewed as the duty or responsibility of other societal institutions, including public safety, housing, education, and even industry. It is somewhat ironic that activities that focus on the state of health and that seek to maintain and promote health are not commonly perceived to be "health services." To some extent, this is also true for the other category of health-maintaining strategies—specific protection activities.

Specific protection activities provide individuals with resistance to factors (such as microorganisms like viruses and bacteria) or modify environments to decrease potentially harmful interactions of health-influencing factors (such as toxic exposures in the workplace). Examples of specific protection include activities directed toward specific risks (e.g., the use of protective equipment for asbestos removal), immunizations, occupational and environmental engineering, and regulatory controls and activities to protect individuals from environmental carcinogens (such as exposure to second-hand or side-stream smoke) and toxins. Several of these are often identified with settings other than traditional healthcare settings. Many are implemented and enforced through governmental agencies. Table 3-2 presents a catalog of health-related prevention organizations, agencies, and institutions.

Early Case Finding and Prompt Treatment, Disability Limitation, and Rehabilitation

Although health promotion and specific protection both focus on the healthy state and seek to prevent disease, a different set of strategies and activities is necessary if the interaction of factors results in disease or injury. When disease occurs, the strategies that become necessary are those facilitating early detection, rapid control, or rehabilitation, depending on the stage of development of the disease.

In general, early detection and prompt treatment reduce individual pain and suffering and are less costly to both the individual and society than treatment initiated only after a condition has reached a more advanced state. Interventions to achieve early detection and prompt treatment include screening tests, case-finding efforts, and periodic physical exams. Screening tests are increasingly available to detect illnesses before they become symptomatic. Case-finding efforts for both infectious and noninfectious conditions are directed at populations at greater risk for the condition on the basis of criteria appropriate for that condition. Periodic physical exams and other screenings, consistent with the age-specific recommendations of the U.S. Preventive Services Task Force,[3] incorporate these practices and are best provided through an effective primary medical care system. Primary care providers who are sensitive to disease patterns and predisposing factors can play substantial roles in the early identification and management of most medical conditions.

Another strategy targeting disease is disability limitation through effective and complete treatment. It is this set of activities that most Americans equate with the term health care, largely because this strategy constitutes the lion's share of the U.S. health system in terms of resource deployment. Quite appropriately, these efforts largely aim to arrest or eradicate disease or to limit disability and prevent death. The final intervention strategy focusing on

Table 3-2   Examples of Health-Related Prevention Organizations, Agencies, and Institutions

Federal Agencies
Department of Agriculture
Department of Transportation
Department of Energy
Department of Health and Human Services
Department of Homeland Security
Department of Labor
Department of Education
Department of Justice
Department of the Interior
Department of Veterans Administration
Department of Commerce
Department of Treasury
Department of Housing and Urban Development
Environmental Protection Agency
Consumer Product Safety Commission
Federal Mine Safety and Health Review Commission
National Transportation Safety Board
Nuclear Regulatory Commission
Occupational Safety and Health Review Commission
Federal Emergency Management Agency

State Agencies (different agency names in different states)
Aging
Agriculture
Alcoholism and Substance Abuse
Children and Family Services
Council on Health and Fitness
Emergency Services and Disaster Agency
Energy and Natural Resources
Environmental Protection Agency
Guardianship and Advocacy Commission
Health Care Cost Containment Agency
Health Facilities Planning Board and Agency
Mental Health and Developmental Disabilities
Nuclear Safety
Pollution Control Board
Professional Regulation Agency
Public Health
Rehabilitation Services
State Fire Marshall
State Board of Education
State Board of Higher Education
Veterans Affairs

Miscellaneous Organizations and Sites
Foundations
Corporations
Voluntary Health Associations
United Way of America
Physician Office Visits
HMO Visits
Dental Visits

disease—rehabilitation—is designed to return individuals who have experienced a condition to the maximum level of function consistent with their capacities.

Links with Prevention

An important aspect of this framework is that it emphasizes the potential for prevention inherent in each of the five health service strategies. Prevention can be categorized in several ways. The best known approach classifies prevention in relation to the stage of the disease or condition.

Preventive intervention strategies are considered primary, secondary, or tertiary. Primary prevention involves prevention of the disease or injury itself, generally through reducing exposure or risk factor levels. Secondary prevention attempts to identify and control disease processes in their early stages, often before signs and symptoms become apparent. In this case, prevention is akin to preemptive treatment. Tertiary prevention seeks to prevent disability through restoring individuals to their optimal level of functioning after damage is done. The selection of an intervention point at the primary, secondary, or tertiary level is a function of knowledge, resources, acceptability, effectiveness, and efficiency, among other considerations.

The relationship of health promotion and specific protection to these levels of prevention is also summarized in Table 3-1 and Figure 3-1. Health promotion and specific protection are primary prevention strategies seeking to prevent the development of disease. Early case finding and prompt treatment represent secondary prevention because they seek to interrupt the disease process before it becomes symptomatic. Both disability limitation and rehabilitation are considered tertiary-level prevention in that they seek to prevent or reduce disability associated with disease or injury. Although these are considered tertiary prevention, they receive primary attention under current policy and resource deployment.

Figure 3-2 illustrates each of the three levels of prevention strategies in relationship to population disease status and effect on disease incidence and prevalence. The various potential benefits from the three intervention levels derive from the basic epidemiologic concepts of incidence and prevalence. Prevalence (the number of existing cases of illness, injury, or a health event) is a function of both incidence (the number of new cases) and duration. Reducing either component can reduce prevalence. Primary prevention aims to reduce the incidence of conditions, whereas secondary and tertiary prevention seek to reduce prevalence by shortening duration and minimizing the effects of disease or injury. It should be apparent that there is a finite limit to how much a condition's duration can be reduced. As a result, approaches emphasizing primary prevention have greater potential benefit than do approaches emphasizing other levels of prevention. This basis for understanding the differential impact of prevention and treatment approaches to a particular health problem or condition cannot be overstated.

These same considerations are pertinent to the notion of postponement of morbidity as a prevention strategy, as illustrated in Figure 3-3. As demonstrated in model I, increased life expectancy without postponement of morbidity may actually increase the burden of illness within a population, as measured by

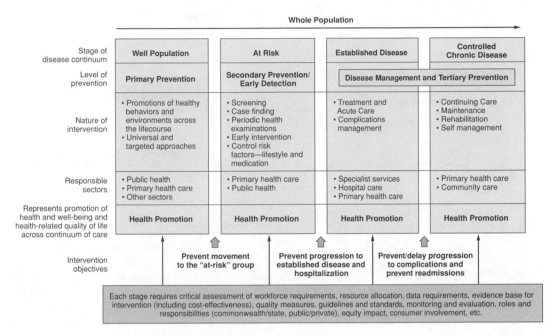

Figure 3-1 Comprehensive model of chronic disease prevention and control. *Source:* From National Public Health Partnership. Preventing Chronic Disease: A Strategic Framework. Background paper; 2001.

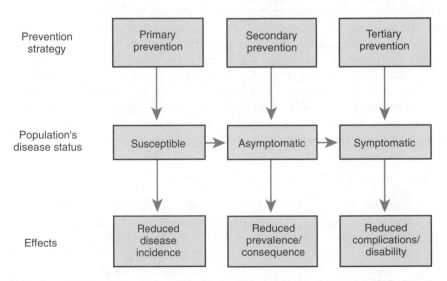

Figure 3-2 Levels of prevention with effects. *Source:* From Brownson RC, Remington PL, Davis J, eds. *Chronic Disease Epidemiology and Control.* 2nd ed. Washington, DC: American Public Health Association; © 1998.

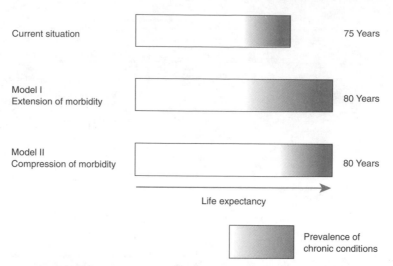

Figure 3-3   Alternative models of extension or compression of morbidity as life expectancy is extended. *Source:* From Brownson RC, Remington PL, Davis J, eds. *Chronic Disease Epidemiology and Control.* 2nd ed. Washington, DC: American Public Health Association; © 1998.

prevalence; however, postponement may result in the development of a condition so late in life that it results in either no or less disability in functioning.

Another approach to classifying prevention efforts groups interventions by the nature of the intervention into clinical, behavioral, or environmental categories. Clinical interventions are provided to individuals, whereas environmental interventions are organized for populations or groups. Behavioral interventions can be provided either for individuals or for populations, including subgroups identified as being at higher risk for a particular condition.

Within this framework for considering intervention strategies aimed at health or illness, the potential for prevention as an element of all strategies is clear. There are substantial opportunities to use primary and secondary prevention strategies to improve health in general and reduce the burden of illness for individuals and for society. As noted in Chapter 2, reducing the burden of illness carries the potential for substantial cost savings. These concepts serve to promote a more rational intervention and investment strategy for the U.S. health system.

Links with Public Health and Medical Practice

Another useful aspect of this framework is its delineation of responsibilities for carrying out the various interventions. Three practice domains can be roughly delineated: public health practice, medical practice, and long-term care practice.[2] The framework assigns public health practice primary responsibility for health promotion, specific protection, and a good share of early case finding. It is important to note that the concept of public health practice here is a broad one that accommodates the activities carried out by many different types of health professionals and workers, not only those working in public health agencies. Although many of these activities are carried out in public health agencies of the federal, state, or local government, many are not. Public health practice occurs in voluntary health agencies, as well as in settings such as schools, social service agencies, industry, and even traditional medical care settings. In terms of prevention, public health practice embraces all of the primary prevention activities in the model, as well as some of the activities for early diagnosis and prompt treatment.

The demarcations between public health and medical practice are neither clear nor absolute. In recent decades, public health practice has been extensively involved in screening and has become an important source of primary medical care for populations with diminished access to care. The mix of population-based and personal health services considered to represent public health practice varies over time and by location and history. The essential public health services framework introduced in Chapter 1 largely focuses on population-based activities, including monitoring health status, investigating health problems and hazards, informing and educating people about health issues, mobilizing community partnerships, developing policies and plans, enforcing laws and regulations, ensuring a competent workforce, evaluating effectiveness and quality of services, and researching for new insights and solutions. One of these essential public health services, however, focuses more on personal health services by linking people with needed health services and ensuring the provision of health care when otherwise unavailable. Public health tracking systems must capture information on both the population-based activities and on the safety-net personal health services provided through the public health system.

Even as public health practice has branched into personal health services, medical practice is now extensively involved with early case finding while traditionally providing the major share of primary care services to most segments of the population. Medical practice, meaning those services usually provided by or under the supervision of a physician or other traditional healthcare provider, can be viewed as including three levels (Table 3-3). Primary medical care has been variously defined but generally focuses on the basic health needs of individuals and families. It is first-contact health care in the view of the patient; provides at least 80% of necessary care; includes a comprehensive array of services, on site or through referral, including health promotion and disease prevention, as well as curative services; and is accessible and acceptable to the patient population. This comprehensive description of primary care differs substantially from what is commonly encountered as primary care in the U.S. health system. Often lacking from current so-called primary care services are those relating to health promotion and disease prevention.

The concept of disease management has evolved from efforts to provide a more integrated approach to healthcare delivery in order to improve health outcomes and reduce costs, often for defined populations such as Medicaid enrollees. Disease management focuses on identifying and proactively monitoring high-risk populations, assisting patients and providers to adhere to treatment plans that are based on proven interventions, promoting provider coordination, increasing patient education, and preventing avoidable medical complications.

Table 3-3   Healthcare Pyramid Levels

- Tertiary medical care
  Subspecialty referral care requiring highly specialized personnel and facilities

- Secondary medical care
  Specialized attention and ongoing management for common and less frequently encountered medical conditions, including support services for people with special challenges caused by chronic or long-term conditions

- Primary medical care
  Clinical preventive services, first-contact treatment services, and ongoing care for commonly encountered medical conditions

- Population-based public health services
  Interventions aimed at disease prevention and health promotion that shape a community's overall health profile

Source: Data from U.S. Public Health Service. *For a Healthy Nation: Return on Investments in Public Health.* Hyattsville, MD: Public Health Service; 1994.

Beyond primary medical care are two more specialized types of care that are often termed secondary care and tertiary care, respectively. Secondary care is specialized care serving the major share of the remaining 20% of the need that lies beyond the scope of primary care. Physicians or hospitals generally provide secondary care, ideally on referral from a primary care source. Tertiary medical care is even more highly specialized and technologically sophisticated medical and surgical care for those with unusual or complex conditions (generally no more than a small percentage of the need in any service category). Tertiary care is frequently provided in large medical centers or academic health centers.

Long-term care is appropriately classified separately because of the special needs of the population requiring such services and the specialized settings where many of these services are offered. This, too, is changing, as specialized long-term care services increasingly move out of long-term care facilities and into home settings.

Within the health services pyramid illustrated in Figure 3-4, primary prevention activities are largely associated with population-based public health services at the base of the pyramid, although some primary prevention in the form of clinical preventive services is also associated with primary medical care services. Secondary prevention activities are split somewhat more evenly between the population-based public health services and primary medical care. Tertiary prevention activities fall largely in the secondary and tertiary medical care components of the pyramid. The use of a pyramid to represent health services implies that each level serves a different proportion of the total population. Everyone should be served by population-wide public health services, and nearly everyone should be served by primary medical care; however, increasingly smaller proportions of the total population require secondary- and tertiary-level medical care services. In any event, the system should be built from the bottom up. It would not be rational to build such a system from the top down; there might not be enough resources to address the lower levels that served as the founda-

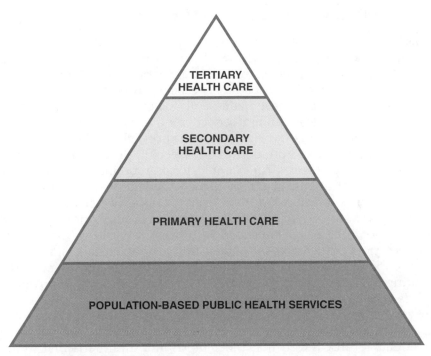

Figure 3-4 Health services pyramid. *Source:* From U.S. Public Health Service. *For a Healthy Nation: Return on Investments in Public Health.* Hyattsville, MD: Public Health Service; 1994.

tion for the system. Nonetheless, there is evidence in later sections of this chapter that this is exactly what has occurred with the U.S. health system.

Targets of Health Service Strategies

A final facet of this model characterizes the targets for the strategies and activities. Generally, primary preventive services are community based and are targeted toward populations or groups rather than individuals. Early case-finding activities can be directed toward groups or toward individuals. For example, many screening activities target groups at higher risk when these are provided through public health agencies. The same screening activities can also be provided for individuals through physicians' offices and hospital out-patient departments. Much of primary and virtually all of secondary and tertiary medical care are appropriately individually oriented. There is a concept, termed community-oriented primary care, in which primary care providers assume responsibility for all of the individuals in a community, rather than only those who seek out care from the provider. Even in this model, however, care is provided on an individual basis. Long-term care involves elements of both community-based service and individually oriented service. These services are tailored for individuals but often in a group setting or as part of a package of services for a defined number of recipients, as in a long-term care facility.

Public Health and Medical Practice Interfaces

This framework also sheds light on the potential conflicts between public health and medical practice. Although the two are presented as separate domains of practice, there are many interfaces that provide a template for either collaboration or conflict. Both paths have been taken over the past century. Public health practitioners have traditionally deferred to medical practitioners for providing the broad spectrum of services for disease and injuries in individuals. Medical practitioners have generally acknowledged the need for public health practice for health promotion and specific protection strategies. The interfaces raise difficult issues. For example, for one specific protection activity—childhood immunizations—it can be argued that the extensive role of public health practice has served to fragment health services for children. It would be logical to provide these services within a well-functioning primary-care system, where they could be better integrated with other services for this population. Despite occasional differences as to roles, in most circumstances, medical practice has supported the role of public health to serve as the provider of last resort in ensuring medical care for persons who lack financial access to private health care. This, too, has varied over time and from place to place.

Advances in bacteriologic diagnoses in public health laboratories, for example, fostered friction between medical practitioners and public health professionals for diseases such as tuberculosis and diphtheria that were often difficult to identify from other common but less serious maladies. Clinicians feared that laboratory diagnoses would replace clinical diagnoses and that, in highly competitive medical markets, paying patients would abandon private physicians for public health agencies. Issues of turf and scope of practice persist in many communities.

Some of the most serious conflicts have come in the area of primary care services, including early case-finding activities. Because of the increased yield of screening tests when these are applied to groups at higher risk, public health practice has sought to deploy more widely risk group or community case-finding methods (including outreach and linkage activities). This has, at times, been perceived by medical practitioners as encroachment on their practice domain for certain primary care services, such as prenatal care. Although there has been no rule that public health practice could not be provided within the medical practice domain and vice versa, the perception that these are separate, but perhaps unequal, territories has been widely held by both groups.

It is important to note that this territoriality is not based only on turf issues. There are significant differences in the world views and approaches of these two domains. Medical practice quite properly seeks to produce the best possible outcome through the development and execution of individualized treatment plans. Seeking the best possible outcome for an individual suggests that decisions are made primarily for the benefit of that individual. Costs and resource availability are secondary considerations. Public health practice, on the other hand, seeks to deploy its limited resources to avoid the worst outcomes (at the level of the group). Some level of risk is tolerated at the collective level to prevent an unacceptable level of adverse outcomes from occurring. These are quite different approaches to practice: maximizing individual positive outcomes, as opposed to minimizing adverse collective outcomes. As a result, differences in perspective and philosophy often underlie differences in approaches that initially appear to be concerns over territoriality.

An example that illustrates these differences is apparent in approaches to widespread use of human immunodeficiency virus (HIV) antibody testing in the mid and late 1980s. Medical practitioners perceived that HIV antibody testing would be very useful in clinical practice and that its widespread use would enhance case finding. As a result, medical practitioners generally opposed restrictions on use of these tests, such as specific written informed consent and additional confidentiality provisions. Public health practitioners perceived that widespread use of the test without safeguards and protections would actually result in fewer persons at risk being tested and decreased case finding in the community. With both groups focusing on the same science in terms of the accuracy of the specific testing regimen, these differences in practice approaches may be difficult to understand; however, in view of their ultimate aims and concerns as to individual versus collective outcomes, the conflict is more understandable.

Perspectives and roles may differ for public health and medical practice, but both are important and necessary. The real question is what blending of these approaches will be most successful in improving health status throughout the population. There is sufficient cause to question current policy and investment strategies. Table 3-4 examines the potential contributions of various strategies (personal responsibility, healthcare services, community action, and social policies) toward reducing the impact of the actual causes of death identified in Chapter 2. Table 3-4 suggests that more medical care services are

Table 3-4   Actual Causes of Death in the United States and Potential Contribution to Reduction

	Deaths		Potential Contribution to Reduction*			
Causes	Estimated Number	Percentage	Personal	Healthcare System	Community Action	Social Policy
Tobacco	435,000	19	++++	+	+	++
Diet/activity patterns	400,000	14	+++	+	+	++
Alcohol	85,000	5	+++	+	+	+
Microbial agents	75,000	4	+	++	++	++
Toxic agents	55,000	3	+	+	++	++++
Motor vehicles	43,000	1	++	+	+	++
Firearms	29,000	2	++	+	+++	+++
Sexual behavior	20,000	1	++++	+	+	+
Illicit use of drugs	20,000	<1	+++	+	++	++

*Plus sign indicates relative magnitude (4+ scale).

Sources: Data from Fielding J, Halfon L. Where is the health in health system reform? *JAMA.* 1994;272:1292–1296, and Mokdad AH, Marks JS, Stroup DF, et al. Actual causes of death in the United States, 2000. *JAMA.* 2004;291:1238–1245.

not as likely to reduce the toll from these causes as are public health approaches (community action and social policies). Nevertheless, there are opportunities available through the current system and perhaps even greater opportunities in the near term as the system seeks to address the serious problems that have brought it to the brink of major reform.

Medicine and Public Health Collaborations

The need for a renewed partnership between medicine and public health generated several promising initiatives in the final years of the 20th century. Just as bacteriology brought together public health professionals and practicing physicians at the turn of the 20th century to battle diphtheria and other infectious diseases, technology and economics may become the driving forces for a renewed partnership at the dawn of the 21st century. In pursuit of this vision, the American Medical Association and the American Public Health Association established the Medicine/Public Health Initiative in 1994 to provide an ongoing forum to define mutual interests and to promote models for successful collaborations. Regional and state meetings followed a National Congress in 1996. A variety of collaborative structures were identified and promoted through the widely circulated monograph, "Medicine & Public Health: The Power of Collaboration."[4] More than 400 examples of collaborations are highlighted in the monograph. General categories of collaboration include coalitions, contracts, administrative/management systems, advisory bodies, and intraorganizational platforms. This initiative represents a major breakthrough for public health interests, one long overdue and welcome; in fact, it represents the first time that these two major professional organizations have met around mutual interests.

Collaborations between public health and hospitals have also gained momentum. Increasingly, hospitals and managed care organizations have begun to pursue community health goals, at times in concert with public health organizations and at other times filling voids that exist at the community level. In many parts of the United States, hospitals have taken the lead in organizing community health planning activities. More frequently, however, they participate as major community stakeholders in health planning efforts organized through the local public health agency. A variety of positive interfaces with managed care organizations have been documented.[5] Hospital boards and executives now commonly include community benefit objectives in their annual performance evaluations. Examples of community health strategies include the following:

- Establishing "boundary spanner" positions that report to the chief executive officer but focus on community-wide, rather than institutional, interests
- Changing reward systems in terms of salaries and bonuses that executives and board members linked to the achievement of community health goals
- Educating staff on the mission, vision, and values of the institution and linking these with community health outcomes
- Exposing board members to the work of community partners
- Engaging board members with the staff and community
- Reporting on community health performance (report cards)[6]

THE HEALTH SYSTEM IN THE UNITED STATES

There are many sources of more complete information on the health system in the United States than are provided in this chapter. Here, the intent is to examine those aspects of the health industry and health system that interface with public health or raise issues of public health significance. There is no shortage of either. This section examines some of the issues facing the health system in the United States, with a special focus on the problems of the system that are fueling reform and change. Interfaces with public health are identified and discussed, as are possible effects of these changes on the various images of public health. Throughout these sections, data from the Health, United States series, published annually by the Centers for Disease Control and Prevention, National Center for Health Statistics, are used to describe the economic, demographic, and resources aspects of the American health system.

Economic Dimensions

The health system in the United States is immense and growing steadily, as illustrated in Figure 3-5. Total national health expenditures in the United States doubled in the first decade of the 21st century to over $2.5 trillion, 2.5 times the sum expended in 1995 and 10 times more than in 1980. Health expenditures are on a pace to reach $4.5 trillion by the year 2020. In order to understand how public health interfaces with other components of the health system in the United States, it is important to consider the context in which these interactions take place—the health sector of modern America. In the first decade of the new century, economic growth and employment in the United States weakened and then deteriorated even further as the decade ended. Nonetheless, through periods of both economic prosperity and retrenchment,

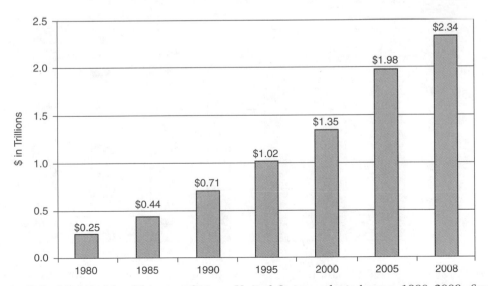

Figure 3-5 National health expenditures, United States, selected years 1980–2008. *Source:* Data from Centers for Medicare and Medicaid Services, Office of the Actuary, National Health Statistics Group.

the health sector has remained a powerful component of the overall U.S. economy, accounting for one sixth of the total national gross domestic product (GDP) in 2008. By the year 2020, it will comprise one fifth of the nation's GDP. Figure 3-6 traces the growth in health expenditures as a proportion of GDP.

The United States spends a greater share of its GDP on healthcare services than any other industrialized nation. Health expenditures in the United Kingdom and Japan are about one half and in Germany and Canada about two thirds the U.S. figure. Per capita expenditures on health show the same pattern, with more than $7,400 per capita spent on health in the United States in 2007, more than twice that of Germany, Canada, Japan, and the United Kingdom. Several factors suggest that this is too much. The current system is reaching the point of no longer being affordable, the U.S. population is no healthier than other nations that spend far less, and the opportunity costs are considerable.

Figures 3-7 and 3-8 trace where the money comes from and what it goes for in the U.S. health system. Expenditures for personal healthcare services comprise 85% of all health expenditures in the United States. A little more than one half of the nation's health expenditures (52%) pay for hospital, physician, and other clinical services; 6% goes for nursing home care, 10% purchases prescription drugs, and 7% supports program administration (Figure 3-7). The remaining 25% covers a wide array of other services, including oral health, home health care, durable medical products, over-the-counter medicines, public health activities, other personal care, research, and facilities, with only 3% devoted to government public health activities (about $69 billion in 2008). Chapters 4 and 6 further examine overall health and public health expenditure trends for the various levels of government in the United States.

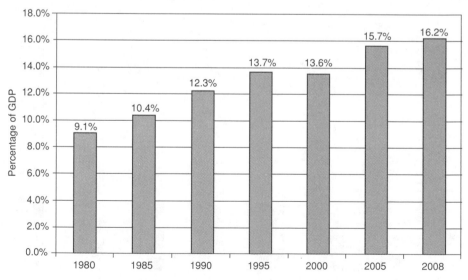

Figure 3-6 Percentage of national gross domestic product (GDP) expenditures spent for health-related purposes, United States, selected years, 1980–2008. *Source:* Data from Centers for Medicare and Medicaid Services, Office of the Actuary, National Health Statistics Group; U.S. Department of Commerce, Bureau of Economic Analysis.

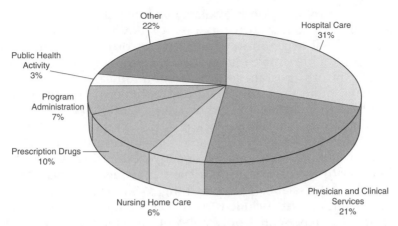

Figure 3-7   Health services purchased by national health expenditures, United States, 2008. *Source:* Data from Centers for Medicare and Medicaid Services, Office of the Actuary, National Health Statistics Group.

There are three general sources for overall national health expenditures, including government at all levels, 48%; private health insurance, 33%; individuals, approximately 12% out of pocket; and the remaining 7%, other private funds (Figure 3-8). Steadily increasing costs for health services have hit all these sources in their pocketbooks, and each is reaching the point at which further increases may not be affordable. The largest single purchaser of health care in the United States remains the federal government, but for all three sources, the ultimate payers are individuals as taxpayers and consumers. Individuals and families covered by health insurance plans are experiencing a steady increase in the triple burden of higher premiums, increased cost sharing, and reduced benefits.

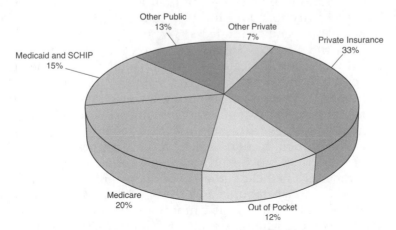

Figure 3-8   Sources of funding for national health expenditures, United States, 2008. *Source:* Data from Centers for Medicare and Medicaid Services, Office of the Actuary, National Health Statistics Group.

Only limited information is available on expenditures for prevention and population-based public health services. A study using 1988 data estimated that total national expenditures for all forms of health-related prevention (including clinical preventive services provided to individuals and population-based public health programs, such as communicable disease control and environmental protection) amounted to $33 billion.[7] The analysis sought to include all activities directed toward health promotion, health protection, disease screening, and counseling. As a result, the $33 billion figure approximates expenditures for primary and secondary prevention efforts. Included in this total, however, was $14 billion for activities not included in the calculation of national health expenditures (such as sewage systems, water purification, and air traffic safety). The remaining $18 billion in prevention-related health expenditures was included in the calculation of total national health expenditures but represented only 3.4% of all national health expenditures for that year. The share of these expenditures that represents population-based public health services cannot be directly determined from this study but appears to be in the $6 to 7 billion range for 1988.

As part of the development of a national health reform proposal in 1994, federal officials developed an estimate of national health expenditures for population-based services.[8] On the basis of expenditures in 1993, this analysis concluded that about 1% of all national health expenditures ($8.4 billion) supported population-based programs and services. U.S. Public Health Service agencies spent $4.3 billion for population-based services in 1993, and state and local health agencies expended another $4.1 billion. Public Health Service officials estimated that achieving an "essential" level of population-based services nationwide would require doubling 1993 expenditure levels to $17 billion and that achieving a "fully effective" level would require tripling (to $25 billion) the 1993 levels.

The 1994 national health reform team likely undercounted the level of population-based public health activity expenditures by state and local governments. The results from a comprehensive examination of public health-related expenditures in nine states for 1994 and 1995, together with federal public health activity spending for 1995, suggest that national population-based public health spending totaled $13.8 billion in that year.

Data from the National Health Accounts identify government public health activity as a distinct category within total national health expenditures. The public health activity category captures the bulk of public health spending funded by government agencies, although it excludes spending for several personal services programs widely considered to be important public health activities, such as maternal and child health, public hospitals, substance abuse prevention, mental health, and Indian health services. Environmental health activities provided through environmental protection agencies are also excluded. Nonetheless, the government public health activity category within the annual national health expenditures total provides useful insights into general public health funding trends over time. Government public health activity spending was $69.5 billion in 2008, $10.5 billion from the federal level, and $59 billion from state and local governments. Figure 3-9 tracks the tenfold increase in federal, state and local, and total government public health activity expenditures between 1980 and 2008.

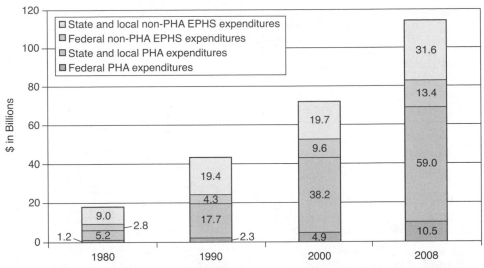

Figure 3-9 Public health activity (PHA) and essential public health services (EPHS) expenditures by government level, United States, selected years, 1980–2008. *Note:* See text for derivation of essential public health services expenditures. *Source:* Data from Centers for Medicare and Medicaid Services, Office of the Actuary, National Health Statistics Group.

Adjustments to public health activity expenditures are necessary in order to include the full array of activities included in the essential public health services framework and to identify the component of essential public health services spending that supports population-based public health efforts. The essential public health services framework (introduced in Chapter 1 and to be more fully examined in Chapters 5 and 6) includes the provision of personal health services when otherwise unavailable in addition to a battery of population-based activities. Figure 3-9 includes an estimate of total essential public health services expenditures developed by adding spending for mental health and substance abuse prevention, Indian health services, maternal and child health services, school health, and public hospitals to the public health activity category in the national health expenditures. For 2008, estimated essential public health services expenditures were $115 billion, about 50% greater than in 2000 and 170% more than in 1990.

A subset of overall public health activity expenditures supports population-based public health activities. Methods for estimating population-based public health expenditures, derived from studies completed in the mid-1990s, calculate national population-based public health expenditures at $28.7 billion in 2008. For comparison purposes, population-based expenditures were $2.9 billion in 1980, $7.8 billion in 1990, and $16.7 billion in 2000.[9,10]

On a per capita basis, expenditures for population-based public health and overall governmental public health activities increased more than 800% between 1980 and 2008 (Figure 3-10). Nonetheless, per capita public health expenditures represented only a tiny fraction of total per capita health spending ($7,681 per person) in the United States in 2008. That fraction varies from 4.9% ($375 per capita) for total essential public health services spending to 3.0%

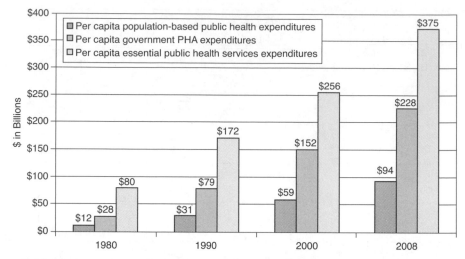

Figure 3-10   Per capita population-based public health, governmental public health activity (PHA) and essential public health services expenditures, United States, selected years, 1980–2008. *Source:* Data from Centers for Medicare and Medicaid Services, Office of the Actuary, National Health Statistics Group.

($228 per capita) for governmental public health activity spending to 1.2% ($94 per capita) for population-based public health activities (Figure 3-11).

The implications of these expenditure patterns are further examined in Chapters 4 and 6 for governmental as well as nongovernmental expenditures for population-based public health activities. Here, however, these gross figures are presented in order to demonstrate the very small slice of the national health

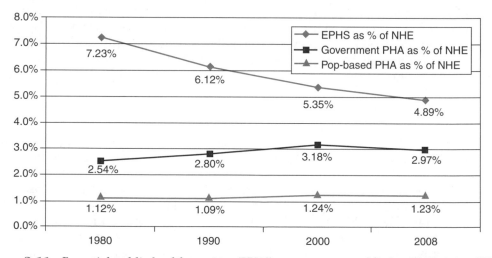

Figure 3-11   Essential public health services (EPHS), government public health activity (PHA) and population-based public health activity expenditures as a percent of total health spending, United States, 1980–2008. NHE, National Health Expenditures. *Source:* Data from Centers for Medicare and Medicaid Services, Office of the Actuary, National Health Statistics Group.

expenditure pie devoted to population-based preventive services and the public health system. As illustrated in Figure 3-11, governmental public health spending as a percent of total national health expenditures grew modestly through the final decades of the 20th century but have declined somewhat since 2000. Population-based public health activity spending as a percent of total national health expenditures shows a similar pattern. The availability of resources from the 1998 settlement between states and the major tobacco companies, together with bioterrorism preparedness funding from Congress beginning in 2002, presented an opportunity to achieve the doubling of expenditures for population-based prevention deemed necessary to achieve an essential level of services by the U.S. Public Health Service in 1994. Although such a doubling would require only a small shift in resource allocation strategies within a $2.5 trillion dollar enterprise, there was little hope for increased resources for population-based public health activities until the tobacco settlement and bioterrorism preparedness funds appeared. Chapters 8 and 9 provide additional information as to the effect these additional resources are having on the public health system.

Macroeconomic trends, however, tell only part of the story. The disparities between rich and poor in the United States are also growing, leaving an increasing number of Americans without financial access to many healthcare services. These and other important aspects are examined as we review the demands on and resources of the U.S. health system.

Demographic and Utilization Trends

Several important demographic trends affect the U.S. healthcare system. These include the slowing population growth rate, the shift toward an older population, the increasing diversity of the population, changes in family structure, and persistent lack of access to needed health services for too many Americans. The changing prevalence of particular diseases is another demographic phenomenon but is not addressed here, although recent history with diseases such as HIV and H1N1 influenza infections illustrates how specific conditions can place increasing demands on fragile healthcare systems.

Census studies document that the growth of the U.S. population has been slowing, a trend that would be expected to restrain future growth in demand for healthcare services; however, this must be viewed in light of projected changes in the age distribution of the U.S. population. Between 2000 and 2030, the population older than age 65 will double, whereas the younger age groups will grow little, if at all.

There is no evidence that excessive utilization or overuse of services contributes significantly to the high cost of health care in the United States. Underuse of care is actually a greater problem than overuse. Quality reviews consistently document that patients fail to receive recommended care almost half the time and that only about 10% of the time do they receive additional care that is not recommended for their specific health problem or condition.[11]

Use of healthcare services, in general, closely correlates with the age distribution of the population. For example, adults age 75 years and older visit physicians three to four times as frequently as do children younger than 17 years old. Because older persons use more healthcare services than do younger people, their expenditures are higher. Obvious reasons for the higher use of healthcare resources by the older population include the high prevalence of chronic conditions, such as arteriosclerosis, cerebrovascular disease, diabetes, senility, arthritis, and mental disorders. As the population ages, it is expected that the prevalence of chronic disorders and the treatment costs associated with them will also increase. This could be minimized through prevention efforts that either avert or postpone the onset of these chronic diseases. Nonetheless, these important demographic shifts portend greater use of healthcare services in the future.

Another important demographic trend is the increasing diversity of the population. The nonwhite population is growing three times faster than the white population, and the Hispanic population is increasing at five times the rate for the entire U.S. population. Between 1980 and 2000, Hispanics increased from 6.4% to 12.5% of the U.S. population. African Americans increased from 11.5% to 14.5% of the total population, whereas the number of Asian/Pacific Islanders more than doubled from 1.6% to 3.7%. The white population declined from 79.7% to 69.1% of the total population over these 2 decades. Figure 3-12 projects these trends through the years 2025 and 2050. These trends reflect differences in fertility and immigration patterns and disproportionately affect the younger age groups, suggesting that services for mothers and children will face considerable challenges in their ability to provide culturally sensitive and acceptable services. At the same time, the considerably less diverse baby boom generation will be increasing its ability to affect

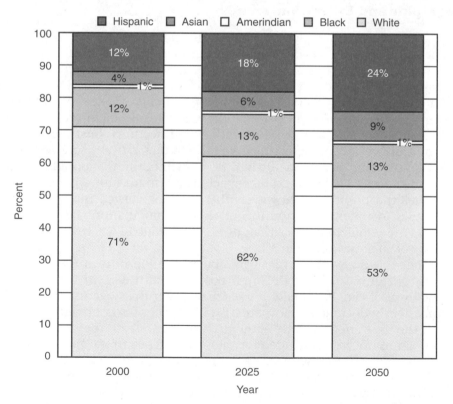

Figure 3-12 Current and projected racial and ethnic composition of U.S. population, 2000, 2025, 2050. *Source:* From U.S. Census Bureau, 2001.

public policy decisions and resource allocations in the early years of the 21st century. These trends also underscore the importance of cultural competence for health professionals. Cultural competence is a set of behaviors and attitudes, as well as a culture within an institution or system that respects and takes into account the cultural background, cultural beliefs, and values of those served and incorporates this into the way services are delivered.

Changes in family structure also represent a significant demographic trend in the United States. There is only a 50% chance that married partners will reach their 25th anniversary. One in three children live part of their lives in a one-parent household; for African American children, the chances are two in three. Labor force participation for women more than doubled from under 25% in 1950 to 54% by 1985. Even more indicative of gender changes in the labor market, the proportion of married women in the workforce with children under age five grew from 44% in 1975 to 64% in 1987. Many American households have maintained their economic status over the past 2 decades with the second paychecks from women in the workforce. As the structure of families changes, so do their needs for access, availability, and even types of services (such as substance abuse, family violence, and child welfare services).

Intermingled with many of these trends are the persistent inequalities in access to services for low-income populations, including African Americans and Hispanics. For example, despite higher rates of self-reported fair or poor health and greater use of hospital inpatient services, low-income persons are 50% more likely to report no physician contacts within the past 2 years than are persons in high-income households. Utilization rates for prenatal care and childhood immunizations are also lower for low-income populations.

Despite outspending other developed countries on health services, the United States leads other industrialized nations by a wide margin in the proportion of its citizens who lack health insurance coverage. Various studies since 2000 place the figure at approximately 45 million Americans and rising. Health insurance coverage of the population has been declining since 1980 for all age groups except those younger than 5 years old, whose access was improved through Medicaid eligibility changes. The age-adjusted percentage of persons who were not covered by health insurance increased from 14% in 1984 to almost 17% in 2000. Young adults 18 to 24 years old were most likely (35%) to be uninsured in 2007.[1]

African Americans were 25% more likely than whites, and Hispanics were two times as likely as whites to be uninsured in 2007. Individuals in households at 200% or less of the poverty level were more than four times more likely to be uninsured than were persons living in households at 200% or more of the poverty level (Figure 3-13). Still, of the 41 million uninsured people younger than age 65, about two thirds are 15 to 44 years of age. Three fourths are white, and one third live in families earning $25,000 or more. Lack of insurance coverage may disproportionately affect minority low-income individuals, but its growth in recent years has affected individuals in almost all groups. About two thirds of uninsured individuals in the United States are either employed or are dependents of an employed family member. Part-time workers and the self-employed are as likely as the unemployed to be uninsured. Access to health services, 1 of the 10 leading indicators of the health status of the United States, is the focus of one of the Public Health Spotlights for this chapter. A prime con-

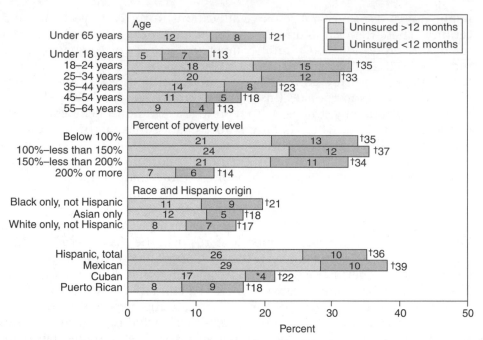

Figure 3-13 Persons under age 65 not covered by health insurance by selected characteristics and length of time uninsured, United States, 2007.

* Includes percentage with unknown length of time uninsured.
† Relative standard error 20–30%.

Source: From Centers for Disease Control and Prevention, National Center for Health Statistics. *Health, United States 2009*, Figure 20. Hyattsville, MD: NCHS; 2009. Data from the National Health Interview Survey.

tributor to the persistently high level of uninsured Americans is the decreasing percentage of business entities that offer health insurance as an employee benefit. Figure 3-14 traces the trend over the past decade.

Healthcare Resources

The supply of healthcare resources is another key dimension of the healthcare system. During the past quarter century, the number of active U.S. physicians increased by more than two thirds, with even greater increases among women physicians and international medical graduates. The specialty composition of the physician population also changed during this period, as a result of many factors, including changing employment opportunities, advances in medical technology, and the availability of residency positions. Medical and surgical subspecialties grew more rapidly than did the primary-care specialties. Recent projections suggest that the early 21st century will see a substantial surplus of physicians, primarily those trained in the surgical and medical specialties. A continuing shortage of registered nurses has reached crisis proportions in some parts of the United States.

Healthcare delivery models have also experienced major changes in recent years. For example, hospital-based resources have changed dramatically. Since

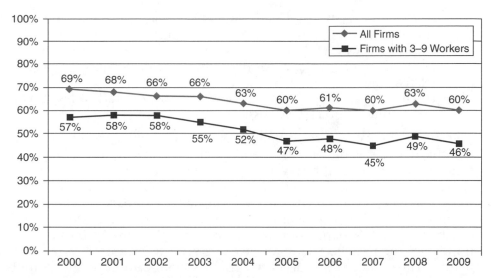

Figure 3-14 Percentage of all firms offering health benefits, United States, 2000–2009. *Source:* Data from Kaiser/HRET Survey of Employer-Sponsored Health Benefits, 2000–2009.

the mid 1970s, the number of community hospitals has decreased, and the numbers of admissions, days of care, average occupancy rates, and average length of stay have all declined as well. On the other hand, the number of hospital employees per 100 average daily patients has continued to increase. Hospital outpatient visits have also been increasing since the mid 1970s.

The growth in the number and types of healthcare delivery systems in recent years is another reflection of a rapidly changing healthcare environment. Increasing competition, combined with cost containment initiatives, has led to the proliferation of group medical practices, health maintenance organizations (HMOs), preferred provider organizations, ambulatory surgery centers, and emergency centers. Common with many of these delivery systems since the early 1990s have been managed care strategies and methods that seek to control the use of services. Managed care represents a system of administrative controls intended to reduce costs through managing the utilization of services. Elements of managed care strategies generally include some combination of the following:

- Risk sharing with providers to discourage the provision of unnecessary diagnostic and treatment services and, to some degree, to encourage preventive measures
- To attract specific groups, designing of tailored benefit packages that include the most important (but not necessarily all) services for that group; cost sharing for some services through deductibles and co-payments can be built into these packages
- Case management, especially for high-cost conditions, to encourage seeking out of less expensive treatments or settings
- Primary-care gatekeepers, generally the enrollee's primary care physician, who control referrals to specialists
- Second opinions as to the need for expensive diagnostic or elective invasive procedures

- Review and certification for hospitalizations, in general, and hospital admissions through the emergency department, in particular
- Continued-stay review for hospitalized patients as they reach the expected number of days for their illness (as determined by diagnostic-related groupings)
- Discharge planning to move patients out of hospitals to less expensive care settings as quickly as possible

One of the Public Health Spotlights for this chapter examines emerging and future issues as public health and managed care seek to coexist in a continuously changing health sector. The growth and expansion of these delivery systems have significant implications for the cost of, access to, and quality of health services. These, in turn, have substantial impact on public health organizations and their programs and services.[5] By the year 2000, more than one half of the U.S. population was served through a managed care organization. Over the next decade, managed care grew to capture 80%–90% of the market. The growth of managed care also has significant implications for both the population-based services of governmental public health agencies and the clinical services that have been provided in the public sector.

CHANGING ROLES, THEMES, AND PARADIGMS IN THE HEALTH SYSTEM

Even a cursory review of the health sector requires an examination of the key participants or key players in the health industry. The list of major stakeholders has been expanding as the system has grown and now includes government, business, third-party payers, healthcare providers, drug companies, and labor, as well as consumers. The federal government has grown to become the largest purchaser of health care and, along with business, has attempted to become a more prudent buyer by exerting more control over payments for services. Government seeks to reduce rising costs by altering the economic performance of the health sector through stimulation of a more competitive healthcare market. At the same time, efforts to expand access through the State Child Health Insurance Program and state initiatives toward universal coverage require more, not less, governmental spending. Still, budget problems at all levels make it increasingly difficult for government to fulfill commitments to provide healthcare services to the poor, the disadvantaged, and older persons. Over recent years, new and expensive medical technology, inflation, and unexpected increases in use forced third parties to pay out more for health care than they anticipated when premiums were determined. As a result, insurers have joined government in becoming more aggressive in efforts to contain healthcare costs. Many commercial carriers are exploring methods to anticipate use more accurately and to control outlays through managed care strategies. Business, labor, patients, hospitals, and professional organizations are all trying to restrain costs while maintaining access to health services.

Reducing the national deficit and balancing the federal budget will look in part to proposals that will control costs within Medicare and Medicaid, as well as in discretionary federal health programs. Except for Medicare, these recommendations are likely to be politically popular, even though the public has little understanding of the federal budget. For example, a 1994 poll[12] found that

Americans believed healthcare costs constituted 5% of the federal budget, although these costs actually constituted 16%. At the same time, Americans believed that foreign aid and welfare constituted 27% and 19%, respectively, of the federal budget when, in fact, they constituted only 2% and 3%, respectively. When the time comes to balance the federal budget and reduce the national deficit, the American public will face difficult choices as to which programs can be reduced. Public health programs, largely discretionary spending, may not fare well in this scenario.

As these stakeholders search for methods to reduce costs and as competition intensifies, efforts to preserve the quality of health care will become increasingly important. An Institute of Medicine study concluded that medical errors account for as many deaths each year as motor vehicle crashes and breast cancer (Figure 3-15).[13] Public debate will continue to focus on how to define and measure quality. Despite the difficulty in measuring quality of medical care, it is likely that quality measurement systems will increase substantially. Dialogue and debate among the major stakeholders in the health system will be influenced by the tension between cost containment and regulation; the interdependence of access, quality, and costs; the call for greater accountability; and the slow but steady acceptance of the need for health reform.

Almost certainly, health policy issues will become increasingly politicized. The debate on healthcare issues will continue to expand beyond the healthcare community. Many health policy issues may no longer be determined by sound science and practice considerations, but rather by political factors. Changes in the health sector may lead to unexpected divisions and alliances on health policy issues. The intensity of economic competition in the health sector is likely to continue to increase because of the increasing supply of healthcare personnel and because of the changes in the financing of care.

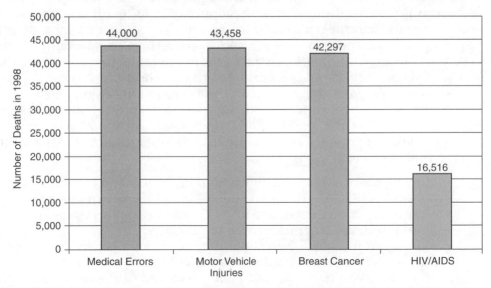

Figure 3-15 Deaths attributed to medical errors, motor vehicle injuries, breast cancer, and HIV/AIDS, United States, 1998. *Source:* Data from Institute of Medicine, *To Err Is Human.* Washington, DC: National Academy of Sciences; 1999.

Increased competition is likely to cause realignments among key participants in the healthcare sector, often depending on the particular issue involved.

The failure of health reform at the national policy level in 1994 did not preclude the implementation of significant improvements in either the public or the private components of the health sector. With or without changes in national health policies, the health system in the United States has been reforming itself for decades. With the persistence of cost and access as the system's twin critical problems, new approaches and models were both needed and expected. The federal, as well as state, governments have moved to control the costs of Medicaid services, primarily through attempts to enroll nondisabled Medicaid populations (largely mothers and children) into capitated managed care programs. The rapid conversion of Medicaid services to managed care operations and the growth of private managed care organizations pose new issues for the delivery of clinical preventive and public health services.[5] Although it is anticipated that these changes will result in fewer clinical preventive and treatment services being provided through public health agencies, both the extent and impact of these shifts remain unclear. In any event, the underlying investment strategy of the U.S. health system appears to remain unchanged, with 95% of the available resources allocated for treatment services, approximately 5% for essential public health services, and 1% for population-based public health services. Without additional investment in prevention and public health approaches, the long-term prospects for controlling costs within the U.S. health system are bleak. The Obama health reform package (see Table 3-5), enacted in 2010, was a significant step toward comprehensive health reform, expecially in terms of serving the 45 million Americans on the fringe of the system, who otherwise would continue to incur excessive costs when accessing the system through hospital emergency departments rather than through primary care providers. Universal access is a prerequisite for eventual control of costs, but it is not clear how comprehensive reform can be affected without concomitant reform of both the medical care and public health subsystems. The Obama health reforms addressed a variety of health insurance gaps but did little to correct the imbalance between treatment and prevention in the U.S. health system.

Although progress along this road has been painfully slow, there is evidence that a paradigm shift is under way. The Pew Health Professions Commission argues that the American healthcare system of the 21st century will be quite different from its 1990s counterpart.[14] The healthcare system of the 21st century will be:

- More managed, with better integration of services and financing
- More accountable to those who purchase and use health services
- More aware of and responsive to the needs of enrolled populations
- More able to use fewer resources more effectively
- More innovative and diverse in how it provides for health
- More inclusive in how it defines health
- Less focused on treatment and more concerned with education, prevention, and care management
- More oriented to improving the health of the entire population
- More reliant on outcomes data and evidence

Table 3-5   Time Line for Selected 2010 Health Reform Provisions

Enhanced Access	
2010	• Establish a temporary national high-risk pool to provide health coverage to individuals with preexisting medical conditions. • Provide dependent coverage for adult children up to age 26 for all individual and group policies. • Prohibit individual and group health plans from placing lifetime limits on the dollar value of coverage. • Prohibit insurers from rescinding coverage except in cases of fraud and prohibit preexisting condition exclusions for children. • Provide tax credits to small employers with no more than 25 employees and average annual wages of less than $50,000 that purchase health insurance for employees. • Create a state option to cover childless adults though a Medicaid State Plan Amendment. • Create a state option to provide Medicaid coverage for family planning services to certain low-income individuals through a Medicaid state plan amendment up to the highest level of eligibility for pregnant women. • Create a new option for states to provide State Children's Health Insurance Program (SCHIP) coverage to children of state government employees eligible for health benefits if certain conditions are met.
2011	• Create a new Medicaid state plan option to permit Medicaid enrollees with at least two chronic conditions, one condition and risk of developing another, or at least one serious and persistent mental health condition to designate a provider as a health home. • Establish a new trauma center program to strengthen emergency department and trauma center capacity. • Improve access to care by increasing funding by $11 billion for community health centers and the National Health Service Corps over 5 years; establish new programs to support school-based health centers and nurse-managed health clinics.
2013	• Create the Consumer Operated and Oriented Plan program to foster the creation of nonprofit, member-run health insurance companies in all 50 states and the District of Columbia to offer qualified health plans. • Increase Medicaid payments for primary care services provided by primary care doctors for 2013 and 2014 with 100% federal funding.
2014	• Require U.S. citizens and legal residents to have qualifying health coverage (phase-in tax penalty for those without coverage) • Assess employers with 50 or more employees that do not offer coverage and have at least one full-time employee who receives a premium tax credit a fee of $2,000 per full-time employee, excluding the first 30 employees from the assessment. (Employers with 50 or more employees that offer coverage but have at least one full-time employee receiving a premium tax credit will pay the lesser of $3,000 for each employee receiving a premium credit or $2,000 for each full-time employee, excluding the first 30 employees from the assessment.)

(continues)

Table 3-5   Time Line for Selected 2010 Health Reform Provisions (continued)

	• Require employers with more than 200 employees to automatically enroll employees into health insurance plans offered by the employer. (Employees may opt out of coverage.) • Create state-based American health benefit exchanges and small business health options program exchanges, administered by a governmental agency or nonprofit organization, through which individuals and small businesses with up to 100 employees can purchase qualified coverage. • Require guaranteed issue and renewability and allow rating variation based only on age (limited to 3 to 1 ratio), premium rating area, family composition, and tobacco use (limited to 1.5 to 1 ratio) in the individual and the small group market and the exchanges. • Reduce the out-of-pocket limits for those with incomes up to 400% of the federal poverty level (FPL). • Limit deductibles for health plans in the small group market to $2,000 for individuals and $4,000 for families unless contributions that offset deductible amounts above these limits are offered. • Limit any waiting periods for coverage to 90 days. • Create an essential health benefits package that provides a comprehensive set of services, covers at least 60% of the actuarial value of the covered benefits, limits annual cost-sharing to the current law HSA limits ($5,950/individual and $11,900/family in 2010), and is not more extensive than the typical employer plan. • Require the Office of Personnel Management to contract with insurers to offer at least two multistate plans in each exchange. At least one plan must be offered by a nonprofit entity and at least one plan must not provide coverage for abortions beyond the provisions of federal law. • Permit states the option to create a basic health plan for uninsured individuals with incomes between 133% and 200% of the FPL who would otherwise be eligible to receive premium subsidies in the exchange. • Allow states the option of merging the individual and small group markets. • Create a temporary reinsurance program to collect payments from health insurers in the individual and group markets to provide payments to plans in the individual market that cover high-risk individuals. • Provide refundable and advanceable premium credits and cost sharing subsidies to eligible individuals and families with incomes between 133% and 400% of the FPL to purchase insurance through the exchanges. • Expand Medicaid to all non-Medicare eligible individuals under age 65 (children, pregnant women, parents, and adults without dependent children) with incomes up to 133% of the FPL based on modified adjusted gross income and provide enhanced federal matching for new eligibles.
2015 and later	• Permit states to form healthcare choice compacts and allow insurers to sell policies in any state participating in the compact.

Table 3-5   Time Line for Selected 2010 Health Reform Provisions (continued)

Prevention/Wellness	
2010	• Require qualified health plans to provide at a minimum coverage without cost-sharing for preventive services rated A or B by the U.S. Preventive Services Task Force, recommended immunizations, preventive care for infants, children, and adolescents, and additional preventive care and screenings for women.
2011	• Eliminate cost sharing for Medicare-covered preventive services that are recommended (rated A or B) by the U.S. Preventive Services Task Force and waive the Medicare deductible for colorectal cancer screening tests. Authorize the Secretary to modify or eliminate Medicare coverage of preventive services based on recommendations of the U.S. Preventive Services Task Force.
	• Provide Medicare beneficiaries access to a comprehensive health risk assessment and creation of a personalized prevention plan and provide incentives to Medicare and Medicaid beneficiaries to complete behavior modification programs.
	• Provide grants for up to 5 years to small employers that establish wellness programs.
	• Establish the National Prevention, Health Promotion and Public Health Council to develop a national strategy to improve the nation's health.
	• Require chain restaurants and vending machine operators to disclose the nutritional content of each food item.
2013	• Provide states that offer Medicaid coverage of and remove cost sharing for preventive services recommended (rated A or B) by the U.S. Preventive Services Task Force and recommended immunizations with a 1 percentage point increase in the federal medical assistance percentage for these services.
2014	• Permit employers to offer employees rewards of up to 30%, increasing to 50% if appropriate, of the cost of coverage for participating in a wellness program and meeting certain health-related standards. Establish 10-state pilot programs to permit participating states to apply similar rewards for participating in wellness programs in the individual market.

Source: Data from Kaiser Family Foundation, Kaiser Commission on Medicaid, and the Uninsured and Health Care Marketplace Project. Publication number: 8060. http://www.kff.org/healthreform/8060.cfm. Accessed May 12, 2010.

These gains, however, are likely to be accompanied by pain. The number of hospitals may decline by as much as 50% and the number of hospital beds by even more than that. There will be continued expansion of primary care in community and other ambulatory settings; this will foster replication of services in different settings, a development likely to confuse consumers. These forces also suggest major traumas for the health professions, with projected deficits of some professions, such as nurses and dentists, and surpluses of others, such as physicians and pharmacists.[14] An estimated 100,000 to 150,000 excess physicians, mainly specialists, could be joined by 200,000 to 300,000 excess nurses as the hospital sector consolidates and by as many as 40,000 excess pharmacists as drug dispensing is automated and centralized. The massive fragmentation among 200 or more allied health fields will cause consolidation into multiskilled professions to meet the changing needs of hospitals and other care settings. One of the few professions likely to flourish in this environment will be public health, with its focus on populations, information-driven planning, collaborative responses, and broad definition of health and health services.

Where these forces will move the health system is not yet known. To blend better the contributions of preventive and treatment-based approaches, several important changes are needed. There must be a new and more rational understanding of what is meant by "health services." This understanding must include a broad view of health promotion and health protection strategies and must afford these equal standing with treatment-based strategies. Once and for all, health services must be seen to include services that focus on health, as well as those that focus on ill health. This should result in support for a more comprehensive approach to defining a basic benefit package that would be provided to all Americans. A second and companion change needed is to finance this enhanced basic benefit package from the same source, rather than funding public health and most prevention from one source (government resources) and treatment and the remaining prevention activities from private sources (business, individuals, insurance). With these changes, a gradual reallocation of resources can move the system toward a more rational and effective investment strategy.

The sheer size and scope of the American health system make it a force to be reckoned with, engendering comparisons with a similar force that existed in the United States in the 1950s and 1960s. At that time and as he left office, President Eisenhower warned the nation of the potentially dangerous influence of the nation's "military industrial complex." His observations were both ominous and insightful as he decried a powerful industry whose self-interest was coloring the nation's view of other countries and their people. The plight of the American health system raises the specter of a modern analogue in a "medical industrial complex." One danger posed by these complexes is their ability to influence the way we address (or even think about) a major public policy problem or issue. This occurs through interpreting and recasting the issues involved, sometimes even to the extent of altering public perceptions as to what is occurring and why.

Public understanding of the meaning of the terms health reform and health care is a case in point. Although, as a society, we have come to substitute the term health care for what is really medical or treatment care, these are simply not the same. The health status of a population is largely determined by a different set of considerations, as discussed in Chapter 2. Those considerations are very much the focus of the public health system. If the ultimate goal is a healthier population and, more specifically, the prevention of disease and disability, the national health system must aggressively balance treatment with population- and community-based prevention strategies.

There is a term for when an organization finds that it is unable to achieve its primary objectives and outcomes (bottom line) and then justifies its existence in terms of how well it does the things it is doing. Outcome displacement is that term; it means that the original outcome (here, improved health status) has been displaced by a focus on how well the means to that end (the organization, provision, and financing of services) are being addressed. These, then, become the new purpose or mission for that system. Instead of "doing the right things" to affect health status, the system focuses on "doing things right" (regardless of whether they maximally affect health). It is possible to have the best medical care services in the world but still have an inadequate health system.

CONCLUSION

Every day in America, decisions are made that influence the health status of individuals and groups of individuals. The aggregate of these decisions and the activities necessary to carry them out constitute our health system. It is important to view interventions as linked with health and illness states, as well as with the dynamic processes and multiple factors that move an individual from one state to another. Preventive interventions act at various points and through various means to prevent the development of a disease state or, if it occurs, to minimize its effects to the extent possible. These interventions differ in their linkages with public health practice, medical practice, and long-term care, as well as in their focus on individuals or groups. The framework represents a rational one, reflecting known facts concerning each of its aspects and their relationships with each other.

As this chapter has described, current health policy in the United States reflects a different view of the factors incorporated in the model. Current policy focuses unduly on disease states and strategies for restoring, as opposed to promoting or protecting, health. It directs the vast majority of human, physical, and financial resources to tertiary prevention, particularly to acute treatment. It focuses disproportionately on individually oriented secondary and tertiary medical care. In so doing, it raises questions as to whether these policies are effective and ethical.

Characterized in the past largely by federalism, pluralism, and incrementalism, the health sector in the United States is undergoing fundamental change, primarily in response to economic realities that have invested more than $2.5 trillion in a model that equates medical care with health care. We are now realizing that this investment strategy is not producing results commensurate with its resource consumption. Health indicators, including those characterizing large disparities in outcomes and access among important minority groups, are not responding to more resources being deployed in the usual ways. The major problems have been widely characterized as cost and access, with the former being considered a cause of the latter. How to fix the cost problem while moving toward universal access will challenge the U.S. health system throughout the second decade of the 21st century, although managed care approaches are serving to place some controls on the utilization of specific services. A better representation of the twin problems facing the U.S. health sector might be excess and access, suggesting a return to the strategic drawing boards for approaches that reduce and redeploy resources, rather than only reducing them. Within this re-examination of purpose and strategies for the health sector, the need to address health, as well as treatment, should be paramount. To accomplish these aims, there must be consensus that basic health services include population-based public health services and clinical preventive services, as well as diagnostic and treatment services. To facilitate rational policy making and investment decisions, these services should be funded from a common source. This does not necessarily require a government-funded, single-payer health system. It could be that health insurance premiums replace governmental appropriations as the source of funding for public sector activities. Whichever course is eventually plotted, these realizations hopefully will take place before the health sector reaches its meltdown point.

DISCUSSION QUESTIONS AND EXERCISES

1. What are the most critical issues facing the healthcare system in the United States today? Before answering this question, see what insights you can find at the websites of these major health organizations: American Medical Association (http://www.ama-assn.org), American Hospital Association (http://www.aha.org), American Nurses Association (http://www.ana.org), and the American Association of Medical Colleges (http://www.aamc.org).

2. What forces are most likely to fuel further movement toward major healthcare reform in America?

3. Why are there even greater concerns over national policy solutions (or "health reform") today than there were in 1994?

4. Select an important health problem (disease or condition) related to maternal and infant health (see the Public Health Spotlight on Access to Health Care for ideas), and describe interventions for this problem across the five strategies of health-related and illness-related interventions (health promotion, specific protection, early detection, disability limitation, rehabilitation) presented in Chapter 3.

5. For the same health problem related to maternal and infant health selected in Question 4, describe interventions for this problem across the three levels of preventive interventions (primary, secondary, and tertiary) presented in Chapter 3.

6. Table 3-2 lists organizations, agencies, and institutions that might be considered part of an overall national prevention effort. Identify those that should be included in a compilation of health-related prevention efforts. On the basis of what you know of these agencies, which of their programs or services should be included? Explain the reasons for your choices in terms of categories of preventive activities (e.g., health promotion, health protection, and clinical preventive services). Identify those that you would include if you had the task of quantifying the scope and cost of all health-related prevention activities and

expenditures in the United States. Which would you choose to leave off this list? Why?

7. Examine the data on the health system in a city or county of interest that are available through a state or local health agency. What elements from this site are most useful?

8. Great Debate: This debate examines contributors to improvement in health status in the United States since 1900. There are two propositions to be considered: proposition A, in which public health interventions are responsible for these improvements, and proposition B, in which medical care interventions are responsible for these improvements. Select one of these positions to argue and submit a summary of arguments.

9. Is an ounce of prevention still worth a pound of cure in the United States? If not, what is the relative value of prevention in comparison with treatment?

10. Has the recent growth of managed care strategies within the health sector had a positive or a negative impact on the public's health? How? Why?

REFERENCES

1. Centers for Disease Control and Prevention, National Center for Health Statistics. *Health, United States, 2009*. Hyattsville, MD: National Center for Health Statistics; 2009.

2. Leavell HR, Clark EG. *Preventive Medicine for the Doctor in His Community*. 3rd ed. New York: McGraw-Hill; 1965.

3. U.S. Preventive Services Task Force. *Guide to Clinical Preventive Services*. 2nd ed. Washington, DC: U.S. Department of Health and Human Services; 1995.

4. Lasker RD. *Medicine & Public Health: The Power of Collaboration*. New York: New York Academy of Medicine; 1997.

5. Halverson PK, Kaluzny AD, McLaughlin CP. *Managed Care & Public Health*. Gaithersburg, MD: Aspen Publishers; 1998.

6. Weil PA, Bogue RJ. Motivating community health improvement: leading practices you can use. *Health Exec*. 1999;14:18–24.

7. Brown RE, Elixhauser A, Corea J, et al. *National Expenditures for Health Promotion and Disease Prevention Activities in the United States*. Washington, DC: Medical Technology Assessment and Policy Research Center; 1991.

8. *Core Functions Project, Public Health Service, Office of Disease Prevention and Health Promotion. Health Care Reform and Public Health: A Paper Based on Population-Based Core Functions*. Washington, DC: U.S. Public Health Service; 1993.

9. Centers for Medicare and Medicaid Services, National Health Accounts, 1960–2000.

10. Frist B. Public health and national security: the critical role of increased federal support. *Health Aff (Millwood)*. 2002;21:117–130.

11. McGlynn EA, Asch SM, Adams J, et al. The quality of health care delivered to adults in the United States. *N Engl J Med*. 2003;348:2635–2645.

12. Blendon RJ. *Kaiser/Harvard/KRC National Election Night Survey*. Menlo Park, CA: Henry J. Kaiser Family Foundation; 1994.

13. Institute of Medicine. *To Err Is Human*. Washington, DC: National Academy of Sciences; 1999.

14. Pew Health Professions Commission. *Critical Challenges: Revitalizing the Health Professions for the Twenty-First Century*. San Francisco: University of California Center for Health Professions; 1995.

Public Health Spotlight on
Managed Care and Public Health

The forces of reform buffeted the U.S. health system during much of the two decades between 1990 and 2010, resulting in significant change in the organization, provision, and financing of health services. These changes certainly constitute reform, although this type of reform takes decades, rather than months or years. Central to these changes are managed care plans and the competitive purchase of health services from large health systems. The links with public health have not always been clear; public health and managed care can appear to be strange bedfellows. What is clear, however, is that public health practitioners need a better understanding of managed care and how it works. The most important reason is that effective partnerships with managed care will be critical to solving many public health problems. In addition, public health surveillance will depend, in part, on the nature and quality of information available from managed care plans. Finally, the mix and match of public health programs and services will depend on what the medical care system does and does not do. For these reasons, the basic concepts and practices of managed care organizations are presented in this Public Health Spotlight.

MANAGED CARE AT THE TURN OF THE CENTURY

Managed care organizations exist for two related purposes: to insure plan members and to furnish and manage the care that they receive. There are many different variations on this theme, but definitions of managed care characterize a system that is under the management of a single entity that insures its members and then furnishes benefits to those members through a defined network of participating providers. Services may be furnished either directly or through intermediaries. In any event, the system strives to manage the healthcare practices of its participating providers. Still, it is the providers who manage the patients. Because it is provider decisions, more than the decisions of patients, that influence service utilization and costs, modern managed care organizations must manage providers.

In the United States, managed care organizations function as corporations. Insurance companies established some, although many are now investor owned. Generally, the largest investors are healthcare providers themselves; the principal stakeholders are hospitals, physicians, and specialized entities that offer a single-service product line, such as behavioral health benefits. The common denominator among managed care organizations is their assumption of risk on a complete or partial basis. Profits are derived from the difference between premium payments and costs of providing services to patients.

HMOs and other forms of managed care grew rapidly in the 1990s. By the end of the decade, more than 80 million privately insured individuals were covered by managed care plans. Managed care has also begun to penetrate governmentally financed health services, with more than one half of all Medicaid beneficiaries and nearly 1 in 10 Medicare recipients receiving services through managed care operations. These numbers will grow rapidly over the next decade.

Many forces are at work to promote the growth of managed care arrangements in the United States. First and foremost are rising costs associated with health care. As costs escalated and because the majority of Americans are covered through employers, businesses moved to control costs. Many businesses had already acted to self-insure their workers and dependents, in an effort to control decisions affecting costs better. They soon began to treat health services as they would other costs of doing business and looked for insurance products that would allow them to control costs through controlling providers. Managed care was an attractive strategy. Managed care also afforded an opportunity for government to control its costs in a manner that would overcome at least some of the obstacles that had traditionally discouraged providers from serving Medicaid recipients (such as delayed payments and extensive paperwork). With predictable reimbursement levels and lower utilization of services, at least in comparison with the greater risk and need, the opportunity for profit margins has attracted interest from managed care organizations in virtually every state. Managed care for Medicare beneficiaries has advanced less rapidly than for the private sector and Medicaid. Official predictions of inadequate resources to serve baby boomers when they reach senior citizenship, however, suggest that managed care will eventually penetrate the Medicare program.

The jargon and terminology of modern managed care confuses even the most knowledgeable individuals. More important than familiarity with the jargon, however, is the understanding of how these plans work. In general, there are both open and closed variations of managed care plans. Open and closed refer to the relationship between the managed care plan and its patients in terms of freedom to choose providers other than those controlled by the managed care organization. Closed plans have tighter control over providers, and enrolled plan members have little ability to secure covered services outside of these panels of providers. Many traditional staff-model HMOs are examples of closed plans. Open panels are looser arrangements that allow members to obtain services from a wider (and less tightly controlled) network of providers. Preferred provider organizations and physician/hospital networks are examples of open panels. In this form of managed care, enrolled members can obtain services at very little additional cost out of pocket, unless that service is received outside the plan. When that occurs, members pay more, although they generally remain partially covered by the plan.

A hybrid arrangement is the point-of-service model. Here, services provided by plan providers are tightly controlled, but services can also be obtained outside of the plan through a looser network of providers for an added fee. This allows for greater consumer choice as to providers, but still provides for some control of costs for basic benefits.

Naturally, the more interested the purchaser is in controlling costs, the less open the plan will be. Medicaid managed care plans and even private plans less concerned over patient freedom to choose among providers find the closed panels more conducive to aggressive cost-control strategies. Decisions to go the closed-panel route require that assessments have been made of the capacity of the managed care organization to provide covered services, including both primary and specialized care services. Unfortunately, methods and tools for such assessments are seldom afforded the same priority as controlling costs.

Methods for controlling costs are straightforward, with utilization control serving as a primary approach. Services and procedures that cannot be quickly and cheaply provided during a provider visit are reviewed for appropriateness in terms of whether such services are actually needed and, if needed, from whom and in what settings they will be provided. In short, the plan determines whether the service is covered and where the member can get it. Denial of approval can be tantamount to denial of care for those who lack the ability to secure the services using their own resources. Until recently, there has been little opportunity for insured individuals to challenge these decisions in the courts.

Sharing of costs between the plan and the enrollee is another approach for controlling costs. When costs are shared, the plan ends up paying less. Such cost sharing also serves to discourage the member from actually receiving the service, another savings for the managed care plan. Other cost-control measures relate to member selection. Marketing to potential members from healthier age groups and populations also serves to control costs down the road. Some marketing efforts are even more explicit in terms of more actively enrolling (even door to door) the healthier members of an eligible group—a practice that has been identified especially with the development of Medicaid managed care programs.

In addition to risk-profiling potential members, similar profiles can be assembled on providers to identify those whose practice patterns and decisions result in "unnecessary" costs for the plan. Patterns for use of screening tests, performance of office procedures, return visits, and hospital admissions are examined to identify providers whose practice patterns might be modified or even whose participation might be excluded. There is some scientific merit to these reviews in the face of numerous studies describing greatly varying rates of medical procedures across the United States, often with no apparent differences in health outcomes.

These approaches to economic credentialing often do not consider differences in the risk mix of populations served. Asthma management of a white teenage male in the suburbs may not be the same as for an innercity black teenager. Identification and consideration of different risk mixes and contributing factors are public health skills that are not widely available in managed care operations.

OPPORTUNITIES FOR IMPROVING PUBLIC HEALTH

Despite the tensions and conflicts that have emerged between managed care organizations and both providers and consumers, aspects of managed care offer opportunities for improving public health. Fragmentation and a lack of coordination of health services have long been a hallmark of the American health system. Managed care imposes some semblance of a structure on this pluralistic "nonsystem" and establishes a framework for effective health services that can reach more individuals. In the past, this could be done only on a provider-by-provider basis. There are now access and leverage points for networks of providers to provide clinical preventive services more extensively and to integrate their activities with community prevention efforts. There are even financial incentives for these to occur. Diseases and conditions prevented today will mean lower expenditures and greater profits tomorrow. Although managed care organizations with a long-term view and a stable base of enrollees recognize this opportunity, many newly established managed care operations focus on shorter-term financial viability concerns, such as expanding enrollment and rapid generation of profits.

Profit orientations cut both ways, however, and public health agencies may find themselves cut out of the picture for many services they have been providing in recent decades. Some services, such as primary and even treatment care services, may shift to managed care organizations for individuals covered by Medicaid or other third-party insurers. Other services are specialized public health services, such as treatment services for tuberculosis, HIV infections, and sexually transmitted diseases. The future for these services is very much an open question. Managed care plans would prefer not to enroll individuals who need specialized, often high-cost services. Providers of specialized services are also worrisome to managed care plans because these might serve to attract more individuals with high-cost needs. Yet these needs will exist, and it is unclear how and by whom they will be addressed.

One approach is to require that managed care plans include specialized public health providers in their networks. Needless to say, this approach is not very popular among managed care organizations. Another option is to tax a portion of the revenues of managed care plans to support specialized public health providers through grants or contracts. The public health agencies would not be formally part of the managed care networks, but they would share information on individuals as referrals were made back and forth. Another approach is to carve out certain services from the managed care plans and let individuals seek out these services on an as-needed basis. This approach, however, fosters fragmentation and lack of continuity of care. The advantages of defining and carving out specific services as public health rather than components of a comprehensive benefit package have not been well established to date.

Another opportunity is afforded by the information systems necessary to manage networks of providers and services. Traditionally, public health surveillance has been not been able to access and use information on health status and health conditions of living persons captured in the ambulatory care system. Combining this information with other data sources can greatly benefit public health surveillance efforts, as well as inform the needs of managed care plans and providers; however, public health interests are not the only ones likely to be seeking access to health plan data and information. The very same stakeholders whose priorities promoted the expansion of managed care will be looking for information that proves that their resources are being used effectively and efficiently. Businesses and the government will be demanding information that demonstrates the value that their health dollars are realizing and that allows them and their employees to evaluate and compare health plan performance. Ideally, health outcome concerns should drive these developments, but financial concerns are more likely to dictate what information is collected and how it is used.

The managed care industry has developed a data set for use in evaluating and comparing health plan performance, the Health Plan Employer Data and Information Set (HEDIS). Revisions of HEDIS have sought to incorporate community and public health performance measures; the public health community is actively seeking to build on HEDIS so that public health data needs might be better addressed. At least three categories of data may have applications for public health purposes:

1. Administrative data sets, such as provider names and payments
2. Enrollment data, such as basic demographic information that can be useful in identifying high-risk individuals and communities
3. Encounter data profiling what their providers order and the frequency of hospital admissions

Encounter data, however, tend to be limited because these are the most expensive form of data to obtain, especially if onsite inspection and abstracting information from medical records are required. Also, managed care plans do not rely on encounter data for reimbursement, as is common with fee-for-service systems.

There has been little agreement to date as to which information from encounter data would be both useful for public health purposes and appropriate for managed care plans to provide. The many issues surrounding data questions are only beginning to be explored. It is likely that additional opportunities will surface as they are discussed and developed. For example, school health may represent another opportunity for forging closer working relationships between managed care plans and public health organizations. In many parts of the country, school health programs are being dismantled because of financial pressures on state and local government. School health nurses have long been the linchpins of school health programs. These, too, are declining in numbers, even while new mandates and expectations are being established in areas such as compliance with immunization requirements, vision and hearing screenings, medical assessments for special education students, medication administration, and crisis intervention services. With these duties, their involvement in health curriculum issues is greatly diluted; however, as Medicaid managed care conversions develop and as managed care penetrates further into the private sector, school health may represent an opportunity to integrate managed care plans with public health objectives. For example, children at a single school may be served by 10 to 20 managed care plans currently and in the future perhaps by only 5 to 10. These plans could contribute proportionately to the funding of school nurses and support staff to carry out the duties described previously here in ways that would be less expensive than either providing them at plan provider sites or not providing them and dealing with preventable disease outbreaks or asthma attacks requiring hospitalization.

The many opportunities afforded by the expansion of managed care call for new thinking and new roles, such as those suggested in Table 3-6. Both managed care plans and public health agencies must approach these challenges with common objectives in order for reform of the medical care system to be accompanied by reform within the public health system.

Table 3-6 Managed Care and Public Health Issues for the Future

Public health goals and Medicaid services	How these can be merged • To increase the focus on health • To simplify and increase access for Medicaid recipients • To incorporate health services (broadly defined) essential for good health outcomes
Case management and enabling services	How to ensure • Inclusion of these services in view of evidence that they improve access and yield better health outcomes for enrollees than systems that only coordinate medical treatment
System capacity and the roles of providers	How these can be clearly articulated • To clarify the sometimes conflicting case management roles of both patient advocates and cost-containment agents
Fluctuations in enrollment	How these will • Complicate efforts to supply case management to Medicaid populations • Affect provider accountability for continuity of care • Increase the likelihood that public health agencies will maintain a significant role in delivering services as "providers of last resort"
Assurance of quality	How to deal with issues of quality so that • Quality will not be compromised • Quality will be monitored by government • There is a public health focus on access and clinical care, as well as a financial focus on solvency and enrollment composition • There is a careful analysis of broad outcome data • Encounter data will facilitate consumer choice and identify problems in the shift from fee-for-service care delivery to managed care with capitated payments • The appropriate roles of government, employers, and consumers are identified
Data	How to address • The need for data essential for a successful "outcome-oriented" approach to continuing quality processes within managed care systems • Integration in systems that collect, make meaningful, and disseminate data to facilitate decision making

(continues)

Table 3-6   Managed Care and Public Health Issues for the Future (continued)

Provider and consumer acceptance	How to resolve • Dependence on the degree to which provider concerns regarding practice autonomy and consumer perceptions of diminished choice are addressed • The need for a consumer-oriented approach to quality, requiring consumer support, and independent access to medical advice, such as second opinions

Source: Data from *Challenge and Opportunity: Public Health in an Era of Change.* Springfield, IL: Illinois Department of Public Health; 1996.

Public Health Spotlight on Access to Health Care

Both medical and public health strategies have contributed to the impressive improvement in maternal and infant health measures achieved over the 20th century. Reducing infant mortality, for example, calls for either decreasing the proportion of infants born at low birth weight (prevention) or by improving the chances of those infants to survive through more effective medical care. Prevention and treatment should not be considered mutually exclusive strategies.

These noteworthy advances reflect an ongoing need to ensure access to needed healthcare services. There has been little progress in recent decades toward improving access to primary healthcare services, one of the 10 leading indicators for Healthy People 2010. This Public Health Spotlight reviews the progress of the 20th century, discusses the status of current efforts, and highlights effective population-based interventions that are needed to achieve the national health objectives for the year 2010.

PUBLIC HEALTH ACHIEVEMENTS IN 20TH CENTURY AMERICA[1]

Improved Pregnancy Outcomes[1]

At the beginning of the 20th century, for every 1,000 live births, six to nine women in the United States died of pregnancy-related complications, and approximately 100 infants died before the age of 1 year.[2,3] From 1915 through 2000, the infant mortality rate declined greater than 90%, and from 1900 through 1997, the maternal mortality rate declined almost 99%[4] (see Figures 3-16 and 3-17). Environmental interventions, improvements in nutrition, advances in clinical medicine, improvements in access to health care, improvements in surveillance and monitoring of disease, increases in education levels, and improvements in standards of living contributed to this remarkable decline.[2] Despite these improvements in maternal and infant mortality rates, significant disparities by race and ethnicity persist.

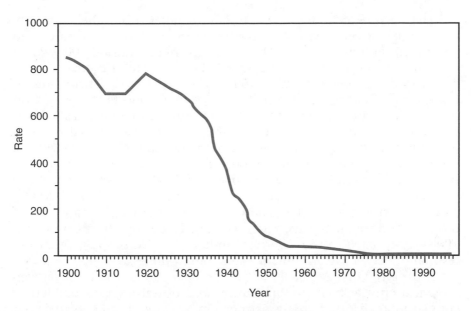

Figure 3-16 Maternal mortality rates (per 100,000 live births) by year, United States, 1900–1997. *Source:* From Centers for Disease Control and Prevention. Public health achievements, United States, 1900–1999: healthier mothers and babies. *MMWR.* 1999;48(38):849–858.

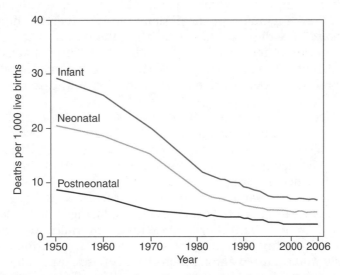

Figure 3-17 Infant, neonatal, and postneonatal mortality rates, United States, 1950–2006. *Source:* From Centers for Disease Control and Prevention, National Center for Health Statistics. *Health, United States, 2009*, Figure 17. Hyattsville, MD: NCHS; 2009. Data from the National Vital Statistics System.

The decline in infant mortality is unparalleled by other mortality reduction this century. If turn-of-the-century infant death rates had continued, an estimated 500,000 live-born infants during 2000 would have died before age 1 year; instead, 525,000 fewer infants died.[4]

In 1900, in some U.S. cities, up to 30% of infants died before reaching their first birthdays.[2] Efforts to reduce infant mortality focused on improving environmental and living conditions in urban areas.[2] Urban environmental interventions (e.g., sewage and refuse disposal and safe drinking water) played key roles in reducing infant mortality. Rising standards of living, including improvements in economic and education levels of families, helped to promote health. Declining fertility rates also contributed to reductions in infant mortality through longer spacing of children, smaller family size, and better nutritional status of mothers and infants.[2] Milk pasteurization, first adopted in Chicago in 1908, contributed to the control of milk-borne diseases (e.g., gastrointestinal infections) from contaminated milk supplies.

During the first 3 decades of the century, public health, social welfare, and clinical medicine (pediatrics and obstetrics) collaborated to combat infant mortality. This partnership began with milk hygiene but later included other public health issues. In 1912, the Children's Bureau was formed and became the primary government agency to work toward improving maternal and infant welfare until 1946, when its role in maternal and child health diminished; the Bureau was eliminated in 1969.[2] The Children's Bureau defined the problem of infant mortality and shaped the debate over programs to ameliorate the problem. The Children's Bureau also advocated comprehensive maternal and infant welfare services, including prenatal, natal, and postpartum home visits by healthcare providers. By the 1920s, the integration of these services changed the approach to infant mortality from one that addressed infant health problems to an approach that included infant and mother and prenatal care programs to educate, monitor, and care for pregnant women.

The discovery and widespread use of antimicrobial agents (e.g., sulfonamide in 1937 and penicillin in the 1940s) and the development of fluid and electrolyte replacement therapy and safe blood transfusions accelerated the declines in infant mortality; from 1930 through 1949, mortality rates declined 52%.[5]

The percentage decline in postneonatal (age 28 to 364 days) mortality (66%) was greater than the decline in neonatal (age 0 to 27 days) mortality (40%). From 1950 through 1964, infant mortality declined more slowly.[1] An increasing proportion of infant deaths was attributed to perinatal causes and occurred among high-risk neonates, especially low birth weight and preterm babies. Although no reliable data exist, the rapid decline in infant mortality during earlier decades probably was not influenced by decreases in low birth weight rates because the decrease in mortality was primarily in postneonatal deaths that are less influenced by birth weight. Inadequate programs during the 1950s and 1960s to reduce deaths among high-risk neonates led to renewed efforts to improve access to prenatal care—especially for the poor—and to a concentrated effort to establish neonatal intensive-care units and to promote research in maternal and infant health, including research into technologies to improve the survival of low birth weight and preterm babies.

During the late 1960s, after Medicaid and other federal programs were implemented, infant mortality (primarily postneonatal mortality) declined substantially.[6] From 1970 to 1979, neonatal mortality plummeted 41% (Figure 3-17) because of technologic advances in neonatal medicine and in the regionalization of perinatal services; postneonatal mortality declined 14%. During the early to mid 1980s, the downward trend in U.S. infant mortality slowed[7]; however, during 1989 to 1991, infant mortality declined slightly faster, probably because of the use of artificial pulmonary surfactant to prevent and treat respiratory distress syndrome in premature infants.[8] During 1991 to 1997, infant mortality continued to decline primarily because of decreases in sudden infant death syndrome and other causes.

Although improvements in medical care were the main force for declines in infant mortality during the second half of the century, public health actions played a role. During the 1990s, a greater than 50% decline in sudden infant death syndrome rates (attributed to the recommendation that infants be placed to sleep on their backs) has helped to reduce the overall infant mortality rate.[9] The reduction in vaccine-preventable diseases (e.g., diphtheria, tetanus, measles, poliomyelitis, and *Haemophilus influenzae* type b meningitis) has reduced infant morbidity and has had a modest effect on infant mortality.[10] Advances in prenatal diagnosis of severe central nervous system defects, selective termination of affected pregnancies, and improved surgical treatment and management of other structural anomalies have helped to reduce infant mortality attributed to these birth defects.[11,12] National efforts to encourage reproductive-aged women to consume foods or supplements containing folic acid could reduce the incidence of neural tube defects by half.[13]

Family Planning[14]

During the 20th century, the hallmark of family planning in the United States has been the ability to achieve desired birth spacing and family size. Fertility decreased as couples chose to have fewer children; concurrently, child mortality declined, people moved from farms to cities, and the age at marriage increased.[15] Smaller families and longer birth intervals have contributed to the better health of infants, children, and women and have improved the social and economic role of women.[16,17] Despite high failure rates, traditional methods of fertility control contributed to the decline in family size.[18] Modern contraception and reproductive healthcare systems that became available later in the century further improved couples' ability to plan their families.

Publicly supported family planning services prevent an estimated 1.3 million unintended pregnancies annually.[19]

Family size declined between 1800 and 1900 from 7.0 to 3.5 children.[18] In 1900, 6 to 9 of every 1,000 women died in childbirth, and 1 in 5 children died during the first 5 years of life. Distributing information and counseling patients about contraception and contraceptive devices was illegal under federal and state laws; the timing of ovulation, the length of the fertile period, and other reproductive facts were unknown.[20,21]

Maternal Mortality[1]

Maternal mortality rates were highest in this century during 1900 to 1930[3] (Figure 3-16). Poor obstetric education and delivery practices were mainly responsible for the high numbers of maternal deaths, most of which were preventable.[3] Obstetrics as a specialty was shunned by many physicians, and obstetric care was provided by poorly trained or untrained medical practitioners. Most births occurred at home with the assistance of midwives or general practitioners. Inappropriate and excessive surgical and obstetric interventions (e.g., induction of labor, use of forceps, episiotomy, and Caesarean deliveries) were common and increased during the 1920s. Deliveries, including some surgical interventions, were performed without following the principles of asepsis. As a result, 40% of maternal deaths were caused by sepsis (half after delivery and half associated with illegally induced abortion), with the remaining deaths primarily attributed to hemorrhage and toxemia.[3]

The 1933 White House Conference on Child Health Protection, Fetal, Newborn, and Maternal Mortality and Morbidity report demonstrated the link between poor aseptic practice, excessive operative deliveries, and high maternal mortality.[22] This and earlier reports focused attention on the state of maternal health and led to calls for action by state medical associations.[22] During the 1930s and 1940s, hospital and state maternal mortality review committees were established. During the ensuing years, institutional practice guidelines and guidelines defining physician qualifications needed for hospital delivery privileges were developed. At the same time, a shift from home to hospital deliveries was occurring throughout the country; during 1938 to 1948, the proportion of infants born in hospitals increased from 55% to 90%.[23] This shift, however, was slow in rural areas and southern states. Safer deliveries in hospitals under aseptic conditions and improved provision of maternal care for the poor by states or voluntary organizations led to decreases in maternal mortality after 1930. Medical advances (including the use of antibiotics, oxytocin to induce labor, and safe blood transfusion and better management of hypertensive conditions during pregnancy) accelerated declines in maternal mortality. During 1939 to 1948, maternal mortality decreased by 71%.[23]

The legalization of induced abortion, beginning in the 1960s, contributed to an 89% decline in deaths from septic illegal abortions during 1950 to 1973.[24]

Since 1982, maternal mortality has not declined[25]; however, more than half of maternal deaths can be prevented with existing interventions.[26] In 1997, 327 maternal deaths were reported based on information on death certificates; however, death certificate data underestimate these deaths, and the actual numbers are two to three times greater. The leading causes of maternal death are hemorrhage, including hemorrhage associated with ectopic pregnancy, pregnancy-induced hypertension (toxemia), and embolism.[26]

21ST CENTURY PUBLIC HEALTH CHALLENGES

These noteworthy improvements are the result of efforts to improve access to care for women and infants and underscore the need to ensure access to quality healthcare services on an ongoing basis. As illustrated in Figures 3-18 and 3-19, strong predictors of access to quality health care include having health insurance, a higher income level, and a regular primary care provider or other source of ongoing health care. In 2008, approximately 9.1% of persons (27.4 million) delayed medical care during the preceding year because of worry about the cost, and another 6.4% (19.5 million) did not receive needed medical care because they could not afford it. Persons whose health was assessed as fair or poor were four to five times as likely as persons whose health was assessed as excellent or very good to delay or not receive needed medical care because of cost.

The use of clinical preventive services, such as early comprehensive prenatal care, is an important benefit of access to quality healthcare services. The U.S. Task Force on Clinical Preventive Services (to be discussed in Chapter 7) has identified a variety of clinical preventive services for pregnant women for which there is strong evidence of effectiveness and improved outcomes, including[27]

- Alcohol misuse screening and behavioral counseling
- Screening for asymptomatic bacteriuria, chlamydial infection, gonorrhea, hepatitis B, HIV, syphilis, and Rh (D) incompatibility
- Behavioral interventions to promote breastfeeding
- Counseling to prevent tobacco use and tobacco-caused diseases

The Task Force on Community Preventive Services systematically reviewed the effectiveness of population-based interventions to improve pregnancy outcomes by reducing the number of pregnancies affected by neural tube defects. The task force concluded that community-wide education campaigns to increase the use of supplements containing folic acid by women of childbearing age and folic acid fortification of food products were effective interventions.[28]

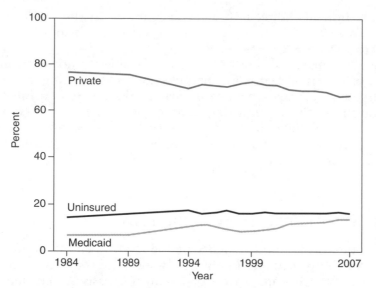

Figure 3-18 Health insurance coverage among people under 65 years old, United States, 1984–2007. *Source:* From Centers for Disease Control and Prevention, National Center for Health Statistics. *Health, United States 2009*, Figure 19. Hyattsville, MD: NCHS; 2009. Data from National Health Interview Survey.

Enhancing access to prenatal care in general and these clinical and community preventive services in particular is a longstanding priority of the Healthy People process. The Healthy People 2010 target of 90% of pregnant women initiating prenatal care in the first trimester was not achieved. Two other sentinel access-related targets were also not achieved. These called for 100% of persons under the age of 65 having some form of healthcare coverage and 90% of persons of all ages having an identified source of ongoing primary care. The lack of progress in recent decades toward improving access is illustrated in Figure 3-20. Expansion of access through the health reform legislation enacted in 2010 holds the promise of meeting these targets by the year 2020.

REFERENCES

1. Reprinted in part and adapted from Centers for Disease Control and Prevention. Achievements in Public Health, United States, 1900–1999: Healthier Mothers and Babies. *MMWR.* 1999;48:849–858.
2. Meckel RA. *Save the Babies: American Public Health Reform and the Prevention of Infant Mortality, 1850–1929.* Baltimore, MD: The Johns Hopkins University Press; 1990.
3. Loudon I. *Death in Childbirth: An International Study of Maternal Care and Maternal Mortality, 1800–1950.* New York, NY: Oxford University Press; 1992.
4. Hoyert DL, Kochanek KD, Murphy SL. *Deaths: Final Data for 1997.* Hyattsville, MD: U.S. Department of Health and Human Services, CDC, National Center for Health Statistics; 1999 (National vital statistics report; vol 47, no 20).
5. Public Health Service. *Vital Statistics of the United States, 1950.* Vol I. Washington, DC: U.S. Department of Health and Human Services, Public Health Service, 1954:258–259.

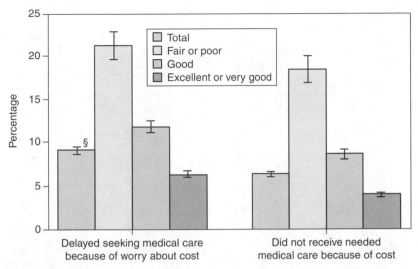

Figure 3-19 Estimated percentage of persons who delayed seeking or did not receive medical care during the preceding year because of cost, by respondent-assessed health status*, National Health Interview Survey, United States, 2008.[†]

* Based on responses to the following questions: "During the past 12 months, has [person] delayed seeking medical care because of worry about the cost?" and "During the past 12 months was there any time when [person] needed medical care but did not get it because [person] could not afford it?" Both questions exclude dental care. Respondents were asked to answer regarding themselves and other family members living in the same household. Health status data were obtained by asking respondents to assess their own health and that of family members living in the same household as excellent, very good, good, fair, or poor.

[†] Estimates are age adjusted using the projected 2000 U.S. population as the standard population and using five age groups: 0–11 years, 12–17 years, 18–44 years, 45–64 years, and ≥65 years. Estimates are based on household interviews of a sample of the civilian, noninstitutionalized U.S. population.

§ 95% confidence interval.

Source: From Centers for Disease Control and Prevention. Estimated percentage of persons who delayed seeking or did not receive medical care during the preceding year because of cost, by respondent-assessed health status*, National Health Interview Survey, United States, 2008. *MMWR.* 2009;58(47):1327. Data from Adams PF, Heyman KM, Vickerie JL. *Summary Health Statistics for the U.S.: National Health Interview Survey, 2008.* U.S. Department of Health and Human Services, Centers for Disease Control and Prevention, National Center for Health Statistics, Division of Health Interview Statistics; Hyattsville, MD, 2009.

6. Pharoah POD, Morris JN. Postneonatal mortality. *Epidemiol Rev.* 1979;1:170–183.

7. Kleinman JC. The slowdown in the infant mortality decline. *Pediatr Perinat Epidemiol.* 1990;4:373–381.

8. Schoendorf KC, Kiely JL. Birth weight and age-specific analysis of the 1990 US infant mortality drop: was it surfactant? *Arch Pediatr Adolesc Med.* 1997;151:129–134.

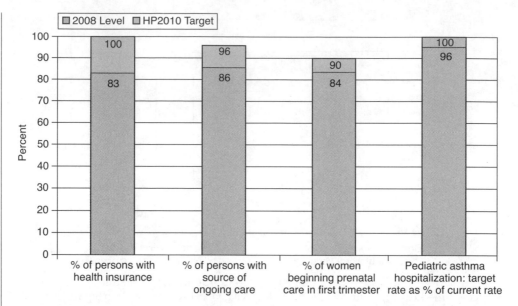

Figure 3-20   Scorecard for selected Healthy People 2010 leading indicators related to access comparing 2008 levels with 2010 targets. *Source:* Data from Data 2010, Healthy People 2010 database. http://wonder.cdc.gov/data2010/ftp selec.htm. Accessed May 31, 2010.

9. Willinger M, Hoffman H, Wu K, et al. Factors associated with the transition to non-prone sleep positions of infants in the United States: the National Infant Sleep Position Study. *JAMA*. 1998;280:329–339.

10. Centers for Disease Control and Prevention. Status report on the Childhood Immunization Initiative: reported cases of selected vaccine-preventable diseases: United States, 1996. *MMWR*. 1997;46:667–671.

11. Centers for Disease Control and Prevention. Trends in infant mortality attributable to birth defects: United States, 1980–1995. *MMWR*. 1998;47:773–777.

12. Montana E, Khoury MJ, Cragan JD, et al. Trends and outcomes after prenatal diagnosis of congenital cardiac malformations by fetal echocardiography in a well defined birth population, Atlanta, Georgia, 1990–1994. *J Am Coll Cardiol*. 1996;27:1805–1809.

13. Johnston RB Jr. Folic acid: new dimensions of an old friendship. *Adv Pediatr*. 1997;44: 231–261.

14. Centers for Disease Control and Prevention. Public Health Achievements, United States, 1900–1999: Family Planning. *MMWR*. 1999;48:1073–1080.

15. Bongaarts J. A framework for analyzing the proximate determinants of fertility. *Population Devel Rev*. 1978;4:105–132.

16. Maine D, McNamara R. *Birth Spacing and Child Survival*. New York: Columbia University Center for Population and Family Health; 1985.

17. Potts M, Thapa S. *Child Survival: The Role of Family Planning*. Research Triangle Park, NC: Family Health International; 1991.

18. Commission on the Population Growth and the American Future. Population growth. Chapter 2 (pp. 9–21) in: *Population and the American Future*. New York: New American Library; 1972.

19. Forrest JD, Samara R. Impact of publicly funded contraceptive services on unintended pregnancies and implications for Medicaid expenditures. *Fam Plann Perspect.* 1996;28: 188–195.

20. Connell EB. Contraception in the prepill era. *Contraception.* 1999;59:7S–10S.

21. Wardell D. Margaret Sanger: birth control's successful revolutionary. *Am J Public Health.* 1980;70:736–742.

22. Wertz RW, Wertz DC. *Lying-In: A History of Childbirth in America.* New Haven, CT: Yale University Press; 1989.

23. Children's Bureau. *Changes in Infant, Childhood, and Maternal Mortality Over the Decade of 1939–1948: A Graphic Analysis.* Washington, DC: Children's Bureau, Social Security Administration; 1950.

24. Centers for Disease Control and Prevention, National Center for Health Statistics. *Vital Statistics of the United States, 1973.* Vol II, mortality, part A. Rockville, MD: U.S. Department of Health, Education, and Welfare; 1977.

25. CDC. Maternal mortality: United States, 1982–1996. *MMWR.* 1999;47:705–707.

26. Berg CJ, Atrash HK, Koonin LM, et al. Pregnancy-related mortality in the United States, 1987–1990. *Obstet Gynecol.* 1996;88:161–167.

27. U.S. Preventive Services Task Force. *Guide to Clinical Preventive Services.* Washington, DC: U.S. Department of Health and Human Services; 2006.

28. Task Force on Community Preventive Services. *The Community Guide.* http://www.the communityguide.org. Accessed May 31, 2010.

Law, Government, and Public Health

OBJECTIVES

After completing Chapter 4, learners will be proficient in describing the role of law and government in promoting and protecting the health of the public and in identifying specific functions and roles of governmental public health agencies in ensuring population health. Key aspects of this competency expectation include the following:

- Identifying strategies used by governments to influence the health status of their citizens

- Describing how various forms of law contribute to government's ability to influence health

- Describing the basic administrative law processes carried out by public health agencies

- Identifying the various federal health agencies and describing their general purpose and major activities

- Identifying different approaches to organizing health responsibilities within state government

- Describing common features of local health departments (LHDs) in the United States

- Discussing implications of different approaches among states to carrying out public health's roles

Public health is not limited to what governmental public health agencies do, although this is a widely held misperception among those inside and outside the field. Still, particular aspects of public health rely on government. For example, the enforcement of laws remains one of those governmental responsibilities important to the public's health and public health practice. Nevertheless, law and the legal system are important for public health purposes above and beyond the enforcement of laws and regulations. Laws at all levels of government bestow the basic powers of government and distribute these powers among various agencies, including public health agencies. Law represents governmental decisions and their underlying collective social values; it provides the basis for actions that influence the health of the public.

Decisions and actions that take place outside the sphere of government also influence the health of the public, perhaps even more than those made by our elected officials and administrative agencies. Private sector and voluntary organizations play key roles in identifying factors important for health and advancing actions to promote and protect health for individuals and groups. Public health involves collective decisions and actions, rather than purely personal ones; however, it is often governmental forums that raise issues, make decisions, and establish priorities for action. Many governmental actions reflect the dual roles of government often portrayed on official governmental seals and vehicles of local public safety agencies—to protect and to serve. As they relate to health, the genesis of these two roles lies in separate, often conflicting, philosophies and legacies of government. This chapter examines how these roles are organized in the United States. This examination particularly emphasizes the relationships among law, government, and public health, seeking answers to the following questions:

- What are the various roles for government in serving the public's health?
- What is the legal basis for public health in the United States?
- How are public health responsibilities and roles structured at the federal, state, and local levels?

To review the organization and structure of governmental public health, this chapter, unlike the history briefly traced in Chapter 1, begins with federal public health roles and activities, to be followed, in turn, by those at the state and local levels. The focus is primarily on form and structure, rather than function. In most circumstances, it is logical for form to follow function. Here, however, it is necessary to understand the legal and organizational framework of governmental public health as part of the context for public health practice. The framework established through law and governmental agencies is a key element of the public health's infrastructure and one of the basic building blocks of the public health system. Other important building blocks, including human, informational, fiscal, and other aspects of organizational resources, are examined in Chapter 6. The topics in this chapter have been separated from the other public health system structures somewhat arbitrarily; however, the legal basis of public health and the governmental agencies that have been created to serve the public health are basic and important concepts in their own right. This structure is a product of our uniquely American approach to government.

AMERICAN GOVERNMENT AND PUBLIC HEALTH

Former Speaker of the U.S. House of Representatives Tip O'Neill frequently observed, "All politics is local." If this is so, public health must be considered primarily a local phenomenon as well because politics are embedded in public health processes. After all, public health represents collective decisions as to which health outcomes are unacceptable, which factors contribute to those outcomes, which unacceptable problems will be addressed in view of resource limitations and which participants need to be involved in addressing the problems. These are political processes, with different viewpoints and values being brought together to determine which collective decisions will be made. All too often, the term politics carries a very different connotation, one frequently associated with overtones of partisan politics; however, political processes are necessary and productive and perhaps the best means devised by humans to meet our collective needs.

The public health system in the United States is a product of many forces that have shaped governmental roles in health. The framers of the U.S. Constitution did not plan for the federal government to deal directly with health or, for that matter, many other important issues. The word health does not even appear in that famous document, relegating health to the group of powers reserved to the states or the people. The Constitution explicitly authorized the federal government to promote and provide for the general welfare (in the Preamble and Article I, Section 8) and to regulate commerce (also in Article I, Section 8). Federal powers evolved slowly in the area of health on the basis of these explicit powers and subsequent U.S. Supreme Court decisions that broadened federal authority by determining that additional powers are implied in the explicit language of the Constitution.

The initial duties to regulate international affairs and interstate commerce led the federal government to concentrate its efforts on preventing the importation of epidemics and assisting states and localities, on request, with their episodic needs for communicable disease control. The earliest federal health unit, the Marine Hospital Service, was established in 1798, partly to serve merchant seamen and partly to prevent importation of epidemic diseases; it evolved over time into what is now the U.S. Public Health Service (PHS).

The power to promote health and welfare, however, did not always translate into the ability to act. The federal government acquired the ability to raise significant financial resources only with the authority to levy a federal tax on income, provided by the 16th Amendment in the early 20th century. The ability to raise vast sums generated the capacity to address health problems and needs through transferring resources to state and local governments in various forms of grants-in-aid. Despite its powers to provide for the general welfare and regulate commerce, the federal government could not act directly in health matters; it could act only through states as its primary delivery system. After 1935, the power and influence of the federal government grew rapidly through its financial influence over state and local programs, such as the Hospital Survey and Construction (Hill-Burton) Act of 1946 and, after 1965, through its emergence as a major purchaser of health care through Medicare and Medicaid. As for a public health presence at the federal level, the best known and most widely respected federal public health agency, now known as the Centers for Disease Control and Prevention (CDC), was not established until 1946.[1]

The emergence of the federal government as a major influence in the health system displaced states from a position they had held since before the birth of the American republic. States were sovereign powers before agreeing to share their powers with the newly established federal government; their sovereignty included powers over matters related to health emanating from two general sources. First, they derived from the so-called police powers of states, which provide the basis for government to limit the actions of individuals in order to control and abate hazards and nuisances. A second source for state health powers lay in the expectation for government to serve those individuals unable to provide for themselves. This expectation had its roots in the Elizabethan Poor Laws and carried over to states in the new American form of government. Despite this common heritage, states assumed these roles quite differently and at different points in time because the evolution of states themselves during the 19th century took place unevenly.

States developed structures and organizations needed to use their police powers to protect citizens from communicable diseases and environmental hazards, primarily from wastes, water, and food. State health agencies developed first in Massachusetts and then across the country during the latter half of the 19th century. When federal grants became available, especially after 1935, states eagerly sought out federal funding for maternal and child health services, public health laboratories, and other basic public health programs. In so doing, states surrendered some of their autonomy over health issues. Priorities were increasingly dictated by federal grants tied to specific programs and services. It is fair to say that the grantor–grantee arrangement has never been fully satisfactory to either party, and the results in terms of health, welfare, education, and environmental policy suggest that better frameworks may be possible.

States possess the ultimate authority to create the political subunits that provide various services to the residents of a particular jurisdiction. In this manner, counties, cities, and other forms of municipalities, townships, boroughs, parishes, and the like are established. Special-purpose districts for every conceivable purpose—from library services and mosquito control to emergency medical services and education—have also abounded. The powers delegated to or authorized for all of these local jurisdictions are established by state legislatures for health and other purposes. Although many big-city health departments were established before the establishment of their respective state health agencies, states are free to use a variety of approaches to structuring public health roles at the local level. Because most states use the county form of subdividing the state, counties became the primary local governmental jurisdictions with health roles after 1900.

State constitutions and statutes impart the authority for local governments to influence health. This authority comes in two forms: those responsibilities of the state specifically delegated to local governments and additional authorities allowed through home rule powers. Home rule options permit local jurisdictions to enact a local constitution or charter and to take on additional authority and powers, such as the ability to levy taxes for local public health services and activities.

Counties generally carry out duties delegated by the state. More than two thirds of U.S. counties have a county commission form of government, with anywhere from 2 to 50 elected county commissioners (supervisors, judges, and other titles are also used).[2] These commissions carry out both legislative and executive branch functions, although they share administrative authority with other local elected officials, such as county clerks, assessors, treasurers, prosecuting attorneys, sheriffs, and coroners. Some counties—generally the more populous ones—have a county administrator accountable to elected commissioners, and a small number of counties (less than 5%) have an elected county executive. Elected county executives often have veto power over the county legislative body; home rule jurisdictions are more likely to have an elected county executive than are other counties.

Local governments in U.S. cities were first on the scene in terms of public health activities, as noted in Chapter 1. Big-city health agencies remain an important force in the public health system in the United States; however, after about 1875, when states became more extensively involved, the relative role of municipal governments began to erode. Both local and state governments were overwhelmed by the availability of federal funding in comparison with their own resources, finding it easier to take what they could get from the federal government rather than generating their own revenue to finance needed services.

Many forces have been at work to alter the initial relationships among the three levels of government for health roles, including the following:

- Gradual expansion and maturation of the federal government
- Staggered addition of new states and variability in the maturation of state governments
- Population growth and shifts over time
- The ability of the various levels of government to raise revenues commensurate with their expanding needs
- Growth of science and technology as tools for addressing public health and medical care needs
- Rapid growth of the U.S. economy
- Expectations and needs of American society for various services from their government[3,4]

The last of these factors is perhaps the most important. For the first 150 years of U.S. history, there was little expectation that the federal government should intervene in the health and welfare needs of its citizenry. The massive need and economic turmoil of the Great Depression years drastically altered this long-standing value as Americans began to turn to government to help deal with current needs and future uncertainties.

The complex public health network that exists today evolved slowly, with many different shifts in relative roles and influence. Economic considerations and societal expectations, both reaching a critical point in the 1930s, set the tone for the rest of the 20th century. In general, power and influence were initially greatest at the local level, residing there until states began to develop their own machinery to carry out their police power and welfare roles. States then served as the primary locus for these health roles until the federal government began to use its vast resource potential to meet changing public expectations in the 1930s. Federal grant programs for public health and eventually personal healthcare service programs soon drove state actions, especially after the 1960s. It was then that several new federal health and social service programs were targeted directly to local governments, bypassing states.

At the same time, a new federal–state partnership for the medically indigent (Medicaid) was established to address the national policy concern over the plight of the medically indigent.

Political and philosophical shifts since about 1980 are altering roles once again.[3] Debates over federal versus state roles continued throughout the decades between 1980 and 2010, initially resulting in some diminution of federal influence and enhancement of state influence, and then in substantial expansion of the federal role in the Obama health care reform legislation enacted in 2010. In the end, the federal government has amassed considerable ability to influence the health system through its fiscal muscle power, as well as its research, regulatory, technical assistance, and training roles.

PUBLIC HEALTH LAW

One of the chief organizing forces for public health lies in the system of law. Law has many purposes in the modern world, and these are evident in public health laws. Unfortunately, there is no one repository where the entire body of law, even the body of public health law, can be found. This has occurred because laws are products of the legal system, which in the United States includes a federal system and 50 separate state legal systems. These developed at different times in response to somewhat different circumstances and issues. Common to each is some form of a state constitution, a considerable amount of legislation, and a substantial body of judicial decisions. If there is any road map through this maze, it lies in the federal and state constitutions, which establish the basic framework dividing governmental powers among the various branches of government in ways that allow each to create its own laws.

As a result, four different types of law can be distinguished by virtue of their form or authority:

- Constitutionally based law
- Legislatively based law
- Administratively based law
- Judicially based law

This framework still allows latitude for judicial interpretation and oversight. A brief description of each of these forms of law follows.

Types of Law

Constitutional law is ultimately derived from the U.S. Constitution, the legal foundation of the nation, in which the powers, duties, and limits of the federal government are established. States basically gave up certain powers (e.g., defense, foreign diplomacy, and printing money), ceding these to the federal government while retaining all other powers and duties. Health is not one of those powers explicitly bestowed on the federal government. The federal constitution also included a Bill of Rights intended to protect the rights of individuals from abuses by their government. States, in turn, have developed their own state constitutions, often patterned after the federal framework, although state constitutions tend to be more clear and specific in their language, leaving less room and need for judicial interpretation. State constitutions provide the broad framework from which states determine which activities will be undertaken and how those activities will be organized and funded. These decisions and actions come in the form of state statutes.

Statutory (legislatively based) law includes all of the acts and statutes enacted by Congress and the various state and local legislative bodies. This collection of law represents a wide range of governmental policy choices, including the following:

- Simple expressions of preferences in favor of a particular policy or service (such as the value of home visits by public health nurses)
- Authorizations for specific programs (such as the authority for local governments to license restaurants)
- Mandates or requirements for an activity to occur or, alternatively, to be prohibited (such as requiring all newborns to be screened for specific metabolic diseases or prohibiting smoking in public places)
- Providing resources for specific purposes (such as the distribution of medications to patients with acquired immune deficiency syndrome [AIDS])

If the legislative intent is for something to occur, the most effective approaches are generally to require or prohibit an activity.

The basic requirement for statutory-based laws is that they must be consistent with the U.S. Constitution and, for state and local statutes, with state constitutions as well. State laws also establish the various subunits of the state and delineate their responsibilities for carrying out state mandates, as well as the limits of what they can do. At the local level, the legislative bodies of these subunits (e.g., city councils and county commissions) enact ordinances and statutes setting forth the duties and authorizations of local government and its agencies. Laws affecting public health are created at all levels in this hierarchy, but especially at the state and local levels. Among other purposes, these laws establish state and local boards of health and health departments, delineate the responsibilities of these agencies, including their programs and budgets, and establish health-related laws and requirements. Many of these laws are enforced by governmental agencies.

Administrative law is law promulgated by administrative agencies within the executive branch of government. Rather than enact statutes that include extensive details of a professional or technical nature and to allow greater flexibility in their design and subsequent revision, administrative agencies are provided with the authority to establish law through rule-making processes. These rules, administrative law, carry the force of law and represent a unique situation in which legislative, judicial, and executive powers are carried out by one agency. Administrative agencies include cabinet-level departments, as well as other boards, commissions, and the like that are granted this power through an enactment of the legislative body. Because of its importance and pervasiveness for public health practice, this chapter examines administrative law in some depth.

The fourth type of law is judicial law, also known as common law. This includes a wide range of tradition, legal custom, and previous decisions of federal and state courts. To ensure fairness and consistency, previous decisions are used to guide judgments on similar disputes. This form of law becomes especially important in areas in which laws have not been codified by legislative bodies. In public health, nuisances (unsanitary, noxious, or otherwise potentially dangerous circumstances) are one such area in which few legislative bodies have specified exactly what does and what does not constitute a public health nuisance. In this situation, the common law for nuisances is derived from previous judicial decisions. These determine under what circumstances and for what specific conditions a public health official can take action, as well as the actions that can be taken.

Purposes of Public Health Law

Two broad purposes for public health law can be described: protecting and promoting health and ensuring the protection of rights of individuals in the processes used to protect and promote health. Public health powers ultimately derive from the U.S. Constitution, which bestows the authority to regulate commerce and provide for the general welfare, and from the various state constitutions, which often provide clear but broad authorities, based largely on the police power of the state. States often have reasonably well-defined public health codes; however, there is considerable diversity in their content and scope, despite similarities in their basic sources of power and authority.

Many public health laws are enacted and enforced under what is known as the state's "police power." This is a broad concept that encompasses the functions historically undertaken by governments in protecting the health, safety, welfare, and general well-being of their citizens. A wide variety of laws derive from the police power of the state, a power that is considered one of the least limitable of all governmental powers. The police power of the state can be vested in an administrative agency, such as a state health agency, which becomes accountable for the manner in which these responsibilities are executed. In these circumstances, its use is a duty, rather than a matter of choice, although its form is left to the discretion of the user.

The courts have upheld laws that appear to limit severely or restrict the rights of individuals where these were found to be reasonable, rather than arbitrary and capricious attempts to accomplish government's ends. The state's police power is not unlimited, however. Interference with individual liberties and the taking of personal property are considerations that must be balanced on a case-by-case basis. At issue is whether the public interest in achieving a public health goal outweighs the public interest in protecting civil liberties. Public health laws requiring vaccinations or immunizations to protect the community have generally withstood legal challenges claiming that they infringed on the rights of individuals to make their own health decisions. A precedent-setting judicial opinion upheld a Massachusetts ordinance authorizing local boards of health to require vaccinations for smallpox to be administered to residents if deemed necessary by the local boards.[5] Such decisions argue that laws that place the common good ahead of the competing rights of individuals should govern society. Similarly, courts have weighed the power of the state to appropriate an individual's property or limit the individual's use of it if the best interests of the community make such an action desirable. In some circumstances, equitable compensation must be provided. Issues of community interest and fair compensation are commonly encountered in dealing with public health nuisances in which an individual's private property can be found to be harmful to others.

The various forms of law and the changing nature of the relationships among the three levels of government have created a patchwork of public health laws. Despite its relatively limited constitutionally based powers, the federal government can preempt state and local government action in key areas of public health regulation involving commerce and aspects of communicable disease control. States also have authority to preempt local government actions in virtually all areas of public health activity. Although this legal framework allows for a clear and rational delineation of authorities and responsibilities, a quite variable set of arrangements has arisen. Often, the higher level of government chooses not to exercise its full authority and shifts that authority to a lower level of government. This can be accomplished in some instances by delegating or requiring, and in other instances by authorizing (with incentives), the lower level of government to exercise authorities of the higher level. This has made for a complex set of relationships among the three levels of government and for 50 variations of the theme to be played in the 50 states. These relationships and their impact on the form and structure of governmental public health agencies are evident in subsequent sections of this chapter.

There have been many critiques of the statutory basis of public health in the United States. A common one is that public health law, not unlike law affecting other areas of society, simply has not kept pace with the rapid and extensive changes in science and technology. Laws have been enacted at different points in time in response to different conditions and circumstances. These laws have often been enacted with little consideration as to their consistency with previous statutes and their overall impact on the body of public health law. For example, many states have different statutes and legal frameworks for similar risks, such as general communicable diseases, sexually transmitted diseases, and human immunodeficiency virus (HIV) infections. Confidentiality and privacy provisions, which trace their origins to the vow in the Hippocratic oath not to reveal patients' secrets, are often inconsistent from law to law, and enforcement provisions vary as well. Beyond these concerns, public health laws often lack clear statements of purpose or mission and are not linked to public health core functions and essential public health services.

In view of these criticisms, recommendations have been advanced calling for a complete overhaul and recodification of public health law. Recommendations for improvement of the public health codes often call for the following:

- Stronger links with the overall mission and core functions of public health
- Uniform structures for similar programs and services
- Confidentiality provisions to be reviewed and made more consistent
- Clarification of police power responsibilities to deal with unusual health risks and threats

- Greater emphasis on the least restrictive means necessary to achieve the law's intent through use of intermediate sanctions and compulsive measures, based on proven effectiveness
- Fairer and more consistent enforcement and administrative practices

Although these recommendations have been advanced for several decades, little progress has been made at either the federal or state level. At times, states have sought to recodify public health statutes by relocating their placement in the statute books, rather than dealing with the more basic issues of reviewing the scope and allocation of their public health responsibilities so that these are clearly presented and assigned among the various levels of government. The intricacies of public health law often drive the inner workings of federal and state health departments, as well as LHDs. Administrative law demonstrates this point.

Administrative Law

The most frequently encountered legal interactions for most people, affecting both health professionals and consumers, are not associated with constitutional, judicial, or even statutory laws. Rather, they occur through the subsystem of administrative law, which develops and enforces rules and regulations through an administrative agency. Administrative law affects people in their daily lives in many ways. It affects people personally (even in very intimate ways) through such requirements as up-to-date immunizations before entering school or identification of sexual contacts of persons with certain sexually transmitted diseases. Administrative law also affects our property. For example, specific requirements for septic fields can prevent us from building our dream vacation home on the perfect lakefront lot. It also affects many of us professionally, most notably in the licensing of health and other professions. These are but a few examples of how pervasive administrative law has become in modern American society.

At first glance, it appears that administrative law violates, or at least circumvents, one of the most fundamental principles of American government—the separation of powers among the legislative, executive, and judicial branches—with its elaborate system of checks and balances. The development and promulgation of administrative law represents the legislative function. The enforcement of the law, through inspections and other means, represents the executive function. Finally, the determination of compliance, often involving hearings and appeals within the agency before a final decision is rendered by the agency, represents the judicial function. Although the life cycle of administrative rules can be complex, it presents an interesting picture of governmental processes in public health.

The process begins with the enactment of a statute, which provides the administrative agency with the authority to develop rules and regulations to implement the intent of the newly enacted law. This authority may be limited to specific aspects of the statute, or the law may only broadly declare the legislative intent, leaving the agency considerable latitude in terms of the scope and content of rule making needed for implementation. The agency then initiates its rule-making processes, which involve technical experts from the field or program affected by the statute and legal staff from the agency or from the legal office of government (such as the attorney general's office at the state level, state's attorney office of the county, or corporation counsel office of the city). Increasingly, agency staffs involved in intergovernmental affairs participate in this process because rule making requires collaboration with the legislative branch. Interested parties, especially those organizations or industries likely to be affected by the law and regulations, may be involved in early stages of drafting rules and regulations through either standing boards, advisory bodies, or ad hoc groups brought together to gain different perspectives. Draft rules are developed and submitted as proposed rules.

There may be public hearings held on the proposals or a specific period in which interested parties and the public can comment on the proposed rules. The agency then must formally respond to public comments and indicate why proposed rules were or were not changed in response to those comments. Revisions are made to the rules, and depending on the requirements of that level of government, the revised rules are submitted to a legislative oversight commission or committee, which then has its opportunity to comment on whether the proposed rules are consistent with the intent of the legislative body and whether the scope of the rules exceeds the authority conferred in the statute. The oversight commission also reviews the agency's response to the comments received. This presents another opportunity for interest groups and affected constituencies to influence the shape of the final regulations. After the legislative oversight comments and objections are made, the agency finalizes the rules and begins enforcement. If the agency chooses not to make changes suggested by the legislative oversight body, it faces the possibility of more specifically worded amendments to the statute or an adversarial relationship between the agency and the legislature. When final rules are adopted, they are widely circulated to the affected groups, and enforcement begins as specified in the new rules. These can be lengthy processes, taking 6 to 18 months (or longer) after enactment of a statute.

Implementation and enforcement of rules often rest with specific program staff of the agency. For licensing programs, these staff members may be surveyors or inspectors. For other programs, they may be professional or administrative personnel. For many licensing programs, the evidence of compliance with statutory and regulatory requirements is compiled through routine or complaint-related inspections. Based on the seriousness and, to a lesser extent, on the number of violations, a determination of noncompliance may lead to demands that specific actions take place to correct violations and that specific sanctions (as provided in the law or rules) be imposed. There is generally an opportunity for these decisions and actions to be challenged before they become final. If they are challenged, a hearing is held before a hearing officer within the administrative agency, and testimony and evidence are presented. The lawyers of the agency (or of that level of government) serve as the prosecutors. Program staff members, some of whom may have been involved with the development of the rules in question, serve as witnesses. A formal record is compiled, and the hearing officer makes a recommendation to the agency head, who issues the final decision.

Several factors justify the circumvention of the principle of separation of powers. The basic rationale for permitting one agency to carry out these functions is that these agencies often operate in a narrow and discrete area that requires a high level of technical expertise to ensure that the intent of the legislative body is fulfilled. With the rapid expansion of science and technology in many areas, and certainly in the health system, there is an increasing need for technologic and professional expertise to develop and apply the details needed to implement the legislative intent. The growth of regulatory responsibilities for government has also served to expand the need for administrative law because it is becoming increasingly unwise for legislative bodies to attempt to put extensive details into statutes. Often these details reflect technical or practice standards that are updated or revised periodically, otherwise necessitating revisions and amendments to existing laws. All of these reasons relate to the growing complexity of society and the need for special expertise to be applied in narrow discrete areas in a timely and professional manner.

Administrative law, however, is not completely exempt from checks and balances, as illustrated in Figure 4-1. Control points exist both for the rule-making process and for judicial review of final administrative decisions. In general, a committee or commission of legislators oversees the development and promulgation of rules to ensure that the legislative intent is being addressed and that the agency is not going beyond the authority provided to it in the statute. This oversight often includes provisions for public notice as to proposed rules and regulations and for written agency responses to public comments received as a result of hearings or public postings of proposed rules. Proposed rules can then be modified or withdrawn, if necessary. The legislative oversight also serves to alert the agency that actual or perceived transgressions may be met with more explicit statutes that would limit the agency's autonomy in developing rules and regulations in a particular area.

The second control point involves judicial review of final agency decisions. Any decision of the agency that adversely affects a party can be challenged through judicial review. This brings the agency's actions and decisions into the formal court system, where administrative actions, including fines and other sanctions, are either upheld or overturned by the courts and appeals are possible to even higher levels of review. These proceedings generally focus on procedural as opposed to evidentiary issues, relying on the record of facts and findings from the agency adjudication process. Most challenges brought for judicial review argue that the agency did not properly follow its own rules. There are instances in which judicial review is sought to require the agency to make a decision when it has not done so; however, these claims are more difficult to sustain unless the agency has completely failed to act in a situation specifically mandated by the legislative body. Agencies are granted considerable discretion in determining when and where to exercise their authorities and responsibilities, and courts are reluctant to step in and second guess the experts. The net result is that the courts often presume that the agency's actions are proper and prefer to focus, instead, on issues of procedural propriety. This suggests that those involved with compliance decisions, from inspectors to administrative hearing officers, must be as concerned over procedural matters as they are with factual issues of health

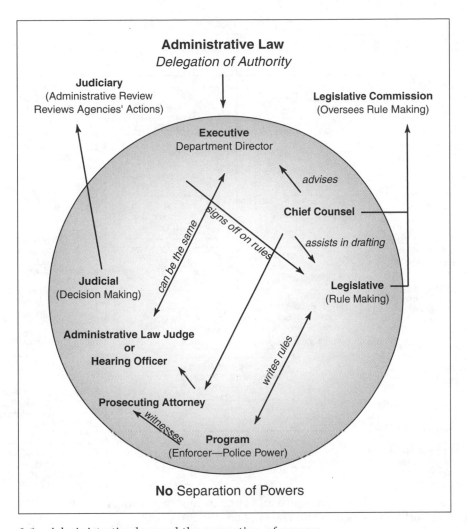

Figure 4-1   Administrative law and the separation of powers.

and safety. After the initial judicial review makes its determination, appeals and higher appeals can bring these issues to state and federal supreme courts.

Law provides an important foundation for key aspects of public health practice and the inner workings of federal, state, and local public health agencies. We now turn to the form and structure of these agencies.

GOVERNMENTAL PUBLIC HEALTH: FEDERAL HEALTH AGENCIES

The U.S. PHS serves as the focal point for health concerns at the federal level. Although there have been frequent reorganizations affecting the structure of PHS and its placement within the massive Department of Health and Human Services (DHHS), the restructuring completed in 1996 was the most

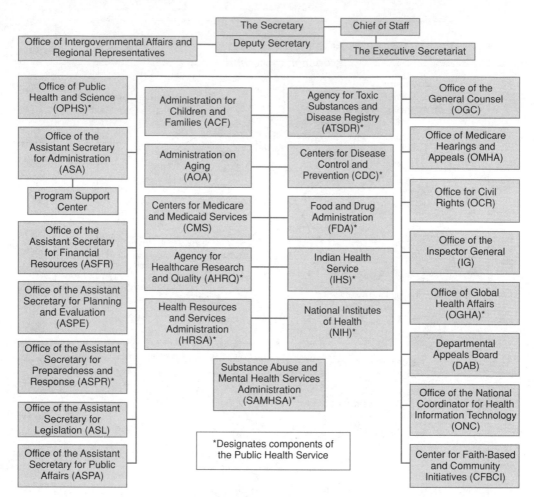

Figure 4-2   U.S. Department of Health and Human Services organization chart, 2010. *Source:* From U.S. Department of Health and Human Services, 2010.

significant in recent decades. The changes were undertaken as part of the federal Reinvention of Government Initiative to bring expertise in public health and science closer to the secretary of the DHHS. In the restructuring, the line authority of the Assistant Secretary for Health over the various agencies within PHS was abolished, with those agencies now reporting directly to the Secretary of DHHS, as illustrated in Figure 4-2. The Assistant Secretary for Health became the head of the Office of Public Health and Science, a new division reporting to the Secretary that also includes the Office of the Surgeon General. Each of the former PHS agencies became a full DHHS operating division. These eight operating agencies, the Office of Public Health and Science, and the regional health administrators for the 10 federal regions of the country now constitute the PHS. In effect, the PHS has become a functional rather than an organizational unit of the DHHS. In 2003, several activities related to emergency preparedness and response were moved into the newly established Department of Homeland Security (see Chapter 8). An Office of Public Health Emergency Preparedness and Response remained at the DHHS to coordinate bioterrorism and other public health emergency activities managed by various PHS agencies.

The PHS agencies address a wide range of public health activities, from research and training to primary care and health protection, as described in Table 4-1. The key PHS agencies are

- Health Resources and Services Administration
- Indian Health Service
- Centers for Disease Control and Prevention (CDC)
- National Institutes of Health (NIH)
- Food and Drug Administration (FDA)
- Substance Abuse and Mental Health Services Administration
- Agency for Toxic Substances and Disease Registry
- Agency for Healthcare Research and Quality

Table 4-1 U.S. Public Health Service Agencies

Health Resources and Services Administration (HRSA)	The HRSA helps provide health resources for medically underserved populations. The main operating units of HRSA are the Bureau of Primary Health Care, Bureau of Health Professions, Maternal and Child Bureau, and the HIV/AIDS Bureau. A nationwide network of 643 community and migrant health centers, plus 144 primary care programs for the homeless and residents of public housing, serve 8.1 million Americans each year. The HRSA also works to build the healthcare workforce and maintains the National Health Service Corps. The agency provides services to people with AIDS through the Ryan White Care Act programs. It oversees the organ transplantation system and works to decrease infant mortality and improve maternal and child health. The HRSA was established in 1982 by bringing together several existing programs. The HRSA has more than 1,850 employees at its headquarters in Rockville, Maryland, and its 10 regional offices throughout the United States.
Indian Health Service (IHS)	The IHS is responsible for providing federal health services to American Indians and Alaska Natives. The provision of health services to members of federally recognized tribes grew out of the special government-to-government relationship between the federal government and Indian tribes. This relationship, established in 1787, is based on Article I, Section 8 of the Constitution and has been given form and substance by numerous treaties, laws, Supreme Court decisions, and Executive

(continues)

Table 4-1 U.S. Public Health Service Agencies (continued)

	Orders. The IHS is the principal federal healthcare provider and health advocate for Indian people, and its goal is to raise their health status to the highest possible level. The IHS currently provides health services to approximately 1.9 million American Indians and Alaska Natives who belong to more than 564 federally recognized tribes in 35 states. The IHS was established in 1924; its mission was transferred from the Interior Department in 1955. Agency headquarters are in Rockville, Maryland. IHS has more than 15,000 employees.
Centers for Disease Control and Prevention (CDC)	Working with states and other partners, the CDC provides a system of health surveillance to monitor and prevent disease outbreaks, including bioterrorism events and threats, and maintains national health statistics. The CDC also provides for immunization services, supports research into disease and injury prevention, and guards against international disease transmission, with personnel stationed in more than 54 foreign countries. The CDC was established in 1946; its headquarters are in Atlanta, Georgia. The CDC has 9,000 employees.
National Institutes of Health (NIH)	Begun as a one-room Laboratory of Hygiene in 1887, the NIH today is one of the world's foremost medical research centers and the federal focal point for health research. The NIH is the steward of medical and behavioral research for the nation. Its mission is science in pursuit of fundamental knowledge about the nature and behavior of living systems and the application of that knowledge to extend healthy life and reduce the burdens of illness and disability. In realizing its goals, the NIH provides leadership and direction to programs designed to improve the health of the nation by conducting and supporting research in the causes, diagnosis, prevention, and cure of human diseases; in the processes of human growth and development; in the biological effects of environmental contaminants; in the understanding of mental, addictive, and physical disorders; and in directing programs for the collection, dissemination, and exchange of information in medicine and health, including the development and support of medical libraries and the training of medical librarians and other health information specialists. Although the majority of NIH resources sponsor external research, there is also a large in-house research program. The NIH includes 27 separate health institutes and centers; its headquarters are in Bethesda, Maryland. The NIH has more than 19,000 employees.
Food and Drug Administration (FDA)	The FDA ensures that the food we eat is safe and wholesome, that the cosmetics we use will not harm us, and that medicines, medical devices, and radiation-transmitting products such as microwave ovens are safe and effective. The FDA also oversees feed and drugs for pets and farm animals.

(continues)

Table 4-1   U.S. Public Health Service Agencies (continued)

	Authorized by Congress to enforce the Federal Food, Drug, and Cosmetic Act and several other public health laws, the agency monitors the manufacture, import, transport, storage, and sale of $1 trillion worth of goods annually at a cost to taxpayers of about $3 a person. The FDA has over 11,000 employees located in 167 U.S. cities. Among its staff, the FDA has chemists, microbiologists, and other scientists, as well as investigators and inspectors who visit 16,000 facilities a year as part of their oversight of the businesses that the FDA regulates. The FDA, established in 1906, has its headquarters in Rockville, Maryland.
Substance Abuse and Mental Health Services Administration (SAMHSA)	The SAMHSA was established by Congress under Public Law 102-321 on October 1, 1992, to strengthen the nation's healthcare capacity to provide prevention, diagnosis, and treatment services for substance abuse and mental illnesses. The SAMHSA works in partnership with states, communities, and private organizations to address the needs of people with substance abuse and mental illnesses as well as the community risk factors that contribute to these illnesses. The SAMHSA serves as the umbrella under which substance abuse and mental health service centers are housed, including the Center for Mental Health Services, the Center for Substance Abuse Prevention, and the Center for Substance Abuse Treatment. The SAMHSA also houses the Office of the Administrator, the Office of Applied Studies, and the Office of Program Services. SAMHSA headquarters are in Rockville, Maryland; the agency has about 600 employees.
Agency for Toxic Substances and Disease Registry (ATSDR)	Working with states and other federal agencies, the ATSDR seeks to prevent exposure to hazardous substances from waste sites. The agency conducts public health assessments, health studies, surveillance activities, and health education training in communities around waste sites on the U.S. Environmental Protection Agency's National Priorities List. The ATSDR also has developed toxicologic profiles of hazardous chemicals found at these sites. The agency is closely associated administratively with the CDC; its headquarters are also in Atlanta, Georgia. The ATSDR has more than 400 employees.
Agency for Healthcare Research and Quality (AHRQ)	The AHRQ supports cross-cutting research on healthcare systems, healthcare quality and cost issues, and effectiveness of medical treatments. Formerly known as the Agency for Health Care Policy and Research, AHRQ was established in 1989, assuming broadened responsibilities of its predecessor agency, the National Center for Health Services Research and Health Care Technology Assessment. The agency has about 300 employees; its headquarters are in Rockville, Maryland.

PHS agencies actually represent only a small part of the DHHS. Other important operating divisions within the DHHS include the Administration for Children and Families, the Centers for Medicare and Medicaid Services (CMS) (previously known as the Health Care Financing Administration), and the Office of the Assistant Secretary for Aging. In addition, there are several administrative and support units within the DHHS for management and the budget, intergovernmental affairs, legal counsel, civil rights, the inspector general, departmental appeals, public affairs, legislation, and planning and evaluation.

Beyond the DHHS, health responsibilities have been assigned to several other federal agencies, including the federal Environmental Protection Agency and the Departments of Homeland Security, Education, Agriculture, Defense, Transportation, and Veterans Affairs, just to name a few. The importance of some of these other federal agencies should not be underestimated in terms of the level and proportion of their resources devoted to health purposes. Health-specific agencies at the federal level are a relatively new phenomenon. The PHS itself remained a unit of the Treasury Department until 1944, and the first cabinet-level federal human services agency of any kind was the Federal Security Agency in 1939. This historical trivia demonstrates that federal powers and authority in health and public health are a relatively recent phenomenon in U.S. history.

The federal government is the largest purchaser of health-related services, with spending on health purposes representing approximately one fourth of the total federal budget. Figure 4-3 compares total national health expenditures with health expenditures attributed to the federal government and to state local governments. Health expenditures constituted 26% of total federal expenditures in 2007, up from 12% in 1980, and only 3% in 1960 (Figure 4-4). Escalating costs for healthcare services seriously constrain efforts to reduce the federal budget deficit, and there is little public or political support for additional taxes for health purposes.

It is no simple task to describe the federal budget development and approval process that determines funding levels for federal health programs. Although one fourth of the federal budget supports health activities, the major share is spent on Medicare and Medicaid. These and other entitlement programs constitute two thirds of the federal budget; this spending is mandatory and cannot be easily controlled. The remaining one third represents discretionary spending; half of this is related to national defense purposes. Spending for discretionary programs is more readily controlled. Nondefense discretionary spending for health purposes competes with a wide array of programs, including education, training, science, technology, housing, transportation, and foreign aid. Despite a small increase caused by national terrorism preparedness initiatives, nondefense discretionary funding for health purposes has declined as a proportion of all federal spending.

Decisions authorizing and funding health programs are made in an annual budget approval process. The current process is a complex one that establishes ceilings for broad categories of expenditures and then reconciles individual programs and funding levels within those ceilings in omnibus budget reconciliation acts. For discretionary programs, Congress must act each year to provide spending authority. For mandatory programs, Congress may

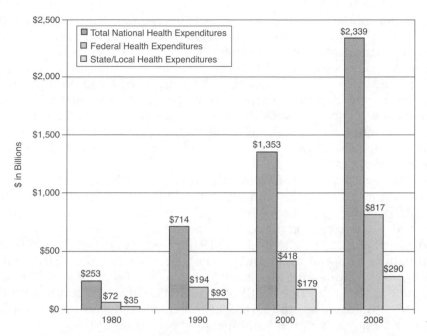

Figure 4-3 Total national health expenditures, and federal and state/local government expenditures for health-related purposes, United States, 1980–2008. *Source:* Data from Centers for Disease Control and Prevention, National Center for Health Statistics. *Health, United States, 2009.* Hyattsville, MD: NCHS; 2009.

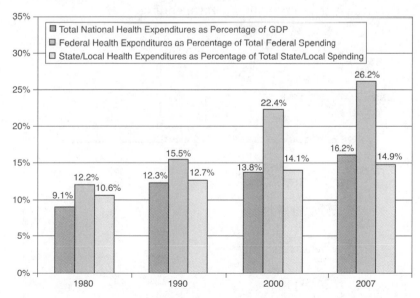

Figure 4-4 National health expenditures as percent of gross domestic product (GDP), and federal and state/local government health expenditures as percent of total government expenditures, United States, 1980–2007. *Source:* Data from Centers for Disease Control and Prevention, National Center for Health Statistics. *Health, United States, 2009.* Hyattsville, MD: NCHS; 2009.

act to change the spending that current laws require. The result is a mixture of substantive decisions as to which programs will be authorized and what they will be authorized to do, together with budget decisions as to the level of resources to be made available through more than a dozen annual appropriations bills. In recent years, federal law has imposed a cap on total annual discretionary spending and requires that spending cuts must offset increased mandatory spending or new discretionary programs. This budgetary environment presents major challenges for new public health programs and, not infrequently, threatens continued funding for programs that have been operating for decades.

The organization of federal health responsibilities within the DHHS is quite complex fiscally and operationally. In federal fiscal year 2011, the overall DHHS budget is about $900 billion.[6] The DHHS has nearly 73,000 employees and is the largest grant-making agency in the federal government, with some 60,000 grants each year. The DHHS manages more than 300 programs through its 11 operating divisions. The major share of the DHHS budget supports the Medicare and Medicaid programs within the CMS. PHS activities account for less than one tenth of the DHHS budget. In addition to the CMS and the PHS agencies, the DHHS also includes the Administration for Children and Families and the Administration on Aging.

Budgets for PHS operating divisions in federal fiscal year 2011 range from $32 billion for the NIH to $600 million for the AHRQ (Figure 4-5). Just over 50 percent of all PHS funds support NIH research activities, and another $32 billion supports the remaining PHS agencies. The HRSA and the CDC together account for about $18 billion, which represents about 2% of total DHHS resources and about 0.5% of all federal spending.

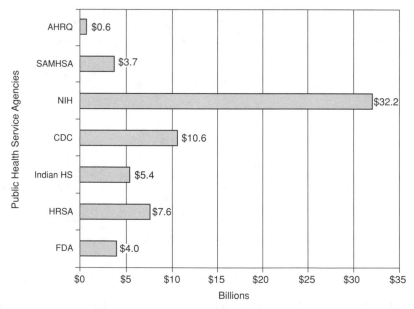

Figure 4-5 Fiscal Year 2011 U.S. Public Health Service Agency program level budgets. *Source:* Data from the fiscal year 2011 budget, U.S. Department of Health and Human Services, 2010.

Since the late 1970s, the Office of Health Promotion and Disease Prevention within the Office of the Assistant Secretary for Health has coordinated the development of the national agenda for public health and prevention efforts. Results of these efforts are apparent in the establishment of national health objectives that targeted the years 1990, 2000, 2010, and 2020 (see Chapter 2). Only 1 of more than 500 objectives from the 1990 and 2000 processes related to the public health system; that objective called for 90% of the population to be served by an LHD that was effectively carrying out public health's core functions.[7] Current estimates are that approximately 95% of the U.S. population is served by an LHD functioning at some level of capability. Baseline data on how many local agencies were effectively carrying out the core functions were not available when this objective was established in 1990. Several studies of core function-related performance in the 1990s suggest that the nation fell far short of achieving its year 2000 target. Chapter 5 describes public health core functions and performance measures used in these assessments as well as some of the issues impeding progress toward this important national objective. Chapter 6 then examines an extensive panel of public health infrastructure objectives developed as part of the Healthy People 2020 initiative.

PHS agencies have promoted greater use of performance measures in key federal health programs, including immunizations, tuberculosis control, sexually transmitted diseases, substance abuse, and mental health services. As previously described, federal grants-in-aid have long been the prime strategy and mechanism by which the federal government generates state and local action toward important health problems. A variety of approaches to grant making have been used over recent decades. These can be categorized by the extent of restrictions or flexibility imparted to grantees. The greatest flexibility and lack of requirements are associated with revenue-sharing grants. Block grants, including those initiated in the early 1980s, consolidate previously categorical grant programs into a block that generally comes with fewer restrictions than the previous collection of categorical grants. Formula grants are awarded on the basis of some predetermined formula, often based at least partly on need, which determines the level of funding for each grantee. Project grants are more limited in availability and are generally intended for a specific demonstration program or project.

In the 1990s, the DHHS proposed a series of federal partnership performance grants to address some of the shortcomings attributed to block grants implemented in the early 1980s. At that time, restrictions were relaxed for the categorical programs folded into the block grants, including the Maternal and Child Health Block Grant and the Prevention Block Grant. Lessons learned from the previous experience suggest the need for a cautious approach to new federal block grant proposals. In the 1980s, the new block grants indeed came with fewer strings attached; however, they also came at funding levels that were reduced approximately 25% from the previous arrangement. The blocking of several categorical programs into one mega grant also served to dissipate the constituencies for the categorical programs. Without active and visible constituencies advocating for programs, restoration or even maintenance of previous funding levels proved difficult. In addition, the reduction in reporting requirements made it more difficult to justify budget requests. Any new federal approaches to overcome these obstacles will be watched closely by advocates, as well as by state and local public health officials.

In addition to being a prime strategy to influence services at the state and local level, federal grants also serve to redistribute resources to compensate for differences in the ability of states to fund and operate basic health services. They have also served as a useful approach to promoting minimum standards for specific programs and services. For example, federal grants for maternal and child health promoted personnel standards in state and local agencies that fostered the growth of civil service systems across the country. Other effects on state and local health agencies will be apparent as these are examined in the following sections.

GOVERNMENTAL PUBLIC HEALTH: STATE HEALTH AGENCIES

Several factors place states at center stage when it comes to health. The U.S. Constitution gives states primacy in safeguarding the health of their citizens. From the mid 19th century until the 1930s, states largely exercised that leadership role with little competition from the federal government and only occasional conflict with the larger cities. Federal funding turned the table on states after 1935, reaching its peak influence in the 1960s and 1970s. At that time, numerous federal health and human service initiatives (such as model cities, community health centers, and community mental health services) were funded directly to local governments and even to community-based organizations. This practice greatly concerned state capitals and served to damage tenuous relationships among the three levels of government. The relative influence of states began to grow once again after 1980, with both increasing rhetoric and federal actions restoring some powers and resources to states and their state health agencies. Although states were finding it increasingly difficult to finance public health and medical service programs, they demanded more autonomy and control over the programs they managed, including those operated in partnership with the federal government. At the same time, local governments were making demands on state governments similar to those that states were making on the federal government. States have found themselves uncomfortably in the middle between the two other levels of government. At the same time, states are one step removed from both the resources needed to address the needs of their citizens and the demands and expectations of the local citizenry. For health issues, especially those affecting oversight and regulation of health services and providers, states often appear unduly influenced by large, politically active lobbies representing various aspects of the health system.

States carry out their health responsibilities through many different state agencies, although the overall constellation of health programs and services within all of state government is similar across states. Table 4-2 outlines 28 state agencies that carry out health responsibilities or activities in a typical state. Somewhere in the maze of state agencies is an identifiable lead agency for health. These official health agencies are often freestanding departments reporting to the governor of the state. In about one half of the states, the state health agency relates or reports to a state board of health, although the preva-

Table 4-2   Typical State Agencies with Health Roles (Names Vary from State to State)

- Official State Health Agency (Department of Health/Public Health)
- Department of Aging
- Department of Agriculture
- Department of Alcoholism and Substance Abuse
- Asbestos Abatement Authority
- Department of Children and Family Services
- Department of Emergency and Disaster Services
- Department of Energy and Natural Resources
- Environmental Protection Agencies
- Guardianship and Advocacy Commissions
- Health and Fitness Council
- Health Care Cost Containment Council
- Health Facilities Authority
- Health Facilities Planning Board
- Department of Homeland Security
- Department of Mental Health and Developmental Disabilities
- Department of Mines and Minerals
- Department of Nuclear Safety
- Pollution Control Board
- Department of Professional Regulation
- Department of Public Aid
- Department of Rehabilitation Services
- Rural Affairs Council
- State Board of Education
- State Fire Marshall
- Department of Transportation
- State University System
- Department of Veterans Affairs

lence of this relationship is declining. Another approach to the organizational placement of state health agencies finds them within a multipurpose human service agency, often with the state's social services and substance abuse responsibilities. This approach has waxed and waned in popularity, although its popularity increased in the 1990s with the hopes of fostering better integration of community services across the spectrum of health and social services. State health agencies are freestanding agencies in 28 states and are part of multipurpose health and/or human services agencies in the others.

The public official with statutory authority to carry out public health laws and declare public health emergencies is generally the state health official who directs the state health department. In some states, however, this statutory authority resides with other public officials, such as the governor or director of the superagency in which the state health department is a component, or with the state board of health (Figure 4-6).

As identified in a recent profile of state public health agencies compiled by the Association of State and Territorial Health Officials (ASTHO), key activities performed by state public health agencies include[8]:

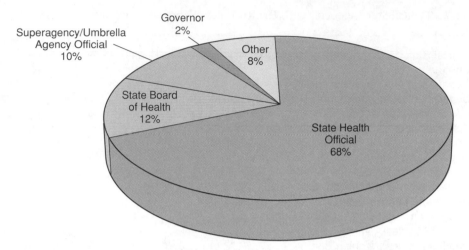

Figure 4-6   Primary statutory public health authority in states. *Source:* Data from Association of State and Territorial Health Officials (ASTHO). *Profile of State Public Health, Volume One.* Washington, DC: ASTHO; 2009.

- Running efficient statewide prevention programs like tobacco quit lines, newborn screening programs, and disease surveillance.
- Ensuring a basic level of community public health services across the state, regardless of the level of resources or capacity of LHDs.
- Providing the services of professionals with specialized skills, such as disease outbreak specialists and restaurant and food service inspectors, who bring expertise that is otherwise hard to find, too expensive to employ at a local level, or involve overseeing local public health functions.
- Collecting and analyzing statewide vital statistics, health indicators, and morbidity data to target public health threats and diseases such as cancer.
- Providing statewide investigations of disease outbreaks, environmental hazards such as chemical spills and hurricanes, and other public health emergencies.
- Monitoring the use of funds and other resources to ensure they are used effectively and equitably throughout the state.
- Conducting statewide health planning, improvement, and evaluation.
- Licensing and regulating health care, food service, and other facilities.

The range of responsibilities for the official state health agency varies considerably in terms of specific programs and services. Staffing levels and patterns also show a wide range, reflecting the diversity in agency responsibilities. The data presented on state health agencies in this chapter are from the most recent surveys of state health officials conducted by ASTHO in 2005 and 2007.[8–11] Figure 4-7 illustrates the variability in state health agencies' responsibilities for programs.[11] In 2005, for example, 90% of the official state health agencies administered the Supplemental Food Program for Women, Infants,

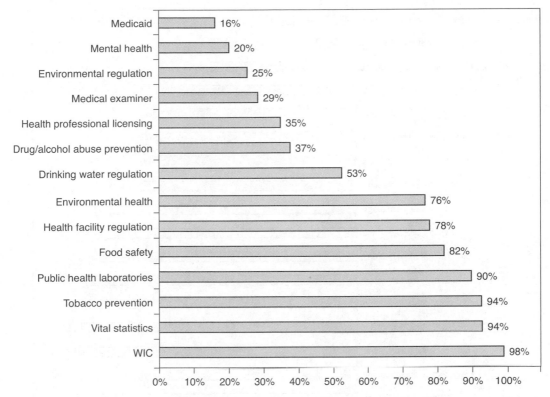

Figure 4-7 Selected organizational responsibilities of state health agencies, 2005. *Source:* Data from Association of State and Territorial Health Officials. Washington, DC: ASTHO; 2006.

and Children, vital statistics systems, public health laboratories, and emergency preparedness and response programs. Less than one half of the state health agencies administered the state Medicaid Program, mental health and substance abuse services, and health professional licensing. Many state health agencies administered programs for environmental health services, most frequently involving food and drinking water safety; however, only 20% of the state health agencies served as the environmental regulatory agency within their state, which often includes responsibility for clean air, resource conservation, clean water, superfund sites, toxic substance control, and hazardous substances.

State health agency responsibilities are anything but fixed in stone; they change with the times. The 1990s witnessed several changes in the public health responsibilities of state health agencies. More state health agencies took on preparedness responsibilities and expanded their health planning and development roles during the decade. On the other hand, fewer state health agencies were carrying out environmental health and institutional licensing functions and some lost responsibility for natural disaster preparedness to state emergency management agencies. Figure 4-8 catalogs new and emerging roles and responsibilities for state health agencies.[9] Notably, bioterrorism preparedness and response is the most prevalent of these emerging roles.

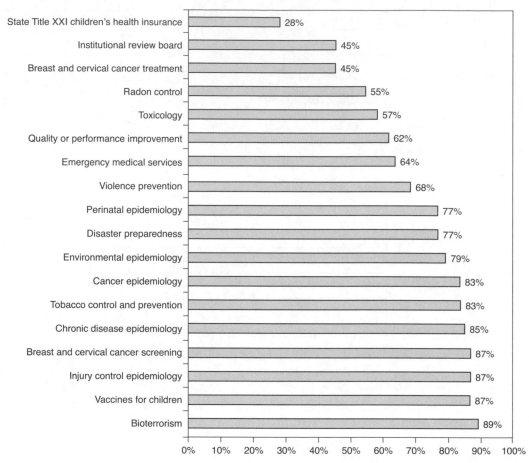

Figure 4-8 States with responsibilities in emerging areas of public health practice: United States, 2001. *Source:* Data from Beitsch LM, Brooks RG, Grigg M, Menchemi N. Structure and functions of state public health agencies. *Am J Public Health.* 2006;96:167–172.

Nearly one in two states relies on regional or district offices to carry out state responsibilities and to assist LHDs.[10] Staff assigned to district offices often provide consultation and technical assistance to local health agencies within that district, especially for purposes of medical oversight, budgetary management, inspectional activities and code enforcement, provision of education and training, and general planning and coordination for activities such as emergency preparedness. More than one half of the 100,000 full-time equivalent (FTE) employees of state health departments perform their duties from regional, district, or local sites.

As illustrated in Figure 4-3, state and local governments spent nearly $300 billion on health-related purposes in 2007. Health expenditures have comprised 13% to 15% of state and local government expenditures since 1990 (Figure 4-4). The burden on states is especially heavy, with approximately 30% of total state budgets expended on health purposes. Before the advent of

Medicaid and Medicare in 1965, state and local governments actually spent more for health purposes than did the federal government.

With public health responsibilities allocated differently across the various states, data on state health agency expenditures are both difficult to interpret and incomplete in several important respects. These data do not allow for meaningful comparison across states because of the variation in responsibilities assigned to the official state health agency and those assigned to other state agencies. More importantly, these data often do not differentiate between population-based public health activities and personal health services. Also lacking is a composite picture of resource allocations for important public health purposes across all state and local agencies with health roles, including substance abuse, mental health, and environmental protection agencies. This limitation is especially apparent for environmental health and protection roles. Chapter 6 examines public health expenditures and financial resources from the perspective of the infrastructure of public health. For this reason, only general information on state health agency expenditures is discussed here.

The organizational placement and specific responsibilities of state health agencies largely determine the size of their budgets and workforce. Just over 50% of the state health agencies have 1,500 or fewer employees; these agencies have budgets approximating $250 million. This group includes many free-standing agencies that have responsibility for traditional public health services but not for Medicaid, mental health, substance abuse, and environmental regulation. As these other responsibilities are added, the budgets and workforce of state health agencies increase substantially. Nine state health agencies have more than 4,500 employees and average expenditures of almost $6 billion.

In order to identify state government expenditures for public health activities, it is necessary to examine the budgets of multiple state agencies. The official state health agency is not the only unit of state government supporting population-based public health activities. Data on state health expenditures for fiscal year 2003 indicate that states spent about $10 billion from state sources on population-based public health activities. This represents about 5.4% of state health expenditures and 1.7% of the total state budget. In addition, states expended another $9 billion of federal funding to support population-based services. Breakdowns for different types of population-based public health activities are provided in Figure 4-9. A higher percentage of state funds supported environmental protection, injury prevention, and infrastructure activities while a higher percentage of federal funds went for disaster preparedness and chronic disease prevention activities. State and federal funds equally supported prevention of epidemics and spread of disease. State health agency expenditures include grants and contracts to LHDs, although the current level of these intergovernmental transfers is not known. In 1991, an estimated $2 billion was transferred from state to LHDs.[12]

At the federal level, more than a dozen federal departments, agencies, and commissions (Transportation, Labor, Health and Human Services, Commerce, Energy, Defense, Environmental Protection Agency, Homeland Security, Interior, Consumer Product Safety Commission, Agriculture, Nuclear Regulatory Commission, and Housing and Urban Development) have environmental health roles. State and local governments have largely replicated this web of

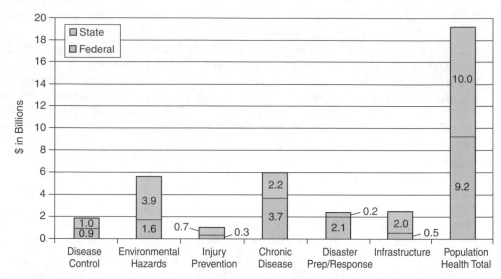

Figure 4-9 State population-based public health expenditures for public health functions, United States, 2002–2003. *Source:* Data from Milbank Memorial Fund, National Association of State Budget Officers, and the Reforming States Group. *2002-2003 State Health Expenditures Report*, June 2005. www.milbank.org/reports/05NSBO/index.html. Accessed May 31, 2010.

environmental responsibility, creating a complex system often poorly under-stood by the private sector and general public. Federal statutes have driven the organization of state responsibilities. Key federal environmental statutes include the following:

- Clean Air Act
- Clean Water Act
- Comprehensive Environmental Response, Competition, and Liability Act and Superfund Amendments and Reauthorization Act
- Federal Insecticide, Fungicide, and Rodenticide Act
- Resource Conservation and Recovery Act
- Safe Drinking Water Act
- Toxic Substance Control Act
- Food, Drug, and Cosmetic Act
- Federal Mine Safety and Health Act
- Occupational Safety and Health Act

States, however, have responded in no consistent manner in assigning implementation of federal statutes among various state agencies. The focus of federal statutes on specific environmental media (water, air, and waste) has fostered the assignment of environmental responsibilities to state agencies other than official state health agencies, as demonstrated in Table 4-3. The implications of this diversification are important for public health agencies. State health agencies are becoming less involved in environmental health pro-grams; only a handful of states use their state health agency as the state's lead agency for environmental concerns. This role has shifted to state environmen-

Table 4-3 Number and Type of State Agencies Responsible for Implementation of Federal Environmental Statutes

Statute	Agriculture	Environment	Health	Labor	Total
Clean Air Act	0	41	10	1	52
Clean Water Act	1	41	11	1	54
CERCLA (Superfund) Act	3	38	25	1	67
Federal Insecticide, Fungicide, and Rodenticide Act	0	41	11	2	54
Resource Conservation and Recovery Act	0	36	33	3	72
Safe Drinking Water Act	0	12	23	3	38
Toxic Substance Control Act	37	4	5	0	46
Food, Drug, and Cosmetic Act	1	1	15	39	56
Federal Mine Safety and Health Act	0	0	0	12	12
Occupational Safety and Health Act	15	1	13	0	29

Source: Data from Health Resources and Services Administration. *Environmental Web: Impact of Federal Statutes on State Environmental Health and Protection—Services, Structure and Funding.* Rockville, MD: Health Resources and Services Administration; 1995.

tal agencies, although many other state agencies are also involved. Still, the primary strategy has shifted from a health-oriented approach to a regulatory approach. Despite their diminished role in environmental concerns, state health agencies continue to address a very diverse set of environmental health issues and maintain epidemiologic and quantitative risk assessment capabilities not available in other state agencies. Linking this important expertise to the workings of other state agencies is a particularly challenging task, and there are other implications of this scenario, as well.

The shift toward regulatory strategies is clearly reflected in resource allocation at the state level. In the mid 1990s, approximately $6 billion was spent on environmental health and regulation by states, with only about $1 billion of that total for environmental health (as opposed to environmental regulation) activities.[13] Public health considerations often take a back seat to regulatory concerns when budget decisions are made. In addition, the fact that many environmental health specialists are working in nonhealth agencies poses special problems for both their training and their practice performance.

The wide variation in organization and structure of state health responsibilities suggests that there is no standard or consistent pattern to public health practice among the various states. An examination of enabling statutes and state public agency mission statements provides further support for this conclusion. Only 11 of 43 state agency mission statements address the majority of the concepts related to public health purpose and mission in the *Public Health in America* document.[14,15] When state public health enabling statutes are examined for references to the essential public health services framework in the *Public Health in America* document, the majority of the essential public health services can be identified in only one fifth of the states. The most frequently identified essential public health services reflect traditional public health activities, such as enforcement of laws, monitoring of health status, diagnosing and investigating health hazards, and informing and educating the public. The essential public health services least frequently referenced in these enabling statutes reflect more modern concepts of public health practice, including mobilizing community partnerships, evaluating the effects of health services, and research for innovative solutions. Only three states had both enabling statutes and state health agency mission statements highly congruent with the concepts advanced in the *Public Health in America* document.[14]

State-based public health systems blend the roles of the state health agency and the LHDs in that state. In more than 40 states, all areas of the state are served by an LHD. Where there is no LHD to provide public health services, the state health agency generally provides basic public health coverage. Increasingly, states are using regional or district structures to provide oversight and support for LHDs. In more than two thirds of states, local boards of health also provide direction and oversight of local public health activities.

In summary, state health agencies face many challenges related to the fragmentation of public health roles and responsibilities among various state agencies. Central to these are two related challenges: how to coordinate public health's core functions and essential services effectively and how to leverage changes within the health system to instill greater emphasis on clinical prevention and population-based services. As the various chapters of this text suggest, these are related aims.

GOVERNMENTAL PUBLIC HEALTH: LOCAL HEALTH DEPARTMENTS

In the overall structuring of governmental public health responsibilities, LHDs are where the "rubber meets the road." These agencies are established to carry out the critical public health responsibilities embodied in state laws and local ordinances and to meet other needs and expectations of their communities. Although some cities had local public health boards and agencies before 1900, the first county health department was not established until 1911. At that time, Yakima County, Washington created a permanent county health unit, based on the success of a county sanitation campaign to control a serious typhoid epidemic. The Rockefeller Sanitary Commission, through its support for county hookworm eradication efforts, also stimulated the development of county-based LHDs. The number of LHDs grew rapidly during the 20th century, although in recent decades, expansion has been tempered by closures and consolidations.

LHDs should not be considered separately from the state network in which they operate. It is important to remember that states, through their state legislative and executive branches, establish the types and powers of local governmental units that can exist in that state. In this arrangement, the state and its local subunits, however defined, share responsibilities for health and other state functions. How health duties are shared in any given state depends on a complex set of factors that include state and local statutes, history, need, and expectations.

Local health agencies relate to their state public health systems in one of three general patterns.[4] In most states, LHDs are formed and managed by local government, reporting directly to some office of local government, such as a local board of health, county commission, or city or county executive officer. In this decentralized arrangement, LHDs often have considerable autonomy, although they may be required to carry out specific state public health statutes. Also, there are some states that share oversight of LHDs with local government through the power to appoint local health officers or to approve an annual budget. In some states with decentralized LHDs, some areas of the state lack coverage because the local government chooses not to form a local health agency and the state must provide services in those uncovered areas. This mixed arrangement occurs in fewer than 10 states. Another 15 states use a more centralized approach, in which local health agencies are directly operated by the state or there are no LHDs and the state provides all local health services.

Classifying these arrangements as decentralized, centralized, or mixed is useful from the perspective of the state–local public health system. From the perspective of the LHD and the population that it serves, however, the LHD is either a unit of local government or a unit of state government.

LHDs are established by governmental units, including counties, cities, towns, townships, and special districts, by one of two general methods. The legislative body may create an LHD through enactment of a local ordinance or resolution, or the citizens of the jurisdiction may create a local board and agency through a referendum. Both patterns are common. Resolution health agencies are often funded from the general funds of the jurisdiction, whereas referendum health agencies often have a specific tax levy available to them. There are advantages and disadvantages to either approach. Resolution health agencies are simpler to establish and may develop close working relationships with the local legislative bodies that create them. Referendum agencies reflect the support of the local electorate and may have access to specific tax levies that preclude the need to compete with other local government funding sources.

Counties represent the most common form of subdividing states. In general, counties are geopolitical subunits of states that carry out various state responsibilities, such as law enforcement (sheriffs and state's attorneys) and public health. Counties largely function as agents of the state and carry out responsibilities delegated or assigned to them. In contrast, cities are generally not established as agents of the state. Instead, they have considerable discretion through home rule powers to take on functions that are not prohibited to them by state law. Cities can choose to have a health department or to rely on the state or their county for public health services. City health departments often have a wider array of programs and services because of this autonomy. As described previously, the earliest public health agencies developed in large urban centers before the development of either state health agencies or county-based LHDs. This status also contributes to their sense of autonomy. These considerations, as well as the increased demands and expectations to meet the needs of those who lack adequate health insurance, have made many city-based, especially big city-based, LHDs qualitatively different from other LHDs.

Both cities and counties have resource and political bases. Both rely heavily on property and sales taxes to finance health and other services, and both are struggling with the limitations of these funding sources. Political resistance to increasing taxes is the major limitation for both. Relatively few counties and cities have imposed income taxes, the form of taxation relied on by federal and state governments; however, both generally have strong political bases, although cities are generally more likely than counties to be at odds with state government on key issues.

Counties play a critical role in the public sector, the extent and importance of which is often overlooked. More than three fourths of all LHDs are organized at the county level, serving a single county, a city–county, or several counties. As a result, counties provide a substantial portion of the community prevention and clinical preventive services offered in the United States. Counties provide care for about 40 million persons who access LHDs and other facilities; they spend more than $30 billion of their local tax revenues on health and hospital services annually through some 4,500 sites that include hospitals, nursing homes, clinics, health departments, and mental health facilities. Counties play an explicit role in treatment, are legally responsible for indigent health care in over 30 states, and pay a portion of the nonfederal share of Medicaid in about 20 states. In addition, counties purchase health care for several million employees.

The National Association of County and City Health Officials tracks public health activities of LHDs with periodic national surveys beginning in the early 1990s.[16-18] The most recent survey of LHDs took place in 2008. Most of the data provided in this chapter, including the basic information on LHDs in Table 4-4, are derived from this 2008 survey.[19]

One limitation of information on LHDs is that there is neither a clear nor a functional definition of what constitutes an LHD. The most widely used definitions call for an administrative and service unit of local government, concerned with health, employing at least one full-time person, and carrying responsibility for health of a jurisdiction smaller than the state. By this definition, more than 3,200 local health agencies operate in 3,042 U.S. counties.[19] The number of LHDs varies widely from state to state; Rhode Island has none, whereas neighboring Connecticut and Massachusetts each report more than 100 LHDs.

Nearly 60% of LHDs are single-county health agencies, and over 80% operate out of a county base (single county, multicounty, or city–county).[19] Other LHDs function at the city, town, or township levels; some state-operated units also serve local jurisdictions. Although the precise number is uncertain, it appears that the total number of LHDs has been increasing, from about 1,300 in 1947 to about 2,000 in the mid 1970s to somewhere over 3,000 today.

Several reports going back more than 60 years have proposed extensive consolidation of small LHDs because of perceived lack of efficiency and coordination of services, inconsistent administration of public health laws, and the inability of small LHDs to raise adequate resources to carry out their prime functions effectively. Consolidations at the county level would appear to be the most rational approach, but only limited progress has been achieved in recent decades.

Table 4-4   Vital Statistics for Local Health Departments (LHDs)

Definition	• An administrative and service unit of state or local government, concerned with health, employing at least one full-time person, and carrying responsibility for health of a jurisdiction smaller than the state
Number	• Approximately 3,200 using the above definition; 2,800 in NACCHO sampling frame • Functional definition would reduce number considerably • Varies from 0 in Rhode Island and Hawaii to more than 100 in seven states
Jurisdiction Type	• 60%—single county • 9%—multicounty • 11%—city-county • 11%—town/township • 7%—city • 2%—other
Jurisdiction Population	• 64%—<50,000 • 31%—50,000–499,999 • 5%—500,000 and greater
Services Most Frequently Provided in LHD Jurisdictions	• 88%—adult immunizations • 88%—communicable disease surveillance • 86%—childhood immunizations • 81%—tuberculosis screening • 77%—food service establishment inspection • 75%—environmental health surveillance • 74%—food safety education • 72%—tuberculosis treatment • 70%—tobacco use prevention • 68%—schools and day care center inspection
Expenditures	• Median—$1,120,000 • 25%—<$500,000 • 17%—>$5,000,000 • Median per capita expenditures: $28 (excluding clinical revenue); $36 (all sources)
Source of Funds	• 25%—local • 20%—state • 17%—federal funds passed through state • 2%—federal direct to local agency • 10%—Medicaid reimbursement • 5%—Medicare reimbursement • 11%—fees • 7%—other • 2%—not specified

Employees	• Median Number of Employees = 18
	• Median Full-Time Equivalent (FTE) Employees = 15
	  ° 63% of LHDs with <25 FTE
	  ° 12% of LHDs with >100 FTEs
	• Median FTEs in Selected Occupational Categories Employed by LHDs

Table 4-4   Vital Statistics for Local Health Departments (LHDs) (continued)

	<10,000	10,000–24,999	25,000–49,999	50,000–99,999	100,000–499,999	500,000+
			Population Served			
All LHD Staff	3	8	15	31	81	359
Manager	1	1	1	1	5	13
Nurse	1	3	5	8	17	57
Physician	0	0	0	0	1	3
Environmental Health Specialist	0	1	2	3	9	21
Other Environmental Health Scientist	0	0	0	0	0	3
Epidemiologist	0	0	0	0	1	2
Health Educator	0	0	0	1	2	6
Nutritionist	0	0	0	1	3	10
Information Systems Specialist	0	0	0	0	1	3
Public Information Specialist	0	0	0	0	0	1
Emergency Preparedness Coordinator	0	0	0	1	1	1
Behavioral Health Professional	0	0	0	0	1	8
Administrative/Clerical	1	2	2	7	18	79

Governance
- 80% of LHDs relate and/or report to a local board of health
- For 66% of local boards of health, members of the board are appointed to their positions

Leadership
- More than one half of local health officers are women
- One fifth of all local health officers have doctoral level degrees
- Mean tenure = 8.7 years

Source: Data from National Association of County and City Health Officials. *2008 National Profile of Local Health Departments.* Washington, DC: NACCHO; 2009.

Most LHDs are relatively small organizations; as illustrated in Figure 4-10, 64% serve populations of 50,000 or less, whereas 31% of LHDs serve populations of 50,000 to 499,999. Only 5% of LHDs serve populations of 500,000 or more residents.[19] Nearly 90% of the U.S. population is served by an LHD in the large or medium category.

Some states set qualifications for local health officers or require medical supervision when the administrator is not a physician. About four fifths of LHDs employ a full-time health officer. Health officers have a mean tenure of about 8 years and a median tenure of about 9 years. Approximately 15% are physicians, and less than one fourth of all LHD executives have graduate degrees in public health. LHDs serving larger populations are more likely to have full-time health officers than are smaller LHDs.

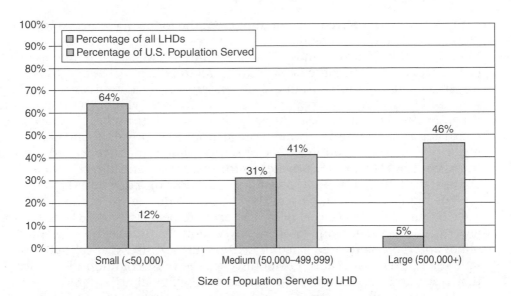

Figure 4-10   Small, medium, and large LHDs; percentage of all LHDs and percentage of population served, United States, 2008. *Source:* Data from National Association of County and City Health Officials. *2008 National Profile of Local Health Departments*. Washington, DC: NACCHO; 2009.

Local boards of health are associated with most LHDs; in 2008, 80% of LHDs reported working with a local board of health. About 35 states have some form of a local board of health. There are an estimated 3,200 local boards of health; approximately 85% reported an affiliation with an LHD. However, 15% exist independently of any LHD; this is most common in Massachusetts, Pennsylvania, New Hampshire, Iowa, and New Jersey. The pattern for size of population, type of jurisdiction, and budget mirrors that for LHDs. Virtually all local boards of health establish local health policies, fees, ordinances, and regulations. Most also recommend and/or approve budgets, establish community health priorities, and hire the director of the local health agency. Although four fifths of LHDs relate to a board of health, only 56% report only to that board rather than some other office of local government. In recent decades, the role of local boards of health has shifted away from policy making to advisory roles as local governments have become more directly involved with oversight of their LHDs.

Similar to the situation with state health agencies, data on LHD expenditures lack currency and completeness. Annual LHD expenditures in 2008 ranged from less than $10,000 to over $1 billion. One half of LHDs had budgets of $1 million or less, and 29% had budgets over $5 million. Total expenditures increase with size of population. LHDs located in metropolitan areas had substantially higher expenditures than their nonmetropolitan area counterparts. The median per capita LHD expenditure level in 2008 was $28, excluding clinical services. Despite concerns as to shrinking public health agencies, 75% of LHDs reported increased budgets in 2005 as compared with the previous year.

In 2008, LHDs derived their funding from the following sources: local funds (26%), the state (37%, including 17% that were federal funds passing through the state), direct federal funds (2%), Medicaid and Medicare reimbursements (15%), fees (12%), and other sources (8%). Metropolitan LHDs and those serving smaller populations are more dependent on local sources of funding, whereas LHDs in nonmetropolitan areas and those serving larger populations depend more on state sources. Virtually all revenue sources for LHDs have been increasing in recent years, including regulatory fees, private foundation funding, city and county funding, federal sources, and patient-generated revenue from Medicaid, Medicare, private health insurance, and direct patient fees. Direct state funding is the sole revenue source showing a downward trend.

The number of FTE employees also increases with the size of the population served. Only 11% of LHDs employ 125 or more persons, and 68% have 24 or fewer employees. The number of employees and the number of different disciplines and professions are related to LHD population size. Clerical staff, nurses, sanitarians, physicians, and nutritionists are the most common disciplines (in that order) and are all found in more than one half of all LHDs.

There is considerable variety in the services provided by LHDs. Later chapters examine in greater detail the functions and services of LHDs, but several general categories of services are notable. Top priority areas for LHDs overall are communicable disease control, environmental health, and child health. LHDs serving both large and small populations report similar priorities, although community outreach replaces environmental health as a top priority for the largest local health jurisdictions (those over 500,000 population). Slight differences in priorities are also apparent between metropolitan and nonmetropolitan area LHDs. LHDs in metropolitan areas often include inspections as a high priority, while nonmetropolitan LHDs are more likely to include family planning and home healthcare services as priorities.

Many LHDs provide a common core battery of services that generally includes adult and childhood immunizations, communicable disease control, community assessment, community outreach and education, environmental health services, epidemiology and surveillance programs, food safety and restaurant inspections, health education, and tuberculosis testing. Less commonly, LHDs provide services related to primary care and chronic disease, including cardiovascular disease, diabetes, and glaucoma screening; behavioral and mental health services; programs for the homeless; substance abuse services; and veterinary public health.[19]

LHDs do not always provide these services themselves; increasingly, they contract for these services or contribute resources to other agencies or organizations in the community. Community partners for LHDs include state health agencies, other LHDs, hospitals, other units of government, nonprofit and voluntary organizations, academic institutions, community health centers, the faith community, and insurance companies. LHDs increasingly interact with managed care organizations, although most do not have either formal or informal agreements governing these interactions.[16] Where agreements existed, they were more likely to be formal, to cover clinical and case management services, and to involve the provision (rather than the purchase) of services. More than one fourth of LHDs had formal agreements for clinical services for Medicaid clients in 1996. Chapters 5, 6, and 7 provide additional details on other key aspects of modern community public health practice.

INTERGOVERNMENTAL RELATIONSHIPS

In terms of public health, no level of government has complete authority and autonomy. Optimal outcomes result from collaborative and complementary efforts. One of this chapter's Public Health Spotlights tells the story of improved workplace safety in the United States during the 20th century, an achievement that relied heavily on effective laws and their enforcement by all levels of government. Future reductions in other forms of worker health and safety will likely require even higher levels of intergovernmental collaboration.

The relationships between and among the three levels of government have changed considerably over time in terms of their relative importance and influence in the health sector. This is especially true for the federal and local roles. The federal government had little authority and little ability to influence health priorities and interventions until after 1930. Since that time, it has exercised its influence primarily through financial leverage on both state and local government, as well as on the private medical care system. The massive financing role of the federal government has moved it to a position of preeminence among the various levels of government in actual ability to influence health affairs. This is evident in the federal share of total national health expenditures and the federal government's substantial support of prevention activities; however, federal public health spending represents only 1.3% of total federal health spending, one fourth less than in 1980 (Figure 4-11). This suggests that the federal commitment to public health has declined over recent decades. The federal proportion for total public health activity spending shows a similar

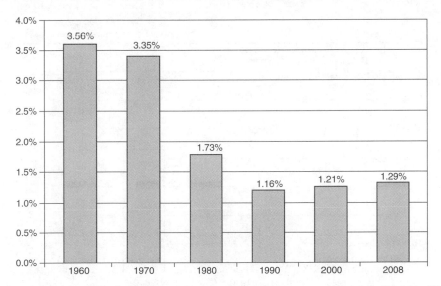

Figure 4-11 Federal public health activity spending as a percent of total federal health spending, United States, 1960–2008. *Source:* Data from Centers for Medicare and Medicaid Services, National Health Accounts (NHA), selected years, 1960–2008.

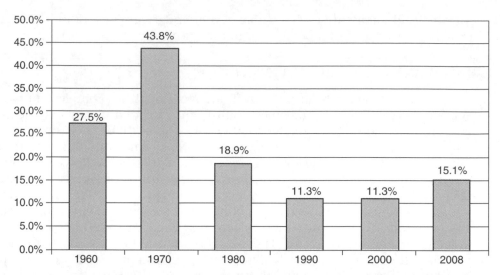

Figure 4-12 Federal public health activity spending as a percent of total public health activity spending, United States, 1960–2008. *Source:* Data from Centers for Medicare and Medicaid Services, National Health Accounts (NHA), selected years, 1960–2008.

pattern (Figure 4-12), declining from nearly 44% in 1970 to 15% in 2008. Although federal bioterrorism preparedness funds beginning in 2002 have slightly reversed this trend, the financial influence of the federal government on public health activities nationally was lower in 2008 than it had been throughout most of the second half of the 20th century. Figure 4-13 traces public health activity spending levels from 1980 to 2008.

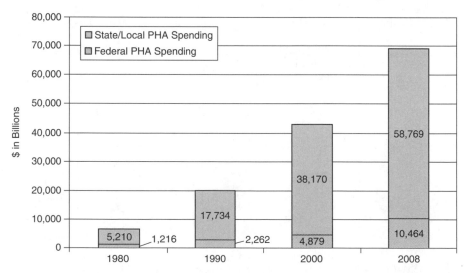

Figure 4-13 Federal and state/local public health activity spending, United States, 1980–2008. *Source:* Data from Centers for Medicare and Medicaid Services, National Health Accounts (NHA), selected years, 1980–2008.

In recent decades, political initiatives have sought to diminish the powerful federal role and return some of its influence back to the states; however, little in the form of true transfer of authority or resource control has taken place through 2010. It is likely that the federal government's fiscal muscle will enable it to continue its current dominant role in its relationships with state and local government.

Local government has experienced the greatest and most disconcerting change in relative influence over the 20th century. Before 1900, local government was the primary locus of action, with the development of both population-based interventions for communicable disease control and environmental sanitation and locally provided charity care for the poor; however, the massive problems related to simultaneous urbanization and povertization of the big cities spawned needs that could not be met with local resources alone. Outside the large cities, local government responses generally took the form of LHDs organized at the county level at the behest of state governments. This was viewed by states as the most efficient manner of executing their broad health powers. States often viewed local governments in general and LHDs in particular as their delivery system for important programs and services. In any event, the power of states and the growing influence of financial incentives through grant programs of both federal and state government acted to influence local priorities greatly. Priorities were being established by higher levels of government more often than through local determinations of needs. Although the demands and expectations were being directed at local governments, key decisions were being made in state capitals and in Washington, DC. Unfortunately, there are signs that local governments across the country are looking for opportunities to reduce their health roles for both clinical services and population-based interventions where they can. The perception is that the responsibility for clinical services lies with federal and state government or the private sector and that even traditional public health services can be effectively outsourced. How these actions will comport with the widespread belief that services are best provided at the local level raises serious questions regarding new roles of oversight and accountability that are not easily answered. Local governments have lost control over priorities and policies; they bridle under the regulations and grant conditions imposed by state and federal funding sources. As costs increase, grant awards fail to keep pace; however, growing numbers of wholly or partly uninsured individuals now look to local government for services. These rising expectations and increasing costs are occurring at a time when local governments are unable and unwilling to seek additional tax revenues. The complexities of organizing and coordinating community-wide responses to modern public health problems and risks also push local governments to look elsewhere for solutions.

States were slow to assume their extensive powers in the health sector but have been major players since the latter half of the 19th century. Although the growing influence of the federal government since 1930 displaced states as the most important level of government, their relative role has strengthened since about 1980. Still, states have become secondary players in the health sector. Most states lack the means, political as well as statutory, to intervene effectively in the portion of the health sector located within their jurisdictional boundaries. This is further complicated by their tradition of imitating the federal health bureaucracy whenever possible through the decentralization of health roles and responsibilities throughout dozens of administrative agencies. Coordination of programs, policies, and priorities has become exceedingly difficult within state government. Outside of state government, it has become virtually impossible. Still, the widely disparate circumstances from state to state make for laboratories of opportunity in which innovative approaches can be developed and evaluated.

The relationship between state and local government in public health has traditionally been tenuous and difficult. Just as the federal government views the states as one of many possible agents, states themselves have come to view local governments as just another way to get things done. As a result, states have turned to other parties, such as community-based organizations, and have begun to deal directly with them, leaving local government on the sidelines. This undervaluing of LHDs, when coupled with the declining appreciation among local governments for their health agencies, presents major challenges for the future of public health services in the United States. Instead of becoming stronger allies, these forces are working to pull apart the fabric of the national public health network.

These ever-changing and evolving relationships call into question whether the governmental public health network can be strengthened through a more centralized approach involving greater federal leadership and direction.[20] In decentralized approaches, some states may truly be laboratories of innovation and provide better services than can be achieved through a centralized approach. There are many examples of creative policies and programs at the state level, but there are also many examples of state creativity being stifled by the federal government. The history of state requests for waivers of Medicaid requirements is a case in point. Many states waited 2 or more years for federal approval of the waivers necessary to begin innovative programs, and some of the more creative proposals were actually rejected. Still, it can be argued that state political processes are more reflective of the different political values that must be reconciled for progressive policies to develop.

CONCLUSION

The structural framework for public health in the United States includes a network of state and LHDs working in partnership with the federal government. This framework is precariously balanced on a legal foundation that gives primacy for health concerns to states, a financial foundation that allows the federal government to promote consistent and minimum standards across 50 diverse states, and a practical foundation of LHDs serving as the point of contact between communities and their three-tiered government. Over time, the relative influence of these partners has shifted dramatically because of changes in needs, resources, and public expectations. The challenges to this organizational structure are many. Those related to the public health emergency preparedness and response are addressed in the next chapter, and those emerging from the rapid changes within the health system and in the expansion of community public health practice are addressed in Chapters 3, 5, and 6. There are increasing calls for government to turn over many public programs to private interests and growing concern over the role of government in general. These developments make it easy to forget that many of the public health achievements of the past century would not have been possible without a serious commitment of resources and leadership by those in the public sector. In any event, it is clear that the organizational structure of public health—its form—intimately reflects the structure of government in the United States. As a result, the success or failure of these public health organizations will be determined by our success in governing ourselves.

DISCUSSION QUESTIONS AND EXERCISES

1. What is the legal basis for public health in the United States, and what impact has that had on the public health powers of federal, state, and local governments?

2. How can the enforcement of nuisance control regulations work for as well as against public health agencies?

3. What is meant by a state's police power, and how is that used in public health?

4. What is the basis for the historic tension between the powers of the federal government and the powers of states in public health matters?

5. How extensive is administrative law in public health, and how does it work? Cite a recent example of important public health rules or regulations in the news media.

6. Describe the basic structure of a typical LHD in the United States in terms of type and size of jurisdiction served, budget, staff, and agency head. (The National Association of County and City Health Officials' website may be useful here!) How does this compare with the typical LHD in your own state?

7. For the prevention of workplace injuries (see the Public Health Spotlight on Occupational and Environmental Health and Safety), how are responsibilities assigned or delegated among the three levels of government (federal, state, and local) and among various agencies of those levels of government? Who is responsible for what?

8. What are the primary federal roles and responsibilities for public health in the United States? How do those roles and responsibilities comport with PHS agency budget requests for federal fiscal year 2011 (Figure 4-5)?

9. Consider the lessons from the Public Health Spotlight on the History of Public Health in Chicago (Chapter 1) and this chapter's Public Health Spotlight on the CDC. Has the evolution of both local and federal public health agencies taken parallel pathways? How have their developments differed in terms of roles and responsibilities? What are the implications of these similarities and differences for public health problems that require more than one level of government?

10. Access the websites of any two U.S. state health departments and compare and contrast the two organizations in terms of their structure, general functions, specific services, resources, and other important features. (The ASTHO link to state health agency websites may be useful here.)

REFERENCES

1. Centers for Disease Control and Prevention. History of CDC. *MMWR*. 1996;45:526–528.
2. Centers for Disease Control and Prevention. *Profile of State and Local Public Health Systems 1990*. Atlanta, GA: Centers for Disease Control and Prevention; 1991.
3. Shonick W. Government and Health Services: *Government's Role in the Development of the U.S. Health Services 1930–1980*. New York: Oxford University Press; 1995.
4. Pickett G, Hanlon JJ. *Public Health Administration and Practice*. 9th ed. St. Louis, MO: Mosby; 1990.
5. *Jacobson v Massachusetts*. 197 US 11 (1905).
6. U.S. Department of Health and Human Services. *The Fiscal Year 2007 Budget*. Washington, DC: U.S. Department of Health and Human Services; 2006.
7. U.S. Department of Health and Human Services. *Healthy People 2000*. Washington, DC: U.S. Public Health Service; 1990.
8. Association of State and Territorial Health Officials. *Profile of State Public Health, Volume One*. Washington, DC: Association of State and Territorial Health Officials; 2008.
9. Beitsch LM, Brooks RG, Grigg M, et al. Structure and functions of state public health agencies. *Am J Public Health*. 2006;96:167–172.
10. Beitsch LM, Grigg M, Menachemi N, et al. Roles of local public health agencies within the state public health system. *J Public Health Manage Pract*. 2006;12:232–241.
11. Beitsch LM, Brooks RG, Menachemi N, et al. Public health at center stage: new roles, old props. *Health Aff*. 2006;25:911–922.
12. Public Health Foundation. Characteristics of state health agencies. *Public Health Macroview*. 1995;7:1–8.
13. Burke TA, Shalauta NM, Tran NL, et al. The environmental web: a national profile of the state infrastructure for environmental health and protection. *J Public Health Manage Pract*. 1997;3:1–12.
14. Gebbie KM. State public health laws: an expression of constituency expectations. *J Public Health Manage Pract*. 2000;6:46–54.
15. Core Public Health Functions Steering Committee. *Public Health in America*. Washington, DC: U.S. Department of Health and Human Services, Public Health Service; 1994.
16. National Association of County and City Health Officials. *Profile of Local Health Departments 1992–1993*. Washington, DC: National Association of County and City Health Officials; 1995.
17. National Association of County and City Health Officials. *Profile of Local Health Departments 1996–1997 Data Set*. Washington, DC: National Association of County and City Health Officials; 1997.
18. National Association of County and City Health Officials. *Local Public Health Agency Infrastructure: A Chartbook*. Washington, DC: National Association of County and City Health Officials; 2001.
19. National Association of County and City Health Officials. *2008 National Profile of Local Health Departments*. Washington, DC: National Association of County and City Health Officials; 2009.
20. Turnock BJ, Atchison C. Governmental public health in the United States: the implications of federalism. *Health Aff*. 2002;6:68–78.

Public Health Spotlight on the CDC

HISTORY OF THE CDC[1]

The CDC, an institution synonymous around the world with public health, was 65 years old on July 1, 2011. The Communicable Disease Center was organized in Atlanta, Georgia on July 1, 1946; its founder, Dr. Joseph W. Mountin, was a visionary public health leader who had high hopes for this small and comparatively insignificant branch of the PHS. It occupied only one floor of the Volunteer Building on Peachtree Street and had fewer than 400 employees, most of whom were engineers and entomologists. Until the previous day, they had worked for Malaria Control in War Areas, the predecessor of the CDC, which had successfully kept the southeastern states malaria-free during World War II and, for approximately 1 year, from murine typhus fever. The new institution would expand its interests to include all communicable diseases and would be the servant of the states, providing practical help whenever called.

Distinguished scientists soon filled the CDC's laboratories, and many states and foreign countries sent their public health staffs to Atlanta for training. Any tropical disease with an insect vector and all those of zoological origin came within its purview. Dr. Mountin was not satisfied with this progress, and he impatiently pushed the staff to do more. He reminded them that except for tuberculosis and venereal disease, which had separate units in Washington, DC, the CDC was responsible for any communicable disease. To survive, it had to become a center for epidemiology.

Medical epidemiologists were scarce, and it was not until 1949 that Dr. Alexander Langmuir arrived to head the epidemiology branch. He saw the CDC as "the promised land," full of possibilities. Within months, he launched the first-ever disease surveillance program, which confirmed his suspicion that malaria, on which the CDC spent the largest portion of its budget, had long since disappeared. Subsequently, disease surveillance became the cornerstone on which the CDC's mission of service to the states was built and in time changed the practice of public health.

The outbreak of the Korean War in 1950 was the impetus for creating the CDC's Epidemic Intelligence Service. The threat of biological warfare loomed, and Dr. Langmuir, the most knowledgeable person in the PHS about this arcane subject, saw an opportunity to train epidemiologists who would guard against ordinary threats to public health while watching out for alien germs. The first class of Epidemic Intelligence Service officers arrived in Atlanta for training in 1951 and pledged to go wherever they were called for the next 2 years. These "disease detectives" quickly gained fame for "shoe-leather epidemiology" through which they ferreted out the cause of disease outbreaks.

The survival of the CDC as an institution was not at all certain in the 1950s. In 1947, Emory University gave land on Clifton Road for a headquarters, but construction did not begin for more than a decade. The PHS was so intent on research and the rapid growth of the NIH that it showed little interest in what happened in Atlanta. Congress, despite the long delay in appropriating money for new buildings, was much more receptive to the CDC's pleas for support than either the PHS or the Bureau of the Budget.

Two major health crises in the mid 1950s established the CDC's credibility and ensured its survival. In 1955, when poliomyelitis appeared in children who had received the recently approved Salk vaccine, the national inoculation program was stopped. The cases were traced to contaminated vaccine from a laboratory in California; the problem was corrected, and the inoculation program, at least for first and second graders, was resumed. The resistance of these 6 and 7 year olds to polio, compared with that of older children, proved the effectiveness of the vaccine. Two years later, surveillance was used again to trace the course of a massive influenza epidemic. From the data gathered in 1957 and subsequent years, the national guidelines for influenza vaccine were developed.

The CDC grew by acquisition. The venereal disease program came to Atlanta in 1957 and with it the first Public Health Advisors, non-science college graduates destined to play an important role in making the CDC's disease-control programs work. The tuberculosis program moved in 1960, immunization practices and the *Morbidity and Mortality Weekly Report* (*MMWR*) in 1961. The Foreign Quarantine Service, one of the oldest and most prestigious units of the PHS, came in 1967; many of its positions were soon switched to other uses as better ways of doing the work of quarantine, primarily through overseas surveillance, were developed. The long-established nutrition program also moved to the CDC, as well as the National Institute for Occupational Safety and Health (NIOSH), and work of already established units increased. Immunization tackled measles and rubella control; epidemiology added family planning and surveillance of chronic diseases. When the CDC joined the international malaria-eradication program and accepted responsibility for protecting the earth from moon germs and vice versa, the CDC's mission stretched overseas and into space.

The CDC played a key role in one of the greatest triumphs of public health: the eradication of smallpox. In 1962, it established a smallpox surveillance unit and a year later tested a newly developed jet gun and vaccine in the Pacific island nation of Tonga. After refining vaccination techniques in Brazil, the CDC began work in Central and West Africa in 1966. When millions of people there had been vaccinated, the CDC used surveillance to speed the work along. The World Health Organization used this "eradication escalation" technique elsewhere with such success that global eradication of smallpox was achieved by 1977. The United States spent only $32 million on the project, about the cost of keeping smallpox at bay for 2.5 months.

The CDC also achieved notable success at home tracking new and mysterious disease outbreaks. In the mid 1970s and early 1980s, it found the cause of Legionnaires' disease and toxic-shock syndrome. A fatal disease, subsequently named AIDS, was first mentioned in the June 5, 1981, issue of *MMWR*. Since then, *MMWR* has published numerous follow-up articles about AIDS, and one of the largest portions of the CDC's budget and staff is assigned to address this disease.

Although the CDC succeeded more often than it failed, it did not escape criticism. For example, television and press reports about the Tuskegee study on long-term effects of untreated syphilis in black men created a storm of protest in 1972. This study had been initiated by the

PHS and other organizations in 1932 and was transferred to the CDC in 1957. Although the effectiveness of penicillin as a therapy for syphilis had been established during the late 1940s, participants in this study remained untreated until the study was brought to public attention. The CDC also was criticized because of the 1976 effort to vaccinate the U.S. population against swine flu, the infamous killer of 1918–1919. When some vaccinees developed Guillain-Barre syndrome, the campaign was stopped immediately; the epidemic never occurred.

As the scope of the CDC's activities expanded far beyond communicable diseases, its name had to be changed. In 1970, it became the Center for Disease Control, and in 1981, after extensive reorganization, Center became Centers. The words "and Prevention" were added in 1992, but by law, the well-known three-letter acronym was retained. In health emergencies, the CDC means an answer to SOS calls from anywhere in the world, such as the recent one from Zaire where Ebola fever raged.

New Responsibilities Bring New Challenges[2]

The growing momentum toward expanding the CDC's responsibilities beyond infectious diseases gained strength during the 1980s. Tremendous advances in controlling infectious diseases had dramatically reduced illness and death from many long-standing health threats. In addition, the detrimental effects of chronic and other noncommunicable diseases on the nation's health were rapidly increasing. Programs to address cancer, heart disease, diabetes, and other leading killers became central to the CDC's focus. Nevertheless, for much of this decade, a newly emerging infectious disease would demand the skills and talents of persons across the agency. These new responsibilities led to additional funding, programs, staff, and partnerships for the growing agency, while introducing a host of new challenges.

Emergence of AIDS Brings Unprecedented Public Health Conflict

The formidable challenges presented by the CDC's broadening responsibilities underscored the importance of strictly adhering to science in presenting findings and developing policy. This lesson would prove even more critical as a new infectious disease began emerging in young, homosexual men in the United States, challenging the public health community in unforeseen ways and eventually changing world health. Fully entrenched by the time it was recognized in 1981, the disease, eventually given the name AIDS, reintroduced the public to fear of infectious diseases and divided the country across social, religious, and political lines.

Before AIDS, public fear of infectious diseases had largely subsided because of the availability and widespread use of vaccines and antibiotics. Many believed most infectious diseases were curable and no longer life threatening, affording a new level of health not enjoyed by previous generations. AIDS abruptly corrected this misperception, emerging as a new health threat with devastating consequences and a host of medical, ethical, legal, and economic implications.

Developing Evidence-Based Guidelines

Not only was the new condition baffling, the myriad of associated diseases, termed "opportunistic infections" because they were usually only seen in persons with drug-suppressed or otherwise severely compromised immune systems, were unfamiliar to most physicians and scientists; however, within 1 year of the first case reports, a case definition had been developed and all major routes of transmission had been identified. In March 1983, the CDC published the first set of guidelines for preventing the disease. Based on the best available science at the time, these recommendations proved essentially correct and have not been revised significantly.

In 1984, the cause of the disease was determined to be a previously unrecognized retrovirus, first termed human T-lymphotropic virus type III/lymphadenopathy-associated virus (HTLV-III/LAV) and later renamed human immunodeficiency virus (HIV). In March 1985, a test to detect antibodies to the virus was licensed by the FDA for use in screening donated blood and plasma. Although the test was not approved for individual testing, public health officials recognized that many at-risk persons would seek testing at blood banks to learn their infection status. By this time, sufficient funds had been authorized by Congress to enable the CDC to begin funding AIDS prevention activities in state and LHDs. Through cooperative agreements, the CDC awarded funds to 55 state and LHDs to establish alternate testing sites for at-risk persons to obtain antibody tests free of charge outside the blood-bank setting. Such sites were established both to decrease potential false-negative donations and to ensure that persons wishing to be tested would receive appropriate pre- and post-test counseling and referrals. The use of the antibody test for individual testing was approved by the FDA in 1986. The ability to test persons for the virus offered new opportunities for prevention and for treatment to possibly delay the onset of the disease. Unfortunately, this medical advancement also unleashed a new set of fears among an already stigmatized population, especially regarding increased discriminatory actions related to education, employment, health care, and insurance.

Scientifically, these early years of AIDS were characterized by unprecedented progress toward understanding a new, highly complex infectious disease. In 1985, the first AIDS conference was held, and the World Health Organization formed a network of AIDS collaborating centers. By the end of 1986, the CDC had published nearly 100 *MMWR* reports related to AIDS. These reports included recommendations to prevent transmission of the virus through transfusions, transplants, patient care, and perinatal exposure; workplace and school-based guidelines; and critical reports from state and LHDs outlining the epidemic's impact in their areas. The CDC's AIDS surveillance programs were among the most comprehensive disease-tracking measures ever undertaken. These programs yielded data that highlighted growing epidemics outside of major metropolitan areas and among minority populations, allowing for more targeted prevention measures and funding.

Fear Affects Public Policy

Despite solid scientific advances, no epidemic in history has engendered a greater level of controversy. Divisive views over the epidemic's earliest and most severely affected populations, homosexual/bisexual men and intravenous drug users, undoubtedly hindered progress on many fronts, including risk communication and funding for prevention and research. Some in Congress claimed that AIDS spending was exorbitant, disproportional to the magnitude of the problem, whereas others argued that inadequate funding was slowing research on testing, treatment, and vaccine development. The public also became involved in these disputes, disagreeing on transmission risks, populations that should be tested, and restrictions on infected persons. The media fueled their interests. In describing results from a 1985 poll of more than 2,000 persons, the New York Times reported that "51 percent of the respondents supported a quarantine of acquired immune deficiency syndrome patients, 48 percent would approve identity cards for those who have taken tests indicating the presence of AIDS antibodies, and 15 percent supported tattooing those with AIDS."

Although these arguments were vocalized as focusing on rights of the public versus rights of AIDS patients, in reality they were driven by fear. The medical and scientific community had difficulty communicating the risks associated with this new disease with the same level of certainty demanded by the public. Studies conducted among family members of AIDS patients had provided strong evidence of the lack of transmission from casual contact; however, many persons, including lawmakers, believed otherwise and were not readily dissuaded.

In particular, school attendance by children with AIDS was the subject of intense debate. The CDC's 1985 recommendations on education and foster care for children with HIV/AIDS stated that decisions regarding the type of education and care setting for infected children should be made on an individual basis but that "for most infected school-aged children, the benefits of an unrestricted setting would outweigh the risks of their acquiring potentially harmful infections in the setting and the apparent nonexistent risk of transmission of HTLV-III/LAV." Soon after the release of these guidelines in late August 1985, the *Washington Post* ran an op-ed piece entitled, "Worry about the Survival of Society First; Then AIDS Victims' Rights," which was picked up by newspapers across the country. Playing to the public's fear and skepticism, the editorial argued that many of the laws that had been enacted to protect AIDS patients from discrimination were misguided and cited the CDC's recent guidelines as remiss.

In many areas of the country, these recommendations were met with staunch opposition. In Florida, the parents of three HIV-infected hemophilic sons, Ricky, Robert, and Randy Ray, were plaintiffs in a federal lawsuit against their local school board to allow their children to attend public school. A week after the court's ruling in favor of the Rays, their home was burned. In Indiana, the experiences endured by a young man named Ryan White would ultimately change public opinion on AIDS throughout the world and lead to specifically designated federal resources for AIDS patients through the 1990 Ryan White Comprehensive AIDS Resources Emergency Act.

At the CDC, measures to expand surveillance and case reporting and to develop new prevention guidelines required dedicated consensus building that went beyond the medical and scientific community to include affected persons, special interest and political groups, and the public. Throughout these processes, the CDC worked to ensure that these new recommendations and guidelines reflected the best available science, a commitment that has served public health well. For example, the CDC's 1988 recommendations for preventing HIV transmission in healthcare settings recommended that blood and certain body fluids from every single patient be viewed as potentially infectious for HIV or other bloodborne pathogens. These guidelines became known as "universal blood and body fluid precautions" or "universal precautions" and led to permanent changes in healthcare practices throughout the world.

Strengthening State and Local Public Health Infrastructures

By the mid 1980s, both funding and political support were available to launch widespread public information campaigns, viewed as critical in stemming the epidemic and enabling those already infected to receive treatment and other services. The CDC's National AIDS Hotline was started in 1983 to enhance surveillance for the disease, but its role quickly expanded to address the urgent need for disseminating accurate and timely information. In 1987, the CDC established the National AIDS Clearinghouse to distribute printed materials on AIDS. The same year, the CDC launched America Responds to AIDS, a substantial, nationwide public information campaign that had been developed through extensive formative research. Over the next 4 years, five separate phases of informational materials were developed and released to the general public, ranging from basic information on the disease to specific information for different risk groups. The largest of these came in 1988, when more than 107 million copies of the brochure "Understanding AIDS" were delivered to homes and residential post office boxes in the United States. A Spanish version also was distributed in Puerto Rico and other predominantly Spanish-speaking areas. The brochure, developed by the CDC in consultation with Surgeon General C. Everett Koop, other health experts, and public citizens, marked the first time the federal government had attempted to contact every resident directly by mail regarding a public health problem. Koop's open stance against smoking had made him a well-recognized public health official, and his commitment to educating the public on HIV/AIDS made him a highly effective and credible spokesperson in this effort.

In addition to expanded funding for AIDS surveillance and prevention activities at state and LHDs, the CDC began funding national and regional minority organizations, community-based organizations, and the faith-based community for these activities in 1988 to 1989. This increased funding for extramural activities is reflected in the CDC's budget for those years, which nearly tripled from fiscal years 1983 to

1989 without a commensurate increase in full-time employees. The systems and services developed and implemented in response to the AIDS epidemic helped build and maintain public health infrastructures at multiple levels and would improve capabilities and serve as a model for other disease detection and prevention measures.

During 1981 to 1989, more than 100,000 cases of AIDS in the United States were reported to the CDC, approximately one third of them in 1989 alone. Although cases were reported from all 50 states, the District of Columbia, and four U.S. territories, two thirds of the cases were reported from five states: New York, New Jersey, Florida, Texas, and California. In addition, although the epidemic had spread beyond the earliest risk groups of homosexual/bisexual men and intravenous drug users, these groups continued to account for nearly 90% of cases.

Today, the epidemic's global impact is staggering, with nearly 40 million persons living with HIV throughout the world in 2006. The fear of the disease that so adversely affected the U.S. response during the early years of the epidemic has largely subsided in this country, dissolving much of the resistance to new policies and procedures and enabling better acceptance and delivery of new prevention and treatment strategies. A clear example of this change is reflected in the CDC's new HIV testing recommendations. Published in September 2006, these evidence-based recommendations call for nearly universal testing of patients in healthcare settings, a strategy that would not have been possible to put forward as recently as a decade ago.

In many of the world's most heavily affected regions, however, fear and lack of education about the disease continue to impede prevention measures and stigmatize infected persons. As new funding and partners are united globally to address the pandemic, primary prevention measures must first focus on ending the fear.

An Expanded Agency

Change, expansion, and growing domestic and international visibility characterized the CDC's recent decades. Exacting science and honest risk communication proved to be the agency's most effective prevention tools. Lessons learned from past successes and challenges will serve the CDC well as its roles and responsibilities toward protecting the nation's health continue to expand.

Sixty years ago the CDC's agenda was noncontroversial (hardly anyone objected to the pursuit of germs), and Atlanta was a backwater. Today, the CDC's programs are often tied to economic, political, and social issues, and Atlanta is as near Washington as the tap of a keyboard.

REFERENCES

1. Reprinted in part and adapted from Centers for Disease Control and Prevention. History of CDC. *MMWR*. 1996:45:426–430.
2. Reprinted in part and adapted from Mason JO. CDC's 60th anniversary: director's perspective. *MMWR*. 2006;55:1354–1359.

Public Health Spotlight on Occupational and Environmental Health and Safety

PUBLIC HEALTH ACHIEVEMENTS IN 20TH CENTURY AMERICA[1]

At the beginning of this century, workers in the United States faced remarkably high health and safety risks on the job. Through efforts by individual workers, unions, employers, government agencies, scientists, and others, considerable progress has been made in improving these conditions. Despite these successes, much work remains, with the goal for all workers being a productive and safe working life and a retirement free from long-term consequences of occupational disease and injury. Using the limited data available, this report documents large declines in fatal occupational injuries during the 1900s, highlights the mining industry as an example of improvements in worker safety, and discusses new challenges in occupational safety and health.

Decreases in Fatal Occupational Injuries

Data from multiple sources reflect the large decreases in work-related deaths from the high rates and numbers of deaths among workers during the early 20th century. The earliest systematic survey of workplace fatalities in the United States in this century covered Allegheny County, Pennsylvania from July 1906 through June 1907; that year in the one county, 526 workers died in "work accidents"—195 of these were steelworkers.[2] In contrast, in 1997, 17 steelworker fatalities occurred nationwide.[3] The National Safety Council estimated that in 1912, 18,000 to 21,000 workers died from work-related injuries.[4] In 1913, the Bureau of Labor Statistics documented approximately 23,000 industrial deaths among a workforce of 38 million, equivalent to a rate of 61 deaths per 100,000 workers.[5] Under a different reporting system, data from the National Safety Council from 1933 through 1997 indicate that deaths from unintentional work-related injuries declined 90%, from 37 per 100,000 workers to 4 per 100,000.[4] The corresponding annual number of deaths decreased from 14,500 to 5,100; during this same period, the workforce more than tripled, from 39 million to approximately 130 million.[4]

More recent and probably more complete data from death certificates were compiled from the CDC's NIOSH National Traumatic Occupational Fatalities surveillance system.[6] These data indicate that the annual number of deaths declined 28%, from 7,405 in 1980 to 5,314 in 1995 (the most recent year for which complete National Traumatic Occupational Fatalities data are available). The average rate of deaths from occupational injuries decreased 43% during the same time, from 7.5 to 4.3 per 100,000 workers. Industries with the highest average rates for fatal occupational injury during 1980 to 1995 included mining (30.3 deaths per 100,000 workers), agriculture/forestry/fishing (20.1), construction (15.2), and transportation/communications/public utilities (13.4) (Figure 4-14). Leading causes of fatal occupational injury during the period include motor vehicle-related injuries, workplace homicides, and machine-related injuries (Figure 4-15).

Factors Contributing to Worker Safety

The decline in occupational fatalities in mining and other industries reflects the progress made in all workplaces since the beginning of the century in identifying and correcting the etiologic factors that contribute to occupational health risks. If today's workforce of approximately 130 million had the same risk as workers in 1933 for dying from injuries, then an additional 40,000 workers would have died in 1997 from preventable events. The declines can be attributed to multiple, interrelated factors, including efforts by labor and management to improve worker safety and by academic researchers such as Dr. Alice Hamilton. Other efforts to improve safety were developed by state labor and health authorities and through the research, education, and regulatory activities undertaken by government agencies (e.g., U.S. Bureau of Mines, the Mine Safety and Health Administration [established as the Mining Enforcement and Safety Administration in 1973], the Occupational Safety and Health Administration [OSHA] [established in 1970], and NIOSH). Efforts

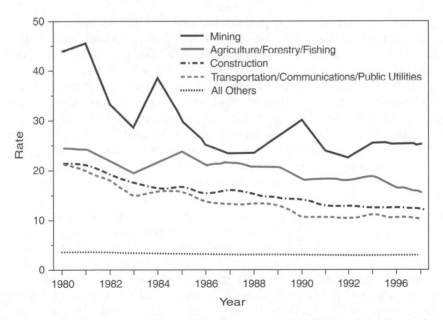

Figure 4-14 Occupational injury death rates (per 100,000 workers), by industry division and year, United States, 1980–1995. *Source:* From Achievements in public health, United States, 1900–1999: improvements in workplace safety. *MMWR.* 1999;48(22):461–469.

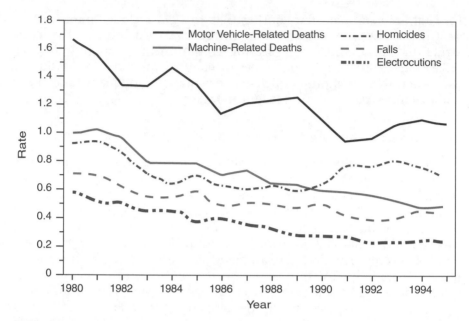

Figure 4-15   Rates (per 100,000 workers) for leading causes of occupation injury deaths, by cause and year, United States, 1980–1995. *Source:* From Achievements in public health, United States, 1900–1999: improvements in workplace safety. *MMWR.* 1999;48(22):461–469.

by these groups led to physical changes in the workplace, such as improved ventilation and dust suppression in mines, safer equipment, development and introduction of safer work practices, and improved training of health and safety professionals and of workers. The reduction in workplace deaths has occurred in the context of extensive changes in U.S. economic activity, the U.S. industrial mix, and workforce demographics.[7] Society-wide progress in injury control also contributes to safer workplaces—for example, the use of safety belts and other safety features in motor vehicles and improvements in medical care for trauma victims.[7]

Only in some instances do data permit association of declines in fatalities with specific interventions. Before 1920, using permissible explosives and electrical equipment (which can be operated in an explosive methane-rich environment without igniting the methane), applying a layer of rock dust over the coal dust (which creates an inert mixture and prevents ignition of coal dust), and improving ventilation, such as reversible fans, led to dramatic reductions in fatalities from explosions[8] (Figure 4-16). New technologies in roof support and improved mine design reduced the number of deaths from roof falls; however, technology also introduced new hazards, such as fatalities associated with machinery. An approximately 50% decrease in coal mining fatality rates occurred from 1966 to 1970 to 1971 to 1975 (Figure 4-17); 1971 to 1975 is the period immediately following passage of the 1969 Federal Coal Mine Health and Safety Act, which greatly expanded enforcement powers of

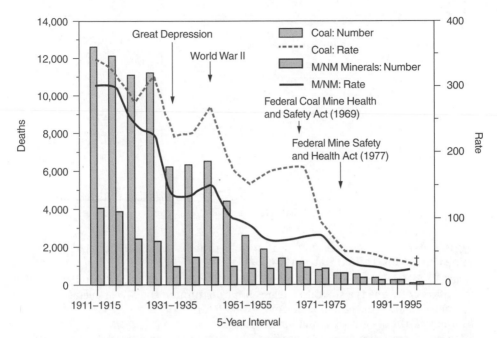

Figure 4-16 Number of deaths and fatality rates (per 100,000 workers) in mining coal and metal/nonmetallic (N/NM) minerals, by 5-year interval, United States, 1911–1997. *Source:* From Achievements in public health, United States, 1900–1999: improvements in workplace safety. *MMWR.* 1999;48(22):461–469.

federal inspectors and established mandatory health and safety standards for all mines. The act also served as the model for the 1970 Occupational Safety and Health Act. Following the 1977 Federal Mine Safety and Health Act, a 33% decrease in fatalities occurred in metal and nonmetallic minerals mining (1976 to 1980 compared with 1981 to 1985).

Similarly, the impact of more recent targeted efforts to reduce workplace fatalities can be illustrated by data on work-related electrocutions. During the 1980s, there were concerted research and dissemination efforts by NIOSH, changes to the National Electrical Code and occupational safety and health regulations, and public awareness campaigns by power companies and others. During this decade, work-related electrocution rates declined 54%, from 0.7 per 100,000 workers per year in 1980 to 0.3 in 1989; the number of electrocutions decreased from 577 to 329.[7]

Although the decline in injuries in general industry since 1970 seems to have resulted from a variety of factors, some sources point to the Occupational Safety and Health Act of 1970, which created NIOSH and OSHA.[7,9] Since 1971, NIOSH has investigated hazardous work conditions, conducted research to prevent injury, trained health professionals, and developed educational materials and recommendations for worker protection. OSHA's regulatory authority for worksite inspection and development of safety standards has brought about safety regulations, mandatory workplace safety controls, and worker training. Dur-

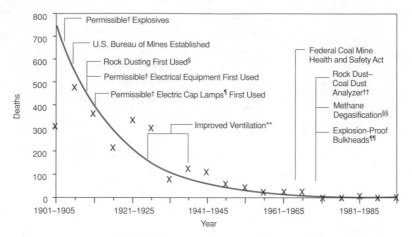

Figure 4-17 Five-year averages of annual number of deaths related to coal mine explosions, United States, 1901–1995.

Notes: Each X represents the 5-year average of the number of deaths resulting from explosions; the line is a smoothed regression line through the 5-year averages.
† Explosives and equipment that can be used in an explosive methane-rich environment without causing a methane explosion.
§ The process of applying a layer of rock dust over the coal dust, which creates an inert mixture and inhibits a coal dust explosion.
¶ Lamps worn on miners' caps.
** Ventilation improvements, including the use of reversible fans, reduce the concentration of methane and remove the explosive gas from the mine.
†† A hand-held monitor that provides instantaneous readings of the rock-to-coal dust mixture to ensure that it is inert.
§§ Techniques to remove methane from the coal bed before mining the coal.
¶¶ Explosion-proof walls used to seal abandoned (mined-out) areas to protect workers in active parts of the mine.
Source: From Achievements in public health, United States, 1900–1999: improvements in workplace safety. *MMWR.* 1999;48(22):461–469.

ing 1980 to 1996, research findings indicated that training creates safer workplaces through increased worker knowledge of job hazards and safe work practices in a wide array of worksites.[10]

21ST CENTURY PUBLIC HEALTH CHALLENGES

Despite the accomplishments described in this report, workers continue to die from preventable injuries sustained on the job. Ongoing efforts to address important workplace hazards include conducting field investigations of fatalities in high-risk occupations and industries, such as the Fire Fighter Fatality Investigation and Prevention Program, establishing a research center to facilitate childhood agricultural injury prevention (National Children's Center for Rural and Agricultural Health and Safety), and developing educational materials for worker protection, such as *Preventing Homicide in the Workplace*.[11] Despite major gains in workplace safety, mining remains the most dangerous industry, and mining safety research remains a national priority.

The National Occupational Research Agenda (NORA), developed by NIOSH and approximately 500 organizations and persons nationwide, identified traumatic injuries as one of its public health priorities. NORA was developed in recognition of the rapidly changing nature of the workplace and workforce and provides the framework for research to improve worker safety in the 21st century. The NORA Traumatic Injuries Team sponsored the first National Occupational Injury Symposium in 1997 and outlined priority needs.[12] These include the need to identify new sources of surveillance data, to improve identification of work-related injuries and illnesses in existing databases, to link data from existing sources for improved information about injuries, and to assess injury exposures and intervention outcomes better. Increased attention to other NORA priority areas, such as intervention effectiveness research, surveillance research methods, and organization of work, should guide continued national efforts to reduce both occupational illnesses and injuries in the next century.

The Task Force on Community Preventive Services selected worksite health promotion as a topic for systematic review, to highlight the importance of the worksite in promoting health.[13] The use of selected worksite policies and programs can reduce health risks and improve the quality of life of the 160 million full- and part-time workers in the United States. The systematic reviews on various aspects of worksite health promotion are intended to give employers and organizations an evidence base to determine which available approaches are effective in promoting healthy lifestyles, preventing disease, and increasing the number of people who receive appropriate preventive counseling and screening. These reviews offer recommendations on worksite-specific policies and activities that can help employers choose those health promotion program components proven effective in changing the behavior and improving the health of employees.

Included in the worksite health promotion reviews were interventions that can be offered at the worksite (e.g., onsite health education classes or posting signs to encourage stair use), made available to employees at work or at other locations (e.g., reducing out-of-pocket costs for gym memberships or flu shots), or incorporated into employees' benefits plans (e.g., vouchers for nicotine patches or to participate in exercise classes). The Task Force on Community Preventive Services found insufficient evidence to determine the effectiveness of assessments of health risks with feedback when implemented alone in achieving improvements in one or more health behaviors and conditions among participating workers. Evidence was considered insufficient largely because of inconsistent effects and concerns about the lack of controlled studies.

The task force, however, does recommend the use of assessments of health risks with feedback when combined with health education programs, with or without additional interventions, on the basis of strong evidence of effectiveness in improving one or more health behaviors or conditions in populations of workers. Additionally, the task force recommends the use of assessments of health risks with feedback when combined with health education programs to improve the following outcomes among participants:

- Tobacco use (strong evidence of effectiveness)
- Excessive alcohol use (sufficient evidence of effectiveness)
- Seat belt use (sufficient evidence of effectiveness)
- Dietary fat intake (strong evidence of effectiveness)
- Blood pressure (strong evidence of effectiveness)
- Cholesterol (strong evidence of effectiveness)
- Number of days lost from work because of illness or disability (strong evidence of effectiveness)
- Healthcare services use (sufficient evidence of effectiveness)
- Summary health risk estimates (sufficient evidence of effectiveness)

The task force found insufficient evidence for several other assessments of health risks when combined with health education programs, including body composition, consumption of fruits and vegetables, and fitness.

For the Healthy People 2010 process, workplace health and safety was not afforded leading health indicator status, although several environmental quality indicators were identified as leading health indicators. Figure 4-18 summarizes the extent to which targets established for these indicators for the year 2010 were achieved. An estimated 25% of

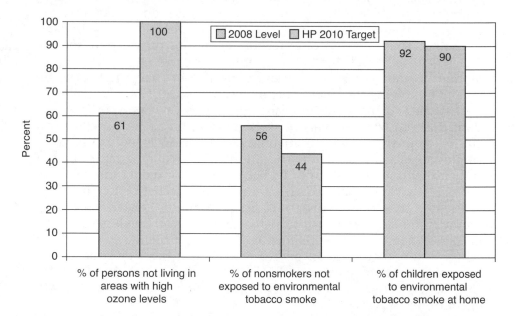

Figure 4-18 Scorecard for selected Healthy People 2010 leading indicators related to environmental exposures comparing 2008 levels with 2010 targets. *Source:* Data from Data 2010, Healthy People 2010 database. http://wonder .cdc.gov/data2010/ftpselec.htm. Accessed May 31, 2010.

preventable illnesses worldwide can be attributed to poor environmental quality. In the United States, air pollution alone is estimated to be associated with 50,000 premature deaths and an estimated $40 billion to $50 billion in health-related costs annually. Two sentinel indicators of air quality are ozone (outdoor) and environmental tobacco smoke (indoor).

In 1997, approximately 43% of the U.S. population lived in areas designated as nonattainment areas for established health-based standards for ozone. During the years 1988 to 1994, 65% of nonsmokers were exposed to environmental tobacco smoke. The nation has already surpassed its target for environmental tobacco smoke exposure but is moving slowly on improving other markers of environmental quality.

REFERENCES

1. Reprinted in part and adapted from Centers for Disease Control and Prevention. Achievements in public health, United States, 1900–1999: improvements in workplace safety. *MMWR*. 1999;48:461–469.

2. Eastman C. *Work-Accidents and the Law*. New York, NY: Russell Sage Foundation, Charities Publications Committee; 1910.

3. Bureau of Labor Statistics, U.S. Department of Labor. Fatal occupational injuries by industry and event or exposure. Table A-1, 1997 Census of Fatal Occupational Injuries. Washington, DC: BLS; 1998.

4. National Safety Council. *Accident Facts, 1998 Edition*. Itasca, IL: National Safety Council; 1998.

5. Corn JK. *Response to Occupational Health Hazards: A Historical Perspective*. New York, NY: Nostrand Reinhold; 1992.

6. Centers for Disease Control and Prevention. Fatal occupational injuries: United States, 1980–1994. *MMWR*. 1998;47:297–302.

7. Stout NA, Jenkins EL, Pizatella TJ. Occupational injury mortality rates in the United States: changes from 1980 to 1989. *Am J Public Health*. 1996;86:73–77.

8. Skow ML, Kim AG, Duel M. Creating a safer environment in U.S. coal mines: the Bureau of Mines methane control program, 1964–79. Washington, DC: U.S. Department of the Interior, Bureau of Mines; May 1981 (report no. 5-81).

9. Bonnie RJ, Fulco CE, Liverman CT, eds. *Reducing the Burden of Injury: Advancing Prevention and Treatment*. Washington, DC: Institute of Medicine, National Academy Press; 1999.

10. National Institute for Occupational Safety and Health. *Assessing Occupational Safety and Health Training: A Literature Review*. Cincinnati, OH: U.S. Department of Health and Human Services, Centers for Disease Control, 1998; DHHS publication no. (NIOSH) 98-145.

11. National Institute for Occupational Safety and Health. *Preventing Homicide in the Workplace*. Cincinnati, OH: U.S. Department of Health and Human Services, Centers for Disease Control; 1993; DHHS publication no. (NIOSH) 93-109.

12. National Institute for Occupational Safety and Health. *Traumatic Occupational Injury Research Needs and Priorities*. Cincinnati, OH: U.S. Department of Health and Human Services, Centers for Disease Control; 1998; DHHS publication no. (NIOSH) 98-134.

13. Task Force on Community Preventive Services. *The Community Guide*. http://www.the communityguide.org. Accessed May 31, 2010.

Core Functions and Public Health Practice

The Institute of Medicine's (IOM) landmark report in 1988[1] initiated important changes in the U.S. public health system. The report rearticulated the mission, substance, and core functions of public health and challenged the public health community to think more strategically, plan more collectively, and perform more effectively. Exciting opportunities afforded by broader participation in community-wide health planning, heightened public expectations for emergency preparedness and response roles, and better integration of public health and medical care activities have energized these efforts, accompanied by new hope for achieving improved health outcomes through the public health system.

These developments have clearly brought change to the public health system and public health practice over the past two decades. It is less clear, however, whether these developments have improved public health practice and, more importantly, the results of the public health system—health outcomes. This chapter examines the link between public health's functions and public health practice, including different understandings as to what constituted public health functions at various points in time over the past century. It also traces efforts to measure the performance of these functions. These tracings help us to understand how well public health addresses its main functions and which of its aspects need improvement. Key questions to be addressed in this chapter are as follows:

- What have been public health's main functions over the past century?
- What are the core functions of public health today?
- How are these functions translated into practice?
- How well are these functions being carried out by the public health system?
- How can public health practice performance be improved?

Continuous quality management concepts argue that results reflect the systems that produce them. In other words, every system is perfectly designed to achieve the exact results it gets. This somewhat elliptical wisdom identifies a major challenge confronting efforts to enhance the results of public health practice: Improving health outcomes calls for improving the basic processes of public health practice; however, as some additional reasoning from the continuous quality management movement warns, to improve something, we must be able to control it; to control it, we must be able to understand it; and to understand it, we must be able to measure it. Measurement relies on operational definitions for the concepts under study. Improving the performance of public health functions calls for an agenda that defines, measures, understands, and controls the processes that constitute public health practice.

For nearly 100 years, the public health community has been grappling with this agenda, with only limited success along the way.[2] Throughout much of the 20th century, an adequate conceptual framework for defining the public health system was lacking. As a result, past efforts generally focused on measuring aspects of the public health system that only indirectly or partially characterized the functions carried out in public health practice. This limited opportunities for understanding, controlling, and improving public health practice and health outcomes. Nonetheless, these efforts set the stage for developments since the 1988 IOM report and for opportunities that lie ahead.

PUBLIC HEALTH FUNCTIONS AND PRACTICE BEFORE 1990

Over much of the past century, the mission and purpose of public health (what it is) and its functions (how it addresses its mission) were viewed as synonymous with the provision of public health services. In fact, public health's services were frequently characterized as its functions. Public health was known more by its deeds than its intent. As a result, early efforts to describe and measure public health practice focused primarily on measuring aspects of important public health services.

The earliest attempts to define and measure public health practice in the United States date back to 1914. Before that time, public health functions were primarily those identified in the broad statutes of state and local governments, centering on the prevention and control of infectious diseases. In 1914, however, a survey catalogued the various services of state health agencies, as well as their role in fostering the development of local health departments (LHDs). This study concluded that even though public health agencies were carrying out a wide variety of programs and services, they were missing their mark. Much of what was being done through public health agencies had little effect on community health status, and there was actually much that these agencies could have been doing that would have reduced mortality and morbidity.[3] Public health practice was evaluated using a scoring system that placed greater weight on some public health activities and services than on others, allowing a basis for comparisons across agencies. Key elements of this approach were soon incorporated into local public health assessment initiatives orchestrated by the American Public Health Association (APHA).

In 1921, the first report of APHA's Committee on Municipal Health Department Practice called for the systematic collection and analysis of information on local public health practice to support the development of standards for LHDs serving the nation's largest municipalities. The committee had determined that LHDs and the communities they served would benefit from standards that would ensure a consistent level of public health services from jurisdiction-to-jurisdiction. The committee also sought to identify characteristics of LHD practice that produce the best results. An elaborate survey instrument and process were established; more than 80 big-city health departments were reviewed in the initial effort.

The need to examine public health practice outside the nation's large cities, especially in the growing number of county-based LHDs, was soon apparent. In 1925, the committee was reconstituted as the Committee on Administrative Practice to assess more broadly the status of public health practice in the United States. The new committee developed the first version of an "Appraisal Form" to be used as a self-assessment tool by local health officers. The intent was to measure the immediate results attained from local public health services. Examples of these immediate results follow:

- Birth and death records adequately catalogued and analyzed
- Various vaccinations provided for specific age groups
- Health problems in school-aged children identified and treated
- Tuberculosis cases hospitalized and treated
- Laboratory tests performed[4]

Successive iterations of the Appraisal Form appeared through the 1920s and 1930s; these were well received by the public health community, although there were occasional concerns that quantity was being emphasized over quality. Local health officers were able to compare their ratings with those of other public health agencies. The basis for comparison was a numerical rating score, based on aggregated points awarded across key administrative and service areas. Comparative ratings were used to improve health programs, advocate for resources, summarize health agency activities in annual reports, and engage other health interests in the community. Agency ratings often attracted considerable public interest, resulting in both good and bad publicity for local agencies. Despite the initial intent to emphasize immediate results, however, the major focus of the ratings remained on measuring the more concrete aspects of public health practice, such as staff, clinic sites, patient visits, and the number of services rendered.

In 1943, a new instrument, the "Evaluation Schedule," which was scored centrally by the APHA Committee on Administrative Practice, replaced the self-assessment approach used in the Appraisal Form. The scores for health agencies of varying size and type were widely disseminated so that individual LHDs could directly compare their performance in meeting community needs with that of their peers. Table 5-1 illustrates some of the key performance measures included in the 1947 version of the Evaluation Schedule.

Table 5-1   Public Health Practice Performance Measures from 1947 Evaluation Schedule

1. Hospital beds: percentage in approved hospitals
2. Practicing physicians: population per physician
3. Practicing dentists: population per dentist
4. Water: percentage of population in communities over 2,500 served with approved water
5. Sewerage: percentage of population in communities over 2,500 served with approved sewerage systems
6. Water: percentage of rural school children served with approved water supplies
7. Excreta disposal: percentage of rural school children served with approved means of excreta disposal
8. Food: percentage of food handlers reached by group instruction program
9. Food: percentage of restaurants and lunch counters with satisfactory facilities
10. Milk: percentage of bottled milk pasteurized
11. Diphtheria: percentage of children under 2 years given immunizing agent
12. Smallpox: percentage of children under 2 years given immunizing agent
13. Whooping cough: percentage of children under 2 years given immunizing agent
14. Tuberculosis: newly reported cases per death, 5-year period
15. Tuberculosis: deaths per 100,000 population, 5-year period
16. Tuberculosis: percentage of cases reported by death certificate
17. Syphilis: percentage of cases reported in primary, secondary, and early latent stage
18. Syphilis: percentage of reported contacts examined
19. Maternal: puerperal deaths per 1,000 total births, 5-year rate
20. Maternal: percentage of antepartum cases under medical supervision seen before the sixth month
21. Maternal: percentage of women delivered at home under postpartum nursing supervision
22. Maternal: percentage of births in hospital
23. Infant: deaths under 1 year of age per 1,000 live births, 5-year rate
24. Infant: deaths from diarrhea and enteritis under 1 year per 1,000 live births, 2-year rate
25. Infant: percentage of infants under nursing supervision before 1 month
26. School: percentage of elementary children with dental work neglected
27. Accidents: deaths from motor accidents per 100,000 population, 5-year rate
28. Health department budget: cents per capita spent by health department

Source: Data from American Public Health Association, Committee on Administrative Practice. *Evaluation Schedule for Use in Study and Appraisal of Community Health Programs.* New York, NY; APHA; 1947.

To develop a blueprint for a national network of LHDs that would provide every American with coverage, the Committee on Administrative Practice established a Subcommittee on Local Health Units. The subcommittee's major report (widely known as the Emerson Report) in 1945 was a landmark for recommendations regarding local public health practice. The Emerson Report became the postwar plan for public health in the United States. The report's far-reaching recommendations called for a minimum population base of 50,000 people for each LHD and included state-by-state proposals for networks of LHDs that would cover all Americans while reducing the number of LHDs by about 50% through consolidation of smaller units.[5]

The Emerson Report gave increased prominence to six basic services believed to represent local government's public health responsibilities to its citizens: vital statistics, environmental sanitation, communicable disease control, maternal and child health services, public health education, and public health laboratory services.[5] This was not a new formulation for local public health services. Rather, it was essentially the same package of services that had been considered the standard of practice among LHDs for several decades and that had been assessed since the early years of the Appraisal Form. Over time, these services had become widely known as the six basic functions of public health ("Basic Six"); Table 5-2 describes the Basic Six. With the added impetus of the Emerson Report, they became the cornerstone for structuring local public health practice. Although the report's extensive recommendations never became national public policy, they promoted positive changes in many states.

The Committee on Administrative Practice stimulated considerable interest in local public health practice. After about 1950 and continuing into the 1980s, there were repeated efforts to reexamine and redefine the boundaries of local public health practice. This search for mission redefinition is evident in a series of APHA policy statements from 1950 to 1970.[6] In a 1950 APHA statement on LHD services and responsibilities, the Basic Six were presented as desirable minimal services, and several new "optimal" responsibilities were identified: recording and analysis of health data, health education and information, supervision and regulation, provision of direct environmental health

Table 5-2   Basic Six Services of Local Public Health

1. Vital statistics—collection and interpretation
2. Sanitation
3. Communicable disease control, including immunization, quarantine, and other measures, such as identifying communicable disease carriers and distributing vaccines to physicians, as well as doing immunizations directly
4. Maternal and child health, consisting of prenatal and postpartum care for mothers and babies and supervision of the health of school children; in some places, immunization of children was handled by the maternal and child health program
5. Health education, including instruction in personal and family hygiene, sanitation, and nutrition, given in schools, at neighborhood health center classes, and in home visits
6. Laboratory services to physicians, sanitarians, and other interested parties

Source: Data from Shonick W. *Government and Health Services: Government's Role in the Development of U.S. Health Services 1930–1980.* New York: Oxford University Press; 1995.

services, administration of personal health services, and coordination of activities and services within the community. Another APHA policy statement in 1963 added the seventh and eighth services to the Basic Six: operation of health facilities and area-wide planning and coordination. Then, in 1970, APHA adopted yet another policy statement, expanding on these concepts and calling for increased involvement of state and LHDs in coordinating, monitoring, and assessing the adequacy of health services in their jurisdictions. The evolution of these various characterizations of public health practice is traced in Table 5-3.

After World War II, important new expectations for local public health practice emerged. A lack of medical care was increasingly identified as a significant impediment to promoting and improving community health. This resulted in LHDs increasingly serving a safety-net function. This expanded direct service provision role moved LHDs into new territory, beyond the boundaries of the expanded Basic Six model. There was considerable debate as to whether this new role was appropriate, as well as whether LHDs were serving leadership roles within their communities in integrating medical and community health services. The movement into medical care was controversial from its inception. Hanlon, in examining the future of LHDs in 1973, called for official public health agencies to withdraw from the business of providing personal health services (whether preventive or therapeutic) and

Table 5-3   Expansion of the Basic Six Public Health Services, 1920–1980

Initial "Basic Six"
- Vital statistics
- Sanitation
- Communicable disease control
- Maternal and child health
- Health education
- Laboratory services

"Optimal" Services in 1950s
- Basic Six as minimal level
- Analysis and recording of health data
- Health education and information
- Supervision and regulation
- Provision of direct environmental health services
- Administration of personal health services
- Coordination of activities and services within the community

Added in 1960s
- Operation of health facilities
- Area-wide planning and coordination

Added in the 1970s
- Coordinating, monitoring, and assessing the adequacy of health services

Source: Data from Shonick W. *Government and Health Services: Government's Role in the Development of U.S. Health Services 1930–1980.* New York: Oxford University Press; 1995.

instead to "concentrate upon [their] important and unique potential as community health conscience and leader"[7(p901)] in promoting the establishment of sound social policy. Despite these admonitions, direct medical care services increased among LHDs throughout the 1960s, 1970s, and 1980s, largely as a result of new federal and state grant programs. LHDs were becoming significant providers of safety-net medical services, joining public hospitals and community health centers in this important role.

Steadily evolving through these developments was a unique concept that began to shift the emphasis from the services of public health to its mission and functions. This concept, often characterized as "a governmental presence at the local level" (AGPALL),[8] emerged in the 1970s in the process of fashioning "model standards" for communities to participate in achievement of the 1990 national health objectives (Table 5-4). AGPALL means that local government, acting through various means, is ultimately responsible and accountable for ensuring that minimum standards are met in the community. Every locality is served by a unit of government that has responsibility for the health of that locality and population. This responsibility can be executed through an organization other than the official public health agency, but government, through its presence and interest in health, is responsible to see that necessary, agreed-on services are available, accessible, acceptable, and of good quality.

The AGPALL concept emphasizes the leadership and change-agent aspects of community public health practice; however, exercising leadership to serve the community's health is neither simple nor straightforward. The complexities of health problems and their contributing factors call for collaborative, rather than command-and-control solutions. Key to identifying and solving

Table 5-4 Governmental Presence at the Local Level

This concept is based on a multifaceted, multitiered governmental responsibility for ensuring that standards are met—a responsibility that often involves agencies in addition to the public health agency at any particular level. Regardless of the structure, every community must be served by a governmental entity charged with that responsibility, and general-purpose government must assign and coordinate responsibility for providing and assuring public health and safety services. Where services in any area covered by standards are readily available, government may also (but need not) be involved in the responsibility of government to have, or to develop, the capacity to deliver such services. Where county and municipal responsibilities overlap, agreements on division of responsibility are necessary.

In summary, government at the local level has the responsibility for ensuring that a health problem is monitored and that services to correct that problem are available. The state government must monitor the effectiveness of local efforts to control health problems and act as a residual guarantor of services where community resources are inadequate—recognizing, of course, that state resources are also limited.

Source: From Preamble to Original Model Standards. U.S. Conference of City Health Officials, National Association of County Health Officials, Association of State and Territorial Health Officials, American Public Health Association, and U.S. Department of Health, Education and Welfare, Public Health Service, Centers for Disease Control and Prevention. Model Standards for Community Preventive Health Services. Public Health Service: Atlanta, GA; 1978.

important community health problems is the ability to deal with diverse interests and build constituencies. The AGPALL concept suggests that public health practice involves more than the provision of services. This broader view of public health's functions was powerfully reinforced by the IOM report.

PUBLIC HEALTH PRACTICE AND CORE FUNCTIONS AFTER 1990

The picture of the state of the public health system painted in the 1988 IOM report[1] was more dismal than many had expected. After all, the infrastructure of the national public health system had grown substantially throughout the century, especially in terms of LHD coverage of the population. There was widespread acceptance that appropriate community services should include chronic disease prevention and medical care, in addition to the Basic Six. Also, notably, health status had never been better. Nevertheless, the human immunodeficiency virus (HIV)/acquired immune deficiency syndrome (AIDS) epidemic had emerged, and there was no shortage of intractable health and social issues now being placed on the public health agenda. Resources to meet these challenges were greatly limited, in part because of the insatiable appetite of the medical care delivery system for every available health dollar. These forces acted together to dissipate public appreciation and support for public health, and the IOM feared that public health would not be able to meet these challenges without a new vision that would engender the support of the public, policy makers, the media, the medical establishment, and other key stakeholders.

The vision articulated in the IOM report was founded in a broader view of public health functions than had existed in the past. Throughout earlier decades, the services provided by public health agencies had come to be viewed by many as public health's "functions." In characterizing three core functions, the IOM report suggested that the function "to serve"—whether described in terms of specific services or as the more abstract concept of "assurance"—inadequately characterizes the unique role of public health in our society. Public health interventions represent the products of carrying out public health's core functions, rather than the functions themselves. The IOM examination described three public health core functions: assessment, policy development, and assurance.[1]

> Assessment calls for public health to regularly and systematically collect, assemble, analyze, and make available information on the health of the community, including statistics on health status, community health needs, and epidemiologic and other studies of health problems. Not every agency is large enough to conduct these activities directly; intergovernmental and interagency cooperation is essential. Nevertheless, each agency bears the responsibility for seeing that the assessment function is fulfilled. This basic function of public health cannot be delegated.[1(p7)]

> Policy development calls for public health to serve the public interest in the development of comprehensive public health policies by promoting the use of the scientific knowledge base in decision making about public health and by leading in developing public health pol-

icy. Agencies must take a strategic approach, developed on the basis of a positive appreciation for the democratic political process.[1(p8)]

Assurance calls for public health to assure their constituents that services necessary to achieve agreed-on goals are provided, either by encouraging actions by other entities (private or public), by requiring such action through regulation or by providing services directly. Each public health agency is to involve key policy makers and the general public in determining a set of high-priority personal and community-wide health services that government will guarantee to every member of the community. This guarantee should include subsidization or direct provision of high-priority personal health services for those unable to afford them.[1(p8)]

The core function framework resonated was widely accepted within the public health community;[9] its broader characterization of the important functions of public health led to the definition and measurement of their operational aspects, permitting assessment of their performance. Several key aspects of the assessment, policy development, and assurance functions are processes that identify and address health problems; others are processes (e.g., services and other interventions) generated to ensure that these problems are addressed. To explicate the core functions and provide a framework for characterizing modern public health practice, a work group representing the national public health organizations developed the essential public health services framework.[10] Since 1995, virtually all national and state public health initiatives have used the essential public health services framework in efforts to characterize, measure, and improve the performance of public health practice. Unfortunately, the use of the term services in the essential public health services framework can be a source of confusion. Although they are not services in the same sense that most people view clinical services (e.g., immunizations) or community preventive services (e.g., fluoridated water), the essential public health services are important processes that operationalize the core functions—assessment, policy development, and assurance—into measurable elements of public health practice.

Public health functions involve identifying health problems and their causative factors, developing strategies to address these problems, and seeing that these strategies are implemented in a way that achieves the desired goals. In this light, public health practice is the development and application of preventive strategies and interventions to promote and protect the health of the public. Whereas the complete description for public health practice is yet to be agreed on, the best depiction of what contemporary public health practice is all about can be found in the mission, vision, and functions outlined in the *Public Health in America* statement.[11] This one-page document includes a vision (healthy people in healthy communities), a mission (promoting physical and mental health and preventing disease, injury, and disability), and statements of what public health practice does and how it accomplishes these ends. As presented in Table 5-5, these statements establish high standards for public health practice as well as a framework for measuring the attainment of those standards. The processes embodied in the essential public health services and their links to the three core functions are critical to an understanding of public health practice.

Table 5-5   Relationship of Public Health in America Statement to Public Health Practice

Public Health in America Elements*	Relationship to Public Health Practice
Healthy people in healthy communities	Vision and mission statements for public health practice
Promote physical and mental health, and prevent disease, injury, and disability	
Public Health • Prevents epidemics and the spread of disease • Protects against environmental hazards • Prevents injuries • Promotes and encourages healthy behaviors • Responds to disasters and assists communities in recovery • Assures the quality and accessibility of health services	*Statements of the broad categories of outcomes affected by public health practice, sometimes viewed as what public health does*
Essential Public Health Services 1. Monitor health status to identify community health problems 2. Diagnose and investigate health problems and health hazards in the community 3. Inform, educate, and empower people about health issues 4. Mobilize community partnerships to identify and solve health problems 5. Develop policies and plans that support individual and community health efforts 6. Enforce laws and regulations that protect health and ensure safety 7. Link people with needed personal health services and assure the provision of health care when otherwise unavailable 8. Assure a competent public health and personal healthcare workforce 9. Evaluate effectiveness, accessibility, and quality of personal and population-based health services 10. Research for new insights and innovative solutions to health problems	*Statements of the processes of public health practice that affect public health outcomes, sometimes viewed as how public health does what it does*

Source: *From *Public Health in America,* Public Health Functions Steering Committee, U.S. Public Health Service: Washington, DC; 1994.

Assessment in Public Health

Two important processes (or essential public health services) characterize the assessment function of public health: (1) monitoring health status to identify community health problems and (2) diagnosing and investigating health problems and health hazards in the community.

Monitoring health status to identify community health problems encompasses the following:

- Accurate, ongoing assessment of the community's health status
- Identification of threats to health
- Determination of health service needs
- Attention to the health needs of groups that are at higher risk than the total population
- Identification of community assets and resources that support the public health system in promoting health and improving quality of life
- Use of appropriate methods and technology to interpret and communicate data to diverse audiences
- Collaboration with other stakeholders, including private providers and health benefit plans, to manage multisectoral integrated information systems

Diagnosing and investigating health problems and health hazards in the community encompass the following:

- Access to a public health laboratory capable of conducting rapid screening and high-volume testing
- Active infectious disease epidemiology programs
- Technical capacity for epidemiologic investigation of disease outbreaks and patterns of infectious and chronic diseases and injuries and other adverse health behaviors and conditions

Policy Development for Public Health

The assessment function and its related processes provide a foundation for policy development and its key processes, including (1) informing, educating, and empowering people about health issues; (2) mobilizing community partnerships to identify and solve health problems; and (3) developing policies and plans that support individual and community health efforts.

Informing, educating, and empowering people about health issues encompass the following:

- Community development activities
- Social marketing and targeted media public communication
- Provision of accessible health information resources at community levels
- Active collaboration with personal healthcare providers to reinforce health promotion messages and programs
- Joint health education programs with schools, churches, worksites, and others

Mobilizing community partnerships to identify and solve health problems encompasses the following:

- Convening and facilitating partnerships among groups and associations (including those not typically considered to be health related)
- Undertaking defined health improvement planning process and health projects, including preventive, screening, rehabilitation, and support programs
- Building a coalition to draw on the full range of potential human and material resources to improve community health

Developing policies and plans that support individual and community health efforts encompasses the following:

- Leadership development at all levels of public health
- Systematic community-level and state-level planning for health improvement in all jurisdictions
- Development and tracking of measurable health objectives from the community health plan as a part of continuous quality improvement strategy plan
- Joint evaluation with the medical healthcare system to define consistent policy regarding prevention and treatment services
- Development of policy and legislation to guide the practice of public health

Assurance of the Public's Health

Whereas assessment and policy development set interventions into motion, the assurance function keeps them on track through five important processes: (1) enforcing laws and regulations that protect health and ensure safety; (2) linking people to needed personal health services and ensuring the provision of health care when otherwise unavailable; (3) ensuring a competent public health and personal healthcare workforce; (4) evaluating effectiveness, accessibility, and quality of personal and population-based health services; and (5) researching for new insights and innovative solutions to health problems.

Enforcing laws and regulations that protect health and ensure safety encompasses the following:

- Enforcement of sanitary codes, especially in the food industry
- Protection of drinking water supplies
- Enforcement of clean air standards
- Animal control activities
- Follow-up of hazards, preventable injuries, and exposure-related diseases identified in occupational and community settings
- Monitoring quality of medical services (e.g., laboratories, nursing homes, and home healthcare providers)
- Review of new drug, biologic, and medical device applications

Linking people to needed personal health services and ensuring the provision of health care when otherwise unavailable (sometimes referred to as outreach or enabling services) encompass the following:

- Assurance of effective entry for socially disadvantaged people into a coordinated system of clinical care
- Culturally and linguistically appropriate materials and staff to ensure linkage to services for special population groups
- Ongoing "care management"
- Transportation services
- Targeted health education/promotion/disease prevention to high-risk population groups

Ensuring a competent public and personal healthcare workforce encompasses the following:

- Education, training, and assessment of personnel (including volunteers and other lay community health workers) to meet community needs for public and personal health services
- Efficient processes for licensure of professionals
- Adoption of continuous quality improvement and lifelong learning programs
- Active partnerships with professional training programs to ensure community-relevant learning experiences for all students
- Continuing education in management and leadership development programs for those charged with administrative/executive roles

Evaluating effectiveness, accessibility, and quality of personal and population-based health services encompasses the following:

- Assessing program effectiveness
- Providing information necessary for allocating resources and reshaping programs

Researching for new insights and innovative solutions to health problems encompasses the following:

- Full continuum of innovation, ranging from practical field-based efforts to fostering change in public health practice to more academic efforts to encourage new directions in scientific research
- Continuous linkage with institutions of higher learning and research
- Internal capacity to mount timely epidemiologic and economic analyses and conduct health services research

The important processes embodied in the essential public health services framework underscore the complexities of public health practice. These processes are important aspects to both problem identification and problem solving. In this sense, the essential public health services framework is relevant to both programs and organizations and is evident in virtually any public health intervention (although in different degrees), constituting what might be considered generic public health practice. The core functions and essential services frameworks demonstrate that public health practice is more than a collection of programs and services; it embodies the AGPALL concept and the tools to carry out that role.

POST-IOM REPORT INITIATIVES

The delineation of core functions and essential public health services fortified the foundation for public health practice.[12] In the decade after the appearance of the IOM report, new tools for public health practice came onto the scene to build on this foundation.

Assessment Protocol for Excellence in Public Health and Mobilizing for Action through Planning and Partnerships

Among the post-IOM report initiatives, the Assessment Protocol for Excellence in Public Health (APEXPH), developed by the National Association of County and City Health Officials (NACCHO), in collaboration with other national public health organizations, has had the most extensive and positive influence on public health practice. Even more promising is the second generation of this tool, Mobilizing for Action through Planning and Partnerships (MAPP).

The original APEXPH was a tool for organizational self-assessment and improvement for LHDs, as well as a simple and effective community needs assessment process. APEXPH provided a means for LHDs to enhance their organizational capacity and strengthen their leadership role in their community. APEXPH guided health department officials in two principal areas of activity: (1) assessing and improving the organizational capacity of the agency and (2) working with the local community to improve the health status of its citizens. There were three principal parts to this process:[13]

- An organizational capacity assessment—self-assessed key aspects of operations, including authority to operate, community relations, community health assessment, public policy development, assurance of public health services, financial management, personnel management, and program management, resulting in an organizational action plan that set priorities for correcting perceived weaknesses.
- A community process—guided formation of a community advisory committee that identified health problems requiring priority attention and then set health status goals and programmatic objectives. The aim was to mobilize community resources in pursuit of locally relevant public health objectives consistent with the Healthy People objectives.
- Completing the cycle—ensured that the activities from the organizational and community processes were effectively carried out and that they accomplished the desired results through policy development, assurance, monitoring, and evaluation activities.

After its appearance in 1991, APEXPH steadily gained acceptance; more than one half of all LHDs used all or part of APEXPH during the 1990s. Although the decade's experience with APEXPH was highly positive, opportunities for strengthening the tool were apparent. Heightened interest in community health improvement efforts, widespread acceptance of the essential public health services as the framework for public health practice, the need to strategically engage a wider range of community interests, and the opportunity to formalize and activate local public health systems converged to suggest that a strategic approach to community health improvement was needed.

The development of MAPP addressed these needs, envisioning and designing a robust tool of public health practice to be used by communities with effective LHD leadership to create a local system that ensures the delivery of health services essential to protecting the health of the public.[14] Distinguishing features of MAPP include the following:

- Incorporation of strategic planning concepts—to assist LHDs in more effectively engaging their communities, securing resources, and managing the process of change. Visioning, contextual environment assessment, strategic issue identification, and strategy formulation principles are among the strategic planning concepts embedded in MAPP.
- Grounding in local public health practice—to ensure that the process is practical, flexible, and user friendly. The instruments rely heavily on the previous experiences and successes of typical communities through vignettes, case studies, and other examples.
- A focus on the local public health system—to broaden community health improvement efforts by recognizing and including all public and private organizations contributing to public health at the local level.

Because public health involves more than what public health agencies do, MAPP provides a framework for actualizing this assertion through the following:

- A common approach for assessing local public health systems—to promote consistent quality of public health practice from community to community and state to state. The essential public health services framework provides the measures used to assess local public health systems consistent with other national and state efforts to promote a basic set of public health performance standards.
- Expansion of the basic indicators for health status—to reflect better the demographic and socioeconomic determinants of health, community assets, environmental and behavioral risks, and quality of life. MAPP includes a core set of measures for all communities and an extended menu of additional measures for use, where appropriate.
- Recognition that community themes and strengths play an important role in community health improvement efforts—to balance overreliance on data and expert opinion, provide new insights into factors affecting community health, and increase buy-in and active participation as stakeholders feel their concerns and opinions are important to the process.

The model developed for MAPP involves interrelated and interactive components. To be practical for use in widely diverse communities and to meld basic strategic planning concepts with public health and community health improvement concepts, MAPP is both simple and complex, as illustrated in Figure 5-1.

Figure 5-1   MAPP model. *Source:* From National Association of County and City Health Officials, 2000.

There is no fixed or even preferred sequencing of its components. The boundaries of the model identify the four assessments that comprise the MAPP process; these are usually completed after visioning has taken place but before strategic issues are identified in the steps indicated in the center of the model. Each element of the model is briefly described here:

- Organizing for success/partnership development—involves establishing values and outcomes for the process and determining the scope, form, and timing for planning process, as well as its participants.
- Visioning—involves developing a shared vision of the ideal future for the community, which serves to provide the process with focus, purpose, direction, and buy-in.
- Four MAPP assessments—these inform the planning process and drive the identification of strategic issues. All are critical to the success of the process, although there is no prescribed order in which they need to be undertaken. The four strategic assessments are as follows:
  - Community themes and strengths—involves the collection of inputs and insights from throughout the community in order to understand issues that residents feel are important.
  - Local public health assessment—involves an analysis of mission, vision, and goals through the use of performance measures for the essential public health services. Both strengths and areas for improvement are identified.

- Community health status assessment—involves an extensive assessment of indicators in 11 domains, including asset mapping and quality of life; environmental health; socioeconomic, demographic, and behavioral risk factors; infectious diseases; sentinel events; social and mental health; maternal and child health; health resource availability; and health status indicators
- Forces of change—identifies broader forces affecting the community, such as technology and legislation.
- Identify strategic issues—involves fundamental policy questions for achieving the shared vision, arising from the information developed in the previous phases. Some are more important than others and require action.
- Formulate goals and strategies—involves developing and examining options for addressing strategic issues, including questions of feasibility and barriers to implementation. Preferred strategies are selected.
- The action cycle—involves implementation, evaluation, and celebration of achievements after strategies are selected and agreed on.

As depicted in Figure 5-2, MAPP serves as a virtual road map for community public health systems. Widespread use of MAPP began in 2001, and after only a few years its impact was apparent in an evaluation of 130 early adopters.[15]

Figure 5-2   MAPP as a road map for community public health systems. *Source:* From National Association of County and City Health Officials, 2000.

Active interest by agency leadership and past experience with APEXPH were strong influences on decisions of early adopters to use MAPP. One third of all MAPP users reported using MAPP primarily as a reference and resource. Among the LHDs that actually implemented MAPP, only about one fourth strictly followed the MAPP model whereas three fourths reported modifying MAPP while implementing it, most frequently by attempting to simplify the process. The local public health system assessment, for which the National Public Health Performance Standards local instrument is often used, was the step most frequently modified by LHDs.

LHDs, other local government agencies, hospitals, and social service providers were the most frequently cited community participants in the MAPP process. Educational institutions, nonprofit organizations, community residents, local business and employers, and civic interest groups were the most frequently identified new partners. Managed care organizations, health professional organizations, environmental agencies, and neighborhood organizations were substantially less likely to be engaged in the MAPP process. In about three of four MAPP implementations, LHDs organized or convened the process. Although LHD staff was generally assigned to MAPP implementation, it was uncommon for there to be a dedicated budget for the process.

LHDs reported that the most frequent results from MAPP were the strengthened existing partnerships, an increased understanding of community health problems, and greater community engagement. The least frequently reported results related to influencing budgets and priorities and making significant changes in LHD programs. LHDs cited maintaining participant engagement, the complexity of MAPP, and the total time involved as the most significant barriers to implementing MAPP. Important to success were support and participation of LHD leadership and participation of key community stakeholders.

About one half of the LHDs rated MAPP as the best tool available for public health planning, although more than three fourths found it effective, flexible, comprehensive, and worth the effort and would recommend it to other LHDs. Very few MAPP users reported undesirable consequences.

Planned Approach to Community Health, Model Standards, and Community Health Improvement Processes

In addition to the essential public health services framework and the APEXPH/MAPP processes, the IOM report stimulated several other important initiatives to promote core function-related performance, especially for the assessment and policy development functions. As described in Chapter 2, new national health objectives and a panel of leading health indicators were established for the year 2020, based on 3 decades of experience with the year 1990, 2000, and 2010 national health objectives. Broader participation in their design and more concerted strategies for their implementation in community settings distinguish the year 2020 objectives from the three earlier efforts.

One of the first community health planning tools to be widely used was the Planned Approach to Community Health (PATCH), a process for community organization and community needs assessment that emphasizes community mobilization and constituency building. PATCH focuses on orienting and training community leaders and other community participants in all aspects of the community needs assessment process and includes excellent documentation and resource materials. Although originally developed by the Centers for Disease Control and Prevention (CDC) to focus on chronic health conditions and stimulate health promotion and disease prevention interventions, PATCH is flexible enough to be used in a wide variety of community health needs assessment applications.

Another important tool for addressing public health core functions and their associated processes is Model Standards, Healthy Communities.[8] The steps outlined for implementation of the Model Standards process in the community link many of the various core function-related tools; they represent, in effect, a pathway for organizations to participate in community health improvement activities.

1. Assessment of organizational role. Communities are organized and structured differently. As a result, the specific roles of local public health organizations will vary from community to community. An essential first step is to reexamine organizational purpose and mission and develop a long-range vision through strategic planning involving its internal and external constituencies. The resulting mission statement and long-range vision serve to guide the organization (leadership and board, as well as employees) and to define it for its community partners. This critical step should be completed before the remaining steps can be successfully addressed. Part I of APEXPH and the expanded strategic planning elements of MAPP are useful in accomplishing this task.

2. Assessment of organizational capacity. After mission and role have been defined, it is necessary to examine an organization's capacity to carry out its role in the community. This calls for an assessment of the major operational elements of the organization, including its structure and performance for specific tasks. This type of organizational and local public health system self-assessment is best carried out through broad participation from all levels. Both APEXPH and MAPP include hundreds of indicators that can be used in this capacity assessment. These indicators can be modified or eliminated if deemed inappropriate, and additional indicators can also be used. This step serves to identify strengths and weaknesses relative to mission and role.

3. Development of a capacity-building plan. The development of a capacity-building plan incorporates the organization's strengths and prioritizes its weaknesses so that the most important are addressed first. As in any plan, specific objectives for addressing these weaknesses are developed, responsibilities are assigned, and a process for tracking progress over time is established. Again, APEXPH and MAPP are valuable tools for accomplishing this task.

4. Assessment of community organizational structure. Having looked internally at its capacity and ability to exercise its leadership role for

identifying and addressing priority health needs in the community, the public health organization must assess the key stakeholders and necessary participants for a community-wide needs assessment and intervention initiative. This is often a long-term and continuous process in which the relationship of all important community stakeholders and partners (e.g., the health agency, community providers of health-related services, community organizations, community leaders, interest groups, the media, and the general public) is assessed. This step determines how and under whose auspices community health planning will take place within the community. Both APEXPH/MAPP and PATCH processes support the successful completion of this step.

5. Organization of community. This step calls for organizing the community so that it represents a strong constituency for public health and will participate collaboratively in partnership with the health agency. Specific strategies and activities will vary from community to community but will generally include hearings, dialogues, discussion forums, meetings, and collaborative planning sessions. The specific roles and authority of community participants should be clarified so that the process is not perceived as one driven largely by the health agency and so-called experts. Both APEXPH/MAPP and PATCH are useful for completing this step.

6. Assessment of community health needs. The actual process of identifying health problems of importance to the community is one that must carefully balance information derived from data sets with information derived from the community's perceptions of which problems are most important. Often, community readiness to mitigate specific problems greatly increases the chances for success, as well as support for the overall process within the community. In addition to generating information on possible health problems, this step gathers information on resources available within the community. This step serves to provide the information necessary for the community's most important health problems to be identified. The community needs assessment tools provided in both APEXPH/MAPP and PATCH can be used to accomplish this step.

7. Determination of local priorities and community health resources. After important health problems are identified, decisions must be made as to which are most important for community action. This step requires broad participation from community participants in the process so that priorities will be viewed as community rather than agency-specific priorities. Debate and negotiation are essential for this step, and there are many approaches to coming to consensus around specific priorities. Both APEXPH/MAPP and PATCH support this step.

8. Selection of outcome objectives. After priorities are determined, the process must establish a target level to be achieved for each priority problem. For this step, the Model Standards process is especially useful in linking community priorities to national health objectives

and establishing targets that are appropriate for the current status and improvement possible from a community intervention. This step also calls for negotiation within the community because deployment and reallocation of resources may be needed to achieve the target outcomes that are agreed upon. In addition to Model Standards, both APEXPH/MAPP and PATCH can be useful in accomplishing this step.

9. Development of intervention strategies. This step is one of determining strategies and methods of achieving the outcome objectives established for each priority health problem. This can be quite difficult and, at times, contentious. For some problems, there may be few or even no effective interventions. For others, there may be widely divergent strategies available, some of which may be deemed unacceptable or not feasible. After agreement is reached as to strategies and methods, responsibilities for implementing and evaluating interventions will be assigned. With community-wide interventions, overall coordination of efforts may also need to be addressed as part of the intervention strategy.

10. Implementation of intervention strategies. After the establishment of goals, objectives, strategies, and methods, specific plans of action for the intervention are developed, and specific tasks and work plans are developed. Clear delineation of responsibilities and time lines is essential for this step.

11. Continuous monitoring and evaluation of effort. The evaluation strategy for the intervention will track performance related to outcome objectives, as well as process objectives and activity measures over time. If activity measures and process objectives are being accomplished, there should be progress toward achieving the desired outcome objectives. If this does not occur, the selected intervention strategy needs to be reconsidered and revised.

Since 1990, numerous communities have used PATCH, Model Standards, and other tools (such as Healthy Cities and Healthy Communities, two similar community needs assessment processes) in community health-improvement initiatives.

In 1996, and again in 2002, the IOM revisited issues addressed in *The Future of Public Health* report, concluding that different organizations, leadership, and political and economic realities were transforming how public health carried out its core functions and essential services.[16,17] On one hand, market-driven health care was forcing public health to clarify and strengthen its public role in a predominately private system. On the other, public health was increasingly identifying and working with a variety of entities within the community that shape community health and well-being. Another important IOM report[18] in 1997 advanced an expanded CHIP model that extends the tools developed earlier in the decade and the steps described previously here. Its main features are its expanded perspective on the wide variety of factors that influence health, its support for broad participation by community stakeholders, and its emphasis on the use of performance measures to ensure accountability of partners and track progress over time.

Community health assessments leading toward community health improvement plans increased in quantity as well as quality during the two decades between 1990 and 2010. A survey conducted by NACCHO in 2008 found that nearly two thirds of local health jurisdictions (LHJs) nationwide had conducted a community health assessment in the past 3 years and nearly 70% planned to complete one within the next 3 years (Figure 5-3).[19] Those not planning to conduct assessments were primarily the smallest LHJs with few full-time employees (Figure 5-4). Similar patterns were identified for community health improvement plans.

The most widely used tools for assessment and planning are APEXPH/MAPP and state-specific tools. Metropolitan LHJs are more likely to develop their own assessment tools, whereas nonmetropolitan LHJs are somewhat more prone to use tools developed at the state level. The expanded use of these tools underscores the importance of community health improvement indicatives as a hallmark of 21st century community public health practice. As documented in Figure 5-5, LHDs play leadership or partnership roles in nearly all LHJs involved with community health planning.

21ST CENTURY COMMUNITY PUBLIC HEALTH PRACTICE

Communities remain the battlefields on which public health threats are met and public health challenges are addressed in the 21st century. There has been steady growth in the armamentarium of community public health practice during the late 20th century. This movement gained pace in the 1990s and promises to be the new public health of the early 21st century. It is grounded in the notion that more doctors, more clinics, and more sophisti-

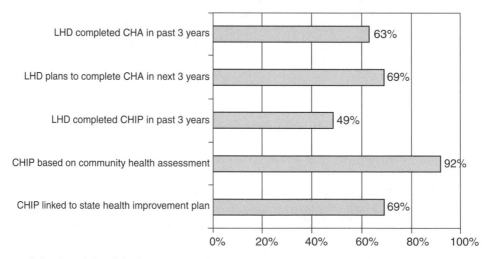

Figure 5-3 Local health department participation in community health assessment (CHA) and community health improvement planning (CHIP) activities, United States, 2008. *Source:* National Association of County and City Health Officials. Data from *2008 National Profile of Local Health Departments*. Washington, DC: NACCHO; 2009.

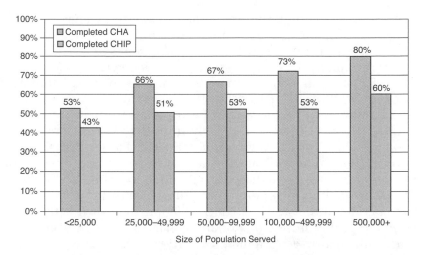

Figure 5-4 Percentage of local health departments with completed community health assessment and community health improvement plans, by local health jurisdiction population, United States, 2008. *Source:* Data from National Association of County and City Health Officials. *2008 National Profile of Local Health Departments.* Washington, DC: NACCHO; 2009.

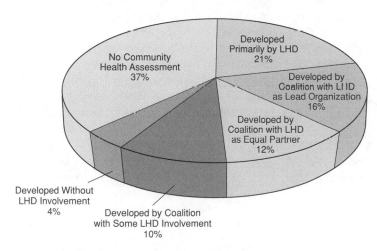

Figure 5-5 Percentage distribution of LHDs, by roles in community health assessments, United States, 2008. *Source:* Data from National Association of County and City Health Officials. *2008 National Profile of Local Health Departments.* Washington, DC: NACCHO; 2009.

cated diagnostic and treatment advances will not alleviate the major health problems facing Americans. Instead, the greatest gains will come from what people do or do not do for themselves, individually and collectively. Acting collectively can take place at many levels; at the community level, it often works best. This section examines the approaches, tools, and opportunities of modern community public health practice.

The notion of community is an elusive concept. Generally, communities are aggregates of individuals who share common characteristics or other bonds. One person can be part of many different communities. One definition views community as the associative, self-generated gathering of common people who have sufficient resources in their lives to cope with life's demands and not suffer ill health. This definition of community focuses on the capacity of communities to achieve their health goals through the effective use of their own assets. It differs considerably from the view of communities as the location in which health services are delivered. Rather than focusing on the level of individual actions and behaviors, it recognizes the importance of social determinants of health and of the environmental and policy levels for public health responses. Community public health practice revolves around engaging communities to work collectively on their own behalf. Community engagement is the process of working collaboratively with groups of people who are affiliated by geographic proximity, special interests, or similar situations, with respect to issues affecting their well-being. For public health workers in government agencies, healthcare organizations, educational institutions, voluntary organizations, or corporate settings, community engagement is essential.

Although community engagement is a relatively recent phenomenon for many governmental public health organizations, health education specialists have been using these principles for more than 4 decades, based on the fundamental admonition to start where the people are. The early experience of community health educators is well expressed in the "Ten Commitments for Community Health Education"[20] (Table 5-6).

This positive approach emphasizes that all communities have assets. Although obvious, all too often communities have been viewed solely in terms of their needs and problems. The implication of these different perspectives is important. If communities are viewed from their needs, the policies and interventions will be based on needs. If they are to be viewed from their assets, the policies and interventions will be based on the community's capacities, skills, and assets. Community health improvement seldom occurs from the actions of outside interests alone; the most successful

Table 5-6   Ten Commitments for Community Health Education

1. Start where the people are.
2. Reorganize and build on community strengths.
3. Honor thy community, but do not make it holy.
4. Foster high-level community participation.
5. Laughter is good medicine and good health education.
6. Health education is educational but is also political.
7. Thou shall not tolerate the bad "isms" (such as racism, sexism, agism).
8. Think globally, act locally.
9. Foster individual and community empowerment.
10. Work for social justice.

Source: Data from Minkler M. Ten commitments for community health education. *Health Educ Res Theory Pract.* 1994;9:527–534.

community development efforts are driven by the commitment of those investing themselves and their resources in the effort. Identifying community assets is possible through approaches that catalog and actually map the basic building blocks that will be used to address important community health problems.[21] Primary building blocks include those community assets that are most readily available for community health improvement, including both individual and organizational assets. Individual assets include the skills, talents, and experiences of residents, individual businesses, and home-based enterprises, as well as personal income. Organizational assets include associations of businesses, citizen associations, cultural organizations, communications organizations, and religious organizations. Secondary building blocks are private, public, and physical assets, which can be brought under community control and used for community improvement purposes. These include private and nonprofit organizations (higher educational institutions, hospitals, social service agencies), public institutions and services (public schools, police, libraries, fire department, parks), and physical resources (vacant land, commercial and industrial structures, housing, energy, and waste resources).

In addition to community engagement and asset-mapping strategies, performance measurement offers another tool for community health improvement activities. Performance measures are also not new to public health practice. The use of performance measures to track progress toward community or national health objectives and to monitor programs has long been standard practice. The CHIP proposed by the IOM in its report on performance monitoring, however, takes performance measurement to a new level. In these processes, performance measures serve to hold communities (acting through stakeholders and partnerships) accountable for actions for which they have accepted responsibility.[18] This supports the development of a shared vision and a collaborative and integrative approach to community problem solving for the purpose of improving health status. It offers a pathway for stakeholders and partners to assume responsibility collectively and to marshal their resources and assets in pursuit of agreed-on objectives.

The CHIP model includes a problem identification and prioritization cycle, followed by an analysis and implementation cycle. This second cycle develops, implements, and evaluates health intervention strategies that address priority community health problems. The distinguishing feature of this approach is the emphasis on measurement to link performance and accountability on a community-wide basis, rather than solely on the LHD or another public entity. Several recommendations were developed to operationalize the community health improvement concept[18]:

- Communities should base a health improvement process on a broad definition of health and a comprehensive conceptual model of how health is produced within the community.
- A CHIP should develop its own set of specific, quantitative performance measures, linking accountable entities to the performance of specific activities expected to lead to the production of desired health outcomes in the community.

- A CHIP should seek a balance between strategic opportunities for long-term health improvement and goals that are achievable in the short term.
- Community conditions guiding CHIPs should strive for strategic inclusiveness, incorporating individuals, groups, and organizations that have an interest in health outcomes, can take actions necessary to improve community health, or can contribute data and analytic capabilities needed for performance monitoring.
- A CHIP should be centered in a community health coalition or similar entity.

To enable the widespread adoption of the CHIP concept, the IOM made additional recommendations.[18]

- State and LHDs should ensure that an effective CHIP is in place in all communities. These agencies should, at a minimum, participate in CHIP activities and, in some communities, should provide the leadership and/or organizational home.
- In support of community-level health improvement processes, state health agencies, in cooperation and collaboration with LHDs, should ensure the availability of community-level data needed for health profiles.
- States and the federal government, through health departments or other appropriate channels, should require that health plans, indemnity insurers, and other private entities report standard data on the characteristics and health status of their enrolled populations, on services provided, and on outcomes of those services, as necessary for performance monitoring in the CHIP.

Numerous useful tools and guides are available via the Internet (including the website resources for this book) to support the expanded community health improvement efforts in models such as CHIP, MAPP, and similar initiatives. Prominent among these tools are the CDC's Principles of Community Engagement,[22] the Community Tool Box (developed by the University of Kansas),[23] and the Healthy People Tool Kit (produced by the Public Health Foundation).[24] Geographic information system tools are emerging as important techniques for assessment of community health problems, needs, and assets.

Governmental public health agencies, especially LHDs, have steadily increased their partnerships with business, nonprofit, and other governmental organizations.[15] Top participant categories participating in the MAPP process are presented in Figure 5-6 and include other units of local government, social service providers, schools, community organizations, hospitals, civic groups, and faith institutions. Schools, nonprofit organizations, elected officials, local businesses, and public safety agencies appear to be more recent partners for LHDs. Participation levels of the board of health and environmental health organizations were relatively low considering how close these categories are to LHD functions.

The need for new community-driven models of public health practice was also reflected in the National Turning Point Initiative.[25] Funded jointly by the

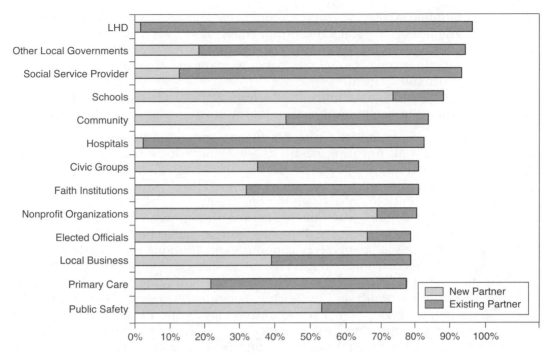

Figure 5-6 Top participant categories for communities using MAPP. *Source:* Data from Lenihan DP, Landrum LB, Turnock BJ. *An Evaluation of MAPP and NPHPS in Local Health Jurisdictions.* Chicago, IL: Illinois Public Health Institute; 2006.

Kellogg and Robert Wood Johnson Foundations, Turning Point sought to transform and strengthen the public health infrastructure at the state and local levels, in effect, reforming public health practice. More than 21 states participated in Turning Point through statewide and local partnerships that brought together a broad spectrum of health interests to develop a shared vision and strategic plans to improve statewide public health systems. CHIPs, performance measurement, and health statute reform received special attention as Turning Point states move from planning into implementation. The collaborations in the various Turning Point sites varied significantly, nurturing and developing many different models for systems change. Broad strategies include the following:

- Developing sustainable and appropriate capacity and infrastructure to support a population-based approach to health improvement
- Developing sustainable partnerships for decision making and policy development related to health improvement at the community and state levels
- Creating ongoing evaluation processes that highlight best practices in public health systems design
- Emphasizing prevention, health protection, and health promotion programs and activities that focus on the broad health determinants

- Building systems that engage proactive and aggressive actions to direct and protect the population from emerging threats to health
- Clearly defining roles and responsibilities for the public health core functions and essential services of all state and community entities that contribute to health
- Focusing on community health improvement models at the local level and using system-level health improvement models at the state level

Healthy Communities represents another successful model for community health improvement, using health as a metaphor for a broader approach to building community.[26] Because health cuts across lines of race, ethnicity, class, culture, and sector, the focus on a healthy community enables the entire community to collaborate in community renewal. Healthy Communities believes that only when people act together to participate directly in the public work of our society will change in our public policies and problems occur. A key to success involves community institutions using their organizational skills, relationships, in-kind resources, and credibility to engage the rest of the community in mobilizing the creativity and resources of the community to improve health and well-being. Focusing on systems change, Healthy Communities seeks to build broad citizen participation that encourages new players and honors diversity. It looks to build true collaborations between business, government, nonprofit organizations, and citizens stimulating the community and political will to act together.

Community-based health policy development is also receiving greater attention in these collaborations and partnerships. Public policy serves as a guide to influence governmental decisions and action at any jurisdictional level, thereby affecting what would otherwise occur.[27] For the health and well-being of communities, policies indicate broad directions toward important goals, cutting across many different stakeholders and affecting large populations. Policies focus on both goals and the means to achieve those goals, often affecting the decisions and actions of individual organizations. At the community level, health policy has many options, such as more and better health services to address unmet needs in the community or advocacy for broader support to improve the conditions influencing health in the community. Increasingly, community-driven public health initiatives are tackling the broader social and community factors, even as they seek to ensure that gaps in services are somehow met. The experiences are many and varied, although one accounting of key lessons learned to date includes the following[27]:

- The need to monitor the policy environment continuously because every issue exists in a historical context, involving past experiences on similar issues and current circumstances that limit possibilities
- The importance of choosing appropriate frames, forums, and channels for debate so that issues are framed in the public interest in ways that are sensitive to the current environment
- The art of designing policy proposals that offer clear gains, even after trade-offs are made with other stakeholders in the process
- The value of negotiating with allies and opponents alike because both are major stakeholders in the policy development process

• The necessity of influencing the social climate of the community through effective use of public opinion and the media

Little research is available to illuminate the value of community-driven health policy development initiatives. There is some evidence that widespread initiation of CHIPs increases the frequency that key policy development components take place. Policy development may be the public health core function most heavily impacted by CHIPs. The increase in performance of specific practices related to the core functions has been greatest for those related to policy development, and generally, the baseline level of measures of policy development lags behind that of assessment and assurance where CHIPs have not been implemented.

Together, these strategies, initiatives, and tools can make substantial contributions to improving public health practice in the United States. In addition, there is reason to believe that improvement is needed in view of assessments of performance that were completed over the next decade.

CORE FUNCTION PERFORMANCE

Much of what is known about public health performance in the United States has been developed within the context of initiatives established after the appearance of the IOM report. Unfortunately, many of these experiences remain unpublished, and few are readily transported and replicated elsewhere; however, more than a dozen reports on various aspects of public health performance were published during the 1990s. Using somewhat different panels of performance measures, they provided significant insight into the performance of public health core functions and essential public health services.

Public health practice performance data, focused on process performance (including outputs), were reported by NACCHO in six surveys of LHJs undertaken between 1990 and 2008. For 48 measures associated with the three core functions from the 1990 NACCHO survey, mean LHD performance was 50%.[28] For 96 measures linked with the core functions in the 1992/1993 NACCHO survey, mean performance was similar, at 46%.[29] Other studies, using practice measures based on the core functions, reported performance scores of 57% performance for 14 LHDs in 1992, 56% for 370 LHDs in 1993, and 50% for 208 LHDs in 1993.[30–33] When similar performance measures were used on a statewide basis in Iowa in 1995, the overall performance score was 61%.[34]

Based on field tests and performance studies completed in the early 1990s, a consensus set of 20 practice performance measures (Table 5-7) was established. Using these 20 measures with a random sample of 298 LHDs stratified by population size and type of jurisdiction,[34] one study assessed the extent to which the U.S. population in 1995 was being effectively served by the public health core functions identified in the IOM report (assessment, policy development, and assurance). Performance of these 20 measures ranged from 23% to 94%. The most frequently performed measures related to investigating adverse health events, maintaining necessary laboratory services, implementing mandated programs, maintaining a network of relationships, and regularly providing information to the public.

Table 5-7   Core Function-Related Practice Performance Measures, 1995

Assessment

1. For the jurisdiction served by your local health department, is there a community needs assessment process that systematically describes the prevailing health status in the community?
2. In the past 3 years in your jurisdiction, has the local public health agency surveyed the population for behavioral risk factors?
3. For the jurisdiction served by your local health agency, are timely investigations of adverse health events, including communicable disease outbreaks and environmental health hazards, conducted on an ongoing basis?
4. Are the necessary laboratory services available to the local public health agency to support investigations of adverse health events and meet routine diagnostic and surveillance needs?
5. For the jurisdiction served by your local public health agency, has an analysis been completed of the determinants and contributing factors of priority health needs, adequacy of existing health resources, and the population groups most impacted?
6. In the past 3 years, in your jurisdiction, has the local public health agency conducted an analysis of age-specific participation in preventive and screening services?

Policy Development

7. For the jurisdiction served by your local public health agency, is there a network of support and communication relationships that includes health-related organizations, the media, and the general public?
8. In the past year, in your jurisdiction, has there been a formal attempt by the local public health agency at informing elected officials about the potential public health impact of decisions under their consideration?
9. For the jurisdiction served by your local public health agency, has there been a prioritization of the community health needs that have been identified from a community needs assessment?
10. In the past 3 years, in your jurisdiction, has the local public health agency implemented community health initiatives consistent with established priorities?
11. For the jurisdiction served by your local public health agency, has a community health action plan been developed with community participation to address priority community health needs?
12. During the past 3 years, in your jurisdiction, has the local public health agency developed plans to allocate resources in a manner consistent with the community health action plan?

Assurance

13. For the jurisdiction served by your local public health agency, have resources been deployed as necessary to address the priority health needs identified in the community health need assessment?
14. In the past 3 years, in your jurisdiction, has the local public health agency conducted an organizational self-assessment?
15. For the jurisdiction served by your local public health agency, are age-specific priority health needs effectively addressed through the provision of or linkage to appropriate services?
16. In the past 3 years, in your jurisdiction, has there been an instance in which the local public health agency has failed to implement a mandated program or service?
17. For the jurisdiction served by your local public health agency, have there been regular evaluations of the effect that public health services have on community health status?
18. In the past 3 years, in your jurisdiction, has the local public health agency used professionally recognized process and outcome measures to monitor programs and to redirect resources as appropriate?
19. For the jurisdiction served by your local public health agency, is the public regularly provided with information about current health status, healthcare needs, positive health behaviors, and healthcare policy issues?
20. In the past year, in your jurisdiction, has the local public health agency provided reports to the media on a regular basis?

Source: Data from Turnock BJ, Handler AS, Miller CA. Core function-related local public health performance. *J Public Health Manage Pract.* 1998;4(5):26–32.

The least frequently performed measures related to assessing use of preventive and screening services in the community, conducting behavioral risk factor surveys, regularly evaluating the effect of services in the community, allocating resources consistent with community action plans, and deploying resources to meet identified needs. The overall weighted mean performance score for all 20 measures was 56%. Subscores for assessment, policy development, and assurance measures were similar to the overall mean. City and county-based LHD jurisdictions with populations greater than 50,000 performed these measures more frequently (65%) than did other LHDs in this study.

Another study[35] using these 20 measures in 1998 found similar levels of performance (65%) in 356 jurisdictions with populations of 100,000 or more. These jurisdictions include only about 20% of LHDs but serve about 70% of the U.S. population. Although the performance of the more populous jurisdictions was somewhat higher than the combination of large and small jurisdictions included in the 1995 national study, both the relative rankings and the population size-specific scores were consistent across these two studies.

The most extensive use of these 20 measures took place as part of the Department of Justice's initial efforts to assess national bioterrorism preparedness. More than 2,000 local jurisdictions provided information relative to these 20 measures between mid 2000 and early 2002. The overall score for all jurisdictions was 65% with scores varying by jurisdiction population and type. Jurisdictions serving populations of less than 25,000 had a mean score of 58%, whereas jurisdictions serving populations of more than 500,000 had a mean score of 74%. Scores for LHJs organized at the city or municipal level were lower than those organized at the city/county, county, district, regional, or state levels.[36]

Although the various studies conducted between 1992 and 2002 used somewhat different methods and measures, they appear to show steady improvement in public health practice performance. These studies also consistently demonstrate performance in the 50% to 70% range and paint a picture of less than optimal functioning of the public health system nationally and in many states. Interestingly, this range is consistent with conclusions of the Emerson Report a half century earlier as to effective public health coverage of the nation, based on an assessment of capacity factors. Although the precise status is not known, it appears that the United States fell well short of its year 2000 target of having 90% of the population residing in jurisdictions in which public health's core functions are being effectively addressed. The findings of two studies of practice performance conducted nationally in the 1990s concluded that only about one third of the U.S. population was effectively served.[33,35]

In addition to the extent of performing core functions and essential services, several other dimensions of performance are important. One relates to the level of adequacy and assesses how well communities are served. Another characterizes the contribution made by the LHD and other community partners. The limited information available on these dimensions of performance says much about the current state of public health practice.

The perceived adequacy for 20 measures of public health practice was 35% in the nation's most populous health jurisdictions in 1998.[36] Assessment activities and assurance activities were rated higher (41% and 38%, respectively) than policy development activities (28%). The highest rated activities were implementation of mandated programs (91%), investigations of adverse health events (75%), and laboratory services (73%). The lowest rated activities were plans for resource allocation (10%), analysis of preventive services (12%), evaluation of services (16%), community action plans (16%), and allocating resources for priorities (18%).

The perceived share of effort contributed by LHDs for 20 measures of public health practice was 67% in the nation's most populous health jurisdictions in 1998.[36] LHDs were responsible for 80% of the total effort for assurance activities, 60% for assessment activities, and 58% for policy development activities. LHDs contributed most heavily to organizational self-assessment (87%), provision of information to the media (77%), investigations of adverse health events (76%), information for elected officials (74%), and monitoring and evaluation of programs (71%). LHDs contributed least to support and communication networks (46%), provision or linkage of services (48%), allocating resources for priority needs (50%), community action plans (50%), and laboratory services (50%).

Consistent with the information on community participants in MAPP implementation (Figure 5-6), many different organizations partner with LHDs in carrying out public health's core functions and essential services. These include state health agencies, hospitals, nonprofit agencies, other agencies of local government, private healthcare providers, universities, health centers, managed care plans, and federal agencies. The participation of these partners varies from activity to activity. Overall, they appear to contribute about one third of the activities that comprise local public health practice in LHJs with populations over 100,000.

Together, these findings suggest that performance of core functions and essential public health services can be improved. Because the concepts used to assess performance were basically standards of public health practice, these measurement and surveillance activities served to promote their adoption by the public health community. These same performance expectations are also advanced in several other initiatives that trace their roots to the IOM report.

Public Health Standards Based on Core Functions

Standards are basically performance expectations. Public health standards, when used before 1990, primarily related to the structural and output aspects of public health practice, rather than the key processes necessary to carry out the public health core functions characterized in the IOM report. Standards for public health practice developed after 1990 have focused both on key processes and outputs and have proven useful in a variety of applications, including agency self-assessment for capacity building, measures of performance in state/local public health systems, and state and national surveillance of practice performance.[37] Still, these standards are in an early stage of development.

The 1990s witnessed many public health organizations conducting organizational self-assessments, identifying strengths and weaknesses, and channeling this information into organizational capacity building plans. The panel of performance expectations for local public health practice in APEXPH and MAPP served as a blueprint for many public health agencies seeking to focus and strengthen their roles in their communities. APEXPH and MAPP adoption and implementation experience have been substantial, although not universal. Where these tools have been implemented widely, public health practice performance has been found to be substantially higher than where it is less frequently used. Despite the availability of APEXPH and MAPP, states are using a variety of approaches and tools based on core functions and the essential public health services framework to establish standards for public health practice and improve performance. The following examples from Washington State and Illinois illustrate some of these approaches.

The state legislature in Washington adopted a framework for a statewide public health improvement plan in 1994 and directed the public health community to identify the capacities needed to carry out core functions, the total cost associated with these capacities, the extent to which the capacities were in place, the difference between current and necessary capacity, and the funding needed to close the gap. Capacity categories needed to address public health core functions were identified, and capacity standards were developed. Subsequent concerns emerged that these capacity standards were overly subjective and not equally applicable for LHJs with different characteristics. This prompted the development of process and output standards for state and LHDs organized around community health assessment and four broad output-related categories (preventing illness and injury, protecting against environmental risks, promoting healthy behaviors, and ensuring quality health services).[38] These performance standards are described in Table 5-8; they are to be used as the basis for contracts between the state and its LHDs.

LHDs in Illinois have been subject to performance standards established by the state since the 1970s. After a series of strategic planning activities, beginning about 1985, these performance standards were revised, effective in 1993, changing the basis of certification by the state to standards based on processes (including outputs) related to public health core functions[39,40] (Table 5-9). The revised certification requirements call for LHDs to implement an adaptation of APEXPH known as Illinois Plan for Local Assessment of Needs, including both the organizational self-assessment and community health improvement planning components of APEXPH. This produced substantial change in patterns of performance of core function-related practices, nearly doubling performance scores over a 2-year period from 1992 to 1994.[41] Performance measures for Illinois LHDs are similar to those described in Table 5-7. There is explicit authority in state law for the state health agency to establish performance standards for LHDs. The standards are promulgated through the state rule-making process, with compliance reviews conducted every 5 years by the state health agency. Longitudinal assessments of performance of these practices in 1992, 1994, and 1999 have been linked with selected capacity factors, as well as with outcomes related to community health priorities identified in the first round of Illinois Plan for Local Assessment of Needs implementation.

Experiences such as those found in these states, as well as Missouri, California, Oregon, Florida, North Carolina, Michigan, South Carolina, and

Table 5-8   Washington State Public Health Standards, 2001

Understanding Health Issues
1. Public health assessment skills and tools are in place in all public health jurisdictions and their level is continuously maintained and enhanced.
2. Information about environmental threats and community health status is collected, analyzed, and disseminated at intervals appropriate for the community.
3. Public health program results are evaluated to document effectiveness.
4. Health policy decisions are guided by health assessment information, with involvement of representative community members.
5. Health data are handled so that confidentiality is protected and health information systems are secure.

Protecting People from Disease
1. A surveillance and reporting system is maintained to identify emerging health threats.
2. Response plans delineate roles and responsibilities in the event of communicable disease outbreaks and other health risks that threaten the health of people.
3. Communicable disease investigation and control procedures are in place and actions are documented.
4. Urgent public health messages are communicated quickly and clearly and actions are documented.
5. Communicable disease and other risk responses are routinely evaluated for opportunities for improving public health system response.

Assuring a Safe, Healthy Environment for People
1. Environmental health education is a planned component of public health programs.
2. Services are available throughout the state to respond to environmental events or natural disasters that threaten the public's health.
3. Both environmental health risks and environmental health illnesses are tracked, recorded, and reported.
4. Compliance with environmental health regulations is sought through enforcement actions.

Prevention Is Best: Promoting Healthy Living
1. Policies are adopted that support prevention priorities and that reflect consideration of scientifically based public health literature.
2. Active involvement of community members is sought in addressing prevention priorities.
3. Access to high-quality prevention services for individuals, families, and communities is encouraged and enhanced by disseminating information about available services and by engaging in and supporting collaborative partnerships.
4. Prevention, early intervention, and outreach services are provided directly or through contracts.
5. Health promotion activities are provided directly or through contracts.

Helping People Get the Services They Need
1. Information is collected and made available at both the state and local level to describe the local health system, including existing resources for public health protection, healthcare providers, facilities, and support services.
2. Available information is used to analyze trends that over time affect access to critical health services.
3. Plans to reduce specific gaps in access to critical services are developed and implemented through collaborative efforts.
4. Quality measures that address the capacity, process for delivery, and outcomes of critical healthcare services are established, monitored, and reported.

(continues)

Table 5-8   Washington State Public Health Standards, 2001 (continued)

Example of Local and State Performance Measures

Protecting People from Disease and Injury: Standard 3—Communicable disease investigation and control procedures are in place and actions documented.

Local Measures
1. Lists of private and public sources for referral to treatment are accessible to LHJ staff.
2. Information is given to local providers through public health alerts and newsletters about managing reportable conditions.
3. Communicable disease protocols require that investigations begin within 1 working day, unless a disease-specific protocol defines an alternate time frame. Disease-specific protocols identify information about the disease, case investigation steps, reporting requirements, contact and clinical management (including referral to care), use of emergency biologics, and the process for exercising legal authority for disease control (including nonvoluntary isolation). Documentation demonstrates staff member actions are in compliance with protocols and state statutes.
4. An annual evaluation of a sample of communicable disease investigations is done to monitor timeliness and compliance with disease-specific protocols.
5. LHJs identify key performance measures for communicable disease investigation and enforcement actions.
6. Staff members conducting disease investigations have appropriate skills and training as evidenced in job descriptions and resumes.

State Measures
1. Consultation and staff time are provided to LHJs for local support of disease intervention management during outbreaks or public health emergencies, as documented by case write-ups. Recent research findings relating to the most effective population based methods of disease prevention and control are provided to LHJs. Laboratories are provided written protocols for the handling, storage, and transportation of specimens.
2. Department of Health leads statewide development and use of a standardized set of written protocols for communicable disease investigation and control, including templates for documentation. Disease-specific protocols identify information about the disease, case investigation steps, reporting requirements, contact and clinical management (including referral to care), use of emergency biologics, and the process for exercising legal authority for disease control (including nonvoluntary isolation). Documentation demonstrates staff member actions are in compliance with protocols and state statutes.
3. An annual evaluation of a sample of state communicable disease investigations and consultations is done to monitor timeliness and compliance with disease-specific protocols.
4. DOH identifies key performance measures for communicable disease investigations and consultation.
5. Staff members conducting disease investigations have appropriate skills and training as evidenced in job descriptions and resumes.

Source: Data from *Standards for Public Health in Washington State*. Olympia, WA: Washington State Department of Health; 2001.

others, laid the foundation for development of a national public health performance standards program. The overall lack of uniformity and consistency among these various state efforts reflects the different needs, values, and circumstances of the relatively autonomous state/local public health networks across the United States. In part because of this diversity in type

Table 5-9   Requirements for Certification of Local Health Departments in Illinois Before and After July 1993

Before July 1993, to Be Certified as a Local Health Department in Illinois	After July 1993, to Be Certified as a Local Health Department in Illinois
A local health agency must carry out the following programs:	A local health agency must:
1. Food sanitation	1. Assess health needs of the community
2. Potable water	2. Investigate health effects and hazards
3. Maternal health/family planning	3. Advocate and build community support
4. Child health	4. Develop policies and plans to address needs
5. Communicable disease control	5. Manage resources
6. Private sewage	6. Implement programs
7. Solid waste	7. Evaluate and provide quality assurance
8. Nuisance control	8. Inform and educate the public
9. Chronic disease	
10. Administration	

and focus of performance standards, the CDC's Public Health Practice Program Office promoted the development of national public health performance standards for use in several complementary applications. These applications include the following:

1. Self-assessment and continuous improvement of local public health systems as part of the MAPP process
2. Surveillance of the public health system nationally and longitudinally
3. Accreditation of public health organizations
4. Performance standards for use in state/local systems

The National Public Health Standards Program represents a partnership among national and state public health organizations to improve the public health delivery system through the development of local and state-based performance standards focused on capacity and processes, the systematic collection and analysis of performance-based data, and a national leadership effort to improve system-wide performance. NACCHO coordinated the development of standards for local public health systems, the Association of State and Territorial Health Officials led the development of standards for state health agencies, and the National Association of Local Boards of Health guided the development of governance standards for local boards of health. Complementary to these standards is the panel of national health objectives for the public health infrastructure that is included in *Healthy People 2010* and *2020* (see Chapter 6).[42] Primary goals across all these efforts are to improve quality, enhance accountability, and strengthen the science base of public health practice.

Potential benefits of a nationwide public health performance standards initiative are many. They include improved accountability; better resource deployment; enhanced capacity building for community, state, and national public health systems; widespread use of best practices; and greater focus on mission and goals.[43] Depending on the lens used, each of these can be viewed as quality improvement, although widespread implementation of national public health performance standards presents formidable challenges.

The establishment of a national accreditation initiative for LHDs has only recently received serious consideration. Absent a federal initiative to support and fund core functions and essential public health services in state/local public health systems through block grants to states, a voluntary national accreditation program for state and local public health agencies is now the most realistic approach to promoting widespread adoption of practice standards related to the core functions. After several years of discussion and developmental efforts, the national Exploring Accreditation Initiative advanced consensus recommendations for a voluntary national program for local public health organization accreditation.[44] Funded by the Robert Wood Johnson Foundation and spearheaded by NACCHO and the Association of State and Territorial Health Officials, Exploring Accreditation adopted recommendations for the standards, financing, governance and evaluation of a national LHD accreditation program. Two developments hastened progress toward this national program. One was consensus as to an appropriate operational definition of a functional LHD, to be discussed later in this chapter. The other was the experience with the implementation of a national certification program, NACCHO's Public Health Ready initiative, which focuses on bioterrorism and emergency readiness standards for LHDs (see Chapter 8).

A national public health accreditation board began pilot testing standards for state and local public health agnecies at 30 sites in 2010 (see Table 5-10). The full program launched in 2011.

The basis for proposing an operational definition of a functional LHD traces its roots to the concept of AGPALL described earlier in this chapter. The basic premise is that every person, regardless of where they live, should reasonably expect their LHD to meet certain basic standards. Table 5-11 outlines these basic expectations and provides the conceptual definition of a functional LHD.[45] Table 5-12 extends this definition from a conceptual to an operational level and offers a panel of standards against which LHDs can be assessed for improvement or accreditation purposes. One of the key recommendations of the Exploring Accreditation project is to utilize the operational definition standards as the basis for the national voluntary accreditation program.

NEW OPPORTUNITIES FOR IMPROVING PUBLIC HEALTH PRACTICE

Measuring performance of public health core functions and essential public health services is necessary but not sufficient to understand, control, and improve public health practice. Figure 5-7 expands the simple model presented in Chapter 1 (Figure 1-2), illustrating a practical approach to describing and measuring key aspects of the public health system. Because a system is a set of interdependent elements with a common purpose, the interdependencies

Table 5-10   Public Health Accreditation Board—Summary of Local Health Department Standards

---

Part A: Administrative Capacity and Governance
- Standard A1: Develop and maintain an operational infrastructure to support the performance of public health functions.
- Standard A2: Establish effective financial management systems.
- Standard A3: Maintain current operational definitions and statements of the public health roles and responsibilities of specific authorities.
- Standard A4: Provide orientation and regular information to members of the governing entity regarding their responsibilities and those of the public health agency.

Part B: Practice Standards
Domain 1: Conduct and disseminate assessments focused on population health status and public health issues facing the community.
- Standard 1.1: Collect and maintain reliable, comparable, and valid data that provide information on conditions of public health importance and on the health status of the population.
- Standard 1.2: Analyze public health data to identify health problems, environmental public health hazards, and social and economic risks that affect the public's health.
- Standard 1.3: Provide and use the results of health data analysis to develop recommendations regarding public health policy, processes, programs, or interventions.

Domain 2: Investigate health problems and environmental public health hazards to protect the community.
- Standard 2.1: Conduct timely investigations of health problems and environmental public health hazards in coordination with other governmental agencies and key stakeholders.
- Standard 2.2: Contain/mitigate health problems and environmental public health hazards in coordination with other governmental agencies and key stakeholders.
- Standard 2.3: Maintain access to laboratory and epidemiologic/environmental public health expertise and capacity to investigate and contain/mitigate public health problems and environmental public health hazards. Propose local domains, standards, and measures.
- Standard 2.4: Maintain a plan with policies and procedures required for urgent and nonurgent communications.

Domain 3: Inform and educate about public health issues and functions.
- Standard 3.1: Provide health education and health promotion policies, programs, processes, and interventions to support prevention and wellness.
- Standard 3.2: Provide information on public health issues and functions through multiple methods to a variety of audiences.

Domain 4: Engage with the community to identify and address health problems.
- Standard 4.1: Engage the public health system and the community in identifying and addressing health problems through an ongoing, collaborative process.
- Standard 4.2: Promote understanding of and support for policies and strategies that will improve the public's health.

Domain 5: Develop public health policies and plans.
- Standard 5.1: Serve as a primary resource to governing entities and elected officials to establish and maintain public health policies, practices, and capacity based on current science and/or promising practice.

(continues)

Table 5-10 Public Health Accreditation Board—Summary of Local Health Department Standards (continued)

- Standard 5.2: Develop and implement a health department organizational strategic plan.
- Standard 5.3: Conduct a comprehensive planning process resulting in a community health improvement plan [CHIP].
- Standard 5.4: Maintain All Hazards/Emergency Response Plan (ERP).

Domain 6: Enforce public health laws and regulations.
- Standard 6.1: Review existing laws and work with governing entities and elected officials to update as needed.
- Standard 6.2: Educate individuals and organizations on the meaning, purpose, and benefit of public health laws and how to comply.
- Standard 6.3: Conduct and monitor enforcement activities for which the agency has the authority and coordinate notification of violations among appropriate agencies.

Domain 7: Promote strategies to improve access to healthcare services.
- Standard 7.1: Assess healthcare capacity and access to healthcare services.
- Standard 7.2: Identify and implement strategies to improve access to healthcare services.

Domain 8: Maintain a competent public health workforce.
- Standard 8.1: Recruit, hire, and retain a qualified and diverse public health workforce.
- Standard 8.2: Assess staff competencies and address gaps by enabling organizational and individual training and development opportunities.

Domain 9: Evaluate and continuously Improve processes, programs, and interventions.
- Standard 9.1: Evaluate public health processes, programs, and interventions provided by the agency and its contractors.
- Standard 9.2: Implement quality improvement of public health processes, programs, and interventions.

Domain 10: Contribute to and apply the evidence base of public health.
- Standard 10.1: Identify and use evidence-based and promising practices.
- Standard 10.2: Promote understanding and use of the current body of research results, evaluations, and evidence-based practices with appropriate audiences.

Source: Data from Public Health Accreditation Board. Proposed Local Domains, Standards and Measures. Final Draft—July 2009. http://www.phaboard.org/assets/documents/PHABLocalJuly2009-finaleditforbeta.pdf. Accessed May 7, 2010.

are as much a part of the system as are the elements themselves. Interest in a system's "results" requires attention to the interdependencies generating that result. Measures of core function performance further an understanding of the relationships between and among key dimensions of the public health system when linked with measures of capacity and outcomes. This understanding is essential to improve public health practice.

A few studies have already shed light on some of these relationships. For example, the relationship between capacity and process performance (including outputs) has been examined in several studies. One study linked practice performance measures from a 1993 national survey with NACCHO Profile

Table 5-11   Operational Definition of a Functional Local Health Department

A Functional Local Health Department
- Understands the specific health issues confronting the community, and how physical, behavioral, environmental, social, and economic conditions affect them.
- Investigates health problems and health threats.
- Prevents, minimizes, and contains adverse health effects from communicable diseases, disease outbreaks from unsafe food and water, chronic diseases, environmental hazards, injuries, and risky health behaviors.
- Leads planning and response activities for public health emergencies.
- Collaborates with other local responders and with state and federal agencies to intervene in other emergencies with public health significance (e.g., natural disasters).
- Implements health promotion programs.
- Engages the community to address public health issues.
- Develops partnerships with public and private healthcare providers and institutions, community-based organizations, and other government agencies (e.g., housing authority, criminal justice, education) engaged in services that affect health to collectively identify, alleviate, and act on the sources of public health problems.
- Coordinates the public health system's efforts in an intentional, noncompetitive, and nonduplicative manner.
- Addresses health disparities.
- Serves as an essential resource for local governing bodies and policy makers on up-to-date public health laws and policies.
- Provides science-based, timely, and culturally competent health information and health alerts to the media and to the community.
- Provides its expertise to others who treat or address issues of public health significance.
- Ensures compliance with public health laws and ordinances, using enforcement authority when appropriate.
- Employs well-trained staff members who have the necessary resources to implement best practices and evidence-based programs and interventions.
- Facilitates research efforts, when approached by researchers, which benefit the community.
- Uses and contributes to the evidence base of public health.
- Strategically plans its services and activities, evaluates performance and outcomes, and makes adjustments as needed to continually improve its effectiveness, enhance the community's health status, and meet the community's expectations.

Source: Data from National Association of County and City Health Officials. *Operational Definition of a Functional Local Health Department.* Washington, DC; National Association of County and City Health Officials; 2005.

information for 264 LHDs. Capacity factors linked to higher levels of practice performance included full-time agency head, larger annual expenditures, a greater number of total and part-time staff, budgets derived from multiple funding sources, private health insurance as a significant budget component, and female agency heads.[46]

A 1998 study of LHDs in the most populous jurisdictions identified several capacity factors associated with higher levels of core function performance. These were population size, presence of a local board of health, existence of mixed or shared arrangements with state health agency, and participation

Table 5-12   Standards for Operational Definition of a Functional Local Health Department

1. Monitor health status and understand health issues facing the community.
   a. Obtain and maintain data that provide information on the community's health (e.g., provider immunization rates; hospital discharge data; environmental health hazard, risk, and exposure data; community-specific data; number of uninsured; and indicators of health disparities such as high levels of poverty, lack of affordable housing, limited or no access to transportation, etc.).
   b. Develop relationships with local providers and others in the community who have information on reportable diseases and other conditions of public health interest and facilitate information exchange.
   c. Conduct or contribute expertise to periodic community health assessments.
   d. Integrate data with health assessment and data collection efforts conducted by others in the public health system.
   e. Analyze data to identify trends, health problems, environmental health hazards, and social and economic conditions that adversely affect the public's health.
2. Protect people from health problems and health hazards.
   a. Investigate health problems and environmental health hazards.
   b. Prevent, minimize, and contain adverse health events and conditions resulting from communicable diseases; food-, water-, and vector-borne outbreaks; chronic diseases; environmental hazards; injuries; and health disparities.
   c. Coordinate with other governmental agencies that investigate and respond to health problems, health disparities, or environmental health hazards.
   d. Lead public health emergency planning, exercises, and response activities in the community in accordance with the National Incident Management System, and coordinate with other local, state, and federal agencies.
   e. Fully participate in planning, exercises, and response activities for other emergencies in the community that have public health implications, within the context of state and regional plans and in a manner consistent with the community's best public health interest.
   f. Maintain access to laboratory and biostatistical expertise and capacity to help monitor community health status and diagnose and investigate public health problems and hazards.
   g. Maintain policies and technology required for urgent communications and electronic data exchange.
3. Give people information they need to make healthy choices.
   a. Develop relationships with the media to convey information of public health significance, correct misinformation about public health issues, and serve as an essential resource.
   b. Exchange information and data with individuals, community groups, other agencies, and the general public about physical, behavioral, environmental, social, economic, and other issues affecting the public's health.
   c. Provide targeted, culturally appropriate information to help individuals understand what decisions they can make to be healthy.
   d. Provide health promotion programs to address identified health problems.
4. Engage the community to identify and solve health problems.
   a. Engage the local public health system in an ongoing, strategic, community-driven, comprehensive planning process to identify, prioritize, and solve public health problems; establish public health goals; and evaluate success in meeting the goals.

(continues)

Table 5-12   Standards for Operational Definition of a Functional Local Health Department (continued)

  b. Promote the community's understanding of, and advocacy for, policies and activities that will improve the public's health.

  c. Support, implement, and evaluate strategies that address public health goals in partnership with public and private organizations.

  d. Develop partnerships to generate interest in and support for improved community health status, including new and emerging public health issues.

  e. Inform the community, governing bodies, and elected officials about governmental public health services that are being provided, improvements being made in those services, and priority health issues not yet being adequately addressed.

5. Develop public health policies and plans.

  a. Serve as a primary resource to governing bodies and policy makers to establish and maintain public health policies, practices, and capacity based on current science and best practices.

  b. Advocate for policies that lessen health disparities and improve physical, behavioral, environmental, social, and economic conditions in the community that affect the public's health.

  c. Engage in LHD strategic planning to develop a vision, mission, and guiding principles that reflect the community's public health needs, and to prioritize services and programs.

6. Enforce public health laws and regulations.

  a. Review existing laws and regulations and work with governing bodies and policy makers to update them as needed.

  b. Understand existing laws, ordinances, and regulations that protect the public's health.

  c. Educate individuals and organizations on the meaning, purpose, and benefit of public health laws, regulations, and ordinances and how to comply.

  d. Monitor, and analyze over time, the compliance of regulated organizations, entities, and individuals.

  e. Conduct enforcement activities.

  f. Coordinate notification of violations among other governmental agencies that enforce laws and regulations that protect the public's health.

7. Help people receive health services.

  a. Engage the community to identify gaps in culturally competent, appropriate, and equitable personal health services, including preventive and health promotion services, and develop strategies to close the gaps.

  b. Support and implement strategies to increase access to care and establish systems of personal health services, including preventive and health promotion services, in partnership with the community.

  c. Link individuals to available, accessible personal healthcare providers (i.e., a medical home).

8. Maintain a competent public health workforce.

  a. Recruit, train, develop, and retain a diverse staff.

  b. Evaluate LHD staff members' public health competencies, and address deficiencies through continuing education, training, and leadership development activities.

  c. Provide practice- and competency-based educational experiences for the future public health workforce, and provide expertise in developing and teaching public health curricula, through partnerships with academia.

  d. Promote the use of effective public health practices among other practitioners and agencies engaged in public health interventions.

  e. Provide the public health workforce with adequate resources to do their jobs.

(continues)

Table 5-12   Standards for Operational Definition of a Functional Local Health Department (continued)

9. Evaluate and improve programs and interventions.
   a. Develop evaluation efforts to assess health outcomes to the extent possible.
   b. Apply evidence-based criteria to evaluation activities where possible.
   c. Evaluate the effectiveness and quality of all LHD programs and activities and use the information to improve LHD performance and community health outcomes.
   d. Review the effectiveness of public health interventions provided by other practitioners and agencies for prevention, containment, and/or remediation of problems affecting the public's health, and provide expertise to those interventions that need improvement.
10. Contribute to and apply the evidence base of public health.
   a. When researchers approach the LHD to engage in research activities that benefit the health of the community,
      1. Identify appropriate populations, geographic areas, and partners.
      2. Work with them to actively involve the community in all phases of research.
      3. Provide data and expertise to support research.
      4. Facilitate their efforts to share research findings with the community, governing bodies, and policy makers.
   b. Share results of research, program evaluations, and best practices with other public health practitioners and academics
   c. Apply evidence-based programs and best practices where possible.

Source: Data from National Association of County and City Health Officials. *Operational Definition of a Functional Local Health Department.* Washington, DC: National Association of County and City Health Officials; 2005.

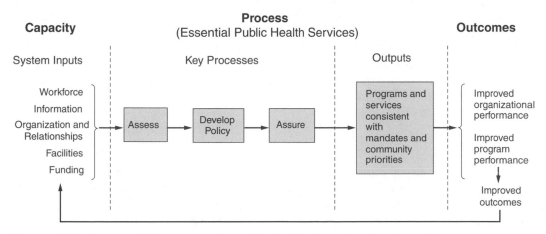

Figure 5-7   Framework for measuring public health system performance.

in public health activities by managed care plans and universities.[36] This study also documented the substantial contribution (one third of the total effort) to practice performance made by parties other than the governmental health agency in these jurisdictions. The most important contributors to process performance were state agencies, hospitals, local government agencies, nonprofit organizations, physicians and medical groups, universities, federally funded community health centers, managed care plans, and federal agencies.

The link between key processes and programs and services (outputs) offered by LHDs can also be examined. One study linked higher levels of performance of key processes with a greater percentage of services directly provided, as well as with the following specific services: personal preventive treatment in maternal and child health, chronic disease personal prevention, health education, injury control, dental health, case management services, and HIV/AIDS testing.[46] In another study, only the provision of behavioral health services was linked with higher levels of performance of key public health processes.[36] Only recently have studies linking process performance and community health outcomes appeared in the public health literature.

Ultimately, the important processes of public health practice will result in improved health status and other important outcomes. The level of current knowledge as to how capacity influences public health processes and how public health processes influence public health outputs and how those outputs influence outcomes makes it difficult to know exactly what works and why. Several studies have taken up this challenge, however, and the early results are encouraging. One study found that states that had more completely adopted the core functions and essential services model experienced greater improvement in population health status than did states with less complete adoption of this model.[47] Another study examined community health status at the LHJ level and found that LHD performance was a primary contributor to predicting county health status for most health outcomes considered.[48] A clear causal link between better health outcomes and high levels of performing public health's core functions and essential services has not yet been found, but continuous improvement in the measures of public health practice used to establish that link bring us closer to the day when we know what works and what does not.

CONCLUSION

Several lessons are apparent after nearly 100 years of trial and error. Early efforts to characterize and measure public health practice were limited by a narrower view of public health's core functions than that articulated in the IOM report. Performance of six specific services—components of the assurance function—was emphasized over more basic public health processes, such as community assessment and constituency building, linked to the assessment and policy development functions. In part, this was a result of the lack of a comprehensive conceptual framework that links public health practice to capacity, process, and outcome measures.

The IOM report identified assessment and policy development functions to complement the longstanding view that public health's role is one of assurance. The essential public health services framework provides operational definitions for these concepts and establishes new standards for public health practice. Additional strategies and tools are now available to promote these practice standards and to measure their performance in public health systems. Despite these advances, there is only limited evidence of significant improvement in core function-related performance since the appearance of the IOM report and little progress toward a comprehensive examination of the links among capacity, processes, and outcomes and their relationship to an effective governmental presence. The clearest lesson after decades of efforts is that it has always been easier to measure specific aspects of public health practice and its core functions than to develop consensus as to what these measurements tell us about public health performance.

DISCUSSION QUESTIONS AND EXERCISES

1. What are the three core functions of public health, and how are these operationalized by public health organizations?
2. Explain the relationships among capacity, processes, and outcomes in Figure 5-7.
3. What features are similar among MAPP, PATCH, and Model Standards? What features are different?
4. Determine whether your LHD has completed APEXPH or MAPP. If it has, what were the results? If it has not, why? What other approaches or tools were used?
5. Obtain the community health plan (or a summary) for your city or county and review the process that developed it for consistency with the 11 steps of Model Standards and with the essential public health services framework. In what ways did the process and plan differ from these frameworks?
6. Review the organization of health responsibilities in the state of your choice and describe how the three core functions of public health are delegated and carried out among various offices and agencies of state government beyond the state health department. The URL for a state is usually http://www.state.stateinitials.us. For example, Illinois would be http://www.state.il.us.
7. What role do tools such as PATCH, APEXPH, and MAPP play in carrying out public health's core functions at the local level?
8. How do current community-driven health planning models differ from resource-based planning models of the past?

9. You are the administrator of a typical county-based LHD in a largely rural state. Your newly elected county board president has ordered you to come up with new health-related initiatives that will improve the health of the county's residents. How would you approach this charge?

10. Review the progress of the past century related to reducing the toll from cardiovascular diseases (CVDs) (see this chapter's Public Health Spotlight on Cardiovascular Disease). To what extent is there a constituency group for these issues? Why would it be beneficial to the public's health to build or strengthen a constituent group for these issues?

11. What arguments can be made in support of national standards for public health organizations and systems? What arguments can be made against them?

REFERENCES

1. Institute of Medicine, Committee on the Future of Public Health. *The Future of Public Health*. Washington, DC: National Academy Press; 1988.

2. Turnock BJ, Handler AS. From measuring to improving public health practice. *Annu Rev Public Health*. 1997;18:261–282.

3. Vaughan HF. Local health services in the United States: the story of CAP. *Am J Public Health*. 1972;62:95–108.

4. American Public Health Association, Committee on Administrative Practice. Appraisal form for city health work. *Am J Public Health*. 1926;16(Suppl):1–65.

5. Emerson H, Luginbuhl M. *Local Health Units for the Nation*. New York: Commonwealth Fund; 1945.

6. Shonick W. *Government and Health Services: Government's Role in the Development of U.S. Health Services 1930–1980*. New York, NY: Oxford University Press; 1995.

7. Hanlon JJ. Is there a future for local health departments? *Health Serv Rep*. 1973;88:898–901.

8. American Public Health Association. Healthy Communities 2000: Model Standards. Washington, DC: American Public Health Association; 1991.

9. Scutchfield FD, Hiltabiddle SE, Rawding N, et al. Compliance with the recommendations of the IOM report, the future of public health: a survey of local health departments. *J Public Health Policy*. 1997;18:155–166.

10. Harrell JA, Baker EL. The essential services of public health. *Leadership Public Health*. 1994;3: 27–31.

11. Public Health Functions Steering Committee. *Public Health in America*. Washington, DC: U.S. Public Health Service; 1994.

12. Corso LC, Wiesner PJ, Halverson PK, et al. Using the essential services as a foundation for performance measurement and assessment of local public health systems. *J Public Health Manage Pract*. 2000;6:1–18.

13. National Association of County and City Health Officials. *Assessment Protocol for Excellence in Public Health*. Washington, DC: National Association of County and City Health Officials; 1991.

14. National Association of County and City Health Officials. *Mobilizing for Action Through Planning and Partnerships*. Washington, DC: National Association of County and City Health Officials; 2000.

15. Lenihan DP, Landrum LB, Turnock BJ. *An Evaluation of MAPP and NPHPS in Local Public Health Jurisdictions*. Chicago, IL: Illinois Public Health Institute; 2006.

16. Institute of Medicine. *Healthy Communities: New Partnerships for the Future of Public Health*. Washington, DC: National Academy Press; 1996.

17. Committee on the Future of the Public's Health in the 21st Century, Institute of Medicine. *The Future of the Public's Health in the 21st Century*. Washington, DC: National Academy Press; 2003.

18. Institute of Medicine. *Improving Health in the Community: A Role for Performance Monitoring*. Washington, DC: National Academy Press; 1997.

19. National Association of County and City Health Officials. *2005 National Profile of Local Health Departments*. Washington, DC: National Association of County and City Health Officials; 2006.

20. Minkler M. Ten commitments for community health education. *Health Educ Res Theory Pract*. 1994;9:527–534.

21. McKnight JL, Kretzmann J. Mapping community capacity. *New Designs*. 1992;Winter:9–15.

22. Centers for Disease Control/ATSDR Committee on Community Engagement. *Principles of Community Engagement*. Atlanta, GA: Centers for Disease Control; 1997.

23. University of Kansas. Community Tool Box. http://ctb.lsi.ukans.edu. Accessed May 31, 2010.

24. Public Health Foundation. *Healthy People 2010 Tool Kit*. Washington, DC: American Public Health Foundation; 1999.

25. Berkowitz B. Collaboration for health improvement: models for state, community, and academic partnerships. *J Public Health Manage Pract*. 2000;6:67–72.

26. Norris T. Healthy Communities. *Natl Civic Rev*. 1997;86:3–10.

27. Milio N. Priorities and strategies for promoting community-based prevention policies. *J Public Health Manage Pract*. 1998;4:14–28.

28. National Association of County and City Health Officials. *1990 National Profile of Local Health Departments*. Washington, DC: National Association of County and City Health Officials; 1992.

29. National Association of County and City Health Officials. *1992–1993 National Profile of Local Health Departments*. Washington, DC: National Association of County and City Health Officials; 1995.

30. Miller CA, Moore KS, Richards TB, et al. A proposed method for assessing the performance of local public health functions and practices. *Am J Public Health*. 1994;84:1743–1749.

31. Richards TB, Rogers JJ, Christenson GM, et al. Assessing public health practice: application of ten core function measures of community health in six states. *Am J Prev Med*. 1995;11(Suppl 6):36–40.

32. Richards TB, Rogers JJ, Christenson GM, et al. Evaluating local public health performance at a community level on a statewide basis. *J Public Health Manage Pract*. 1995;1:70–83.

33. Turnock BJ, Handler AS, Hall W, et al. Local health department effectiveness in addressing the core functions of public health. *Public Health Rep*. 1994;109:653–658.

34. Rohrer JE, Dominguez D, Weaver M, et al. Assessing public health performance in Iowa's counties. *J Public Health Manage Pract*. 1997;3:10–15.

35. Turnock BJ, Handler AS, Miller CA. Core function-related local public health performance. *J Public Health Manage Pract*. 1998;4:26–32.

36. Mays GP, Miller CA, Halverson PK, et al. Availability and perceived effectiveness of public health activities in the nation's most populous communities. *Am J Public Health*. 2004;94:1019–1026.

37. Suen J, Gadsden-Knowles K, Sohani M. *Public Health Jurisdiction Capabilities: Assessment of Core Function Related Performance*. Philadelphia, PA: APHA 130th Annual Meeting Abstract Session 4109; 2002.

38. Washington State Department of Health. *Standards for Public Health in Washington State*. Olympia, WA: Washington State Department of Health; 2001.

39. Illinois Roadmap Implementation Task Force. *Improving the Public Health System: The Road to Better Health for All of Illinois*. Springfield, IL: Illinois Department of Public Health; 1990.

40. Illinois Local Health Liaison Committee. *Project Health: The Reengineering of Public Health in Illinois*. Springfield, IL: Illinois Department of Public Health; 1994.

41. Turnock BJ, Handler AS, Hall W, et al. Capacity-building influences on Illinois local health departments. *J Public Health Manage Pract*. 1995;1:50–58.

42. U.S. Department of Health and Human Services. *Healthy People 2020*. Chapter 23 Public Health Infrastructure. Washington, DC: U.S. Department of Health and Human Services-Public Health Service; 2010.

43. Halverson PK, Nicola RM, Baker EL. Performance measurement and accreditation of public health organizations: a call to action. *J Public Health Manage Pract.* 1998;4:5–7.

44. Issue Focus: Accreditation of Public Health Departments. *J Public Health Manage Pract.* 2007;13(4):329–434.

45. National Association of County and City Health Officials. *Operational Definition of a Functional Local Health Department.* Washington, DC: National Association of County and City Health Officials; 2005.

46. Handler AS, Turnock BJ. Local health department effectiveness in addressing the core functions of public health: Essential ingredients. *J Public Health Policy.* 1996;17:460–483.

47. Ford EW, Duncan WJ, Ginter PM. Health departments' implementation of public health's core functions: an assessment of health impacts. *Public Health.* 2005;119:11–21.

48. Kanarek N, Stanley J, Bialek R. Local public health agency performance and community health status. *J Public Health Manage Pract.* 2006;12:522–527.

Public Health Spotlight on Screening for Antibody to the Human Immunodeficiency Virus

(This case study was adapted and expanded by Bernard J. Turnock from one developed in 1987 for CDC by Lyle Peterson, Guthrie Birkhead, and Richard Dicker. Dr. Turnock served as Director of the Illinois Department of Public Health from 1985 through 1990 when the events described in this case study occurred in Illinois.)

After completing this case study, learners will be able to do the following:

- Define and perform calculations of sensitivity, specificity, predictive-value positive, and predictive-value negative
- Describe the relationship between prevalence and predictive value
- Discuss the trade-offs between sensitivity and specificity
- List the principles of a good screening program
- Identify political and policy implications of the use of screening tests in populations with different levels of prevalence

In December 1982, a report in the *Morbidity and Mortality Weekly Report* (*MMWR*) described three persons who had developed AIDS but who had neither of the previously known risk factors for the disease: homosexual/bisexual activity with numerous partners and intravenous drug use. These three persons had previously received whole-blood transfusions. By 1983, widespread recognition of the problem of transfusion-related AIDS led to controversial recommendations that persons in known high-risk groups voluntarily defer from donating blood. In June 1984, after the discovery of HIV, five companies were licensed to produce enzyme-linked immunosorbent assay (EIA, then called ELISA) test kits for detecting HIV antibody. A Food and Drug Administration (FDA) spokesman stated that "getting this test out to the blood banks is our No. 1 priority. . . ." Blood bank directors anxiously awaited the availability of the first test kit for screening blood. The first test kit was approved by the FDA in early March 1985.

In the prelicensure evaluation, sensitivity and specificity of the test kits were estimated using blood samples from four groups: those with AIDS by CDC criteria, those with other symptoms and signs of HIV infection, those with various autoimmune disorders and neoplastic diseases that could give a false-positive test result, and presumably healthy blood and plasma donors. Numerous complex issues were discussed even before licensure. Among them were understanding the magnitude of the problem of false-positive test results and determining whether test-positive blood donors should be notified.

It is now March 1985. The first HIV antibody test kits will arrive in blood banks in the state in a few hours. Meeting to discuss the appropriate use of this test are the State Health Director, the State Epidemiologist, the medical director of the regional blood bank, and the Director of the State Department of Alcohol and Substance Abuse.

To help in the discussions, the group reviews the prelicensure information regarding the sensitivity and specificity of test kit A. The information indicates that the sensitivity of test kit A is 95% (0.95), and the specificity is 98% (0.98). These and related measures are defined in Table 5-13.

Question 1: With this information, by constructing a 2-by-2 table, calculate the predictive-value positive and predictive-value negative of the EIA in a hypothetical population of 1,000,000 blood donors. Using a separate 2-by-2 table, calculate PVP and PVN for a population of 1,000 drug users. Assume that the actual prevalence of HIV antibody among blood donors is 0.04% (0.0004) and that of intravenous drug users is 10% (0.10).

The blood bank medical director wants assistance in evaluating the EIA as a test for screening donor blood in the state. In particular, she is concerned about the possibility that some antibody-positive units will be missed by the test, and she wonders about false-positive test results because she is under pressure to develop a notification procedure for EIA-positive donors.

Question 2: Do you think that the EIA is a good screening test for the blood bank? What would you recommend to the blood bank medical director about notification of EIA-positive blood donors?

The director of the Department of Alcohol and Substance Abuse has noticed a dramatic increase in AIDS among clients in his intravenous-drug-abuse treatment programs. For planning purposes, he wants to do a voluntary HIV antibody seroprevalence survey of intravenous drug-abuse clients and would like to assess the feasibility of using the test results as part of behavior-modification counseling.

Question 3: Do you think that the EIA performs well enough to justify informing test-positive clients in the drug abuse clinics that they are positive for HIV?

Table 5-13 Relationship of Antibody Status to Test Results: Definitions for Sensitivity, Specificity, Predictive-Value Positive, and Predictive-Value Negative

		Actual Antibody Status		
		Present	*Absent*	*Total*
Test result	Positive	True positive (A)	False positive (B)	All positive tests (A + B)
	Negative	False negative (C)	True negative (D)	All negative tests (C + D)
	Total	All with antibody (A + C)	All without antibody (B + D)	Total (A + B + C + D)

- Sensitivity: the probability that the test result will be positive when administered to persons who actually have the antibody. Sensitivity = true positives/all with antibody. Algebraically, sensitivity = $A/(A + C)$.
- Specificity: the probability that the test result will be negative when administered to persons who are actually without the antibody. Specificity = true negatives / all without antibody. Algebraically, specificity = $D/(B + D)$.
- Predictive-value positive (PVP): the probability that a person with a positive screening test result actually has the antibody. PVP = true positives / all with positive test. Algebraically, PVP = $A/(A + B)$.
- Predictive-value negative (PVN): the probability that a person with a negative screening test result actually does not have the antibody. PVN = true negatives/all with negative test. Algebraically, PVN = $D/(C + D)$.

Question 4: If sensitivity and specificity remain constant, what is the relationship of prevalence to predictive-value positive and predictive-value negative?

EIA results are recorded as optical-density (OD) ratios. The OD ratio is the ratio of absorbance of the tested sample to the absorbance of the control sample. The greater the OD ratio, the more "positive" is the test result. The EIA, as with most other screening tests, is not perfect; there is some overlap of OD ratios of samples that are actually antibody positive and those that are actually antibody negative. Establishing the cutoff value to define a positive test result from a negative one can be somewhat arbitrary. Suppose that the test manufacturer initially considered that an OD ratio of 2.0 or higher would be considered positive.

Question 5: In terms of sensitivity and specificity, what happens if you raise the cutoff from 2.0 to 3.0?

Question 6: In terms of sensitivity and specificity, what happens if you lower the cutoff from 2.0 to 1.0?

Question 7: From what you know now, what is the relationship between sensitivity and specificity of a screening test?

Question 8: If the scenario above described HIV antibody test results for normals and persons with HIV/AIDS, where might the blood bank medical director and the head of drug treatment want the cutoff point to be for each program? Who would probably want a lower cutoff value? Why?

The blood bank medical director is concerned that because of the low predictive-value positive of the EIA in the blood donor population, the blood bank personnel cannot properly inform those who are EIA positive of their actual antibody status. For this reason, she wishes to evaluate the Western blot test as a confirmatory test for HIV antibody. The Western blot test identifies antibodies to specific proteins associated with HIV. The Western blot is the most widely used secondary test to detect HIV antibody because its specificity exceeds 99.99%; however, it is not used as a primary screening test because it is expensive and technically difficult to perform. Its sensitivity is thought to be lower than that of the EIA.

Because the Western blot test is not yet generally available, the blood bank medical director is wondering whether the initial EIA-positive results can be confirmed by repeating the EIA and by considering persons to have the antibody only if results of both tests are positive. The state epidemiologist suggests that they compare the performance of the repeat EIA and the Western blot as confirmatory tests. To do this, they will use the earlier hypothetical sample of 1,000,000 blood donors. They assume that serum specimens that are initially positive by EIA are then split into two portions; a repeat EIA is performed on one portion and a Western blot test on the other portion.

Question 9: What is the actual antibody prevalence in the population of persons whose blood samples will undergo a second test?

Question 10: Calculate the predictive-value positive of the two sequences of tests: EIA-EIA and EIA-Western blot. Assume that the sensitivity and specificity of the EIA are 95% and 98%, respectively. Assume that the sensitivity and specificity of the Western blot are 80% and 99.99%, respectively. Also assume that the tests are independent, even though they may not be (e.g., those with cross-reactive proteins are likely to cross-react each time).

Question 11: Why does the predictive-value positive increase so dramatically with the addition of a second test? Why is the predictive value positive higher for the EIA-WB sequence than for the EIA-EIA sequence?

The combination of EIA and Western blot testing is quickly implemented by blood donation centers, and the number of new AIDS cases attributed to blood donations declines rapidly. The use of these screening tests for the purpose of safeguarding the blood supply appears to be very successful.

AIDS remains a major public health concern as the number of new cases, especially among men having sex with men and IV drug users, continues to grow in Illinois and elsewhere. Despite the growth of the epidemic, there is little political activity in the way of new laws to deal with AIDS in 1985 and 1986. Only a few legislative proposals are introduced into the state legislature during that period. In early 1987, however, more than 60 legislative proposals are introduced into the state legislature. About three fourths of these call for testing various subgroups in the population, including food handlers, teachers, public safety personnel, and marriage license applicants.

Question 12: What might have happened in 1986/1987 to prompt increased political and legislative attention to the AIDS epidemic? Why do you think so many proposals focused on testing various subgroups in the population?

It is now 1987 and the governor has asked the state health director to evaluate a proposed premarital HIV-antibody-screening program. A bill to establish the program is to be voted on by the state legislature tomorrow. It will amend a long-standing state law requiring marriage license applicants to submit information from a physician that they are free from transmissible syphilis. An estimated 200,000 people will get married in the state in the next year. The proposed legislation requires that each prospective bride and groom submit a blood sample for EIA testing. Samples that test positive by EIA will undergo confirmatory Western blot testing.

The legislation describes the goal of the screening program to be to decrease inadvertent perinatal or sexual HIV transmission by determining who among those to be married are probably infected with the virus.

Question 13: What criteria are used in evaluating mass screening programs? Which of these criteria would you consider to be most important in evaluating this proposed screening program?

Table 5-14 shows the possible results of the testing, assuming that persons getting married have the same actual HIV antibody prevalence as blood donors (0.04%). In 1987, the sensitivity and specificity of the improved EIA Test Kit A available at the time were 97% and 99.8%, respectively. The Western blot sensitivity and specificity were 95% and 99.99%, respectively.

Question 14: Compute the cost of the screening program. Assume a cost of $90.00 for every initial EIA test ($30.00 laboratory fee and $60.00 health-care-provider visit) and an additional $100.00 for EIA-positive persons who will need additional testing. What is the cost of the screening program in the next year? What is the cost per identified antibody-positive person?

These results do not fully reflect some of the qualitative impacts of what took place in Illinois in 1988 to 1989. As noted previously here, the prevalence rate for premarital tests in Illinois was found to be about one half of that used in the example above (2 per 10,000). The research literature on HIV testing identifies an important additional consideration: the background false-positivity rate that occurs even when serial testing protocols are used. For example, it may be that 1 person per 10,000 will have

Table 5-14   Case Study Test Results

		Actual Antibody Status		
		Present	*Absent*	*Total*
Test	Positive	78	400	478
result	Negative	2	199,520	199,522
	Total	80	199,920	200,000

Note: 478 positive tests to undergo Western blot testing.
Follow-Up Western Blot Test

		Actual Antibody Status		
		Present	*Absent*	*Total*
Test	Positive	74	0	74
result	Negative	4	400	404
	Total	78	400	478

Note: With sequential tests, sensitivity = 92% (74/80); specificity = 100% (199,920/199,920);
predictive-value positive = 100% (74/74).

a falsely-positive result even after serial tests are performed. That may not be a serious problem when testing is performed on populations in which the prevalence is high such as those attending testing and counseling centers (where the prevalence is over 300 per 10,000). In this situation, more than 99% of positive tests would occur to people who really had the antibody, but in a population with a prevalence of 4 per 10,000, one fourth of those who test positive would not actually carry the antibody. In a population with a prevalence of 2 per 10,000, approximately half would not actually carry the antibody; however, they would be given the same information ("you are positive") as those who actually were positive, and they might make important life decisions (to marry, to have children, to continue with a pregnancy, etc.) based on information that has a 25% probability (at 4 per 10,000 prevalence) or 50% probability (at 2 per 10,000 prevalence) to be incorrect.

Question 15: What is your final recommendation to the Governor? What are the three strongest arguments in support of your recommendation?

Despite the opposition of the public health and medical community (among many others), a law is enacted that requires all marriage license applicants to submit evidence of having been tested for HIV antibodies. This law is part of a package of 17 bills addressing a wide variety of AIDS issues that was considered the most comprehensive AIDS legislative package in the nation. Virtually all of the bills included in this package were supported by public health advocates and officials, except for the one that would require all marriage license applicants to provide evidence of having been tested for HIV antibody. That particular provision took effect on January 1, 1988, and continued through August 1989.

Question 16: Review the data summarized in Table 5-15. Does the information from this experience support your initial recommendation and arguments? Are there other factors that you would not have predicted that eventually may have contributed to the legislature's and governor's decision to repeal this law?

Question 17: It is now the current year and a new bill has been introduced into the state legislature that would require all elementary and secondary school teachers in the state to provide evidence of having been tested for HIV antibody as a requirement for securing teacher certification. All teachers must be certified in order to be hired or continued by a school district, public or private. Because of your expertise in HIV screening tests, the governor has asked you to write a memo outlining whether he should sign this bill into law if it reaches his desk.

Table 5-15   Twenty-Month Experience with Illinois Premarital HIV Testing Law

56 positives out of 260,000 tests (2 per 10,000) for comparison purposes (at that time)
    1,530 per 10,000—IV drug users
    318 per 10,000—counseling/testing sites
    11 per 10,000—military recruits
    9 per 10,000—women of childbearing age
    3 per 10,000—blood donors statewide
    4 per 10,000—blood donors, Cook and collar counties
    2 per 10,000—marriage license applicants
37 males, 19 females
26 white, 23 black, 6 Hispanic
23 from Cook County, 17 from collar counties, 14 from down-state Illinois
    2 per 10,000 Cook County
    3 per 10,000 DuPage County
    4 per 10,000 Lake County
    7 per 10,000 Will County
28 reported risk factors (10 sexual contact, 14 IV drug use, 4 transfusion)
Marriage Licenses issued by year:
    1987—99,000
    1988—77,000 (premarital HIV testing law in effect all year)
    1989—87,000 (premarital HIV testing law in effect 8 months of year)
    1990—100,000
Number of marriage licenses issued to Illinois residents in selected counties of bordering states, 1987 versus 1988:
    Scott County (Iowa) 240 versus 560
    Lake County (Indiana) 210 versus 1000
    Kenosha County (Wisconsin) 110 versus 1210
    Paducah County (Kentucky) 320 versus 1710

Source: Data from Turnock BJ and Lokar K, unpublished data.

REFERENCES

McKilip J. The effect of mandatory premarital HIV testing on marriage: the case of Illinois. *Am J Public Health*. 1991;81:650–653.

Peterson LR, White CR, the Premarital Screening Study Group. Premarital screening for antibodies to human immunodeficiency virus in the United States. *Am J Public Health*. 1990;80:1087–1090.

Turnock BJ, Kelly CJ. Mandatory premarital testing for human immunodeficiency virus: the Illinois experience. *JAMA*. 1989;261:3415–3418.

Public Health Spotlight on Cardiovascular Disease

Heart disease has been the leading cause of death in the United States since 1921, and stroke has been the third leading cause since 1938; together they account for approximately 40% of all deaths. Between 1950 and 2000, age-adjusted death rates from CVD have declined 60%, representing one of the most important public health achievements of the 20th century. This Public Health Spotlight summarizes 20th century trends for CVD, advances in the understanding of risk factors for CVD, development of prevention interventions to reduce these risks, and improvements in therapy for persons who develop CVD. Current status and 21st century challenges are also highlighted.

PUBLIC HEALTH ACHIEVEMENTS IN 20TH CENTURY AMERICA[1]

Age-adjusted death rates per 100,000 persons (standardized to the 1940 U.S. population) for diseases of the heart (i.e., coronary heart disease, hypertensive heart disease, and rheumatic heart disease) decreased from a peak of 307.4 in 1950 to 134.6 in 1996, an overall decline of 56%[2] (Figure 5-8). Age-adjusted death rates for coronary heart disease (the major form of CVD contributing to mortality) continued to increase into the 1960s and then declined. In 1996, 621,000 fewer deaths occurred from coronary heart disease than would have been expected had the rate remained at its 1963 peak.[2]

Age-adjusted death rates for stroke have declined steadily since the beginning of the century. Since 1950, stroke rates have declined more than 60%, from 88.8 in 1950 to 26.5 in 1996. Total age-adjusted CVD death rates have declined 60% since 1950 and accounted for approximately 73% of the decline in all causes of deaths during the same period.[2]

Intensive investigation into the CVD epidemic largely began in the 1940s after World War II, although causal hypotheses about CVD and recognition of geographic differences in disease rates occurred earlier.[3–5] Landmark epidemiologic investigations, such as the Framingham Heart

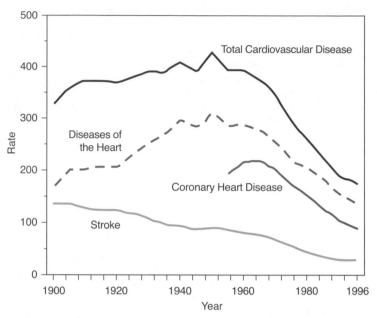

Figure 5-8   Age-adjusted death rates for total CVD, diseases of the heart, coronary heart disease, and stroke by year, United States, 1900–1996. *Source:* From Centers for Disease Control and Prevention. Achievements in public health, 1900–1999: decline in deaths for heart disease and strokes. *MMWR.* 1999;48: 649–656.

Study,[6] established the major risk factors of high blood cholesterol, high blood pressure, and smoking and dietary factors (particularly dietary cholesterol, fat, and sodium). The risk factor concept—that particular biologic, lifestyle, and social conditions were associated with increased risk for disease—developed out of CVD epidemiology.[4,5] In addition to the major risk factors (i.e., high blood pressure, high blood cholesterol, and smoking), other important factors include socioeconomic status, obesity, and physical inactivity.[7] Striking regional differences were noted particularly for stroke mortality, with the highest rates observed in the southeastern United States.[2] Cross-national and cross-cultural studies highlighted the importance of social, cultural, and environmental factors in the development of CVD.

Coronary heart disease and stroke, the two major causes of CVD-related mortality, are not influenced to the same degree by the recognized risk factors. For example, elevated blood cholesterol is a major risk factor for coronary heart disease, and hypertension is the major risk factor for stroke. Physical activity, smoking cessation, and a healthy diet, which can lower the risk for heart disease, can also help lower the risk for stroke.[8]

Early intervention studies in the 1960s sought to establish whether lowering risk factor levels would reduce risk for CVD.[3–5] During the

1970s and 1980s, along with numerous clinical trials demonstrating the efficacy of antihypertensive and lipid-lowering drugs, community trials sought to reduce risk at the community level.[9] Public health interventions to reduce CVD have benefitted from a combination of the "high-risk" approach—aimed at persons with increased risk for CVD—and the population-wide approach—aimed at lowering risk for the entire community.[10] National programs that combine these complementary approaches and that are aimed at healthcare providers, patients, and the general public include the National High Blood Pressure Education Program,[11] initiated in 1972, and the National Cholesterol Education Program, initiated in 1985.[12] Although earlier CDC community demonstration projects focused on cardiovascular health, the CDC established its National Center for Chronic Disease Prevention and Health Promotion in 1989, with a high priority of promoting cardiovascular health.[9]

Reasons for the declines in heart disease and stroke may vary by period and across region or socioeconomic groups (e.g., age, gender, and racial/ethnic groups). Prevention efforts and improvements in early detection, treatment, and care have resulted in a number of beneficial trends (Table 5-16), which may have contributed to declines in heart disease and stroke. These trends include the following:

- A decline in cigarette smoking among adults aged greater than or equal to 18 years from approximately 42% in 1965 to 25% in 1995.[13] Substantial public health efforts to reduce tobacco use began soon after recognition of the association between smoking and CVD and between smoking and cancer and the first Surgeon General's report on smoking and health published in 1964.
- A decrease in mean blood pressure levels in the U.S. population.[11,13,14]
- An increase in the percentage of persons with hypertension who have the condition treated and controlled.[11,13,14]
- A decrease in mean blood cholesterol levels.[12–14]
- Changes in the U.S. diet. Data based on surveys of food supply suggest that consumption of saturated fat and cholesterol has decreased since 1909.[15] Data from the National Health and Nutrition Examination surveys suggest that decreases in the percentage of calories from dietary fat and the levels of dietary cholesterol coincide with decreases in blood cholesterol levels.[16]
- Improvements in medical care, including advances in diagnosing and treating heart disease and stroke, development of effective medications for treatment of hypertension and hypercholesterolemia, greater numbers of specialists and healthcare providers focusing on CVD, an increase in emergency medical services for heart attack and stroke, and an increase in coronary-care units.[13,17] These developments have contributed to lower case-fatality rates, lengthened survival times, and shorter hospital stays for persons with CVD.[2,17]

Table 5-16   Estimated Change in Risk Factors and Correlates for Heart Disease and Stroke, by Selected Characteristics—United States

Characteristic	Baseline Year	Baseline Estimate	Follow-Up Year	Follow-Up Estimate
Adults aged 20 to 74 years with hypertension	1960–1962	37%	1988–1994	23%
Persons with hypertension who are taking action to control their blood pressure (e.g., medication, diet, reducing salt intake, and exercise)	1985	79%	1990	90%
Persons with hypertension whose blood pressure is controlled	1976–1980	11%	1988–1991	29%
Adults aged 20–74 with high blood cholesterol	1960–1962	32%	1988–1994	19%
Mean serum cholesterol levels mg/dL of adults aged >18 years	1960–1962	220	1988–1994	203
Adults aged ≥18 years who are current smokers	1965	42%	1995	25%
Persons who are overweight	1960–1962	24%	1988–1994	35%
Percentage of calories in the diet from fat	1976–1980	36%	1988–1994	34%
Percentage of calories in the diet from saturated fat	1976–1980	13%	1988–1994	12%
Number of physicians indicating cardiovascular diseases as their primary area of practice	1975	5,046	1996	14,304

Source: From Achievements in Public Health, United States, 1900–1999: Decline in Deaths for Heart Disease and Strokes. *Morbidity and Mortality Weekly Report.* Vol. 48, No. 36. The Centers for Disease Control and Prevention; 1999:649–656.

21ST CENTURY PUBLIC HEALTH CHALLENGES[1]

Despite remarkable progress, heart disease and stroke remain leading causes of disability and death. Estimated costs for morbidity and mortality from CVD, including health expenditures and lost productivity, were $286.5 billion in 1999.[18] In addition, the overall declines in heart disease and stroke mortality mask important differences in rates of decline by race/ethnicity, gender, socioeconomic status, and geographic region. During 1985 to 1996, for example, heart disease age-adjusted mortality declined 29% among white men, but only 10% among American Indian/Alaskan Native women.[13] Persons of lower socioeconomic status have higher mortality, morbidity, and risk factor levels for heart disease and stroke than persons of higher socioeconomic status.[13,19] In addition, the social class gap in heart disease deaths may be increasing as the rates of heart disease decline faster among higher social classes.[19] Geographically, declines in heart disease deaths did not occur at the same time for all communities. Areas with poorer socioeconomic profiles were more likely to experience a later onset of the decline of heart disease.[19]

Public health programs at the state level for heart disease and stroke have been limited. In fiscal year 1999, through a new program, the CDC funded 11 states with the highest CVD mortality rates to plan, develop, and implement state-based efforts for CVD prevention. In addition to activities such as surveillance, these programs will emphasize policy and environmental interventions, both social and physical, aimed at sustaining positive health behavior change.

Although many trends have been positive, including steadily declining hospitalization rates for heart disease (Figure 5-9), trends for some important indicators have not improved substantially, have leveled off, or are reversing. For example, approximately 70% of persons with hypertension do not have the condition controlled at levels below 140/90 mm Hg, and death rates for stroke have not declined in recent years.[2,11,13] Heart failure has emerged as a health concern for older adults, and adults who survive a myocardial infarction or other hypertension-related diseases remain at increased risk for heart failure.[20] In addition, the prevalence of obesity has increased dramatically among both children and adults in the United States.[13] Figure 5-10 summarizes recent levels of major risk factors for CVD among Americans.

Major public health challenges for the 21st century include the following:

- Reducing risk factor levels and preventing the development of adverse risk factors. Continued research is needed to understand the determinants (social, psychological, environmental, physiologic, and genetic) of CVD risk factors.
- Reducing the racial/ethnic disparities in heart disease and stroke mortality.
- Increasing the ability to reach underserved groups with appropriate and effective public health messages.
- Promoting policy and environmental strategies that enhance healthy behavior.
- Determining the relation between genetics and disease. The associations of genetic variants with CVD, and especially the interplay between genetic and environmental factors, may play increasingly important roles in the nation's efforts to prevent CVD.
- Identifying new or emerging risk factors and determining their potential for public health intervention. New or emerging risk factors that have been associated with CVD include elevated levels of

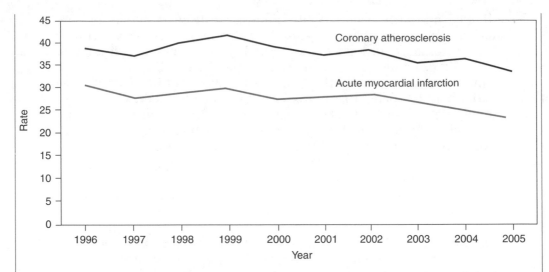

Figure 5-9 Rate* of hospitalizations† for coronary atherosclerosis and acute myocardial infarction (MI),§ by year, National Hospital Discharge Survey, United States, 1996–2005.

* Per 10,000 population.

† Hospitalizations in general hospitals, children's general hospitals, and hospitals with an average stay of <30 days.

§ Coronary atherosclerosis hospitalizations were those with a first-listed diagnosis code 414.0 based on the *International Classification of Diseases*, 9th Revision, Clinical Modification. Acute MI hospitalizations were those with a first-listed diagnosis code 410.0–410.9.

Source: From Centers for Disease Control and Prevention. Rate of hospitalizations for coronary atherosclerosis and acute myocardial infarction (MI), by year, National Hospital Discharge Survey, United States, 1996—2005. *MMWR.* 2007; 56(26):659.

total homocysteine, fibrinogen, and C-reactive protein, and infectious agents such as *Helicobacter pylori* and *Chlamydia pneumoniae*.

- Focusing on secondary prevention and disability. An aging U.S. population and an increasing number of persons surviving life-threatening cardiovascular conditions require public health programs to focus on issues such as disability and quality of life. Persons with existing cardiovascular conditions are at increased risk for future life-threatening events related to those conditions.
- Addressing the needs of the global community. Although CVD death rates are higher in developed nations, most cases occur in developing nations.[8] Developing countries may face a double burden of infectious and chronic diseases. International collaboration to improve cardiovascular health will need to continue to reduce the burden of CVD worldwide.[9]

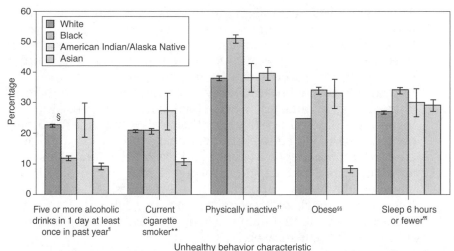

Figure 5-10 Prevalence of selected unhealthy behavior characteristics among adults aged ≥18 years, by race*, National Health Interview Survey, United States, 2005–2007[†].

* Racial categories include persons who indicated a single race only.

[†] Estimates are age adjusted using the projected 2000 U.S. population as the standard population and using three age groups: 18–44 years, 45–64 years, and ≥ 65 years. Estimates are based on household interviews of a sample of the civilian, noninstitutionalized U.S. adult population. Denominators for each percentage exclude persons with unknown health behavior characteristics.

[§] 95% confidence interval.

[¶] The question regarding consumption of five or more drinks in 1 day at least once in the past year was asked of only current drinkers; however, estimates reflect percentage of all adults who engaged in this behavior.

** Smoked at least 100 cigarettes in lifetime and currently smokes.

[††] Never engage in any light, moderate, or vigorous leisure-time physical activity.

[§§] Defined as a body mass index (weight [kg]/height [m^2]) ≥30.

[¶¶] Usual number of hours of sleep in a 24-hour period.

Source: From Centers for Disease Control and Prevention. Prevalence of selected unhealthy behavior characteristics among adults aged ≥18 years, by race, National Health Interview Survey, United States, 2005–2007. *MMWR.* 2010;59(16):495. Data from Schoenborn CA, Adams PF. Health behaviors of adults—United States, 2005–2007. *Vital Health Stat.* 2010;10(245). http://www.cdc.gov/nchs/data/series/sr_10/sr10_245.pdf. Accessed May 12, 2010.

To assist in meeting these modern challenges, the Task Force on Community Preventive Services completed systematic reviews of the effectiveness of selected population-based interventions designed to increase levels of physical activity. Effective community preventive interventions for increasing physical activity include:[21]

- Community-wide campaigns to increase physical activity that involve many community sectors, include highly visible, broad-based, multicomponent strategies (e.g., social support, risk factor screening, or health education), and that may also address other CVD risk factors, particularly diet and smoking.
- Individually adapted health behavior change programs to increase physical activity that teach behavioral skills to help participants incorporate physical activity into their daily routines; these programs are best tailored to each individual's specific interests, preferences, and readiness for change and teach behavioral skills such as: goal-setting and self-monitoring of progress toward those goals; building social support for new behaviors; behavioral reinforcement through self-reward and positive self-talk; structured problem solving to maintain the behavior change; and prevention of relapse into sedentary behavior.
- Social support interventions that focus on changing physical activity behavior through building, strengthening, and maintaining social networks that provide supportive relationships for behavior change (e.g., setting up a buddy system, making contracts with others to complete specified levels of physical activity, or setting up walking groups or other groups to provide friendship and support).
- Programs that increase the length of, or activity levels in, school-based physical education classes based on strong evidence of their effectiveness in improving both physical activity levels and physical fitness among school-aged children and adolescents.

The Task Force on Community Preventive Services concluded there was insufficient evidence to determine the effectiveness of classroom-based health education focused on providing information in increasing physical activity levels and physical fitness as a result of inconsistent findings.

Healthy People 2020 gives high visibility to several leading indicators related to physical activity in order to reduce the burden of CVD. Figures 5-11 and 5-12 illustrate physical activity levels by educational attainment for U.S. adults compared with HP2010 targets and suggest that much remains to be accomplished.

REFERENCES

1. Adapted from Centers for Disease Control and Prevention. Achievements in public health, United States, 1900–1999: decline in deaths for heart disease and strokes. *MMWR*. 1999;48:649–656.

2. National Heart, Lung and Blood Institute. *Morbidity & Mortality: 1998 Chartbook on Cardiovascular, Lung, and Blood Diseases*. Rockville, MD: U.S. Department of Health and Human Services, National Institutes of Health; 1998.

3. Epstein FH. Contribution of epidemiology to understanding coronary heart disease. In: Marmot M, Elliott P, eds. *Coronary Heart Disease Epidemiology: From Aetiology to Public Health*. New York, NY: Oxford University Press; 1992:20–32.

4. Epstein FH. Cardiovascular disease epidemiology: a journey from the past into the future. *Circulation*. 1996;93:1755–1764.

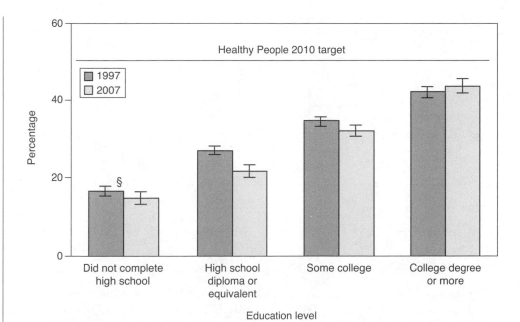

Figure 5-11   Percentage of adults aged >25 years who reported regular leisure-time physical activity,* by education level, National Health Interview Survey, United States, 1997 and 2007.†

* Defined as at least 30 minutes of moderate activity, five times per week, or at least 20 minutes of vigorous physical activity, three times per week.

† Data were age adjusted to the 2000 standard population.

§ 95% confidence interval.

Source: From Centers for Disease Control and Prevention. Percentage of adults aged >25 years who reported regular leisure-time physical activity, by education level, National Health Interview Survey, United States, 1997 and 2007. *MMWR.* 2009;58(10):261. National Health Interview Surveys, 1997 and 2007. http:// www.cdc.gov/nchs/nhis.htm. U.S. Department of Health and Human Services. Objective 22-2. *Healthy People 2010 (midcourse review).* Washington, DC: U.S. Department of Health and Human Services; 2000. http://www.healthypeople .gov/data/midcourse/pdf/fa22.pdf. Accessed May 12, 2010.

5. Stamler J. Established major coronary risk factors. In: Marmot M, Elliott P, eds. *Coronary Heart Disease Epidemiology: From Aetiology to Public Health.* New York, NY: Oxford University Press; 1992:35–66.

6. Dawber TR. *The Framingham Study: The Epidemiology of Atherosclerotic Disease.* Cambridge, MA: Harvard University Press; 1980.

7. National Heart, Lung and Blood Institute. *Report of the Task Force on Research in Epidemiology and Prevention of Cardiovascular Diseases.* Rockville, MD: National Institutes of Health; 1994.

8. Labarthe DR. *Epidemiology and Prevention of Cardiovascular Diseases: A Global Challenge.* Gaithersburg, MD: Aspen; 1998.

9. CDC/Stanford University School of Medicine. *Worldwide Efforts to Improve Heart Health: A Follow-Up of the Catalonia Declaration: Selected Program Descriptions.* Atlanta, GA: U.S. Department of Health and Human Services, Centers for Disease Control; 1997.

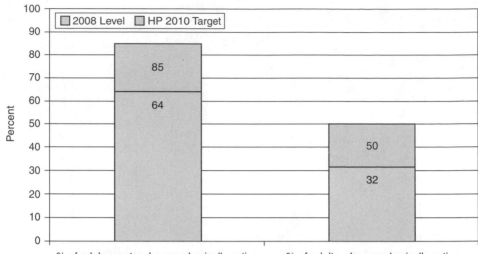

Figure 5-12 Scorecard for selected Healthy People 2010 leading indicators for physical activity comparing 2008 levels with 2010 targets. *Source:* Data from Data 2010, Healthy People 2010 database. http://wonder.cdc.gov/data2010/ftpselec.htm. Accessed May 31, 2010.

10. Rose G. *The Strategy of Preventive Medicine.* New York, NY: Oxford University Press; 1992.

11. National Institutes of Health. *The Sixth Report of the Joint National Committee on Prevention, Detection, Evaluation, and Treatment of High Blood Pressure.* Rockville, MD: US Department of Health and Human Services, National Institutes of Health, National Heart, Lung, and Blood Institute; November 1997. (NIH publication no. 98-4080).

12. National Cholesterol Education Program. *Second Report of the Expert Panel on Detection, Evaluation and Treatment of High Blood Cholesterol in Adults.* Rockville, MD: U.S. Department of Health and Human Services, National Institutes of Health; 1993. (NIH publication no. 93-3095).

13. Centers for Disease Control and Prevention, National Center for Health Statistics. *Health, United States, 1998 with Socioeconomic Status and Health Chartbook.* Hyattsville, MD: U.S. Department of Health and Human Services, Centers for Disease Control; 1998.

14. Centers for Disease Control and Prevention, National Center for Health Statistics. *Healthy People 2000 Review, 1997.* Hyattsville, MD: U.S. Department of Health and Human Services, Centers for Disease Control; 1997.

15. Gerrior S, Bente L. *Nutrient Content of the U.S. Food Supply, 1909–94.* Washington, DC: U.S. Department of Agriculture; 1997. (Home economics research report no. 53).

16. Ernst ND, Sempos ST, Briefel RR, et al. Consistency between US dietary fat intake and serum total cholesterol concentrations: the National Health and Nutrition Examination surveys. *Am J Clin Nutr.* 1997;66:965S–972S.

17. Higgins M, Thom T. Trends in CHD in the United States. *Int J Epidemiol.* 1989;18: S58–S66.

18. American Heart Association. *1999 Heart and Stroke Statistical Update*. Dallas, TX: American Heart Association; 1998.

19. Kaplan GA, Keil JE. Socioeconomic factors and cardiovascular disease: a review of the literature. *Circulation*. 1993;88:1973–1798.

20. Centers for Disease Control and Prevention. Changes in mortality from heart failure: United States, 1980–1995. *MMWR*. 1998;47:633–637.

21. Task Force on Community Preventive Services. *The Community Guide*. http://www.the communityguide.org. Accessed May 31, 2010.

The Infrastructure of Public Health

OBJECTIVES

After completing Chapter 6, learners will be proficient in identifying, measuring, and assessing components of the public health infrastructure in the community. Key aspects of this competency expectation include the following:

- Identifying the major components of public health's infrastructure
- Describing the public health workforce in terms of numbers, distribution, and skills
- Listing five or more major categories of universal competencies for public health professionals
- Describing the current status of public health organizational resources
- Defining the term coalition and describe key steps in their development and operation
- Describing several major categories of public health information systems
- Describing the current status of the financial resources of the public health system
- Identifying strategies for enhancing the infrastructure of public health

---

After the violin virtuoso had finished her concert presentation and was attempting to slip out of the orchestra hall through the delivery entrance, some adoring fans mobbed her. One particularly aggressive young man pushed his way to the front of the throng and grabbed the musician's hand, shaking it furiously. "Maestro, you played those notes just brilliantly tonight," he said. Taken a little aback by these circumstances, the violinist replied, "Young man, anyone can play the notes correctly. It's the spaces between the notes that present the real challenge."

Similar to the maestro's music, public health derives its effectiveness from both its notes and how they are blended together. This chapter examines the basic ingredients of public health that are integrated to carry out its work. This ground-level view of public health focuses on infrastructure, a concept that is more easily understood outside the field of public health. When we think of infrastructure, we routinely think of roads, bridges, sewers, power lines, and water supplies. It is not easy to see the similarities between these concrete and visible structures in our communities and their counterparts in public health, although it can be useful to picture the public health infrastructure as a bridge over which trucks delivering public health services must pass. Needs and expectations are met by using more and bigger trucks to deliver more and better public health services, as illustrated in Figure 6-1; however, this approach has limitations in terms of the ability of the infrastructure to accommodate those trucks, just as the state of the nation's roads, bridges, and tunnels limits the effectiveness of the national transportation system. Attention to the infrastructure is essential for public health services to be delivered effectively.[1] There are, however, different views as to what the concept of public health infrastructure actually represents.

Infrastructure can be described in terms of both static and dynamic attributes. In a static representation, such as the bridge described previously, public health infrastructure is the basic foundation for public health activities; this foundation consists of building blocks and other basic materials. In a more dynamic representation, infrastructure is the capacity or capability of that foundation to carry out its main functions. Both of these views—what the infrastructure is and what the infrastructure does—provide useful insights into the public health system and derive from the governmental presence in health concept described in Chapter 5. Importantly, both also portray infra-

Figure 6-1 Public health infrastructure. *Source:* From Centers for Disease Control and Prevention, Public Health Practice Program Office, 1999.

structure as essential for carrying out public health's core functions and essential public health services.

The public health infrastructure serves as the nerve center of the public health system, representing the capacity necessary to carry out public health's core functions and essential services, but it is also a composite that can be broken down to reveal the basic building blocks of the public health system. What makes the system's infrastructure difficult to describe fully is that public health itself is not neatly partitioned within our complex society. Nonetheless, this chapter presents a broad description of the public health infrastructure in the first decade of the new century. The key questions addressed are as follows:

- What are the critical components of public health's infrastructure?
- What is the current status of these components?
- How can public health's infrastructure be enhanced?

INFRASTRUCTURE, INGREDIENTS, AND INPUTS

In simple terms, the public health infrastructure consists of the resources and relationships necessary to carry out the core functions and essential services of public health. Contributing to the system's capacity are some relatively recognizable resources: human, informational, financial, and organizational, including aspects of organizational relationships (such as statutes, leadership, and partnerships) that specify how the building blocks relate to each other—similar to the spaces between the notes in the maestro's response.

It is no simple task to separate the elements of the public health infrastructure into discrete categories. For example, drawing lines between the knowledge and skills of the workforce and information resources calls for an arbitrary distinction between what people do and what they are able to do after accessing information that is readily available to them. Other distinctions between organizational relationships within a community and individual leadership skills also lack clear boundaries. Financial resources can be considered as system resources or as a means of measuring the other resources in economic terms. Still, it is useful to categorize the elements of the public health infrastructure, realizing that they can be lumped or split in many different ways.

Human resources include the workforce of public health and the knowledge, skills, and abilities of public health workers. Organizational resources include the relationships among the various system participants—public and private—and the mechanisms that manage the system practices, including their statutory aspects, leadership components, and collaborative strategies. Information resources include various data, information, and communication systems. Fiscal resources are the funding levels and sources for the work of public health. Each of these elements contributes to the system's capacity to perform, and each is examined in turn. Physical resources, such as equipment and physical facilities, are also necessary to carry out the work of public health; however, these are not examined here.

HUMAN RESOURCES IN PUBLIC HEALTH

Understanding and appreciating the public health workforce underlie efforts directed at improving public health practice. The public health workforce is by far the most important component of public health's infrastructure. Consistent with the concepts embodied in the core functions and essential services of public health, it is the people performing these functions who comprise the public health workforce.

Chapter 1 introduces the framework of public health's core functions and essential services, and Chapter 5 more fully explains these constructs. The "Public Health in America" statement summarized in Table 1-5 summarizes this framework. In it, the practice of public health is described in terms of both its ends (vision, mission, and six broad responsibilities) and how it accomplishes those ends (10 essential public health services).[2] These constitute an aggregate job description for the entire public health workforce, with the workload divided among the many different professional and occupational categories composing the total public health workforce.

This functional perspective clearly links public health workers to public health practice. Unfortunately, this does not simplify the practical task of determining who is and who is not part of the public health workforce. There has never been any specific academic degree, even the master's of public health (MPH) degree, or unique set of experiences that distinguish public health's workers from those in other fields. Many public health workers have a primary professional discipline in addition to their attachment to public health. Physicians, nurses, dentists, social workers, nutritionists, health educators, anthropologists, psychologists, architects, sanitarians, economists, political scientists, engineers, epidemiologists, biostatisticians, managers, lawyers, and dozens of other professions and disciplines carry out the work of public health. This multidisciplinary workforce, with somewhat divided loyalties to multiple professions, blurs the distinctiveness of public health as a unified profession. At the same time, however, it facilitates the interdisciplinary approaches to community problem identification and problem solving, which are hallmarks of public health practice.

Size and Distribution of the Public Health Workforce

There is little agreement as to the size of the public health workforce in the United States today, except that it is only a small subset of the 15 million persons employed in the health sector of the American economy. Enumerations and estimates of public health workers in general and public health professionals in particular suffer from several limitations—the definition of a public health worker is unclear; public health workers employed outside governmental public health agencies are difficult to identify, and not all employees of governmental public health agencies have public health responsibilities associated with their jobs. Enumerating specific types of public health workers is also difficult because many have other professional affiliations.

Because of these limitations, a composite picture of the public health workforce is lacking, but it is clear that efforts to identify and categorize public health workers must take into account three important aspects of public health practice[3]:

- Work setting: Public health workers work for organizations actively engaged in promoting, protecting, and preserving the health of a defined population group. The organization may be public or private, and its public health objectives may be secondary or subsidiary to its principal objectives. In addition to governmental public health agencies, other public and private organizations employ public health workers. For example, school health nurses working for the local school district and health educators employed by the local Red Cross chapter are part of the public health workforce.
- Work content: Public health workers perform work addressing one or more of the essential public health services. Many job descriptions for public health workers are tailored from the essential public health services, and the scope of tasks can be very broad. A focus on populations, as opposed to individuals, is often a distinguishing characteristic of these job descriptions. For example, an individual trained as a health educator who works for a community-based teen pregnancy-prevention program is clearly a public health worker, but the same cannot be said of a health educator working for a commercial advertising firm promoting cosmetics.
- Worker: The individual must occupy a position that conventionally requires at least 1 year of postsecondary specialized public health training and that is (or can be) assigned a professional, administrative, or technical occupational title. This distinction may seem artificial but rests on the notion that public health practice relies on a foundation of knowledge, skills, and attitudes that, in most circumstances, cannot be imparted through work experiences alone.

If public health workers cannot be counted from the ground up, maybe they can be approximated from the top down. As described in Chapter 3, estimates for public health activity expenditures, including both clinical and population-based services, fall in the range of 3% to 5% of all health expenditures. If public health workers comprised a similar percentage of the 15 million health workers in the United States, the number of public health workers would be between 450,000 and 750,000. Because expenditures for some public health activities, such as those for many environmental and occupational health services, are not captured in the total for national health expenditures, the actual number of public health workers may range as high as 500,000 to 800,000.

That range is consistent with a crude enumeration of the public health workforce conducted in the year 2000, which identified 450,000 public health workers.[4] The year 2000 enumeration did not include most public health workers employed by nongovernmental agencies as well as many public health workers employed by government agencies other than official public health agencies. As a result, the actual total exceeds the 450,000 workers identified in the enumeration.

Data from another source, the ongoing employment census of federal, state, and local health agencies, indicated that there were 586,000 full-time equivalent (FTE) governmental public health workers in 2008.[5] There were 446,000 workers in state and local governments, and another 140,000 were employed by federal agencies (Table 6-1). Adding in even the admittedly low estimate of 64,000 nongovernmental public health workers from the year 2000 enumeration study, the size of the public health workforce in 2008, using these figures, was nearly 650,000 FTE positions.

The overall workforce in the health sector of the American economy has more than doubled in size since 1975 and has increased by more than 30% since 1990.[6] Table 6-1 indicates that the number of public health workers employed by federal, state, and local health agencies has also been steadily increasing, largely among workers of local health departments (LHDs). Unquestionably, the number of public health workers employed by non-governmental agencies also grew during this period. The number of FTE employees working for governmental health agencies was 487,000 FTEs in 1994 (126,000 federal, 158,000 state, 203,000 local). By 2008, the total was 586,000 (140,000 federal, 186,000 state, 260,000 local). Figure 6-2 demonstrates that the ratio of FTE workers of state and local health agencies to population has changed little during this period, although there is evidence that it may be declining somewhat since reaching its highest levels (approximately

Table 6-1 Full-Time Equivalent (FTE) Workers of Federal, State, and Local Government Health* Agencies, 1994–2008, United States

Year	Federal Health FTE	State Health FTE	Local Health FTE	State + Local FTE	Total (F+S+L) FTE
1994	126,292	157,962	202,732	360,694	486,986
1995	125,048	160,031	208,588	368,619	493,667
1997	119,921	162,605	214,824	377,429	497,350
1998	119,846	166,930	219,655	386,585	506,431
1999	121,033	169,213	223,999	393,212	514,245
2000	120,362	172,678	236,496	409,174	529,536
2001	122,999	172,414	251,399	423,813	546,812
2002	124,979	176,345	252,326	428,671	553,650
2003	124,828	176,868	253,888	430,756	555,584
2004	127,933	174,301	249,857	424,128	552,061
2005	125,163	178,465	246,300	424,765	549,918
2006	126,775	182,694	250,163	432,857	559,632
2007	130,952	183,227	251,207	434,760	565,712
2008	140,026	185,667	260,404	446,071	586,097

*Health: public health services, emergency medical services, mental health, alcohol and drug abuse, outpatient clinics, visiting nurses, food and sanitary inspections, animal control, other environmental health activities (e.g., pollution control), etc.

Source: Data from U.S. Bureau of the Census, federal, state, and local governments, and public employment and payroll data. www.census.gov/govs/apes/. Accessed June 14, 2010.

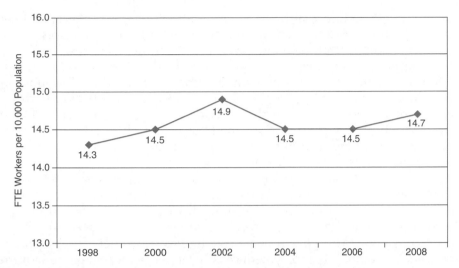

Figure 6-2   Full-time equivalent (FTE) workers for state and local health* agencies per 10,000 population, selected years, 1998–2008, United States.

* Health: public health services, emergency medical services, mental health, alcohol and drug abuse, outpatient clinics, visiting nurses, food and sanitary inspections, animal control, other environmental health activities (e.g., pollution control), etc.

Source: Data from U.S. Bureau of the Census. Federal, state, and local governments, and public employment and payroll data. www.census.gov/govs/apes/. Accessed June 14, 2010.

15 per 10,000) in 2001 and 2003. Any downward trend after 2003 and before 2009 would be surprising in view of a substantial influx of federal funding for state and local health departments since 2002 discussed in Chapters 4 and 8. The severe economic recession in 2009 did, however, impact the number of governmental health agency workers.

Like most health sector workers, public health workers are more likely to be found in urban and suburban settings rather than rural communities. The public health worker to population ratio, however, is often higher in rural areas than in urban areas. States show significant variation as well, with a six-fold difference between the highest and lowest ratios for states. Higher ratios are found in many of the smaller and less urban states in the East and West with lower ratios in the Central states.

In 1980, Health Resources and Services Administration (HRSA) estimated the size of the public health workforce at 500,000 workers, including a primary public health workforce of 250,000 professional workers, most working in governmental public health agencies.[7] More than 50,000 occupational health physicians, nurses, and specialists working in the private sector, as well as 20,000 health educators working in schools and 45,000 administrators working in nursing homes, hospitals, and medical group practices were included in the 250,000 professionals characterized by the HRSA as the primary public health workforce at the time. If only those working for governmental public health agencies had been included, the number would have been closer to 140,000.

The year 2000 public health enumeration identified 40,000 fewer occupational health professionals and did not seek to include health educators working in schools or administrators in nongovernmental clinical settings.

Comparing the overall 1980 estimate (500,000 workers) with the year 2000 public health workforce enumeration suggests that the public health workforce is shrinking. Comparing the 1980 HRSA estimate with current employment census data, on the other hand, suggests that the public health workforce is growing. Because the methods used for the 1980 estimation were considerably different from those in the more recent studies, a direct comparison of the results is of questionable value.

The public health workforce enumeration completed in 2000 found one third of public health workers employed by state agencies and another one third employed by agencies of local government, with less than 20% working at the federal level and 14% outside government entirely.[4] Chapter 4 examines key characteristics of the governmental public health agencies that employ these workers. Government employment census data, which excludes nongovernmental workers, also classify one third as state workers but 44% as employees of local government and 24% as working for federal agencies. Some of these differences can be attributed to state public health systems in which state employees work at the local level and may be counted as state employees in the employment census data and as LHD employees in the public health enumeration study. These differences may also be partly attributed to the inclusion of workers in state and local governmental agencies other than the LHD in the government employment census data but not in the year 2000 public health enumeration study. For example, substance abuse and mental health prevention services, school health services, or restaurant inspections may operate from local mental health agencies, school districts, or consumer affairs agencies rather than from the LHD. The National Association of County and City Health Officials (NACCHO) estimated that LHDs employed 155,000 workers in 2008.[8]

Although recent decades have witnessed an increase in the number of public health workers employed by nongovernmental agencies as a result of expanded partnerships for public health priorities, governmental public health workers are often considered the primary public health workforce. Their number, composition, distribution, and competence are issues of public concern. The government employment census data provide useful insights into overall trends at the national level and among the various levels of government. The year 2000 public health enumeration study, however, provides richer information on the composition of the public health workforce, such as the proportion and types of professional occupational categories within that workforce. Both sources enrich understanding of the size and composition of the public health workforce today.

Composition of the Public Health Workforce

Public health is multidisciplinary, with many different professions and occupations involved in its work. In recent years, there has been an effort to identify standard occupational classifications for public health workers, resulting in nearly 30 different job categories. Because the total number of public health workers is not clear, the precise proportion of the various subgroups cannot be determined. It is clear that nurses and environmental health practitioners constitute the largest subgroups of public health workers. Managers, epidemiologists, health educators, and laboratory workers are also significant subgroups. Table 6-2 provides information on occupational categories and titles from the public health workforce enumeration study completed in 2000. Specific categories and titles were not reported for one fourth of the workers in this study, necessitating the use of an adjustment process to allow for better estimates for public health worker categories and occupational titles.

Despite the lack of precise information, it appears that professional occupational categories comprise more than 300,000, or one half, of the estimated 620,000 workers in the public health workforce. For comparison purposes, there were approximately 2.3 million nurses, 800,000 physicians, 200,000 pharmacists, 170,000 dentists, and 90,000 dietitians/nutritionists working in the United States at the turn of the 21st century.[6]

Studies of LHDs indicate that three positions are found in more than two thirds of all LHDs—public health nurse, administrator, and sanitarian/environmental health specialist.[8] These positions are present in large and small agencies alike. The next most frequent positions (emergency preparedness coordinator, nutritionist, health educator, physician, other environmental health scientist, information system specialist, and epidemiologist) are found in only 25% to 60% of LHDs. There is considerable variation in the proportion of LHDs with these positions, associated with agency size (Table 6-3). For example, health educators are employed in only 25% of LHDs serving populations under 10,000 persons but in 97% of agencies serving 500,000 or more.

Two general patterns of LHD staffing exist around a core set of employees. One pattern focuses on clinical services, the other on more population-based programs.[9] The core employees consist of dietitian/nutritionists, sanitarians/environmental specialists, administrators, laboratory specialists, and health educators. The clinical pattern adds physicians, nurses, and dental health workers. The population-based pattern includes epidemiologists, public health nurses, social workers, and program specialists.

The availability of information on public health workers at the state and local level varies from state to state and is often inconsistent and incomplete. Detailed information from the official state health departments has not been available since the late 1980s and even then did not include public health workers employed by state agencies other than the official state health department. The periodic profiles of LHDs completed by the NACCHO before 2005 provided only general data on the proportion of responding agencies that employ specific public health job titles, either directly or through contracted services. The national profile of LHDs completed in 2008 included the estimates of the number of workers in key job titles presented in Table 6-4.

The lack of information on the public health workforce extends to some of the most basic and important characteristics of that workforce. For example, there is very little information available on the racial and ethnic characteristics of the overall public health workforce. Although important, information on cultural competency is also lacking.

Table 6-2   Number of Public Health Workers in Selected Occupational Categories and Titles, United States, 2000

Government Public Health Workers	Reported Number	Adjusted Number
Administrators	15,920	21,247
Professionals	176,980	236,202
Technicians	61,088	81,530
Other support	59,085	69,283
Unreported	104,763	
Total	417,836	417,836
Occupational Categories		
Health administrators	15,920	21,247
Administration support staff	37,805	62,981
Administration/business professional	4,725	7,306
Attorney/hearing officer	601	929
Biostatistician	1,164	1,800
Environmental engineer	4,549	7,034
Environmental specialist	14,882	23,013
Epidemiologist	927	1,433
Policy analyst/plan/economist	3,678	5,687
Disease investigator	783	1,211
License/inspection specialist	13,780	21,309
Social, behavioral, mental	3,762	5,817
Occ. health and safety specialist	5,593	8,649
Public health dental worker	2,032	3,142
Public health educator	2,230	3,448
Public health laboratory professional	14,088	21,785
Public health nurse	41,232	63,759
Public health nutritionist	6,680	10,330
Public health pharmacist	1,496	2,313
Public health physician	6,008	9,290
Public health program specialist	7,820	12,092
Public health veterinarian/animal control specialist	2,037	3,150
Public relations/public information	563	871
Other public health professional	14,119	21,833
Computer specialist	4,326	6,210
Environmental engineering technician	414	594
Environmental health technician	501	719
Health information system/data analyst	605	868
Occupational health and safety technician	95	136
Public health laboratory technician	5,700	8,182
Other public health technician (LPN, etc.)	26,953	38,690
Community outreach/field worker	676	902
Other paraprofessional	18,902	25,227

Source: Reported column data from Health Resources and Services Administration, Bureau of Health Professions, National Center for Health Workforce Information and Analysis and Center for Health Policy, Columbia School of Nursing. *The Public Health Workforce Enumeration 2000.* Washington, DC: Health Resources and Services Administration; 2000.

Table 6-3 Local Health Departments with Employees in Selected Occupations, by Size of Population Serviced, United States, 2008

	All LHDs	Under 10,000	10,000 to 24,999	25,000 to 49,999	50,000 to 99,999	100,000 to 249,999	250,000 to 499,999	500,000 to 999,999	1 million +
Clerical staff	95%	85%	95%	97%	97%	100%	99%	100%	100%
Nurse	94%	82%	94%	96%	97%	98%	100%	97%	100%
Manager/director	91%	79%	89%	94%	96%	97%	100%	97%	100%
Environmental health specialist (sanitarian)	80%	54%	78%	86%	90%	92%	93%	88%	88%
Emergency preparedness coordinator	57%	38%	43%	52%	66%	77%	94%	96%	100%
Health educator	56%	25%	40%	57%	70%	78%	87%	96%	97%
Nutritionist	51%	23%	35%	50%	64%	76%	85%	85%	88%
Physician	42%	15%	24%	41%	52%	69%	79%	85%	94%
Behavioral health professional	33%	6%	22%	26%	47%	49%	68%	80%	71%
Other environmental health scientist	27%	7%	17%	24%	32%	41%	65%	69%	70%
Information system specialist	24%	4%	9%	16%	24%	49%	69%	86%	88%
Epidemiologist	23%	4%	7%	11%	19%	50%	78%	91%	100%
Public information specialist	19%	6%	7%	12%	20%	30%	50%	80%	88%

Source: Data from National Association of County and City Health Officials. 2008 National Profile of Local Health Departments. Washington, DC: NACCHO; 2009.

Table 6-4 Estimated Size and Composition of Local Health Department (LHD) Workforce, United States, 2008

	Best Estimate	95% Confidence Interval	Percentage of All LHD Staff
Clerical staff	36,000	31,000–40,000	23.1%
Nurse	33,000	29,000–36,000	21.3%
Environmental health specialist (sanitarian)	12,000	10,000–13,000	7.5%
Manager/director	9,500	8,400–11,000	6.2%
Behavioral health professional	7,100	5,400–8,700	4.6%
Health educator	4,400	3,800–4,900	2.8%
Nutritionist	4,300	3,700–4,900	2.8%
Other environmental health scientist	3,200	2,400–3,900	2.0%
Physician	2,000	1,500–2,400	1.3%
Information system specialist	1,600	1,100–2,000	1.0%
Emergency preparedness coordinator	1,400	1,300–1,500	0.9%
Epidemiologist	1,200	900–1,500	0.8%
Public information specialist	430	350–510	0.3%
All LHD staff	155,000	135,000–174,000	100%

Source: Data from National Association of County and City Health Officials. *2008 National Profile of Local Health Departments*. Washington, DC: NACCHO; 2009.

Public Health Worker Ethics and Skills

Public health workers may come from different academic, professional, and experiential backgrounds, but they share a common bond. All are committed to a common mission and share common ethical principles, as exemplified by the following list advanced by the American Public Health Association:[10]

- Public health should address principally the fundamental causes of disease and requirements for health, aiming to prevent adverse health outcomes.
- Public health should achieve community health in a way that respects the rights of individuals in the community.
- Public health policies, programs, and priorities should be developed and evaluated through processes that ensure an opportunity for input from community members.
- Public health should advocate and work for the empowerment of disenfranchised community members, aiming to ensure that the basic resources and conditions necessary for health are accessible to all.
- Public health should seek the information needed to implement effective policies and programs that protect and promote health.
- Public health institutions should provide communities with the information they have that is needed for decisions on policies or programs and should obtain the community's consent for their implementation.

- Public health institutions should act in a timely manner on the information they have within the resources and the mandate given to them by the public.
- Public health programs and policies should incorporate a variety of approaches that anticipate and respect diverse values, beliefs, and cultures in the community.
- Public health programs and policies should be implemented in a manner that most enhances the physical and social environment.
- Public health institutions should protect the confidentiality of information that can bring harm to an individual or community if made public. Exceptions must be justified on the basis of the high likelihood of significant harm to the individual or others.
- Public health institutions should ensure the professional competence of their employees.
- Public health institutions and their employees should engage in collaborations and affiliations in ways that build the public's trust and the institution's effectiveness.

Information from national and state surveys indicates that the majority of public health workers lack formal education and training in public health. In 1980, HRSA determined that only 20% of the 250,000 professionals in the primary public health workforce had formal training in public health.[7] More than 2 decades later, there is little evidence that this situation has improved. Although the proportion of those who have formal training varies by category of worker, the lack of formal training is striking in even some of the most critical categories. For example, the NACCHO profile completed in 2005 found that 81% of LHD leaders had no formal public health education or training.[8] This reflects virtually no change from similar studies completed 15 years earlier.[11] A survey of Illinois local health jurisdictions in the year 2000 yielded similar results, with 79% of local health agency administrators lacking formal preparation in public health.[12]

Formal training for many public health workers focuses only on a specific aspect of public health practice such as environmental health or community or school health nursing. Environmental health practitioners, nurses, administrators, and health educators account for the majority of public health workers with formal training in public health. Even among those with formal training in public health, public health workers with graduate degrees from schools of public health or other graduate public health programs represent only a small fraction of the total. In view of the number of master's-level graduates of schools of public health and other graduate-level public health degree programs—about 10,000 in 2008—this is not surprising.

Evidence of the lack of formal training within this workforce, however, does not necessarily lead to the conclusion that public health workers are unprepared.[13] Instead, public health workers enter the field having earned a wide variety of degrees and professional training credentials from academic programs and institutions unrelated to public health. Often overlooked, these institutions produce the bulk of the public health workforce and represent major assets for addressing unmet needs. On-the-job training and work experience contribute substantially to the overall competency and preparedness of the public health workforce. For example, public health workers are frequently involved in responses to earthquakes, floods, and other disasters and have increasingly acquired and demonstrated skills in assessing community health needs and devising community health improvement plans. These are skills that most public health workers acquired through real-world work experience rather than through their formal training.

Continuing education and career development for public health workers has long been a cottage industry involving many different parties. Academic institutions certainly are contributors, but public health agencies at the state and local level, public health associations (national, state, and local), and other voluntary-sector health organizations participate as well. Many different entities offer credits for continuing education, including professional organizations, academic institutions, and hospitals, among others. Public health workers value continuing education credits as a means to satisfy requirements of their core disciplines in order to maintain some level of credentialing status (such as licensed physicians and nurses, certified health education specialists, and so on). A few states, such as New Jersey, enforce continuing education requirements for the public health disciplines licensed by that state. There is no formal system of public health-specific continuing education units and only fledgling efforts toward credentialing public health workers.

Public Health Practice Profiles

Individual workers, as well as occupational categories, produce work important to achieving public health goals and objectives. As discussed in previous chapters, key public health goals and objectives address preventing disease and injury, promoting healthy behaviors, protecting against health risks and threats, responding to emergencies, and ensuring the quality of health services.[2] This overall public health practice framework provides the basis for channeling contributions both by individuals and organizations toward common goals. The specific work tasks of different occupations and individuals generally fall into one or more of the 10 essential public health services. Chapters 1 and 5 characterized the essential public health services as the means to achieving public health ends or how the work of public health is accomplished. It is useful to view these functions and essential public health services as an aggregate job description for the entire public health workforce, with the workload then divided among the many different professional and occupational categories composing the total public health workforce.

In that light, Table 6-5 identifies several purposes and essential public health services that form the core of the duties and job descriptions for selected public health occupations. In Table 6-5, the assignment of specific public health purposes and essential public health services may appear somewhat arbitrary. In each case, however, judgments are made as to which purposes and essential services are most closely associated with each occupational category. Some occupational categories may appear to have a relatively limited focus (e.g., public health laboratory workers) in comparison with others (e.g., public health nurses) that may have very broad roles that could conceivably cover all purposes and services. For each occupational category and title,

Table 6-5 Composite Public Health Practice Profile for Public Health Occupations and Titles Addressed in Chapters 7–13

	PH Adm	Env Hlth	PH Nurs	Epi	PH Ed	Nutr	Soc Beh MH	PH Lab	MD DVM Phar	Dent Wkrs	Adm Law Jdg	PH Prog Spec	ERC	PH Pol An	Hlth Info	Out Wkrs
Public health purposes																
Preventing epidemics and the spread of disease	✓	✓	✓	✓	✓		✓	✓	✓	✓	✓			✓	✓	✓
Protecting against environmental hazards		✓	✓	✓							✓	✓	✓	✓	✓	
Preventing injuries	✓	✓		✓		✓					✓	✓				
Promoting and encouraging healthy behaviors		✓			✓		✓	✓	✓	✓	✓	✓	✓			✓
Responding to disasters and assisting communities in recovery	✓		✓				✓				✓			✓	✓	
Ensuring the quality and accessibility of health services	✓	✓				✓	✓	✓	✓	✓					✓	
Essential public health services																
Monitoring health status to identify community health problems		✓		✓		✓		✓	✓	✓		✓				
Diagnosing and investigating health problems and health hazards in the community		✓	✓	✓				✓	✓			✓	✓			
Informing, educating, and empowering people about health issues					✓	✓	✓			✓				✓	✓	✓
Mobilizing community partnerships to identify and solve health problems	✓				✓		✓						✓	✓		✓
Essential public health services																
Developing policies and plans that support individual and community health efforts	✓				✓		✓	✓		✓		✓	✓	✓	✓	
Enforcing laws and regulations that protect health and ensure safety	✓	✓									✓					

(continues)

Table 6-5   Composite Public Health Practice Profile for Public Health Occupations and Titles Addressed in Chapters 7–13 (continued)

Essential public health services	PH Adm	Env Hlth	PH Nurs	Epi	PH Ed	Nutr	Soc Beh MH	PH Lab	MD DVM Phar	Dent Wkrs	Adm Law Jdg	PH Prog Spec	ERC	PH Pol An	Hlth Info	Out Wkrs
Linking people with needed personal health services and ensuring the provision of health care when otherwise unavailable	✓										✓					
Ensuring a competent public health and personal healthcare workforce			✓		✓	✓	✓		✓	✓			✓		✓	
Evaluating effectiveness, accessibility, and quality of personal and population based health services	✓	✓	✓	✓		✓	✓	✓	✓	✓	✓	✓	✓	✓	✓	
Researching new insights and innovative solutions to health problems			✓	✓		✓		✓	✓		✓				✓	✓

Notes: PH Adm, Public Health Administrator; Env Hlth, Environmental Health Practitioner; PH Nurs, Public Health Nurse; EPI, Epidemiologist; PH Ed, Public Health Educator; Nutr, Nutritionist; Soc Beh MH, Public Health Social, Behavioral, and Mental Health Workers; PH Lab, Public Health Laboratory Worker; MD DVM Phar, Public Health Physicians, Veterinarians, and Pharmacists; Dent Wkrs, Dental Health Workers; Adm Law Jdg, Administrative Law Judge; PH Prog Spec, Public Health Program Specialist; ERC, Emergency Response Coordinator; PH Pol An, Public Health Policy Analyst; Hlth Info, Health Information Specialist; and Out Wkrs, Outreach Workers.

however, the number of purposes and essential services identified for each occupational category is limited to no more than one half the number possible (3 of 6 purposes, 5 of 10 essential public health services).

Characterizing the work of an occupational category in this manner proves a functional view of the work performed. It also facilitates an understanding of how the work of one occupational category relates to the work of another category and how it relates to the overall work performed across all public health occupational categories.

Public Health Workforce Growth Prospects

Will the public health workforce increase or decrease in size over the next 10 years? There should be little debate over this question, but there is. One reason for controversy derives from the lack of accurate information on the size of the public health workforce between 1980 and 2000. Another relates to the many complex forces within public health and the broader economy that influence the number of public health workers needed.

In hindsight, it is clear that the frequently cited figure that the workforce numbered 500,000 in 1980 lacked precision in terms of what was included and how it was generated. This is unfortunate, because the 500,000 figure from 1980 is often used to argue that the public health workforce must be shrinking because only 450,000 public health workers were enumerated in 2000. As previously discussed, the HRSA 1980 estimate actually indicated that only 250,000 of the 500,000 public health workers were in the primary public health workforce consisting of federal, state, and LHD workers and selected others who devoted most of their work efforts on public health activities.[7] Within this 250,000 figure, there were faculty and researchers at academic institutions; occupational health physicians and nurses working for various private companies; health educators teaching in schools; and administrators working in hospitals, nursing homes, and other medical care settings. The actual number of public health professionals working for federal health departments, state health departments, and LHDs in 1980, after adjusting for these inclusions, was closer to 140,000. The total for the comparable categories from the Public Health Workforce Enumeration 2000 was 260,000. This figure indicates that the public health workforce is growing rather than shrinking. Data from the employment census of governmental agencies support this conclusion, showing there has been a steady increase in FTE workers of governmental health agencies over the past decade (Table 6-1).

These findings indicate that the public health workforce has been increasing since 1980, throughout the 1990s, and into the early years of the current decade. This is consistent with the documented expansion of the health sector within the overall economy, which continues to grow at a more rapid rate than the rest of the economy. If public health activities continue to maintain their small share of total health spending, funding for public health activities and public health workers will grow commensurately. It is conceivable that public health activities could even increase their share of overall health spending, fostering even more rapid growth of employment opportunities.

There are concerns, however, that the growth of the public health workforce may be slowing or even reversing. It is somewhat surprising that the infusion of bioterrorism preparedness funding after 2001 didn't result in even greater numbers of state and local public health workers than are reflected in Table 6-1. It appears that state and local governments initially shifted some workers onto federal bioterrorism grant payrolls, thereby saving state and local resources or possibly shifting resources from public health to other priorities such as education. The severe national economic downturn in 2009 forced many states and localities to suspend hiring and even lay off workers. The impact of this recession on the national public health workforce will be clearer after 2011, although surveys conducted by the Association of State and Territorial Health Officials and NACCHO in 2009 and 2010 suggest that state and LHDs suffered significant staff reductions.

This example illustrates how federal funding to states and localities for bioterrorism preparedness serves as a temptation to replace or supplant state and local support for public health with federal money. The funding of epidemiologists further illustrates this phenomenon. In 2004, federal bioterrorism funds paid the salaries of 460 epidemiologists; among 390 epidemiologists working on bioterrorism and emergency response activities, 62% were funded by the federal government. Infectious disease epidemiologists did not increase between 2001 and 2004, but in 2004 nearly 20% were paid through federal bioterrorism funds.[14] This scenario may also be true for several other public health occupational categories, such as laboratory workers and emergency response coordinators. It underscores the important role of the underlying financial health of state and local governments in determining the size of the public health workforce.

Two additional modern forces affect public health workforce size. These are the expansion of information technology and the resulting increase in worker productivity. Public health practice, by its very nature, is information dependent and information driven, as is discussed later in this chapter. Enhanced information technology tools and increased individual worker productivity mean fewer workers are needed to support the work of administrators, professionals, and technical staff. This trend would tend to increase the proportion of professionals within the public health workforce; however, these trends also mean fewer professionals are needed to perform the same volume of work. The net effect is therefore difficult to predict in terms of the number and types of workers needed.

The impact of these trends will be affected by events and forces within the overall economy, the health system, and the public sector in general. Public health workers and public health agencies are key components of the public health system, but it is important to consider the larger context in which they operate. This larger environment is in constant flux, undergoing changes that impact the public health system and its components. For example, information and communication technologies advance continuously. These developments enable public health agencies and workers to carry out their duties in a more efficient and effective manner. The work of public health is especially information dependent. The speed at which information is accessed and communicated significantly affects how well public health achieves its mission and objectives. Advances in information and communications technology improve public health practice and public health outcomes. There is every reason to believe that these advances will continue at least at levels achieved in recent decades. The net effect is to make public health workers more effective and productive. The challenge is to ensure that public health workers have access to the education and training resources that ensure this happens.

Trends within the health sector will also continue to affect public health workers. Health is highly valued both as a personal and societal goal. The economic value placed on health exceeds $2.5 trillion annually, approaching $8,000 per person for every man, woman, and child in the United States. There is no indication that health will assume a lower priority within the American social value system. In recent years, for example, expenditures for health purposes have grown faster than the rate for the overall economy. In effect, health is becoming an even greater priority. Between the two general strategies to achieve health—preventive and therapeutic approaches—the balance may be slowly shifting toward more prevention. The imbalance remains sizable, with a 20 to 1 ratio; however, this shift is likely to continue. Taken together with an increased priority on health itself, public health activities, including those carried out by public health agencies and workers, should continue to increase in size, importance, and value to society.

The value placed on public health activities can be measured in economic terms, such as funding levels for programs, services, and the workers who implement public health programs and services. To sustain or even enhance public health funding, national leadership is necessary. Federal health agencies such as the Centers for Disease Control and Prevention (CDC) and HRSA within the Department of Health and Human Services are especially important in the area of public health workforce development. In addition to national leadership, state and local governments must remain committed to and invested in public health objectives; however, states and local governments face difficult economic circumstances and tough choices across the United States and are looking to cut back services that are either low priority or that have other funding sources. If state and local governments supplant their own funding with the new federal funds, the overall effort will be less than it should be.

Beyond funding, administrative and bureaucratic obstacles challenge public health workforce development efforts in the public sector. State and local agencies are often the source of some of the most significant recruitment and retention problems facing the public health workforce. These include slow hiring by governmental agencies, civil service systems, hiring freezes, budget crises affecting state and local government, and the lack of career ladders, competitive salary structures, and other forms of recognition that value workers for their skill and performance.

Despite the uncertainties inherent in these influences, past trends and current forces suggest that professional and administrative jobs and careers in public health are likely to grow over the next decade. Unfortunately, it will be difficult to measure the progress that has been made without deployment of a standard taxonomy for public health occupations and more comprehensive enumeration strategies and tools that provide better information on the key dimensions of the public health workforce, including its size and distribution in official agencies and private and voluntary organizations.

In addition to the size of the public health workforce, its distribution and composition are important to current and future public health workers. Key questions include the following: (1) where will public health job opportunities be most abundant, and (2) which occupational categories are likely to grow most rapidly and be in greatest demand?

Job opportunities generally track with population density and demographic shifts. Within the health sector, job opportunities cluster around metropolitan areas. Public health positions also follow this pattern. There are more positions, and therefore more opportunities, in metropolitan areas than there are in rural areas. General demographic trends indicate a continuing shift of population from the Northeast and Midwest regions of the United States to the South, Southwest, and West Coast. It is likely that health sector jobs and public health positions will also follow this pattern.

The ratio of positions to population, however, can be higher in rural areas (and states that have higher proportions of their population living in nonmetropolitan areas). This occurs because there is a basic core staffing that must be present regardless of the size of the population and because rural and remote communities often lack other public health resources and assets. For example, LHDs in small as well as large communities will have an agency administrator, director of nursing, and environmental director. Public health agencies serving larger communities may have more total workers, but the ratio of workers to population is often lower because of the effect of core (or overhead) staffing. In addition, nongovernmental resources are often lacking in rural communities. Governmental agencies may constitute a larger proportion of a rural community's overall resources than for urban or suburban communities. A higher public health worker to population ratio in rural areas raises issues of efficiency in terms of scarce resources, including public health professionals, and can be used as an argument for consolidation of several small LHDs into one large agency.

Table 6-5 provides a snapshot describing the distribution and composition of the public health workforce from a different perspective by aggregating their public health practice profiles. This composite profile illustrates the breadth of roles in addressing public health's broad purposes and essential services as well as the contribution of the various public health occupational categories and titles.

This composite highlights the importance of preventing the spread of disease and ensuring the quality of health services as public health purposes. The majority of public health occupations place significant emphasis on these purposes. Only a few public health occupations and titles focus on emergency response as a primary duty. Virtually all, however, have roles in responding to public health emergencies as a secondary-level responsibility.

Among the 10 essential public health services, nearly all public health occupations and titles are actively involved in evaluating the effectiveness, accessibility, and quality of personal and population-based health services.

Eight other essential public health services are widely distributed across the various occupational categories and titles. Only a few public health occupations focus extensively on ensuring a competent workforce.

Some health sector occupations will grow more rapidly than others, even while the health sector grows more rapidly than the rest of the economy. Among the many public health occupations, several appear to be growing rapidly and several others appear to be in danger of their supply not keeping pace with anticipated demand.

It is not surprising that public health nurses and environmental health practitioners are repeatedly identified as the positions in greatest demand. Indeed, these occupational categories are the largest in the public health workforce, and it is only natural that these categories undergo greater turnover than others. For registered nurses, there is substantial evidence of a current national shortage. For environmental health practitioners, this is not so clear.

The demand for several public health professional occupations is growing steadily. Between 1990 and 2005, an increasing number of LHDs are employing epidemiologists, health educators, and public information officers (Table 6-6). The aftermath of terrorist events of 2001, including the series of anthrax spore attacks through the postal system, spotlighted the need for two professional positions in particular. The first, emergency response coordinators, is new to the list of public health occupations; the second, epidemiologists, is one of the oldest public health professional occupations. State health departments and LHDs are rapidly hiring emergency response coordinators. These people come to these new positions with a wide range of academic and experiential qualifications. Epidemiologists, on the other hand, have more restrictive qualifications in terms of academic preparation such as master's and doctoral degrees. Concerns over the past few decades that epidemiologists were in short supply and great demand are now heightened as agencies seek to hire these specialists quickly. The number of epidemiologists coming out of graduate programs does not appear to be keeping pace with the need, despite an increase in interest as measured by the number of applications for epidemiology training programs.

Before 2001, health educators and community health planners were steadily growing professional categories in the public health workforce. Expansion of health education and promotion services and an increase in community health planning and community health improvement activities account for this trend. It is not clear whether this trend will continue in view of the current emphasis on bioterrorism and public health emergency preparedness.

Public Health Practitioner Competencies

Beyond workforce size, distribution, and composition are issues related to the core competencies and skills that will be most important in public health practice and how these skills are best acquired. Establishing and promoting competencies for public health workers is tricky business. For one thing, public health workers come from a variety of professional backgrounds, many of which have their own core competencies. For example,

Table 6-6 Percentage of LHDs Employing Selected Professional Occupations: 1989–1990 and 2005 Profile Data

	1989 (%)	2005 (%)
Physicians—All LHDs	62	43
<50,000	51	27
50,000–499,999	75	62
500,000+	99	91
Epidemiologists—All LHDs	11	25
<50,000	3	7
50,000–499,999	8	41
500,000+	87	94
Health Educators—All LHDs	37	55
<50,000	22	37
50,000–499,999	54	78
500,000+	95	94
Public Information Specialists—All LHDs	6	18
<50,000	2	5
50,000–499,999	5%	29%
500,000+	52%	78%

Source: Data from National Association of County and City Health Officials. *2005 National Profile of Local Health Departments.* Washington, DC: National Association of County and City Health Officials; 2006.

public health nursing has a set of core competencies, and health educators use a sophisticated competency framework for purposes of certification.[15] The same can be said for public health physicians, administrators, epidemiologists, and several other public health professional occupations. Identifying a common core for these various professional categories generally leads to a framework with very general and nonspecific competencies that are difficult to relate to a specific situation or problem. The Council on Linkages between Academia and Public Health Practice spent 2 decades grappling with this problem before arriving at the set of core competencies for public health professionals presented in Table 6-7.

The national public health organizations endorsed and adopted these core competencies, which track to the essential public health services framework, as the basis for assessing and enhancing the skills of public health workers. Core public health practice competencies serve as a useful benchmark for competency frameworks developed to serve state or local public health systems or to guide the development of more focused skills, such as in public health law, informatics, genomics, and emergency preparedness.

There are several important and practical uses for competency frameworks. Core competencies can serve as models whenever an agency's job descriptions are developed, updated, or revised. As competency-oriented job descriptions become more widely used, core competencies can guide orientation and training activities for new employees. Core competencies are also useful in employee self-assessment activities as well as in personnel evaluation activities when supervisors review the past performance of employees and set

Table 6-7 Core Competencies for Tier 1 (Entry-Level) Public Health Workers

Analytic/Assessment Skills
- Identifies the health status of populations and their related determinants of health and illness
- Describes the characteristics of a population-based health problem
- Uses variables that measure public health conditions
- Uses methods and instruments for collecting valid and reliable quantitative and qualitative data
- Identifies sources of public health data and information
- Recognizes the integrity and comparability of data
- Identifies gaps in data sources
- Adheres to ethical principles in the collection, maintenance, use, and dissemination of data and information
- Describes the public health applications of quantitative and qualitative data
- Collects quantitative and qualitative community data
- Uses information technology to collect, store, and retrieve data
- Describes how data are used to address scientific, political, ethical, and social public health issues

Policy Development/Program Planning Skills
- Gathers information relevant to specific public health policy issues
- Describes how policy options can influence public health programs
- Explains the expected outcomes of policy options
- Gathers information that will inform policy decisions
- Describes the public health laws and regulations governing public health programs
- Participates in program planning processes
- Incorporates policies and procedures into program plans and structures
- Identifies mechanisms to monitor and evaluate programs for their effectiveness and quality
- Demonstrates the use of public health informatics practices and procedures
- Applies strategies for continuous quality improvement

Communication Skills
- Identifies the health literacy of populations served
- Communicates in writing and orally, in person, and through electronic means, with linguistic and cultural proficiency
- Solicits community-based input from individuals and organizations
- Conveys public health information using a variety of approaches
- Participates in the development of demographic, statistical, programmatic, and scientific presentations
- Applies communication and group dynamic strategies in interactions with individuals and groups

Cultural Competency Skills
- Incorporates strategies for interacting with persons from diverse backgrounds
- Recognizes the role of cultural, social, and behavioral factors in the accessibility, availability, acceptability, and delivery of public health services
- Responds to diverse needs that are the result of cultural differences
- Describes the dynamic forces that contribute to cultural diversity
- Describes the need for a diverse public health workforce
- Participates in the assessment of the cultural competence of the public health organization

Community Dimension of Practice Skills
- Recognizes community linkages and relationships among multiple factors (or determinants) affecting health
- Demonstrates the capacity to work in community-based participatory research efforts
- Identifies stakeholders
- Collaborates with community partners to promote the health of the population
- Maintains partnerships with key stakeholders
- Uses group processes to advance community involvement
- Describes the role of governmental and nongovernmental organizations in the delivery of community health services

(continues)

Table 6-7   Core Competencies for Tier 1 (Entry-Level) Public Health Workers (continued)

- Identifies community assets and resources
- Gathers input from the community to inform the development of public health policy and programs
- Informs the public about policies, programs, and resources

Public Health Sciences Skills
- Describes the scientific foundation of the field of public health
- Identifies prominent events in the history of the public health profession
- Relates public health science skills to the core public health functions and 10 essential services of public health
- Identifies the basic public health sciences (including, but not limited to biostatistics, epidemiology, environmental health sciences, health services administration, and social and behavioral health sciences)
- Describes the scientific evidence related to a public health issue, concern, or intervention
- Retrieves scientific evidence from a variety of print and electronic sources
- Discusses the limitations of research findings
- Describes the laws, regulations, policies, and procedures for the ethical conduct of research
- Partners with other public health professionals in building the scientific base of public health

Financial Planning and Management Skills
- Describes the local, state, and federal public health and healthcare systems
- Describes the organizational structures, functions, and authorities of local, state, and federal public health agencies
- Adheres to the organization's policies and procedures
- Participates in the development of a programmatic budget
- Operates programs within current and forecasted budget constraints
- Identifies strategies for determining budget priorities based on federal, state, and local financial contributions
- Reports program performance
- Translates evaluation report information into program performance improvement action steps
- Contributes to the preparation of proposals for funding from external sources
- Applies basic human relations skills to internal collaborations, motivation of colleagues, and resolution of conflicts
- Demonstrates public health informatics skills to improve program and business operations
- Participates in the development of contracts and other agreements for the provision of services
- Describes how cost-effectiveness, cost-benefit, and cost-utility analyses affect programmatic prioritization and decision making

Leadership and Systems Thinking Skills
- Incorporates ethical standards of practice as the basis of all interactions with organizations, communities, and individuals
- Describes how public health operates within a larger system
- Participates with stakeholders in identifying key public health values and a shared public health vision as guiding principles for community action
- Identifies internal and external problems that may affect the delivery of essential public health services
- Uses individual, team, and organizational learning opportunities for personal and professional development
- Participates in mentoring and peer review or coaching opportunities
- Participates in the measuring, reporting, and continuous improvement of organizational performance
- Describes the impact of changes in the public health system and larger social, political, and economic environment on organizational practices

Note: Tier 1 core competencies apply to public health professionals who carry out the day-to-day tasks of public health organizations and are not in management positions. Responsibilities of these public health professionals may include basic data collection and analysis, fieldwork, program planning, outreach activities, programmatic support, and other organizational tasks. In general, an individual at the Tier 1 level may be educated at the baccalaureate level or educated at a higher level with limited experience as a public health professional.

Source: From Council on Linkages between Academia and Public Health Practice, 2010.

performance expectations for the next cycle. The use of competencies within personnel and human resources systems is growing slowly within the public sector, although widespread implementation could take decades.

The identification of core competencies for public health practice and for emergency preparedness and response demonstrate the support for competency-based training among practice organizations. A companion effort to identify a panel of core competencies for graduates of MPH programs in schools of public health was completed in 2006 under the auspices of the Association of Schools of Public Health. This panel of competencies addresses discipline-specific competencies for behavioral sciences, health administration, epidemiology, biostatistics, environmental health, and public health biology as well as cross-cutting competencies in the areas of communication, informatics, cultural proficiency, ecologic determinants of health, leadership, policy development, professionalism, program development and evaluation, and systems thinking.

Despite this progress, formidable challenges lie ahead.[16,17] These include the establishment of mechanisms to support workforce planning and training in all states and local jurisdictions, and refinement and validation of public health practice competencies associated with each of the various disciplines that compose the workforce. Enhanced competencies are necessary to improve basic, advanced, and continuing education curricula for public health workers. Also needed are strategies to certify competencies among practitioners. In addition, large-scale assessments of current levels of workforce preparedness as measured by core competencies are lacking. For education and training of the public health workforce to be taken seriously, both academic and practice interests must view public health workforce development as an important priority.

Education and training opportunities for public health workers are widely available today and are likely to expand even further over the next decade. The first school of public health was established in 1916 at the Johns Hopkins School of Hygiene and Public Health with the support of the Rockefeller Foundation. In 1969, there were only 12 schools of public health, but that number grew to 43 by mid 2010, with a dozen new schools in the pipeline. The number of accredited programs offering the MPH and equivalent degrees exceeded 80 in 2010. Many unaccredited programs also exist.

Before 1970, students in public health training were primarily physicians or members of other disciplines with professional degrees. In recent decades, however, more than two thirds of the students enter public health training in order to obtain their primary postgraduate degrees. Public health training evolved from a second degree for medical professionals to a primary health discipline. Schools of public health that initially emphasized the study of hygiene and sanitation have expanded their curricula to address five core disciplines—biostatistics, epidemiology, health services administration, health education/behavioral science, and environmental science.

The number of individuals earning graduate degrees in public health tripled between 1975 and 2010, from 3,000 to more than 10,000.[6] Ironically, this increase has not had a significant impact on the number and proportion of professionals trained in public health in the primary public health workforce. In the 1970s, about one half of MPH graduates took jobs with governmental public health agencies, the primary public health workforce. Currently, only approximately one in five MPH graduates take jobs with governmental public health agencies.

Despite this impressive growth of public health schools and programs, most public health workers continue to receive their professional preparation elsewhere. This is not surprising in view of the number of training programs for key occupational categories in the public health workforce. There are more than 1,500 basic registered nurse training programs at the bachelor, associate, or diploma level; well in excess of 1,000 licensed practical nurse training programs; more than 150 programs in health administration; and several hundred programs offering training in environmental health sciences.

In summary, educational resources contribute to a national network of nearly 150 accredited schools and other graduate programs of public health, and as many as 500 other graduate-level education programs in areas related to public health, such as health administration, public health nursing, and environmental engineering.

Training activities that focus on public health workers rather than students are also extensive. HRSA has long been the primary federal health agency supporting development of the various health professions, although the public health workforce has never been a priority for that agency. Because many public health workers come from other health disciplines, however, HRSA support for training other health professionals also benefits the public health workforce. Throughout the 1990s, HRSA training activities for public health focused increasingly on strengthening links between schools of public health and public health agencies. Early in the 1990s, HRSA initiated support for the Council on Linkages between Academia and Public Health Practice, which has grown to include representation from many prominent public health academic and practice organizations. Since 1999, HRSA has funded Public Health Training Centers, which are multistate training collaborations involving schools of public health and health agencies, with 14 such centers (with approximately $5 million in annual funding) operating in late 2010. Beginning in 2002, HRSA also funded states and several large cities to support hospital bioterrorism planning and provided funds for curriculum development and training for healthcare professionals and for community-wide planning related to bioterrorism and other public health emergencies.

During the 1990s, the CDC became increasingly engaged in supporting capacity development and improving state-based public health systems through the establishment of national and regional leadership development projects in the early 1990s. The CDC also provided direct financial assistance to state public health systems for emergency preparedness later in that decade. The CDC encouraged states and large cities to utilize this funding to improve the capacity of their public health infrastructures in order to respond to a wide range of both emergency and routine threats, including bioterrorism preparedness. The CDC increasingly emphasized and supported public health workforce development as the cornerstone of infrastructure improvement. Between 2000 and 2010, through its cooperative agreement with the Association of Schools of Public Health, the CDC awarded substantial grants (approximately

$1 million per center per year) to more than 2 dozen academic Centers for Public Health Preparedness.

Since 1998, funding for public health workforce development through schools of public health has increased dramatically, from under $1 million (primarily from HRSA) in 1997 to more than $30 million (mainly from the CDC) in 2007. Approximately another $70 to $80 million for public health training is available in the bioterrorism grants awarded to states and several large cities, an estimated 10% of those grants. A total of more than $100 million is being programmed specifically for public health workforce development in 2010 in addition to resources that prepare other health professionals to participate in responses to public health emergencies.[13]

The extent of organized workforce development activities within state and LHDs and other public health organizations is unknown. Nonetheless, virtually all public health organizations provide some form of orientation, training, and support of continuing education for their workers. Costs for these activities are often buried in agency budgets as human resources, administrative support, and employee travel expenditures encompassing both direct and indirect, or opportunity costs for time spent away from performing official duties. Aggregating these costs would likely represent a significant pool of resources.

Efforts to forge links between academic and training partners and public health practice agencies at all levels of government are advancing, although unevenly from state to state. Comprehensive approaches that serve the entire public health workforce with an extensive menu of options for workers at varying stages of career development are lacking. More limited approaches that increase the number of workers who can acquire formal public health training through degree programs or that provide advanced skills to specific categories of workers within the public health workforce are useful but not sufficient. These efforts serve a relatively small portion of the overall public health workforce. More comprehensive and systems-based approaches are needed.

Public Health Workforce Development

Although education and training are key components of public health workforce strategies, they are not by themselves sufficient. Comprehensive public health workforce development efforts assess and promote competencies in addition to enhancing them (Figure 6-3). Efforts to promote the acquisition of public health competencies focus on several fronts but necessarily emphasize the workplace and the organizations that employ workers. Critical skills and core competencies are promoted in the workplace through job descriptions and performance appraisals that are organized around those skills and competencies. Managers and supervisors work with their employees to manage the professional development of workers and build skills that are necessary for career advancement. These administrative and personnel policies and practice create a culture that values competent performance and the acquisition of new skills.

A complementary approach to promote competencies relies on external bodies to validate and recognize skill levels through credentialing programs.

1. Assess Competency Using
   Consistent Methods and Tools

2. Enhance Specific Competencies
   Based on Assessment

3. Verify Competent Performance in
   Workplace Via Human Resource
   Management

4. Recognize Competent Performance
   Via System Incentives Such as
   Credentialing

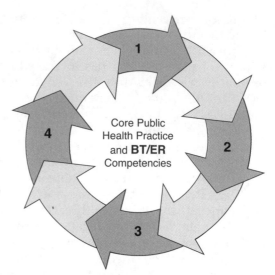

Figure 6-3   Components of a public health workforce preparedness management system.

Previous chapters identify many different forms of credentials for various categories of public health workers. For example, nutritionists may earn the registered dietitian credential, health educators may become certified health education specialists, physicians may achieve board certification in preventive medicine and public health, and many different credentials are available to environmental health practitioners. With discipline-specific credentials available to so many different public health worker occupational categories, it should come as no surprise that there are now efforts to develop credentials specific to public health.

The intent of any credential is to distinguish someone who is eligible for some status from others who are not. Identifying individuals who have demonstrated practice-relevant competencies at a specified level (from frontline workers to senior professionals, specialists, and leaders) provides an incentive for individuals to enhance their skills. Health professions have taken various approaches to credentialing that include licensing (for physicians and nurses), certification (for health education specialists), and registration (for dietitians and sanitarians). These examples suggest that credentialing is already widely used for public health workers; examples include board-certified preventive medicine physicians, certified community health nurses and health education specialists, and certified, registered environmental health practitioners. There is still a need for credentials for those who would not fit into these specialty-specific credentials, such as public health physicians not certified in preventive medicine, or health educators who are not certified health education specialists. Because many, indeed most, workers will not be able to meet the specific requirements for specialty credentialing, such as the 3-year residency for physicians or completion of a health education degree at the undergraduate or graduate level for certified health educators, a midlevel public health-specific credential could be attractive to many public health disciplines. Fledgling competency-based credentialing programs for public health managers and for public health emergency response coordinators exist in one state using an independent certification board.[18] The newly established Board of Public Health Examiners initiated a credential (Certified in Public Health) for graduates of MPH degree programs based on a national test, beginning in 2008. These and other models focus more on public health practice competencies rather than on a worker's core discipline, making them fertile ground for turf battles with professional organizations. Considerable input from these professional organizations and professionals in practice will be needed, however, for any framework to be valued and widely used. A three-prong credentialing strategy emerged from the National Public Health Workforce Development Conference in early 2003 calling for recognition of public health competency at a basic or Public Health 101 level and at a leadership level as well as expansion of existing credentialing activities for public health disciplines to cover those not now included.[19]

For workers to value credentials and the competencies on which they are based, employers and health agencies must find value in them as well and base decisions about hiring, promotion, salaries, and the like on an individual worker's demonstration of those competencies. Improving workers' ability to perform their functions competently relies on both worker training and work-management strategies; these relationships are illustrated in Figure 6-4.[3] As performance standards for public health organizations and public health systems gain headway through initiatives such as the National Public Health

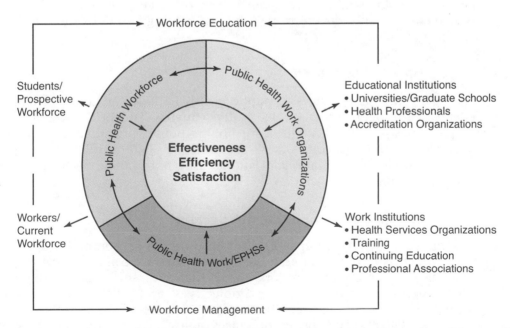

Figure 6-4 The structure of a public health work-doing system. *Source:* From Centers for Disease Control and Prevention, Public Health Practice Program Office, 2002.

Performance Standards Program and the NACCHO's Mobilizing for Action through Planning and Partnerships (MAPP) process, competency-based performance standards for workers will increasingly be viewed as key ingredients of organizational and system performance.

An innovative NACCHO program, Public Health Ready, contributed significantly to promoting public health workforce preparedness. Public Health Ready recognizes public health agencies that meet standards for worker competency, agency preparedness plans, and regular exercises of those plans.[20] Workers can demonstrate preparedness competencies during those drills and simulations, furthering the ability of the agency to verify and document the preparedness levels of the organization and its staff. As this approach expands, it could serve to focus public health workforce development efforts through its emphasis on the work, workers, and work organizations that constitute the governmental public health enterprise.

Although several forms of incentives are slowly advancing, one key element of a system of incentives remains lacking—there is no common currency in the form of a public health continuing-education unit that ensures quality and consistency of training activities nationally. Neither the CDC nor any of the national public health organizations has sought to serve in this capacity. A common currency that has credibility in the practice sector and is linked with organized workforce development strategies and funding from recent bioterrorism preparedness legislation would provide a considerable incentive for competency-based approaches to public health workforce development. Nonetheless, the obstacles and inertia that have accrued over several decades remain formidable challenges for the public health system. As demonstrated in Figure 6-4, comprehensive workforce development strategies must focus not only on the worker, but on the organizations in which the work is performed.

ORGANIZATIONAL RESOURCES

Organizational resources in public health include the complex web of federal health agencies, state health departments, and LHDs described in Chapter 4, as well as mechanisms for linking public, private, and voluntary organizations through collaborative relationships. Before collaboration patterns are addressed, several organizational aspects of public health agencies merit discussion.

Organizational Aspects of Public Health Systems

Organizations are groups of individuals linked by common goals and objectives. This implies that each organization has a specific mission or purpose, resources appropriate to work toward that purpose, the ability to determine progress toward its goals and objectives, and a defined process for making decisions that change the direction or speed of the organization in pursuit of its goals. Each organization takes on a structure to delegate its activities to specific units or individuals and to coordinate the tasks among them. Communication pathways facilitate the accomplishment of the organization's goals and objectives. In one respect, communication channels define the organization, even as the organizational structure defines the communication pathways. A variety of forces shape an organization's ability to succeed, including its ability to survive in a changing environment. These include the organization's mission and leadership, as well as key aspects of its operations, such as planning, collaboration, and communications. The specifics of these organizational arrangements are best left to texts in health administration and organizational behavior; only selected pertinent issues are addressed in this section.

Public-sector organizations differ in many important respects from their private- and voluntary-sector counterparts. The most obvious, and perhaps most important, difference is apparent in their bottom lines. The bottom line of public health agencies is measured in health outcomes, with efficiency and effectiveness valued, but not nearly as much. For the private sector, the bottom line is often profits and customer satisfaction, and efficiency and effectiveness are viewed as means to those ends. Many community and voluntary organizations address missions that resemble those of public agencies; however, public agencies often have political and bureaucratic environments that are unique among organizations. It should not be forgotten that employment itself is an important public objective, although the public sector lacks the ability to expand or contract its workforce rapidly in response to market conditions. In fact, public-sector jobs and services become even more important during times of economic recession.

The presence of a civil service-based workforce in many public health agencies is often cited as an impediment to getting things done, although the real problem may be more related to inadequate management practices than to institutionalized inertia. Civil service personnel systems were established in state and local governments, in large part through personnel standards fostered by Maternal and Child Health funding with the enactment of Title V of the Social Security Act in 1935. Although the initial intent was to provide added security for government workers, there has been long-standing discontent with the system and tension and conflict between government workers and elected officials ever since. Civil service employees generally lack the power to strike, unlike their private-sector counterparts who are organized into unions.

For many years, public health organizations operated under a command-and-control approach to management. If a problem was assigned to the public health agency, the agency sought to acquire the resources needed to deal with that problem. Resources were deployed directly from the agency; this approach worked well when the major problems called for environmental engineering solutions or communicable disease control expertise. As problems became more complex, however, encroaching on the territory of other health and human service agencies, command-and-control approaches became problematic. To resolve delicate turf issues, cooperating with other agencies and collaborative approaches began to supplement more directly controlled strategies.

These added to the challenges of public agency managers, which also included promoting workers' efficiency and effectiveness. Management training has never been well supported in the public sector, certainly not to the extent that it has been in the private sector. As a result, public health agencies often are poorly managed; this generates tensions and conflicts between professional staff and administrators brought into an agency to maximize efficiency and effectiveness, as well as between the agency and its community collaborators. For example, there has been a declining proportion of LHD heads with medical degrees. For larger health departments (especially those serving populations of 100,000 or more), this trend is partly explained by the employment of non-physician agency heads to manage the increasingly complex array of community and clinical services. Clinical professionals in health departments have not always adjusted well to these changes, and the result has sometimes been management and morale problems.

Public health agencies at the state and local levels often have boards to guide their efforts. Eighty percent of LHDs reported the presence of a local board of health in the 2008 NACCHO profile with a notably higher prevalence in smaller local health jurisdictions (Figure 6-5). During the past century, boards have assumed roles less involved with direct agency operations than when initially established. Agency leadership today has assumed much of the direction of professional staff, and boards have retained roles of approving regulations, advising/approving agency budgets, and often hiring the agency director. The role of many local boards of health has become unclear and largely advisory to the agency, prompting debate as to their role in the modern practice of public health. In response to concerns over past and current roles, the Institute of Medicine report calls for public health councils so

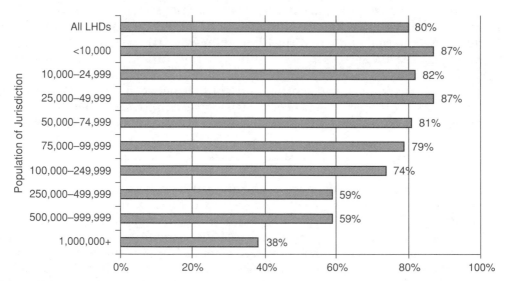

Figure 6-5 Percentage of LHDs with a local board of health in the jurisdiction, by size of population served, United States, 2008. *Source:* Data from National Association of County and City Health Officials. *2008 National Profile of Local Health Departments*. Washington, DC: NACCHO; 2009.

that any historic baggage attached to boards of health will be minimized. Public health agencies often have a plethora of advisory boards and committees developed for specific programs or activities. Although the proliferation of these advisory bodies can be seen as unwieldy and sometimes conflicting with the roles of more formally established bodies, such as the board of health itself, these groups also serve to greatly expand participation and communication with professional constituencies. Superfluous from a management perspective, these are, nevertheless, often effective constituency-building activities. Boards of health and various forms of advisory committees provide a link between the agency and the community it serves. Agency and community interests are better served by fostering the utilization of these relationships than by limiting or controlling them.

Within public health agencies, leadership positions carry several different responsibilities. The leader manages the agency, interacts with the major stakeholders and constituency groups, and carries out some largely ceremonial functions. The specific authorities of the agency are vested in its director through statutes or ordinances; these are the only legal powers of that leader. Within state and LHDs, there has been a steady move away from physician directors of agencies, although approximately one sixth of all LHDs continue to hire physicians as chief executive officers. An evolving literature on leadership is developing within the public health community. The CDC has established a national public health leadership institute, and nearly two dozen regional and state-based leadership development initiatives were in place in the year 2010.

Leadership development programs are often organized around concepts such as envisioning the future, inspiring others to act, and generally acting through others. Public health leaders used these skills a century ago to foster public perceptions of sound science in action in deploying culture tubes and laboratory diagnostic capabilities in the war against infectious disease risks.

Leadership in public health, however, involves more than individual leaders or individuals in leadership positions. Public health is intimately involved in leadership as an agent of social change by identifying health problems and risks and stimulating actions toward their elimination. Because the work of public health emphasizes both collective and individual leadership, the battery of leadership principles and practices is pertinent throughout public health organizations and systems. In many respects, the tools described in Chapter 5 (accreditation standards, MAPP, Healthy Communities, etc.) are tools of and for public health leadership.

Nongovernmental organizations have played major roles in public health activities since 1900. As the national network of federal, state, and local public agencies expanded and government assumed more responsibility for health issues, it assimilated public health initiatives that were initiated and supported by nongovernmental organizations. The modern public health system represents the work of both government and nongovernmental organizations. The Rockefeller Sanitary Committee's Hookworm Eradication during 1910 to 1920 stimulated the development of LHDs; other foundations sponsored health department development and medical education reform. The National Tuberculosis Association worked for tuberculosis (TB) prevention and treatment. The National Consumers League championed maternal and infant health initiatives in the 1920s. The American Red Cross supported nutrition programs during the Depression years of the 1930s, and in the 1940s and 1950s, the March of Dimes led the national effort to develop a successful polio vaccine. More recently, Mothers Against Drunk Driving began in 1980 through the efforts of a group of women in California (after a young girl was killed by an intoxicated driver) and grew into a national campaign for stronger laws against drunk driving. Professional organizations and labor unions also worked to promote public health. The American Medical Association advocated better vital statistics and safer foods and drugs. The American Dental Association endorsed water fluoridation, despite the economic consequences to its members. Labor organizations worked for safer workplaces in industry. Today, nongovernmental organizations sponsor diverse public health research projects and programs, including family planning, human immunodeficiency virus (HIV) prevention, violence prevention, vaccine development, and heart disease and cancer prevention.

Coalitions and Consortia

An increasingly important aspect of organizational resources is the ability to work through collaborative links with other agencies and organizations. Often, these arrangements are described as coalitions or consortia, although other terms are frequently used, and distinctions are often blurred (Table 6-8).[21] Coalitions can be formed for short-term efforts or established to address ongoing problems on a long-term basis. They are most likely to be successful when they include representation from all groups affected by the problem and making efforts to deal with that problem. In general, coalitions and consortia are formal partnerships involving two or more groups working together to achieve specific goals according to a common plan. The rationale for a consortia approach is that the goals are believed to be beyond the capacity of any one participating organization. Goals can take various forms, from communication among members, to public and professional education, to advocating and lobbying for particular policy changes. It is essential that coalition members be in agreement that the problem is best addressed through a coalition approach and that they be comfortable with the scope of activities planned. Building on mutual interests allows a coalition to place expectations and demands on its member organizations. Most important, coalitions must do things that are important for their members; they must help their members, as well as the group.

There are many advantages to working through coalitions and consortia. Collaborative efforts can function more efficiently than single organizations because work plans are shared among collaborating organizations rather than carried out by a single group. This serves to conserve limited resources and provides a pathway for reaching a larger part of the community. When organizations band together around specific goals, their efforts carry greater credibility than when only one or a few organizations are involved. Collaborative efforts are also excellent mechanisms for ensuring a broad range of inputs and perspectives into the policy development process and for facilitating commu-

Table 6-8 Characteristics of Collaborative Organizations

Organization	Characteristics
Advisory committees	Generally respond to organizations or programs by providing suggestions and technical assistance
Commissions	Usually consist of citizens appointed by official bodies
Consortia and alliances	Tend to be semiofficial, membership organizations; typically have broad policy-oriented goals and may span large geographic areas; usually consist of organizations and coalitions, as opposed to individuals
Networks	Are generally loosely knit groups, formed primarily for the purpose of resource and information sharing
Task forces	Most often come together to accomplish a specific series of activities, often at the request of an overseeing body

Source: Data from Contra Costa County Health Services Department Prevention Program. *Developing Effective Coalitions: An Eight Step Guide.* Martinez, CA: Contra Costa County Health Department; 1994.

nication and information across agencies and organizations. This has the added benefit of helping staff from one organization to view problems and possible solutions from a broader perspective than their usual vantage point. By building trust and personal relationships around one issue, collaborative approaches facilitate future collaborations around other issues.

There are no set rules for developing coalitions and consortia, but some general principles and approaches are useful after the decision is made to use a collaborative approach (Table 6-9). That decision may come from a lead agency determining that a coalition would facilitate achievement of some goal or, in some instances, being required to establish one by a funding organization. On other occasions, an organization may be requested by community leaders or other agencies to organize a collaborative effort. Unmet community needs, scandals, and service breakdowns all serve to promote the development of coalitions, as do both informal and formal ties that exist among members.

Most coalitions have an agency or organization that leads the effort. Lead agencies must have both the credibility and the resources necessary for a coalition to succeed.

If it is determined that a coalition is the best mechanism to address a particular goal, the resources needed from the lead agency and other coalition members should be assessed to determine whether the coalition represents the best use of those resources to accomplish that goal. This requires examination of objectives and implementation strategies that might facilitate achievement of the coalition's goals. A range of implementation strategies is available to coalitions, including making advocacy efforts to influence policy and legislation, changing organizational behavior, promoting networks,

Table 6-9   Key Steps for Coalitions and Other Collaborative Organizations

Step 1: Analyze the program's objectives and determine whether to form a coalition.
Step 2: Recruit the right people.
Step 3: Develop a set of preliminary objectives and activities.
Step 4: Convene the coalition.
Step 5: Anticipate the necessary resources.
Step 6: Define elements of a successful coalition structure.
Step 7: Maintain coalition vitality.
Step 8: Make improvements through evaluation.

Source: Data from Contra Costa County Health Services Department Prevention Program. *Developing Effective Coalitions: An Eight Step Guide.* Martinez, CA: Contra Costa County Health Department; 1994.

educating providers, educating the community, and increasing individual knowledge and skills. One or more implementation strategies should be adopted by the coalition on the basis of how well these fit with the community's strengths and weaknesses.

After the decision is made to develop a coalition, recruitment of the appropriate members is necessary to advance the process. Questions to be addressed include whether membership will consist of individuals or organizations and, if the latter, who should represent a particular organization on the coalition. In some cases, it is desirable to have agency leaders; in others, lower-level staff more familiar with the issues and programs may make better members. The size of the coalition also requires careful consideration. After these issues are decided, preliminary objectives and work plans are developed, and the coalition is convened. At this point, the role of the lead agency in chairing or staffing the coalition should be determined, and resources needed to carry out the coalition's work plan should be identified and made available. Early decisions of the coalition should establish its expected life span, criteria for membership and decision making, and expectations for participation at and between meetings. Constant vigilance is necessary to identify problems internal to the coalition's operation. These can include a loss of interest and participation from some members, tension and conflict over power and leadership of the coalition, a lack of community representativeness, and turnover of coalition members. Frequently, coalition members perceive threats to their organizational autonomy or come to disagree about service priorities or, more specifically, about which members will provide specific services.

Careful assessment of a coalition's strengths and weaknesses (Table 6-10), together with a commitment to make a good process even better, is often necessary to maintain the vitality and momentum of even the best coalition. Many of these steps and issues appear to be straightforward and noncontroversial until they are addressed within the context of an actual coalition experience. In virtually all instances, however, coalitions rely on information as well as relationships to achieve their ends.

Table 6-10 Sample Questions for Partnership Self-Assessment

Synergy	• Ability to identify new and creative ways to solve problems • Ability to include the views and priorities of the people affected by the partnership's work • Ability to develop goals that are widely understood and supported among partners • Ability to identify how different services and programs in the community relate to the problems the partnership is trying to address • Ability to respond to the needs and problems of the community • Ability to implement strategies that are most likely to work in the community • Ability to obtain support from individuals and organizations in the community that can either block the partnership's plans or help move them forward • Ability to carry out comprehensive activities that connect multiple services, programs, or systems • Ability to communicate to people in the community clearly how the partnership's actions will address problems that are important to them
Leadership	• Taking responsibility for the partnership • Inspiring or motivating people involved in the partnership • Empowering people involved in the partnership • Communicating the vision of the partnership • Working to develop a common language within the partnership • Fostering respect, trust, inclusiveness, and openness in the partnership • Creating an environment where differences of opinion can be voiced • Resolving conflict among partners • Combining the perspectives, resources, and skills of partners • Helping the partnership be creative and look at things differently • Recruiting diverse people and organizations into the partnership
Efficiency	• Using the partners' financial resources • Using the partners' in-kind resources (e.g., skills, expertise, information, data, connections, influence, space, equipment, goods) • Using the partners' time
Administration and management	• Coordinating communication among partners • Coordinating communication with people and organizations outside the partnership • Organizing partnership activities, including meetings and projects • Applying for and managing grants and funds • Preparing materials that inform partners and help them make timely decisions • Performing secretarial duties • Providing orientation to new partners as they join the partnership • Evaluating the progress and impact of the partnership • Minimizing the barriers to participation in the partnership's meetings and activities (e.g., by holding them at convenient places and times and by providing transportation and childcare)

(continues)

Table 6-10   Sample Questions for Partnership Self-Assessment (continued)

Nonfinancial resources	• Skills and expertise (e.g., leadership, administration, evaluation, law, public policy, cultural competency, training, and community organizing) • Data and information (e.g., statistical data, information about community perceptions, values, resources, and politics) • Connections to target populations • Connections to political decision makers, government agencies, other organizations/groups • Legitimacy and credibility • Influence and ability to bring people together for meetings and activities
Financial and other capital resources	• Money • Space • Equipment and goods
Decision making	• Comfort with the way decisions are made in the partnership • Support of decisions made by the partnership • Frequency of feeling left out of the decision-making process
Benefits of participation	• Enhanced ability to address an important issue • Development of new skills • Heightened public profile • Increased utilization of your expertise or service • Acquisition of useful knowledge about services, programs, or people in the community • Enhanced ability to affect public policy • Development of valuable relationships • Enhanced ability to meet the needs of your constituency or clients • Ability to have a greater impact than you could have on your own • Ability to make a contribution to the community • Acquisition of additional financial support
Drawbacks of participation	• Diversion of time and resources away from other priorities or obligations • Insufficient influence in partnership activities • Viewed negatively because of association with other partners or the partnership • Frustration or aggravation • Insufficient credit given to you for contributing to the accomplishments of the partnership • Conflict between your job and the partnership's work • Comparison of the benefits of participating in this partnership to the drawbacks
Satisfaction with participation	• Satisfaction with the way the people and organizations in the partnership work together • Satisfaction with your influence in the partnership • Satisfaction with your role in the partnership • Satisfaction with the partnership's plans for achieving its goals • Satisfaction with the way the partnership is implementing its plans

Source: Data from Center for the Advancement of Collaborative Strategies in Health, 2002.

INFORMATION RESOURCES

In addition to human, organizational, and collaborative resources, information and access to information represent important elements of the public health infrastructure. The information resources that support public health practice include both the scientific basis of public health and the network of data and information needed to assess and address health problems. In large part, this knowledge base is outlined in the competencies for public health professionals presented in the discussion of the public health workforce. It includes elements from the public health sciences consisting of epidemiology, biostatistics, environmental health sciences, health administration, and behavioral sciences. This knowledge base contributes to the development of competencies across a broad range of analytical, communication, policy development and planning, cultural, basic public health science, and management skills. Although this knowledge base is provided through graduate-level public health education, it can also be acquired through other educational, training, and experiential opportunities.

Information resources to carry out the activities of public health are increasingly abundant and accessible. Several important principles[22] that underlie the effective use of information sets in public health are highlighted in Table 6-11. The need to ensure both flexibility and compatibility within information systems creates a tension that is not always readily resolved. In addition, two general categories of data sets are commonly encountered in public health practice. It is important to recognize their differences, although there is often great value in using both categories in efforts to identify and address health problems.

One category includes service- or encounter-based data, which are collected for a variety of purposes, such as reimbursement, eligibility, and evaluation of care. These data sets are common to programs that provide primary or episodic healthcare services, nutrition services for women, infants, and children, mental health and substance abuse treatment, and many other services.

Table 6-11   Principles of Public Health Information

1. Recognize different types of data: encounter-based data on individuals as they encounter providers and universal data on populations from surveys and environmental monitoring systems.
2. Provide for integrated management to improve meeting of individual needs and to portray fully individual participation in multiple, categorical programs.
3. Maintain a service orientation to address the overriding concern of public health information systems.
4. Ensure flexibility so as to adapt to differences in data collection resources at the local level while accommodating data needs to support a broad range of public health programs and objectives.
5. Achieve system compatibility to allow data flow and functioning across systems in a fully compatible fashion.
6. Protect confidentiality to provide better service and to preserve privacy.

Source: Data from Lumpkin JR. Six principles of public health information. *J Public Health Manage Pract.* 1995;1:40–42.

The information is collected for individual recipients of these services, which may include important clinical preventive services, such as immunizations or cancer screening. Aggregate data from these service encounters provide useful information on health needs and the health status of a population, including program coverage and penetration rates; however, the population is limited to those seeking services and may not be representative of the larger population.

Another category of data sets describes populations, rather than individuals. Examples include many of the federal surveys of health status and service utilization, as well as behavioral risk factor surveys of the population that collect information on population samples (composed of individual respondents) that are representative of the entire population. For these data sets, the population is described through the use of sampling techniques. Other data sets capture information on specific health events and outcomes for a defined population, such as cancer incidence registries and vital records systems. For these, data are collected on individuals and aggregated in comparison with a reference population, often derived from census information (e.g., the rate of newly diagnosed lung cancers among women aged 45 to 64 years in a state). Data sets that describe risks or hazards common to a population, such as environmental monitoring data, represent yet another form of population-based data.

The limitations of encounter-based information systems are apparent when individuals participate in more than one service program. A prenatal care program may have its own information system; the women, infants, and children program serving the same person may have another system, and the lead screening program yet another. The communicable disease program may have separate systems for general communicable diseases, HIV infections, TB, and sexually transmitted diseases. Beyond these health information systems, an individual may also be receiving services from other agencies for mental health, substance abuse, spousal abuse, and Medicaid. The information systems are often problem specific, but individuals generally have multiple problems. Integration of information systems across the entire spectrum of human services programs and needs is essential both to promote efficiency in programs and to characterize the health status and needs of individuals and populations.

Confidentiality issues can be especially difficult to address in information systems. State statutes for the collection, sharing, and confidentiality of health statistics should make it impossible for individuals to be identified unless they have consented. Disclosure of personal identifiers should be permitted only to a government entity or research project that had a written agreement to protect the confidentiality of the information or to a governmental entity for the purpose of conducting an audit, evaluation, or investigation of the agency.

Information and Analytic Techniques

The capacity of the public health system to use information more effectively expanded during the 20th century. Advances occurred in both study design and periodic standardized health surveys. Methods of data collection evolved from simple measures of disease prevalence, such as field surveys, to more complex studies and precise analyses, such as case-control studies, cohort studies, and randomized clinical trials. The first well-developed, longitudinal cohort study was conducted in 1947 among the 28,000 residents of Framingham, Massachusetts, many of whom volunteered to be followed over time to determine incidence of heart disease. The Framingham Heart Study has served as a model for other longitudinal cohort studies, advancing understanding of the multiple risk factors that contribute to disease. The age of modern clinical trials began in 1948 with a study of streptomycin therapy for TB; this study involved randomization, selection criteria, predetermined evaluation criteria, and ethical considerations. In 1950, the first convincing evidence of an association between lung cancer and tobacco use was provided in a case-control study, adding credibility to this important study design. Subsequently, high-powered statistical tests and analytic computer programs enabled multiple variables collected in large-scale studies to be measured and tools to be developed for mathematical modeling. Advances in epidemiology contributed to the elucidation of risk factors for heart disease and other chronic diseases and the development of effective interventions.

The first periodic standardized health surveys in the United States began in 1921. In 1935, the first national health survey was conducted among U.S. residents. In 1956, these efforts culminated in the National Health Survey, a population-based survey that evolved from focusing on chronic disease to estimating disease prevalence for major causes of death, measuring the burden of infectious diseases, assessing exposure to environmental toxicants, and measuring the population's vaccination coverage. Other population-based surveys, such as the Behavioral Risk Factor Surveillance System, Youth Risk Behavior Survey, and the National Survey of Family Growth, were developed to assess risk factors for chronic diseases and other conditions. Survey methods used in epidemiologic studies were enhanced by new approaches to sampling and interviewing developed by social scientists and statisticians.

Information and the Assessment Function of Public Health

Information drives the assessment function of public health in at least three ways. First, public health agencies commonly use surveillance data to monitor community health status and trends and to identify any new health risks or hazards. Second, after health needs and problems are identified, information is needed on the community's resources that are available to address those needs and problems and on the effectiveness of those resources. Third, information from assessments of health needs and current efforts must be tailored to the needs of decision and policy makers to facilitate more effective interventions.[23] Data sources for the various facets of the assessment function monitor health status and risk factors, identify and evaluate resources, and inform and advise managers, policy makers, and the public. These interrelated purposes demonstrate that information is a resource widely used throughout public health practice in applications involving surveillance, planning processes, selection of scientifically based interventions, and health communications.

Information and Surveillance

Public health surveillance activities monitor health status and risk factors in the population. Although surveillance data sets have become both more sophisticated and more accessible in recent years, the most important consideration for their establishment relates to why and how they will be used. The very first collection of health statistics dates back to the work of John Graunt in England in the mid 17th century.

Health data in the United States have had the benefit of national enumerations of the population every 10 years, although the decennial census was established to ensure fair representation in the Congress, rather than to serve as a source of health or even demographic information on the population. National disease monitoring was first conducted in the United States in 1850 when the federal government first published mortality statistics based on death registrations. In the late 19th century, Congress authorized the collection of morbidity reports on cholera, smallpox, plague, and yellow fever for use in quarantine measures and provided funding to expand weekly reporting from states and municipal authorities. The first annual summary of notifiable diseases appeared in 1912 with reports of 10 diseases from 19 states, the District of Columbia, and Hawaii. By 1928, all states were reporting on 29 diseases. In 1950, state and territorial health officers authorized the Council of State and Territorial Epidemiologists to determine which diseases should be reported to the U.S. Public Health Service (PHS). The CDC assumed responsibility for collecting and publishing national data on notifiable diseases in 1961. As of 2008, more than 60 infectious diseases were notifiable at the national level (Table 6-12).

Numerous sources of data are available for epidemiologic surveillance data. These range from well-known data sets, such as birth and death records, to lesser known sources, such as school and work absenteeism reports. Similar information is available for surveillance of environmental health risks. Several important data sources are operated through the CDC's National Center for Health Statistics, which maintains systems for the following:

- Vital Statistics (births, deaths, fetal deaths, induced abortions, marriages, divorces, follow-back surveys to gather additional information)
- National Health Interview Survey (amount, distribution, and effects of illness and disability, using a multistage probability sample)
- National Medical Care, Utilization, and Expenditure Survey (use of and expenditures for medical services, done in 1980 but not repeated since)
- National Ambulatory Medical Care Survey (location, setting, and frequency of ambulatory care encounters)
- National Health and Nutrition Examination Survey (direct physical, physiologic, and biochemical data from national sample)
- National Hospital Discharge Survey (characteristics of patients, lengths of stay, diagnoses, procedures, and patterns of patient use by type of hospital)

Surveillance is a multifaceted operation in that information is collected at a variety of levels. Surveillance information used in environmental public health applications illustrates this point. For any environmental agent that is

Table 6-12   Nationally Notifiable Infectious Diseases, United States, 2008

Acquired immune deficiency syndrome (AIDS)
Anthrax
Arboviral neuroinvasive and nonneuroinvasive diseases
- California serogroup virus disease
- Eastern equine encephalitis virus disease
- Powassan virus disease
- St. Louis encephalitis virus disease
- West Nile virus disease
- Western equine encephalitis virus disease
Botulism
- Botulism, food-borne
- Botulism, infant
- Botulism, other (wound and unspecified)
Brucellosis
Chancroid
Chlamydia trachomatis, genital infections
Cholera
Coccidioidomycosis
Cryptosporidiosis
Cyclosporiasis
Diphtheria
Ehrlichiosis/anaplasmosis
- *Ehrlichia chaffeensis*
- *Ehrlichia ewingii*
- *Anaplasma phagocytophilum*
- Undetermined
Giardiasis
Gonorrhea
Haemophilus influenzae, invasive disease
Hansen's disease (leprosy)
Hantavirus pulmonary syndrome
Hemolytic uremic syndrome, postdiarrheal
Hepatitis, viral, acute
- Hepatitis A, acute
- Hepatitis B, acute
- Hepatitis B virus, perinatal infection
- Hepatitis C, acute
Hepatitis, viral, chronic
- Chronic hepatitis B
- Hepatitis C virus infection (past or present)
HIV infection
HIV infection, adult (≥13 years)
HIV infection, pediatric (<13 years)
Influenza-associated pediatric mortality
Legionellosis
Listeriosis
Lyme disease
Malaria
Measles

(continues)

Table 6-12   Nationally Notifiable Infectious Diseases, United States, 2008 (continued)

Meningococcal disease
Mumps
Novel influenza A virus infections
Pertussis
Plague
Poliomyelitis, paralytic
Poliovirus infection, nonparalytic
Psittacosis
Q fever
Rabies
- Rabies, animal
- Rabies, human
Rocky Mountain spotted fever
Rubella
Rubella, congenital syndrome
Salmonellosis
Severe acute respiratory syndrome-associated coronavirus (SARS-CoV) disease
Shiga toxin-producing *Escherichia coli* (STEC)
Shigellosis
Smallpox
Streptococcal disease, invasive, group A
Streptococcal toxic shock syndrome
Streptococcus pneumoniae, drug resistant, invasive disease
Streptococcus pneumoniae, invasive disease nondrug resistant, in children less than 5 years of age
Syphilis
- Syphilis, primary
- Syphilis, secondary
- Syphilis, latent
- Syphilis, early latent
- Syphilis, late latent
- Syphilis, latent, unknown duration
- Neurosyphilis
- Syphilis, late, nonneurological
- Syphilitic stillbirth
Syphilis, congenital
Tetanus
Toxic shock syndrome (other than streptococcal)
Trichinellosis (trichinosis)
Tuberculosis
Tularemia
Typhoid fever
Vancomycin-intermediate *Staphylococcus aureus* (VISA)
Vancomycin-resistant *Staphylococcus aureus* (VRSA)
Varicella (morbidity)
Varicella (deaths only)
Vibriosis
Yellow fever

Source: Data from Centers for Disease Control and Prevention, 2010.

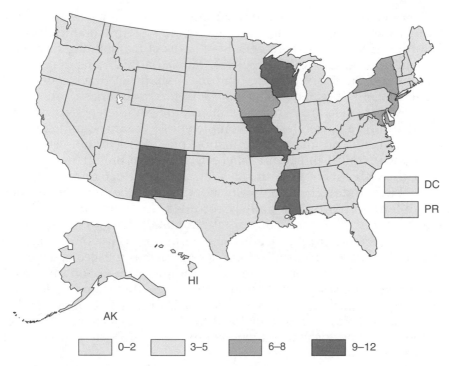

| 0–2 | 3–5 | 6–8 | 9–12 |

Figure 6-6 Number of environmental public health surveillance systems, by jurisdiction, United States, 1997. *Source:* From Centers for Disease Control and Prevention, 2001.

considered to be a hazard, surveillance efforts can measure its effects at various steps in its chain of causation. For example, the agent's presence in the environment can be assessed, and its route of exposure can be measured through surveillance efforts that can be considered hazard surveillance. Beyond hazard surveillance, exposure surveillance can track actual exposures between the host and agent, the frequency in which the agent reaches its target tissue, and the early production of adverse effects. In addition, outcome surveillance can measure the actual adverse effects after these become clinically apparent.

Together, these three levels of surveillance activities provide a more complete picture of the problem and allow for a more rational strategy for its control and for evaluating whether control strategies are working.

There is wide variability in the capacity of state and local health agencies to maintain and use surveillance information. A CDC survey in 1997 identified 174 environmental public health surveillance systems from 51 jurisdictions[24] (Figure 6-6). The mean number of systems per jurisdiction was three; the median was two. Of the 174, a total of 79 systems (45%) monitored lead exposure, with most systems monitoring childhood blood lead levels. The remaining 28 systems monitored nonoccupational adult lead exposures. The environmental diseases least frequently monitored were heatstroke and hypothermia (four systems each). One state had surveillance systems for all 12 of the environmental public health conditions covered by the survey. One state did not have any surveillance systems. Nine percent of the surveillance systems collected data only; 27% collected data and conducted reviews; and

64% collected data and conducted both reviews and case investigations. Asthma was the only condition for which no systems conducted case investigations. LHDs also vary considerably in terms of maintaining surveillance data on common public health problems. More than 80% maintain surveillance data on communicable diseases, but fewer than half track water quality, air quality, chronic diseases, behavioral risk factors, or injuries.

Most data sets are neither complete nor completely accurate. Each has problems and issues related to completeness, accuracy, and timeliness. For example, key denominator information provided through census enumerations under counts important subpopulations that are often at greater risk of adverse health effects. Even the data set often considered to be the most complete—birth and death records—includes some important data elements that are underreported or inaccurately recorded, including maternal behaviors, length of gestation, and congenital anomalies of newborn infants. Death records also suffer from variability in determining cause of death and, specifically, in identifying true underlying causes, such as tobacco or alcohol.

Vital records represent yet another example of an important federal health policy being operationalized through the states; there is no national mandate for uniform reporting of birth and deaths. Through a voluntary and cooperative effort with the states, a national model of these records is implemented by the states and localities, stimulated in part by federal grants for a national cooperative health statistics system.

Access to information and data for surveillance purposes has improved steadily with improved technology for electronic management and transfer. Today, reports including a mix of text, tables, and figures are available from an increasing number of federal and state sources through a variety of electronic modes: telephone, fax, CD-ROM and diskettes, modem, and the Internet.[25] Increasingly, electronic systems are used in ongoing surveillance activities of federal health departments, state health departments, and LHDs. These include the following:

- National Electronic Telecommunications System for Surveillance, which is used to collect, transmit, and analyze weekly reports of notifiable diseases from state and local health agencies; the system reports on a common set of diseases, using standard protocols for formatting and transmitting data, standard case definitions, a common record format, and designated individuals responsible for reporting from each agency.
- HIV/acquired immune deficiency syndrome (AIDS) Reporting System, which collects detailed demographic, risk, and clinical information on persons diagnosed with either AIDS or HIV infection; since 1985, the CDC has provided state and local health agencies with standardized case report forms and microcomputer-based software for managing HIV and AIDS surveillance in their areas.
- Public Health Laboratory Information System, which reports laboratory isolates to the CDC to reduce the enormous paper burden in state laboratories, to facilitate cluster identification, to provide states with better access to data, and to reduce the lag time between identification and reporting to the CDC.
- CDC WONDER, which is also used as a vehicle for transmission of surveillance files by a number of CDC surveillance systems.

Surveillance systems are a major component of the public health preparedness activities that are described in Chapter 8.

Information and Planning

Although there are various forms of planning, each relies heavily on information resources. In public health, planning information is widely employed for purposes of community health planning, agency strategic and operational planning, and program planning and management.

The community health planning role is new for many local governmental public health agencies. From the mid 1960s through the mid 1980s, community health planning was carried out through a national program of state and local planning agencies. The Comprehensive Health Planning Act of 1966 and the National Health Planning and Resource Development Act of 1974 established the framework for these structures and activities. At the state level, state health departments generally coordinated the development of state health plans, in part through the generation of local health plans. These local plans were developed by agencies known as health systems agencies, whose role was to organize community participation in the development and implementation of the local plans. In large part, this form of planning focused on resources within the health system, assessing the availability of facilities, health manpower, and specific services. Where resources were lacking, plans were established to increase supply. Where resources were underused, plans sought to increase demand. As consumer majorities sat on planning boards at both the state and local levels, the focus was on resource planning, rather than needs-based planning.

Largely because of their focus on resources, inability to make change happen, and widespread provider resentment of consumer-dominated processes, political support for this effort waned, and the federal program was repealed. Very soon thereafter most of the local health planning agencies also disappeared, leaving a significant void. LHDs, with a few exceptions, had not been very involved in community health planning and found it difficult to pick up the slack. LHDs often lacked staff with the skills and expertise in community health planning: Many information sources resided at levels of government outside their direct control, and they simply did not see it as part of their job description at a time when demands for serving the uninsured and the AIDS epidemic were at their doorsteps. These factors contributed to the need for the development of tools such as Assessment Protocol for Excellence in Public Health (APEXPH) and MAPP, the Planned Approach to Community Health, Model Standards, and the series of national Healthy People initiatives described in earlier chapters.

The framework of planning objectives in the Healthy People process encouraged states to develop more consistent state health plans. Most states used measures drawn directly from Healthy People 2020; however, this also meant that states replicated the lack of emphasis on mental health, substance abuse, environmental health, and occupational health issues that have marked the various iterations of Healthy People. In some states, these objectives are addressed in separate planning processes or not at all. States found that baseline data were generally available for state planning efforts modeled on Healthy People 2020, but they also found that such data were generally not available at the county or city level. Planning efforts relied heavily on vital records and, to a lesser extent, behavioral risk factor and notifiable disease data. Only infrequently were sources such as youth behavioral surveys, hospital discharge data, or morbidity data such as that provided in Table 6-13 used in state planning processes during the early 2000s. Stimulated by renewed interest in community-level health planning in the latter part of the decade, however, this situation has gradually improved.

APEXPH/MAPP and other community needs assessment processes call for a variety of mortality, morbidity, and risk factor information, as well as data and information on available resources to address priority health problems. Information describing the health status and needs of the local population is often available from federal and state sources, but more often, these sources must be supplemented with more locally developed information. The lessons from earlier attempts at consumer-directed local health planning demonstrate that community health planning is as much a political process as it is an objective process based on statistical data. Diversity in values and perspectives within a community cannot be homogenized through the use of what some consider objective data. These past failures make it all the more difficult for LHDs seeking to reenter this minefield. Managerial planning improvements, however, have emerged, including planning-programming-budgeting systems, operations research, systems analysis, and program evaluation and review techniques.

Information resources also support the strategic and operational planning activities of an organization. Strategic planning seeks to identify external and internal trends that might influence the agency's ability to carry out its mission and role. Operational planning looks to maximize the use of available resources to achieve specific objectives that have been established for a specific period of time, generally 2 years.

Information and Scientifically Based Interventions

At the heart of public health interventions for improving the quality of life and reducing preventable mortality and morbidity are scientifically sound strategies and approaches. Although the scientific basis for public health interventions has always been highly valued, the formal application of rigorous assessments to the evidence for effectiveness is a relatively new undertaking for public health. Considerable progress has been made on this front since 1990; Chapter 7 presents principles, strategies, and tools that will drive public health interventions in the early 21st century. These build on public health achievements throughout the 20th century, such as the efforts to ensure safer and healthier foods described in one of the Public Health Spotlights for this chapter.

FISCAL RESOURCES

The fiscal resources available for public health activities can be viewed as both inputs and outputs of the system. They are clearly inputs in that they represent an economic measure of the human, organizational, and informational resources described earlier, as well as the physical facilities, equipment, and other inputs that do not fit nicely into any of the other categories. The fiscal

Table 6-13 Injuries Associated with Selected Sports and Recreation Equipment Treated in Emergency Departments, 1994

Estimated Number of Product-Related Injuries Per 100,000 Population in the United States That Were Treated in Hospital Emergency Departments

Product Groupings	Estimated Number of Cases	AGE (YEAR)						DISPOSITION	
		All Ages	0–4	5–14	15–24	25–64	65+	Treated and Released	Hospitalized or Dead on Arrival
ATVs, mopeds, etc.	125,136	48.1	14.5	111.7	116.8	27.0	6.5	45.1	3.0
Baseball, softball	404,364	155.3	45.0	410.7	294.4	100.1	3.3	153.4	1.7
Basketball	716,114	275.1	13.4	584.0	955.3	111.6	3.2	272.9	1.8
Bicycles and accessories	604,455	232.2	247.8	908.2	243.2	87.5	28.2	223.3	8.6
Exercise and exercise equipment	155,231	59.6	45.2	68.8	134.6	49.6	16.6	58.5	1.0
Football	424,622	163.1	5.0	484.7	557.1	30.4	1.3	160.8	2.2
Hockey	81,885	31.5	5.4	85.1	81.9	14.4	0.3	30.9	0.5
Horseback riding	71,162	27.3	7.9	38.7	41.0	29.4	3.0	25.1	2.2
Lacrosse, rugby, miscellaneous ball games	90,252	34.7	18.4	126.4	63.4	11.9	1.1	34.2	0.3
Playground equipment	266,810	102.5	386.1	468.7	16.4	5.9	1.6	99.5	2.9
Skateboards	25,486	9.8	7.3	37.5	24.0	1.0	—	9.7	0.1
Skating (excludes in-line)	146,082	56.1	15.6	226.8	57.3	27.1	2.6	54.8	1.3
In-line skating	75,994	29.2	2.3	115.6	40.4	12.9	0.7	28.3	0.8
Soccer	162,115	62.3	2.7	190.6	180.7	18.5	0.6	61.4	0.8
Swimming, pools, equipment	115,139	44.2	62.4	128.8	63.3	21.1	10.1	42.5	1.7
Track and field activities, equipment	18,774	7.2	—	24.3	24.2	0.5	1.0	7.1	0.1
Trampolines	52,892	20.3	27.7	93.5	20.6	3.6	0.1	19.8	0.5
Volleyball	97,523	37.5	2.0	52.4	111.4	27.7	0.6	37.2	0.2

Source: From National Electronic Injury Surveillance System, U.S. Consumer Product Safety Commission.

resources provided for public health programs, however, also represent the perceived worthiness of these activities in comparison with other public policy goals. In this light, fiscal resources are a product of public health activities and an expression of their value in the eyes of society. In either interpretation, however, it is useful to quantify their levels and assess changes over time.

It is no simple task to link financial expenditures to the core functions and essential public health services framework. As we have seen in Chapters 1 and 5, the essential public health services framework includes both population-based and personal health services as well as some activities that don't resemble health services at all. For example, maintaining a competent workforce through training and continuing education is generally not considered a health service. Nor is research intended to improve services or health outcomes. The public sector sponsors many but not all the activities included in the essential public health services framework. Some personal health services provided through public sector resources fall into the essential public health services framework, such as those assuring the provision of care when otherwise unavailable, while others do not. In the public sector, agencies other than official health agencies provide essential public health services. For example, mental health, substance abuse, environmental protection, and emergency management agencies contribute as well. As a result, the essential public health services framework is not easy to measure through the use of government financial and accounting systems. Although precise determinations may not be possible, national health expenditure tracking systems do allow for reasonable approximations of public health activity expenditures in the United States.

Chapter 3 outlines the economic dimensions of the overall health system in the United States, including total national health expenditures ($2.3 trillion in 2008) and the amount identified for government public health activities ($69 billion in 2008).[6,26] These data provide the basis for the estimated population-based public health activity spending figure ($31 billion) also presented in that chapter. The figure for government public health activity captures much of the nation's spending for essential public health services, although there are additional essential public health service activities imbedded in several other government-sponsored programs and in entities outside government altogether. Examples of the latter include public information and education campaigns of voluntary health organizations such as heart, lung, cancer, and diabetes associations. Examples of the former include maternal and child health programs, environmental health activities, school health, and mental health, alcohol, and substance abuse programs operated by federal and state agencies. These activities are included in categories other than the public health activity category of the national health accounts.

Adjustments to the total government public health activity spending figures are necessary to approximate essential public health services expenditures. The rationale for computing an adjusted total government public health activity spending level is that several important public health programs and services that fall within the essential public health services framework are not captured in the government public health activity category. These include maternal and child health services, mental health, substance abuse prevention, Indian health services, and environmental protection activities, all of which contribute to the spectrum of essential public health services in many communities.

An important subset of the essential public health services framework is population-based public health activities, which are activities directed toward the community or an entire population rather than toward specific individuals. Population-based public health activities are a core component of the public health system. The basis for estimating the population-based component of total essential public health services expenditures derives from a series of studies of public health expenditure patterns that occurred at the state and local level in the mid-1990s.[27–29] Especially useful are two comprehensive examinations of essential public health services expenditures in nine state-local public health systems in 1994/1995 and in Florida in 2005/2006.[27,30] Findings from these studies shed light on the proportion of public health spending devoted to the various essential public health services as well as the sources of financial support for each service.

Of the total government expenditures for essential public health services in the nine states, 69% were directed toward individuals (personal health services) while 31% supported population-based public health activities. Extrapolations to all 50 states for 1994 yielded an estimate that about $36 billion was spent by the 50 states on essential public health services in that year. An additional $5 billion was expended by federal agencies in that year, excluding research funding, resulting in a total of $41 billion in essential public health services expenditures. Of this total, $16 billion went for population-based public health activities. For comparison purposes, expenditures for the government public health activity category in the national health expenditures in 1994 totaled $30 billion. It is important to note that environmental agency spending is not captured in the government public health activity category or in the overall national health expenditures, although it was included in the nine-state study.

The findings of the nine-state study offer a basis for developing estimates of population-based public health activities based on the ratio of population-based activities to total government public health activity expenditures. Only a few comparison points are available for purposes of validating this approach for estimating population-based public health spending levels. An examination by the National Association of State Budget Officers (NASBO) of state spending for the 2002–2003 fiscal year identified $19.2 billion in population-based public health spending by the 50 states, $10.0 billion from state funds and $9.2 from federal funds (see Chapter 4). This study included state environmental agency spending but did not incorporate all public health funding of local governments in these states. For comparison purposes, the population-based public health activity levels estimated for 2002 and 2003 amount to $24.1 and $25.3 billion, respectively. The NASBO study did not include all federal agency and local public health expenditures. It is likely that these differences would result in the national estimate of population-based public health activity spending being several billion dollars higher than the population-based spending reported in the study.

Both the nine-state study and the NASBO data offer important insights into the types of population-based public health activities that are funded through federal, state, and local sources. Of the total expenditures by state and local health, substance abuse, mental health, and environmental agencies in the nine-state study, 79% was expended on essential public health services (EPHS) while more than twice as much was spent on linkage and safety net personal health services as on population-based public health activities. Expenditures for population-based services accounted for one fourth of the total spending for state and local health, environmental protection, mental health, and substance abuse agencies. For population-based public health activities in these states:

- Approximately one fourth involved enforcing laws and regulations related to protection of the environment, housing, food, water, and the workplace.
- State health departments and LHDs accounted for approximately two thirds of all population-based service expenditures and, together with environmental health agencies, expended about 90% of the total.
- 50% to 60% of expenditures for state and LHDs were for population-based services; for environmental health and substance abuse agencies, 30% to 40% supported population-based activities.

Population-based expenditures in the nine states were derived from a combination of federal, state, and local funds. State sources accounted for 50%, federal agencies provided 32%, and local sources were responsible for 16%. Medicaid and other sources accounted for only 2% of the total expended by state and local governments for population-based public health activities. The nine-state study also documented that federal agencies spend proportionately more on informing and educating the public (EPHS 4), linking to personal health services (EPHS 7), and research (EPHS 10). State and local governments spend proportionately more on monitoring health status (EPHS 1), diagnosing and investigating health risks (EPHS 2), enforcing laws and regulations (EPHS 3), mobilizing community partnerships (EPHS 5), policy and planning (EPHS 6), evaluation (EPHS 8), and training (EPHS 9).

An assessment of essential public health services spending in Florida for 2005–2006 demonstrated similar findings. Expenditures for enabling access and assuring care (EPHS 7) again comprised 69% of state and local public health spending with the remaining 31% split among the other nine essential public health service categories. Federal sources supported the majority of expenditures only for EPHS 7. Federal and state-local sources equally shared the burden for mobilizing partnerships (EPHS 4), while state-local sources supported the majority of spending for the other eight essential public health service categories. Figure 6-7 summarizes these findings.[30]

NASBO data, as described previously in Chapter 4 (see Figure 4-9), document that protecting against environmental hazards and preventing chronic disease and encouraging healthy behaviors are the highest funded population-based public health functions and that states provide the majority of funding for epidemic prevention, environmental hazard prevention, and health infrastructure. Federal funding supports the major share of preventing chronic diseases and encouraging healthy behaviors, as well as disaster preparedness and response. The NASBO data does not include expenditures of local governments for population-based public health activities and therefore does not provide a precise and complete accounting of essential public health services spending by states.

In sum, more than two thirds of population-based service expenditures in the states are derived from nonfederal sources, reinforcing the observation that state and local governments bear the brunt of the burden for funding

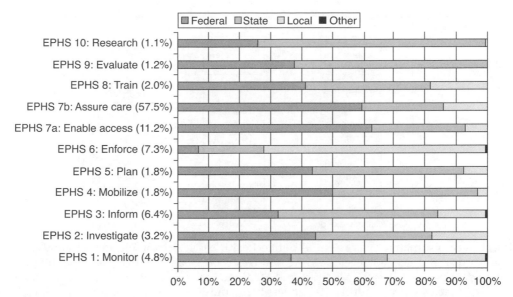

Note: Percent in parenthesis for each EPHS indicates percent of total EPHS spending for that EPHS (e.g., expenditures for EPHS 1 (monitor) comprise 4.8% of total EPHS spending).

Figure 6-7 Federal, state, local, and other funds supporting essential public health services, Florida, 2005–2006. *Source:* Data from Brooks RG, Beitsch LM, Street P, Chukmaitov A. Aligning public health financing with essential public health service functions and national public health performance standards. *J Public Health Manage Pract.* 2009;15(4):299–306.

public health activities in the United States. Who currently pays the bills says much about the likelihood for expansion of public health efforts in the future. Tax bases of state and especially local governments and political opposition to tax increases of any kind do not augur well for increased state and local public health resources in the future.

Identifying expenditures for all population-based public health activities or even for all essential public health services does not capture all public health expenditures because this does not include spending by nongovernmental public health agencies for core functions and essential public health services. It is estimated that nongovernmental organizations are responsible for performing approximately one fourth to one third of the total performance of essential public health services in the community.[31] The costs of these activities must also be factored into estimating total expenditures for public health.

Using the year 2008 as an example, Figure 6-8 and Table 6-14 summarize estimates of the fiscal resources supporting public health core functions and essential services, using the findings and assumptions described in this section. All factors considered, a reasonable estimate is that approximately $163 billion—or nearly 7% of national health expenditures—supports activities related to public health core functions and essential services. About $31 billion funds population-based services, and the remaining $132 billion supports

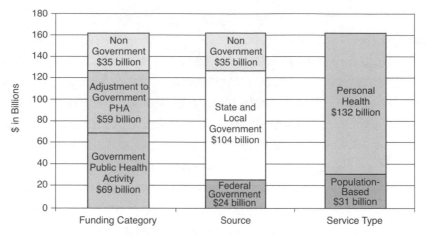

Figure 6-8 Estimated total essential public health services expenditures by funding category, source, and type of service. United States, 2008. *Sources:* Government public health activity data from Centers for Medicare and Medicaid Services, Office of the Actuary, National Health Statistics Group. Additional government public health spending categories from Sensenig AL. Refining estimates of public health spending as measured in national health expenditure accounts: the United States experience. *J Public Health Manage Pract.* 2007;13(2): 103–114. Nongovernment public health contribution data from Mays GP, Miller CA, Halverson PK, Baker EL, Stevens R, Vann JJ. Availability and perceived effectiveness of public health activities in the nation's most populous communities. *Am J Public Health.* 2004;94(6):1019–1026.

personal care. This amounts to about $102 per person per year (or 28 cents per person per day) for population-based services and about $584 per person per year (or $1.46 per person per day) for the entire package of essential public health services. Public health's infrastructure serves the entire population for the cost of one can of cola per day.

HEALTHY PEOPLE 2020 INFRASTRUCTURE OBJECTIVES

Only 1 of the more than 500 national health objectives included in the Healthy People 1990 and Healthy People 2000 processes directly addressed the national public health system. That objective (from *Healthy People 2000*) called for 90% of the population to be served by an LHD that was effectively carrying out public health's three core functions. The pursuit of this objective during the 1990s focused attention on the infrastructure capacity that must be in place for this target to be achieved. As a result, a more comprehensive panel of objectives related to the public health infrastructure was established for the Healthy People 2010 and 2020 national health objectives. These infrastructure objectives address the human, organizational, informational, and financial aspects of the public health infrastructure described in this chapter. One of this chapter's Public Health Spotlights traces the attainment status of the panel of infrastructure objectives included in *Healthy People 2010*.[32,33] The inability to develop the information systems to track progress for 12 of the 17 public health infrastructure objectives for 2010 suggests that the

Table 6-14 Estimated Expenditures (in Billions of Dollars) for Essential Public Health Services, by Source of Funds, United States, 2008

	Federal	State and Local	Nongovernment Partners	Total
Government public health activity	$10.4	$59.0	NA	$69.4
Additional government public health spending (maternal and child health, substance abuse, mental health, Indian health service, public hospitals, etc.)	$13.4	$45.1	NA	$58.5
Nongovernment public health contribution (estimated)			$35	$35
Total public health spending	$23.8	$104.1	$35	$162.9
Percent of total	14.6%	63.9%	21.4%	100%
Population-based public health				$30.7
Nonpopulation-based public health				$132.2

Sources: Government public health activity data from Centers for Medicare and Medicaid Services, Office of the Actuary, National Health Statistics Group. Additional government public health spending categories from Sensenig AL. Refining estimates of public health spending as measured in national health expenditure accounts: the United States experience. *J Public Health Manage Pract.* 2007;13(2):103–114. Nongovernment public health contribution data from Mays GP, Miller CA, Halverson PK, Baker EL, Stevens R, Vann JJ. Availability and perceived effectiveness of public health activities in the nation's most populous communities. *Am J Public Health.* 2004;94(6):1019–1026.

national agenda for strengthening the public health infrastructure has a long way to go.

CONCLUSION

Public health infrastructure includes the inputs and ingredients of the public health system that are blended together to carry out public health's core functions and essential public health services. Although these can be presented in various categories, several key elements are easily recognized. The first of these is the workforce of public health, an army of individuals committed to improving the public health, although relatively few have had other than on-the-job training for their roles. The diversity of this workforce in terms of educational and experiential backgrounds represents both a major strength and a potential weakness for efforts to focus and direct their collective efforts. Facilitating the contributions of the workforce are the organizations in which they work. These organizations exist at all levels of government, as well as in all corners of the community. The relationships between and among the agencies, organizations, institutions, and individuals committed to this work are more often informal and collaborative than formalized and centrally directed. Leadership within and across organizations to assess and address health issues and needs in the community is essential to initiate the community problem identification and problem-solving activities that can foster the changes necessary for improved health outcomes. The workforce, the organizations, and their leadership rely heavily on information for identifying problems, determining interventions, and tracking progress toward agreed-on objectives. Together, these essential ingredients of the public system formulate the system's capacity to act in serving the public health. The public health infrastructure has evolved to provide the elements necessary for successful public health interventions: organized and systematic observations through morbidity and mortality surveillance, well-designed epidemiologic studies and other data to facilitate the decision-making process, and individuals and organizations to advocate for resources and to ensure that effective policies and programs were implemented and conducted properly. In the 21st century, public health is a complex partnership among federal agencies, state and local governments, nongovernmental organizations, academia, and community members. This infrastructure, and the essential public health services that it provides, represents a small portion of the national economy and only approximately 5% of all health-related expenditures, but its contribution to improved health status and its potential for realizing further gains and closing current gaps suggest that it is worth its weight in gold.

DISCUSSION QUESTIONS AND EXERCISES

1. Choose a recent (within the last 3 years) outbreak or other public health emergency situation that has drawn significant media attention. Describe how specific aspects of the public health infrastructure contributed to either the emergency situation or its solution. *The Morbidity and Mortality Weekly Report* (*MMWR*) contents for recent weeks would be a good place to look for recent outbreaks; various print and electronic media may also be useful sources of information.
2. What distinguishes a public health professional from a professional working for a public health organization?
3. Are public health professionals viewed as change agents in their communities today? Why or why not? Do you hold the same opinion for public health organizations? Why or why not?
4. What factors determine the optimum size for a coalition?
5. How have the roles of local boards of health changed over the past century? What would be the most useful roles for such boards in the future?
6. What factors limit our ability to use the extensive amount of data and information that is currently available? How can these obstacles be overcome?

7. Is health planning at the community level necessary? If so, who should be responsible? How can duplication and replication of community health planning be averted?
8. Examine the data provided in Table 6-13, and in small groups, prioritize the various injuries to determine which should be the target of a statewide injury-reduction campaign focusing on sports and recreation equipment injuries. Which three should be targeted? Why?
9. Review the status of the national health objectives for the public health infrastructure in this chapter's Public Health Spotlight on the Public Health System. What important information on the status of the public health infrastructure did we know in 2010? What are the implications?
10. Describe how the various components of the public health infrastructure have contributed to the gains described in the Public Health Spotlight on Safer and Healthier Foods. Which components were most important?

REFERENCES

1. Roper WL, Baker EL, Dyal WW, et al. Strengthening the public health system. *Public Health Rep*. 1992;107:609 615.
2. Public Health Functions Steering Committee. *Public Health in America*. Washington, DC: U.S. Public Health Service; 1995.
3. Kennedy VC, Moore FI. A systems approach to public health workforce development. *J Public Health Manage Pract*. 2001;7:17–22.
4. Health Resources Services Administration, U.S. Department of Health and Human Services. *Public Health Enumeration 2000*. Washington, DC: Government Printing Office; December 2000.
5. U.S. Bureau of the Census. Federal, State, and Local Governments, Public Employment and Payroll Data. http://www.census.gov/govs/www/apes.html. Accessed January 8, 2008.
6. Centers for Disease Control and Prevention, National Center for Health Statistics. *Health United States, 2009*. Hyattsville, MD: National Center for Health Statistics; 2009.
7. Health Resources and Services Administration, U.S. Department of Health and Human Services. *Health Personnel in the United States: Eighth Report to Congress*. Washington, DC: U.S. Public Health Service; 1992.
8. National Association of County and City Health Officials. *2005 National Profile of Local Health Departments*. Washington, DC: National Association of County and City Health Officials; 2006.
9. Gerzoff RB, Baker EL. The use of scaling techniques to analyze U.S. local health department staffing structures, 1992–1993. *Proceedings of the Section on Government Statistics and Section on Social Statistics of the American Statistical Association*. 1998;209–213.
10. American Public Health Association. Public health code of ethics. http://www.apha.org/NR/rdonlyres/1CED3CEA-287E-4185-9CBD-BD405FC60856/0/ethicsbrochure.pdf. Accessed January 8, 2008.

11. Gerzoff RB, Richards TB. The education of local health department top executives. *J Public Health Manage Pract*. 1997;3:50–56.

12. Turnock BJ, Hutchison KD. *The Local Public Health Workforce: Size, Distribution, Composition, and Influence on Core Function Performance, Illinois 1998–1999*. Chicago IL: Illinois Center for Health Workforce Studies; 2000.

13. Turnock BJ. Roadmap for Public Health Workforce Preparedness. *J Public Health Manage Pract*. 2003;9:471–480.

14. Council of State and Territorial Epidemiologists. 2004 National Assessment of Epidemiologic Capacity: Findings and Recommendations. Washington, DC: Council of State and Territorial Epidemiologists; 2004. http://www.cste.org/Assessment/ECA/pdffiles/ECAfinal05.pdf. Accessed January 8, 2008.

15. Turnock BJ. *Public Health: Career Choices That Make a Difference*. Sudbury, MA: Jones and Bartlett; 2006.

16. Tilson H, Gebbie KM. The public health workforce. *Annu Rev Public Health*. 2004;25:341–356.

17. Gebbie KM, Turnock BJ. The public health workforce, 2006: new challenges. *Health Aff (Millwood)*. 2006;25:923–933.

18. Turnock BJ. Competency-based credentialing of public health administrators in Illinois. *J Public Health Manage Pract*. 2001;7:74–82.

19. Cioffi JP, Lichtveld MY, Thielen L, et al. Credentialing the public health workforce: an idea whose time has come. *J Public Health Manage Pract*. 2003;6:451–458.

20. National Association of County and City Health Officials. Project Public Health Ready. http://www.naccho.org/topics/emergency/pphr.cfm. Accessed January 8, 2008.

21. *Developing Effective Coalitions: An Eight Step Guide*. Martinez, CA: Contra Costa County Health Services Department; 1994.

22. Lumpkin JR. Six principles of public health information. *J Public Health Manage Pract*. 1995;1: 40–42.

23. Keppel KG, Freedman MA. What is assessment? *J Public Health Manage Pract*. 1995;1:1–7.

24. CDC. Monitoring environmental disease—United States, 1997. *MMWR*. 1998;47:522–525.

25. Friede A, O'Carroll PW. CDC and ATSDR electronic information resources for health officers. *J Public Health Manage Pract*. 1996;2:10–24.

26. Sensenig AL. Refining estimates of public health spending as measured in national health expenditure accounts: the United States experience. *J Public Health Manage Pract*. 2007;13:103–114.

27. Eilbert KW, Barry M, Bialek R, et al. *Measuring Expenditures for Essential Public Health Services*. Washington, DC: Public Health Foundation; 1996.

28. Eilbert KW, Barry M, Bialek R, et al. Public health expenditures: developing estimates for improved policy making. *J Public Health Manage Pract*. 1997;3:1–9.

29. Barry M, Centra L, Pratt E, et al. *Where Do the Dollars Go? Measuring Local Public Health Expenditures*. Washington, DC: Public Health Foundation; 1998.

30. Brooks RG, Beitsch LM, Street P, Chukmaitov A. Aligning public health financing with essential public health service expenditures and national public health performance standards. *J Public Health Manage Pract*. 2009;15(4):299–306.

31. Mays GP, Miller CA, Halverson PK, et al. Availability and perceived effectiveness of public health activities in the nation's most populous communities. *Am J Public Health*. 2004;94: 1019–1026.

32. U.S. Department of Health and Human Services. *Healthy People 2020*. Washington, DC: Department of Health and Human Services–Public Health Service; 2010.

33. U.S. Department of Health and Human Services. *Healthy People 2010: Mid-Course Review, Chapter 23, Public Health Infrastructure*. Washington, DC: Department of Health and Human Services–Public Health Service; 2006.

Spotlight on the Public Health System

PUBLIC HEALTH ACHIEVEMENTS IN 20TH CENTURY AMERICA[1]

The 10 public health achievements highlighted in the 1999 *MMWR* series reflect the successful response of public health to the major causes of morbidity and mortality of the 20th century.[2-12] In addition, these achievements demonstrate the ability of public health to meet an increasingly diverse array of public health challenges. This report highlights critical changes in the U.S. public health system this century.

In the early 1900s in the United States, many major health threats were infectious diseases associated with poor hygiene and poor sanitation (e.g., typhoid), diseases associated with poor nutrition (e.g., pellagra and goiter), poor maternal and infant health, and diseases or injuries associated with unsafe workplaces or hazardous occupations.[5,6,8,9] The success of the early public health system to incorporate biomedical advances (e.g., vaccinations and antibiotics) and to develop interventions such as health education programs resulted in decreases in the impact in these diseases; however, as the incidence of these diseases decreased, chronic diseases (e.g., cardiovascular disease and cancer) increased.[7,11] In the last half of the century, public health identified the risk factors for many chronic diseases and intervened to reduce mortality. Public efforts also led to reduced deaths attributed to a new technology, the motor vehicle.[4] These successes demonstrated the value of community action to address public health issues and have fostered public support for the growth of institutions that are components of the public health infrastructure. The focus of public health research and programs shifted to respond to the effects of chronic diseases on the public's health.[13-18] While continuing to develop and refine interventions, enhanced morbidity and mortality surveillance helped to maintain these earlier successes. The shift in focus led to improved capacity of epidemiology and to changes in public health training and programs.

Quantitative Analytic Techniques

Epidemiology, the population-based study of disease and an important part of the scientific foundation of public health, acquired greater quantitative capacity during the 20th century. Improvements occurred in both study design and periodic standardized health surveys.[13,19-22] Methods of data collection evolved from simple measures of disease prevalence (e.g., field surveys) to complex studies of precise analyses (e.g., cohort studies, case-control studies, and randomized clinical trials).[13] The first well-developed, longitudinal cohort study was conducted in 1947 among the 28,000 residents of Framingham, Massachusetts, many of whom volunteered to be followed over time to determine incidence of heart disease.[13] The Framingham Heart Study served as the model for other longitudinal cohort studies and for the concept that biologic, environmental, and behavioral risk factors exist for disease.[7,13]

In 1948, modern clinical trials began with publication of a clinical trial of streptomycin therapy for TB, which employed randomization, selection criteria, predetermined evaluation criteria, and ethical considerations.[20,22] In 1950, the case-control study gained prominence when this method provided the first solidly scientific evidence of an association between lung cancer and cigarette smoking.[23] Subsequently, high-powered statistical tests and analytic computer programs enabled multiple variables collected in large-scale studies to be measured and to the development of tools for mathematical modeling. Advances in epidemiology permitted elucidation of risk factors for heart disease and other chronic diseases and the development of effective interventions.

Periodic Standardized Health Surveys

In 1921, periodic standardized health surveys began in Hagerstown, Maryland.[13] In 1935, the first national health survey was conducted among U.S. residents.[13,24] In 1956, these efforts resulted in the National Health Survey, a population-based survey that evolved from focusing on chronic disease to estimating disease prevalence for major causes of death, measuring the burden of infectious diseases, assessing exposure to environmental toxicants, and measuring the population's vaccination coverage. Other population-based surveys (e.g., Behavioral Risk Factor Surveillance System, Youth Risk Behavior Survey, and the National Survey of Family Growth) were developed to assess risk factors for chronic diseases and other conditions.[25–27] Methods developed by social scientists and statisticians to address issues such as sampling and interviewing techniques have enhanced survey methods used in epidemiologic studies.[13]

Morbidity and Mortality Surveillance

National disease monitoring was first conducted in the United States in 1850, when mortality statistics based on death registrations were first published by the federal government.[24,28] During 1878 to 1902, Congress authorized the collection of morbidity reports on cholera, smallpox, plague, and yellow fever for use in quarantine measures, to provide funds to collect and disseminate these data, to expand authority for weekly reporting from states and municipal authorities, and to provide forms for collecting data and publishing reports.[16,24,28] The first annual summary of The Notifiable Diseases in 1912 included reports of 10 diseases from 19 states, the District of Columbia, and

Hawaii. By 1928, all states, the District of Columbia, Hawaii, and Puerto Rico were participating in the national reporting of 29 diseases. In 1951, state and territorial health officers authorized the Council of State and Territorial Epidemiologists to determine which diseases should be reported to the U.S. PHS.[28] In 1961, the CDC assumed responsibility for collecting and publishing nationally notifiable diseases data. As of January 1, 1998, 52 infectious diseases were notifiable at the national level.

In the early 1900s, efforts at surveillance focused on tracking persons with disease; by mid century, the focus had changed to tracking trends in disease occurrence.[29,30] In 1947, Alexander Langmuir at the newly formed Communicable Disease Center, the early name for the CDC, began the first disease surveillance system.[28] In 1955, surveillance data helped to determine the cause of poliomyelitis among children recently vaccinated with an inactivated vaccine.[29] After the first polio cases were recognized, data from the national polio surveillance program confirmed that the cases were linked to one brand of vaccine contaminated with live wild poliovirus. The national vaccine program continued by using supplies from other polio vaccine manufacturers.[29] Because of these initial disease surveillance efforts, morbidity tracking has become a standard feature of public health infectious disease control.[30]

Public Health Training

In 1916, with the support of the Rockefeller Foundation, the Johns Hopkins School of Hygiene and Public Health was started.[31,32] By 1922, Columbia, Harvard, and Yale universities had established schools of public health. In 1969, the number of schools of public health had increased to 12, and in 1999, 29 accredited schools of public health enrolled approximately 15,000 students.[32,33] Besides the increase in the number of schools and students, the types of student in public health schools changed. Traditionally, students in public health training already had obtained a medical degree; however, increasing numbers of students entered public health training to obtain a primary postgraduate degree. In 1978, 3753 (69%) public health students enrolled with only baccalaureates. The proportion of students who were physicians declined from 35% in 1944 to 1945 to 11% in 1978.[29,32] Thus, public health training evolved from a second degree for medical professionals to a primary health discipline.[34] Schools of public health initially emphasized the study of hygiene and sanitation; subsequently, the study of public health has expanded into five core disciplines: biostatistics, epidemiology, health services administration, health education/behavioral science, and environmental science.[31,35]

Programs also were started to provide field training in epidemiology and public health. In 1948, a board was established to certify training of physicians in public health administration, and by 1951, approximately 40 LHDs had accredited preventive medicine and public residency programs. In 1951, the CDC developed the Epidemic Intelligence Service (EIS) to guard against domestic acts of biologic warfare during the Korean conflict and to address common public health threats. Since 1951, more than 2000 EIS officers have responded to requests for epidemiologic assistance within the United States and throughout the world. In 1999, 149 EIS officers were on duty.

Nongovernment and Government Organizations

At the beginning of the century, many public health initiatives were started and supported by nongovernment organizations; however, as federal, state, and local public health infrastructure expanded, government's role increased and assumed more responsibility for public health research and programs. Today, public health represents the work of both government and nongovernment organizations.

Nongovernment Organizations

The Rockefeller Sanitary Committee's Hookworm Eradication Project conducted during 1910 to 1920 was one of the earliest voluntary efforts to engage in a campaign for a specific disease.[36] During 1914 to 1933, the Rockefeller Foundation also provided $2.6 million to support county health departments and sponsored medical education reform. Other early efforts to promote community health include the National Tuberculosis Association work for TB treatment and prevention, the National Consumers League's support of maternal and infant health in the 1920s, the American Red Cross's sponsorship of nutrition programs in the 1930s, and the March of Dimes' support of research in the 1940s and 1950s that led to a successful polio vaccine. Mothers Against Drunk Driving started in 1980 by a group of women in California after a girl was killed by an intoxicated driver and grew into a national campaign for stronger laws against drunk driving.

Professional organizations and labor unions also worked to promote public health. The American Medical Association advocated better vital statistics and safer foods and drugs.[18] The American Dental Association endorsed water fluoridation despite the economic consequences to its members.[10] Labor organizations worked for safer workplaces in industry.[5] In the 1990s, nongovernment organizations sponsored diverse public health research projects and programs (e.g., family planning, HIV prevention, vaccine development, and heart disease and cancer prevention).

State Health Departments

The 1850 Report of the Sanitary Commission of Massachusetts, authored by Lemuel Shattuck, outlined many elements of the modern public health infrastructure including a recommendation for establishing state and local health boards.[14,15] Massachusetts formed the first state health department in 1889. By 1900, 40 states had health departments that made advances in sanitation and microbial sciences available to the public. Later, states also provided other public health interventions: personal health services (e.g., disabled children and maternal and child health care and sexually transmitted disease treatment), environmental health (e.g., waste management and radiation control), and health resources (e.g., health planning, regulation of health care and emergency services, and health statistics). All states have public health laboratories that provide direct services and oversight functions.[37]

County Health Departments

Although some cities had local public health boards in the early 1900s, no county health departments existed.[34] During 1910 to 1911, the success of a county sanitation campaign to control a severe typhoid epidemic in Yakima County, Washington, created public support for a permanent health service, and an LHD was organized on July 1, 1911.[34] Concurrently, the Rockefeller Sanitary Commission began supporting county hookworm eradication efforts.[18,36] By 1920, 131 county health departments had been established; by 1931, 599 county health departments were providing services to one fifth of the U.S. population;[34] in 1950, 86% of the U.S. population was served by an LHD, and 34,895 persons were employed full-time in public health agencies.[38]

LHDs

In 1945, the American Public Health Association proposed six minimum functions of LHDs.[39] In 1988, the Institute of Medicine defined these functions as assessment, policy development, and assurance, and the PHS has proposed 10 organizational practices to implement the three core functions.[40,41] The national health objectives for 2000, released in 1990, provided a framework to monitor the progress of LHDs.[42] In 1993, 2888 LHDs, representing county, city, and district health organizations operated in 3042 U.S. counties. Of the 2079 LHDs surveyed in 1993, nearly all provided vaccination services (96%) and TB treatment (86%); fewer provided family planning (68%) and cancer-prevention programs (54%).[43]

Federal Government

In 1798, the federal government established the Marine Hospital Service to provide health services to seamen.[16] To recognize its expanding quarantine duties, in 1902, Congress changed the service's name to the Public Health and Marine Hospital Service and, in 1912, to the Public Health Service. In 1917, the PHS's support of state and local public health activities began with a small grant to study rural health.[36] During World War I, the PHS received resources from Congress to assist states in treating venereal diseases. The Social Security Act of 1935, which authorized health grants to states, and a second Federal Venereal Diseases Control Act in 1938,[14,15] expanded the federal government's role in public health.[16,36] In 1939, the PHS and other health, education, and welfare agencies were combined in the Federal Security Agency, forerunner of the Department of Health and Human Services. In the 1930s, the federal government began to provide resources for specific conditions, beginning with care for crippled children. After World War II, the federal role in public health continued to expand with the Hospital Services and Construction Act (Hill-Burton) of 1946.[16] In 1930, Congress established the National Institutes of Health (formerly the Hygiene Laboratories of the PHS) and the Food and Drug Administration. The CDC was established in 1946.[30] Legislation to form Medicare and Medicaid was enacted in 1965, and the Occupational Safety and Health Administration and the Environmental Protection Agency (EPA) were organized in 1970.

Although federal, state, and local health agencies and services have increased throughout the century, public health resources represent a small proportion of overall healthcare costs. In 1993, federal, state, and local health agencies spent an estimated $14.4 billion on core public health functions, 1% to 2% of the $903 billion in total healthcare expenditure.[44]

21ST CENTURY PUBLIC HEALTH CHALLENGES[45]

Healthy People 2010 included a Public Health Infrastructure focus area with objectives to ensure that federal, tribal, state, and local health agencies have the infrastructure to provide essential public health services effectively. The Public Health Infrastructure focus area supported the goals and objectives of all other focus areas in *Healthy People 2010*, particularly those that address preparedness and prevention or management of chronic disease or emphasize healthy behavioral choices. The public health infrastructure objectives encompass tribal, rural, and urban populations focusing on four components: data and information systems, workforce, public health organizations, and prevention research.

Initially, 17 public health infrastructure objectives were developed with 15 of these objectives classified as developmental, meaning that there was the potential for identifying a data source to measure the objective but that none was available in 2000. By the midcourse review in 2005, only 5 of these 15 had become measurable. Of the remaining 10 objectives, 3 were dropped entirely and 7 remain classified as developmental (Table 6-15).

As a result, at the time of the midcourse review in 2005, data were available to measure progress for only two objectives. Timely release of data for Healthy People 2010 objectives (Objective 23-7) moved toward its target for the year 2010. The use of geocoding in health data systems (Objective 23-3) showed no change. Progress on 15 objectives could not be assessed because of insufficient data. Of these, three were deleted because data were unavailable (Objectives 23-1, 23-5, and 23-16). Five objectives became measurable and are anticipated to have data for

Table 6-15   Healthy People 2010 Revised Public Health Infrastructure Objectives with Attainment Status as of 2005 Midcourse Review

Healthy People 2010 Public Health Infrastructure Objectives	Midcourse Review Status
DATA AND INFORMATION SYSTEMS	
23.1 Increase the proportion of public health agencies that provide Internet and e-mail access for at least 75 percent of their employees and that teach employees how to use the Internet and other electronic information systems to apply data and information to public health practice.	Dropped (Cannot Be Measured)
23.2 Increase the proportion of federal, tribal, state, and local health agencies that have made information available for internal or external public use in the last year based on health indicators related to Healthy People 2010 objectives.	May Be Tracked: Baseline by 2010?
23.3 Increase the proportion of major national health data systems that use geocoding to promote the development of geographic information system (GIS) at all levels.	Being Tracked: No Change through 2004
23.4 Increase the proportion of population-based Healthy People 2010 objectives for which national data are available for all population groups identified for the objective.	May Be Tracked: Baseline by 2010?
23.5 Increase the proportion of leading health indicators, health status indicators, and priority data needs for which data—especially for select populations—are available at the tribal, state, and local levels.	Dropped (Cannot Be Measured)
23.6 Increase the proportion of Healthy People 2010 objectives that are tracked regularly at the national level.	May Be Tracked: Baseline by 2010?
23.7 Increase the proportion of Healthy People 2010 objectives for which national data are released within one year of data collection.	Being Tracked: 41% of target achieved by 2004
SKILLED WORKFORCE	
23.8 Increase the proportion of tribal and local agencies that incorporate specific competencies in the essential public health services into job descriptions and performance evaluations.	May Be Tracked: Baseline by 2010?
23.9 Increase the proportion of CEPH-accredited schools for public health, CEPH-accredited academic programs, and schools of nursing (with public health or community health components) that integrate core competencies in the essential public health services into curricula.	May Be Tracked: Baseline by 2010?

(continues)

Table 6-15 Healthy People 2010 Revised Public Health Infrastructure Objectives with Attainment Status as of 2005 Midcourse Review (continued)

23.10 Increase the proportion of tribal, state, and local personnel who receive continuing education consistent with the core competencies in the essential public health services.	Will Be Tracked: Trend by 2010
EFFECTIVE PUBLIC HEALTH ORGANIZATIONS **23.11** Increase the number of state and local public health systems that meet national performance standards for essential public health services.	Will Be Tracked: Trend by 2010
23.12 Increase the proportion of tribal, state, and local health agencies that have implemented a health improvement plan and increase the proportion of local health jurisdictions that have implemented a health improvement plan linked with their state plan.	May Be Tracked: Baseline by 2010?
23.13 Increase the proportion of tribal, state, and local public health agencies that provide or ensure comprehensive laboratory services to support essential public health services.	Will Be Tracked: Trend by 2010
23.14 Increase the proportion of tribal, state, and local public health agencies that provide or ensure comprehensive epidemiology services to support essential public health services.	Will Be Tracked: Trend by 2010
23.15 Increase the proportion of states that review and evaluate their public health laws using tools such as Turning Point's Model State Public Health Act and the Model State Emergency Health Powers Act.	Will Be Tracked: Trend by 2010
RESOURCES **23.16** Increase the proportion of federal, state, and local public health agencies that gather accurate data on public health expenditures, categorized by essential public health service.	Dropped (Cannot Be Measured)
PREVENTION RESEARCH **23.17** Increase the proportion of federal, tribal, state, and local health agencies that conduct or collaborate on population-based prevention research.	May Be Tracked: Baseline by 2010?

Source: Data from U.S. Department of Health and Human Services, Office of Disease Prevention and Health Promotion. *Healthy People 2010 Midcourse Review.* Public Health Infrastructure. Rockville, MD: Office of Disease Prevention and Health Promotion; 2006.

trend assessment by the end of the decade (Objectives 23-10, 23-11, 23-13, 23-14, and 23-15). Seven were retained as developmental, with data for assessment anticipated by the end of the decade (Objectives 23-2, 23-4, 23-6, 23-8, 23-9, 23-12, and 23-17). Table 6-16 identifies public health infrastructure objectives proposed for the Healthy People 2020 process.

The public health infrastructure evolved in the 20th century to provide the elements necessary for successful public health interventions: organized and systematic observations through morbidity and mortality surveillance, well-designed epidemiologic studies, and other data to

Table 6-16   Public Health Infrastructure Objectives Proposed for Healthy People 2020

Objectives Retained As Is from Healthy People 2010

1   Increase the proportion of tribal, state, and local public health agencies that provide or ensure comprehensive laboratory services to support essential public health services.
2   Increase the proportion of tribal, state, and local public health agencies that provide or ensure comprehensive epidemiology services to support essential public health services.

Objectives Retained but Modified from Healthy People 2010

3   Increase the proportion of population-based Healthy People 2020 objectives for which national data are available for all major population groups.
4   Increase the proportion of Healthy People 2020 objectives that are tracked regularly at the national level.
5   Increase the proportion of Healthy People 2020 objectives for which national data are released within 1 year of the end of data collection.
6   Increase the proportion of federal, tribal, state, and local public health agencies that incorporate core competencies for public health professionals into job descriptions and performance evaluations.
7   Increase the proportion of Council on Education for Public Health (CEPH) accredited schools of public health, CEPH accredited academic programs, and schools of nursing (with a public health or community health component) that integrate core competencies in public health into curricula.
8   (Developmental) Increase the proportion of tribal, state, and local public health personnel who receive continuing education consistent with the core competencies for public health professionals.
9   Increase the proportion of state and local public health jurisdictions that conduct performance assessment and improvement activities in the public health system using national standards.
10   Increase the proportion of tribal, state, and local public health agencies that have implemented a health improvement plan and increase the proportion of local health jurisdictions that have implemented a health improvement plan linked with their state plan.

Objectives Moved from Another Healthy People Topic

11   (Developmental) Increase the proportion of all degrees awarded to members of underrepresented racial and ethnic groups among the health professions, allied and associated health profession fields, the nursing field, and the public health field.

(continues)

Table 6-16   Public Health Infrastructure Objectives Proposed for Healthy People 2020 (continued)

Objectives New to Healthy People 2020
12 Increase the number of states that record vital events using the latest U.S. standard certificates and report.
13 Increase the percentage of vital events reported using the latest U.S. standard certificates of birth and death and the report of fetal death.
14 Increase the proportion of 4-year colleges and universities that offer public health or related majors and/or minors.
15 (Developmental) Increase the proportion of 4-year colleges and universities that offer public health or related majors and/or minors that are consistent with the core competencies of undergraduate public health education.
16 (Developmental) Increase the proportion of 2-year colleges that offer public health or related associate degrees and/or certificate programs.
17 (Developmental) Increase the proportion of tribal, state, and local public health agencies that are accredited.
18 (Developmental) Increase the proportion of tribal, state, and local public health agencies that have implemented an agency-wide quality improvement process.
19 (Developmental) Increase the proportion of public health laboratory systems (including state, tribal, and local) that perform at a high level of quality in support of the 10 essential public health services.

Objectives Archived from Healthy People 2010. Archived objectives are Healthy People 2010 objectives that are not included in the proposed set of Healthy People 2020 objectives for data, target, or policy reasons.
23-2 (Developmental) Increase the proportion of federal, tribal, state, and local health agencies that have made information available for internal and external public use in the past year based on health indicators related to Healthy People 2010 objectives.
23-3 Increase the proportion of major national health data systems that use geocoding to promote nationwide use of geographic information systems.
23-15 (Developmental) Increase the number of states that review and evaluate their public health laws using tools such as the Turning Point Model State Public Health Act and the Model State Emergency Health Powers Act.
23-17 (Developmental) Increase the proportion of federal, tribal, state, and local public health agencies that conduct or collaborate on population-based prevention research.

Source: Data from U.S. Department of Health and Human Services. http://www.healthypeople.gov/hp2020/Objectives/TopicArea.aspx?id=40&TopicArea=Public+Health+Infrastructure. Accessed May 21, 2010.

facilitate the decision-making process, and individuals and organizations to advocate for resources and to ensure that effective policies and programs were implemented and conducted properly.

Unfortunately, the ability to measure key aspects of the public health infrastructure has not advanced to where meaningful measures can be tracked over time. Despite being added as a specific focus area of Healthy People 2010, little progress has occurred in identifying appropriate measures and using these to fuel change. The inability to track key aspects of the public health infrastructure speaks volumes as to priorities and leadership for public health systems improvement at the national level.

In the first decade of the 21st century, public health is a complex partnership among federal agencies, state and local governments, nongovernment organizations, academia, and community members. The success of the U.S. public health system in the 21st century will depend on its ability to change to meet new threats to the public's health.

REFERENCES

1. Adapted from the Centers for Disease Control and Prevention. Changes in the public health system: United States, 1900–1999. *MMWR*. 1999;48:1141–1147.
2. Centers for Disease Control and Prevention. Ten great public health achievements: United States, 1900–1999. *MMWR*. 1999;48:241–243.
3. Centers for Disease Control and Prevention. Impact of vaccines universally recommended for children: United States, 1990–1998. *MMWR*. 1999;48:243–248.
4. Centers for Disease Control and Prevention. Motor-vehicle safety: a 20th century public health achievement. *MMWR*. 1999;48:369–374.
5. Centers for Disease Control and Prevention. Improvements in workplace safety: United States, 1900–1999. *MMWR*. 1999;48:461–469.
6. Centers for Disease Control and Prevention. Control of infectious diseases. *MMWR*. 1999;48:621–629.
7. Centers for Disease Control and Prevention. Decline in deaths from heart disease and stroke: United States, 1900–1999. *MMWR*. 1999;48:649–656.
8. Centers for Disease Control and Prevention. Healthier mothers and babies. *MMWR*. 1999;48:849–857.
9. Centers for Disease Control and Prevention. Safer and healthier foods. *MMWR*. 1999; 48:905–913.
10. Centers for Disease Control and Prevention. Fluoridation of drinking water to prevent dental caries. *MMWR*. 1999;48:933–940.
11. Centers for Disease Control and Prevention. Tobacco use: United States, 1900–1999. *MMWR*. 1999;48:986–993.
12. Centers for Disease Control and Prevention. Family planning. *MMWR*. 1999;48: 1073–1080.
13. Susser M. Epidemiology in the United States after World War II: the evolution of technique. *Epidemiol Rev*. 1985;7:147–177.
14. Turnock BJ. The organization of public health in the United States. In: Turnock BJ, ed. *Public Health: What It Is and How It Works*. Gaithersburg, MD: Aspen Publishers, 1997:1121–1168.
15. Last JM. Scope and method of prevention. In: Last JM, Wallace RB, eds. *Maxcy-Rosenau-Last Public Health and Preventive Medicine*. 13th ed. Norwalk, CT: Appleton & Lange, 1992:11–39.
16. Hanlon JJ, Pickett GE. Public *health: administration and practice*. 8th ed. St. Louis, MO: Times Mirror/Mosby College Publishing, 1984:22–44.
17. Koplan JP, Thacker SB, Lezin NA. Epidemiology in the 21st century: calculation, communication, and intervention. *Am J Public Health*. 1999;89:1153–1155.
18. Terris M. Evolution of public health and preventive medicine in the United States. *Am J Public Health*. 1975;65:161–169.
19. Vandenbroucke JP. Clinical investigation in the 20th century: the ascendancy of numerical reasoning. *Lancet*. 1998;352(suppl 2):12–16.
20. Vandenbroucke JP. A short note on the history of the randomized controlled trial. *J Chronic Dis*. 1987;40:985–986.
21. Doll R. Clinical trials: retrospect and prospect. *Stat Med*. 1982;1:337–344.
22. Armitage P. The role of randomization in clinical trials. *Stat Med*. 1982;1:345–352.

23. Doll R, Hill AB. Smoking and carcinoma of the lung. *Br Med J*. 1950;2:740–748.

24. Teutsch SM, Churchill RE, eds. *Principles and Practice of Public Health Surveillance*. New York: Oxford University Press; 1994.

25. Remington PL, Smith MY, Williamson DF, et al. Design, characteristics and usefulness of state-based behavioral risk factor surveillance, 1981–87. *Public Health Rep*. 1988;103:366–375.

26. Kann L, Kinchen SA, Williams BI, et al. Youth risk behavior surveillance: United States, 1997. In: CDC surveillance summaries (August 14). *MMWR*. 47(no. SS-3).

27. Mosher WD. Design and operation of the 1995 national survey of family growth. *Fam Plann Perspect*. 1998;30:43–46.

28. Centers for Disease Control and Prevention. Summary of notifiable diseases, United States, 1997. *MMWR*. 1997;46(no. SS-54).

29. Langmuir AD. The surveillance of communicable diseases of national importance. *N Engl J Med*. 1963;268:182–192.

30. Centers for Disease Control and Prevention. History perspectives: history of CDC. *MMWR*. 1996;45:526–528.

31. Roemer MI. Preparing public health leaders for the 1990s. *Public Health Rep*. 1988;103: 443–451.

32. Winkelstein W, French FE. The training of epidemiologists in schools of public health in the United States: a historical note. *Int J Epidemiol*. 1973;2:415–416.

33. Association of Schools of Public Health. Enrollment of U.S. schools of public health 1987–1997. http://www.asph.org/webstud1.gif. Accessed December 14, 1999.

34. Crawford BL. Graduate students in U.S. schools of public health: comparison of 3 academic years. *Public Health Rep*. 1979;94:67–72.

35. Association of Schools of Public Health. Ten most frequently asked questions by perspective students. http://www.asph.org/10quest.htm. Accessed December 14, 1999.

36. U.S. Treasury Department/Public Health Service. History of county health organizations in the United States 1908–1933. In: Public Health Bulletin (No. 222). Washington, DC: Public Health Service, 1936.

37. Altman D, Morgan DH. The role of state and local government in health. *Health Aff*. 1983;2;7–31.

38. Mountin JW, Flook E. *Guide to Health Organization in the United States, 1951*. Washington, DC: Public Health Service, Federal Security Agency, Bureau of State Services, 1951; Public Health Service publication no. 196.

39. Emerson H, Luginbuhl M. 1200 local public school departments for the United States. *Am J Public Health*. 1945;35:898–904.

40. Dyal WW. Ten organizational practices of public health: a historical perspective. *Am J Prev Med*. 1995;11(suppl 2):6–8.

41. Institute of Medicine. *The Future of Public Health*. Washington, DC: National Academy Press, 1988.

42. Public Health Service. *Healthy People 2000: National Health Promotion and Disease Prevention Objectives: Full Report, With Commentary*. Washington, DC: U.S. Department of Health and Human Services, Public Health Service, 1991; Department of Health and Human Services publication no. (Public Health Service) 91-50212.

43. Centers for Disease Control and Prevention. Selected characteristics of local health departments: United States, 1992–1993. *MMWR*. 1994;43:839–843.

44. Centers for Disease Control and Prevention. Estimated expenditures for core public health functions: selected states, October 1992–September 1993. *MMWR*. 1995;44: 421:427–429.

45. Adapted from U.S. Department of Health and Human Services. *Healthy People 2010 Midcourse Review: Chapter 23, Public Health Infrastructure*. Washington, DC: Department of Health and Human Services–Public Health Service; 2006.

Public Health Spotlight on Safer and Healthier Foods

PUBLIC HEALTH ACHIEVEMENTS IN 20TH CENTURY AMERICA[1]

During the early 20th century, contaminated food, milk, and water caused many food-borne infections, including typhoid fever, TB, botulism, and scarlet fever. In 1906, Upton Sinclair described in his novel *The Jungle* the unwholesome working environment in the Chicago meat-packing industry and the unsanitary conditions under which food was produced. Public awareness dramatically increased and led to the passage of the Pure Food and Drug Act.[2] After the sources and characteristics of food-borne diseases were identified—long before vaccines or antibiotics—they could be controlled by handwashing, sanitation, refrigeration, pasteurization, and pesticide application. Healthier animal care, feeding, and processing also improved food supply safety. In 1900, the incidence of typhoid fever was approximately 100 per 100,000 population; by 1920, it had decreased to 33.8 and by 1950 to 1.7 (Figure 6-9). During the 1940s, studies of autopsied muscle samples showed that 16% of persons in the United States had trichinellosis; 300 to 400 cases were diagnosed every year, and 10 to 20 deaths occurred.[3] Since then, the rate of infection has declined markedly; from 1991 through 1996, three deaths and an average of 38 cases per year were reported.[4]

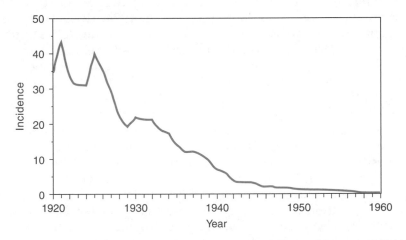

Figure 6-9   Incidence of typhoid fever, by year, United States, 1920–1960. *Source:* From Centers for Disease Control and Prevention. Achievements in public health, United States, 1900–1999: safer and healthier foods. *MMWR.* 1999;48 (40):905–913.

Nutritional sciences also were in their infancy at the start of the century. Unknown was the concept that minerals and vitamins were necessary to prevent diseases caused by dietary deficiencies. Recurring nutritional deficiency diseases, including rickets, scurvy, beriberi, and pellagra, were thought to be infectious diseases. By 1900, biochemists and physiologists had identified protein, fat, and carbohydrates as the basic nutrients in food. By 1916, new data had led to the discovery that food contained vitamins, and the lack of "vital amines" could cause disease. These scientific discoveries and the resulting public health policies, such as food fortification programs, led to substantial reductions in nutritional deficiency diseases during the first half of the century. The focus of nutrition programs shifted in the second half of the century from disease prevention to control of chronic conditions, such as cardiovascular disease and obesity.

Food Safety

Perishable foods contain nutrients that pathogenic microorganisms require to reproduce. Bacteria such as *Salmonella* sp., *Clostridium* sp., and *Staphylococcus* sp. can multiply quickly to sufficient numbers to cause illness. Prompt refrigeration slows bacterial growth and keeps food fresh and edible.

At the turn of the 20th century, consumers kept food fresh by placing it on a block of ice or, in cold weather, burying it in the yard or storing it on a window sill outside. During the 1920s, refrigerators with freezer compartments became available for household use. Another process that reduced the incidence of disease was invented by Louis Pasteur—pasteurization. Although the process was applied first in wine preservation, when milk producers adopted the process, pasteurization eliminated a substantial vector of food-borne disease. In 1924, the PHS created a document to assist Alabama in developing a statewide milk sanitation program. This document evolved into the Grade A Pasteurized Milk Ordinance, a voluntary agreement that established uniform sanitation standards for the interstate shipment of Grade A milk and now serves as the basis of milk safety laws in the 50 states and Puerto Rico.[5]

Along with improved crop varieties, insecticides and herbicides have increased crop yields, decreased food costs, and enhanced the appearance of food. Without proper controls, however, the residues of some pesticides that remain on foods can create potential health risks.[6] Before 1910, no legislation existed to ensure the safety of food and feed crops that were sprayed and dusted with pesticides. In 1910, the first pesticide legislation was designed to protect consumers from impure or improperly labeled products. During the 1950s and 1960s, pesticide regulation evolved to require maximum allowable residue levels of pesticides on foods and to deny registrations for unsafe or ineffective products. During the 1970s, acting under these strengthened laws, the newly formed EPA removed DDT and several other highly persistent pesticides from the marketplace. In 1996, the Food Quality Protection Act set a stricter safety standard and required the review of older allowable residue levels to determine whether they were safe. In 1999, federal and state laws required that pesticides meet specific safety standards; the EPA reviews and registers each product before it can be used and sets levels and restrictions on each product intended for food or feed crops.

Newly recognized food-borne pathogens have emerged in the United States since the late 1970s; contributing factors include changes in agricultural practices and food processing operations and the globalization of the food supply. Seemingly healthy food animals can be reservoirs of human pathogens. During the 1980s, for example, an epidemic of egg-associated Salmonella serotype Enteritidis infection spread to an estimated 45% of the nation's egg-laying flocks, which resulted in a large increase in egg-associated food-borne illness within the United States.[7,8] *Escherichia coli O157:H7*, which can cause severe infections and death in humans, produces no signs of illness in its nonhuman hosts.[9] In 1993, a severe outbreak of *E. coli O157:H7* infections attributed to consumption of undercooked ground beef resulted in 501 cases of illness, 151 hospitalizations, and 3 deaths and led to a restructuring of the meat inspection process.[10] The most common food-borne infectious agent may be the calicivirus (a Norwalk-like virus), which can pass from the unwashed hands of an infected food handler to the meal of a consumer. Animal husbandry and meat production improvements that have contributed to reducing pathogens in the food supply include pathogen eradication campaigns, the Hazard Analysis and Critical Control Point,[11] better animal feeding regulations,[12] the use of uncontaminated water in food processing,[13] more effective food preservatives,[14] improved antimicrobial products for sanitizing food processing equipment and facilities, and adequate surveillance of food-handling and preparation methods.[15] Hazard Analysis and Critical Control Point programs also are mandatory for the seafood industry.[16]

Improved surveillance, applied research, and outbreak investigations have elucidated the mechanisms of contamination that are leading to new control measures for food-borne pathogens. In meat-processing plants,[17] the incidence of Salmonella and Campylobacter infections has decreased; however, in 1998, apparently unrelated cases of Listeria infections were linked when an epidemiologic investigation indicated that isolates from all cases shared the same genetic DNA fingerprint; approximately 100 cases and 22 deaths were traced to eating hot dogs and deli meats produced in a single manufacturing plant.[18] In 1998, a multistate outbreak of shigellosis was traced to imported parsley.[19] During 1997 to 1998 in the United States, outbreaks of cyclosporiasis were associated with mesclun mix lettuce, basil/basil-containing products, and Guatemalan raspberries.[20] These instances highlight the need for measures that prevent food contamination closer to its point of production, particularly if the food is eaten raw or is difficult to wash.[21]

Any 21st century improvement will be accelerated by new diagnostic techniques and the rapid exchange of information through use of electronic networks and the Internet. PulseNet, for example, is a network of laboratories in state health departments, the CDC, and food-regulatory agencies. In this network, the genetic DNA fingerprints of specific pathogens can be identified and shared electronically among laboratories, enhancing the ability to detect, investigate, and control geographically distant yet related outbreaks. Another example of technology is DPDx, a computer network that identifies parasitic pathogens. By combining PulseNet and DPDx with field epidemiologic investigations, the public health system can rapidly identify and control outbreaks. The CDC, the Food and Drug Administration, the U.S. Department of Agriculture (USDA), other federal agencies, and private organizations are enhancing food safety by collaborating in education, training, research, technology, and transfer of information and by considering food safety as a whole—from farm to table.

Nutrition

The discovery of essential nutrients and their roles in disease prevention has been instrumental in almost eliminating nutritional deficiency diseases such as goiter, rickets, and pellagra in the United States. During 1922 to 1927, with the implementation of a statewide prevention program, the goiter rate in Michigan fell from 38.6% to 9%.[22] In 1921, rickets was considered the most common nutritional disease of children, affecting approximately 75% of infants in New York City.[23] In the 1940s, the fortification of milk with vitamin D was a critical step in rickets control.

Because of food restrictions and shortages during World War I, scientific discoveries in nutrition were translated quickly into public health policy; in 1917, the USDA issued the first dietary recommendations based on five food groups; in 1924, iodine was added to salt to prevent goiter. The 1921 to 1929 Maternal and Infancy Act enabled state health departments to employ nutritionists, and during the 1930s, the federal government developed food relief and food commodity distribution programs, including school feeding and nutrition education programs, and national food consumption surveys.

Pellagra is a good example of the translation of scientific understanding to public health action to prevent nutritional deficiency. Pellagra, a classic dietary deficiency disease caused by insufficient niacin, was noted in the South after the Civil War. Then considered infectious, it was known as the disease of the four Ds: diarrhea, dermatitis, dementia, and death. The first outbreak was reported in 1907. In 1909, more than 1000 cases were estimated based on reports from 13 states. One year later, approximately 3000 cases were suspected nationwide based on estimates from 30 states and the District of Columbia. By the end of 1911, pellagra had been reported in all but nine states, and prevalence estimates had increased nearly ninefold.[24] During 1906 to 1940, approximately 3 million cases and approximately 100,000 deaths were attributed to pellagra.[25] From 1914 until his death in 1929, Joseph Goldberger, a PHS physician, conducted groundbreaking studies that demonstrated that pellagra was not infectious but was associated with poverty and poor diet. Despite compelling evidence, his hypothesis remained controversial and unconfirmed until 1937. The near elimination of pellagra by the end of the 1940s has been attributed to improved diet and health associated with economic recovery during the 1940s and to the enrichment of flour with niacin. Today, most physicians in the United States have never seen pellagra, although outbreaks continue to occur, particularly among refugees and during emergencies in developing countries.[26]

The growth of publicly funded nutrition programs was accelerated during the early 1940s because of reports that 25% of draftees showed evidence of past or present malnutrition; a frequent cause of rejection from military service was tooth decay or loss. In 1941, President Franklin D. Roosevelt convened the National Nutrition Conference for Defense, which led to the first recommended dietary allowances of nutrients and resulted in issuance of War Order Number One, a program to enrich wheat flour with vitamins and iron. In 1998, the most recent food-fortification program was initiated; folic acid, a water-soluble vitamin, was added to cereal and grain products to prevent neural tube defects.

Although the first half of the century was devoted to preventing and controlling nutritional deficiency disease, the focus of the second half has been on preventing chronic disease with initiation of the Framingham Heart Study in 1949. This landmark study identified the contribution of diet and sedentary lifestyles to the development of cardiovascular disease and the effect of elevated serum cholesterol on the risk for coronary heart disease. With increased awareness, public health nutrition programs have sought strategies to improve diets. By the 1970s, food and nutrition labeling and other consumer information programs stimulated the development of products low in fat, saturated fat, and cholesterol. Since then, persons in the United States have significantly decreased their dietary intakes of total fat from approximately 40% of total calorie intake in 1977 to 1978 to 33% in 1994 to 1996, approaching the recommended 30%;[27] saturated fat intake and serum cholesterol levels also have decreased.[28] Prevention efforts, including changes in diet and lifestyle and early detection and improved treatment, have contributed to impressive declines in mortality from heart disease and stroke.[29,30]

Populations with diets rich in fruits and vegetables have a substantially lower risk for many types of cancer. In 1991, the National Cancer Institute and the Produce for Better Health Foundation launched a program to encourage eating at least five servings of fruits and vegetables daily. Although public awareness of the "5 A Day" message has increased, only approximately 36% of persons in the United States aged greater than or equal to 2 years achieved the daily goal of five or more servings of fruits and vegetables.[29] A diet rich in fruits and vegetables that provide vitamins, antioxidants (including carotenoids), other phytochemicals, and fiber is associated with additional health benefits, including decreased risk for cardiovascular disease.

21ST CENTURY PUBLIC HEALTH CHALLENGES

The most urgent challenge to nutritional health during the 21st century will be obesity. In the United States, with an abundant, inexpensive food supply and a largely sedentary population, overnutrition has become an important contributor to morbidity and mortality in adults. As early as 1902, USDA's W.O. Atwater linked dietary intake to health, noting that "the evils of overeating may not be felt at once, but sooner or later they are sure to appear—perhaps in an excessive amount of fatty tissue, perhaps in general debility, perhaps in actual disease."[31] In U.S. adults, overweight (body mass index [BMI] of greater than or equal to 25 kg/m^2) and obesity (BMI greater than or equal to 30 kg/m^2) have increased markedly, especially since the 1970s. Figure 6-10 tracks changes since 1960 using National Health and Nutrition Examination Survey data.[32] Figure 6-11 demonstrates that this phenomenon is not limited to a few states or regions of the United States. Obesity rates doubled among American adults between

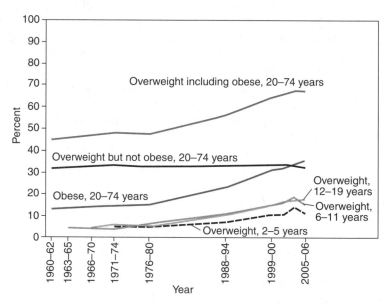

Figure 6-10 Overweight and obesity, selected age categories, United States, 1960–2006. *Source:* From Centers for Disease Control and Prevention, National Center for Health Statistics, *Health, United States 2009*, Figure 7. Hyattsville, MD: NCHS; 2009. Data from the National Health Examination Survey and the National Health and Nutrition Examination Survey.

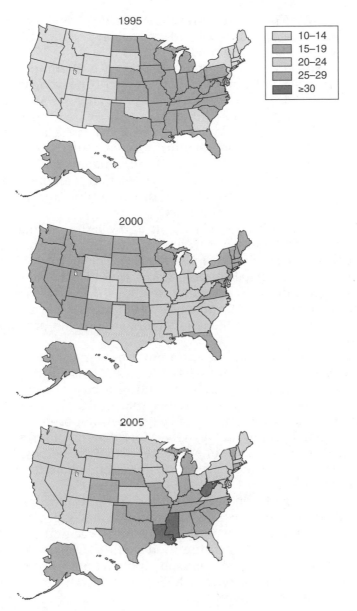

Figure 6-11   Percentage of adults aged 18 years or over who were obese,* by state—Behavioral Risk Factor Surveillance System, United States, 1995, 2000, and 2005.

Note: *Persons with a body mass index (BMI) greater than or equal to 30.0; self-reported weight and height were used to calculate BMI.

Source: From Centers for Disease Control and Prevention. State-specific prevalence of obesity among adults, United States, 2005. *MMWR.* 2006;55(36): 985–988.

1980 and 2000, whereas the prevalence of overweight and obesity combined increased nearly 40%. More than two thirds of American adults are overweight and/or obese.

Overweight and obesity increase risk for and complications of hypertension, hyperlipidemia, diabetes, coronary heart disease, osteoarthritis, and other chronic disorders; total costs attributable to obesity are an estimated $100 billion annually.[33] Obesity also is a growing problem in developing countries where it is associated with substantial morbidity and where malnutrition, particularly deficiencies of iron, iodine, and vitamin A, affects approximately 2 billion people. Increasing physical activity in the U.S. population is an important step, but effective prevention and control of overweight and obesity will require concerted public health action.[34]

Factors contributing to overweight and obesity are many but in the end result from consuming more calories than are expended through physical activity. Genes, metabolism, behavior, environment, culture, and socioeconomic status can all play roles in determining energy imbalance and body weight. The rapid increase in the prevalence of overweight and obesity among all age groups over recent decades argues that genetic factors are not the primary factor involved.

Social, behavioral, cultural, and environmental factors are more likely contributors. American society has undergone major changes in food options and eating habits, including increased portion sizes, prepackaged foods, fast food restaurants, soft drinks, and more frequent snacking. Increased consumption of calories has not been accompanied by increased levels of physical activity. More than one fourth of American adults report no leisure-time physical activity. One positive trend, however, has been a steady decline in adult blood cholesterol levels, as demonstrated in Figure 6-12.

As the U.S. population ages, attention to both nutrition and food safety will become increasingly important. Challenges will include maintaining and improving nutritional status, because nutrient needs change with aging, and ensuring food quality and safety, which is important to an older, more vulnerable population. Continuing challenges for public health action include reducing iron deficiency, especially in infants, young children, and women of childbearing age; improving initiation and duration of breastfeeding; improving folate status for women of childbearing age; and applying emerging knowledge about nutrition on dietary patterns and behavior that promotes health and reduce risk for chronic disease. Behavioral research indicates that successful nutrition promotion activities focus on specific behaviors, have a strong consumer orientation, segment and target consumers, use multiple reinforcing channels, and continually refine the messages.[35] These techniques form a paradigm to achieve public health goals and to communicate and motivate consumers to change their behavior.

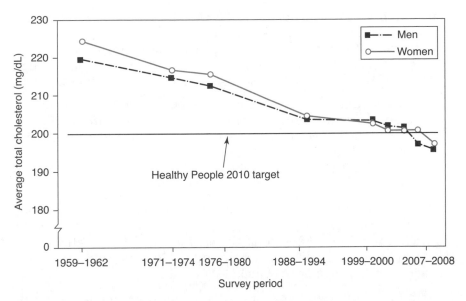

Figure 6-12 Average total cholesterol level among men and women aged 20–74 years, National Health and Nutrition Examination Survey, United States, 1959–1962 to 2007–2008.

Note: Graph points represent serum total cholesterol levels at the midpoint of the survey years for the National Health Examination Survey conducted during 1959–1962 and the National Health and Nutrition Examination Surveys conducted during 1971–1974, 1976–1980, 1988–1994, 1999–2000, 2001–2002, 2003–2004, 2005–2006, and 2007–2008. Data were age adjusted by the direct method to the 2000 Census population estimates using the age groups 20–39 years, 40–59 years, and 60–74 years.

Sources: From Centers for Disease Control and Prevention. Average total cholesterol level among men and women aged 20–74 years, National Health and Nutrition Examination Survey, United States, 1959–1962 to 2007–2008. *MMWR.* 2009;58(37):1045. Data from National Health Examination Survey, 1959–1962; National Health and Nutrition Examination Surveys, 1971–1974, 1976–1980, 1988–1994, 1999–2000, 2001–2002, 2003–2004, 2005–2006, and 2007–2008.

In the *Guide to Community Preventive Services* (*Community Guide*), the Task Force on Community Preventive Services assessed the effectiveness of selected population-based interventions aimed at promoting healthy growth and development in children and adolescents and supporting healthy weights among adults.[36] Only a few interventions are recommended; others lacked sufficient evidence. In general, the task force found multicomponent counseling or coaching interventions to be effective in achieving or maintaining weight loss. Also effective were behavioral interventions to reduce screen time (time spent watching TV, videotapes, or DVDs; playing video or computer games; and surfing the Internet). These could be single-component or multicomponent interventions that often focus on changing screen time through classes aimed at improving children's or parents' knowledge, attitudes, or skills. Components of these interventions may include:

- Skills building, tips, goal setting, and reinforcement techniques.
- Parent or family support through provision of information on environmental strategies to reduce access to television, video games, and computers.
- A TV turnoff challenge in which participants are encouraged not to watch TV for a specified number of days.

Another effective community intervention strategy involves work-site nutrition and physical activity programs that include one or more approaches to support behavioral change including informational and educational, behavioral and social, and policy and environmental strategies. Such programs may include:

- Informational and educational strategies designed to increase knowledge about a healthy diet and physical activity using lectures, written materials (provided in print or online), or educational software.
- Behavioral and social strategies that target the thoughts (e.g., awareness, self-efficacy) and social factors that affect behavior changes through individual or group behavioral counseling, skill-building activities such as cue control, rewards or reinforcement, or inclusion of coworkers or family members to build support systems.
- Policy and environmental approaches designed to make healthy choices easier and target the entire workforce by changing physical or organizational structures through improving access to healthy foods (e.g., changing cafeteria options and vending machine content) and/or providing more opportunities to be physically active (e.g., providing on-site facilities for exercise).
- Modifying rules and procedures for employees such as health insurance benefits or costs or money for health club membership.
- Worksite weight control strategies that may occur separately or as part of a comprehensive worksite wellness program that addresses several health issues (e.g., smoking cessation, stress management, cholesterol reduction).

The recognition of the obesity epidemic greatly influenced the Healthy People process. One of the 2010 national health objectives called for the prevalence of adult obesity to be reduced to less than 15% by 2010. Recent data, however, indicate the situation is getting worse rather than better, both for children (Figure 6-13) and older age groups (Figure 6-14). The prevalence of overweight among children has been climbing steadily since 2000, while rates among adults show no improvement since 2000, and have even been increasing for men.

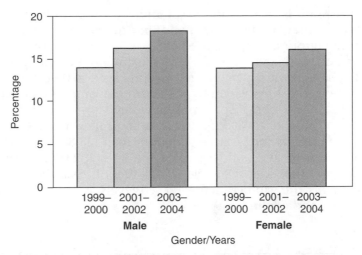

Figure 6-13 Prevalence of overweight* among persons aged 2–19 years, by sex, National Health and Nutrition Examination Survey (NHANES), United States, 1999–2000 through 2003–2004.

* Defined as having a body mass index (weight [kg]/height [m²]) at or above the 95th percentile for age and sex based on the reference population of the CDC 2000 growth charts.

Source: From Centers for Disease Control and Prevention. Prevalence of overweight among persons aged 2–19 years, by sex, National Health and Nutrition Examination Survey, United States, 1999–2000 through 2003–2004. *MMWR.* 2006;55(45):1229.

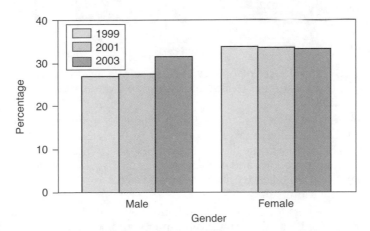

Figure 6-14 Prevalence of obesity* among adults aged more than 20 years by gender, National Health and Nutrition Examination Survey, United States, 1999–2000 through 2003–2004.

* Defined as having a body mass index (weight [kg]/height [m²]) >30.

Source: From Centers for Disease Control and Prevention. Prevalence of obesity among adults aged >20 years, by sex, National Health and Nutrition Examination Survey, 1999–2000 through 2003–2004. *MMWR.* 2006;55(44):1206.

The net result is that the lofty aspirations for obesity in the Healthy People process may not be realized and that the nation is losing, rather than gaining, ground in the battle being waged in the early decades of the 21st century. Figures 6-15 and 6-16 illustrate the challenges that lie ahead. The age-adjusted percentage of adults aged ≥20 years who were obese during 2003–2006 varied by race/ethnicity among women, ranging from 53.3% for non-Hispanic black women to 41.8% for Mexican American women and 31.6% for non-Hispanic white women. Obesity levels were more similar for Mexican American men (28.8%), non-Hispanic black men (35.0%), and non-Hispanic white men (32.0%). None of the groups had met the Healthy People 2010 target of 15%. Figure 6-16 further documents the gap between achieved levels and year 2010 targets for adolescent and adult obesity.

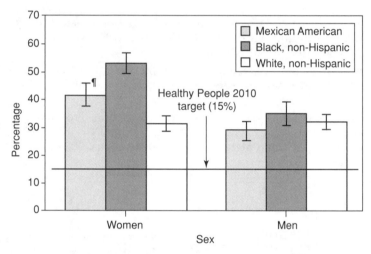

Figure 6-15   Prevalence* of obesity[†] among adults aged ≥20 years, by race/ethnicity[§] and sex, National Health and Nutrition Examination Survey, United States, 2003–2006.

* Prevalence estimates are age adjusted to the 2000 U.S. standard population.
[†] Defined as having a body mass index (weight [kg]/height [m^2]) ≥30.
[§] The categories non-Hispanic black and non-Hispanic white include persons who reported only one race and exclude persons of Hispanic ethnicity. Persons of Mexican American ethnicity might be of any race.
[¶] 95% confidence interval.

Sources: From Centers for Disease Control and Prevention. Prevalence of obesity among adults aged ≥20 Years, by race/ethnicity and sex, National Health and Nutrition Examination Survey, United States, 2003–2006. *MMWR.* 2009;58 (Data from National Health and Nutrition Examination Survey, 2003–2006. http://www.cdc.gov/nchs/nhanes.htm. Healthy People 2010 database. http://wonder.cdc.gov/data2010. US Department of Health and Human Services. Healthy People 2010. 2nd ed. With understanding and improving health and objectives for improving health. 2 vols. Washington, DC: U.S. Government Printing Office; 2000. http://www.health.gov/healthypeople. Accessed May 31, 2010.

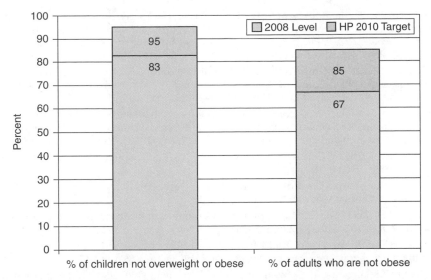

Figure 6-16 Scorecard for Healthy People 2010 leading indicators for overweight and obesity comparing 2008 levels with 2010 targets. *Source:* Data from Data 2010, Healthy People 2010 database. http://wonder.cdc.gov/data2010/ftpselec.htm. Accessed May 31, 2010.

In summary, this is a story of an epidemic in our midst and one nation overweight. The national obesity epidemic threatens to disrupt the trends of improved life expectancy and years of healthy life realized during the 20th century. Safer and healthier foods certainly carry a different connotation in this century than it did in the previous one.

REFERENCES

1. Adapted from Centers for Disease Control and Prevention. Achievements in public health, United States, 1900–1999: safer and healthier foods. *MMWR*. 1999;48: 905–913.
2. Young JH. *Pure Food: Securing the Federal Food and Drugs Act of 1906*. Princeton, NJ: Princeton University Press; 1989.
3. Schantz PM. Trichinosis in the United States: 1947–1981. *Food Technol*. 1983;March: 83–86.
4. Moorhead A. Trichinellosis in the United States, 1991–1996: declining but not gone. *Am J Trop Med Hyg*. 1999;60:66–69.
5. Public Health Service. *1924 United States Proposed Standard Milk Ordinance*. Public Health Reports, Washington, DC: Public Health Service; November 7, 1924.
6. Fan AM, Jackson RJ. Pesticides and food safety. *Regul Toxicol Pharmacol*. 1989;9: 158–174.
7. St. Louis ME, Morse DL, Potter ME, et al. The emergence of grade A eggs as a major source of Salmonella enteritidis infections: new implications for the control of salmonellosis. *JAMA*. 1988;259:2103–2107.
8. Ebel ED, Hogue AT, Schlosser WD. Prevalence of Salmonella enterica serovar enteritidis in unpasteurized liquid eggs and aged laying hens at slaughter: implications on epidemiology and control of the disease. In: Saeed AM, Gast RK, Potter ME, Wall PG, eds. *Salmonella enterica serovar enteritidis in humans and animals; epidemiology, pathogenesis and control*. Ames, IA: Iowa State University Press; 1999:341–352.

9. Griffin PM. Epidemiology of shiga toxin-producing *Escherichia coli* infections in humans in the United States. In: Kaper JB, O'Brien AD, eds. *Escherichia Coli O157:H7 and Other Shiga-Toxin Producing E. Coli Strains*. Washington, DC: American Society for Microbiology; 1998:15–22.

10. Bell BP, Goldoft M, Griffin PM, et al. A multistate outbreak of *Escherichia coli* O157: H7-associated bloody diarrhea and hemolytic uremic syndrome from hamburgers: the Washington experience. *JAMA*. 1994;272:1349–1353.

11. Amendment to the Federal Meat Inspection Act and the Poultry Products Inspection Act to Ensure the Safety of Imported Meat and Poultry Products. Ensuring the Safety of Imported Meat and Poultry Act of 1999. H. R. 2581, July 21, 1999.

12. Centers for Disease Control and Prevention. Trichinella spiralis infection: United States, 1990. *MMWR*. 1991;40:35.

13. Centers for Disease Control and Prevention. Outbreaks of cyclosporiasis: United States and Canada, 1997. *MMWR*. 1997;46:521.

14. Binkerd EF, Kolari OE. The history and use of nitrate and nitrite in the curing of meat. *Food Cosmetics Toxicol*. 1975;13:655–661.

15. Centers for Disease Control and Prevention. Multistate surveillance for food handling, preparation, and consumption. *MMWR*. 1998;47(no. SS-4):33–57.

16. Shapiro RL, Altekruse S, Hutwagner L, et al. The role of Gulf Coast oysters harvested in warmer months in Vibrio vulnificus infections in the United States, 1988–1996. *J Infect Dis*. 1998;178:752–759.

17. Centers for Disease Control and Prevention. Incidence of foodborne illnesses: preliminary data from the Foodborne Disease Active Surveillance Network (FoodNet): United States, 1998. *MMWR*. 1999;48:189–194.

18. Centers for Disease Control and Prevention. Update: Multistate outbreak of listeriosis: United States, 1998–1999. *MMWR*. 1999;47:1117–1118.

19. Centers for Disease Control and Prevention. Outbreaks of Shigella sonnei infection associated with eating fresh parsley: United States and Canada, July-August, 1998. *MMWR*. 1999;48:285–289.

20. Herwaldt BL, Ackers ML, the Cyclospora Working Group. An outbreak in 1996 of cyclosporiasis associated with imported raspberries. *N Engl J Med*. 1997;336: 1548–1556.

21. Osterholm MT, Potter ME. Irradiation pasteurization of solid foods; taking food safety to the next level. *Emerging Infectious Dis*. 1997;3:575–577.

22. Langer PL. History of goitre. In: *Endemic Goitre*. Geneva, Switzerland: World Health Organization, 1960:9–25 (WHO Monograph Series No. 44).

23. Hess AF. Newer aspects of some nutritional disorders. *JAMA*. 1921;76:693–700.

24. Lanska DJ. Stages in the recognition of epidemic pellagra in the United States: 1865–1960. *Neurol*. 1996;47:829–834.

25. Bollet AJ. Politics and pellagra: the epidemic of pellagra in the US in the early twentieth century. *Yale J Biol Med*. 1992;65:211–221.

26. CDC. Outbreak of pellagra among Mozambican refugees: Malawi, 1990. *MMWR*. 1991;40:209–213.

27. Tippett KS, Cleveland LE. How current diets stack up: comparison with dietary guidelines. In: Frazao E, ed. *America's Eating Habits: Changes and Consequences*. Washington, DC: U.S. Department of Agriculture, Economic Research Service, Food and Rural Economics Division; 1999:51–70 (Agricultural Information Bulletin no. 750).

28. Ernst ND, Sempos ST, Briefel RR, Clark MB. Consistency between US dietary fat intake and serum total cholesterol concentrations: the National Health and Nutrition Examination surveys. *Am J Clin Nutr*. 1997;66:965S–972S.

29. Crane NT, Hubbard VS, Lewis CJ. American diets and year 2000 goals. In: U.S. Department of Agriculture. *America's Eating Habits: Changes and Consequences*. Washington,

DC: U.S. Department of Agriculture, Economic Research Service, Food and Rural Economics Division; 1999:111–132 (Agricultural Information Bulletin no. 750).

30. Centers for Disease Control and Prevention. Decline in deaths from heart disease and stroke: United States, 1900–1999. *MMWR*. 1999;48:649–656.

31. Atwater WO. Foods: nutritive value and cost. Washington, DC: U.S. Department of Agriculture, 1894 (Farmers' Bulletin no. 23).

32. Flegal KM, Carroll MD, Kuczmarski RJ, Johnson CL. Overweight and obesity in the United States: prevalence and trends, 1960–1994. *Int J Obesity*. 1998;22:39–47.

33. Wolf AM, Colditz GA. Current estimates of the economic cost of obesity in the United States: whither? *Obesity Res*. 1998;6:97–106.

34. Centers for Disease Control. Physical activity and health: a report of the Surgeon General. Atlanta, GA: U.S. Department of Health and Human Services, Centers for Disease Control; 1996.

35. Contento I, Balch GI, Bronner YL, et al. The effectiveness of nutrition education and implications for nutrition education policy, programs and research: a review of research. *J Nutr Edu*. 1995;27:279–283.

36. Task Force on Community Preventive Services. *The Community Guide*. Available at www.thecommunityguide.org. Accessed May 31, 2010.

Public Health Interventions

Public health practice affects everyone in the community in one way or another. Still, the image that the public most commonly associates with public health is the provision of medical care—mostly treatment—to low-income populations. Although this image is understandable, for public health professionals, it is disconcerting.

There are several reasons why this image is prevalent. Many people equate public health with what public health agencies do, and public-sector agencies play an important safety-net role in serving individuals who otherwise lack access to care. This vital safety-net role often overshadows the population-based activities of these agencies. In fact, the major share of public health resources supports personal care, as opposed to population-based interventions. Public perceptions as to the primary products of public health practice differ from those of most public health practitioners who believe that population-based interventions are the heart and soul of public health practice; however, public health professionals also know that public health is broader than what public health agencies do and that both the public and private sectors provide preventive as well as treatment interventions.

Preventive interventions that target individuals are considered clinical prevention; those that target populations are considered community prevention. Although population-based prevention is usually ascribed to public sector efforts, this should not imply that disease prevention and health promotion are offered only through the public sector or that future shifts in the level and proportion of these strategies offered by public and private providers are unlikely; however, the public appears to understand and highly value personal care, both curative and preventive. Its understanding of population-based interventions is much less complete, although public opinion polls provide evidence that these interventions are also highly valued.

Just as people wish to be known as much for their aspirations as for their deeds, public health seeks to be identified with the wide variety of strategies that promote, protect, and maintain health. These strategies, in the form of various interventions, are often organized as programs. Programs represent identifiable products of the public health system's functioning. This chapter examines various forms of public health interventions, as well as key steps in their planning, development, and evaluation. Key questions addressed in this chapter include the following:

- What are the important interventions and programs of public health?
- What characteristics distinguish clinical preventive interventions from population-based interventions?
- How are public health interventions planned and evaluated?

INTERVENTIONS, PROGRAMS, AND SERVICES

The outcomes of the public health system result from carrying out the system's important processes. The important processes of public health, embodied in the essential public health services framework, affect outcomes both directly and indirectly. They directly affect outcomes by identifying important health problems and mobilizing efforts to address those problems. Interventions occur in a variety of forms, including statutes, regulations, policies, and programs intended to improve health status. Many interventions are organized into programs consisting of component processes that together seek to achieve specific outcomes. In this light, public health processes contribute to both the generation and operation of programs. As such, programs are understandable and useful constructs that link public health practice with specific outcomes.

Programs are collections of activities that have common objectives; lumping and splitting otherwise discrete programs can result in different formulations. For example, measles immunizations and measles surveillance can be considered as either separate programs or as components of a single program, depending on the formulation of their program objectives. A separate measles immunization program might have an objective to achieve a 90% immunization rate among 2- to 3-year-old children in a particular community. A separate measles surveillance program's objective might be to investigate newly reported cases of measles within 48 hours. Both of these could be considered as part of a more comprehensive measles prevention and control program whose objective might be stated as seeking a reduction in the incidence of measles by some percentage from the current rate.

Programs also provide an understandable framework for describing the scope and content of public health practice and for cataloging public health expenditures. Organizations generally develop budgets and track expenditures on a program-by-program basis. As a result, information on the economic dimensions of public health programs, similar to that presented in Chapters 4 and 6, is available at a variety of levels. Nevertheless, public health practice is more than an aggregation of programs, and public health organizations are more than 40 different companies under one roof, as one health officer described his agency in the early 1990s before re-engineering the agency from a program focus to one emphasizing public health's core functions.

Programs and their component processes are sometimes referred to as services if some benefit is bestowed on the individual or groups targeted for those interventions. Other processes of programs may be performed to support the provision of services. Some public health services, such as childhood immunizations, can be classified as clinical services if directly aimed at protecting or improving individual well-being. Others, such as the fluoridation of public water supplies, can be considered population-based services if directed toward a group of individuals or the entire population.

This connotation of services represents one aspect of what programs do, although programs are often known for the services that are provided through them. For example, immunization programs are commonly thought of as vaccinations given to individuals, although the actual shots given represent only one activity of that program. Public education, provider education, outreach, compliance determination, recordkeeping, and follow-up are also activities of immunization programs. Together, these make up a program whose best known services are vaccinations. The terms programs and services are often used interchangeably when public health activities are reported. The use of the term services in the essential public health services framework further muddies the water because these are not services in the same way as the clinical preventive and population-based services described previously here.

Data from the National Association of County and City Health Officials (NACCHO) profiles of local health departments (LHDs) provide one measure of the prevalence of public health activities and services as well as the level of involvement by LHDs.[1] Table 7-1 summarizes information from NACCHO's 2008 survey as to the prevalence of specific public health activities and services in jurisdictions served by LHDs. The percentage of jurisdictions in which a particular activity or service is available does not imply that the LHD is the entity providing that service. A variety of configurations are possible: the LHD directly providing the service; the LHD contracting with another organization to provide the service; the LHD both directly providing and contracting for the service; another local governmental agency providing the services; a state

Table 7-1   Public Health Activities and Services Provided in Local Health Jurisdictions (LHJs), United States, 2008

Category	Provided in 20%–39% of LHJs	Provided in 40%–59% of LHJs	Provided in 60%–79% of LHJs	Provided in 80%–100% of LHJs
Immunizations				• Adult immunizations • Childhood immunizations
Screening for diseases and conditions		• Diabetes • Cancer • Cardiovascular disease	• High blood pressure • Blood lead • STDs • HIV/AIDS	• Tuberculosis
Communicable disease treatment		• HIV/AIDS	• STDs	• Tuberculosis
Maternal and child health		• Prenatal care • Early Periodic Screening Diagnosis and Treatment (EPSDT) • Well-child care	• WIC • Family planning • MCH home visits	
Other health services	• Oral health • Home health • Primary care • Behavioral/mental health • Substance abuse			
Population-based primary prevention services			• Injury • Violence • Substance abuse • Mental illness	• Tobacco use • Nutrition/obesity • Unintended pregnancy • Chronic disease • Physical activity
Surveillance and epidemiology			• Syndromic • Injury	• Environmental health • Communicable/infectious disease • Behavioral risk factors • Maternal and child health • Chronic disease

Table 7-1 Public Health Activities and Services Provided in Local Health Jurisdictions (LHJs), United States, 2008 (continued)

Category	Provided in 20%–39% of LHJs	Provided in 40%–59% of LHJs	Provided in 60%–79% of LHJs	Provided in 80%–100% of LHJs
Environmental health			• Collection of unused pharmaceuticals	• Food safety education • Vector control • Groundwater protection • Surface water protection • Hazardous waste disposal • Land use planning • Hazardous materials response • Indoor air quality • Pollution prevention • Noise pollution • Radiation control
Regulation, inspection, and/or licensing centers				• Food service establishments • Public swimming pools • Septic tank installation • Schools/day care • Public drinking water • Hotels/motels • Lead inspection • Solid waste haulers • Solid waste disposal sites • Food processing • Health-related facilities • Public drinking water • Campgrounds/RVs • Smoke-free ordinances • Mobile homes • Housing inspections

(continues)

Table 7-1   Public Health Activities and Services Provided in Local Health Jurisdictions (LHJs), United States, 2008 (continued)

Category	Provided in 20%–39% of LHJs	Provided in 40%–59% of LHJs	Provided in 60%–79% of LHJs	Provided in 80%–100% of LHJs
Other public health activities		• School-based clinics	• Correctional health • Laboratory services • Asthma prevention and/or management	• Tobacco retailers • Cosmetology businesses • Milk processing • Vital records • Animal control • Emergency medical services • School health • Outreach and enrollment for medical insurance • Veterinary public health • Occupational safety and health • Medical examiner's office

Source: Data from National Association of County and City Health Officials. *2008 National Profile of Local Health Departments.* Washington, DC: National Association of County and City Health Officials; 2009.

agency providing the services; multiple governmental agencies providing the service; nongovernmental organizations providing the service; or the LHD and nongovernmental organizations providing the service.

The services most frequently provided directly by LHDs are highlighted in Figure 7-1. These include a variety of immunization, infectious disease prevention and control, and environmental health activities. Tobacco use prevention and school and daycare inspections are also among the most frequently provided services by LHDs.

Figure 7-2 identifies the most frequent public health activities that are provided through a contract involving the LHD and another entity. Although increasing somewhat in recent years, the level of contracting for public health activities is far below that of the LHD directly offering these services. Laboratory services are the only public health activity for which contracting is used in more than 10% of jurisdictions.

The activities and services most frequently provided by other local governmental agencies are presented in Figure 7-3. Animal control, land use planning, hazmat response, and emergency medical services lead this list with more than half of jurisdictions relying on a local governmental agency other than the health department for these services.

Nongovernmental agencies play major roles in providing a variety of public health activities and services in the community (Figure 7-4). These agencies are especially critical for comprehensive primary care, obstetrical care, home health services, oral health care, mental health, and substance abuse services.

There are many different combinations and permutations of service delivery from one community to another. These patterns also change over time, as demonstrated in Figure 7-5, which compares the involvement of LHDs in specific activities and services from NACCHO surveys performed in 1992 to 1993

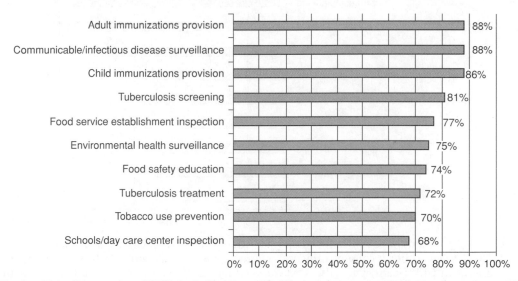

Figure 7-1 Percentage of LHD jurisdictions with 10 most frequent activities and services available through LHDs directly. *Source:* Data from National Association of County and City Health Officials. *2008 National Profile of Local Health Departments.* Washington, DC: NACCHO; 2009.

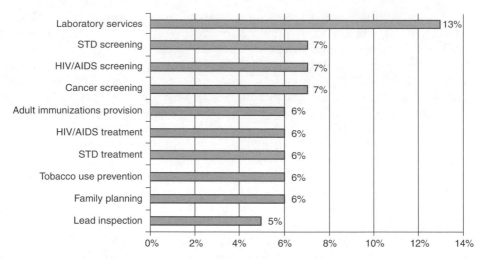

Figure 7-2　Percentage of LHD jurisdictions with 10 most frequent activities and services available through LHD contracts. *Source:* Data from National Association of County and City Health Officials. *2008 National Profile of Local Health Departments.* Washington, DC: NACCHO; 2009.

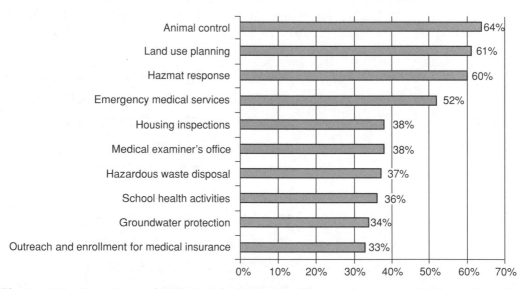

Figure 7-3　Percentage of LHD jurisdictions with 10 most frequent activities and services available through other local governmental agencies. *Source:* Data from National Association of County and City Health Officials. *2008 National Profile of Local Health Departments.* Washington, DC: NACCHO; 2009.

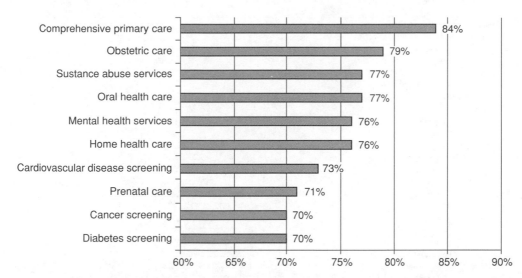

Figure 7-4 Percentage of LHD jurisdictions with 10 most frequent activities and services available through nongovernmental organizations. *Source:* Data from National Association of County and City Health Officials. *2008 National Profile of Local Health Departments.* Washington, DC: NACCHO; 2009.

and a dozen years later in 2005.[1,2] LHDs in 2005 were more likely to provide surveillance for behavioral risk factors, injuries, and communicable diseases than in the early 1990s. Notably, LHDs were less likely to offer laboratory services, home health care, animal control, Early Periodic Screening Diagnosis and Treatment (EPSDT) services, prenatal care, and public drinking water protection services. Several recent trends explain the lower levels of involvement of LHDs in many of these activities. One is that fewer LHDs are now involved in providing clinical services as other healthcare providers have become more engaged with serving low income populations through expansions of Medicaid eligibility and State Child Health Insurance Programs. Another trend is the increased involvement of nongovernmental organizations in addressing community health problems as a result of the growth and maturation of community-wide planning initiatives. More than 80% of LHDs offer community assessment and community outreach activities. Together, Table 7-1 and Figures 7-1 though 7-5 document a constellation of local public health programs and services that are noteworthy for both their extensive scope and their local variability.

Categorizing Programs and Services of Public Health

Aggregating programs into categories that focus on broad outcomes provides additional insights into the products of public health practice. External audiences who think of public health in terms of programs and services, rather than internal processes, readily understand this approach. The mega-outcome categories included in the Public Health in America statement (see

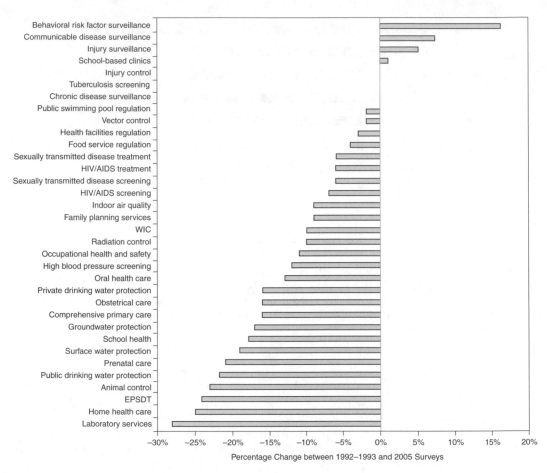

Figure 7-5 Change in percentage of LHDs active in selected program areas between 1992 to 1993 and 2005.

Notes:

1992–93 survey: Please indicate whether your local health department provides each of the services listed below. It is recognized that this is a fairly exhaustive list; please mark "no activity" where appropriate. (Responses: directly provides service; contracts to provide service; no activity.)

2005 survey: For each activity in the charts below and on the following pages, check the boxes that describe who has conducted that activity in your jurisdiction during the past year. Indicate whether your LHD performs the activity, contracts for it, or both.

Source: Data from National Association of County and City Health Officials. *2005 National Profile of Local Health Departments.* Washington, DC: NACCHO; 2006.

Table 1-5) represent what public health does.[3] The six categories of programs provide a clear and comprehensive aggregation of the products of the public health system that seek to

- Prevent epidemics
- Protect the environment, workplaces, housing, food, and water

- Prevent injuries
- Promote healthy behaviors
- Respond to disasters
- Ensure the quality, accessibility, and accountability of health services

Each of these categories includes a mixture of preventive interventions targeted both to populations and to individuals. Preventing epidemics includes efforts such as disease surveillance, disease investigation, contact tracing, case management, prophylactic treatment, laboratory services, and immunizations. Environmental protection includes air and water quality monitoring and permitting, food, housing and workplace safety standards enforcement, toxic waste permitting and hazardous conditions monitoring, environmental risk assessment services, toxicology evaluation services, laboratory services, and enforcement activities. Injury prevention includes injury surveillance, trauma network services, public education and awareness campaigns, child car seat loaner programs, and so forth. Promoting healthy behaviors includes behavioral risk factor monitoring, fitness programs, comprehensive school health education, work-site health promotion, community-wide risk reduction programs, media involvement, health education, parenting education, and information clearinghouses and other referral sources. Disaster response includes disaster planning, emergency medical system maintenance, trauma networks, disaster management drills, and emergency information system establishment. Ensuring the quality, accessibility, and accountability of health services can include health professions licensing and certification, medical facilities licensing and certification, laboratory services quality assurance, hospital outcomes monitoring, personal services outcomes monitoring, personal services availability assessment, patient satisfaction assessment, cost-effectiveness studies, and automated and linked database management.

Using the framework presented earlier in Chapter 3, these programs and services can also be described in terms of their intervention strategy, level of prevention, practice domain, and target population. Intervention strategies include health promotion, specific protection, early identification and treatment, disability limitation, and rehabilitation. By level of prevention, interventions can be classified as primary, secondary, or tertiary. By practice domain, interventions can be furnished by either public health or medical care practitioners. Interventions are also grouped by their target population, either individuals or populations.

As demonstrated in Table 7-1, the activities available to carry out public health's core functions are extensive. Some are clinically oriented preventive services for individuals; others are population-based programs and services. The clinical preventive services emphasize early case finding and other aspects of primary care, whereas population-based programs and services largely involve a variety of health promotion and specific protection services. There is considerable overlap between the two, especially for specific protection and early case-finding services.

Clinical Preventive Services

Clinical preventive services include screening tests, counseling interventions, immunizations, and prophylactic regimens for individuals of all age groups and risk categories. Although many of these interventions have been widely accepted and deployed by practitioners, there have been increasing concerns as to whether they truly improved clinical outcomes. Since the 1980s, both the Canadian Task Force on Preventive Health Care and the U.S. Preventive Services Task Force (USPSTF) have reviewed information on the effectiveness of specific clinical preventive services.[4] At the heart of this examination are five key questions:[5]

- How important is the target condition?
- How important is the risk factor?
- How accurately can the risk factor or target population be identified?
- Is the preventive service effective?
- Do the benefits of implementation outweigh the costs?

Importance of the target condition is assessed using measures of frequency and severity. Incidence and prevalence are two key measures of frequency, whereas mortality, morbidity, and survival rates are useful measures of severity. The importance of a risk factor is determined by its frequency (incidence and prevalence) and measures of the magnitude of the relationship between the risk factor and the target condition, such as absolute and attributable risk. Absolute risk measures the incidence of the target condition in the population with the risk factor. Attributable risk measures the amount of the risk that is attributable to one particular risk factor.

Risk factor or target population accuracy depends on measures of sensitivity (the proportion of persons with a condition who correctly test positive), specificity (the proportion of persons without a condition who correctly test negative), and positive predictive value (proportion of positive test results that are correct). For screening tests, the criteria consider the accuracy and effectiveness of early detection. For counseling interventions, the criteria relate to the efficacy of risk reduction and the effectiveness of counseling. Efficacy of vaccines is the primary criterion for evaluating these biologic interventions. For chemoprophylaxis, the criteria relate to efficacy, as well as to the effectiveness of counseling. Recommendations for clinical preventive services were first published in 1989 and revised periodically for the various age and risk status groups. The second Task Force Guide to Clinical Preventive Services was published in 1996 and became the basis for the 1998 Clinicians Handbook of Preventive Services and the Put Prevention into Practice national implementation program. The third edition of these recommendations is an ongoing process involving re-examination of previous recommendations and consideration of new ones. In order to expedite their translation into practice, recommendations are now released soon after the task force concludes its examination of a specific clinical preventive service.

The USPSTF grades its recommendations (A, B, C, D, or I) based on the strength of evidence and magnitude of net benefit (benefits minus harms). An "A" grade means the USPSTF strongly recommends that clinicians provide the service to eligible patients. The USPSTF found good evidence that the service improves important health outcomes and concluded that benefits substantially outweigh harms. A grade of "B" means that the task force recommends that clinicians provide the service to eligible patients based on at least fair evidence that the service improves important health outcomes and that benefits outweigh harms. A grade of "C" means the USPSTF makes no recommendation for or against routine provision of the service based on at least fair evidence that the service can improve health outcomes but after concluding that the balance of benefits and harms is too close to justify a general recommendation. A "D" grade means the task force recommends against routinely providing the service to asymptomatic patients based on at least fair evidence that the service is ineffective or that harms outweigh benefits. Finally, an "I" grade means that the USPSTF concludes that the evidence is insufficient to recommend for or against routinely providing the service. In these cases, evidence that the service is effective is lacking, of poor quality, or conflicting, and the balance of benefits and harms cannot be determined.

Assessments of the effectiveness of preventive services are made in part by examining the quality of the scientific evidence available for specific interventions. Evidence from properly designed randomized controlled trials is most heavily weighted in this process followed, in order, by evidence from controlled trials without randomization, well-designed cohort or case control studies (preferably multicenter studies), multiple time series or uncontrolled studies, and expert clinical opinion.

This grading scheme became even more important with the enactment of comprehensive health reform legislation in 2010 affecting individuals in private health insurance plans as well as those served by Medicare and Medicaid. One provision of the health reform package stipulates that group health plans and health insurance issuers offering group or individual health insurance coverage shall provide coverage for but cannot impose any cost-sharing requirements for evidence-based items or services that carry a rating of A or B in the current recommendations of the USPSTF. Similarly, other health reform provisions waive any coinsurance requirements for most preventive services for Medicare recipients, resulting in Medicare paying 100% of these costs. These include personalized prevention plan services, initial preventive physical examinations, and any recommended preventive services that are graded A or B by the USPSTF. Medicaid state options for diagnostic, screening, preventive, and rehabilitation services now include all clinical preventive services graded A or B by the USPSTF, as well as all immunizations recommended by the Advisory Committee on Immunization Practices of the Centers for Disease Control and Prevention (CDC). States covering these services in their state Medicaid plans would have the percentage of federal support for their state Medicaid programs increased by 1%.

A summary of the recommendations made by the task force as of 2010 is provided in Table 7-2. These recommendations were not intended to serve as standards of care; rather, they stand as statements as to the quality of the evidence available to justify the use of practices as effective preventive interventions. The USPSTF recommends that clinicians discuss these preventive services with eligible patients and offer them as a priority. All of these services have received an "A" (strongly recommended) or a "B" (recommended) grade from the task force.

Table 7-2 Clinical Preventive Services Recommended by the U.S. Preventive Services Task Force as of June 2010

Recommendation	Adults		Special Populations	
	Men	Women	Pregnant Women	Children
Abdominal aortic aneurysm, screening[1]	X			
Alcohol misuse screening and behavioral counseling interventions	X	X	X	
Aspirin for the prevention of cardiovascular events[2]	X	X		
Asymptomatic bacteriuria in adults, screening[3]			X	
Breast cancer, screening[4]		X		
Breast and ovarian cancer susceptibility, genetic risk assessment, and BRCA mutation testing[5]		X		
Breastfeeding, behavioral interventions to promote[6]		X	X	
Cervical cancer, screening[7]		X		
Chlamydial infection, screening[8]		X	X	
Colorectal cancer, screening[9]	X	X		
Congenital hypothyroidism, screening[10]				X
Dental caries in preschool children, prevention[11]				X
Depression (adults), screening[12]	X	X		
Diet, behavioral counseling in primary care to promote a healthy diet[13]	X	X		
Gonorrhea, screening[14]		X	X	
Gonorrhea, prophylactic medication[15]				X
Hearing loss in newborns, screening[16]				X
Hepatitis B virus infection, screening[17]			X	
High blood pressure, screening	X	X		
HIV, screening[18]	X	X	X	X
Iron deficiency anemia, prevention[19]				X
Iron deficiency anemia, screening[20]			X	
Lipid disorders in adults, screening[21]	X	X		
Major depressive disorder in children and adolescents, screening[22]				X
Obesity in adults, screening[23]	X	X		
Osteoporosis in postmenopausal women, screening[24]		X		
Phenylketonuria, screening[25]				X
Rh (D) incompatibility, screening[26]			X	
Sexually transmitted infections, counseling[27]	X	X		X
Sickle cell disease, screening[28]				X
Syphilis infection, screening[22]	X	X	X	
Tobacco use and tobacco-caused disease, counseling[30]	X	X	X	
Type 2 diabetes mellitus in adults, screening[31]	X	X		
Visual impairment in children younger than age 5 years, screening[32]				X

(continues)

Table 7-2 Clinical Preventive Services Recommended by the U.S. Preventive Services Task Force as of June 2010 (continued)

1. One-time screening by ultrasonography in men aged 65–75 who have ever smoked.
2. When the potential harm of an increase in gastrointestinal hemorrhage is outweighed by a potential benefit of a reduction in myocardial infarctions (men aged 45–79 years) or in ischemic strokes (women aged 55–79 years).
3. Pregnant women at 12–16 weeks gestation or at first prenatal visit, if later.
4. Mammography every 1–2 years for women 40 and older.
5. Refer women whose family history is associated with an increased risk for deleterious mutations in BRCA1 or BRCA2 genes for genetic counseling and evaluation for BRCA testing.
6. Interventions during pregnancy and after birth to promote and support breastfeeding.
7. Women aged 21–65 who have been sexually active and have a cervix.
8. Sexually active women 24 and younger and other asymptomatic women at increased risk for infection. Asymptomatic pregnant women 24 and younger and others at increased risk.
9. Adults aged 50–75 using fecal occult blood testing, sigmoidoscopy, or colonoscopy.
10. Newborns.
11. Prescribe oral fluoride supplementation at currently recommended doses to preschool children older than 6 months whose primary water source is deficient in fluoride.
12. In clinical practices with systems to ensure accurate diagnoses, effective treatment, and follow-up.
13. Adults with hyperlipidemia and other known risk factors for cardiovascular and diet-related chronic disease.
14. Sexually active women, including pregnant women 25 and younger, or at increased risk for infection.
15. Prophylactic ocular topical medication for all newborns against gonococcal ophthalmia neonatorum.
16. Newborns.
17. Pregnant women at first prenatal visit.
18. All adolescents and adults at increased risk for HIV infection and all pregnant women.
19. Routine iron supplementation for asymptomatic children aged 6–12 months who are at increased risk for iron deficiency anemia.
20. Routine screening in asymptomatic pregnant women.
21. Men aged 20–35 and women over age 20 who are at increased risk for coronary heart disease; all men aged 35 and older.
22. Adolescents (age 12–18) when systems are in place to ensure accurate diagnosis, psychotherapy, and follow-up.
23. Intensive counseling and behavioral interventions to promote sustained weight loss for obese adults.
24. Women 65 and older and women 60 and older at increased risk for osteoporotic fractures.
25. Newborns.
26. Blood typing and antibody testing at first pregnancy-related visit. Repeated antibody testing for unsensitized Rh (D)-negative women at 24–28 weeks' gestation unless biological father is known to be Rh (D) negative.
27. All sexually active adolescents and adults at increased risk for STIs.
28. Newborns.
29. Persons at increased risk and all pregnant women.
30. Tobacco cessation interventions for those who use tobacco. Augmented pregnancy-tailored counseling to pregnant women who smoke.
31. Asymptomatic adults with sustained blood pressure greater than 135/80 mm Hg.
32. To detect amblyopia, strabismus, and defects in visual acuity.

Source: Data from U.S. Preventive Services Task Force, 2010.

The effectiveness of immunizations has been well established through reductions of more than 99% for diseases that include poliomyelitis, rubella, diphtheria, and pertussis. Several screening tests have also contributed to reductions in disease mortality and morbidity. For example, hypertension screening has contributed to the 67% reduction in stroke mortality since 1968, and newborn screening for both congenital hypothyroidism and phenylketonuria and cervical cancer screening through Pap tests have greatly reduced the burden of these diseases. Chemoprophylaxis, especially for diseases such as tuberculosis, has also contributed to reductions in mortality and morbidity in recent decades. Despite the successes with these forms of clinical preventive services, the greatest potential lies in changing personal behaviors. In the clinical setting, counseling, often supported with screening tests, appears to be the clinical preventive service with the greatest potential.[4]

Complementing the scientific assessment of efficacy (answering the question "does it work?"), the task force has increasingly focused on assessment of economic benefits and costs (answering the question "is it worth it?"). These economic evaluations provide an additional dimension to the review of clinical preventive services that takes on greater importance in a world of finite resources, conflicting claims, and competing demands on decision makers.

Notwithstanding the demonstrated effectiveness of many clinical preventive interventions, they remain underused. Reasons for the failure to provide clinical preventive interventions often relate to reimbursement practices, provider education and practice patterns, and the pluralistic and fragmented health system in the United States. In addition to these factors, the proliferation of recommendations as to appropriate use of these interventions has created confusion and uncertainty among many health providers as to exactly what should be done and when. Further complicating the picture are underlying suspicions and uncertainty among health providers as to whether interventions such as counseling are effective in the first place. The process developed by the USPSTF sought to address these last two concerns directly.

The review of evidence leading to the age- and risk group-specific recommendations of the task force was accompanied by several important findings. The task force concluded that interventions addressing patients' personal health practices are vitally important, in view of the major health risks and problems currently facing the U.S. population. Providers must take on a greater role in assisting their patients to reduce risks in their daily lives. In short, personal health behaviors are a legitimate and important clinical concern, and both clinicians and patients should share decision making regarding possible interventions. In determining that many screening tests are effective, the task force also found that many are not. These unproved and ineffective services must be avoided and their costs averted as clinicians become more selective in ordering tests and providing preventive services. Most important, the task force concluded that many opportunities for delivering preventive services were being missed, especially for persons with limited access to care.

Another important conclusion of the USPSTF was that, for some health problems and risks, community-wide preventive interventions are more effective than clinical services. This does not diminish the role of clinical providers, however, because their standing in the community can do much to advance community interventions and link them more effectively with the provision of clinical services.

Additional insights into the scope and extent of public health interventions are provided through information on clinical preventive services. Until relatively recently, very little information on these services has been available. Through national surveys conducted by the CDC's National Center for Health Statistics (see Chapter 6), information on the general population has been generated. This information is increasingly available at the local level.

Evidence-Based Community Preventive Services

Scientifically sound strategies and approaches are essential for public health interventions to be successful in improving quality of life and reducing preventable mortality and morbidity. Public health practitioners have always highly valued the science base for public health practice, but only recently has the evidence for the effectiveness of community-based interventions been subjected to rigorous scrutiny. This effort is modeled on the work of the USPSTF, which reviewed data and information related to the provision of clinical preventive services to assess what works and what does not. The clinical practice guidelines that emerged from that process have been widely accepted and have served to raise the standard of practice for clinical preventive services for specific age groups.

For preventive interventions, the job only begins with demonstrating efficacy: that an intervention works well under ideal circumstances. Although an intervention may be efficacious, it may not work somewhere else because of the particular conditions and circumstances that exist there. Such an intervention would not be considered effective: that is, it would not have the impact intended. Many different social, ethical, legal, and distributional factors may limit effectiveness in a particular setting.[6] Figure 7-6 illustrates the life cycle of a preventive intervention, from its development through basic research to its eventual widespread intervention. In between, applied research activities and community demonstrations are necessary to provide a complete picture of its effectiveness in terms of its impact on outcomes, economic considerations, and safety.

Although these analyses have been applied to clinical preventive services for more than a decade, efforts to apply them to community prevention activities are of more recent vintage. In 1995, the first steps were taken toward the development of practice guidelines for public health, using similar principles.[6] An assessment of the feasibility of such an undertaking was completed through the Council on Linkages between Academia and Public Health Practice. The conclusions and recommendations of this assessment are presented in Table 7-3; they indicate strong support for developing population-based practice guidelines. The primary purpose of guidelines for community preventive services is to provide public health practitioners, their community partners, and policy makers with information needed for informed decision making on the most effective public health strategies, policies, and programs for their communities. Where interventions are found to be effective, this process then

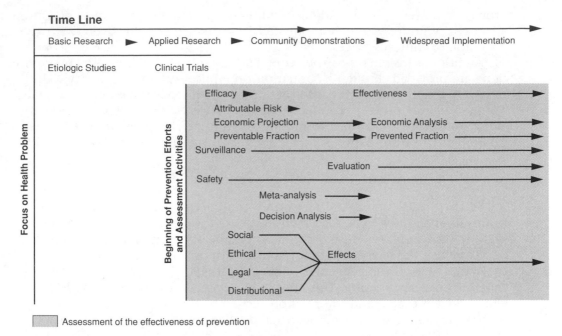

Figure 7-6   Natural history of the development of an effective prevention strategy and temporal relationship to the types of assessment activities. *Source:* From Teutsch S. A framework for assessing the effectiveness of disease and injury prevention. *MMWR.* 1992;41(RR-3).

examines their cost-effectiveness, benefits and harms, generalizability, and barriers to implementation. This information provides the basis for evidence-based recommendations on the use of specific community preventive interventions.

Population-based community prevention focuses on assessing and addressing common, as well as emergent, health problems and needs. It is both an investment strategy and a tool for protecting and enhancing community health status. Several forces have accelerated interest in a more evidence-based approach to community prevention that complements recent advances in evidence-based medicine and clinical preventive services in order to assess what works and what does not. The increasing chronic disease burden is one of those forces necessitating greater interest in preventive (reducing incidence and prevalence) strategies that focus on education and behavioral change rather than on new treatment modalities. Lessons learned in terms of environmental interventions and public policy changes in laws, regulations, and enforcement can be extended to new threats and other conditions. Changes in the healthcare system are also needed in order to promote and target effective clinical preventive services to reach more of those who would benefit from such services.

The progress made after 1950 in identifying risk factors associated with chronic diseases and injuries is sometimes called the second epidemiologic revolution. With the importance of heart disease, stroke, cancer, diabetes, chronic lung diseases, and injuries as major contributors to morbidity and

Table 7-3   Practice Guidelines for Public Health: Recommendations for Assessment of Scientific Evidence, Feasibility, and Benmefits

1. Public health practice guidelines are feasible, based on scientific evidence and other empirical information.
2. The potential benefits of public health practice guidelines are immediate and far reaching.
3. Each set of guidelines should have a carefully circumscribed scope.
4. Guidelines should be flexible, rather than proscriptive.
5. Guidelines should be dynamic.
6. All major stakeholders should be involved as the guidelines are developed.
7. Critical questions are an efficient tool to structure the evidence-collection process.
8. A database search for scientific studies is a useful first step.
9. Additional sources of documentary evidence should be tapped and systematically evaluated.
10. Empiric evidence from state and local public health programs should be sought, evaluated, and incorporated into the guidelines.
11. Development of guidelines will stimulate needed research.
12. Guidelines should be pilot tested before dissemination, then continuously evaluated.

Source: Data from Council on Linkages Between Academia and Public Health Practice. *Practical Guidelines for Public Health: Assessment of Scientific Evidence, Feasibility and Benefits*. Washington, DC: Council on Linkages, U.S. Public Health Services; October 1995.

mortality, health promotion programs have grown in number and scope over the past two decades. Examples include injury risk reduction through seat belts, education to prevent tobacco use, campaigns against drinking and driving, nutrition education (fat intake), fitness campaigns, smokeless tobacco use, stress management, and programs promoting safe sex and abstinence. Risk or harm reduction strategies often seek to reduce, rather than totally eliminate, risk factors in a population by focusing on multiple strategies and by not considering the risk behavior from a moral or value-laden perspective.

Commercial marketing concepts and techniques are increasingly used in community prevention efforts. Often termed social marketing, target audiences are identified for purposes of influencing voluntary behaviors or policy makers. Social marketing techniques promote the acceptance, rejection, maintenance, or modification of specific health or care-seeking behaviors by offering or reinforcing incentives and/or consequences that serve the self-interest of individuals in the target group.[7] This consumer-driven focus is rapidly gaining acceptance among public health professionals and organizations.

Although viewed as important for health purposes, and increasingly emphasized by public and voluntary organizations, these services have not been widely embraced by providers and organizations in the private sector. To some extent, this has occurred because insurance plans have not covered these services and because they are not viewed as valued by the public. As a result, providers have not sought to advertise or otherwise promote them. Instead, disease-specific services emphasizing sophisticated, high-technology services, including screening tests, have been used to attract patients and market share.

The convergence of these considerations led to the development of the Task Force on Community Preventive Services and the establishment of the *Guide to Community Preventive Services*[8] (*Community Guide*). The *Community*

Guide identifies strategies that work to promote healthy lifestyles, prevent disease, and increase the number of people who receive appropriate preventive counseling and screening. The *Community Guide* provides decision makers with recommendations regarding population-based interventions to promote health and to prevent injury, disease, disability, and premature death. These recommendations target communities and healthcare providers and focus on changing risk behaviors, reducing the prevalence of diseases, injuries and impairments, and addressing environmental and ecosystem challenges.

Systematic reviews are conducted for specific interventions within each health topic and organized as a chapter of the *Community Guide*. The assessment evaluates evidence of effectiveness and translates that into a recommendation or a finding of insufficient evidence. Importantly, a determination that evidence is insufficient does not mean that there is evidence of ineffectiveness. Table 7-4 provides a summary of some of the task force's initial conclusions regarding community preventive services that work. Current recommendations for preventing infectious diseases, tobacco use, cardiovascular disease, obesity, and injuries and for promoting access to health services are included in the Public Health Spotlight accompanying each chapter.

Community preventive services embody the two basic strategies for primary prevention: health promotion and specific prevention and foster appropriate use of various tools for secondary prevention. These strategies are largely targeted to populations—the entire population or specific groups. These services constitute public health practice regardless of whether they are provided by public- or private-sector organizations and providers. It is not essential that all community preventive services be provided by the public sector, although some specific services can be organized and provided only through that route (e.g., fluoridation of water supplies).

It is likely that, as more communities become engaged in community-wide health improvement initiatives across the United States, there will be greater recognition of the need for community prevention services geared toward chronic diseases and a variety of behavioral health problems. During the 20th century, public health priorities have shifted away from communicable disease control, environmental hazards, and maternal and child health services toward chronic disease prevention, injuries, violence, mental health, and substance abuse as community health priorities. Evidence of this shift is reflected in the categories of community health priorities that were established as a result of all certified LHDs in Illinois completing a community needs assessment process and community health plan (an adaptation of the Assessment Protocol for Excellence in Public Health, described in Chapter 5) in 1993/1994 followed by a second round of assessments in 1999/2000.[9] More than 90 local health jurisdictions completed developed community health plans with thousands of community participants across the state. In each round, more than 335 health priorities were identified in nine categories. As illustrated in Figure 7-7, there were changes in the leading categories for priorities during the 1990s, with more local health jurisdictions in 1999/2000 identifying priories related to access to care, chronic diseases, and mental health and fewer identifying environmental hazards, communicable disease control, and maternal and child health as priorities than in 1993/1994. Mental health,

Table 7-4 Guide to Community Preventive Services: What Works?

	Community Preventive Interventions That Work
Community interventions	• Community-wide information and enhanced enforcement to increase child safety seat use • Community water fluoridation • School-based dental sealant delivery programs • Community-wide education campaigns to increase physical activity • Early childhood development programs • Mass media campaigns to reduce alcohol-impaired driving • Mass media campaigns to reduce tobacco use • Tobacco cessation telephone support systems • Community mobilization when combined with additional interventions to reduce tobacco use initiation
Education and behavior change	• Reducing exposure to ultraviolet radiation and increasing sun-protective behaviors in children • Diabetes self-management education in community gathering places and in the home • Incentive and education programs to increase child safety seat use • Distribution and education programs for child safety seats • Individually adapted behavior change programs to increase physical activity • School-based physical education • Point of decision prompts to increase physical activity • Social support interventions in community settings to increase physical activity • Publicly funded, center-based comprehensive early childhood development programs for children 3 to 5 years old
Environmental interventions	• Create or enhance access to places for physical activity combined with informational outreach • Point of decision prompts to increase physical activity • Use of tenant-based rental assistance vouchers improves household safety by giving qualified families a choice in moving to neighborhoods that offer reduced exposure to violence
Healthcare system interventions	• Diabetes disease management and case management programs • Tobacco cessation provider reminders + provider education • Reduce out-of-pocket costs for tobacco cessation therapies • Reduce patients' out-of-pocket costs for vaccinations • Client and provider reminder systems for vaccinations • Standing orders for vaccinations
Legislation, regulation, and enforcement	• Sobriety checkpoints • Reduce legal blood alcohol levels to <0.08% • Lower blood alcohol for young or inexperienced drivers • Maintain legal drinking age at 21 years • Intervention training for servers of alcoholic beverages • Child-safety seat laws • Safety-belt laws • Primary enforcement laws (rather than secondary enforcement laws) • Enhanced enforcement of safety belt use laws • Increase the unit price of tobacco products • Smoking bans and restrictions

Source: Data from the Task Force on Community Preventive Services. *The Community Guide.* http://www.thecommunityguide.org. Accessed October 10, 2007.

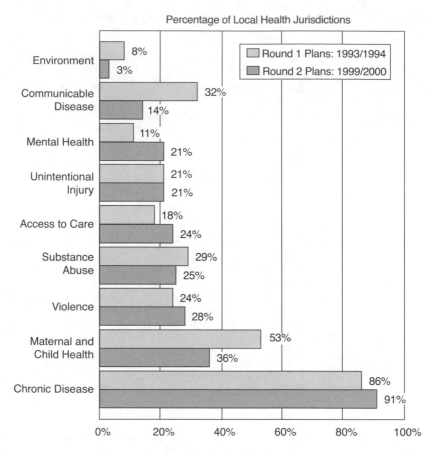

Figure 7-7   Categories of health problems identified as priority community health problems through community needs assessments, Illinois, 1993 to 1994 and 1999 to 2000. *Source:* Data from Illinois Department of Public Health, IPLAN Objective Summary, 2002.

substance abuse, violence and injuries were more frequently identified as priorities than communicable disease control or environmental hazards in the 1999/2000 community health assessments.

Evidence-based public health practice presents formidable challenges for several important reasons. Frequently relying on cross-sectional and quasi-experimental designs that lack a true comparison or control group, the quality of evidence for public health interventions is often limited, in comparison with the evidence for medical interventions. In addition, there is a longer time period between intervention and outcome for many public health activities. Still, there is a variety of tools available to public health practitioners to assist in determining when public health action is warranted, including meta-analysis, risk assessment, economic evaluation, public health surveillance, and expert panels and consensus conferences.[10,11] Basic steps useful for enhancing evidence-based public health practice are illustrated in Figure 7-8 and Table 7-5. These include the following:

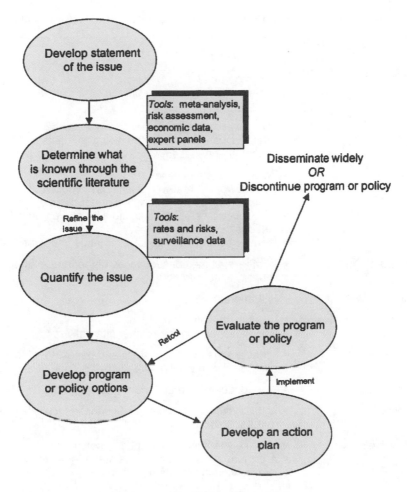

Figure 7-8 A sequential framework for enhancing evidence-based public health. *Source:* From Brownson RC, Gurney JG, Land GH. Evidence-based decision making in public health. *J Pub Health Manage Pract.* 1999;5(5):86–97.

- Developing an initial, concise, operation statement of the issue
- Determining what is known through the scientific literature
- Quantifying the issue
- Developing program or policy options
- Developing an action plan for the program or policy
- Evaluating the program or policy[10]

It is clear that the needs of science and public policy differ in terms of their standards of evidence. Scientists would prefer that many true hypotheses go unproven rather than to "prove" one false hypothesis. Public health professionals, however, often cannot wait until definitive evidence is available. Evidence-based practice does not demand that judgment be suspended until all of the evidence is in or that only "gold standard" evidence is acceptable.

Table 7-5   Quantitative and Qualitative Factors in Public Health Decision Making

Factor	Specific Questions
Size of the problem	• Is it important? • What is the public health burden?
Problem preventability	• What is the efficacy? • Can it work at least in ideal circumstances? • What do we know about the biological plausibility? Is it logical (theory based)?
Intervention effectiveness	• What is the effectiveness? • Does it work in real-world settings? Would it work in the settings being considered (is it generalizable)? • How much less effective would it be compared with ideal settings? • Is there better evidence for alternative interventions?
Benefits and harms	• What are all the consequences of the intervention? • What are the trade-offs?
Intervention cost	• Is it affordable?
Comparison of benefits and costs	• What is the value? • How does it compare to other alternatives?
Incremental gain	• What are the additional costs and benefits (value) compared with what is already being done (if anything)?
Feasibility	• Are adequate time and money available?
Acceptability	• Is it consistent with community priorities, culture, values, and the political situation?
Appropriateness	• Is it likely to work in this specific setting? • Are there ways to better understand the context for intervention in various populations?
Equitability	• Does it distribute resources fairly?
Sustainability	• Are resources and incentives likely to support conditions to maintain the intervention?

Source: Data from Anderson LM, Brownson RC, Fullilove MT, et al. Evidence-based public health policy and practice: promises and limits. *Am J Prev Med.* 2005;28:226–230.

For decades, the tobacco industry dismissed evidence of the causal link between tobacco use and lung cancer as inconclusive because it was based largely on observational studies. This objection resonated with research scientists but did not deter public health activists from planning and implementing antitobacco interventions or deploying both population-based and individual-oriented preventive interventions in reducing dental caries through fluoridation of public water supplies during the second half of the 20th century (see the Public Health Spotlight on Oral Health at the end of Chapter 8).

PROGRAM MANAGEMENT IN PUBLIC HEALTH

Program management in public health includes the myriad activities involved with the development, implementation, and evaluation of interventions addressing public health problems. Effective program management is an organized response requiring a carefully designed problem statement, the availability of an appropriate intervention, and the capacity to deliver that intervention in a specific setting. Each of these is an essential component of an organized response. The task is to bring these elements together and direct them toward the solution of problems. Public health program management seeks to organize and direct public health workers, scientifically sound interventions, and appropriate strategies toward specific health problems.[12] The ultimate aim is to eliminate or reduce these problems to the maximum extent possible (effectiveness) and to achieve these results with the minimum resources necessary (efficiency). Effectiveness and efficiency are the primary criteria by which programs are judged or evaluated.

Management revolves around resource allocation and utilization. The resources of public health as described in Chapter 6 include the human, organizational, informational, fiscal, and other supportive resources. To use these resources both effectively and efficiently, there must be a process that carefully examines the problem for the pathways most likely to yield successful results. There are two cardinal sins of program management: failing to achieve program objectives when adequate resources are available and using more resources than are necessary to achieve a program's objectives. The first situation is more commonly viewed as poor management than the second, although from a management point of view each results in resources being wasted. When program management is improperly or only partially applied, resources and technology are underused, and problems are not fully addressed or resources and technology are inefficiently used, resulting in excess resource consumption and opportunity costs.

Program management calls for the development of a program hypothesis. This is best understood when programs are considered at the level of their basic elements, namely, the specific activities or tasks that are undertaken. The program hypothesis in its simplest form is a logic model; if the designated activities are successfully undertaken, the program's goals and objectives will be successfully addressed. For health programs, we expect that these activities will change characteristics of individuals or populations, such that factors contributing to the level of the health problem will improve. With improvements in these various factors affecting the health problem, we expect that the level of the health problem itself will also be improved. Depending on how many intervening levels of factors there might be, we expect that improvement at one level will result in improvements in higher levels. These terms will be defined and clarified later here; the major point here is that rational programs use logic models in order to address directly the chain of causation that creates the health problem being targeted by the program.

The management cycle is often described as consisting of three phases: planning (deciding what to do and how to do it), implementation (acting to accomplish what has been planned), and evaluation (comparing the results of what was accomplished with what was intended).[12] Very often, planning, implementation, and evaluation have been viewed as linear processes. First we plan. Then we implement. Finally, we evaluate what has occurred. In this linear model, we stop planning when we begin implementing, and we do not evaluate until after we have implemented our program. This approach views planning and evaluation as discrete, independent functions carried out at different points in the life span of a program. There are few fallacies more dangerous to sound management than this one! It is critical that planning and evaluation be viewed as interrelated and interdependent processes working together at varying levels of emphasis throughout the life of a program. Rather than a linear process, program management should be viewed as a cyclical process in which one step logically leads to the next and feedback obtained at all steps is used to revise the directions established in preceding steps. This relationship is illustrated in Figure 7-9, which is reprinted from Michele Issel's excellent text on public health program planning and development.[13]

Program management centers on the development of objectives. Unfortunately, objectives are all too often viewed as the products of planners alone. Program management in public health and other areas is simply too important for objectives to be left to the planners! Objectives are more than abstract targets for achievement. Although they are often characterized as the blueprint of a program, they actually serve more as a road map than as a blueprint. Objectives point the program toward a specific destination and, at the same time, set its speed and establish its mile markers. Objectives guide program administration and establish the framework and strategy for program evaluation. Rather than serving primarily as a tool for program planning, they guide all aspects of program planning, administration, and evaluation.

Linking Planning and Evaluation

A practical definition of planning views it as the application of rational decision making to the commitment of future resources. Planning is as much an art as it is a science. Planners do not have any special abilities to predict or foresee the future, and planning does not result in certainty as to what will happen. Rational planning serves to reduce but not entirely eliminate risk. The management purpose behind planning must be kept in mind: it is to make the most efficient use of resources. As a result, planning should not be judged solely by the accuracy of its predictions or even by whether planning targets, such as objectives, are met. Instead, planning should be judged on the basis of whether it helps an organization to achieve the best possible results in a changing environment. It is rare for programs to be carried out exactly as they were designed. Change occurs constantly among the external and internal factors that affect both the problem and programs designed to address the problem. Ongoing planning serves to recognize changes and modify implementation strategies accordingly. The ability of a program to evaluate itself continuously determines how quickly and effectively it can respond to changing conditions.

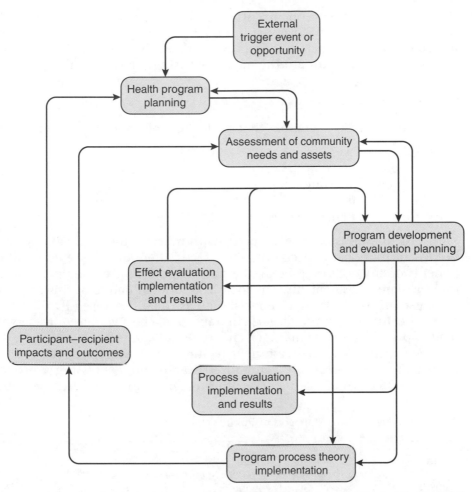

Figure 7-9 The planning and evaluation cycle. *Source:* From Issel LM. *Public Health Program Planning and Evaluation: A Practical, Systematic Approach for Community Health.* Sudbury, MA: Jones and Bartlett; 2004.

The key to the process of evaluation is the ability to ask the right questions. All too often, little thought is given to an evaluation strategy until the program is already in place and decision makers or funders begin to ask for evidence of its benefit. In short, evaluation is an afterthought. As a result, programs scurry around, asking this question: What are we doing that we can measure? Unfortunately, often very little can be done at this point. Evaluation strategies should be developed and agreed on before programs are implemented, and they should be based on asking a quite different question: What do we need to measure to know what we are doing? We return to these issues in greater detail as we discuss planning and evaluation in subsequent sections of this chapter. The point here is that these are not to be considered as bookends for program implementation; rather, they should be carried out concurrently and continuously. When this is done, planning and evaluation contribute substantially to a rational decision-making system in which managers are more likely to ask the right questions and direct resources toward the most promising intervention activities.

Key Questions for Managers

There are five key questions that guide the program management process[12]:

- Where are we?
- Where do we want to be?
- Should we do something?
- What should we do?
- How do we know that we are getting there?

These questions provide managers with much of the essential information needed to make better decisions. They focus attention on the essential components of any decision process: the starting point, the ending point, and the intermediate measurements. The logic and rational nature of this process can be tracked through decision models, such as those developed by the CDC for public health program managers. In Table 7-6, the five questions serve as a roadmap of the program manager's major duties and tasks.

Even with a road map, journeys require a destination or goal. For public health programs, goals are generalized statements expressing a program's intended effect on one or more health problems. Goals are often described as

Table 7-6   Key Questions for Managers of Public Health Programs

Where are we?	• State problem. • Identify appropriate intervention. • Specify resources. • Project future level of problem.
Where do we want to be?	• Identify desired outcome objective.
Should we do something?	• Discontinue current efforts? • Maintain current efforts? • Implement new intervention?
What should we do?	• Analyze problem for determinants and contributing factors. • Determine intervention point most likely to succeed. • Develop impact and process objectives, activity measures, work plan, and budget. • Develop expected outcome objective.
How do we know that we are getting there?	• Track progress toward achieving activity measures and process objectives (doing things right). • Track progress toward achieving impact and outcome objectives (doing the right things).

Source: Adapted from Dyal WW. *Program Management: A Guide for Improving Program Decisions.* Atlanta, GA: USPHS-SDC-PHPPO; 1990.

timeless statements of overall aspirations; these generally serve to establish boundaries for the program's operational activities, but they also serve as the philosophic justification for a program's existence. It is unusual for program managers to be involved in the establishment of goals. Higher authorities, such as boards, legislative bodies, or even funding sources, usually establish these. Despite being somewhat abstract and externally developed, goals serve a valuable purpose for public health programs. Goals need to be clearly stated, and they need to be understood by all program staff, if only to serve as a common bond and continuous reminder of the program's aspirations.

Where Are We?

The essence of decision making at any level is deciding either to do something or to do nothing. A rational decision to do or not do something calls for a thorough assessment of the current situation, based on asking this question: Where are we? Determining the current status of things assists the manager in several ways. It provides information that can be later used to decide whether action should be taken. It also serves to describe the dimensions of a potential problem in terms of which groups might be more affected and establishes a baseline for comparisons over time.

In examining where things stand, it is important to assess in detail the problem, the interventions capable of addressing the problem, and the resources available to deploy those interventions. Although these three elements need to be considered together in determining the current situation, the availability of an effective intervention is absolutely essential from the program management perspective. Without a potentially effective intervention, it makes little sense to plan and implement a program. The availability of an effective intervention refers to the current level of sophistication of the knowledge and techniques for its coordinated application. It is the science and knowledge base for developing and justifying a technical approach for accomplishing a goal. The specific intervention approach could be drawn from any of the categories of health interventions strategies described in Chapter 3 (health promotion, specific protection, early case finding and treatment, disability limitation, and rehabilitation) and from recommendations as to effectiveness from the U.S. Task Force on Clinical Preventive Services and the Task Force on Community Preventive Services discussed in earlier sections of this chapter. As a result, the intervention could be based on medical sciences, physical sciences, or social sciences. Sometimes referred to as the state of the art, this knowledge or technical information convinces program managers that a particular health problem can be addressed.

In addition to the capability to intervene, there are two other considerations in assessing where things currently stand. These are the level of a health problem and the capacity or resources to intervene. A health problem is defined here as a situation or condition of people (expressed in health outcome terms, such as mortality, morbidity, or disability) that is considered undesirable and is likely to exist in the future unless additional interventions are implemented. The heart of any intervention strategy lies in the definition of the problem. The development of objectives and intervention strategies flows naturally from a careful and precise statement of the problem. Problem statements come in all formats and lengths, and they vary significantly in their complexity. Still, all good problem statements present a clear, concise, and accurate description of the condition to be controlled or prevented. The more carefully that a problem is stated, the more likely it is that it can be accurately measured.

Planning processes look to the future. Above all, planning is concerned with future resource allocation; therefore, decisions will need to address the anticipated future level of problems, rather than their current levels. It makes little sense to throw additional resources at a problem if that problem's level is declining and the level of the problem in the future may not be deemed unacceptable. This would constitute at least a partial waste of resources, something that is to be avoided with good management practices. Even a decreasing level of a problem may merit additional resource allocation if that level is judged to be unacceptable or if additional resources might accelerate the decrease.

Looking to both the past and the future is necessary to describe a problem adequately because its trends are an important aspect of its description. Tracking problems over time also helps to project their future levels through trend analysis techniques. Often, however, tracking the level of a problem provides only an incomplete picture of changes over time. It is also important to track changes and trends in the problem's major determinants. For example, changes in low birthweight (a major determinant of infant mortality) should be examined alongside infant mortality rates, and changes in tobacco use should be tracked alongside lung cancer rates. Projecting future levels of a problem on the basis of trends in the problem and its determinants is fraught with uncertainty and is imprecise at best. Nonetheless, it is both useful and rational in informing decisions that will allocate resources to achieve specific results.

In addition to trends and projections of levels, the process of problem specification calls for assessment of the size, scope, and distribution of a problem, beginning with a clear definition of the problem in terms of its nature and etiology, its magnitude and extent in terms of its incidence and prevalence, its affected populations in terms of specific populations at risk (by age, gender, race, occupation, or other risk factors), and its time and place of occurrence. In some respects, this reads like the major components of a news story in terms of who, what, when, where, and how much.

Just as problems need to be carefully specified in determining where we are, resources also need to be assessed for their trends over time in terms of financial resources, as well as human resources (number, types, and skills), organizational resources, information resources, facilities, equipment, and other materials. Tracking both the problem and the resources over time allows for reasonable predictions to be made as to the effects (if any) of resources on the problem and what might be expected at various future resource levels. This information facilitates the development of realistic outcomes.

Where Do We Want to Be?

Determining where you are allows for a comparison with where you want to be. In answering this question, we make an effort to identify the level at which a problem will be considered acceptable at some point in the future. This is the level at which a current problem will no longer be considered a problem, and it is very much dependent on how carefully and comprehensively the problem has been described. If a problem is well defined in terms of what, how much, who, when, and where, priorities can be established so that resources can be most efficiently used to achieve program results. Specific measurable objectives can also be established on the basis of these components of the problem description. The term *desired outcome objective* refers to the level to which a health problem should be reduced and/or maintained within a specified time period. It is meant to be of long term (generally 2 or more years), realistic (achievable through the intervention strategies proposed), and measurable. Outcome objectives are designed to measure directly the level of the health problem; they include a statement of how much and when the program should affect the health problem. An outcome objective is a quantitative measurement of the health problem at some future date and is something that the manager believes the program can and should accomplish. To establish meaningful outcome objectives, the three key ingredients are the availability of effective interventions, the resources and capacity to implement these interventions, and projections for the future level of the health problem. By assessing the past and current relationships among capability, capacity, and outcomes, we can project realistic and measurable outcome objectives for various levels of program activity.

Should We Do Something?

The purpose of asking the first two questions (where are we? and where do we want to be?) is to force a decision as to whether something additional needs to be done. When where you are (and are likely to be) differs from where you would like to be, change is indicated. Change can take one of two forms, doing more or doing less. As a result, there are three options in terms of resource allocation and deployment: reduce (or even eliminate) current efforts, maintain current efforts, or implement a new intervention.

Discontinuing current efforts may be called for if the health problem has already reached or is projected to reach desirable levels, such that further resource allocation is unnecessary. From a manager's point of view, this represents an opportunity to save or redirect resources, rather than to waste them.

A second option is to continue to provide the same level of resources if that level will achieve the desired outcome level by the target achievement date. The decision for a maintenance level should never become automatic; an active, analytic decision-making process should precede it. If the expected level of the problem falls within the acceptable range and resources are available, maintenance of the current level of effort is appropriate.

Interventions are called for when the projected level of the problem exceeds the desired outcome objective and when the capability and capacity to intervene are available. With the availability of technology and resources, the trick is to determine the best implementation strategy that will use these to achieve the desired outcome. How a program gets from where it is to where it wants to be requires that decisions be made as to which specific strategies and activities are to be used. There are generally at least several strategies for affecting the level or extent of a health problem. The decisions to be made are based on which options are likely to be most successful and how much of the program's resources should be devoted to each strategy. A program's intervention strategy determines how a program's resources are to be deployed to achieve the desired outcome objective. The logic behind this is simple: If the strategies and activities are carried out as planned, the problem will be reduced to the expected level on schedule. Many uncertainties and unforeseen circumstances can prevent an intervention strategy from succeeding as planned. These can be viewed as analogous to the difference between efficacy (will it work?) and effectiveness (will it work here?). In any event, an intervention strategy is as much a hypothesis as it is a plan. It remains to be proven, and the likelihood of unforeseen problems and obstacles increases when the problem is inadequately defined and analyzed.

What Should We Do?

When the problem has been clearly and concisely stated, when the capability to intervene exists, and when the capacity to deploy the interventions is on hand, an intervention strategy can succeed. Success will further depend on how thoroughly the problem has been analyzed so that its major determinants and their contributing factors are identified. This analysis provides information as to which approaches are most likely to be effective and allows for matching of program resources with activities that will address key contributing factors.

Consistent with the health problem analysis model described in Chapter 2, measures of health problems should be stated in terms of health outcomes, such as mortality, morbidity, incidence, and prevalence. Determinants are risk factors that, on the basis of scientific evidence or theory, are thought to influence directly the level of a specific health problem. Contributing factors are those factors that directly or indirectly influence the level of determinants. Analysis should continue until all pertinent direct determinants and their associated contributing factors have been identified. The direct determinants are then examined to determine which offer the greatest chance of success in achieving the desired outcome. For some determinants, there are either no or only partly effective interventions. Those that offer the best chances for success are selected as points of intervention.

In addition to the expected outcome objective, other levels of objectives guide the intervention process. The outcome objective relates to the level of the health problem. Similarly, some objectives relate to determinants, and still others relate to the contributing factors (Tables 7-7 and 7-8).

Impact objectives address the level to which a direct determinant is to be reduced within a specified time period. They are generally intermediate (1 to 5 years) in terms of time, and they are both realistic and measurable. An impact objective measures a determinant and states how much and when the program will affect the determinant. It is the quantitative measurement of the determinant at some future date.

Just as impact objectives measure determinants, process objectives measure contributing factors. For a program to function as planned, achieving process objectives will lead to achieving impact objectives, which, in turn, will

Table 7-7 Levels of Program Management and Planning

Goal	Defined Operational and Philosophical Parameters
• Outcome objective	• Projected future level of the health problem
• Impact objective	• Projected future level of a direct determinant
• Process objective	• Projected future level of a contributing factor
• Activities	• Actual tasks performed by program personnel

Source: Adapted from Dyal WW. *Program Management: A Guide for Improving Program Decisions.* Atlanta, GA: USPHS-CDC-PHPPO; 1990.

Table 7-8 Characteristics of Program Objectives

Term	Time Period	Description	Measurement
Outcome objective	Usually long-term	Related to health problem	Degree of accomplishment; addresses doing the right things
Impact objective	Intermediate	Related to direct determinants and risk factors	Degree of accomplishment; addresses doing the right things
Process objective	Short-term	Related to contributing factors	Degree of accomplishment; addresses doing things right
Activities	Usually short-term	Describes the use of program resources	Accomplishment (yes/no); addresses doing things right

Source: Adapted from Dyal WW. *Program Management: A Guide for Improving Program Decisions.* Atlanta, GA: USPHS-CDC-PHPPO; 1990.

result in achieving of the outcome objective. Process objectives are shorter term than outcome or impact objectives. They are of short term (usually one year), realistic, and measurable.

The establishment of process objectives initiates two additional steps, one focusing on developing a work plan for the activities necessary to address the process objectives and one revisiting the outcome objective. The former activity is seldom overlooked because it is essential in order to complete the program planning process. The latter activity, however, is often forgotten, resulting in programs operating with outcome objectives that cannot be achieved. The rationale for revisiting the outcome objective is that the intervention strategy selected, together with its process objectives and activity measures, is likely to be only partially successful in reducing the outcome objective to the desired level. Programs are seldom able to achieve the entire improvement called for in the desired outcome objective. As a result, an expected outcome objective is established by reassessing the probability of achieving the desired outcome objective within the estimated time frame for the program. The expected outcome objective represents an estimate of an important future event that can and should be accomplished through the program's actual efforts and within the resources available.

Completing the program-planning process requires the establishment of a work plan with specific activities and tasks that carry out the program's process objectives. Program resources are attached to these activities, and tasks and activity measures are used to track progress. Activity measures are generally very short term (often expressed in weeks or months) but are also realistic and measurable. The program budget is expended in carrying out these activities and tasks. These work statements are short term (less than 1 year), realistic, and measurable, and they describe what is to be done, by whom, when, and where. A budget is very much an operational plan for financial expenditures to support the actions agreed upon in the program plan.

As noted previously, the program plan is based on a logic model, a set of theoretical links or assumptions involving the problem and its determinants, contributing factors, activities, and resources. Program resources are deployed through specific activities that serve to modify contributing factors, resulting in achievement of process objectives. Achievement of the process objectives affects the determinants, resulting in the achievement of impact objectives. Achievement of the impact objectives reduces the level of the health problem, resulting in the achievement of the expected outcome objective.

How Do We Know That We Are Getting There?

To answer the last question, "how do we know that we are getting there?" we examine the effectiveness of program design and implementation. Key to any evaluation strategy is the establishment of measurable checkpoints, or milestones, in both time and direction. These assist the manager in determining whether the program is moving in the right direction and whether it will arrive at its destination on time. Both the strategy and the importance of continuously assessing the effectiveness of a program are summed up in the well-known observation that it is more important to be doing the right things than it is to be doing things right. Evaluation focuses on both.

Evaluation was previously characterized as asking the right questions. With a well-analyzed problem statement and the selection of an appropriate intervention strategy, asking the right questions should be straightforward. The key questions are as simple as this: Was the outcome objective achieved? Were the impact objectives achieved? Were process objectives achieved? Were program activities performed as planned? Evaluation within this framework calls for measuring the actual results and comparing them with the intended results. Information on intended results is derived from the program plan, whereas data and information on the actual result must be provided by the program's information system. Goals, objectives, activities, and other standards establish the level of the intended result for comparison.

The intervention strategy represents a causal hypothesis that must be continuously reassessed because circumstances and conditions may change in ways that affect the initial assumptions and links. Evaluation is essential before decisions are made as to whether efforts should be expanded, reduced, or even maintained. In 1999, the CDC developed guidelines for public health professionals to use in program evaluations.[14] These guidelines focus less on the technical aspects of program evaluation than on six essential elements and four broad standards for program evaluations. The six steps include the following:

- Identify stakeholders, including program implementers, those served or affected, and those who will use the results of the program evaluation.
- Describe the program, including a clear description of need, expectations for the program, the logic model behind the program, resources to be used, activities to be implemented, and its stage of development and how it fits into the larger organizational and community context.
- Focus the evaluation design, including a clearly stated purpose for the evaluation (its uses and users), as well as its specific evaluation questions and methods.
- Gather credible evidence, including indicators that translate the general concepts of the program into specific measures; consider important sources of evidence, collect only what is needed, and use accepted data gathering and management techniques.
- Justify conclusions, including analysis, synthesis, interpretation, and recommendations consistent with values of stakeholders.
- Ensure the use of and share lessons learned, including preparation for addressing both positive and negative findings and adequate mechanisms for feedback, follow-up, and dissemination with stakeholders.

The broad evaluation standards help determine whether an evaluation is well designed and working to its full potential. They are very much interrelated to the essential steps in the evaluation, as illustrated in Table 7-9. The standards address four key questions:

1. Is the evaluation useful (utility)?
2. Is the evaluation practical (feasibility)?
3. Is the evaluation ethical (propriety)?
4. Is the evaluation correct (accuracy)?

There are several dimensions for evaluating preventive interventions. These include a program's reach (proportion of the target population that participated in the intervention), efficacy (success rate if implemented as intended), adoption (proportion of all potential settings that will adopt this intervention), implementation (extent to which the intervention is implemented as intended in the real world), and maintenance (extent to which a program is sustained over time).[15] Failure to assess impact in all five dimensions can contribute to inefficient use of resources, suboptimal influence on health outcomes, and limited research opportunities.

Effectiveness represents the ability to produce an intended result and achieve expected outcomes. When a program fails to achieve its expected outcomes, the cause of that failure must be identified. Programs may not be effective for several reasons that relate to the various levels of the program's objectives and activities: its outcome objectives, its impact objectives, its process objectives, and its activity measures.

Table 7-9   Centers for Disease Control and Prevention Evaluation Steps and Relevant Standards

	Utility	Feasibility	Propriety	Accuracy
1. Identify stakeholders	✓		✓	
2. Describe program			✓	✓
3. Focus evaluation design		✓	✓	✓
4. Gather credible evidence	✓			✓
5. Justify conclusions	✓			✓
6. Ensure use, share lessons learned	✓		✓	✓

Source: Adapted from Centers for Disease Control and Prevention. *Framework for program evaluation in public health. MMWR.* 1999;48(RR-11):1–41.

In reverse order, activity measures may not be achieved if resources are lacking or if personnel fail to carry out their tasks. This results in activity measures not being met. If the activity measures are closely linked to their associated process measures, these also will not be met. Failure to address a program's activity measures and process objectives successfully means that a program is not doing things right. Successfully carrying out activity measures and achieving process objectives, on the other hand, means that a program is doing things right. Even when a program is doing things right, however, it may not be doing the right things. Doing the right things means that program outcome and impact objectives are achieved. Four combinations of program effectiveness can occur:

1. Programs can be doing the right things and doing things right. These are well-designed and well-managed programs that merit emulation.
2. Programs can be doing the right things, even though things are not being done right. The link between the program's process objectives and activity measures and the program's outcome and impact objectives has been poorly identified. These programs are neither well designed nor well managed. It is not possible to link program activities and resources to the outcomes achieved.
3. Programs can be neither doing the right things nor doing things right. These programs are poorly designed and executed on all accounts.
4. Programs can be doing things right but not doing the right things. Here, activity measures and process objectives are achieved, but impact and outcome objectives are not. Although the program staff may be satisfied with its performance, the program as a whole cannot be satisfactory. This situation occurs when a problem is inadequately analyzed. It can be argued that these programs, although poorly designed, are at least partly well managed.

As suggested in these alternatives, programs can suffer from invalid assumptions or incomplete strategies linking process objectives to impact objectives or linking impact objectives to an expected outcome objective. Pinpointing the location of a program's weaknesses in design or implementation calls for continuously assessing the validity, reliability, and completeness of the intervention strategy.

"Doing things right" refers to the performance of activities and the achievement of process objectives. It is measured through process evaluation. Process objectives can be unmet for two reasons: (1) lack of resources, which calls for reassessing the impact and process objectives in order to align them with the available resources (lower expectations or locate additional resources), or (2) lack of performance, which calls for reassessing the program personnel in terms of motivation, skills, and knowledge (hire, fire, train, or motivate). If process objectives are being met, the program is doing things right.

"Doing the right things" refers to the achievement of impact and outcome objectives and measures the program's effectiveness. If the impact objectives are not being achieved but the process objectives are, the manager must reexamine the assumed relationship between contributing factors and the determinants, revise the intervention strategy, and develop a new work plan. If the expected outcome objective is not being achieved but the impact objective is, the manager must re-examine the assumed link between the determinants and the health problem, revise the intervention strategy, and develop a new work plan. If a program is doing things right (activities and process objectives) but is not achieving its projected impact or outcome, the only conclusion is that the program is not doing the right things. If the expected outcome objective is being achieved, the manager must reassess the need for the program and begin the management cycle again.

The three-level objective and evaluation procedure (process, impact, and outcome) facilitates locating the source of problems when a program does not achieve its expected outcome[12] (Figure 7-10). Many programs start off with a focus on achieving outcomes but rapidly shift to a focus on accomplishing their activities and process measures. This is an example of outcome displacement, in that outcomes are displaced as the driving force of programs by lower-level activities. Because every program needs to succeed, a program defines its success by doing things right, even if those things do not lead to the outcomes that the program was designed to produce. If a program cannot succeed in terms of outcome, it will shift its objectives to those it can achieve. Activities and processes then become the program's purpose and are accepted as surrogates for achieving the program's objectives. An analogous situation is apparent in the larger health system, where health outcomes have been displaced as objectives by processes such as access to medical care or the perceived quality of specific medical services.

This simple program management system works well in public health for many reasons. It is rational, flexible, and adaptable to most programs and allows for easily understood comparisons between programs. In addition, it fosters communications within an organization and serves to prevent outcome displacement. Most important, it provides a road map and mile markers for managers so that they can maintain a steady course along the road to achieving the program's stated outcome objectives. One of the Public Health Spotlights for this chapter provides an opportunity to work through this framework.

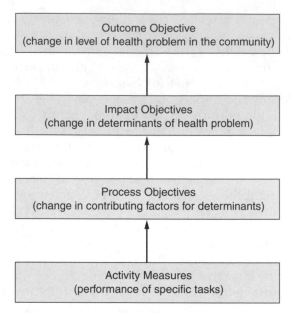

Figure 7-10 Multilevel program evaluation. *Source:* Adapted from Dyal WW. *Program Management: A Guide for Improving Program Decisions*. Atlanta, GA: CDC-PHPPO; 1990.

CONCLUSION

The question "what have you done for me recently?" conveys the expectation for services that permeates society. Interventions and the programs that orchestrate their implementation have become the hallmark of public health. Most people define public health in terms of the interventions that they most frequently encounter. Because personal health services represent such a large share of public health expenditures and because many of public health's population-based services are neither as visible nor as direct as clinical services, a common perception is that public health mainly provides clinical services for those without access to other providers.

There are a number of ways to categorize or classify the interventions and programs that result from collective efforts to identify and address health needs and risks in the community. One approach separates population-based community preventive from clinical preventive interventions. This approach is based largely on the different emphases of public health and medical practitioners. The interfaces between the two modes of practice are extensive and increasing.

Organizing and orchestrating these interventions are accomplished through program-management methods that begin with and revolve around careful definition of health problems. Analysis of carefully defined health problems allows for the establishment of three levels of objectives for the problem, as well as its determinants and contributing factors. Outcome, impact, and process objectives, together with the specific tasks necessary to carry out the process objectives, constitute a framework for tracking progress and modifying program strategies and activities. This program management system helps programs to keep their "eyes on the prize," rather than allowing them to shift their emphases from their intended outcomes to their day-to-day tasks.

DISCUSSION QUESTIONS AND EXERCISES

1. How are planning and evaluation related to program implementation?
2. What are outcome, impact, and process objectives, and how do they contribute to program evaluation?
3. Identify a health problem related to oral health (see the Public Health Spotlight on Oral Health at the end of Chapter 8) and an intervention that can reduce the level of that problem. Provide examples of possible outcome, impact, and process objectives for that intervention.
4. If your program is meeting its activity and process measures but not affecting impact and outcome objectives, what should you do?
5. If a program is not meeting its activity and process objectives, what should be done?
6. Why is the definition of a health problem so important to program management?
7. What is the principle of "outcome displacement," and how does it affect programs and bureaucracies?
8. What is the difference between doing the right things and doing things right in public health?
9. Complete the development of an intervention for one of the injury problems identified in the Public Health Spotlight on Developing a Program Intervention at the end of this chapter.
10. If more extensively used, which of the community preventive services identified as effective in Table 7-4 might serve as useful models for addressing health problems related to oral health?

REFERENCES

1. National Association of County and City Health Officials. *2005 National Profile of Local Health Departments*. Washington, DC: National Association of County and City Health Officials; 2006.
2. National Association of County and City Health Officials. *1992–1993 National Profile of Local Health Departments*. Washington, DC: National Association of County and City Health Officials; 1995.
3. Public Health Functions Steering Committee. *Public Health in America*. Washington, DC: U.S. Public Health Service; 1994.
4. U.S. Preventive Services Task Force. *Guide to Clinical Preventive Services*. 2nd ed. Washington, DC: U.S. Department of Health and Human Services; 1995.
5. Teutsch S. A framework for assessing the effectiveness of disease and injury prevention. *MMWR*. 1992;41:RR-3.
6. *Practice Guidelines for Public Health: Assessment of Scientific Evidence, Feasibility and Benefits*. Baltimore, MD: Council on Linkages between Academia and Public Health Practice; 1995.

7. Grier S, Bryant CA. Social marketing in public health. *Annu Rev Public Health*. 2005;26:319–339.

8. Task Force on Community Preventive Services. Guide to Community Preventive Services. http://www.thecommunityguide.org. Accessed October 10, 2007.

9. Illinois Department of Public Health. *Challenge and Opportunity: Public Health in an Era of Change*. Springfield, IL: Illinois Department of Public Health; 1996.

10. Brownson RC, Gurney JG, Land GH. Evidence-based decision making in public health. *J Public Health Manage Pract*. 1999;5:86–97.

11. Brownson RC, Baker EA, Leet TL, et al. *Evidence-Based Public Health*. New York NY: Oxford University Press, 2002.

12. Dyal WW. *Program Management: A Guide for Improving Program Decisions*. Atlanta, GA: Public Health Service; 1990.

13. Issel LM. *Public Health Program Planning and Evaluation: A Practical Systematic Approach for Community Health*. Sudbury, MA: Jones and Bartlett; 2004.

14. Centers for Disease Control and Prevention. Framework for program evaluation in public health. *MMWR*. 1999;48:RR-11.

15. Glasgow RE, Vogt TM, Boles SM. Evaluating the public health impact of health promotion interventions: the RE-AIM framework. *Am J Public Health*. 1999;89:1322–1327.

Public Health Spotlight on Developing a Program Intervention

PART 1: COALITION-BUILDING EXERCISE

You are the director of the Center for Health Promotion, one of the units of the Office of Community Health within the Lincoln State Department of Public Health. Your office is within a few blocks of the state capitol building, which lies in the heart of the city of Jackson Springs, the capital of Lincoln.

Data indicate that the number of deaths in the state attributable to injury continues to be a problem. The fourth leading cause of death in terms of numbers of deaths, injury, accounts for more years of potential life lost before age 65 than any other cause among Lincoln residents each year. Resources in state government are increasingly scarce. To maximize available resources, you convince your agency director that the Injury Coalition should be formed.

The Injury Coalition would be composed of organizational and individual representatives from throughout Lincoln with an interest in injury control and an influence on potentially affected groups of people. Ideally, this broad participation would not only bring diversity of perspective but would also ensure "buy-in" or commitment by involved organizations to project goals as these are developed. The role of the Injury Coalition would be to determine, on the basis of presentations of data concerning the burden of injury in Lincoln, which populations in the state are at greatest risk of death from injuries and how these groups might best be reached with preventive services. The coalition would help develop a statewide injury control plan, set priorities in areas of greatest concern, and determine future interventions. The annual budget allocated to cover planning and other activities of the Injury Coalition is $100,000.

You and your coworkers at the state health department have had some experience setting up and working with coalitions on tobacco control and maternal and child issues in the past. Contact with legislators is not always easy in Lincoln, because of both political and geographic considerations.

DISCUSSION QUESTIONS

(Note: For these questions, respond as if Lincoln were your home state.)

1. Why should the Injury Coalition be formed? What do you see as potential advantages and potential drawbacks of working with a coalition for this purpose?
2. How can you and the state health department build on prior successful involvement with coalitions?
3. What is the ideal size for such a coalition? What factors might help determine size?
4. Who might you invite to coalition meetings? How would you recruit members? What other facts should be considered when planning on coalition membership? Should members represent organizations or participate on the basis of individual leadership in their fields? Should they be agency heads?
5. Are there organizations that you would not like to have represented on the Injury Coalition?
6. Assuming that you decide on developing such a coalition, who should be in charge?
7. Would you choose Lincoln State Department of Public Health staff to serve as coalition members? Why or why not? Should they be in charge of the coalition? Should they staff the coalition?
8. What powers and authorities should be given to the coalition? How might decision making within the coalition take place? What are the advantages and disadvantages of different styles of decision making?
9. What geographic factors particular to Lincoln need to be considered when planning coalition meetings?
10. What can you expect to be the coalition's major expenses? How might these be reduced?
11. How would you evaluate the coalition's effectiveness?

PART 2: PROGRAM DEVELOPMENT

The statewide injury-control initiative has resulted in a newly funded program in the state of Lincoln. In the meantime, you have taken a new position with the planning unit of the largest LHD in the state. Now your task is to complete the following activities related to program development and evaluation. These call for you to develop an appropriate intervention by formulating a problem statement, analyzing the problem for its determinants and contributing factors, establishing outcome, impact and process objectives, developing a work plan and budget, and designing an evaluation strategy. An executive summary is also required. The completed exhibits (or equivalents) will help you to organize your thinking as you develop the problem statement, desired outcome objective, problem analysis, objective setting, work plan, and evaluation plan. The executive summary will effectively communicate the rationale and arguments for your proposal.

You have been staffing a citywide planning group that has proposed priorities for the city's Health Improvement Plan at the request of the mayor. The priority setting process has progressed well and priorities have been defined. To that end, the mayor and city council have assured an appropriation of $1,000,000 for the next fiscal year to begin an intervention program for "Health Problem X." (Each group will select the health problem that it will address. Consider a health problem identified as a priority in the Module 5 Exercise or some other health problem that you believe is important.) The overall goal is to reduce mortality and morbidity caused by Health Problem X in the City. All of the available resources are to be directed toward this goal.

Task A: State the Health Problem and the Desired Outcome Objective

You should identify and access whatever information and data you believe is necessary for you to be able to

- Characterize the current state of the art for control of Health Problem X
- Develop a carefully designed problem statement that includes the magnitude and extent of the problem, the population at risk, and pertinent trends
- Determine the resources available to address the problem and any additional resources that might be needed
- Develop a desired outcome objective for the health problem

Tasks B and C: Develop an Intervention Strategy and Impact Objectives

After completing the following activities, record your work in a suitable format.

- Analyze Health Problem X in terms of the factors most amenable to intervention.
- Identify the two most important determinants, and for each, two major contributing factors.
- After completion, this logic model should describe potential pathways through which mortality from injury X can be reduced. Record your two determinants and their contributing factors in a

suitable format. (Refer back to Chapter 2 for a description and illustration of this approach.)

- Develop an intervention strategy that would address one or both determinants for the health problem. To do so, select one determinant and its associated contributing factors for which to develop an impact objective and at least two process objectives. Consider the state of the art and available resources in developing your objectives. Record your impact objective and the two process objectives.
- Examine the projected impact objective and the associated process objectives. On the basis of these objectives, evaluate the desired outcome objective and modify it as needed to develop the expected outcome objective. Record the expected outcome objective.

Task D: Develop a Work Plan

After completing the following activity, develop a summary of the work plan to achieve each process objective in a suitable format. For each of the process objectives identified previously here, specify the major tasks (activities) that must be performed by program personnel to achieve the objective, such that

- The tasks are in logical sequence and will lead to the achievement of the process objective
- The person(s) or position(s) generally responsible for each task is identified
- Necessary deadlines are specified
- The budget of $1,000,000 is not exceeded

Task E: Develop an Evaluation Strategy

Prepare a summary report of the evaluation plan as part of your report, addressing questions such as these: "What is the evidence that this intervention approach will really work?" and "How will we know that this valid approach is really working in this situation?"

- Describe how you will evaluate each of the following: activities, process objectives, impact objective, and outcome objective. For each evaluation process include information on items to be measured or counted, sources of information, and periodicity of monitoring.
- Assume that you achieve all of your process objectives and that your outcome objective is 80% achieved and 40% achieved. Discuss the appropriate actions based on these evaluation scenarios.

Task F: Develop an Executive Summary

You may develop your Executive Summary in any way that you choose, but it should summarize the problem (why is this important?), the approach (what will be accomplished?), and how progress and success will be tracked. The Executive Summary should be developed in a format suitable for submission to the health committee of the city council and should be brief (suggested length for the Executive Summary is about 500 words).

Source: Adapted from Translating Science Into Practice. CDC Case Study; 1991.

Public Health Spotlight on Injury Prevention

The 20th century witnessed a substantial decline in the rate of deaths from motor-vehicle crashes, perhaps the most serious injury threat for much of the 1900s. Motor-vehicle–related injuries remain a significant health problem in the 21st century although other forms of injury, including those related to violence and unintentional overdoses, are now emerging on the national health agenda. This Public Health Spotlight reviews the progress of the 20th century, discusses the status of current efforts, and highlights effective population-based interventions that are needed to achieve the national health objectives for the year 2020.

PUBLIC HEALTH ACHIEVEMENTS IN 20TH CENTURY AMERICA[1]

The reduction of the rate of deaths attributable to motor-vehicle crashes in the United States represents the successful public health response to a great technologic advance of the 20th century—the motorization of America. Six times as many people drive today as in 1925, and the number of motor vehicles in the country has increased 11-fold since then to approximately 215 million.[2] The number of miles traveled in motor vehicles is 10 times higher than in the mid 1920s. Despite this steep increase in motor-vehicle travel, the annual death rate has declined from 18 per 100 million vehicle miles traveled in 1925 to 1.7 per 100 million vehicle miles traveled in 1997—a 90% decrease[2] (Figure 7-11).

Systematic motor-vehicle safety efforts began during the 1960s. In 1960, unintentional injuries caused 93,803 deaths;[2] 41% were associated with motor-vehicle crashes. In 1966, after 5 years of continuously increasing motor-vehicle–related fatality rates, the Highway Safety Act created the National Highway Safety Bureau (NHSB), which later became the National Highway Traffic Safety Administration (NHTSA). The systematic approach to motor-vehicle–related injury prevention began with NHSB's first director, Dr. William Haddon.[3] Haddon, a public health physician, recognized that standard public health methods and epidemiology could be applied to preventing motor-vehicle–related and other injuries. He defined interactions between host (human),

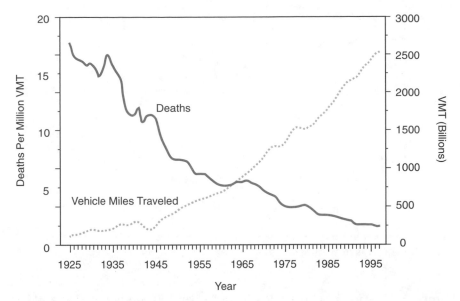

Figure 7-11 Motor vehicle-related death rates per million vehicle miles traveled and annual vehicle miles traveled, by year, United States, 1925 to 1997. *Source:* From Public health achievements, United States, 1900–1999: motor vehicle safety. *MMWR.* 1999;48(18):369–374.

agent (motor vehicle), and environmental (highway) factors before, during, and after crashes resulting in injuries. Tackling problems identified with each factor during each phase of the crash, NHSB initiated a campaign to prevent motor-vehicle–related injuries.

In 1966, passage of the Highway Safety Act and the National Traffic and Motor Vehicle Safety Act authorized the federal government to set and regulate standards for motor vehicles and highways, a mechanism necessary for effective prevention.[3,4] Many changes in both vehicle and highway design followed this mandate. Vehicles (agent of injury) were built with new safety features, including head rests, energy-absorbing steering wheels, shatter-resistant windshields, and safety belts.[4,5] Roads (environment) were improved by better delineation of curves (edge and center line stripes and reflectors), use of breakaway sign and utility poles, improved illumination, addition of barriers separating oncoming traffic lanes, and guardrails.[5,6] The results were rapid. By 1970, motor-vehicle–related death rates were decreasing by both the public health measure (deaths per 100,000 population) and the traffic safety indicator (deaths per vehicle miles traveled) (Figure 7-12).[2]

Changes in driver and passenger (host) behavior also have reduced motor-vehicle crashes and injuries. Enactment and enforcement of traffic safety laws, reinforced by public education, have led to safer behavior choices. Examples include enforcement of laws against driving while intoxicated and underage drinking, and enforcement of safety-belt, child-safety seat, and motorcycle helmet use laws.[6,7]

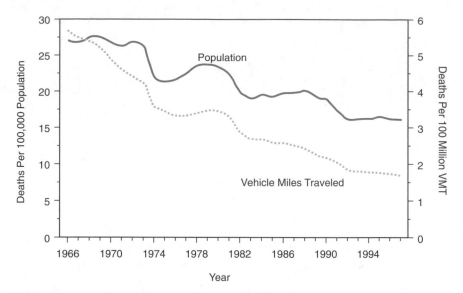

Figure 7-12 Motor vehicle-related deaths per 100,000 population and per 100 million vehicle miles traveled by year, United States, 1996–1997. *Source:* From Public health achievements, United States, 1900–1999: motor vehicle safety. *MMWR.* 1999;48(18):369–374.

Government and community recognition of the need for motor-vehicle safety prompted initiation of programs by federal and state governments, academic institutions, community-based organizations, and industry. NHTSA and the Federal Highway Administration within the U.S. Department of Transportation have provided national leadership for traffic and highway safety efforts since the 1960s.[3] The National Center for Injury Prevention and Control, established at the CDC in 1992, has contributed public health direction.[8,9] State and local governments have enacted and enforced laws that affect motor-vehicle and highway safety, driver licensing and testing, vehicle inspections, and traffic regulations.[3] Preventing motor-vehicle–related injuries has required collaboration among many professional disciplines (e.g., biomechanics has been essential to vehicle design and highway safety features). Citizen and community-based advocacy groups have played important prevention roles in areas such as drinking and driving and child-occupant protection.[7] Consistent with the public/private partnerships that characterize motor-vehicle safety efforts, NHTSA sponsors "Buckle Up America" week, which focuses on the need to always properly secure children in child-safety seats.

High-Risk Populations

Alcohol-Impaired Drivers

Annual motor-vehicle crash-related fatalities involving alcohol have decreased 39% since 1982, to approximately 16,000; these deaths account for 38.6% of all traffic deaths.[10,11] Factors that may have contributed to this decline include increased public awareness of the dangers of drinking and driving; new and tougher state laws; stricter law enforcement; an increase in the minimum legal drinking age; prevention programs that offer alternatives such as safe rides (e.g., taxicabs and public transportation), designated drivers, and responsible alcohol-serving practices; and a decrease in per capita alcohol consumption.[6,7]

Young Drivers and Passengers

Since 1975, motor-vehicle–related fatality rates have decreased 27% for young motor-vehicle occupants (aged 16 to 20 years); however, in 1997 the death rate was 28.3 per 100,000 population—more than twice that of the U.S. population (13.3 per 100,000 population).[10] Teenaged drivers are more likely than older drivers to speed, run red lights, make illegal turns, ride with an intoxicated driver, and drive after drinking alcohol or using drugs.[12] Strategies that have contributed to improved motor-vehicle safety among young drivers include laws restricting purchase of alcohol among underaged youths and some aspects of graduated licensing systems (e.g., nighttime driving restrictions).[7,13]

Pedestrians

From 1975 to 1997, pedestrian fatality rates decreased 41%, from 4 per 100,000 population in 1975 to 2.3 in 1997 but still account for 13% of motor-vehicle–related deaths.[10] Factors that may have reduced pedestrian fatalities include more and better sidewalks, pedestrian paths, playgrounds away from streets, one-way traffic flow, and restricted on-street parking.[7]

Occupant-Protection Systems

Safety Belts

In response to legislation, highly visible law enforcement, and public education, rates of safety belt use nationwide have increased from approximately 11% in 1981 to 68% in 1997.[9] Safety belt use began to increase after enactment of the first state mandatory-use laws in 1984.[7] All states except New Hampshire now have safety-belt use laws. Primary laws (which allow police to stop vehicles simply because occupants are not wearing safety belts) are more effective than secondary laws (which require that a vehicle be stopped for some other traffic violation).[7-14] The prevalence of safety belt use after enactment of primary laws increases 1.5 to 4.3 times, and motor-vehicle–related fatality rates decrease 13% to 46%.[14]

Child-Safety and Booster Seats

All states have passed child passenger protection laws, but these vary widely in age and size requirements and the penalties imposed for noncompliance. Child-restraint use in 1996 was 85% for children aged less than 1 year and 60% for children aged 1 to 4 years.[15] Since 1975, deaths among children aged less than 5 years have decreased 30% to 3.1 per 100,000 population, but rates for age groups 5 to 15 years have declined by only 11% to 13%.[10] Child seats are misused by as many as 80% of users.[16–18] In addition, parents fail to recognize the need for booster seats for children who are too large for child seats but not large enough to be safely restrained in an adult lap-shoulder belt.[19]

21st Century Public Health Challenges

Despite the great success in reducing motor-vehicle–related death rates, motor-vehicle crashes remain the leading cause of injury-related deaths in the United States, accounting for 31% of all such deaths in 1996. Furthermore, motor-vehicle–related injuries led all causes for deaths among persons aged 1 to 24 years. In 1997, motor-vehicle crashes resulted in 41,967 deaths (16 per 100,000 population), 3.4 million nonfatal injuries (1,270 per 100,000 population),[10] and 23.9 million vehicles in crashes; cost estimates are $200 billion.[2]

The challenge for the 21st century is to sustain and improve motor-vehicle safety. Future success will require augmentation of the public health approach to (1) expand surveillance to better monitor nonfatal injuries, detect new problems, and set priorities; (2) direct research to emerging and priority problems; (3) implement the most effective programs and policies; and (4) strengthen interagency, multidisciplinary partnerships. Key public health activities will be to

- Continue efforts shown to reduce alcohol-impaired driving and related fatalities and injuries
- Promote strategies such as graduated licensing that discourage teenage drinking and other risky driving behaviors such as speeding and encourage safety belt use
- Enhance pedestrian safety, especially for children and the elderly, through engineering solutions that reduce exposure to traffic and permit crossing streets safely and by encouraging safer pedestrian behaviors, such as crossing streets at intersections, and increasing visibility to drivers and driver awareness of pedestrians
- Accommodate the mobility needs of persons aged greater than 65 years—a population that will almost double to 65 million by 2030—through a combination of alternative modes of transportation (e.g., walking and better public transportation) and development of strategies to reduce driving hazards[7,20]
- Encourage the 30% of the population who do not wear safety belts to use them routinely
- Encourage proper use of age-appropriate child-safety seats and booster seats, especially for older children who have outgrown their child seats but are too small for adult lap-shoulder belts
- Conduct biomechanics research to better understand the causes of nonfatal disabling injuries, in particular brain and spinal cord injuries, as a foundation for prevention strategies

- Develop a comprehensive public health surveillance system at the federal, state, and local levels that track fatal and nonfatal motor-vehicle-related injuries and other injuries and diseases (i.e., outpatient and emergency department visits, hospitalizations, disabilities, and deaths) as a basis for setting prevention and research priorities

Declines in deaths and injuries related to motor vehicle use now allow for increased attention to be placed on other causes of injury-related deaths. Figure 7-13 tracks the three leading causes of injury deaths from 1979 to 2006 and suggests that injuries related to firearms and poisonings now rival those related to motor vehicle use.

Figure 7-14 provides even more recent trends for deaths due to the leading causes of unintentional injury. Motorcycles, poisonings, and falls appear to be the major injury prevention challenges of the new century.

An interesting sidelight of the emergence of unintentional poisonings as a public health problem is illustrated in Figure 7-15. Many studies suggest that the increased mortality rates caused by unintentional poisoning were primarily because of deaths associated with prescription opioid analgesics (such as oxycodone) and increasing numbers of over-doses of cocaine and prescription sedatives rather than to heroin, amphetamines, and other illegal drugs. In contrast to conventional wisdom, however, the recent increases in prescription drug poisoning mortality appear to be higher in rural communities.

Improved emergency medical services and hospital trauma care may not greatly impact mortality from injuries. For example, as illustrated in Figure 7-16, nearly two thirds of all injury deaths occur outside of a hospital, including 75% of deaths from poisoning or firearm-related injuries and 60% of motor-vehicle–related fatalities. These findings underscore the potential and importance of population-based prevention strategies.

The systematic reviews by the U.S. Task Force on Community Preventive Services (*Community Guide*) assessed the effectiveness of population-based interventions to reduce motor vehicle occupant injuries and prevent violence focused on children and youth.[21] More than a dozen interventions are recommended; others lack sufficient evidence.

The task force identified a number of effective interventions for preventing motor-vehicle–related injuries through strategies that promote child safety seat and general seat belt use and that reduce injuries associated with alcohol-impaired driving. Effective for promoting use of child safety seats are laws mandating their use, community-wide information and enhanced enforcement campaigns, distribution and education programs, and incentive and education programs. Recommended as effective interventions for use of safety belts are laws mandating their use, enhanced enforcement programs and primary (as opposed to secondary) enforcement laws. Interventions found to be effective in reducing motor-vehicle–related injuries associated with alcohol-impaired driving are: 0.08% blood alcohol concentration laws, lower blood alcohol concentration laws for young or inexperienced drivers, maintaining current

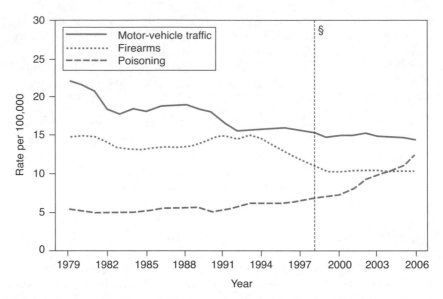

Figure 7-13 Age-adjusted death rates per 100,000 population* for the three leading causes of injury† death, United States, 1979–2006.

* Age-adjusted to the 2000 U.S. standard population.

† Injuries are from all manners, including unintentional, suicide, homicide, undetermined intent, legal intervention, and operations of war. Poisoning deaths include those resulting from drug overdose, those resulting from other misuse of drugs, and those associated with solid or liquid biologic substances, gases or vapors, or other substances such as pesticides or unspecified chemicals.

§ In 1999, *International Classification of Diseases, 10th Revision* (ICD-10) replaced the previous revision of the ICD (ICD-9). This resulted in approximately 5% fewer deaths being classified as motor-vehicle traffic–related deaths and 2% more deaths being classified as poisoning-related deaths. Therefore, death rates for 1998 and earlier are not directly comparable with those computed after 1998. Little change was observed in the classification of firearm-related deaths from ICD-9 to ICD-10.

Sources: From Centers for Disease Control and Prevention. Age-adjusted death rates per 100,000 population for the three leading causes of injury death, United States, 1979–2006. *MMWR.* 2009;58(24):675. Data from National Vital Statistics System, mortality data, http://www.cdc.gov/nchs/deaths.htm (for 2006 rates). Accessed CDC WONDER, compressed mortality file, underlying cause-of-death. http://wonder.cdc.gov/mortsql.html (for 1979–2005 rates). Accessed May 31, 2010.

minimum legal drinking age laws, sobriety checkpoints, intervention training programs for servers of alcoholic beverages, mass media campaigns, ignition interlocks, and multicomponent interventions with community mobilization. The task force also recommends school-based instructional programs to reduce riding with alcohol-impaired drivers but found insufficient evidence to determine whether these programs reduce alcohol-impaired driving or alcohol-related crashes.

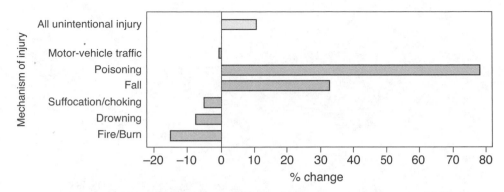

Figure 7-14 Percentage change in death rates for leading causes of unintentional injury, by mechanism of injury, United States, 1999–2005. *Source:* From Centers for Disease Control and Prevention. Percentage change in death rates for leading causes of unintentional injury, by mechanism of injury, United States, 1999–2005. *MMWR.* 2008;57(25):701. Data from National Vital Statistics System (NVSS), 1999–2005. NVSS injury mortality data are available from CDC's Web-Based Injury Statistics Query and Reporting System (WISQARS) at http://www.cdc.gov/ncipc/wisqars. Accessed May 31, 2010.

Recommended as effective interventions for violence prevention focused on children and youth are early childhood home visitation programs to prevent child maltreatment, cognitive-behavioral therapy for individuals and groups after traumatic events, school-based programs to reduce violence, and therapeutic foster care for delinquent juveniles. Notably there was insufficient evidence to support firearms laws and strong evidence against youth transfer to adult criminal courts.

The Healthy People 2010 process also took aim on the injury problem in the United States and included it as one of its leading health indicators. The midcourse review of all objectives in 2005 found little progress toward the motor-vehicle injury indicator and negative movement with respect to the violence indicator. Figure 7-17 demonstrates that only about one-half of the improvement expected for motor vehicle and suicide death rates between the years 2000 and 2010 had been achieved by 2008.

Will 21st century injury prevention strategies necessary to counter the complex factors associated with poisonings and firearms be as successful as those from the 20th century were with motor-vehicle risks? Only time will tell. Nevertheless, progress appears slow toward achieving targets established for injury prevention as one of the leading indicators in the Healthy People 2010 and 2020 efforts.

REFERENCES

1. Reprinted in part and adapted from Centers for Disease Control and Prevention. Achievements in public health, United States 1900–1999: motor vehicle safety. *MMWR.* 1999;48:369–374.

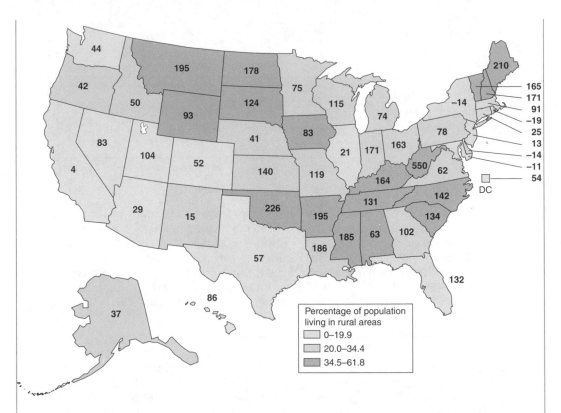

Figure 7-15   Percentage change in unintentional poisoning rates by rural status of state—United States, 1999–2004.

Note: Age-adjusted rates per 100,000 population. Rural status defined as the percentage of the population living in census blocks below a certain population density based on U.S. Census data for 2000.

Source: From Centers for Disease Control and Prevention. Unintentional poisoning deaths, United States, 1999–2004. *MMWR.* 2007;56(05):93–96.

2. National Safety Council. *Accident Facts.* 1998 edition. Itasca, IL: National Safety Council; 1998.

3. Committee on Injury Prevention and Control, Institute of Medicine. *Reducing the Burden of Injury: Advancing Prevention and Treatment.* Washington, DC: National Academy Press; 1999.

4. Transportation Research Board. *Safety Research for a Changing Highway Environment.* Special report no. 229. Washington, DC: National Research Council, Transportation Research Board; 1990.

5. Rice DP, MacKenzie EJ, Jones AS, et al. *The Cost of Injury in the United States: A Report to Congress.* San Francisco, CA: University of California, Institute of Health and Aging; Johns Hopkins University, Injury Prevention Center; 1989.

6. Centers for Disease Control and Prevention/National Highway Traffic Safety Administration. Position papers from the Third National Injury Control Conference: setting the national agenda for injury control in the 1990s. Washington, DC: U.S. Department of Health and Human Services, Public Health Service, Centers for Disease Control; 1992.

7. Graham JD. Injuries from traffic crashes: meeting the challenge. *Annu Rev Public Health.* 1993;14:515–543.

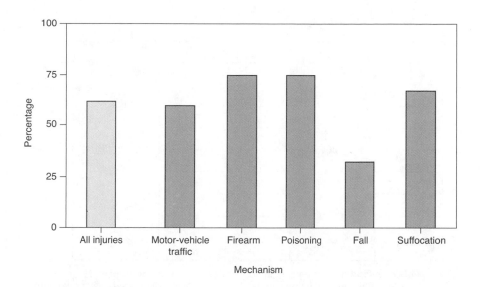

Figure 7-16 Percentage of injury deaths* for which death was pronounced outside of a hospital,[†] by leading mechanisms of injury death,[§] United States, 2005.

* Includes deaths from unintentional injuries, suicides, homicides, deaths of undetermined intent, and deaths attributed to legal intervention.

[†] Includes deaths pronounced in homes, in hospice facilities, in nursing homes, on arrival to hospital, and in other places outside of a hospital, clinic, emergency department, or medical center. Place of death was not specified for 0.5% of all injury deaths; these were excluded from the percentage calculations.

[§] Mechanisms are mutually exclusive.

Source: From Centers for Disease Control and Prevention. Percentage of injury deaths for which death was pronounced outside of a hospital, by leading mechanisms of injury death, United States, 2005. *MMWR*. 2008;57(41):1130. Data from National Vital Statistics System, mortality data (based on death certificate information), 2005. http://www.cdc.gov/nchs/about/major/dvs/vitalstatsonline.htm. Accessed May 31, 2010.

8. Sleet DA, Bonzo S, Branche C. An overview of the National Center for Injury Prevention and Control at the Centers for Disease Control and Prevention. *Injury Prevent.* 1998;4:308–312.

9. National Center for Injury Prevention and Control, Centers for Disease Control. *Prevention of Motor Vehicle-Related Injuries: A Compendium of Articles From the Morbidity and Mortality Weekly Report, 1985–1996.* Atlanta, GA: U.S. Department of Health and Human Services, Centers for Disease Control; 1997.

10. National Highway Traffic Safety Administration. *Traffic Safety Facts, 1997.* Washington, DC: Department of Transportation, National Highway Traffic Safety Administration; 1998.

11. Centers for Disease Control and Prevention. Alcohol involvement in fatal motor-vehicle crashes—United States, 1996–1997. *MMWR.* 1998;47:1055–1063.

12. Hingson R, Howland J. Promoting safety in adolescents. In: Millstein SG, Petersen AC, Nightingale EO, eds. *Promoting the Health of Adolescents: New Directions for the 21st Century.* New York, NY: Oxford University Press; 1993.

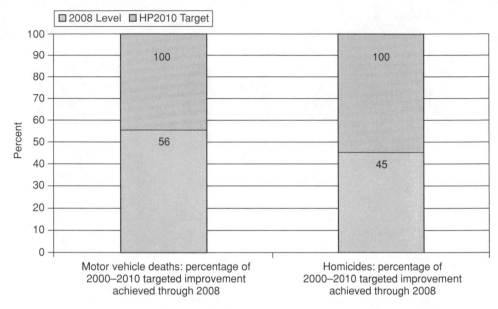

Figure 7-17   Scorecard for selected Healthy People 2010 leading indicators for injury comparing 2008 levels with 2010 targets. *Source:* Data from Data 2010, Healthy People 2010 database. http://wonder.cdc.gov/data2010/ftpselec.htm. Accessed May 31, 2010.

13. Foss RD, Evenson KR. Effectiveness of graduated driver licensing in reducing motor vehicle crashes. *Am J Prev Med.* 1999;16(1 suppl):47–56.

14. Rivara FP, Thompson DC, Cummings P. Effectiveness of primary and secondary enforced seat belt laws. *Am J Prev Med.* 1999;16(1 suppl):30–39.

15. National Highway Traffic Safety Administration. *Research Note. National Occupant Protection Use Survey, 1996—Controlled Intersection Study.* Washington, DC: U.S. Department of Transportation, National Highway Traffic Safety Administration; August 1997.

16. National Highway Traffic Safety Administration. *NHTSA Traffic Tech Note No. 133, Observed Patterns of Misuse of Child Safety Seats.* Washington, DC: U.S. Department of Transportation, National Highway Traffic Safety Administration; September 1996.

17. Centers for Disease Control and Prevention. Improper use of child safety seats—Kentucky, 1996. *MMWR.* 1998;47:541–544.

18. Taft CH, Mickalide AD, Taft AR. *Child Passengers at Risk in America: A National Study of Car Seat Misuse.* Washington, DC: National Safe Kids Campaign; 1999.

19. Centers for Disease Control and Prevention. National Child Passenger Safety Week—February 14–20, 1999. *MMWR.* 1999;48:83–84.

20. Transportation Research Board. *Transportation in an Aging Society: Improving Mobility and Safety for Older Persons.* Vol 1. Special report no. 218. Washington, DC: National Research Council, Transportation Research Board; 1988.

21. Task Force on Community Preventive Services. *The Community Guide.* http://www.thecommunityguide.org. Accessed May 31, 2010.

Chapter 8

Public Health Emergency Preparedness and Response

Public health crossed the threshold of a new century as an admittedly important but poorly understood contributor to the American way of life. Despite its contributions to population health status and quality of life throughout the 20th century, the visibility and economic valuation of public health activities remained low. This situation changed rapidly after the terrorist attacks on the World Trade Center and Pentagon on September 11, 2001, and the bioterrorism events spreading anthrax through the U.S. postal system the following month. The nation responded quickly in the aftermath of these events, elevating international terrorism, bioterrorism preparedness, and emergency response to the top of the national agenda. Within months, more than $2 billion was made available to federal, state, and local health departments (LHDs) for emergency preparedness and response activities, with additional funding allocated annually thereafter. This explosion of attention, resources, and expectations typifies the history of public health in America—a dramatic health-related event spotlights a largely neglected public health infrastructure followed by rapid infusion of resources to resuscitate the system.

This chapter describes the decisions made and actions taken to enhance public health emergency preparedness, as well as some of the successes, failures, and lessons encountered along the way. The intent is to initiate a dialogue as to whether public health preparedness is destined to become one of the great public health achievements in 21st century America. In the process, this chapter focuses on several key questions:

- What is public health preparedness?
- What are the key components of preparedness?
- Is the public health system currently prepared?
- What is needed to become better prepared?

PUBLIC HEALTH ROLES IN EMERGENCY PREPAREDNESS AND RESPONSE

Chapter 1 introduces and Chapter 5 explicates a framework for modern public health responses organized around six major functions[1]:

- Preventing epidemics and the spread of disease
- Protecting against environmental hazards
- Preventing injuries
- Promoting and encouraging healthy behaviors
- Responding to disasters and assisting communities in recovery
- Ensuring the quality and accessibility of health services

Although only one of these functions explicitly refers to public health's role in responding to emergencies, all six drive the public health approach to emergency preparedness and response. Public health emergency preparedness and response efforts seek to prevent epidemics and the spread of disease, protect against environmental hazards, prevent injuries, promote healthy behaviors, and ensure the quality and accessibility of health services. Each of these is expected by the public and each is evident in effective preparedness and response related to public health emergencies. Together they make preparedness and response a special and particularly critical component of modern public health practice.

For public health emergencies, preparedness and response are inextricably linked.[2] Preparedness is based on lessons learned from both actual and simulated response situations. Effective response is all but impossible without extensive planning and thoughtful preparation. Public health roles in health-related emergencies illustrate both facets.

Public Health Surveillance

Many public health emergencies are readily apparent, but others may not manifest themselves immediately. Effective preparedness and response rely on monitoring disease patterns, investigating individual case reports, and using epidemiologic and laboratory analyses to target public health intervention strategies. For example, food-borne illness outbreaks may involve individuals who remain in the same location after being exposed, making it easier to identify a common exposure pattern when these individuals seek medical care. Alternatively, an exposure at a convention or family reunion is more difficult to detect because individuals may present for medical care far from the location of exposure. Whether within the same community or in distant locations, it is often difficult for individual medical practitioners to recognize that an outbreak or widespread epidemic is occurring. Prompt recognition and reporting of cases to health authorities is a critical link in the public health chain of protection. New approaches to public health surveillance include syndromic surveillance and biosurveillance, which involve the early detection of abnormal disease patterns through the use of early disease indicators, such as pharmaceutical sales, school and work absenteeism, and animal disease events. Multiple large data sets can be mined and analyzed for nontraditional markers of disease, which can lead to more rapid detection and response efforts.

Epidemiologic Investigation and Analysis

After a disease event is reported, public health agencies can uncover unusual patterns that help identify outbreaks and continuing risks. Public health professionals may use sophisticated analytic tools, such as pattern recognition software and geographic information systems, to determine patterns in disease cases. These surveillance activities help to ensure that disease outbreaks are identified quickly and that appropriate response actions, such as the issuance of health alerts for area providers and communication with response partners, are initiated. Many current disease surveillance systems act in a passive manner (i.e., they rely on providers to initiate disease reports); however, public health agencies are increasingly using active surveillance activities, such as when public health workers proactively seek information from providers and other sources to monitor disease trends. In the event of an actual or threatened public health emergency, active surveillance activities are deployed and/or expanded.

Surveillance activities trigger more extensive and focused epidemiologic investigations in order to determine the identity, source, and modes of transmission of disease agents. Epidemiologic investigations seek to determine what is causing the disease, how the disease is spreading, and who is at risk. Answers to these questions inform efforts to mount rapid and effective interventions. Methods of obtaining epidemiologic information, often characterized as disease detective activities, include contacting patients, obtaining detailed information on location and types of possible exposures, and examining both clinical specimens (such as blood and urine) and environmental samplings (such as food, water, air, and soil). Epidemiologic investigations require trained personnel and, in many cases, are quite human resource intensive in terms of the quantity and quality of manpower needed. Laboratory capacity to support these investigations is critical.

Laboratory Investigation and Analysis

In many situations, laboratories provide the definitive identification of causative agents, both biologic and chemical, and through various fingerprinting activities link cases to a common source. Capabilities to identify rare or unusual diseases are often not present in every community, necessitating linkages with higher-level laboratories. Specimens may be sent for analysis and confirmation to a regional or state public health laboratory or possibly even to a Centers for Disease Control and Prevention (CDC) reference laboratory. Some specialized capabilities found at these higher level laboratories include serotyping to determine the antigenic profile of a microorganism and DNA fingerprinting to not only identify the type of microorganism causing an infectious disease but to also pinpoint the particular strain of bacterium or virus involved. In this way, public health authorities can determine whether reported disease cases are part of the same outbreak and therefore linked to a common source. Public health laboratories must rely on specialized protective laboratory equipment and facilities because of the dangerous agents with which they work. Some agents, such as smallpox, require special biocontainment equipment and procedures; laboratories are rated in terms of the level of safety they can provide.

Intervention

The primary reason for collecting, analyzing, and sharing information on disease is to control the spread of that disease. Expending resources for surveillance and analysis makes little sense if actions do not follow. Interventions that protect individuals from risks associated with environmental hazards are many, including setting standards for health and safety, inspecting food production and importation facilities, monitoring environmental conditions, abating conditions that foster infectious disease (e.g., insect and animal control), and enforcing private-sector compliance with established standards. Disease and injury risks associated with these biologic and chemical hazards, whether naturally occurring or initiated by man, are reduced through rigorous monitoring and enforcement activities. Public health agencies also play a substantial role in remediation of environmental hazards by decontaminating sites and facilities after they are identified. The extent of remediation necessary can vary greatly, just as the nature and extent of the contamination varies with different disease agents and their ability to remain viable outside a human host or animal/insect vector.

Risk Communication

Epidemiologic and laboratory investigations drive the initiation of actions intended to limit the spread of disease and to prevent additional cases in the community. The range of possible actions can be quite broad, including restraining the activities of individuals through isolation and quarantine and imposing temporary or permanent barriers around sources of contamination (e.g., sealing buildings, closing restaurants, and cutting off water supplies). In severe and unusual circumstances, special emergency powers may be put into effect limiting human and animal travel and/or restricting certain types of business activity. In these situations, the importance of effective public education and information activities to communicate risk to the public cannot be overstated. Commonly encountered examples include notices to boil drinking water when contaminated water supplies are suspected and product recalls and food safety advisories for potentially contaminated food products. The dissemination of information on mail handling practices during the anthrax attacks in late 2001 served both public education and risk communication purposes.

Promoting and encouraging healthy behaviors during public health emergencies represents another public health intervention strategy. It is not uncommon in the event of a natural disaster or terrorist attack for the most devastating effects to take the form of social disruption and infrastructure damage. The psychological effects of fear and terror, together with disruption of infrastructure components such as electricity, water, and safe housing, may create more casualties than any initial terrorist's biologic or chemical assault. Such conditions can also foster toxicity and infectious disease threats, such as occurred with the mass evacuation of the area around the World Trade Center leading to the abandonment of food supplies in surrounding homes and restaurants. Public health officials in New York City took steps to secure these premises to avoid the proliferation of rodents and other pests that otherwise could have resulted in secondary health threats.

Preparedness Planning

Organizing responses to emergencies is another public health role that ensures the availability and accessibility of medical and mental health services. Preparedness and planning cannot eliminate all biologic, chemical, radiation, and mass casualty threats, but coordinated, community-wide planning for emergency medical and public health responses ensures that emergency medical services and medical treatment services are deployed in a rapid and effective manner. Such planning foresees the need for public health measures to be activated in order to ensure the safety of responders and to prevent secondary effects caused by further disease transmission and injury risk. Planning for these coordinated responses includes monitoring available response resources, establishing action protocols, simulating emergency events to improve readiness, training public and private sector personnel, assessing communication capabilities, supplies, and resources, and maintaining relationships with partner organizations to improve coordination.

Figure 8-1 News media ad in early 2002 promoting public health infrastructure as a front line defense against bioterrorism. *Source:* From Health Track Coalition, 2002.

Community-Wide Response

Public health agencies play an important, but not exclusive, role in community-wide responses to emergencies (Figure 8-1). In many response situations, private sector medical care providers deliver the bulk of the triage and treatment services needed when a mass casualty emergency occurs. Although less involved with direct care, public health agencies play key roles in coordinating and overseeing the delivery of services as well as communicating with providers, the media, and the public. Supervision of decontamination and triage often falls to public health authorities. Countermeasures such as antibiotics, antitoxins, and chemical antidotes as well as prophylactic medications and vaccines must be obtained, deployed, and delivered. Public health plays an active role in situations necessitating deployment of Strategic National Stockpile (SNS) pharmaceuticals, supplies, and equipment. In some situations, public health professionals also provide direct medical care. Public health also contributes through mobilization of regional and national assets and resources when local resources are overwhelmed. Some emergency situations, such as the anthrax attacks of 2001, prompted public fear and overreactions resulting in mountains of unknown powdery substances being tested and thousands of individuals unnecessarily initiating prophylactic antibiotic treatments. That situation and others over recent years argue that the worried well can stress response systems even more than those actually affected.

Unique Aspects of Bioterrorism Emergencies

Across the spectrum of possible public health emergency scenarios, bioterrorism threats represent a particularly challenging form of public health emergency. Bioterrorism is the threatened or intentional release of biologic agents (viruses, bacteria, or their toxins) for the purpose of influencing the conduct of government or intimidating or coercing a civilian population to further political or social objectives. These agents (Tables 8-1 and 8-2) can be released by way of the air (as aerosols), food, water, or insects.

Biologic agents with bioterrorism potential in category A are organisms that pose a risk to national security because of several factors. These organisms can be easily disseminated or transmitted from person to person and they result in high mortality rates and have the potential for major public health impact. In addition, these organisms are likely to cause public panic and social disruption, thereby requiring special action for public health preparedness. Category B agents are the second highest priority organisms. These are moderately easy to disseminate, result in moderate morbidity rates and low mortality rates, and require specific enhancements of the CDC's diagnostic capacity and enhanced disease surveillance. The third highest priority agents fall into category C and include emerging pathogens that could be engineered for mass dissemination in the future because of availability, ease of produc-

Table 8-1 Biologic Agents with Bioterrorism Potential

Category A
- Anthrax (*Bacillus anthracis*)
- Botulism (*Clostridium botulinum* toxin)
- Plague (*Yersinia pestis*)
- Smallpox (variola major)
- Tularemia (*Francisella tularensis*)
- Viral hemorrhagic fevers (filoviruses [e.g., Ebola, Marburg] and arenaviruses [e.g., Lassa, Machupo])

Category B
- Brucellosis (*Brucella* species)
- Epsilon toxin of *Clostridium perfringens*
- Food safety threats (e.g., *Salmonella* species, *Escherichia coli* O157:H7, *Shigella*)
- Glanders (Burkholderia mallei)
- Melioidosis (*Burkholderia pseudomallei*)
- Psittacosis (*Chlamydia psittaci*)
- Q fever (*Coxiella burnetii*)
- Ricin toxin from *Ricinus communis* (castor beans)
- Staphylococcal enterotoxin B
- Typhus fever (*Rickettsia prowazekii*)
- Viral encephalitis (alpha viruses [e.g., Venezuelan equine encephalitis, eastern equine encephalitis, western equine encephalitis])
- Water safety threats (e.g., *Vibrio cholerae*, *Cryptosporidium parvum*)

Category C
- Emerging infectious diseases such as Nipah virus and hantavirus

Source: Data from Centers for Disease Control and Prevention. Bioterrorism Agents/Diseases. http://www.bt.cdc.gov/agent/agentlist-category.asp. Accessed June 14, 2010.

Table 8-2   Chemical Agents with Bioterrorism Potential

Biotoxins—Poisons that come from plants or animals
- Abrin
- Brevetoxin
- Colchicine
- Digitalis
- Nicotine
- Ricin
- Saxitoxin
- Strychnine
- Tetrodotoxin
- Trichothecene

Blister Agents/Vesicants—Chemicals that severely blister the eyes, respiratory tract, and skin on contact
- Distilled mustard (HD)
- Mustard gas (H) (sulfur mustard)
- Mustard/lewisite (HL)
- Mustard/T
- Nitrogen mustard (HN-1, HN-2, HN-3)
- Sesqui mustard
- Sulfur mustard (H) (mustard gas)
- Lewisite (L, L-1, L-2, L-3)
- Mustard/lewisite (HL)
- Phosgene oxime (CX)

Blood Agents—Poisons that affect the body by being absorbed into the blood
- Arsine (SA)
- Carbon monoxide
- Cyanogen chloride (CK)
- Hydrogen cyanide (AC)
- Potassium cyanide (KCN)
- Sodium cyanide (NaCN)
- Sodium monofluoroacetate (compound 1080)

Caustics (Acids)—Chemicals that burn or corrode people's skin, eyes, and mucous membranes (lining of the nose, mouth, throat, and lungs) on contact
- Hydrofluoric acid (hydrogen fluoride)

Choking/Lung/Pulmonary Agents—Chemicals that cause severe irritation or swelling of the respiratory tract (lining of the nose, throat, and lungs)
- Ammonia
- Bromine (CA)
- Chlorine (CL)
- Hydrogen chloride
- Methyl bromide
- Methyl isocyanate
- Osmium tetroxide
- Diphosgene (DP)
- Phosgene (CG)
- Phosphine
- Phosphorus, elemental, white or yellow
- Sulfuryl fluoride

(continues)

Table 8-2   Chemical Agents with Bioterrorism Potential (continued)

Incapacitating Agents—Drugs that make people unable to think clearly or that cause an altered state of consciousness (possibly unconsciousness)
* BZ
* Fentanyls and other opioids

Long-Acting Anticoagulants—Poisons that prevent blood from clotting properly, which can lead to uncontrolled bleeding
* Super warfarin

Metals—Agents that consist of metallic poisons
* Arsenic
* Barium
* Mercury
* Thallium

Nerve Agents—Highly poisonous chemicals that work by preventing the nervous system from working properly
* Sarin (GB)
* Soman (GD)
* Tabun (GA)
* VX

Organic Solvents Agents that damage the tissues of living things by dissolving fats and oils
* Benzene

Riot Control Agents/Tear Gas—Highly irritating agents normally used by law enforcement for crowd control or by individuals for protection (e.g., mace)
* Bromobenzylcyanide (CA)
* Chloroacetophenone (CN)
* Chlorobenzylidenemalononitrile (CS)
* Chloropicrin (PS)
* Dibenzoxazepine (CR)

Toxic Alcohols—Poisonous alcohols that can damage the heart, kidneys, and nervous system
* Ethylene glycol

Vomiting Agents—Chemicals that cause nausea and vomiting
* Adamsite (DM)

Source: Data from Centers for Disease Control and Prevention. Chemical Agents. http://www.bt.cdc.gov/agent/agentlistchem.asp. Accessed June 14, 2010.

tion and dissemination, and potential for high morbidity and mortality rates with major public health impact.

Biologic, chemical, radiation, and mass casualty threats that are intentionally inflicted differ from naturally occurring disease and injury threats in a number of important aspects. Central to these differences, bioterrorism is a criminal act requiring its prevention and response to include criminal justice, military, and intelligence agencies that are not likely to be familiar with naturally occurring disease outbreaks. Law enforcement agencies, including the Federal Bureau of Investigation, have lead responsibility for responding to a bioterrorism attack. In addition, bioterrorism attacks may involve disease agents that occur infrequently in nature and with which neither public health officials nor clinicians have had much experience. It is increasingly possible to engineer chimeras genetically to create, for example, microorganisms that blend the pathogenic qualities of multiple disease agents. Because such organisms do not exist in nature, they would be completely unknown to public health and medical experts. Attacks related to biologic or chemical threats initiated by a bioterrorist would not likely follow known epidemiologic patterns, diminishing the value of using past experience with disease transmission and manifestation to identify the source or cause.

It is likely that bioterrorists would seek to be covert, expending great energy and attention to ensure the delayed discovery of the disease to maximize the population's exposure. The time lines and pathways for the anthrax attacks of September and October 2001 illustrated in Figures 8-2 and 8-3 chronicle a recent example of a covert bioterrorist operation. Intentional outbreaks may develop in multiple locations simultaneously, thereby straining local, state, and federal response efforts. With many emerging and reemerging infectious disease threats (e.g., Ebola Virus, Sudden Acute Respiratory Syndrome, West Nile Virus, hantavirus), it is increasingly difficult to predict the precise nature of the next public health emergency. It could result from a chance mutation of a microorganism or it could result from the intentional act of terrorists. Multiple threats are possible, necessitating preparedness and response systems that can address a wide variety of unknown and unanticipated hazards. This concept of multiple threats and unknown hazards has led many experts to advocate for a robust public health infrastructure capable of responding to many different forms of emergencies.

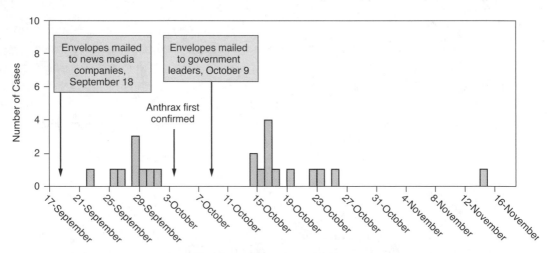

Figure 8-2 Epidemic curve for 22 cases of bioterrorism-related anthrax, United States, 2001. *Source:* From Jernigan DB, Raghunathan PL, Bell BP, et al. Investigation of bioterrorism-related anthrax, United States, 2001: epidemiologic findings. *Emerging Infectious Diseases.* 2002;8(10): 1019–1028.

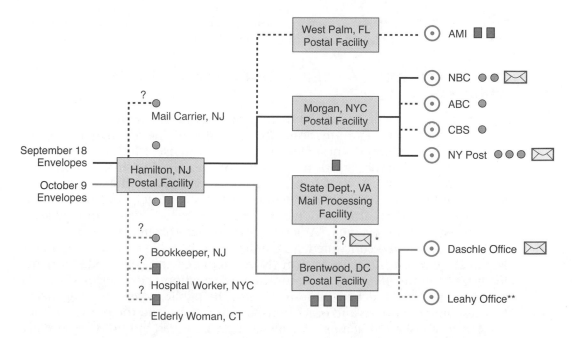

Figure 8-3 Cases of anthrax associated with mailed paths of implicated envelopes and intended target sites, United States, 2001

Notes: NBC = National Broadcasting Company; AMI = American Media Inc.; CBS = Columbia Broadcasting System. Envelope addressed to Senator Leahy, found unopened on November 16, 2001, in a barrel of unopened mail sent to Capitol Hill; **dotted line indicates intended path of envelope to Senator Leahy; shaded circle = cutaneous case; shaded rectangle = inhalational case; circle with central dot = intended target; envelope = recovery site of implicated envelope.

Source: From Jernigan DB, Raghunathan PL, Bell BP, et al. Investigation of bioterrorism-related anthrax, United States, 2001: epidemiologic findings. *Emerging Infectious Diseases.* 2002;8(10): 1019–1028.

Workplace Preparedness

Public health emergencies, including those related to terrorism, have many different visages and many different venues. Nevertheless, most of the direct victims of terrorism in the United States in recent years have been people at work, including the victims of the bombing of the federal building in Oklahoma City, those who died in the World Trade Center and the Pentagon on September 11, 2001, and the victims who contracted anthrax transmitted through the mail later in that same year.

Acts of terrorism intend to make people feel powerless and believe that they cannot take steps to prevent such incidents or mitigate their consequences, but experience to date in battling other workplace safety risks suggests that there are steps that can be taken by employers and employees. The workplace is, in effect, a key line of defense for homeland security. This is recognized formally in the formation and scope of responsibilities for the new federal Department of

Homeland Security (DHS) as well as in the response of the business community after 2001 in taking tangible steps to enhance security.

NATIONAL PUBLIC HEALTH PREPAREDNESS AND RESPONSE COORDINATION

The terrorist events of late 2001 initiated a series of new national policies and priorities to safeguard American citizens at home. The first major development was the creation of a new federal DHS with extensive authority and powers related to domestic terrorism and security. In accord with the Homeland Security Act of 2002, several important public health functions were transferred into the new DHS in 2003, including the SNS of emergency pharmaceutical supplies and medical equipment. This new federal agency immediately became part of the everyday American experience through the color-coded national homeland security alert system described in Table 8-3. In 2011, a new National Terrorism Advisory System (NTAS) replaced the color-coded scheme in order to more effectively communicate information about terrorist threats by providing timely, detailed information to the public, government agencies, first responders, airports and other transportation hubs, and the private sector.

The establishment of a new federal agency, however, did not substantially alter the configuration of homeland safety and public health responsibilities within the system of operational federalism described in Chapter 4. Federal agencies are significant contributors, but public health and safety remain largely a state responsibility, with the bulk of public health activity taking place at the local level. For public health emergencies, including natural disasters such as Hurricane Katrina in 2005 and bioterrorism events or threats, preparedness and coordinated response across all levels of government are critical. Nonetheless, there are significant issues related to intergovernmental relationships, resource deployment, and financing that make public health emergencies especially difficult challenges. The following sections examine key aspects of the structure, operations, and problems in public health emergency preparedness and response at the national, state, and local levels.

Federal Agencies and Assets

More than 20 separate federal departments and agencies play important roles in preparing for or responding to public health emergencies, including bioterrorist attacks. Within this constellation of agencies, the Department of Health and Human Services (DHHS) and the DHS play the most important public health roles.

Before 2003, the DHHS was the primary federal agency responsible for the medical and public health response to emergencies (including major disasters and terrorist events). Beginning in 2003, the DHHS now shares center stage with the new DHS. The DHHS discharges its responsibilities through several operating agencies, including the following:

- CDC: The CDC works with state public health agencies to detect, investigate, and prevent the spread of disease in communities. The CDC provides

Table 8-3   Homeland Security Advisory System: 2002–2011

1. Low Condition (Green)
   This condition is declared when there is a low risk of terrorist attacks. Federal departments and agencies should consider the following general measures in addition to agency-specific protective measures they develop and implement.
   - Refining and exercising as appropriate preplanned protective measures
   - Ensuring personnel receive proper training on the Homeland Security Advisory System and specific preplanned department or agency protective measures
   - Institutionalizing a process to ensure that all facilities and regulated sectors are regularly assessed for vulnerabilities to terrorist attacks and that all reasonable measures are taken to mitigate these vulnerabilities

2. Guarded Condition (Blue)
   This condition is declared when there is a general risk of terrorist attacks. In addition to the protective measures taken in the previous threat condition, federal departments and agencies should consider the following general measures in addition to the agency specific protective measures that they will develop and implement.
   - Checking communications with designated emergency response or command locations
   - Reviewing and updating emergency response procedures
   - Providing the public with any information that would strengthen its ability to act appropriately

3. Elevated Condition (Yellow)
   An elevated condition is declared when there is a significant risk of terrorist attacks. In addition to the protective measures taken in the previous threat condition, federal departments and agencies should consider the following general measures in addition to the agency-specific protective measures that they will develop and implement.
   - Increasing surveillance of critical locations
   - Coordinating emergency plans as appropriate with nearby jurisdictions
   - Assessing whether the precise characteristics of the threat require the further refinement of preplanned protective measures
   - Implementing, as appropriate, contingency and emergency response plans

4. High Condition (Orange)
   A high condition is declared when there is a high risk of terrorist attacks. In addition to the protective measures taken in the previous threat condition, federal departments and agencies should consider the following general measures in addition to the agency-specific protective measures that they will develop and implement.
   - Coordinating necessary security efforts with federal, state, and local law enforcement agencies or any National Guard or other appropriate armed forces organizations
   - Taking additional precautions at public events and possibly considering alternative venues or even cancellation
   - Preparing to execute contingency procedures, such as moving to an alternate site or dispersing their workforce
   - Restricting threatened facility access to essential personnel only

5. Severe Condition (Red)
   A severe condition reflects a severe risk of terrorist attacks. Under most circumstances, the protective measures for a severe condition are not intended to be sustained for substantial periods of time. In addition to the protective measures taken in the previous threat

(continues)

Table 8-3   Homeland Security Advisory System: 2002–2011 (continued)

condition, federal departments and agencies should consider the following general measures in addition to the agency-specific protective measures that they will develop and implement.
- Increasing or redirecting personnel to address critical emergency needs
- Assigning emergency response personnel and prepositioning and mobilizing specially trained teams or resources
- Monitoring, redirecting, or constraining transportation systems
- Closing public and government facilities

Source: From U.S. Department of Homeland Security. Homeland Security Advisory System. Washington, DC: DHS; 2003.

support to state public health agencies in a variety of ways, including financial assistance, training programs, technical assistance and expert consultation, sophisticated laboratory services, research activities, and standards development. The Office of Public Health Preparedness and Response coordinates efforts across the various CDC centers and institutes.
- Health Resources and Services Administration (HRSA): The HRSA administers a state grant program to facilitate regional hospital preparedness planning and to upgrade the capacity of hospitals and other healthcare facilities to respond to public health emergencies. The HRSA is also generally responsible for healthcare workforce development, including grant programs for curriculum development and continuing education for health professionals on bioterrorism preparedness and response.
- Food and Drug Administration (FDA): The FDA has responsibilities both for ensuring the safety of the food supply and for ensuring the safety and efficacy of pharmaceuticals, biologics, and medical devices. The FDA fulfills its food safety responsibilities in partnership with the Department of Agriculture, which is responsible for the safety of meat, poultry, and processed egg products.
- National Institutes of Health (NIH): The NIH conducts and supports biomedical research, including research targeted at the development of rapid diagnostics and new and more effective vaccines and antimicrobial therapies.
- Office of Preparedness and Response within DHHS: Under the Assistant Secretary for Preparedness and Response, this office sets policy direction and coordinates public health emergency preparedness and response activities across the various DHHS agencies and with international agencies and organizations. In addition this office oversees the advanced development and procurement of countermeasures and manages the SNS.

In March 2003, 23 federal agencies, programs, and offices were fashioned into the new federal DHS. The new agency sought to bring a coordinated approach to national security from emergencies and disasters, both natural and man-made. The DHS actively promotes an "all-hazards" approach to disasters

Table 8-4   Robert T. Stafford Disaster Relief and Emergency Assistance Act

The Congress hereby finds and declares that (1) because disasters often cause loss of life, human suffering, loss of income, and property loss and damage and (2) because disasters often disrupt the normal functioning of governments and communities and adversely affect individuals and families with great severity, special measures, designed to assist the efforts of the affected states in expediting the rendering of aid, assistance, and emergency services, and the reconstruction and rehabilitation of devastated areas, are necessary.

It is the intent of Congress, by this act, to provide an orderly and continuing means of assistance by the Federal Government to state and local governments in carrying out their responsibilities to alleviate the suffering and damage which result from such disasters by—

1. Revising and broadening the scope of existing disaster relief programs
2. Encouraging the development of comprehensive disaster preparedness and assistance plans, programs, capabilities, and organizations by the states and by local government
3. Achieving greater coordination and responsiveness of disaster preparedness and relief programs
4. Encouraging individuals, states, and local governments to protect themselves by obtaining insurance coverage to supplement or replace governmental assistance
5. Encouraging hazard mitigation measures to reduce losses from disasters, including development of land use and construction regulations
6. Providing Federal assistance programs for both public and private losses sustained in disasters

Source. P.L. 93–228, as amended.

and homeland security issues. The Federal Emergency Management Agency (FEMA), formerly an independent agency, became one of the major branches of the new DHS responsible for emergency preparedness and response, tasked with responding to, planning for, recovering from, and mitigating against disasters under authority provided by the Stafford Act (Table 8-4).

Within the DHS, the Emergency Preparedness and Response Directorate coordinates emergency medical response in the event of a public health emergency, including the Metropolitan Medical Response Systems (MMRSs) (described later in this chapter). Other major directorates (divisions) of the new DHS include Border and Transportation Security, Science and Technology, Information Analysis and Infrastructure Protection, and Management. Within the DHS, the chief medical officer has primary responsibility for medical issues related to natural and man-made disasters and terrorism. In the aftermath of Hurricane Katrina, the Pandemic and All Hazards Preparedness Act (PAHPA) of 2006 clarified the roles and responsibilities of the DHS and DHHS. Several programs, including the National Disaster Medical System (NDMS), were moved from the DHS to the DHHS.

Other federal agencies also carry out important responsibilities related to bioterrorism and public health emergency preparedness. The Environmental Protection Agency responds to emergencies involving chemicals and other hazardous substances. The Department of Defense indirectly supports public health preparedness through various research efforts on biologic and chemical weapons, intelligence gathering related to terrorism threats, and civil support functions in the event of an emergency that results in severe social unrest. The Department of Justice has lead responsibility for assessing and investigating terrorist threats, including those related to bioterrorism, and provides funds and assistance to emergency responders (police, fire, ambulance, and rescue personnel) at state and local levels. The Department of Veterans Affairs purchases drugs and other therapeutics for the SNS and operates one of the nation's largest healthcare systems, which could provide critical surge capacity in the event of a mass casualty event. Several other federal agencies, including the Departments of Transportation, Commerce, and Energy, also have potential roles to play in preparing for and responding to a public health emergency.

National Incident Management System and National Response Plan

Before the establishment of the new DHS, the management of large-scale health events was complicated by the involvement of so many different federal agencies. States have established a similar web of agencies to manage disasters and other emergencies, with each developing its own form of an incident management system. In order to ensure greater consistency across states and for interfaces between the federal government and states, a National Incident Management System (NIMS) was prescribed by a presidential directive in 2003 to cover all incidents (natural and unnatural) for which the federal government deploys emergency response assets. The Secretary of Homeland Security is responsible for the development and implementation of NIMS. Its success depends in large part on the establishment of consistent approaches within the states as to roles and responsibilities for both public health agencies and the hospital community (including their supporting healthcare systems) in managing emergencies at the state and regional levels and developing and deploying incident management plans at substate levels.

Bioterrorism and other public health incidents fall within the scope of NIMS. To this end, the DHHS has the initial lead responsibility for the federal government and deploys assets as needed within the areas of its statutory responsibility (such as the Public Health Service Act and the Federal Food, Drug, and Cosmetic Act) while keeping the Secretary of Homeland Security apprised regarding the course of the incident and nature of the response operations.

Although NIMS is used for all events; the National Response Plan (NRP) is implemented for incidents requiring federal coordination. The NRP is another key provision of the Homeland Security Act of 2002 and Homeland Security Presidential Directive 5. The purpose of the NRP is to align federal coordinating, structures, capabilities, and resources into a unified, all-discipline, and all-hazards approach to domestic incident management. It is based on the premise that incidents are typically managed at the lowest possible geographic, organizational, and jurisdictional level. The NRP does not alter or impede the ability of federal agencies to carry out their specific authorities under applicable laws, executive orders, and directives. It establishes the coordinating structures, processes, and protocols required to integrate the specific statutory and policy authorities of various federal departments and agencies in a collective framework for action to include prevention, preparedness, response, and recovery activities. The NRP distinguishes between events that require the secretary of the DHS to manage the federal response for incidents of national significance and the majority of incidents occurring each year that are handled by responsible jurisdictions or avenues through other established authorities and existing plans.

Under the NRP, the DHS assumes responsibility for coordinating federal response operations, including those involving public health components, under certain conditions. The DHS coordinates the federal government's resources utilized in response to or recovery from terrorist attacks, major disasters, or other emergencies if and when any of the following four conditions applies[3]:

- A federal department or agency acting under its own authority has requested the assistance
- The resources of state and local authorities are overwhelmed and federal assistance has been formally requested by state and local authorities
- More than one federal department or agency has become substantially involved in responding to the incident
- The DHS has been directed to assume responsibility for managing the domestic incident by the President

For states and local governments to gain full benefit from the emergency response assets of the federal government, states must develop incident management systems that are interoperable with NIMS. Beginning in 2004, adherence to and compatibility with NIMS became a condition of all grants and other awards from federal agencies for any aspect of state or local emergency preparedness and response. NRP compliance was required as well after 2006.

The PAHPA of December 2006 reauthorized and restructured key components of public health preparedness and response efforts in the DHS and the DHHS. PAHPA also addressed lessons learned from the flawed federal response to Hurricane Katrina and growing concerns over a possible global flu pandemic. Central to the restructuring of federal roles and responsibilities was the establishment of a National Health Security Strategy for public health emergency preparedness and response, including a full assessment of federal, state, and local public health and medical capabilities. Key elements of the National Health Security Strategy in PAHPA focused on the following:

- Public health workforce enhancements, including revitalization of the Commissioned Corps and loan repayment programs to increase the number of public health professionals working in shortage areas
- Vaccine tracking and distribution to improve effective distribution of seasonal flu vaccine supplies
- Enhanced all-hazards medical surge capacity through use of mobile medical assets and federal facilities during emergencies, expanding the Medical Reserve Corps and establishing a single nationwide network of systems for the purpose of advance registration of volunteer health professionals

- Biomedical research and development for vaccines and drugs to combat pandemic flu emergencies
- Grants to state and local government to improve detection and response capabilities for pandemic flu

Federal Emergency Medical Assets

Several national emergency response assets are available to state and local governments through the DHS and the DHHS. These include the NDMS, the MMRS, and the SNS.

The NDMS now operates within the Office of Emergency Preparedness and Response within DHHS. When the DHS was initially created, NDMS moved from the Office of the Secretary of DHHS into DHS. After Hurricane Katrina, it was moved back to DHHS. NDMS brings together medical services from DHHS, DHS, Defense, and Veterans Affairs to augment local emergency medical services during a disaster or other large-scale emergency. The NDMS has several operational components, including Disaster Medical Assistance Teams (DMATs), Disaster Mortuary Teams (DMORTs), Federal Coordinating Centers, and Management Support Units.

DMATs are self-sustaining squads of licensed, actively practicing, volunteer professional and paraprofessional medical personnel who provide emergency medical care at the site of a disaster or other emergency. DMAT teams often triage, stabilize, and prepare patients for evacuation in mass casualty situations. They are sent into these situations to supplement, rather than supplant or replace, local capacity. Once activated, these professionals are federalized, allowing them to practice with their current professional licenses in any jurisdiction. DMORTs include mortuary, dental, and forensic specialists who serve to augment the services of local coroners and medical examiners. Portable temporary mortuaries for mass casualty situations are provided when needed. Management support units provide command, coordination, and communication capabilities for DMATs and DMORTs and other federal assets. Federal Coordinating Centers recruit hospitals to participate in the NDMS and recruit health workers for the DMATs and DMORTs.

The MMRS, involving more than 100 metropolitan communities, integrates existing emergency response systems at the local level, including emergency management, medical and mental health providers, public health agencies, law enforcement, fire departments, emergency medical services, and the National Guard. The MMRS seeks to develop a unified regional response to mass casualty events. The MMRS was transferred from DHHS when the new DHS was established in 2003.

The SNS ensures the availability and rapid deployment of life-saving pharmaceuticals, antidotes, other medical supplies, and equipment necessary to counter the effects of nerve agents, biologic pathogens, and chemical agents. The SNS stands ready for immediate deployment to any U.S. location in the event of a terrorist attack using a biologic toxin or chemical agent directed against a civilian population. In the event of possible bioterrorist attack, a 12-hour push package containing 50 tons of stockpile materials can be immediately dispatched to predetermined Receipt, Store, and Storage sites identified in state bioterrorism response plans. There are twelve 12-hour push packages centrally located around the United States for immediate deployment. Detailed deployment activities for SNS materials are prescribed in state and local emergency response plans.

Project BioShield represents another federal asset, one that includes private sector interests that develop drugs, vaccines, and other countermeasures that may be deployed in an emergency. In Project BioShield, the DHS coordinates a strategic plan to encourage the development of chemical, biologic, radiological, and nuclear countermeasures that otherwise would lack commercial markets.

Federal Funding for Public Health Infrastructure

Although multiple agencies provide federal funding for emergency preparedness, federal support for the public health infrastructure at the state and local levels is provided largely from grants and cooperative agreements with the CDC. In 1999, for the first time, the CDC awarded more than $40 million for bioterrorism preparedness to states and cities for enhanced laboratory and electronic communication capacity and another $32 million to establish a national pharmaceutical stockpile to ensure availability of vaccines, prophylactic medicines, chemical antidotes, medical supplies, and equipment needed to support a medical response to a biologic or chemical terrorist incident. At the time, these appeared to be large sums. In the wake of September 11, 2001, and the anthrax attacks the following month, increased concerns regarding homeland security led to a $2.1 billion FY 2002 appropriation for the CDC's antiterrorism activities, over a 20-fold increase from FY 1999 levels. The FY 2002 supplemental appropriations provided $917 million for grants to states and localities to upgrade state and local capacity. Roughly similar levels of funding have been provided in subsequent years. The state and local activities impacted by this funding are described in later sections of this chapter.

STATE AND LOCAL PREPAREDNESS COORDINATION

State Agencies and Assets

Similar to the federal pattern, states rely on a variety of agencies to deliver public health emergency services. Also, similar to the federal model, these functions tend to be concentrated within a limited number of agencies at the state level, with the state health department and state emergency management agency playing the most significant roles. As described in Chapter 4, most state health departments are freestanding agencies (not part of a larger human services agency), and most have responsibility for emergency medical service systems within the state; however, most states have an environmental health agency that is separate from the state health agency. Although these states may have a small environmental health section within the health agency, the environmental health agency is charged with monitoring environmental contaminants and remediation of hazardous conditions. Nearly all states have a separate emergency management agency (patterned after FEMA), although some states have established their own Departments of Homeland Security. In responding to a public health emergency, the state health agency works collaboratively with the state emergency management agency as well as with the state environmental protection, law enforcement, public safety, and transportation agencies and possibly the National Guard.

States derive their powers and authority to act in public health emergencies from their public health laws as described in Chapter 4. There are concerns that existing public health laws may be inadequate in some states because they are obsolete and fragmented. A Model Public Health Emergency Powers Act has been used to assist states in examining and enhancing their legal framework for public health emergencies. The model act addresses key issues related to preparedness, surveillance, protection of persons, management of property, and public information and communications.[4]

Considerable differences exist among states in the breadth and depth of services provided within their jurisdictions and the degree to which public health service delivery responsibilities are delegated to local governments. In general, however, state governments are ultimately responsible for ensuring adequate response to a public health emergency and tend to play certain key roles in preparedness and response, regardless of how decentralized a particular public health system might be. Except in the largest metropolitan local public health departments, local public health officials rely on state personnel and capacity for a number of key functions, including advanced laboratory capacity, epidemiologic expertise, and serving as a conduit for federal assistance.

States maintain an agreement whereby one or more states can provide resources, equipment, services, and other needed support to another state during an emergency incident. This mutual aid agreement, the Emergency Management Assistance Compact (EMAC), covers licensing, credentialing, workers compensation and reimbursement, allowing personnel to focus on the emergency at hand. EMAC personnel integrate into the existing structures of the requesting state. Of the more than 65,000 personnel deployed to Louisiana, Mississippi, and Alabama for Hurricanes Katrina and Rita in 2005, nearly 4,000 were health and medical personnel.

Incident Command Systems

In order to manage resources effectively and facilitate decision making during emergencies, Incident Command Systems (ICSs) are in wide use by police, fire, and emergency management agencies. Initially adopted for the fire service, an ICS eliminates many common problems related to communication, terminology, organizational structure, span of control, and other differences across different disciplines and agencies in response to a critical incident. Critical incidents include any natural or man-made event, civil disturbance, or any other occurrence of unusual or severe nature that threatens to cause or actually causes the loss of life or injury to citizens and/or severe damage to property.

In managing critical incidents, clear goals and objectives are established and communicated to responders, response plans are used, communications are effective, and resources are used in a timely and effective manner. The

ICS should not be considered an additional set of procedures; rather, the system must become part of routine operations, with personnel fully trained in its use and standard operating procedures reflective of the capabilities actually available.

One important key to effective ICS is the ability to size up the incident scene and make the initial call for resources. This allows responders to get control of the incident rather than playing catch-up for the rest of the incident. Appropriate initial sizeup prevents unnecessary injury or loss of life, property or environmental damage, and negative perceptions on the responding agencies.

Key components of ICS include the following:

- Common terminology—Major organizational functions and units are named; in multiple incidents, each incident is named. Common names are used for personnel, equipment, and facilities. Clear terms are used in radio transmissions (e.g., codes, such as "10" codes, are not used).
- Modular organization—An ICS develops "top down" from the first unit involved based on the specific incident's management needs. Each ICS is staffed with a designated incident commander (responsible for safety, liaison, and information) with other functions (operations, planning, logistics, finance/administration) staffed as needed.
- Integrated communications—An ICS uses a common communications plan and redundant two-way communications.
- A unified command structure—This is necessary when the incident is within a single jurisdiction with multiple agencies involved, or the incident is multijurisdictional, or individuals representing different agencies or jurisdictions share common responsibilities. All agencies involved contribute to the unified command process by determining overall goals and objectives, planning jointly for tactical activities, conducting integrated tactical operations, and maximizing the use of assigned resources.
- Consolidated action plans—Written action plans are necessary when the incident is complex and/or when several agencies and/or jurisdictions are involved. Action plans include specific goals, objectives, and support activities.
- A manageable span of control—The number of subordinates one supervisor can manage effectively should be between three and seven, with five being optimal.
- Designated incident facilities—These include the command post from which all incident operations, direction, control, coordination, and resource management are directed. Command posts can be fixed or mobile but need adequate communications capabilities.
- Comprehensive resource management—This maximizes resource use, consolidates control, reduces communications load, provides accountability, and reduces freelancing.

The emergency management team generally functions from the emergency operations center (EOC), managing strategic decisions through the incident command structure. Ideally, the team should be isolated from the confusion, media, and weather during the incident. EOC participants must have adequate authority and decision-making capability. EOC decisions could include issuing curfews, circumventing normal bidding processes, emergency appointments, permanent or temporary relocation, emergency demolition of unsafe properties, or implementation of prophylaxis to populations. The EOC is supported operationally by incident command posts in the field, which are responsible for tactical decisions as well as oversight and command of responders at the scene.

Effective emergency operations plans and standard operating procedures simplify decision making during incidents. Training makes implementation of decisions easier for subordinates. When the level of preparation and practice exercises is inadequate, emergency operations plans can become overwhelmed by common incidents and unable to deal with those that are not fully anticipated. In such circumstances, decision making becomes complex and challenging. A comprehensively planned and frequently exercised organizational system is necessary to overcome these pitfalls.

As an ICS has become increasingly accepted as an effective framework for responding to incidents, its use has extended to other settings. For example, there has been much progress in development and deployment of hospital emergency ICSs and tabletop exercises for hospitals. Several states have expanded on the ICS concept to develop standardized emergency management systems that formally incorporate ICS, mutual aid agreements, and multijurisdictional and interagency cooperation at the substate level, resulting in coordinated and unified decisions throughout the state.

Local Agencies and Assets

The front line of response to public health emergencies is at the local level, where LHDs work collaboratively with other "first responders," such as fire and rescue personnel, emergency medical service providers, law enforcement officers, hazardous materials teams, physicians, and hospitals in preparing for and managing the consequences of health-related emergencies. Although the relationships between state and LHDs vary greatly from state to state and even from local jurisdiction to local jurisdiction within the same state, local government has significant responsibilities for dealing with emergencies in virtually all states. First responders play key roles in the following:

- Recognizing public health emergencies, including those that result from terrorist attacks
- Identifying unique personal safety implications associated with the emergency situation
- Identifying security issues that are unique to the event or to the emergency medical system response
- Understanding basic principles of patient care based upon the type of emergency event encountered

Focusing on the services most directly related to emergency preparedness and response, the vast majority of LHDs carry out activities related to epidemiology and surveillance, communicable disease control, food safety, and restaurant inspections.[5] Only about one fourth of LHDs are involved in emergency responses each year. Relatively few LHDs are responsible for laboratory services or have responsibility for air quality, animal control, or water inspections.[5]

In those cases in which the LHD is not responsible for these services, they are typically delivered by another local government agency (e.g., a fire department or environmental services agency), a private agency (hospital or ambulance service), or the state. Even when services are offered by an LHD, they may be quite limited in terms of scope or hours of availability. For example, although nearly one third of LHDs report providing laboratory services, these services may be quite limited in nature (e.g., to support testing for tuberculosis and sexually transmitted diseases). Many LHDs that report having laboratory services are likely to rely on state public health labs for more specialized diagnostic needs.

The state of readiness among LHDs has increased substantially since 2001, when only approximately one fourth of local public health agencies (LHPAs) had completed a comprehensive emergency response plan with another one fourth indicating their plans were at least 80% complete. LHDs have tailored the national threat advisory guidelines for public health emergencies. In general, LHD threat advisory guidelines describe a spectrum of activities that range from planning through implementation. The activities that are undertaken at each threat level of the national homeland security advisory system used prior to 2011 are summarized in Table 8-5 and roughly equate to the preparedness and response concepts listed here:

- Low threat (green)—creating, developing, identifying
- General threat (blue)—reviewing, updating, distributing
- Significant threat (yellow)—evaluating, testing, verifying
- High threat (orange)—preparing to implement and implementing partially
- Severe threat (red)—fully implementing

Deployment of LHD staff to assist in emergencies is limited by the size and qualifications of the agency's workforce. More than one half of all LHDs have 20 or fewer staff members.[5] Larger agencies generally have much higher staffing levels and a more comprehensive range of expertise, as was described in Chapters 4 and 6.

The configuration of LHPAs within a state or in a multistate metropolitan area also varies across the country. Several states organize local public health activities at a regional or district level. Other states have virtually hundreds of LHPAs that serve towns or townships, some in counties or districts served by a larger LHPA. Some communities have no LHD at all. Organizing preparedness and response efforts in these different circumstances presents special problems in terms of multijurisdictional response, surge capacity, backup, and mutual aid agreements. Increasingly, public health emergency preparedness planning is occurring at the regional level, involving multiple LHPAs. Many states have developed mutual aid agreements or compacts involving all LHPAs in the state, sometimes patterned on key components of the EMAC. Several capacity assessment and enhancement tools are available from the National Association of County and City Health Officials and the CDC to assist local assessment of readiness.[6–8]

Table 8-5   Homeland Security Advisory System Guidelines for Local Public Health Agencies

	Key Activities for Each Threat Condition
Emergency planning, training, staffing	Green (Low) • Ensure personnel receive proper training on Homeland Security Advisory and agency protective measures/disaster plans • Ensure employee emergency notification system is current • Develop and train staff on staffing modification plans including 24/7 duty assignments • Train staff on local and state disaster plans • Develop and review roles and responsibilities in an emergency situation for each employee in the agency (all-hazards plan, which includes bioterrorism) Blue (Guarded) • Review and update disaster plans specific to the agency (local health department medication distribution plan, smallpox pre-event and postevent plans) • Provide training to key personnel on handling inquiries from the media Yellow (Elevated) • Coordinate emergency plans with nearby jurisdictions and review mutual aid agreements • Conduct employee emergency notification system drill • Be aware of large-scale community events (e.g., sports, concerts) and include these in emergency planning • Review technical information on chemical and biologic agents with all staff Orange (High) • Prepare to staff the agency's EOC or provide staff at the city/county EOC • Activate the employee emergency notification system and place staff on full alert • Review medication dispensing plans and mass vaccination plans with all staff Red (Severe) • Staff the agency's EOC or provide staff at the city/county EOC • Activate the agency's disaster preparedness plan • Activate the employee emergency notification system and secure as many additional staff as necessary to implement the agency's disaster preparedness plan • Prepare to implement the medication dispensing and mass vaccination plans • Coordinate preparedness and response activities with all public health partners and local jurisdictions (hospitals, physicians, local law enforcement, neighboring local health departments, emergency management agencies, and state health department) • Conduct a comprehensive disaster plan review with all staff to ensure an effective response in the event of a terrorist attack
Communications	Green (Low) • Ensure all emergency communication systems are in operational condition (Health Alert Network, e-mail, fax, and pagers)

(continues)

Table 8-5 Homeland Security Advisory System Guidelines for Local Public Health
Agencies (continued)

	Key Activities for Each Threat Condition
	• Ensure staff have the technical information on chemical and biologic agents necessary to respond to inquiries from the public or the media (fact sheets) • Review procedure/protocol for disseminating information to the community and media during a public health emergency **Blue (Guarded)** • Alert all agency staff that the threat condition has been raised to Guarded (Blue) • Assign a staff person to routinely monitor for faxes, e-mails, and correspondence from the state health agency • Obtain technical information from the state health agency and the Centers for Disease Control and Prevention on biologic and chemical weapons of mass destruction for possible dissemination to healthcare providers and the public **Yellow (Elevated)** • Alert all agency staff that the threat condition has been raised to Elevated (Yellow) • Review media protocols with key personnel • Brief key personnel at least weekly on threat status, changes in security, and potential action plans **Orange (High)** • Alert all agency staff that the threat condition has been raised to High (Orange) • Ensure that all members of the jurisdiction-wide bioterrorism committee are aware that the threat condition has been raised to High (Orange) • Advise staff of shift modifications if the situation escalates • Test all emergency communication systems **Red (Severe)** • Alert all agency staff that the threat condition has been raised to Severe (Red) • Ensure that all members of the jurisdiction-wide bioterrorism committee are aware that the threat condition has been raised to Severe (Red) • Issue periodic news releases with factual information on chemical and biologic agents to reduce the potential for public panic • Brief key personnel daily on threat status, changes in security, and potential action plans • Check all emergency communications equipment on a daily basis
Administration	**Green (Low)** • Maintain routine operations without security stipulations • Continue to include employee safety and common sense practices in daily routines • Report suspicious circumstances and/or individuals to law enforcement agencies • Ensure all staff have issued current security credentials (ID badges) • Build networking relationships with other agencies, inside and outside the health professions

(continues)

Table 8-5 Homeland Security Advisory System Guidelines for Local Public Health Agencies (continued)

	Key Activities for Each Threat Condition
	Blue (Guarded) • Increase liaison with local and state agencies to monitor the threat • Prohibit casual access by unauthorized personnel • Assess mail-handling procedures Yellow (Elevated) • Ensure security of facility operations • Check all essential equipment for operational readiness • Check inventories of critical supplies and reorder if necessary Orange (High) • Ensure security of the agency's critical infrastructure • Have designated staff continuously monitor for emergency communications from state health agency • Have designated staff continuously monitor radio and TV stations for a possible change in threat condition Red (Severe) • Initiate or augment security staffing at department facilities • Control building access and implement positive identification of all persons, including inspection of all incoming packages, briefcases, and deliveries • Maintain continuous monitoring for emergency communications from state health agency, as well as continuous monitoring of radio and TV stations for breaking news concerning terrorist attacks within state or elsewhere in the United States
Public Health Surveillance	Green (Low) • Review agency procedures for handling reportable infectious diseases in the state Blue (Guarded) • Ensure information concerning reportable infectious diseases is coming into the agency from the healthcare providers within the jurisdiction Yellow (Elevated) • Request that hospitals (infectious control nurses and emergency departments), local laboratories, outpatient clinics, managed care organizations, and physicians report significant increases or clusters of illness of unknown etiology and review mandatory reporting procedures Orange (High) • Contact all hospitals (infectious control nurses and emergency departments), local laboratories, outpatient clinics, managed care organizations, and physicians and emphasize the importance of timely reporting of significant increases or clusters of illness of unknown etiology and review mandatory reporting procedures

Source: Data from Illinois Department of Public Health. Homeland Security Advisory System Guidelines for Local Public Health Agencies. Springfield, IL: IDPH; 2003.

Medical Reserve Corps are locally based volunteer response teams that can be deployed in emergency situations. These multidisciplinary teams often have ongoing relationships with LHDs and other community medical care providers that may include volunteer work on health promotion and screening projects or assistance with mosquito control activities in communities where West Nile Virus presents a risk. During emergencies, Medical Reserve Corps teams play predetermined roles such as providing local surge capacity for triage and medical care or assisting with deployment of SNS materials. It is expected that several hundred communities will participate in the Medical Reserve Corps program, either through start-up funding from the HRSA or through local resources.

Private Healthcare Providers and Other Partners

In nearly all communities, government agencies play a central role in preparing for and responding to public health emergencies. Often overlooked, however, is the critical contribution made by private sector healthcare providers, pharmaceutical manufacturers, agricultural producers, the food industry, and other private sector interests. An important example is the role played by alert health professionals who are trained to recognize potential emergency situations and report these suspicions to public health officials. Clinicians in Florida played a major role in first identifying and then linking anthrax cases with bioterrorism in 2001. Hospital emergency rooms and physicians' offices are where most individuals who have contracted an infectious disease or are exposed to dangerous chemicals encounter their community's emergency response system. That encounter should trigger an appropriate response if the condition is one that represents a threat to others. Every state has incorporated requirements in state statutes that call for physicians, laboratories, and other health providers to notify public health officials when specific notifiable diseases or conditions are encountered. Some states include a general provision that physicians should report "unusual" infectious diseases. Despite these laws and regulations, compliance with disease reporting is well documented to be low among physicians for a variety of reasons. The requirements and the reporting procedures may not be understood by some physicians. Others believe reporting is not worth the time and effort. Reporting from laboratories is more complete, but concerns exist as to whether laboratories serving multiple jurisdictions are fully aware of differences in requirements among the jurisdictions served.

In addition to playing an important role in identifying potential public health emergencies, healthcare providers play a critical role in responding to the medical consequences of those emergencies, especially in mass casualty situations. For the relatively rare disease threats associated with bioterrorism, healthcare providers often have only limited experience dealing with these conditions and look to public health authority for clinical guidance. Through the development of community-wide emergency response plans, public health agencies, private sector delivery systems, hospitals, physicians, pharmacies, nursing homes, and others are mobilized in the event of an emergency to provide needed treatment to those affected by disease and to provide prophylactic care to those at risk for exposure to disease. State and federal laws that confer tax-exempt status on hospitals typically require those institutions to provide significant community benefit, including the provision of emergency medical services and participation in regional emergency medical service planning. Funds for hospital preparedness, including staff training and preparedness planning, are provided by the HRSA and channeled through state health departments. Figure 8-4 provides information during 2003 to 2004 on the percentage of hospitals with emergency department staff members with bioterrorism preparedness training for various potential bioterrorism agents.

Other private sector interests also contribute to public health emergency preparedness. Although the NIH makes significant investments in the development of new vaccines and antimicrobial agents, pharmaceutical manufacturers represent the primary source of funding for research and development. Efforts to encourage industry interest in the development of vaccines and other countermeasures include incentives such as liability protections, antitrust waivers, patent extensions, and long-term contracts. Similarly, activi-

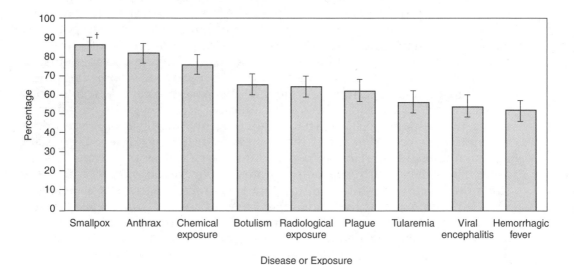

Figure 8-4 Percentage of hospitals with staff members trained to respond to selected terrorism-related diseases or exposures,* National Hospital Ambulatory Medical Care Survey, United States, 2003–2004.

* The staff person responsible for the hospital's emergency response plan for bioterrorism or mass casualties was asked the following question: "Have your hospital staff members received special training (e.g., in-service or other courses, continuing medical education, grand rounds, or self-guided study) since September 11, 2001, in the identification, diagnosis, and treatment of the following diseases/conditions? Smallpox, anthrax, plague, botulism, tularemia, viral hemorrhagic fever, viral encephalitis, chemical exposure, nuclear/radiologic exposure."

† 95% confidence interval.

Source: From Centers for Disease Control and Prevention. Percentage of hospitals with staff members trained to respond to selected terrorism-related diseases or exposures, National Hospital Ambulatory Medical Care Survey, United States, 2003–2004. *MMWR.* 2007;56(16):401.

ties to improve the safety and security of the food supply will rely on the agricultural and food production industries to make necessary upgrades to their processes and to seek innovative ways to minimize disease threats.

Public Perceptions and Expectations

The flurry of activity to improve public health emergency preparedness and response capabilities is understandable. The public is highly concerned over the possibility of terrorist attacks of all types.[9] Fears of possible anthrax or smallpox attacks are nearly as high as concerns of conventional explosives, airline hijacking or bombings, and attacks using radioactive, toxic, or hazardous materials as weapons. Among these potential terrorist weapons, concern is growing that smallpox will be used, related in part to the attention placed on smallpox at the national level with the initiation of smallpox preparedness programs that include vaccinations for key medical and first responder personnel. Although the public believes that the country is better prepared for a biologic or chemical attack than it was before 2002, the public perceives that the current level of preparedness is not high enough and more needs to be done. The public is also concerned that the emphasis on bioterrorism will reduce efforts on other public health problems and issues that are important to the public. The public rates bioterrorism preparedness and response high but no higher than health alerts, immunizations, testing and monitoring for diseases, education, and responses to natural epidemics and chronic diseases.[9]

State and Local Bioterrorism Preparedness Grants

With the public health infrastructure increasingly viewed as a front-line defense against terrorism and homeland security priority, federal funding for public health purposes increased dramatically beginning in 2002. To put this increase into perspective, total governmental spending in 2000 for population-based public health services was $16.7 billion, with the federal government accounting for about 30% of that total, or approximately $5 billion.[10] The federal share of total governmental public health activity spending has been under 30% since the mid-1980s, after having been as high as 44% in 1970.

Beginning in 2002, federal funding increased by more than $2 billion, with about one half of that amount directed to state and local governments for public health infrastructure improvements. Similar levels were funded through 2010 and are expected for at least the next few years. The infusion of this magnitude of resources creates the opportunity to address serious and long-standing gaps in public health protection and foster greater consistency and enhanced quality throughout the national network of governmental public health agencies at the federal, state, and local levels.

Public health infrastructure funding, approximately $1 billion annually, is channeled to the states and several large cities (including New York, Chicago, Los Angeles, and Washington, DC) through the CDC. Each state receives a minimum award of $5 million plus an additional amount based on a population formula.

State Proposals and Work Plans

Activities supported by these funds must be consistent with federal guidance. For funding from the CDC for public health preparedness, grantees must undertake activities that increase capacity in state and LHDs in order to achieve the national preparedness goals identified in Table 8-6.

Key elements of capacity include the following:

- Preparedness planning and readiness assessment—These activities establish strategic leadership, direction, assessment, and coordination of activities (including SNS response) to ensure statewide readiness, interagency collaboration, local and regional preparedness (both intrastate and interstate) for bioterrorism, other outbreaks of infectious disease, and other public health threats and emergencies.

Table 8-6   CDC Preparedness Goals

Goal	Timing	Focus	Intent
1	Preevent	Prevention	Increase the use and development of interventions known to prevent human illness from chemical, biologic, radiological agents, and naturally occurring health threats
2	Preevent	Detection and Reporting	Decrease the time needed to classify health events as terrorism or naturally occurring in partnership with other agencies
3	Preevent	Detection and Reporting	Decrease the time needed to detect and report chemical, biologic, radiological agents in tissue, food, or environmental samples that cause threats to the public's health
4	Preevent	Detection and Reporting	Improve the timeliness and accuracy of information regarding threats to the public's health
5	Event	Investigation	Decrease the time to identify causes, risk factors, and appropriate interventions for those affected by threats to the public's health
6	Event	Control	Decrease the time needed to provide countermeasures and health guidance to those affected by threats to the public's health
7	Postevent	Recover	Decrease the time needed to restore health services and environmental safety to preevent levels
8	Postevent	Recover	Improve the long-term follow-up provided to those affected by threats to the public's health
9	Postevent	Improve	Decrease the time needed to implement recommendations from after-action reports following threats to the public's health

Source: Data from Centers for Disease Control and Prevention. Preparedness Goals. http://www.bt.cdc.gov. Accessed October 10, 2007.

- Surveillance and epidemiology capacity—Surveillance and epidemiologic capacities enable state and LHDs to enhance, design, and develop systems for rapid detection of unusual outbreaks of illness that may be the result of bioterrorism, other outbreaks of infectious disease, and other public health threats and emergencies. These activities assist state and LHDs in establishing expanded epidemiologic capacity to investigate and mitigate such outbreaks of illness as part of a National Electronic Disease Surveillance System (NEDSS). NEDSS is an initiative that promotes the use of data and information system standards to advance the development of efficient, integrated, and interoperable surveillance systems at federal, state, and local levels. NEDSS-based systems can be used by states for the surveillance and analysis of notifiable diseases, providing a platform on which modules can be built to meet state and program area data needs as well as providing a secure, accurate, and efficient way for collecting and processing data.
- Laboratory capacity for biologic agents—These activities ensure that core diagnostic capabilities for bioterrorist agents are available at all state and major city/county public health laboratories in order to conduct rapid and accurate diagnostic and reference testing for select biologic agents likely to be used in a terrorist attack. Given the myriad forms that terrorism might take, emergency preparedness requires not only a variety of different types of analytical laboratories, but also well defined operational relationships among them, especially with respect to routing of samples and sharing of test results. The national Laboratory Referral Network provides this connectivity.
- Laboratory capacity for chemical agents—These activities ensure that all state public health laboratories have the capacity to measure chemical threat agents in human specimens (e.g., blood and urine) or to appropriately collect and ship specimens to qualified Laboratory Referral Network partner laboratories for analysis and further the establishment of a network of public laboratories for analysis of chemical threat agents.
- Health alert network/communications and information technology—Activities for this focus area enable state and LHDs to establish and maintain a network that supports exchange of key information and training over the Internet by linking public health and private partners on a 24/7 basis, provides for rapid dissemination of public health advisories to the news media and the public at large, ensures secure electronic data exchange between public health partners' computer systems, and ensures protection of data, information, and systems, with adequate backup, organization, and surge capacity to respond to bioterrorism and other public health threats and emergencies.
- Health risk communication and health information dissemination—Activities for this focus area ensure that state and local public health organizations develop an effective risk communications capacity that provides for timely information dissemination to citizens during a bioterrorist attack, bioterrorism, outbreak of infectious disease, or other

public health threat and emergency. This includes training for key individuals in communications skills, the identification of key spokespersons (particularly experts in infectious diseases), the development of printed materials, timely reporting of critical information, and effective interaction with the media.

- Education and training—Activities for this focus area ensure that state and local health agencies have the capacity to assess the training needs of key public health professionals, infectious disease specialists, emergency department personnel, and other healthcare (including mental health) providers in preparedness for and response to bioterrorism, other outbreaks of infectious disease, and other public health threats and emergencies and ensure effective provision of needed education and training to key target audiences through multiple channels, including schools of public health, schools of medicine, other academic institutions, healthcare professionals, the CDC, the HRSA, and other sources. Emergency preparedness competencies (Table 8-7) for all public health workers serve as the focal point for these assessment, enhancement, and recognition efforts. A more extensive panel of bioterrorism and emergency readiness competencies for various categories of public health workers is also in wide use.[11]

- Hospital preparedness—Although not a focus area funded by the CDC, hospital preparedness is the primary category of activity supported by HRSA funding to states and large cities. Activities that are supported include development of regional hospital preparedness and response plans; identification of hospital capacity for isolation, quarantine, and decontamination; procedures for receipt and distribution of materials from the SNS; personal protective equipment; communications capabilities; biologic disaster drills; and training.

Several new emphases were injected into guidance for the second and subsequent funding cycles. These included laboratory capacity for chemical agents, integration of mental health services into preparedness planning and response activities, coordination of CDC funding with HRSA-funded hospital preparedness activities, and concurrence of local public health authorities with state spending plans.

In several funding cycles, additional priorities were added, some without additional resources. In 2003, federal guidance incorporated specific smallpox preparedness and response capacities and allowed for costs associated with smallpox preparedness to be covered by grant funds. In 2006, pandemic flu preparedness became a priority with some additional one-time funding provided.

Important issues surfaced in many states during early implementation of bioterrorism preparedness activities. As the cooperative agreement program evolved, the lack of an operational definition of preparedness became apparent. After examining several different approaches, the CDC adopted a panel of performance measures for state and local governments that established clearer performance expectations (Table 8-8).

Table 8-7   Emergency Preparedness Core Competencies for All Public Health Workers

All Public Health Workers must be competent to
- Describe the public health role in emergency response in a range of emergencies that might arise (e.g., "The department provides surveillance, investigation, and public information in disease outbreaks and collaborates with other agencies in geological, environmental, and weather emergencies.")
- Describe the chain of command in emergency response.
- Identify and locate the agency emergency response plan (or the pertinent portion of the plan).
- Describe his or her functional role(s) in emergency response and demonstrate his or her role(s) in regular drills.
- Demonstrate correct use of all communication equipment used for emergency communication (e.g., phone, fax, and radio).
- Describe communication role(s) in emergency response—within the agency using established communication systems, with the media, with the general public, and with personal individuals (family and neighbors).
- Identify limits to own knowledge/skill/authority and identify key system resources for referring matters that exceed these limits.
- Recognize unusual events that might indicate an emergency and describe appropriate action (e.g., communicate clearly within chain of command).
- Apply creative problem solving and flexible thinking to unusual challenges within his/her functional responsibilities and evaluate effectiveness of all actions taken.

Public Health Leaders/Administrators must also be competent to
- Describe the chain of command and management system (Incident Command System) or similar protocol for emergency response in the jurisdiction.
- Communicate the public health information, roles, capacities, and legal authority to all emergency response partners—such as other public health agencies, other health agencies, and other governmental agencies—during planning, drills, and actual emergencies. (This includes contributing to effective community-wide response through leadership, team building, negotiation, and conflict resolution.)
- Maintain regular communication with emergency response partners. (This includes maintaining a current directory of partners and identifying appropriate methods for contacting them in emergencies.)
- Ensure that the agency (or the agency unit) has a written, regularly updated plan for major categories of emergencies that respects the culture of the community and provides for continuity of agency operations.
- Ensure that the agency (or agency unit) regularly practices all parts of emergency response.
- Evaluate every emergency response drill (or actual response) to identify needed internal and external improvements.
- Ensure that knowledge and skill gaps identified through emergency response planning, drills, and evaluation are addressed.

Public Health Professionals must also be competent to
- Demonstrate readiness to apply professional skills to a range of emergency situations during regular drills (e.g., access, use, and interpret surveillance data; access and use laboratory resources; access and use science-based investigation and risk assessment protocols; identify and use appropriate personal protective equipment).
- Maintain regular communication with partner professionals in other agencies involved in emergency response. (This includes contributing to effective community-wide response through leadership, team building, negotiation, and conflict resolution.)
- Participate in continuing education to maintain up-to-date knowledge in areas relevant to emergency response (e.g., emerging infectious diseases, hazardous materials, and diagnostic tests).

(continues)

Table 8-7   Emergency Preparedness Core Competencies for All Public Health Workers (continued)

Public Health Technical and Support Staff must also be competent to
- Demonstrate the use of equipment (including personal protective equipment) and skills associated with his or her functional role in emergency response during regular drills.
- Describe at least one resource for backup support in key areas of responsibility.

Source: Data from Centers for Disease Control and Prevention. Bioterrorism and Emergency Readiness Competencies for All Public Health Workers. http://www.bt.cdc.gov. Accessed October 10, 2007.

Table 8-8   Performance Measures for CDC Public Health Emergency Preparedness Cooperative Agreement

1   Percent of public health employees who have emergency response roles documented in their job descriptions that are trained in incident management.
2   Time to organize a NIMS-compliant medical and public health operations functional area with hospitals that supports:
- Incident epidemiologic profiling
- Prehospital care
- Medical care
- Mental health
- Hazard threat/disease containment
- Mass casualty care
(Target: 3 hours of plan activation)
3   Time from request for mutual aid to acknowledgment that request has been approved.
4   Time to complete the notification/alerting of the initial wave of personnel to staff emergency operations (target: 60 minutes).
5   Time to have initial wave of personnel physically present to staff emergency operations (target: 90 minutes from notification).
6   Time to receive confirmed case reports of immediately notifiable conditions by public health agency (includes Biowatch and BDS).
7   Time for state to notify local or local to notify state of receipt of a suspicious or confirmed case report of an immediately notifiable condition (target: 1 hour from receipt).
8   Time to have a knowledgeable public health professional respond to a disease report call 24/7/365 (target: 15 minutes or less).
9   Percentage of subtyping data submitted to PulseNet within 72 to 96 hours of receiving isolate in the laboratory.
10 Time to recommend public health courses of action to minimize human health threats identified in the jurisdiction's hazard and vulnerability analysis (Target: 60 days from the identification of risk or hazard/120 days from cooperative agreement award).
11 Percent of LRN biologic and chemical laboratories that demonstrate proficiency in
- Confirming category A agents in human clinical specimens
- Confirming category A agents in food samples
- Confirming the identity of and further characterizing Salmonella, Shigella, Shiga toxin-producing *E. coli* and pathogenic vibrios isolated from food samples
- Confirming category A agents in environment samples
- Confirming chemical agents in human clinical specimens
12 Time following initiation of an epidemiologic investigation to begin obtaining or directing the acquisition of specimens/samples for laboratory analysis to support epidemiologic investigation, as needed. (Target: 60 minutes)
13 For clinical specimens, environmental samples and samples of potentially contaminated food collected by public health personnel in an emergency, time to

(continues)

Table 8-8 Performance Measures for CDC Public Health Emergency Preparedness Cooperative Agreement (continued)

- Send clinical specimens to a reference laboratory within the LRN when an incident may involve an infectious biologic agent (target: within 60 minutes of collection)
- Send clinical specimens to the CDC or CDC-designated state laboratory when an incident may involve a hazardous chemical agent (target: within 180 minutes of collection)
- Send environmental samples to a reference laboratory within the LRN when the incident requires biologic or chemical characterization of an incident scene (target: within 60 minutes of collection)
- Send potentially contaminated food samples to a reference laboratory within the LRN or coordinate with Food Emergency Response Network (FERN), as appropriate, when the incident might involve food contaminated with a biologic or chemical agent (target: within 60 minutes of collection)

14 Percentage of local public health agencies using BioSense or other integrated early event detection system data.
15 Percentage of desired nontraditional public health data sources that are currently part of early event detection system (e.g., HMO encounter data, over-the-counter pharmaceutical sales).
16 Time to initiate epidemiologic investigation after the initial detection of a deviation from normal disease/condition patterns.
17 Time from initial detection of a deviation from normal disease/condition patterns or initial report to initiation of intervention (e.g., dissemination of protective action guidance, treatment).
18 Percent of key stakeholders that are notified/alerted using the public health emergency communication system (target: 90%).
19 Time to issue information to the public that emphatically acknowledges the event, explains and informs the public about risk; provides emergency courses of action; commits to continued communication (target: 60 minutes from activation of the response plan).
20 Percent of key stakeholders that are notified/alerted when electricity, telephones, cellular telephone service, and Internet service are unavailable.
21 Percent of level 3/Sentinel labs that can reach a designated contact at an LRN laboratory 24/7/365 by phone within 15 minutes or radio/satellite phone within 5 minutes.
22 Time to obtain message approval and authorization for distribution of public health and medical information to clinicians and other responders (target: 60 minutes from confirmation of health threat).
23 Percent of public health responders that have been trained and cleared to use personal protective equipment appropriate for their response roles.
24 Percentage of isolation orders that are violated.
25 Percentage of quarantine orders that are violated.
26 Current rating on the SNS preparedness functions.
27 Time to provide prophylactic protection and/or immunizations to all responders, including nongovernmental personnel supporting relief efforts.
28 Percentage of volunteers needed to support epidemiologic investigation that has been trained.
29 Percentage of volunteers needed to support mass prophylaxis that has been trained.
30 Time needed to issue interim guidance on risk and protective actions during recovery.
31 Percentage of cases and exposed successfully tracked from identification through disposition to enable short- and long-term follow-up.
32 Time needed to identify deficiencies in personnel, training, equipment, and organizational structure, for areas requiring corrective actions (target: 72 hours after a real event or exercise).
33 Time needed to implement corrective actions (target: 60 days after identification of deficiency).
34 Time needed to retest areas requiring corrective action (target: 90 days after identification of deficiency).

Source: Data from Centers for Disease Control and Prevention. Performance Measures for CDC Public Health Preparedness Cooperative Agreement. http://www.bt.cdc.gov. Accessed October 10, 2007.

Early Lessons

Comprehensive preparedness programs require hazard and vulnerability analyses, forecasts of the probable health effects, analyses of the availability of needed resources, identification of vulnerable populations, and development of detailed plans for both preparedness and response. Many factors influence a state's ability to complete these tasks. Public health preparedness is particularly challenging because public health and public safety roles differ for federal, state, and local governments. The federal government has primary responsibility for national security, whereas state and local governments carry the responsibility and financial burden for most other public health responsibilities. Some of the early lessons from the states reflect these themes.

Preparedness, like public health and politics, is primarily local. In that light, careful attention must be paid to identifying and addressing local needs for public health preparedness and response. Local health officials in many states have raised concerns over the distribution of funding, perceiving that local health jurisdictions should have received more than the share allotted to them. In future years, the proportion of funding shared with local health jurisdictions may need to increase as state level needs are addressed. Some local health jurisdictions would prefer that the CDC directly fund local jurisdictions in a manner similar to what is now done for only a handful of the largest U.S. cities. They argue that political whims at the state level too often result in poor priorities, state money grabs, and inefficient reimbursement mechanisms. States, on the other hand, argue that state control and decision making promotes interoperable equipment, complementary resources across jurisdictions, and avoidance of gaps in coverage. It is not possible to draw conclusions as to the wisdom of separate grants to states and localities within that state. Some differences in approach are apparent for surveillance systems, hospital relationships, and training, but none appear, as yet, to be major. Strong leadership within state and local health agencies should minimize the potential for problems. Furthermore, strong federal leadership and assurance of consistency across jurisdictions could also serve to avert problems; however, federal guidance for interjurisdictional (city–state), multijurisdictional (multistate) regional preparedness has been minimal to date, at least in comparison to that for state-wide and substate regional preparedness. The impact on local public health practice should ultimately be positive as better systems and workforce development advance; however, preparedness competes with other local priorities and may have suffered in recent years because of the need for West Nile Virus- and smallpox-focused activities. Ongoing community health priorities may have fared even worse.

Notable in recent federal guidance for bioterrorism preparedness grants is the requirement for evidence of consensus, approval, or concurrence between state and local public health officials for the proposed use of the funds. States must provide assurance that both state and local capacity development is to be achieved and local public health officials, especially those serving a significant portion of the state's population, concur with the proposed use of funds. The intent of this guidance is to focus more on the benefit that can be achieved rather than the level of government spending the dollars. Whether it will serve to engage state and local public health interests constructively remains to be seen. In states with a long history of collaboration around public health improvement initiatives, it could serve to upset the delicate balance that has evolved over time.

At the local level, public health preparedness must be well coordinated with hospital preparedness. The experience to date suggests that hospitals feel isolated from much of the community-wide planning that is taking place. Nevertheless, hospitals are key players in response to actual events. Lessons from several large-scale national exercises substantiate this concern. Virtually all states have identified a need for exercises and drills (Table 8-9), and there have been a number of national exercises involving the top officials of federal and state government. One of the Public Health Spotlights for this chapter presents an example of a tabletop exercise.

Ideally, the infusion of resources to shore up the sagging public health infrastructure would foster positive structural changes in public health systems at the state and local level. The early evidence supports this contention.

Table 8-9   Types of Emergency Exercises

Exercise	Activities that can be undertaken by an agency or group of agencies to test their readiness to respond to emergencies or to evaluate the adequacy of their response plan and success of their training program
Orientation seminar or workshop	An exercise carried out to familiarize new staff with the agency's emergency response activities or current staff to new or changing information or procedures or to bring together response agencies for better understanding and coordination
Drill	An exercise limited to a specific response activity and conducted to instruct thoroughly through repetition and practice
Tabletop	An exercise conducted in a conference room setting with situations presented as verbal or written problems or questions intended to generate discussion of actions to be taken based on the emergency plan and standard operating procedures. Basic tabletop exercises use group process to solve problems. Advanced play uses prescripted messages.
Functional	An exercise usually conducted at the site where the event would normally take place such as the command center and designed to evaluate the capabilities of the disaster response system.
Full scale	An exercise designed to test a major portion of the emergency operations plan, evaluate the operational capability of emergency responders in an interactive manner over an extended period of time, and mobilize field personnel and resources.

Source: Data from Center for Health Policy, Columbia University School of Nursing. *Defining Emergency Exercises: A Working Guide to the Terminology Used in Practicing Emergency Responses in Communities and Public Health Agencies*. New York, NY: Columbia University School of Nursing, Center for Health Policy; 2004.

More than three fourths (77%) of LHDs received federal preparedness funds in 2008. The nation's largest cities received funding directly from the CDC. Most other LHDs received their funding through their state health agencies. The average award was equivalent to about $1.59 per capita with suburban LHPAs receiving an average of $1.48, and rural LHPAs receiving $2.36 per capita. The median for urban LHDs was $1.07. These resources represent a significant component of the mean expenditures for all LHDs for nonclinical purposes (about $28 per capita; see Chapter 4).

Bioterrorism funding allowed LHDs to support more than 4,000 full-time equivalent positions, although this does not imply that these were new positions added to the agency. In some instances, staff members paid from other sources were switched from local or state funding sources to the bioterrorism grants.

LHDs conduct a wide variety of emergency preparedness activities, as shown in Figure 8-5. Notably, about one fourth responded to an actual public health emergency in the preceding year. Despite fears that the increased focus on public health emergency preparedness would weaken other public health duties, virtually all LHD functions and services were reported to be stronger as a result of federal funding for emergency preparedness and response (Figure 8-6). States also reported that public health emergency preparedness and response funding strengthened other public health programs as well as the public health infrastructure in their states (Figure 8-7).

The impact on core public health practice activities should be measurable, and ultimately, there is a need to assess this impact as preparedness efforts advance. Preparedness should be viewed as an important quality or attribute of an effective public health system rather than as a categorical end in itself. This is the essence of the philosophy that has become to be known as the "dual use," "multiple use," or "all hazards" strategy. Although this has been the public position of federal officials since late 2001, federal actions have not always been consistent with federal rhetoric.

Indeed, credibility is one theme that constantly re-emerges from the early experience of the states with preparedness funding. The CDC's emphasis on smallpox preparedness has both helped and hurt its credibility with the state and local public health community. It hurt in several ways, including the lack of information related to the hazard and risk assessment process. States and localities were to accept the risk assessment undertaken by the federal government based on undisclosed intelligence information. Many public health officials questioned whether a terrorist-generated smallpox attack represents enough of a real risk to justify the harm associated with smallpox vaccination strategies. Second, federal directives on smallpox undermine the credibility of an all-hazards approach through the enormous emphasis placed on one specific threat at the expense of all others. This nurtures the fear that the federal preparedness program may be little more than another federal categorical program. Countering these concerns is the perception that the implementation steps for smallpox provide useful practical experience that may assist future responses to other threats and actual events. In any event, all sides recognize the need to take full advantage of federal funding increases to leverage overall infrastructure improvements. How this can be done when states and localities are tempted to cut back on their own support of public health infrastructure will require vision, leadership, and follow-through beyond anything seen to date.

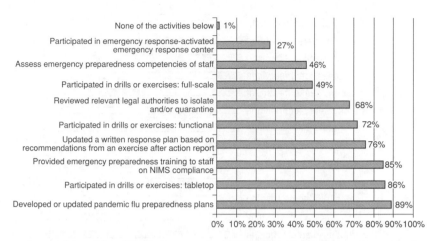

Figure 8-5   Percentage of local health departments with selected emergency preparedness activities in the past year. *Source:* Data from National Association of County and City Health Officials (NACCHO). *2008 National Profile of Local Health Departments*. Washington, DC: NACCHO; 2009.

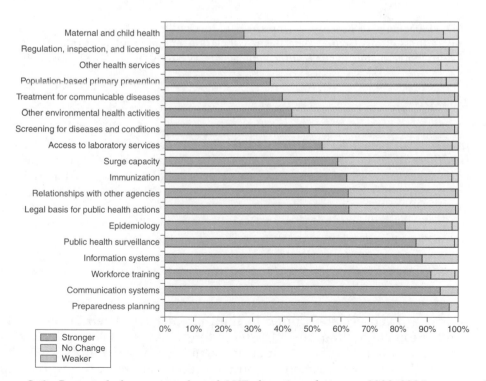

Figure 8-6   Reported change in selected LHD functions between 2002–2005 as a result of efforts to improve emergency preparedness. *Source:* Data from National Association of County and City Health Officials. *2005 National Profile of Local Health Departments*. Washington, DC: NACCHO; 2006.

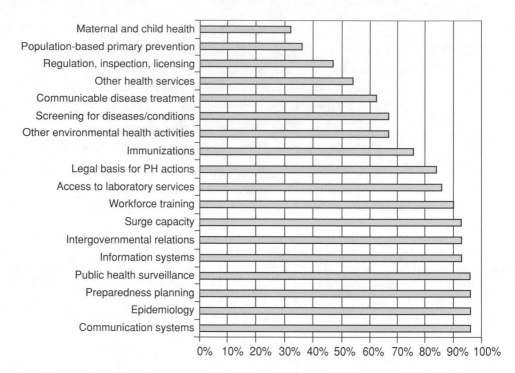

Figure 8-7 Percentage of states reporting stronger infrastructure and programs due to emergency preparedness efforts. *Source:* Data from Association of State and Territorial Health Officials (ASTHO). *Profile of State Public Health, Volume One.* Washington, DC: ASTHO; 2009.

CONCLUSION

Preparing for and responding to emergencies is a well-established role for public health agencies and their workers. This role, highlighted in the *Public Health in America* statement[1] as one of six critical responsibilities, has often been viewed as one of responding to an occasional natural disaster such as an earthquake, hurricane, or flood. Large-scale events that threaten public health and safety have seldom been intentionally inflicted, despite recent examples in contrast, such as the bombing of the federal building in Oklahoma City in the 1990s. Events in the international theater raised the specter of increased risk for terrorist acts, including bioterrorism, directed against the American population and prompted interest in preparedness and response capacities within the federal government in the mid-1990s.

The cycle of progress in public health preparedness has been remarkably consistent over several centuries in the United States. A terrible epidemic or another form of health-related disaster or threat occurs. Public expectations call for such an event to never occur again. Significant new resources are deployed to raise the level of preparedness and protection. The threat seems to dissipate over time. Preparedness, although still important, becomes relatively less important. Eventually, a new threat or event appears, and the cycle repeats itself. This recurring scenario raises the question as to whether current preparedness efforts represent a new and different strategy that could short circuit this chain of events. Past preparedness efforts focused on a specific threat and diminished as that specific threat diminished. Perhaps a more broadly focused preparedness campaign, one that is valued because it battles many different threats, will fare differently. Although still early in the process, some things are clear.

The price for public health preparedness will be high, regardless of how it is calculated. In crude dollar terms, its costs reflect a 20% increase in the federal investment in governmental public health services provided through governmental public health agencies. This increase will need to be sustained indefinitely because it primarily supports information, communications, and workforce development systems that are ongoing in nature, and it will require commensurate commitment and investment on the part of state and local governments. Otherwise, supplanting will occur in one form or another, and the opportunity for federal preparedness funds to leverage other resources will be lost.

If the price is to be calculated in terms of federalism and intergovernmental relationships, it will also be high. States will need to encourage and accept stronger federal leadership on the one hand and generate a better understanding of local needs and priorities on the other. These will need to be fashioned into effective local, regional, state, and multistate efforts in ways that will challenge states to live up to their primary responsibility for the health of their citizens. All of this must be done while navigating through a treacherous obstacle course laden with political, economic, and bureaucratic impediments to sustained progress.

The federal government must avoid the pitfall of merely throwing money at the problem, without fostering a national vision of public health preparedness and nurturing the state–local public health systems that must carry out that vision. This will require the federal agencies to be accountable for meaningful capacity and performance standards, consistent credibility as to ends and means, integration both across focus areas and across federal agencies, and leadership rather than either regulatory or advisory approaches to dealing with state–local public health system issues.

When information from preparedness and response capacity in three states was pooled together and analyzed by population density of the county where the LHDs were located, a clear trend was observed of increasing preparedness with increasing population density, despite rural areas receiving more money per capita from CDC preparedness funding. Such comparisons using common tools can produce valuable results, suggesting the need for adoption of national performance standards, assessment instruments and scoring methods that can be used productively and immediately, and improved based on experience and evidence acquired with use over time.[12]

Although these are formidable challenges, the opportunities (and the opportunity costs) are unprecedented. The boost in federal funding and potential for federal leadership provides a unique opportunity to fashion a more coordinated national public health system. Certainly, the public now expects this,[9] and the price of not being prepared will be high; however, progress often comes at a high price. The history of public health preparedness reflects this lesson. Ironically, failure to seize this opportunity will increase the likelihood that another cycle will occur. We can either learn the lessons of the past, the lessons of public health threats and responses, and the lessons of public health operated within a federalist form of government, or we can relive this history over and over again.

DISCUSSION QUESTIONS AND EXERCISES

1. What constitutes vulnerability in populations living in disaster-prone areas? Give a concrete example from a disaster that has drawn media attention in recent years (several media websites are provided in the Course Resources catalog).
2. Choose a public health discipline or occupational group (either your own or one that you are somewhat familiar with), and describe the range of tasks that groups of public health practitioners may be asked to perform in disaster preparedness and response. Why is public health participation important?
3. Why should public health organizations take a leadership role in emergency and disaster planning?
4. Why is the process of planning more important than the written plan itself? Describe the "paper plan" syndrome and how it can detract from public health emergency preparedness. Identify factors contributing to disaster and other public health emergency planning apathy.
5. What is meant by the term surge capacity, and how is this addressed in public health emergency response plans?
6. Describe three or more elements of public health statutes that are important elements of public health emergency response plans.
7. Describe the role of your agency and at least four other agencies that work in conjunction with your agency in public health emergencies.
8. Describe your own specific role for several different public health emergency situations.
9. What are the basic functions that a health department should perform in response to an emergency or disaster? When should a health department identify these functions?
10. What public health resources are available at the federal, state, or local level in an emergency or disaster? How would you go about requesting these resources?

REFERENCES

1. Public Health Functions Steering Committee. *Public Health in America*. Washington, DC: Public Health Service; 1995.
2. Landesmann LY. *Public Health Management of Disasters: The Practice Guide*. Washington, DC: American Public Health Association; 2001.
3. Presidential Homeland Security Directive No. 5, February 28, 2003.
4. The Center for Law and the Public's Health. *The Model State Emergency Health Powers Act Emergencies Act*. Baltimore, MD: Georgetown and Johns Hopkins Universities; 2001.
5. National Association of County and City Health Officials. *2005 National Profile of Local Health Departments*. Washington, DC: National Association of County and City Health Officials; 2006.
6. National Association of County and City Health Officials. *Elements of Effective Local Bioterrorism Preparedness: A Planning Primer for Local Health Departments*. Washington, DC: National Association of County and City Health Officials; 2001.

7. National Association of County and City Health Officials. *Local Centers for Public Health Preparedness: Models for Strengthening Local Public Health Capacity*. Washington, DC: National Association of County and City Health Officials; 2001.

8. Centers for Disease Control and Prevention. *Local Emergency Preparedness and Response Inventory: A Tool for Rapid Assessment of Local Capacity to Respond to Bioterrorism, Outbreaks of Infectious Disease, and Other Public Health Threats and Emergencies*. Atlanta, GA: Centers for Disease Control; 2001.

9. Lake, Snell, Perry & Associates. *Americans Speak Out on Bioterrorism and U.S. Preparedness to Address Risk*. Princeton, NJ: Robert Wood Johnson Foundation; December 2002.

10. Centers for Medicare and Medicaid Services. *National Health Accounts, 1960–2000*.

11. Columbia University School of Nursing, National Association of County and City Health Officials, and Centers for Disease Control and Prevention. 2003. Bioterrorism & Emergency Readiness: Competencies for All Public Health Workers. http://www.nursing.hs.columbia.edu/institutes-center/chphsr/btcomps.pdf. Accessed June 5, 2007.

12. Pezzino G, Thompson MZ, Edgar M. *A Multi-State Comparison of Local Public Health Preparedness Assessment Using a Common, Standardized Tool*. New Orleans, LA: National Network of Public Health Institutes; 2006.

Public Health Spotlight on Tabletop Exercises

BIOTERRORIST ATTACK ON FOOD: A TABLETOP EXERCISE

This exercise is designed as an opportunity for public health personnel and their local emergency counterparts to gain skills and knowledge in preparing for and responding to a large-scale communicable disease event. Participants will address a hypothetical bioterrorism incident in the form of an infectious disease outbreak to acquire this learning. The exercise enables participants to identify the communication, resources, data, coordination, and organizational elements associated with an emergency response.

This educational tool, originally titled "Hands-on Training for Public Health Emergencies," was prepared by the Northwest Center for Public Health Practice in conjunction with the Washington State Department of Health. Its development was supported by funding from the Health Alert Network and the Bioterrorism Preparedness and Response Program at the CDC, with the understanding that states need to develop an effective public health emergency response infrastructure for bioterrorism events that impact state and local communities.

INTRODUCTION

The exercise is aimed at identifying the policy questions that need to be considered in responding to a bioterrorism event. The depicted exercise scenario will enable participants to understand and experience the shortcomings or gaps in their ability to identify and respond to policy issues (as opposed to operational procedures). Participants will be required to state policy questions such as these: "Who should be responsible? Or what information is needed? Or when is public information given out?" In essence, participants will be identifying the "what" is required in responding to an incident and not necessarily the "how" an agency will actually respond. It is important that the exercise identify policies required to respond effectively to the scenario rather than using only those policies that currently exist. Addressing those policies that need clarification or development will be helpful in eventually strengthening the overall response system and will identify areas in operational policies and procedures that need refinement.

PURPOSE OF THIS EXERCISE

The purpose of this exercise is to provide the participants with an opportunity to respond to a bioterrorism event scenario through a simulated tabletop exercise. Specific objectives are for the learner to be able to

- Understand measures that can be performed at the local level to prepare for a large-scale communicable disease or bioterrorism incident
- Promote interagency collaboration/coordination regarding emergency preparation and responsiveness
- Recognize the roles of a variety of public officials in a large-scale communicable disease or bioterrorism incident
- Recognize need for intense teamwork and communication to prepare for a large-scale communicable disease or bioterrorism incident
- Identify gaps in local preparedness and ability to coordinate
- Identify additional related training/learning needs (an "assessment tool")

TABLETOP EXERCISE: PART 1

Storyboard 1

This incident affects four Counties: Cedar, Dogwood, Pine, and Maple. The incident begins in Cedar County in the month of August. Click here for a map illustrating these counties.
Cedar County

- Total population: 150,000 residents.
- The major city, Watertown, has a population of 40,000 residents.
- There are two area hospitals; one is a children's hospital.
- There are numerous nursing homes and day care centers.
- International trade, tourism, agricultural products, and lumbering are the major industries.
- An economic trade group conference is scheduled to be held in Watertown in 3 weeks. About 100 members will be attending, including foreign economic officials.

- Residents are all served by a regional public water supply system.
- Cedar County Health Department has a staff of 70 employees. The department has a full-time director of public health and a full-time health officer (MD). A full range of public health services, including environmental health, community health nursing, laboratory, and clinical public health services are provided.

Dogwood County

- Located directly to the north of Cedar County.
- Total population: 35,000 residents.
- Noted for its numerous water recreational areas.
- About 10,000 residents are served by small or individual water supply systems.
- Dogwood County Health Department has 25 total staff, including Environmental Health Specialists and Community Health Nurses. A health officer (MD) is part-time.

Pine County

- Located directly to the south of Cedar County.
- Total population: 15,000.
- Serves as a "bedroom community" to Cedar County. Many Pine County residents commute to work in Cedar County's major city.
- Residents receive public water supplied by Cedar County Regional Water Utility.
- Pine County Health Department has a total of 14 staff members (5 are part-time). Two are environmental health specialists and 10 are public health nurses. The remaining staff members provide administrative support. A health officer is a contract physician from the community.

The State Health Department is located in Maple County, 140 miles to the east of Cedar County. The State Health Department's Public Health Laboratory and the state's university are also located in Maple County. The population of Maple County is 1 million.

Event 1

Day 1, Friday

Persons with gastrointestinal illness are beginning to contact their medical care providers through the nurse hotline and patient consultation lines. Individuals with gastrointestinal problems are calling or visiting area emergency rooms and urgent care centers on Friday afternoon and evening. The hospital's patient consultation line is experiencing an increased number of calls with symptoms, including severe diarrhea, fever, chills, headache, nausea, vomiting, abdominal pain, and possibly bloody stools. All cases describe diarrhea as a symptom. Almost all report at least two or more of the additional symptoms. Illnesses have lasted 1 to 2 days without improvement. Most patients are middle-aged adults, but approximately 10% are over the age of 65 years. A total of 30 people are seen in hospital emergency rooms and urgent care centers by late Friday evening. (This means that a total of 400 individuals may actually be exhibiting similar symptoms, but are not seeking medical care. The 30 cases, or 7.5% of the 400, visit a medical care provider for symptoms.) Stool samples are taken on six of the affected cases seen by a physician. Three individuals are hospitalized for dehydration or other gastrointestinal complications.

Day 2, Saturday AM

Patients are still being seen in the emergency room and urgent care centers. By 10 AM, the number of patients exhibiting similar symptoms is up to 45. The decision is made to notify the health department. There is some concern about the capacity of the clinics to handle the increasing number of patients coming in for treatment.

Questions for you to consider and discuss as if you were part of the emergency preparedness response team follow. Please do not skip ahead in the story, but follow the events in the sequence they are presented here.

> How do medical care providers decide when to contact the health officials?
>
> How do medical care personnel determine whom to contact?
>
> How is the health department person contacted (after hours/nonbusiness days)?
>
> What does the health department do with this information?
>
> What additional information does the health department need?
>
> How does the medical care facility address its capacity needs?

Event 2

Day 2, Saturday noon

By noon, the patient count is up to 60. The local health officer decides to convene a meeting to discuss next steps. A local pharmacist calls the local hospital to ask what is happening. The pharmacist reports that the store is almost out of antidiarrheal medicine because of heavy demand.

The questions here are for you to consider and discuss as if you were part of the emergency preparedness response team. Please do not skip ahead in the story, but follow the events in the sequence they are presented here.

> Who should be involved in the meeting?
>
> Would nontraditional partners such as emergency management be brought in at this time?
>
> What should be discussed in the meeting?
>
> What is the health department doing to collect additional information about cases?

Event 3

Day 2, Saturday PM

The health department decides to begin interviewing cases.

Questions for you to consider and discuss as if you were part of the emergency preparedness response team follow. Please do not skip ahead in the story, but follow the events in the order they unfold.

> How do you proceed?
>
> What additional information is needed for further investigation?

Event 4

Day 2, Saturday PM

Medical care providers from Dogwood and Pine Counties are reporting a high number of patients complaining about severe gastrointestinal problems. By 5:00 PM, the total patient count from all three counties is 75. Seventeen stool specimens have been taken. Six people have now been hospitalized.

Questions for you to consider and discuss as if you were part of the emergency preparedness response team follow. Do not skip ahead in the story, but follow the events as they unfold.

> To whom do the medical care providers from Dogwood and Pine Counties report their information, particularly if key health department staff cannot be contacted?
>
> How is information being shared between the health agencies?

Event 5

Day 2, Saturday PM

Hospital personnel have confirmed to the news media about a large number of people being seen with some type of "intestinal illness," but refer callers to the health department.

The following are questions for you to consider and discuss as if you were part of the emergency preparedness response team. Please do not skip ahead but follow the events in the order in which they unfold.

> How does the Health Department respond to news media inquiries?
>
> Does the health department have a designated public information officer?

Event 6

Day 2, Saturday PM

At 5:00 PM, a member of a tour group visiting the county reports to the health department that 35 out of 50 members have become ill with severe diarrhea, vomiting, and nausea. None have seen a doctor. All ate at local restaurants in the area for the past week. The group is primarily non-English speaking tourists from Southeast Asia.

The following are questions for you to consider and discuss as if you were part of the emergency preparedness response team. Please do not skip ahead in the story but proceed through these events in the order they unfold.

What actions should occur to respond to this information?

How are the issues of language translation handled?

TABLETOP EXERCISE: PART 2

Storyboard 2

The focus of attention is being directed toward food service establishments in the three counties as a result of patient interview data. Numerous establishments are being identified as places where interviewed patients have eaten or have purchased foods in the past week. Many are restaurants; however, specialty grocery stores are also being frequently mentioned.

Twelve identified restaurants are in Cedar County. One is in Dogwood County. All restaurants serve a high volume and variety of customers. They range from well-known, moderately priced, national chain restaurants to popular, high-scale dining establishments. Company executives, business leaders, attorneys, and governmental officials often eat at the affected city establishments. All are popular with tourists visiting both counties. Four establishments serve ethnic foods. Two are Mexican. The other two are Asian. Three affected restaurants have a history of poor food handling practices, particularly hand washing and temperature violations. None of the establishments have had violations of foods from unapproved sources.

The three specialty grocery stores are highly popular and have a high turnover of food inventory. All are owned and operated by the same company. Two of the specialty stores are in Cedar County. The third is located in Dogwood County. All food service establishments are served by public water, but from different water utilities.

Event 7

Day 3, Sunday AM

Health department personnel interviewing cases are hearing about 12 restaurants being repeatedly named in Cedar County and one in Dogwood County. Three of the restaurants in Cedar County have had a history of food service violations. A number of people becoming ill, however, have not eaten at any of the 13 named restaurants. Laboratory results on patients will not be available until the next day.

The following are questions for you to consider and discuss as if you were part of the emergency preparedness response team. Do not skip ahead in the chronology of events but proceed through them in the order they unfold.

What is the significance of this information?

What action is taken on the named restaurants, if any?

What information is shared with the news media, if any?

Event 8

Day 3, Sunday AM

Many ill patients have not eaten at a restaurant in the past week; however, food items being commonly named include fresh salsa, pesto dishes, pizzas, Asian soups, and gourmet salads.

The following are questions for you to consider and discuss as if you were part of the emergency preparedness response team. Do not skip ahead in the story but proceed through the events in the order they unfold.

What is the significance of this information?

How is this information shared with the public and first responders?

Event 9

Day 3, Sunday AM

Remember that there is a large economic trade group conference scheduled in Watertown (Cedar County) in 3 weeks, as mentioned in Storyboard 1.

Hospital emergency rooms and medical clinics in the county are getting overwhelmed with patients. Medical facilities are short staffed because many medical personnel are home ill with "gastrointestinal upset." There is concern among medical staff about spread of the illness within the hospital and the urgent care clinics.

The following are questions for you to consider and discuss as if you were part of the emergency preparedness response team. Do not skip ahead in the story, but follow the events in the order they are presented here.

What is the procedure for added capacity to handle the high volume of patients?

What is the policy of infection control (and communication) within the medical care facilities?

Event 10

Day 3, Sunday PM

Patient count up to 250 after news report on disease outbreak. The source is not yet determined, but food is highly suspected with attention focusing on fresh herbs. Most cases are middle-aged adults. The age range of cases is from 5 to 82 years.

The following are questions for you to consider and discuss as if you were part of the emergency preparedness response team. Do not skip ahead in the story, but proceed through the events in the order in which they occur.

What actions are being performed by the health department to determine the cause of the outbreak?

What communication systems are in place?

What resources are available to handle influx of public calls? Phone bank?

What state and national resources are called in?

What is the content of the food safety message to the public?

How and when does this message get out?

Who is dealing with the food industry in the three counties?

Event 11

Day 3, Sunday PM

Early results of diagnostic tests indicate that Shigella sonnei is the causative agent.

The following are questions for you to consider and discuss as if you were part of the emergency preparedness response team. Do not skip ahead in the story but continue through the events in the order they occur.

What actions are needed in response to this result?

Shigellosis Fact Sheet

Typical symptoms of Shigellosis include severe diarrhea often accompanied by fever, chills, headache, nausea, vomiting, abdominal pain, and possibly bloody stools. The incubation period is 1 to 7 days (usually 1 to 3 days). Less than 10% of cases seek medical care, and fewer have confirmatory stool cultures performed. Complications such as dehydration may result in hospitalization but deaths are rare.

Event 12

Day 3, Sunday PM

The city's mayor receives a message from an extremist group taking credit for "contaminating the food supply with an infectious bacterial agent." The group threatens to continue to do so unless the upcoming conference of economic trade group representatives is canceled. Mayor shares message with the health department director and the chief of police.

The following are questions for you to consider and discuss as if you were part of the emergency preparedness response team. Do not skip ahead in the story but follow the events in the order they unfold.

How should the health department handle this information?

Who should be involved in assessing this message?

Who is in charge?

Event 13

Day 3, Sunday PM

Anonymous person calls the local newspaper and says she represents a group who wishes to take credit for "making people sick with food contaminated with botulism."

The following are questions for you to consider and discuss as if you were part of the emergency preparedness response team. Do not skip ahead in the story but follow the events in the order they unfold.

What does the health department do with this information?

Events 14 and 15

Day 3, Sunday PM

The health officer declares a public health emergency. The phone lines are jammed.

The following are questions for you to consider and discuss as if you were part of the emergency preparedness response team. Do not skip ahead in the story but follow the events in the order they unfold.

Has the EOC already been activated?

Where does the health department fit into the EOC command structure?

Event 16

Day 4, Monday AM

Reported patient count is now over 400. Eighty percent of cases are from the largest county. The remaining 20% of the cases come from the two adjacent counties. Thirty cases are restaurant workers. Affected cases range in age from 4 to 87 years. Thirty cases are hospitalized. Five are in serious condition.

The following are questions for you to consider and discuss as if you were part of the emergency preparedness response team. Do not skip ahead in the story but follow the events in the order they unfold.

What actions are taking place to prevent the outbreak from spreading?

Event 17

Day 4, Monday AM

The state university microbiology laboratory located in another part of the state reports to the university campus security that numerous vials of *Shigella sonnei* are missing from the laboratory. The vials were last seen 7 days ago. A few vials from the original batch of the culture are still available. Campus security contacts the county sheriff. The county sheriff contacts its LHD (Maple County Health Department).

The following are questions for you to consider and discuss as if you were part of the emergency preparedness response team. Do not skip ahead in the story but follow the events in the order they unfold.

What does Maple County Health Department do after receipt of this information?

How is it shared with Cedar County?

TABLETOP EXERCISE: PART 3

Storyboard 3

A terrorist group possesses 2 gallons of a liquid broth containing high concentrations of a disease-causing bacterial agent. The cultures of the bacterial agent have been secretly manufactured using stolen vials from a university laboratory. The infectious broth was surreptitiously sprayed onto produce at a food distribution warehouse in Cedar County over a 2-day period. The contaminated produce was then distributed to affected food establishments (13 restaurants and 3 specialty grocery stores): 12 local restaurants and 2 specialty grocery stores in Cedar County and 1 restaurant and a specialty grocery store in Dogwood County. Pine County food establishments were not affected. The produce was used for garnish and seasonings in a variety of different dishes at the restaurants. The contaminated dishes were consumed in all 13 restaurants on Tuesday evening and Wednesday lunch and dinner. The produce was also purchased directly by consumers at the three local specialty grocery stores on Tuesday and Wednesday. Residents in all three counties became ill by consuming the contaminated products. Not all sick have visited their medical care provider.

Event 18

Day 4, Monday PM

Business at area food establishments is dropping significantly.

The following are questions for you to consider and discuss as if you were part of the emergency preparedness response team. Do not skip ahead in the story but follow the events in the order they unfold.

What is the message to food service operators? To food workers?

Who communicates food safety information to the public?

Event 19

Day 4, Monday PM

News media from other states calling for interviews or information.

The following are questions for you to consider and discuss as if you were part of the emergency preparedness response team. Do not skip ahead in the story but follow the events in the order they unfold.

Who responds?

How is the response script developed?

Event 20

Day 4, Monday PM

Reinterviewing of cases and working closely with restaurants to identify common ingredients indicates cilantro and basil as the most likely contaminated products.

The following are questions for you to consider and discuss as if you were part of the emergency preparedness response team. Do not skip ahead in the story but follow the events in the order they unfold.

What is done with this information?

Event 21

Day 4, Monday PM

An older woman (86 years old) dies from complications resulting from Shigellosis. Family threatens lawsuit against responsible agency.

The following are questions for you to consider and discuss as if you were part of the emergency preparedness response team. Do not skip ahead in the story but follow the events in the order they unfold.

How are legal issues handled?

Event 22

Day 14, Friday—recovery period

Nothing more was ever heard from the extremists. No new infections are attributed to the identified food source; however, secondary cases continue to occur including outbreaks in three daycare centers. Public alarm has decreased, but people are still calling about food safety and concerned by the cases that continue to occur—do not understand the meaning of "secondary cases." The trade conference is still scheduled for 1 week from today.

The following are questions for you to consider and discuss as if you were part of the emergency preparedness response team.

How does the health department ensure the public the "outbreak" is over and the new cases are a result of secondary transmission?

What recommendations should be given to the mayor about the risks of holding the annual conference of trade representatives?

Public Health Spotlight on Oral Health

This Public Health Spotlight examines one of the most overlooked public health achievements of the 20th century, improvements in oral health status. The history of this achievement, its current status in the early decades of the 21st century, and the challenges that lie ahead are examined.

PUBLIC HEALTH ACHIEVEMENTS IN 20TH CENTURY AMERICA[1]

At the beginning of the 20th century, extensive dental caries was common in the United States and in most developed countries.[2] No effective measures existed for preventing this disease, and the most frequent treatment was tooth extraction. Failure to meet the minimum standard of having six opposing teeth was a leading cause of rejection from military service in both world wars.[3,4] Pioneering oral epidemiologists developed an index to measure the prevalence of dental caries using the number of decayed, missing, or filled teeth (DMFT) or decayed, missing, or filled tooth surfaces (DMFS) rather than merely presence of dental caries,[5] in part because nearly all persons in most age groups in the United States had evidence of the disease. Application of the DMFT index in epidemiologic surveys throughout the United States in the 1930s and 1940s allowed quantitative distinctions in dental caries experience among communities—an innovation that proved critical in identifying a preventive agent and evaluating its effects.

Soon after establishing his dental practice in Colorado Springs, Colorado, in 1901, Dr. Frederick S. McKay noted an unusual permanent stain or "mottled enamel" (termed "Colorado brown stain" by area residents) on the teeth of many of his patients.[6] After years of personal field investigations, McKay concluded that an agent in the public water supply probably was responsible for mottled enamel. McKay also observed that teeth affected by this condition seemed less susceptible to dental caries.[7]

The effectiveness of community water fluoridation in preventing dental caries prompted rapid adoption of this public health measure in cities throughout the United States. As a result, dental caries declined precipitously during the second half of the 20th century. For example, the mean DMFT among persons aged 12 years in the United States declined 68%, from 4 in 1966 to 1970 to 1.3 in 1988 to 1994[8] (Figure 8-8). The American Dental Association, the American Medical Association, the World Health Organization, and other professional and scientific organizations quickly endorsed water fluoridation. Knowledge about the benefits of water fluoridation led to the development of other modalities for delivery of fluoride, such as toothpastes, gels, mouth rinses, tablets, and drops. Several countries in Europe and Latin America have added fluoride to table salt.

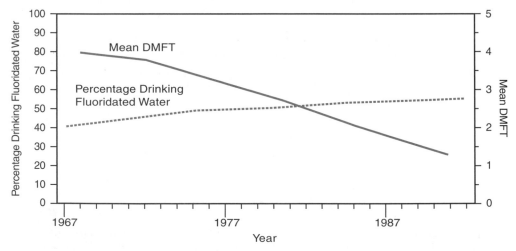

Figure 8-8 Percentage of population residing in areas with fluoridated community water system and mean number of DMFT among children aged 12 years, United States, 1967–1992. *Source:* From Centers for Disease Control and Prevention. Achievements in public health, United States, 1900–1999: fluoridation of drinking water to prevent dental caries. *MMWR.* 1999;48:933–940.

Early studies reported that caries reduction attributable to fluoridation ranged from 50% to 70%, but by the mid-1980s, the mean DMFS scores in the permanent dentition of children who lived in communities with fluoridated water were only 18% lower than among those living in communities without fluoridated water.[8] A review of studies on the effectiveness of water fluoridation conducted in the United States during 1979 to 1989 found that caries reduction was 8% to 37% among adolescents (mean, 26.5%).[9]

Since the early days of community water fluoridation, the prevalence of dental caries has declined in both communities with and communities without fluoridated water in the United States. This trend has been attributed largely to the diffusion of fluoridated water to areas without fluoridated water through bottling and processing of foods and beverages in areas with fluoridated water and widespread use of fluoride toothpaste.[10] Fluoride toothpaste is efficacious in preventing dental caries, but its effectiveness depends on frequency of use by persons or their caregivers. In contrast, water fluoridation reaches all residents of communities and generally is not dependent on individual behavior.

Although early studies focused mostly on children, water fluoridation also is effective in preventing dental caries among adults. Fluoridation reduces enamel caries in adults by 20% to 40% and prevents caries on the exposed root surfaces of teeth, a condition that particularly affects older adults.[9]

Water fluoridation is especially beneficial for communities of low socioeconomic status.[11] These communities have a disproportionate burden of dental caries and have less access than higher income communities to dental-care services and other sources of fluoride. Water fluoridation may help reduce such dental health disparities.

By the end of 1992, 10,567 public water systems serving 135 million persons in 8,573 U.S. communities had instituted water fluoridation.[12] Approximately 70% of all U.S. cities with populations of greater than 100,000 used fluoridated water. In addition, 3,784 public water systems serving 10 million persons in 1,924 communities had natural fluoride levels greater than or equal to 0.7 ppm. In total, 144 million persons in the United States (56% of the population) were receiving fluoridated water in 1992, including 62% of those served by public water systems; however, approximately 42,000 public water systems and 153 U.S. cities with populations greater than or equal to 50,000 have not instituted fluoridation.

Water fluoridation costs range from a mean of 31 cents per person per year in U.S. communities of greater than 50,000 persons to a mean of $2.12 per person in communities of less than 10,000 (1988 dollars).[13] Compared with other methods of community-based dental caries prevention, water fluoridation is the most cost effective for most areas of the United States in terms of cost per saved tooth surface.[14]

Water fluoridation reduces direct healthcare expenditures through primary prevention of dental caries and avoidance of restorative care. Per capita cost savings from 1 year of fluoridation may range from negligible amounts among very small communities with very low incidence of caries to $53 among large communities with a high incidence of disease. One economic analysis estimated that prevention of dental caries, largely attributed to fluoridation and fluoride-containing products, saved $39 billion (1990 dollars) in dental care expenditures in the United States during 1979 to 1989.[15]

Early investigations into the physiologic effects of fluoride in drinking water predated the first community field trials. Since 1950, opponents of water fluoridation have claimed that it increased the risk for cancer, Down syndrome, heart disease, osteoporosis and bone fracture, acquired immune deficiency syndrome, low intelligence, Alzheimer's disease, allergic reactions, and other health conditions.[16] The safety and effectiveness of water fluoridation have been re-evaluated frequently, and no credible evidence supports an association between fluoridation and any of these conditions.[17]

21ST CENTURY PUBLIC HEALTH CHALLENGES[1]

Despite the substantial decline in the prevalence and severity of dental caries in the United States during the 20th century, this largely preventable disease is still common.[18,19] Figure 8-9 demonstrates the persistently high rates of untreated dental caries among all age groups, and especially in poor and near poor populations.

Among the most striking results of water fluoridation is the change in public attitudes and expectations regarding oral health. Tooth loss is no longer considered inevitable, and increasingly adults in the United States are retaining most of their teeth for a lifetime.[20] For example, the percentage of persons aged 45 to 54 years who had lost all their permanent teeth decreased from 20% in 1960 to 1962 to 9.1% in 1988 to 1994.[21] The oldest post-World War II "baby boomers" will reach age 70 years in the second decade of the 21st century, and more of that birth cohort will have a relatively intact dentition at that age than any generation in history. Thus, more teeth than ever will be at risk for caries among older adults. In the new century, water fluoridation will continue to help prevent caries among these older persons in the United States.

Most persons in the United States support community water fluoridation.[22] Although the proportion of the U.S. population drinking fluoridated water increased fairly quickly from 1945 into the 1970s, the rate of increase has been much lower in recent decades. This slowing in the expansion of fluoridation is attributable to several factors: (1) the public, some scientists, and policy makers may perceive that dental caries is no longer a public health problem or that fluoridation is no longer necessary or effective; (2) adoption of water fluoridation can require political processes that make institution of this public health measure difficult; (3) opponents of water fluoridation often make unsubstantiated claims about adverse health effects of fluoridation in attempts to influence public opinion;[16] and (4) many of the U.S. public

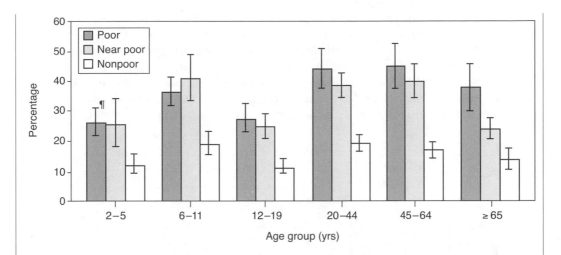

Figure 8-9 Percentage of persons with untreated dental caries,* by age group[†] and poverty status,[§] National Health and Nutrition Examination Survey (NHANES), United States, 2001–2004.

* As determined by NHANES dental examination; excludes persons who are edentulous.

[†] Persons aged 2–5 years: primary teeth only; 6–11 years: both primary and secondary teeth; >12 years: secondary teeth only.

[§] Poor is defined as having an annual family income <100% of the relevant U.S. Census poverty threshold, near poor as 100% to <200% of the threshold, and nonpoor as >200% of the threshold. In 2004, for a family of four (two adults and two children aged <18 years), the poverty threshold was $19,157, and poverty status levels were as follows: poor, <$19,157; near poor, $19,157–$38,314; and nonpoor, >$38,314.

[¶] 95% confidence interval.

Source: From Centers for Disease Control and Prevention. Percentage of persons with untreated dental caries, by age group and poverty status, National Health and Nutrition Examination Survey (NHANES), United States, 2001–2004. *MMWR.* 2007;56(34):889.

water systems that are not fluoridated tend to serve small populations, which increases the per capita cost of fluoridation. These barriers present serious challenges to expanding fluoridation in the United States in the 21st century. To overcome the challenges facing this preventive measure, public health professionals at the national, state, and local level will need to enhance their promotion of fluoridation and commit the necessary resources for equipment, personnel, and training.

None of the leading health indicators for Healthy People 2010 specifically addressed oral health, a serious shortcoming in that indicator panel in the eyes of oral health advocates. Oral health status among

2- to 4-year-olds in particular does not appear to be moving in the right direction, however, possibly because of limited access to services.

Figures 8-10 and 8-11 illustrate the gaps that exist between current measures of oral health status and the national targets established for the year 2010. But even these measures fail to tell the entire story. Mouth and throat diseases, which range from cavities to cancer, also cause pain and disability for millions of Americans each year, yet

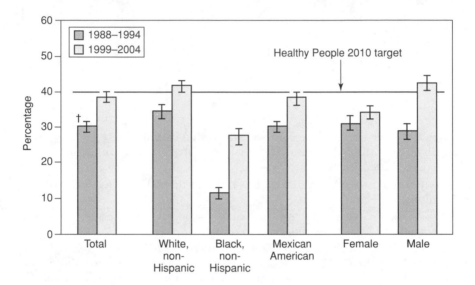

Figure 8-10   Percentage of adults aged 35–44 years with no permanent tooth loss from disease, by race/ethnicity* and sex, National Health and Nutrition Examination Survey, United States, 1988–1994 and 1999–2004.

* Findings based on dental examination of a sample of the civilian, noninstitutionalized population conducted as part of the National Health and Nutrition Examination Survey. Before 1999, respondents were asked to select only one race. For 1999 and later years, respondents were asked to select one or more races. For all years, the categories black and white include persons who reported only one racial group and exclude persons of Hispanic ethnicity. Persons of Mexican American ethnicity might be any race.

† 95% confidence interval.

Sources: From Centers for Disease Control and Prevention. Percentage of adults aged 35–44 years with no permanent tooth loss from disease, by race/ethnicity and sex, National Health and Nutrition Examination Survey, United States, 1988–1994 and 1999–2004. *MMWR.* 2009;58(08):205. Data from: National Health and Nutrition Examination Survey, 1988–2004 data files. http://www.cdc.gov/nchs/nhanes.htm. CDC. Trends in oral health status: United States, 1988–1994 and 1999–2004. *Vital Health Stat.* 2007;11(248). http://www.cdc.gov/nchs/data/series/sr_11/sr11_248.pdf. U.S. Department of Health and Human Services. Healthy People 2010 (2nd ed., in 2 vols). Washington, DC: U.S. Department of Health and Human Services; 2000. http://www.health.gov/healthypeople. Accessed June 3, 2010.

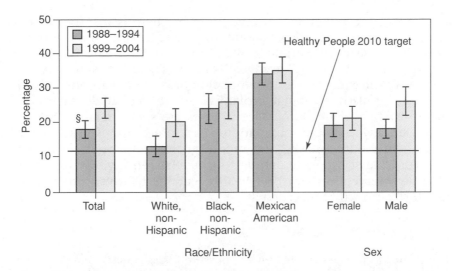

Figure 8-11   Percentage of children aged 2–4 years who ever had caries in primary teeth,* by race/ethnicity[†] and sex, National Health and Nutrition Examination Survey, United States, 1988–1994 and 1999–2004.

* Clinical diagnosis of dental caries or presence of fillings in at least one primary tooth based on a dental examination.

[†] Respondents were asked to select only one race before 1999. For 1999 and later years, respondents were asked to select one or more races. For all years, the categories black and white include persons who reported only one racial group and exclude persons of Hispanic ethnicity. Persons of Mexican American ethnicity might be any race.

[§] 95% confidence interval.

Sources: From Centers for Disease Control and Prevention. Percentage of children aged 2–4 years who ever had caries in primary teeth, by race/ethnicity and sex, National Health and Nutrition Examination Survey, United States, 1988–1994 and 1999–2004. *MMWR.* 2009;58(02):34. Data from National Health and Nutrition Examination Survey, 1988–2004 data files. http://www.cdc.gov/nchs/ nhanes.htm. Healthy People 2010 database. http://wonder.cdc.gov/data2010. U.S. Department of Health and Human Services. Healthy People 2010 (conference ed., in 2 vols). Washington, DC: U.S. Department of Health and Human Services; 2000. http://www.healthypeople.gov. Dye BA, Tan S, Smith V, et al. Trends in oral health status: United States, 1988–1994 and 1999–2004. *Vital Health Stat.* 2007;11(248). http://www.cdc.gov/nchs/data/series/sr_11/sr11_ 248.pdf. Accessed June 3, 2010.

almost all oral diseases are largely preventable. Despite substantial improvements in reducing tooth decay (dental caries) in the United States, tooth decay remains one of the most common childhood diseases. The Task Force on Community Preventive Services has identified community water fluoridation and school-associated sealant delivery programs as recommended interventions.[23] There is insufficient evidence to support statewide or community-wide sealant promotion programs. Each year, an estimated 30,000 people learn that they have mouth (oral) or throat (pharyngeal) cancer. There is insufficient evidence as to the effectiveness of population-based interventions for early detection. Similarly, although as many as one third of all dental injuries and up to 19% of head and face injuries are sports related, there is insufficient evidence that population-based interventions to encourage use of helmets, face masks, and mouth guards have been effective to date. For at least the early decades of the 21st century, the arsenal of effective interventions for oral health remains relatively unchanged from the century that preceded it.

REFERENCES

1. Reprinted in part and adapted from Centers for Disease Control and Prevention. Achievements in public health, United States: fluoridation of drinking water to prevent dental caries. *MMWR*. 1999;48:933–940.
2. Burt BA. Influences for change in the dental health status of populations: an historical perspective. *J Public Health Dent*. 1978;38:272–288.
3. Britten RH, Perrott GSJ. Summary of physical findings on men drafted in world war. *Public Health Rep*. 1941;56:41–62.
4. Klein H. Dental status and dental needs of young adult males, rejectable, or acceptable for military service, according to Selective Service dental requirements. *Public Health Rep*. 1941; 56:1369–1387.
5. Klein H, Palmer CE, Knutson JW. Studies on dental caries. I. Dental status and dental needs of elementary school children. *Public Health Rep*. 1938;53:751–765.
6. McKay FS, Black GV. An investigation of mottled teeth: an endemic developmental imperfection of the enamel of the teeth, heretofore unknown in the literature of dentistry. *Dental Cosmos*. 1916;58:477–484.
7. McKay FS. Relation of mottled enamel to caries. *J Am Dent A*. 1928;15:1429–1437.
8. Brunelle JA, Carlos JP. Recent trends in dental caries in U.S. children and the effect of water fluoridation. *J Dent Res*. 1990;69:723–727.
9. Newbrun E. Effectiveness of water fluoridation. *J Public Health Dent*. 1989;49:279–289.
10. Horowitz HS. The effectiveness of community water fluoridation in the United States. *J Public Health Dent*. 1996;56:253–258.
11. Riley JC, Lennon MA, Ellwood RP. The effect of water fluoridation and social inequalities on dental caries in 5-year-old children. *Int J Epidemiol*. 1999;28:300–305.
12. Centers for Disease Control and Prevention. *Fluoridation Census 1992*. Atlanta, GA: U.S. Department of Health and Human Services, Public Health Service, Centers for Disease Control, National Center for Prevention Services, Division of Oral Health; 1993.
13. Ringelberg ML, Allen SJ, Brown LJ. Cost of fluoridation: 44 Florida communities. *J Public Health Dent*. 1992;52:75–80.
14. Burt BA, ed. Proceedings for the workshop: cost effectiveness of caries prevention in dental public health. *J Public Health Dent*. 1989;49(5, special issue):251–344.
15. Brown LJ, Beazoglou T, Heffley D. Estimated savings in U.S. dental expenditures, 1979–89. *Public Health Rep*. 1994;109:195–203.
16. Hodge HC. Evaluation of some objections to water fluoridation. In: Newbrun E, ed. *Fluorides and dental caries*. 3rd ed. Springfield, IL: Charles C Thomas, 1986:221–255.
17. National Research Council. *Health effects of ingested fluoride*. Washington, DC: National Academy Press; 1993.

18. Kaste LM, Selwitz RH, Oldakowski RJ, Brunelle JA, Winn DM, Brown LJ. Coronal caries in the primary and permanent dentition of children and adolescents 1–17 years of age: United States, 1988–1991. *J Dent Res*. 1996;75:631–641.

19. Winn DM, Brunelle JA, Selwitz RH, et al. Coronal and root caries in the dentition of adults in the United States, 1988–1991. *J Dent Res*. 1996;75:642–651.

20. Burt BA, Eklund SA. *Dentistry, dental practice, and the community*. 5th ed. Philadelphia, PA: WB Saunders; 1999.

21. Centers for Disease Control and Prevention, National Center for Health Statistics. Decayed, missing, and filled teeth in adults—United States, 1960–1962. Rockville, MD: U.S. Department of Health, Education, and Welfare, Public Health Service, Health Resources Administration, 1973. *Vital and Health Statistics*, Vol. 11, no. 23. DHEW publication no. (HRA)74-1278.

22. American Dental Association Survey Center. *1998 Consumers' Opinions Regarding Community Water Fluoridation*. Chicago, IL: American Dental Association; 1998.

23. Task Force on Community Preventive Services. The Community Guide. Available at www.thecommunityguide.org. Accessed May 31, 2010.

Future Challenges for Public Health in America

OBJECTIVES

After completing Chapter 9, learners will be proficient in describing the past achievements, current issues, and future challenges for public health and their implications for improving population health status and quality of life. Key aspects of this competency expectation include the following:

- Identifying and discussing at least three lessons from public health's achievements in the 20th century
- Identifying and discussing at least three current issues and challenges facing public health and public health practitioners in the first decade of the 21st century

This text approaches what public health is and how it works from a unified conceptual framework. Key dimensions of the public health system are examined, including its purpose, functions, capacity, processes, and outcomes. Although a simple framework, many of the concepts addressed are anything but simple. As a result, much has been left unsaid, and many important issues and problems facing the public health system have been addressed only in passing. This may serve to whet the appetite of those eager to move beyond the basics and ready to tackle emerging and more complex issues in greater depth. The basic concepts included in this text seek to facilitate that process and encourage thinking "outside the book." Delving into these other issues without the benefit of a broad understanding of the field and how it works, however, can be an occupational hazard in any field of endeavor. For public health workers, continuously fighting off alligators remains the major deterrent to draining the swamp in order to avert the alligator problem in the first place.

Each of the eight initial chapters spotlights one or more public health achievements of the 20th century, telling the story of how we got where we are today. Together, these stories demonstrate that the problems facing public health have changed over the past century and argue that we can expect them to continue to change throughout the current century. In retrospect, many past problems appear relatively easy to solve in comparison with those on the public health agenda at the beginning of the 21st century; however, we often forget that the last century's problems appeared to be quite formidable to public health advocates back in 1910. Although formidable, they were eventually deemed unacceptable, initiating the chain of events that resulted in the impressive catalog of accomplishments chronicled in earlier chapters.

Each of these achievements provides valuable lessons and insights into the obstacles to achieving even further gains that lie ahead. Challenges reside at many levels, especially at the level of preparedness for unforeseen and previously unanticipated threats to the public's health. Melding the expectations for addressing ongoing health problems in the community with those for preparing and responding to new threats leads us to the three key questions addressed in this chapter:

- What are the lessons learned from the threats and challenges faced by public health in 20th century America?
- What are the limitations and challenges facing public health in the 21st century?
- How can these limitations and challenges be overcome?

LESSONS FROM A CENTURY OF PROGRESS IN PUBLIC HEALTH

The remarkable achievements of the 20th century did not completely eradicate the public health problems faced in 1910. Many of these continue to threaten the health of Americans and impede progress toward realizing the life span projections presented in Figure 9-1. New faces for old enemies have appeared in the form of challenges and obstacles to be overcome in the early decades of the 21st century. Infectious diseases, tobacco, maternal and infant mortality, environmental and occupational health, food safety, cardiovascular disease, injuries, and oral health remain high on the list of leading threats to the public's health. Each presents special challenges.

Infectious Diseases

The continuing battle against infectious diseases will be fought on several fronts because of the emergence of new infectious diseases and the re-emergence of old enemies, often in drug-resistant forms. For example, infections caused by *Escherichia coli* O157:H7 have emerged as a frequent and frightening risk to the public. Initially identified as the cause of hemorrhagic conditions in the early 1980s, this pathogen was increasingly associated with food-borne illness outbreaks in the 1990s, including a major outbreak in the Pacific Northwest related to *E. coli*-contaminated hamburgers distributed through a national fast food chain.[1] The source of the *E. coli* was cattle. Other outbreaks of this pathogen involved swimmers in lake water contaminated by bathers infected with the organism (Figure 9-2). Because many of the illnesses are minor and both medical and public health practitioners fail to perform the tests necessary to diagnose *E. coli* infections properly, current surveillance efforts greatly underreport the extent of this condition. Multidrug-resistant pathogens represent another emerging infectious disease problem for the public health system. The widespread and, at times, indiscriminate use of antibiotics

Figure 9-1   Past and projected female and male life expectancy at birth, United States, 1900–2050. *Source:* From U.S. Dept. of Health and Human Services, Office of Disease Prevention and Health Promotion. *Healthy People 2010: Understanding and Improving Health.* Rockville, MD: ODPHP; 2000.

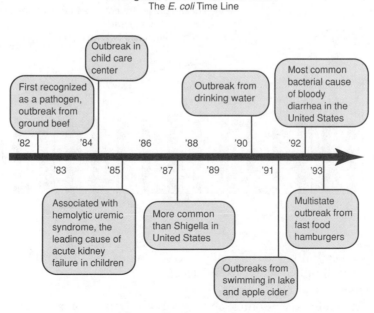

Figure 9-2   Emergence of a public health threat: the *Escherichia coli* O157:H7 time line. *Source:* From *Addressing Emerging Infectious Disease Threats: A Prevention Strategy for the United States*, 1994, U.S. Centers for Disease Control and Prevention, Atlanta, GA.

in agricultural and healthcare settings produces strains of bacteria that are resistant to these drugs. Antimicrobial agents have been increasingly deployed throughout the second half of the 20th century. Slowly, over this period, the consequences of these "miracle drugs" have been experienced in the community, as well as in health facilities. The emergence of drug-resistant strains has reduced the effectiveness of treatment for several common infections, including tuberculosis, gonorrhea, pneumococcal infections, and hospital-acquired staphylococcal and enterococcal infections. For tuberculosis, drug resistance and demographic trends, including immigration policies, played substantial roles in this disease's resurgence in the early 1990s. The changing demographics of tuberculosis infections are illustrated in Figure 9-3.

Pathogens, both old and new, have devised ingenious ways of adapting to and thwarting the weapons used to control them. Many factors in society, the environment, and global interconnectedness continue to increase the risk of emergence and spread of infectious diseases. An outbreak of monkeypox virus affecting several states in the United States in 2003 demonstrates how unusual diseases in remote parts of the world can affect Americans virtually overnight (Figure 9-4).

The potential for global outbreaks and massive pandemics is now on the public health radar screen. An outbreak of severe acute respiratory syndrome hit more than two dozen countries in North America, South America, Europe, and Asia in 2003 before it was contained, but not before taking nearly 800 lives. The possibility of a global pandemic of influenza virus looms as even

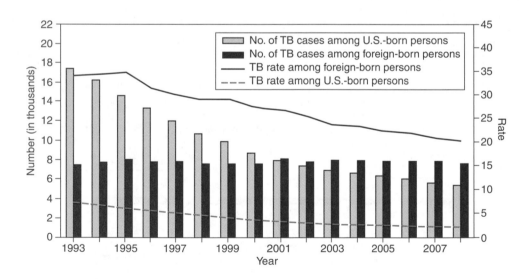

Figure 9-3 Number and rate of tuberculosis cases among U.S.-born and foreign-born persons* by year reported, United States, 1993–2008.

* per 100,000 population

Source: From Centers for Disease Control and Prevention. Trends in tuberculosis, United States, 2008. *MMWR.* 2009;58(10):249–253.

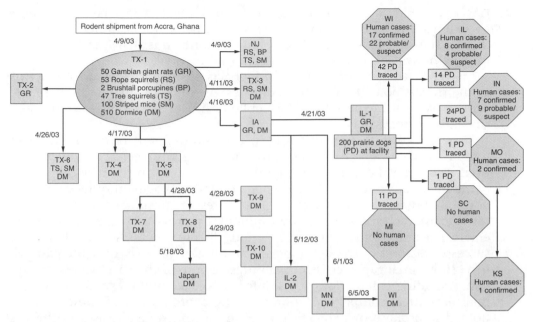

Figure 9-4 Movement of imported African rodents to animal distributors and distribution of prairie dogs from an animal distributor associated with human cases of monkeypox, 11 states, 2003. *Source:* From Centers for Disease Control and Prevention. Update: multistate outbreak of monkeypox—Illinois, Indiana, Kansas, Missouri, Ohio, and Wisconsin, 2003. *MMWR.* 2003:52(27):642–646.

more frightening because it is impossible to predict when the next influenza pandemic will occur or how severe it will be. Wherever and whenever a pandemic starts, everyone everywhere in the world is at risk. Countries might, through measures such as border closures and travel restrictions, delay arrival of the virus, but cannot stop it.

The H1N1 influenza pandemic in 2009 served to test pandemic preparedness and response plans in the United States and internationally. Although never achieving the impact initially feared, the sudden emergence and rapid global sprees left an imprint on public health systems everywhere. Health professionals remain concerned that the possible spread of a highly pathogenic avian H5N1 virus across eastern Asia and other countries represents a significant threat to human health. The H5N1 virus has raised concerns about a potential human pandemic because

- It is especially virulent.
- It is being spread by migratory birds.
- It can be transmitted from birds to mammals and in some limited circumstances to humans.
- Like other influenza viruses, it continues to evolve.

Since 2003, a growing number of human H5N1 cases have been reported in Asia, Africa, and Europe. More than half of the people infected with the

H5N1 virus have died. Most of these cases are all believed to have been caused by exposure to infected poultry. There has been no sustained human-to-human transmission of the disease, but the concern is that H5N1 will evolve into a virus capable of human-to-human transmission.

Heightened concerns over the risk of acts of bioterrorism add a new twist to the threats posed by infectious diseases. As noted in Chapter 8, these concerns have raised expectations for public health to serve both national security and personal safety roles.

The role of infectious diseases in the development of chronic diseases such as diabetes, heart disease, and some cancers further argues that infectious diseases will continue as important health risks in the new century. To battle infectious diseases, the development and deployment of new methods, both in laboratory and epidemiologic sciences, are needed to understand better the interactions among environmental factors as contributors to the emergence and re-emergence of infectious disease processes. Also, despite the successes realized in the development and use of vaccines over the past century, substantial gaps persist in the infrastructure of the vaccine delivery system, including parents, providers, information technology, and biotech and pharmaceutical companies. Improving the coordination of these elements holds the promise of reducing the toll from infectious diseases in the 21st century.

Tobacco Use

The potential gains to be realized from further reduction of tobacco usage are also apparent. Despite the overall decline in tobacco use among adults over the second half of the 20th century, an alarmingly high prevalence of tobacco use among teens persists, and rates among adults are no longer declining, as they did before 1980. These trends suggest that concerns over risks related to exposure to environmental tobacco smoke will continue for many years to come. Disparities in tobacco use by race and ethnicity, together with the growth of demographic groups with high use rates, add yet another dimension to the war against tobacco. New approaches and new products will raise new issues of safety, whereas the increase in tobacco use across the globe will transport old and new challenges around the world.

Maternal and Child Health

Even as maternal and child health outcomes have improved dramatically, there has been little change in the prime determinants of perinatal outcomes—the rate of low birth weight and preterm deliveries. This situation must be addressed to even partially replicate the gains realized in the 20th century. Another important risk factor moving in the wrong direction is the rate of unintended pregnancies. Together, these challenges call for improved understanding of the biologic, social, economic, psychological, and environmental factors that influence maternal and infant health outcomes and in the effectiveness of intervention strategies designed to address these causative factors.

Workplace Safety

Workplaces are now safer than ever before, yet challenges remain on this front as well. Improved surveillance of work-related injuries and illnesses and better methods of conducting field investigations in high-risk occupations and industries remain formidable challenges. Applying new methods of risk assessment to improve assessment of injury exposures and intervention outcomes, as well as improved research into intervention effectiveness, surveillance methods, and organization of work represent additional challenges for public health practice in the 21st century.

Cardiovascular Disease

An aging population less threatened by infectious disease and injury will place even more people at risk of ill health related to cardiovascular diseases. Greater attention to research to understand the various social, psychological, environmental, physiologic, and genetic determinants of cardiovascular diseases is needed in the new century. Reducing disparities that exist in terms of burden of disease, prevalence of risk factors, and ability to reach high-risk populations represents another megachallenge. Identifying new and emerging risk factors and their relationships, including genetic and infectious disease factors, will be necessary in both developed and developing parts of the world.

Food Safety

Our understanding of food safety and nutrition made great strides in the 1900s, but both old and new risks will need to be addressed in the new century. Iron and folate deficiencies continue, and many of the advantages related to breastfeeding remain unrealized. The emergence of obesity as an increasingly prevalent condition throughout the population is one of the most startling developments of the late twentieth century. Persistent challenges include applying new information about nutrition, dietary patterns, and behavior that promote health and reduce the risk of chronic diseases.

Injuries

The impressive gains realized in reducing motor vehicle injuries have uncovered gaps in our understanding of comprehensive prevention. Challenges include expanding surveillance to monitor nonfatal injuries, detect new problems, and set priorities. Greater research into emerging and priority problems, as well as intervention effectiveness, is also needed, as are more effective collaborations and interagency partnerships. Injuries to pedestrians and from vehicles other than automobiles will also challenge public health in the 21st century. The effects of age, alcohol use, seat belt use, and interventions targeting these risks will require greater attention for progress to continue in the battle against motor vehicle injuries.

Oral Health

One of the most overlooked achievements of public health in the 20th century was the dramatic decline in dental caries due to fluoridation of drinking water supplies. Ironically, these advances in oral health have contributed to the perception that dental caries are no longer a significant public health problem and that fluoridation is no longer needed. These battles are likely to be fought in political, rather than scientific, arenas, presenting a substantial challenge to public health in the 21st century.

Unfinished Agenda

For the second decade of the 21st century, Healthy People 2020 articulates the unfinished agenda by identifying important targets and leading indicators of health status for the United States.[2] Various chapters of this text spotlight these leading indicators and targets, including immunizations (Chapter 1), tobacco use (Chapter 2), access to care (Chapter 3), workplace health and safety (Chapter 4), physical activity (Chapter 5), overweight and obesity (Chapter 6), injuries (Chapter 7), and oral health (Chapter 8). Targets for the nation's leading health indicators are examined in these chapters as well. Evidence- and population-based preventive interventions, based on the work of the Community Preventive Services Task Force, are highlighted for each leading indicator.

Key aspects of these health problems are new to the public health agenda. Over the course of recent decades, the public health agenda has expanded to include new issues related to medical care, substance abuse, mental health, long-term care, and violence. These are now categorized as public health problems and have taken their rightful place on the public health agenda. Several of these deserve to be spotlighted here because they are included in Healthy People's panel of leading health indicators.

Spotlight on Behavioral Health[3]

Among the Healthy People 2010 leading health indicators were mental health, substance abuse, alcohol abuse and misuse, and responsible sexual behavior. Although none of these directly relates to the public health achievements of the 20th century spotlighted in previous chapters, these stood among the most important public health issues at the end of the 20th century and remain leading causes of poor health status in the early 21st century. Figure 9-5 reflects progress toward meeting the year 2010 targets established in Healthy People 2010 for these leading indicators. Notably, despite some progress, the year 2010 targets for each of these measures of behavioral health were not achieved.

The landmark study "Global Burden of Disease" identifies mental disorders as the second leading source of disease burden in established market economies.[4] Chief among mental disorders as a leading cause of disability in these countries is major depression, which takes an enormous toll on functional status, productivity, and quality of life and is associated with elevated risk of heart disease and suicide. Increasingly, at least in the United States, the

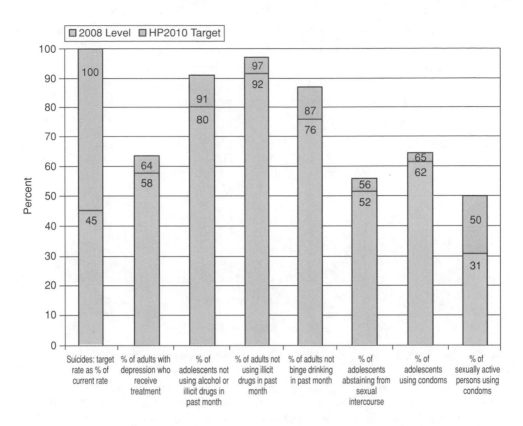

Figure 9-5 Scorecard for selected Healthy People 2010 leading indicators for behavioral health comparing 2008 levels with 2010 targets. *Source:* Data from Data 2010, Healthy People 2010 database. http://wonder.cdc.gov/data2010/ftpselec.htm. Accessed May 31, 2010.

rate of treatment for depression is increasing dramatically. Figures 9-6 and 9-7 provide evidence of the health burden of mental disorders in the United States and of the differences among various racial and ethnic populations. The annual economic burden of depression in the United States (including direct care, mortality, and morbidity costs) has been estimated to total almost $44 billion. This combination of increasing burden and cost has stimulated numerous investigations into population-based strategies to prevent the occurrence of major depression and to encourage more effective treatment of depression, thereby limiting its course and preventing its recurrence.

In the light of this growing body of literature around population-based strategies to improve the primary, secondary, and tertiary prevention of depression and the increasing burden of this debilitating chronic condition, the Task Force on Community Preventive Services has identified several effective interventions. For individuals in all age groups 18 years of age and older, the task force found collaborative care for the management of depressive disorders to be effective in improving short-term depression outcomes. Depression outcomes include response rates (50% reduction in depression

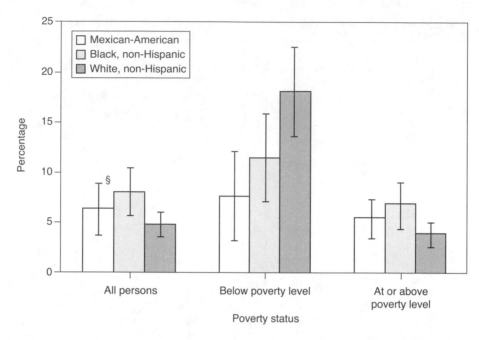

Figure 9-6   Percentage of persons aged >12 years with depression,* by race/ethnicity and poverty status[†], National Health and Nutrition Examination Survey, United States, 2005–2006.

* Depression was measured using the Patient Health Questionnaire (PHQ-9), a nine-item screening instrument that asks questions about the frequency of symptoms of depression during the preceding 2 weeks. Response categories "not at all," "several days," "more than half the days," and "nearly every day" were given a score ranging from 0 to 3. Depression was defined as a total score of 10 or higher on the PHQ-9. This cut point has been well validated and is commonly used in clinical studies that measure depression with the PHQ-9.

[†] Poverty status was defined using the poverty income ratio (PIR), an index calculated by dividing the family income by a poverty threshold that is based on the size of the family. A PIR of less than 1 was used as the cut point for below the poverty level.

[§] 95% confidence interval.

Sources: From Centers for Disease Control and Prevention. Percentage of persons aged >12 years with depression, by race/ethnicity and poverty status, National Health and Nutrition Examination Survey, United States, 2005–2006. *MMWR.* 2008;57(39):1082. Data from National Health and Nutrition Examination Survey data, 2005–2006. http://www.cdc.gov/nchs/nhanes.htm. Accessed May 31, 2010. Pratt LA, Brody DJ. Depression in the United States household population, 2005–2006. NCHS data brief no. 7. Hyattsville, MD: US Department of Health and Human Services, CDC, National Center for Health Statistics; 2008. Available at http://www.cdc.gov/nchs/data/databriefs/db07.htm. Accessed May 31, 2010.

scores), remission (no longer meeting diagnostic criteria), and changes in depression scale scores. This intervention aims to increase primary care providers' knowledge and skills, improve client understanding and awareness of depressive disorders, and to reorganize the system of care into an optimal environment for management of depression and depressive disor-

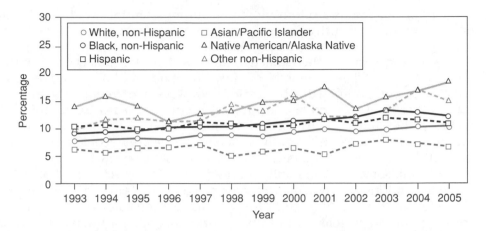

Figure 9-7 Percentage of adults with 14 or more mentally unhealthy days (frequent mental distress), by race, United States, 1993–2005. *Source:* From Centers for Disease Control and Prevention, National Center for Health Statistics, National Household Interview Survey Data.

ders that is systematic, multifaceted, and team based. This intervention creates a collaboration of primary care providers (such as physicians, nurse practitioners, and physician assistants), mental health specialists (such as psychiatrists, psychologists, and psychiatric-mental health nurses), and other providers (such as social workers and nurses) to improve the effectiveness of their engagement with clients in the management of depression. Multicomponent interventions often include client education, provider feedback, case management, provision of information on treatment guidelines/protocols to providers, and use of information technology.

For adults 60 years of age and older with depression, the task force rated both home-based and clinic-based depression care management as effective interventions. Home-based depression care management incorporates active screening for depression, measurement-based outcomes, trained depression care managers, case management, patient education, and a supervising psychiatrist. Clinic-based depression care management involves all of the components included in home-based management plus primary care provider education, antidepressant treatment, and/or psychotherapy.

The task force also assessed the effectiveness of community-based exercise interventions that provide individual or group exercise classes for older adults. These classes may focus on strengthening, endurance, and/or functional training. The task force found insufficient evidence to determine the effectiveness of exercise interventions for reducing depression in older adults. Although the studies reviewed generally found that exercise interventions were associated with improved scores on depression symptom scales, none of the studies reviewed reported results for depressed subjects, so it is unclear whether clinically significant changes can be expected in these populations.

Substance abuse is a priority topic for future attention by the Task Force on Community Preventive Services. In addition to systematic reviews already completed or in progress on reducing the use of tobacco and preventing alcohol abuse and misuse, other addictive drugs will be the subject of future systematic reviews. These reviews explore the evidence on effectiveness of selected population-based interventions to prevent or reduce the abuse of drugs other than tobacco and alcohol. The criteria used to select this topic included the burden of disease, injury, impairment, or exposure, as well as preventability and related initiatives such as the Healthy People process. As of mid-2010, work had not yet begun on this systematic review.

The Task Force on Community Preventive Services selected alcohol use and abuse as a priority for systematic review based on the same criteria described above for substance abuse. Figure 9-8 presents recent data on excessive alcohol consumption, often referred to as binge drinking. Several interventions were identified as effective in preventing excessive alcohol use. These include alcohol outlet density regulations, laws limiting the days and hours when alcohol can be sold, excise taxes on alcohol, and enhanced enforcement of laws prohibiting the sale of alcohol to minors. Alcohol outlet density regulation is defined as applying regulatory authority to reduce alcoholic beverage outlet density or to limit the increase of alcoholic beverage outlet density. Regulation is often implemented through licensing or zoning processes. An alcohol outlet is a place where alcohol may be legally sold for the buyer to drink there (on-premises) or elsewhere (off-premises). Density refers to the number of alcohol outlets in a given area. The task force recommends the use of regulatory authority (e.g., through licensing and zoning) to limit alcohol outlet density on the basis of sufficient evidence of a positive association between outlet density and excessive alcohol consumption and related harms. The task force also recommends maintaining existing limits on the days and hours when alcohol can be sold in order to prevent excessive alcohol consumption and related harms. Most policies limiting days of sale target weekend days (usually Sundays). They may apply to alcohol outlets in which alcohol may be legally sold for the buyer to drink at the place of purchase (on-premises outlets) or elsewhere (off-premises outlets). In the United States, policies may be made at the state level and, where not prohibited by state preemption laws, at local levels. Alcohol excise taxes affect the price of alcohol and are intended to reduce alcohol-related harms, raise revenue, or both. Alcohol taxes are implemented at the state and federal level and are beverage specific (i.e., they differ for beer, wine, and spirits). These taxes are usually based on the amount of beverage purchased (not on the sales price), so their effects can erode over time due to inflation if they are not adjusted regularly. The task force recommends increasing the unit price of alcohol by raising taxes based on strong evidence of effectiveness for reducing excessive alcohol consumption and related harms. Public health effects are expected to be proportional to the size of the tax increase. Enhanced enforcement programs that initiate or increase the frequency of retailer compliance checks for laws against the sale of alcohol to minors were also found to be effective interventions.

With respect to responsible sexual behaviors, prevention of HIV, sexually transmitted infections, and pregnancy, the task force recommends

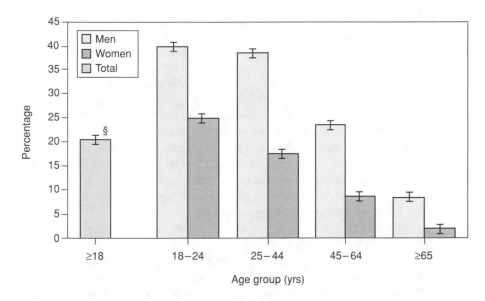

Figure 9-8   Percentage of adults aged >18 years who consumed five or more alcoholic drinks in 1 day at least once in the preceding year,* by sex and age group, National Health Interview Survey, United States, 2007[†].

* Based on responses to the following questions: "In your entire life, have you had at least 12 drinks of any type of alcoholic beverage?" and if "yes," "In the past year, on how many days did you have five or more drinks of any alcoholic beverage?"

[†] Estimates are based on household interviews of a sample of the civilian noninstitutionalized U.S. population.

[§] 95% confidence interval.

Sources: From Centers for Disease Control and Prevention. Percentage of adults aged >18 years who consumed five or more alcoholic drinks in 1 day at least once in the preceding year, by sex and age group, National Health Interview Survey, United States, 2007. *MMWR.* 2008; 57(49):1333. Data from Heyman KM, Schiller JS, Barnes P. Early release of selected estimates based on data from the 2007 National Health Interview Survey. http://www.cdc.gov/nchs/about/major/nhis/released200806.htm. Accessed May 31, 2010.

group-based comprehensive risk reduction (CRR) delivered to adolescents as an effective intervention. The recommendation is based on sufficient evidence of effectiveness in reducing the number of self-reported risk behaviors, including engaging in any sexual activity, frequency of sexual activity, number of partners, and frequency of unprotected sexual activity. CRR also increases self-reported use of protection against pregnancy and sexually transmitted infections (STIs) and reduces the incidence of self-reported or clinically documented SITI. There is limited direct evidence of effectiveness, however, for reducing pregnancy and human immunodeficiency virus (HIV). The task force's review evaluated CRR interventions delivered in school or community settings to groups of adolescents (10–19 years old). These interventions may also include other components such as condom distribution and STI testing.

CRR promotes behaviors that prevent or reduce the risk of pregnancy, HIV, and other STIs. These interventions may suggest a hierarchy of recommended behaviors, identifying abstinence as the best or preferred method but also providing information about sexual risk reduction strategies. CRR may promote abstinence and sexual risk reduction without placing one approach above another, or primarily or solely promote sexual risk-reduction strategies. The task force concluded that there is insufficient evidence to determine the effectiveness of group-based abstinence education delivered to adolescents to prevent pregnancy, HIV, and other STIs. Evidence was considered insufficient because of inconsistent results across studies.

Although much has been achieved, much remains to be done. The public health challenges of the 21st century appear daunting, but those of the preceding century must have seemed even more so. Nevertheless, steady progress came through consistent application of public health approaches and methods, such as those recounted by the public health physician in Table 9-1.

Applying the lessons learned from the recent century of progress in public health to both new and persisting health threats will be necessary to increase the span of healthy life and eliminate the huge disparities in health outcomes that are the overarching goals of the year 2020 national health objectives. The public health challenges of both centuries call for the application of sound science in an environment that supports social justice in health. This remains the most formidable challenge facing public health practice in the 21st century.

LIMITATIONS OF 21ST CENTURY PUBLIC HEALTH

Despite the remarkable achievements of the 20th century, there is much for public health to do in the early years of the new century. Continued progress is by no means assured because of a new constellation of problems and important limitations of conventional public health efforts. Global environmental threats, the disruption of vital ecosystems, global population overload, persistent and widening social injustice and health inequalities, and lack of access to effective care add to the list of health problems left over from the 20th century.[5] Consider, for example, the implications of Figures 9-9 and 9-10 in terms of the link between income, educational attainment, and health, and a nation growing more and more diverse, with a disproportionate burden of poverty falling on children, minorities, and one-parent families. Further gains in health status may be less related to science than to social policies. For some public health professionals, the limitations of conventional public health are difficult to accept because, in large part, they represent the supporting pillars of the public health enterprise. This reluctance to critically self-assess makes future progress less certain. It is useful to examine these limitations in terms of their relationship to the two major forces shaping public health responses—science and social values.

Despite the impressive gains in health status achieved in the 20th century, and the continuing reductions in mortality rates in the early 21st century, not

Table 9-1   A Young Public Health Physician's Story

In 1940, I left private practice to accept a position as a local health officer in Kentucky. After a 3-month course at the University of Kentucky, which included the principles of epidemiology and law, I was assigned to Breckenridge, Hancock, and Meade counties—three rural counties with a county seat as the only town in each and a combined population of approximately 45,000. The staff in each county consisted of a public health nurse, a sanitarian, and a clerk.

During my 2 years in this assignment, there were outbreaks of poliomyelitis, smallpox, typhoid fever, diphtheria, scarlet fever, measles, and whooping cough. Tuberculosis, syphilis, and gonorrhea were widely prevalent. Rabies was endemic in the wild animal and dog populations. Very few women received prenatal care and most were delivered in the home. Most of the wells were polluted. Disposal of human waste was haphazard, and privies were unsanitary. Practically all of the milk consumed was raw, and restaurants were not inspected.

To raise immunity levels quickly, the nurses and I visited every school in the three counties and vaccinated every child we could hold still long enough to give the immunizations. If you were to do today what we did then, you would be sued. Also, I am sure the Food and Drug Administration would not approve the antigens we used.

Weekly venereal disease clinics were set up in each county. Treatment was a year of weekly injections of arsenicals intravenously and bismuth intramuscularly. Keeping patients in treatment was a problem, and I frequently sent the sheriff to bring in patients who missed treatments.

For tuberculosis patients, we set up the best isolation we could achieve in their own homes. Pregnant women were referred by their physicians to the nurses for prenatal nursing care. A sterile pack of sheets and instruments was developed; the nurses accompanied the doctors to assist in home deliveries.

Well deficiencies were corrected and a system of bacterial testing of well water was instituted. The privy program was a problem because the county court had to set up a procedure to collect for building the privies. Instituting the use of pasteurized milk was a problem because a vocal minority predicted all manner of medical problems that would result from the use of processed milk. They exhibited the same mindset we see today in those who rail against the radiation of foods and fluoridation of water supplies.

Restaurant inspection and food handler instruction posed few problems. The transfer of vital records from the county clerk to the health department required a high order of diplomacy, but was achieved and we were able to hand tabulate a report of births and deaths.

These were primitive programs, but that was public health in the early 1940s. Probably more important than the specific program activities was the public health process. The staff gathered information and then made decisions as to what was needed, gave priorities to the problems, and planned the various programs. This is still a hallmark of the public health method.

Source: From Peterson PQ. *Public Health: Its Program Evolution and Future Challenges. Convocation Address.* Chicago, IL: School of Public Health, University of Illinois at Chicago; May 1994.

all indicators are moving in the right direction. Earlier chapters chronicled the modern epidemic of obesity and minimal progress in increasing physical activity for many Americans. Figures 9-11 and 9-12 track even subtler trends in overall health status in the United States. Figure 9-11 shows an increasing percentage of adults reporting fair or poor health status. Figure 9-12 bolsters this contention in terms of the percentage of adults reporting 14 or more days of activity limitation during the past year. These trends suggest that much more is needed to understand and improve health and quality of life in the first decade of the 21st century.

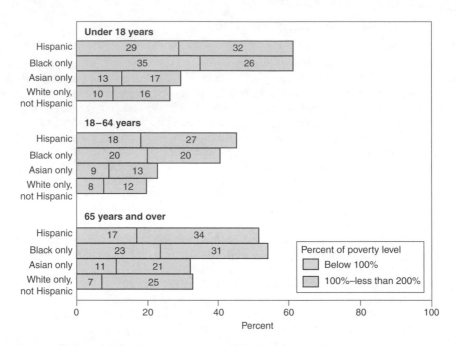

Figure 9-9 Low income by age, race, and Hispanic origin, United States, 2007. *Source:* From Centers for Disease Control and Prevention, Center for Health Statistics. *Health United States, 2009*, Figure 5. Data from U.S. Census Bureau.

These findings also highlight a range of limitations facing modern public health practice. Among the limitations affecting the scientific foundations of public health practice is an undue emphasis on reductionist thinking that seeks molecular-level explanations for social and structural phenomena. Identification of risk factors has been useful for public health efforts, but the emphasis on individual risk factors often obscures patterns that call for multilevel responses within an ecological perspective of health and illness. The persistent identification of the association of social deprivation with many of the important health problems of the last century is a case in point. Approaches for reducing coronary heart disease provide another example. Health interventions targeting a reduction in coronary heart disease frequently focus on risk factors at the physiologic level, such as blood pressure control, cholesterol, and obesity and on lifestyle factors at the individual level, including smoking, nutrition, physical activity, and psychosocial factors; however, there are also environmental influences, such as geographic location, housing conditions, occupational risks, and social structure influences, such as social class, age, gender, and race/ethnicity. In this multilevel view of coronary heart disease, interventions that focus on primary and secondary prevention (those addressing the physiologic and individual levels) need to be supplemented by organization and community-level interventions (addressing environmental influences) and healthy public policy (addressing the social structure level).

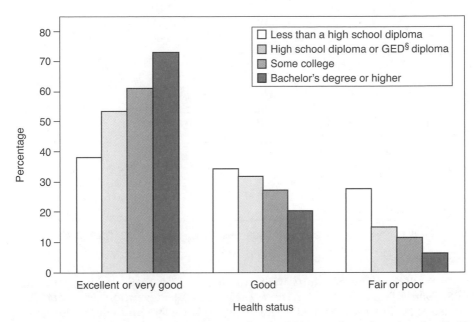

Figure 9-10 Health status* among persons aged >25 years, by education level, National Health Interview Survey, United States, 2007†.

* Health status data were obtained by asking respondents to assess their own health and that of family members living in the same household as excellent, very good, good, fair, or poor. Data are presented only for family members aged >25 years.

† Estimates are based on household interviews of a sample of the noninstitutionalized, U.S. civilian population. Denominators for each category exclude persons for whom data were missing. Estimates are age adjusted using the projected 2000 U.S. population as the standard population and using four age groups: 25–44 years, 45–64 years, 65–74 years, and >75 years.

§ General Educational Development.

Sources: From Centers for Disease Control and Prevention. Health status among persons aged ≥25 years, by education level, National Health Interview Survey, United States, 2007. *MMWR.* 2008;57(47):1282. Data from National Health Interview Survey 2007. http://www.cdc.gov/nchs/nhis.htm. Accessed May 31, 2010. Adams PF, Barnes PM, Vickerie JL. Summary health statistics for the U.S. population: National Health Interview Survey, 2007. *Vital Health Stat.* 2008;10(238).

Nevertheless, another limitation of public health's scientific heritage is the penchant for dichotomous thinking and the failure to view health phenomena as continuous. Again using coronary heart disease as an example, dichotomous thinking draws attention to individual and physiologic level factors, whereas viewing this condition as continuous encourages a population-wide view and development of interventions that reduce overall incidence and prevalence by affecting frequency distributions in the entire population. A view of health problems as continuous phenomena suggests that efforts be made throughout the population to move the entire frequency distribution for coronary heart disease "to the left," rather than to reduce disease burden only among those groups most heavily impacted. Here it is apparent that science and social values are neither pure nor mutually exclusive forces.

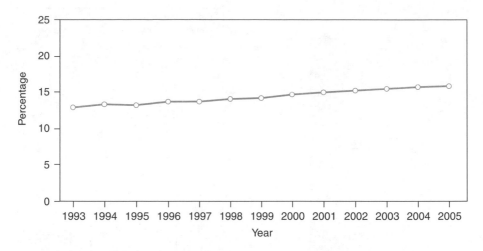

Figure 9-11   Percentage of adults with fair or poor self-rated health, United States, 1993–2005. *Source:* From Centers for Disease Control and Prevention, National Center for Health Statistics, National Behavioral Risk Factor Surveillance System Data 1993–2005.

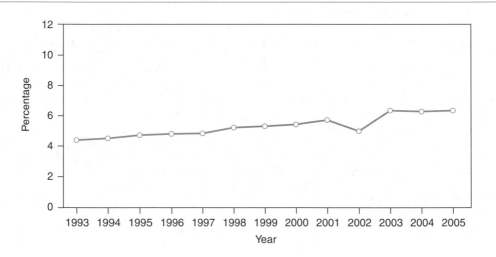

Figure 9-12   Percentage of adults with 14 or more activity limitation days, United States, 1993–2005. *Source:* From Centers for Disease Control and Prevention, National Center for Health Statistics, National Behavioral Risk Factor Surveillance System Data, 1993–2005.

Discussion and debate over scientific approaches to public health problems are not, however, purely scientific in nature. At the heart of collective actions are collective values as to whether issues affecting individuals are more important than issues affecting communities of individuals and as to the meaning of health itself. Should public health emphasize the health of individuals or the health of communities? In part, these reflect the different perspectives of health described in previous chapters. On one hand is a mechanistic view of health as the absence of disease, promoting health interventions that emphasize curative treatment for afflicted individuals. On the other hand is a more holistic view of health that sees health as a complex equilibrium of forces and factors necessary for optimal functioning of that individual. This latter view emphasizes health maintenance and health promotion, often through broad social policies affecting the entire community. Differences in public health systems among societies are largely described by these differences. Some societies, such as the United States, focus on individuals using a largely medical treatment approach. Others are more heavily influenced by collectivism and a holistic view of health. At the core of what can be accomplished, however, are basic values and social philosophies that guide the use of the scientific knowledge available at any time.

These differences in social values also affect perceptions as to what is expected of government and, as a result, the form and leadership of public health efforts. To a large extent, these forces have hastened the development of community public health practice in the United States, a phenomenon previously described in several chapters of this text.

THE FUTURE OF PUBLIC HEALTH IN 1988 AND TWO DECADES LATER

In many respects, the limitations of modern public health are as apparent as its achievements. Persisting, emerging, re-emerging, and newly assigned problems will forever challenge public health as a social enterprise. Success will depend on both the structure and the content of the public health response. A continuous, critical, and comprehensive self-examination of the public health enterprise offers the greatest chance for continued success. A series of such self-examinations began with the 1988 report of the Institute of Medicine (IOM), *The Future of Public Health*.[6] A comprehensive reexamination, *The Future of the Public's Health in the 21st Century*, was published in 2003.[7] A companion study of issues related to educating public health professionals was also published by the IOM in 2003.[8] These examinations outlined the limitations of public health efforts in the 20th century but cast these failings as lessons, challenges, and opportunities for public health in the 21st century.

The Future of Public Health, 1988

The IOM's landmark report, completed in 1988, found much of value in the nation's public health efforts, but it also identified a long list of problems. The most serious problem of all was that Americans were taking their public health system for granted. The nation had come to believe that epidemics of communicable diseases were a thing of the past and that food and water would forever be free of infectious and toxic agents. Americans assumed that workplaces, restaurants, and homes were safe and that everyone had access to the information and skills needed to lead healthy lives. They also assumed that all of this could occur even while public health agencies were being increasingly called on to provide health services to more than 40 million Americans who had no health insurance or were underinsured; however, across the nation, states and localities were failing to provide the resources that would allow both the traditional public health and more recent health service roles to be carried out successfully. When future benefits compete with immediate needs, the results are predictable.

These circumstances fostered the image of a public health system in disarray. Within this system, neither the public nor those involved in the work of public health appreciated the scope and content of public health in modern America. There was little consensus as to the specific responsibilities to be expected from the various levels of government and even less interest in securing such consensus.

Previous chapters document that several formulations in the IOM report have been widely embraced by the public health community. These include statements of the mission, substance, and core functions of public health. The mission has been described simply as ensuring conditions in which people can be healthy. The substance consists largely of organized community efforts to promote health and prevent disease. The IOM report identified an essential role for government in public health in organizing and ensuring that the mission gets addressed. An expanded view of the fundamental functions of governmental public health was articulated in the three core functions of assessment, policy development, and assurance. These represent a more comprehensive view of public health efforts than that conveyed by earlier views that public health primarily furnished services and enforced statutes. The new public health differed in its emphasis on problem identification and resolution as the basis of rational interventions and on working with and through other stakeholders, rather than intervening unilaterally.

Perhaps the most motivating aspect of the IOM report, however, was its characterization of the disarray of public health and the significance of that disarray. The IOM report painted a picture of disjointed efforts in the 1980s to deal with immediate crises, such as the epidemic of HIV infections and an increasing lack of access to health services and enduring problems with significant social impacts, such as injuries, teen pregnancy, hypertension, depression, and tobacco and drug use. With impending crises on the horizon in the form of toxic substances, Alzheimer's disease, and public health capacity, the IOM report found the situation to be grimmer still.

The report found a wide gap between the capabilities of the public health system of the 1980s and those of a public health system capable of rising to modern challenges. It charted a course to move ever closer to an optimally functioning system. Several enabling steps were identified[6]:

- Improving the statutory base of public health
- Strengthening the structural and organizational framework
- Improving the capacity for action, including technical, political, management, programmatic, and fiscal competencies of public health professionals
- Strengthening linkages between academia and practice

In the end, the report concluded that working through a multitude of society's institutions, rather than through only traditional public health organizations, is the key to improving the public health system. It is also a daunting task, calling for entering into partnerships with sectors such as education, law enforcement, media, faith, corrections, and business, and fostering change through leadership and influence, rather than through command and control. The barriers to effecting these collaborations are the major obstacles to achieving the aspirations outlined in Healthy People 2010's national health objectives. These barriers come in all sizes and shapes and from many different sources. Some are perceived as external barriers; others appear to be more internal.

The IOM report identified important barriers inhibiting effective public health action[6]:

- Lack of consensus on the content of the public health mission
- Inadequate capacity to carry out the essential public health functions of assessment, policy development, and assurance of services
- Disjointed decision making without necessary data and knowledge
- Inequities in the distribution of services and the benefits of public health
- Limits on effective leadership, including poor interaction among the technical and political aspects of decisions, rapid turnover of leaders, and inadequate relationships with the medical profession
- Organizational fragmentation or submersion
- Problems in relationships among the several levels of government
- Inadequate development of necessary knowledge across the full array of public health needs
- Poor public image of public health, inhibiting necessary support
- Special problems that unduly limit the financial resources available to public health

The Future of Public Health, Two Decades Later

The IOM advanced these themes through several other reports published in the 1990s and early years of the new century. A brief status report on progress in implementing the 1988 report's major recommendations was completed in the mid-1990s, and a report promoting community health improvement processes (see Chapter 5) appeared later in the decade. A full-scale reexamination of the public health enterprise, titled *The Future of the Public's Health in the 21st Century*, was undertaken after the turn of the century and completed in late 2002. That report focused more extensively on multi-sectoral partnerships with government than had the 1988 report, which emphasized government's role in achieving public health goals.

The 2002 IOM report (although not published until 2003) restated the unique responsibility that government has for promoting and protecting the health of its people. It noted, however, that four factors argue that government alone should not bear full responsibility for the health of the public[7]:

- Public resources are limited, and public health spending must compete with other valid causes.
- Democratic societies expressly limit the powers of government and reserve many activities for private institutions.
- Determinants affecting health derive from multiple sources and sectors, including many social determinants that cannot be addressed by government alone.
- There is growing evidence that multi-sectoral collaborations are more powerful and effective than government acting alone.

In light of these factors, the 2002 IOM report examined both the governmental contributions to the public's health and those from other sectors of American society. Recommendations for the governmental enterprise were complemented by recommendations for healthcare providers, business, media, the faith community, and academia. The report proposed six major areas for action[7]:

- Adopting a population health approach that considers the multiple determinants of health within an ecological framework
- Strengthening the governmental public health infrastructure, which forms the backbone of the public health system
- Building a new generation of intersectoral partnerships that also draw on the perspectives and resources of diverse communities and actively engages them in health actions
- Developing systems of accountability to ensure the quality and availability of public health services
- Making evidence the foundation of decision making and the measure of success
- Enhancing and facilitating communication within the public health system (e.g., among all levels of the governmental public health infrastructure, between public health professionals and community members)

The barriers to future progress are apparent in both major IOM reports. Foremost has been the lack of an ecological view of health that attempts to understand good and poor health in terms of the multiple factors that interact with each other at the personal, family, community, and population level. Another set of important barriers affecting public health is the prevailing values of the American public—in particular, those restricting the ability of government to identify and address factors that influence health. Social values determine the extent to which government can regulate human behavior, such as through controlling the production and use of tobacco products or requiring bicycle or motorcycle helmet use. These values also determine whether and to what extent family planning or school-based clinic services are provided in a community and determine the content of school health education curricula. Some of these social values find strange bedfellows. For example, many Americans oppose control of firearms on the basis of principles of self-protection embodied in the U.S. Constitution; gun companies also oppose control, although on the basis of more direct economic considerations.

Economic and resource considerations are common themes, as well. One obvious issue is that most public health activities remain funded from the discretionary budgets of local, state, and federal government. At all levels, discretionary programs have been squeezed by true entitlement programs, such as Medicaid and Medicare, as well as by some governmental responsibilities that have become near-entitlements, such as public safety, law enforcement, corrections, and education. The Bush Administration's war on terrorism with military campaigns in Iraq and Afghanistan further squeezed the national budget and any chance of significant health or human service initiatives at home. Funding one set of health-related services from governmental discretionary funds while other health services are financed through a competitive marketplace widens the imbalance between treatment and prevention as investment strategies for improved health status. There are powerful economic interests among health sector industries, as well as among industries whose products affect health, such as the tobacco, alcohol, pesticide, and firearms industries. One can only dream that equally powerful lobbies, other than pharmaceutical companies, might develop for hepatitis or drug-resistant tuberculosis.

All too often, the complex problems and issues of public health, with causes and contributing factors perceived to lie outside its boundaries, lead public health professionals to believe that they should not be held accountable for failure or success; however, many facets of public health practice itself could be further improved. These include relationships with the private sector and medical practice and some internal re-engineering of public health processes. Fear and suspicion of the private sector can lead to many missed opportunities. Just as the three most important factors determining real estate values are location, location, and location, it can be argued that the three most important factors for health are jobs, jobs, and jobs. If this is anywhere near true, suspicions of the private sector need to be put to rest. There is little question that employment is a powerful preventive health intervention, in terms of both individual and community health status. Community development activities that bring new businesses and jobs to a community can affect health status more positively than a public health clinic on every corner. Furthermore, businesses have been major forces behind the growth of managed care systems in the United States. Their partnership with public health interests will be essential to secure new resources or to shift the balance between treatment and prevention strategies. Increased partnerships with medical care interests will also be necessary. Unfortunately, there is widespread ignorance of the medical care sector among public health workers.

Among barriers internal to public health agencies is one that often goes unnoticed—the widespread use of categorical approaches to program management, which often fragments and isolates individual programs, one from another. In addition to the unnecessary proliferation of information, management, and other administrative processes, each program tends to develop its own assortment of interest and constituency groups, including those involving program staff members, who often work to oppose meaningful consolidation and integration of programs.

Another limiting factor is the generalized inability to prioritize and focus public health efforts, despite the wealth of information as to which factors most affect health at the national, state, or even local levels. Time and time again, tobacco, alcohol, diet, and violence have been shown to lie at the root of most preventable mortality and years of potential life lost. Ideally, resource allocation decisions would be made on the basis of the most important attributable risks, rather than being spread around to address, ineffectively, risks both large and small. With scores of priorities, there are really none, and without clear priorities, accountability is seldom expected. Public health has always operated at the confluence of science and politics; political issues and compromises are natural. Still, inconsistencies between stated public health priorities and actual program priorities, as demonstrated through funding, are themselves barriers to public understanding and support for public health work. Comprehensive and systematic approaches must replace current silo strategies.

Other factors that influence public understanding and support for public health relate to the transition from conditions caused by microorganisms to those caused by human behaviors. It is more difficult for the public to appreciate the scientific basis for public health interventions when social, rather than physical sciences, guide strategies. This occurs at a time when government is increasingly portrayed as both incompetent and overly intrusive. Largely because governmental processes are considered by the public to be intensely political, the public view of public health processes, including programs and regulations, is that of highly politicized and partly scientific exercises.

There has been considerable debate as to whether the 1988 IOM report accurately captured the problems and needs of the American public health system. In many respects, the report restated the fundamental values and concepts underlying public health in terms of its emphasis on prevention, professional diversity, collaborative nature, community problem solving, loosely attached constituencies, assurance functions, need to draw other sectors into the solution of public health problems, and lack of an identifiable constituency. Taken together, these features appear to represent disarray; however, the cause of this disarray may not lie with public health but rather with our social and governmental institutions, more generally. Posing solutions that restructure the system's components may do little more than rearranging the deck chairs on the Titanic.

It may be necessary to more broadly restructure the tasks and functions of public health to deal with modern public health problems. The larger work of public health is to get the threat protection, disease prevention, and health promotion job done right, rather than to get it done through a traditional structuring of roles and responsibilities. Preventing disease and promoting health must be embraced throughout society and its health institutions, rather than existing in a parallel subsystem. There is no evidence to support the contention that public health activities are best organized through public health agencies of government. It is the mission and the effort that are important and not necessarily the organization from which those efforts are generated.

CONCLUSION: THE NEED FOR A MORE EFFECTIVE PUBLIC HEALTH SYSTEM

The perpetual frustration for public health is the gap between what has been achieved and what could have been achieved. The unfulfilled promise of public health should not be viewed as some unfortunate accident but as a direct result of a series of past decisions and actions undertaken quite purposefully. Sadly, they reflect both a history of disregard and the consequences of battles over the legitimacy, scope, professional authority, and political reach of public health.[9] A recent example is the use of tobacco settlement funds.

The various settlements in 1998 with a group of the major tobacco companies will provide $250 billion to the states over a 25-year period. These settlements were initially viewed as a colossal success for public health over one of its most important enemies. Although still in the early years of this possible quarter-century windfall, state legislative and executive branch leaders have opted to use these funds for a variety of purposes, some for health purposes but much for other ends. It was expected that approaches would vary from state to state, with most using some portion of the money to support tobacco cessation and prevention interventions. Early indications, however, are that as little as one third of the settlement funds were earmarked for health programs through 2002 and that the health share declined rapidly in the face of state budget deficits after 2002.

The tobacco company settlement can be viewed as a success story or as part of a full accounting of the massive failure of public health efforts in the battle against tobacco use. Why did it take 3 decades to change public perceptions and values to the point that settlement became inevitable? Without attention to the lessons of this saga and to strengthening the public health system, tobacco will be the first of many health hazards that are inadequately addressed and for which a negotiated settlement will eventually occur. If we look at the tobacco settlement as a signal of the failure of public health and evidence of a weak public health infrastructure, this windfall becomes, at best, a bittersweet victory. Perhaps the tobacco settlement windfall would best be directed toward averting the next tobacco-like settlement. Difficult questions arise, even in otherwise good times!

In any event, the settlement offered the possibility of a sustained increase in public health resources to the tune of about $10 billion annually for 25 years. Considering that only approximately $17 billion was expended for governmental public health activities in 2000, the tobacco funds represented a possible 70% increase. Additional funding to governmental public health agencies for bioterrorism preparedness on top of the tobacco settlement funds provided for a possible doubling of governmental public health activities in the early years of the 21st century. As we have seen, however, this was an illusion that never materialized.

These circumstances and other key issues and challenges facing the future of public health defy simple summarization. This chapter has examined several, including those offered by the achievements and limitations of public health practice in the 20th century and others offered by the IOM reports; earlier chapters presented many more. Which of these are most important remains a point of contention. It would be useful to have an official list that represents the consensus of policy makers and the public alike; however, because an official list is lacking, several general conclusions as to the critical challenges and obstacles facing the future of public health in the United States are presented. They summarize some of the important themes of this text in describing why we need more effective public health efforts.

The Easy Problems Have Already Been Solved

Major successes have been achieved through public health efforts over the past 150 years, largely related to massive reductions in infectious diseases but also involving substantial declines in death rates for injuries and several major chronic diseases since about 1960. The list of current problems for public health includes the more difficult chronic diseases, new and emerging conditions, including bioterrorism, and broader social problems with health effects (teen pregnancy and violence are good examples) that have identifiable risk and contributing factors that can be addressed only through collective action. The days of command-and-control approaches to relatively simple infectious risks are behind us. In the past, environmental sanitation and engineering could collaborate with communicable disease control expertise to address important public health problems. The collaborations needed for violence prevention or bioterrorism preparedness require very different skills and relationships.

To a Hammer, the Entire World Looks Like a Nail

Behind this aphorism is the perception that common education and work experiences foster common professional perspectives. The danger lies in believing that one's own professional tools are adequate to the task of dealing with all of the problems and needs that are served by the profession. Each profession has its own scientific base and jargon. Problems are given labels or diagnoses, using the profession's specialized language, so that the tools of the profession can be brought to bear on those problems. All too often, however, the problems come to be considered as the domain of that profession, and the potential contributions of other professions and disciplines are underappreciated. Although public health professionals are remarkably diverse in terms of their educational and experiential backgrounds, we can also fall into this trap. When we do, bridges to other partners are not built, and collaborations do not take place. As a result, problems that can be addressed only through collaborative intersectoral approaches flourish unabated.

A Friend in Need Is a Friend Indeed

Finding means to build such bridges can be difficult, but some key collaborations appear to be absolutely essential for the work of public health to succeed. Certainly, links between public health and medical care must be improved for both to prosper in a reforming health system. Links with businesses also represent another avenue for mutually successful collaborations. The key is to find major areas of common purpose. For medical care interests, the common denominator is that prevention saves money and rewards those who use it as an investment strategy. For business interests, the bottom line has to be improved, and businesses must accept the premise that improving health status in the community serves their bottom lines through healthier, more productive workers and healthier and wealthier consumers.

You Get What You Pay For

There is good cause to question the current national investment strategy as it relates to health. The excess capacity that has been established in the American health system is becoming increasingly unaffordable, and the results are nothing to write home about. Still, the competition for additional dollars is intense among the major interests that dominate the health industry, and there is little movement to alter the current balance between treatment and prevention strategies. With less than 5% of all health expenditures supporting public health's core functions and essential services and only about one percent supporting population-based prevention, even small shifts could reap substantial rewards. The argument that resources are limited and that there simply are not adequate resources to meet treatment, as well as prevention purposes, is uniquely American and quite inimical to the public's health. More disconcerting yet are the lost opportunities in securing and using recent tobacco settlement and bioterrorism preparedness funding to shore up a sagging public health infrastructure.

It's Not My Job?

The job description of public health has never been clear. As a result, public health has become quite proficient in delivering specific services, with less attention paid to mobilizing action toward those factors that most seriously affect community health status. Among traditional health-related factors, tobacco, alcohol, and diet are factors responsible for much of modern America's mortality and morbidity. Nonetheless, the resources supporting interventions directed toward these factors are minuscule. Similarly, the primary cause of America's relatively poor health outcomes, in comparison with other developed nations, as well as the most likely source for further health gains in the United States, resides in the huge and increasing gaps between racial and ethnic groups. The public health system, from national to state and local levels, must recognize these circumstances and move beyond them to advocate and build constituencies aggressively for efforts that target the most important of the traditional health risk factors and that promote social policies that will both minimize and equalize risks throughout the population. The task is as simple as following the Golden Rule and doing for others what we want done for ourselves because efforts to improve the health of others make everyone healthier. This does not constitute a new job description for public health in the United States, but rather a recommitment to an old, successful, and necessary one.

DISCUSSION QUESTIONS AND EXERCISES

1. What was the most important achievement of public health in the 20th century? Why?
2. What will be the most important achievement of public health in the 21st century? Why?
3. If randomized clinical trials are considered the gold standard of research, why is there not more emphasis on this approach in assessing community-based interventions?
4. Using a scale from 1 to 10, how effective is the public health system in the United States? How did you arrive at this rating?
5. Do you agree with the IOM assertion that public health is in disarray or with the counterassertion that it is government, not public health, that is in disarray?

6. What impact has *The Future of Public Health* had on the public health community since 1990?
7. What impact has *The Future of the Public's Health in the 21st Century* had on the public health community since 2003?
8. What do you think are the most important new or expanded roles for public health in the 21st century?
9. Your state has $100 million from tobacco settlement funds. What strategies and programs should receive funding? Why?
10. How has your understanding of what public health is and how it works changed after examining the topics in this book?

REFERENCES

1. Centers for Disease Control and Prevention. *Addressing Emerging Infectious Disease Threats: A Prevention Strategy for the United States*. Atlanta, GA: U.S. Public Health Service; 1994.
2. U.S. Department of Health and Human Services. *Healthy People 2010: Understanding and Improving Health*. Washington, DC: U.S. Department of Health and Human Services-Public Health Service; 2000.
3. Task Force on Community Preventive Services. The Community Guide. http://www.the communityguide.org. Accessed May 31, 2007.
4. Murray CJL, Lopez AD, eds. *The Global Burden of Disease: A Comprehensive Assessment of Mortality and Disability from Diseases, Injuries, and Risk Factors in 1990 and Projected to 2020*. Cambridge, MA: Harvard School of Public Health; 1996.
5. McKinlay JB, Marceau LD. To boldly go. . . . *Am J Public Health*. 2000;90:25–33.
6. Institute of Medicine. *The Future of Public Health*. Washington, DC: National Academy Press; 1988.
7. Institute of Medicine. *The Future of the Public's Health in the 21st Century*. Washington, DC: National Academy Press; 2003.
8. Institute of Medicine. *Who Will Keep the Public Healthy? Educating Public Health Professionals for the 21st Century*. Washington, DC: National Academy Press; 2003.
9. Fee E, Brown TM. The unfulfilled promise of public health: déjà vu all over again. *Health Affairs*. 2002;21:31–43.

Glossary

ACCESS

The potential for entry or actual entry of a population into the health system. Entry is dependent on the wants, resources, and needs that individuals bring to the care-seeking process. Ability to obtain wanted or needed services may be influenced by many factors, including travel distance, waiting time, available financial resources, and availability of a regular source of care.

ACTIVITIES

Specific tasks that must be completed for a program's processes to achieve their targets.

ACTIVITY MEASURES

Indicators of whether a program's activities are successfully completed.

ACTUAL CAUSE OF DEATH

A primary determinant or risk factor associated with a pathologic or diagnosed cause of death. For example, tobacco use would be the actual cause for deaths from many lung cancers.

ADJUSTED RATE

The adjustment or standardization of rates is a statistical procedure that removes the effect of differences in the composition of populations. Because of its marked effect on mortality and morbidity, age is the variable for adjustment used most commonly. For example, an age-adjusted death rate for any cause permits a better comparison between different populations and at different times because it accounts for differences in the distribution of age.

ADMINISTRATIVE LAW

Rules and regulations promulgated by administrative agencies within the executive branch of government that carry the force of law. Administrative law represents a unique situation in which legislative, executive, and judicial powers are carried out by one agency in the development, implementation, and enforcement of rules and regulations.

AGE-ADJUSTED MORTALITY RATE

The expected number of deaths that would occur if a population had the same age distribution as a standard population, expressed in terms of deaths per 1,000 or 100,000 persons.

APPROPRIATENESS

Health interventions for which the expected health benefit exceeds the expected negative consequences by a wide enough margin to justify the intervention.

ASSESSMENT

One of the three core functions of public health. Assessment calls for regularly and systematically collecting, analyzing, and making available information on the health of a community, including statistics on health status, community health needs, and epidemiologic and other studies of health problems.

ASSESSMENT PROTOCOL FOR EXCELLENCE IN PUBLIC HEALTH (APEXPH)

A tool and process for local health department involvement in community health improvement initiatives. APEXPH includes organizational self-assessment and community health assessment components. APEXPH was the predecessor to the Mobilizing for Action through Planning and Partnerships (MAPP) process.

ASSETS

Resources available to achieve a specific end, such as community resources that can contribute to community health-improvement efforts or emergency-response resources, including human, to respond to a public health emergency.

ASSOCIATION

The relationship between two or more events or variables. Events are said to be associated when they occur more frequently together than one would expect by chance. Association does not necessarily imply a causal relationship.

ASSURANCE

One of the three core functions of public health. It involves assuring constituents that services necessary to achieve agreed-on goals are provided by encouraging actions on the part of others, by requiring action through regulation, or by providing services directly.

ATTRIBUTABLE RISK

The theoretical reduction in the rate or number of cases of an adverse outcome that can be achieved by elimination of a risk factor. For example, if tobacco use is responsible for 75% of all lung cancers, the elimination of tobacco use will reduce lung cancer mortality rates by 75% in a population over time. The risk of lung cancer attributable to tobacco use is 75%.

BEHAVIORAL RISK FACTORS SURVEILLANCE SYSTEM (BRFSS)

A national data collection system supported in part by the Centers for Disease Control and Prevention (CDC) to assess the prevalence of behaviors that affect health status. Through individual state efforts, BRFSS coordinates the collection, analysis, and distribution of survey data on seat belt use, hypertension, physical activity, smoking, weight control, alcohol use, mammography screening, cervical cancer screening, and AIDS, as well as other health-related information.

BIOTERRORISM

The threatened or intentional release of biologic agents (viruses, bacteria, or their toxins) for the purpose of influencing the conduct of government or intimidating or coercing a civilian population to further political or social objectives. These agents can be released by way of the air (as aerosols), food, water, or insects.

CAPACITY

The capability to carry out the core functions of public health (also see Infrastructure).

CAPITATION

A method of payment for health services in which a provider is paid a fixed amount for each person served, without regard to the actual number or nature of services provided to each person in a set period of time. Capitation is the characteristic payment method in health maintenance organizations.

CASE DEFINITION

Standardized criteria for determining whether a person has a particular disease or health-related condition. Criteria often include clinical and laboratory findings, as well as personal characteristics (age, gender, location, time period, etc.). Case definitions are often used in investigations and for comparing potential cases.

CASE MANAGEMENT

The monitoring and coordinating of services rendered to individuals with specific problems or who require high-cost or extensive services.

CASUALTY

Any person suffering physical and/or psychological damage that leads to death, injury, or material loss.

CAUSALITY

The relationship of causes to the effects they produce; several types of causes can be distinguished. A cause is termed necessary when a particular variable must always precede an effect. This effect need not be the sole result of the one variable. A cause is termed sufficient when a particular variable inevitably initiates or produces an effect. Any given cause may be necessary, sufficient, both, or neither.

CAUSE OF DEATH

For the purpose of national mortality statistics, every death is attributed to one underlying condition, based on the information reported on the death certificate and using the international rules for selecting the underlying cause of death from the reported conditions.

CENTERS FOR DISEASE CONTROL AND PREVENTION (CDC)

The CDC, based in Atlanta, Georgia, is the federal agency charged with protecting the nation's public health by providing direction in the prevention and control of communicable and other diseases and responding to public health emergencies. The CDC's responsibilities as the nation's prevention agency have expanded over the years in response to contemporary threats to health, such as injury, environmental and occupational hazards, behavioral risks, chronic diseases, and emerging communicable diseases, such as the Ebola virus.

CENTERS FOR MEDICARE AND MEDICAID SERVICES

The government agency within the U.S. Department of Health and Human Services that directs the Medicare and Medicaid programs (Titles XVIII and XIX of the Social Security Act) and conducts the research to support those programs.

CERTIFICATION

A process by which an agency or association grants recognition to another party who has met certain predetermined qualifications specified by the agency or association.

CHRONIC DISEASE

A disease that has one or more of the following characteristics: it is permanent, leaves residual disability, is caused by a nonreversible pathologic alteration, requires special training of the patient for rehabilitation, or may be expected to require a long period of supervision, observation, or care.

CLINICAL PRACTICE GUIDELINES

Systematically developed statements that assist practitioner and patient decisions about appropriate health services for specific clinical conditions.

CLINICAL PREVENTIVE SERVICES

Clinical services provided to patients to reduce or prevent disease, injury, or disability. These are preventive measures (including screening tests, immunizations, counseling, and periodic physical examinations) provided by a health professional to an individual patient.

COMMUNITY

A group of people that has common characteristics. Communities can be defined by location, race, ethnicity, age, occupation, interest in particular problems or outcomes, or other common bonds. Ideally, there should be available assets and resources, as well as collective discussion, decision making, and action.

COMMUNITY HEALTH-IMPROVEMENT PROCESS

A systematic effort that assesses community needs and assets, prioritizes health-related problems and issues, analyzes problems for their causative factors, develops evidence-based intervention strategies based on those analyses, links stakeholders to implementation efforts through performance monitoring, and evaluates the effect of interventions in the community.

COMMUNITY HEALTH NEEDS ASSESSMENT

A formal approach to identifying health needs and health problems in the community. A variety of tools or instruments may be used; the essential ingredient is community engagement and collaborative participation.

COMMUNITY PREVENTIVE SERVICES

Population-based interventions to reduce or prevent disease, injury, or disability. Community preventive services target populations, such as the entire population or some subset of that population, rather than individuals.

COMPREHENSIVE EMERGENCY MANAGEMENT

A broad style of emergency management, encompassing prevention, preparedness, response, and recovery.

CONDITION

A health condition is a departure from a state of physical or mental well-being. An impairment is a health condition that includes chronic or permanent health defects resulting from disease, injury, or congenital malformations. All health conditions except impairments are coded according to an international classification system based on their duration. There are two types of conditions: acute and chronic.

CONSEQUENCE MANAGEMENT

An emergency management function includes measures to protect public health and safety, restore essential government services, and provide emergency relief to governments in the event of terrorism.

CONTAMINATION

An accidental release of hazardous chemicals or nuclear materials that pollutes the environment and places humans at risk.

CONTRIBUTING FACTOR

A risk factor (causative factor) that is associated with the presence and/or level of a determinant. Direct contributing factors are linked with the level of determinants; indirect contributing factors are linked with the level of direct contributing factors.

CORE FUNCTIONS

Three basic roles for public health for ensuring conditions in which people can be healthy, as identified in the Institute of Medicine's landmark report, *The Future of Public Health*. These are assessment, policy development, and assurance.

COST-BENEFIT ANALYSIS

An economic analysis in which all costs and benefits are converted into monetary (dollar) values, and results are expressed as dollars of benefit per dollars expended.

COST-EFFECTIVENESS ANALYSIS

An economic analysis assessed as a health outcome per cost expended.

COST-UTILITY ANALYSIS

An economic analysis assessed as a quality-adjusted outcome per net cost expended.

COVERT RELEASES

For biologic agents, an unannounced release of a biologic agent that causes illness or other effects. If undetected, a covert release has the potential to spread widely before it is detected.

CRISIS MANAGEMENT

Administrative measures that identify, acquire, and plan the use of resources needed to anticipate, prevent, and/or resolve a threat to public safety (such as terrorism).

CRUDE MORTALITY RATE

The total number of deaths per unit of population reported during a given time interval, often expressed as the number of deaths per 1,000 or 100,000 persons.

CULTURAL COMPETENCE

The ability to communicate with and provide services to an individual or a group with full respect for the culturally associated values, preferences, language, and experiences of the group.

DECISION ANALYSIS

An analytic technique in which probability theory is used to obtain a quantitative approach to decision making.

DECONTAMINATION

The removal of hazardous chemicals or nuclear substances from the skin and/or mucous membranes by showering or washing the affected area with water or by rinsing with a sterile solution.

DEMOGRAPHICS

Characteristic data, such as size, growth, density, distribution, and vital statistics, that are used to study human populations.

DEMONSTRATION SETTINGS

A population- or clinic-based environment in which prevention strategies are field tested.

DETERMINANT

A primary risk factor (causative factor) associated with the presence and/or level of health problem (i.e., the level of the determinant influences the level of the health problem).

DISABILITY LIMITATION

An intervention strategy that seeks to arrest or eradicate disease and/or limit disability and prevent death.

DISASTER

Any event, typically occurring suddenly, that causes damage, ecological disruption, loss of human life, or deterioration of health and health services and that exceeds the capacity of the affected community on a scale sufficient to require outside assistance.

DISASTER SEVERITY SCALE

A scale that classifies disasters by the following parameters: the radius of the disaster site, the number of dead, the number of wounded, the average severity of the injuries sustained, the impact time, and the rescue time. By attributing a numeric score to each of the variables from 0 to 2, with 0 being the least severe and 2 the most severe, a scale with a range of 0 to 18 can be created.

DISCOUNTING

A method for adjusting for the value of future costs and benefits. Expressed as a present dollar value, discounting is based on the time value of money (i.e., a dollar today is worth more than it will be a year from now, even if inflation is not considered).

DISEASE MANAGEMENT

A set of strategies that focuses on a specific disease or condition (such as diabetes) and attempts to reduce the burden of disease by identifying and proactively monitoring high-risk populations, assisting patients and providers to adhere to treatment plans that are based on proven interventions, promoting provider coordination, increasing patient education, and preventing avoidable medical complications.

DISTRIBUTIONAL EFFECTS

The manner in which the costs and benefits of a strategy affect different groups of people based on various demographics, geographic location, and other descriptive factors.

EARLY CASE FINDING AND TREATMENT

An intervention strategy that seeks to identify disease or illness at an early stage so that prompt treatment will reduce the effects of the process.

ECOLOGICAL MODEL

A framework for considering the multiple determinants of health and the linkages and relationships among those determinants.

ECOLOGICAL PERSPECTIVE

A perspective on health that involves knowledge of the ecologic model of determinants of health and an attempt to understand a specific problem or situation in terms of that model.

EFFECTIVENESS

The improvement in health outcome that a strategy can produce in typical community-based settings; also, the degree to which objectives are achieved, such as for a program or service.

EFFICACY

The improvement in health outcome effect that a strategy can produce in expert hands under ideal circumstances.

EMERGENCY

Any natural or man-made situation that results in severe injury, harm, or loss to humans or property.

EMERGENCY MANAGEMENT AGENCY

The federal, state, or local agency, under the authority of the highest elected official, that coordinates the efforts of the health department, housing and social service agencies, and public safety agencies (such as police) during an emergency or disaster.

EMERGENCY MEDICAL SERVICES (EMS) SYSTEM

The coordination of the prehospital system (including public access, 911 dispatch, paramedics, and ambulance services) and the in-hospital system (including emergency departments, hospitals, and other definitive care facilities and personnel) to provide emergency medical care.

EMERGENCY OPERATIONS CENTER (EOC)

The site from which civil governmental officials (such as municipal, county, state, or federal) direct emergency operations in a disaster.

EPIDEMIC

The occurrence of a disease or condition at higher than normal levels in a population.

EPIDEMIOLOGY

The study of the distribution of determinants and antecedents of health and disease in human populations. The ultimate goal is to identify the underlying causes of a disease and then apply findings to disease prevention and health promotion.

ESCHERICHIA COLI (E. COLI) O57:H7

A bacterial pathogen that can infect humans and cause severe bloody diarrhea (hemorrhagic colitis) and serious renal disease (hemolytic uremic syndrome).

ESSENTIAL PUBLIC HEALTH SERVICES

A formulation of the processes used in public health to prevent epidemics and injuries, protect against environmental hazards, promote healthy behaviors, respond to disasters, and ensure quality and accessibility of health services. Ten essential services have been identified:

1. Monitoring health status to identify community health problems
2. Diagnosing and investigating health problems and health hazards in the community
3. Informing, educating, and empowering people about health issues
4. Mobilizing community partnerships to identify and solve health problems
5. Developing policies and plans that support individual and community health efforts
6. Enforcing laws and regulations that protect health and ensure safety
7. Linking people to needed personal health services and ensuring the provision of health care when otherwise unavailable
8. Ensuring a competent public health and personal healthcare workforce
9. Evaluating effectiveness, accessibility, and quality of personal and population-based health services
10. Conducting research for new insights and innovative solutions to health problems

EVACUATION

The organized removal of civilians from a dangerous or potentially dangerous area.

EXERCISES

A generic term for a range of activities undertaken by an agency or a group of agencies within or between communities to test readiness to respond to emergencies or to evaluate response plans or success of training and development programs. Exercises fall into five basic categories: orientation, drill, tabletop exercise, functional exercise, and full-scale exercise.

FEDERAL RESPONSE PLAN

The plan that coordinates federal resources in disaster and emergency situations in order to address the consequences when there is need for federal assistance under the authority of the Stafford Disaster Relief and Emergency Assistance Act.

FEDERALLY FUNDED COMMUNITY HEALTH CENTER

An ambulatory healthcare program (defined under Section 330 of the Public Health Service Act), usually serving a catchment area that has scarce or nonexistent health services or a population with special health needs, and sometimes known as a neighborhood health center. Community health centers attempt to coordinate federal, state, and local resources in a single organization capable of delivering both health and related social services to a defined population. Although such a center may not directly provide all types of health care, it usually takes responsibility to arrange all medical services for its patient population.

FIELD MODEL

A framework for identifying factors that influence health status in populations. Initially, four fields were identified: biology, lifestyle, environment, and health services. Extensions of this approach have also identified genetic, social, and cultural factors and have related these factors to a variety of outcomes, including disease, normal functioning, well-being, and prosperity in an ecological model of health.

FOOD-BORNE ILLNESS

Illness caused by the transfer of disease organisms or toxins from food to humans.

GENERAL WELFARE PROVISIONS

Specific language in the Constitution of the United States that empowers the federal government to provide for the general welfare of the population. Over time, these provisions have been used as a basis for federal health policies and programs.

GEOCODING

A technique that specifies the geographic location where a specific event occurs. Public health agencies may use geocoding to detect geographic clusters of disease or concentrations of health disparity, for example.

GOALS

For public health programs, goals are general statements expressing a program's aspirations or intended effect on one or more health problems, often stated without time limits.

GOVERNMENTAL PRESENCE AT THE LOCAL LEVEL

A concept that calls for the assurance that necessary services and minimum standards are provided to address priority community health problems. This responsibility ultimately falls to local government, which may use local health departments or other means for its execution.

HARM REDUCTION

Harm reduction represents a set of practical strategies reflecting individual and community needs that meet individuals with risk behaviors where they are to help them reduce any harms associated with their risk behaviors.

HAZARD

A possible source of harm or injury.

HEALTH

The state of complete physical, mental, and social well-being and not merely the absence of disease or infirmity. It is recognized, however, that health has many dimensions (anatomic, physiologic, and mental) and is largely culturally defined. The relative importance of various disabilities will differ, depending on the cultural milieu and on the role of the affected individual in that culture.

HEALTH DISPARITY

Difference in health status between two groups, such as the health disparity in mortality between men and women, or the health disparity in infant mortality between African American and white infants.

HEALTH EDUCATION

Any combination of learning opportunities designed to facilitate voluntary adaptations of behavior (in individuals, groups, or communities) conducive to good health. Health education encourages positive health behavior.

HEALTH MAINTENANCE ORGANIZATIONS

Entities that manage both the financing and provision of health services to enrolled members. Fees are generally based on capitation, and health providers are managed to reduce costs through controls on utilization of covered services.

HEALTH PLANNING

Planning concerned with improving health, whether undertaken comprehensively for an entire community or for a particular population, type of health services, institution, or health program. The components of health planning include data assembly and analysis, goal determination, action recommendation, and implementation strategy.

HEALTH POLICY

Social policy concerned with the process whereby public health agencies evaluate and determine health needs and the best ways to address them, including the identification of appropriate resources and funding mechanisms.

HEALTH PROBLEM

A situation or condition of people (expressed in health outcome measures such as mortality, morbidity, or disability) that is considered undesirable and is likely to exist in the future unless something is done to address it.

HEALTH PROBLEM ANALYSIS

A framework for analyzing health problems to identify their determinants and contributing factors so that interventions can be targeted rationally toward those factors most likely to reduce the level of the health problem.

HEALTH PROMOTION

An intervention strategy that seeks to eliminate or reduce exposures to harmful factors by modifying human behaviors. Any combination of health education and related organizational, political, and economic interventions designed to facilitate behavioral and environmental adaptations that will improve or protect health. This process enables individuals and communities to control and improve their own health. Health promotion approaches provide opportunities for people to identify problems, develop solutions, and work in partnerships that build on existing skills and strengths.

HEALTH PROTECTION

An intervention strategy that seeks to provide individuals with resistance to harmful factors, often by modifying the environment to decrease potentially harmful interactions. Those population-based services and programs control and reduce the exposure of the population to environmental or personal hazards, conditions, or factors that may cause disease, disability, injury, or death. Health protection also includes programs that ensure that public health services are available on a 24-hour basis to respond to public health emergencies and coordinate responses of local, state, and federal organizations.

HEALTH REGULATION

Monitoring and maintaining the quality of public health services through licensing and discipline of health professionals, licensing of health facilities, and enforcement of standards and regulations.

HEALTH STATUS INDICATORS

Measurements of the state of health of a specified individual, group, or population. Health status may be measured by proxies such as people's subjective assessments of their health; by one or more indicators of mortality and morbidity in the population, such as longevity or maternal and infant mortality; or by the incidence or prevalence of major diseases (communicable, chronic, or nutritional). Conceptually, health status is the proper outcome measure for the effectiveness of a specific population's health system, although attempts to relate effects of available medical care to variations in health status have proved difficult.

HEALTH SYSTEM

As used in this text, the health system is the sum total of the strategies designed to prevent or treat disease, injury, and other health problems. The health system includes population-based preventive services, clinical preventive and other primary medical care services, and all levels of more sophisticated treatment and chronic care services.

HEALTHY COMMUNITIES 2010

A framework for developing and tailoring community health objectives so that these could be tracked as part of the initiative to achieve the year 2010 national health objectives included in Healthy People 2010.

HEALTHY PEOPLE 2010

The national disease prevention and health promotion agenda that included 476 national health objectives to be achieved by the year 2010, addressing improved health status, risk reduction, and utilization of preventive health services.

IMPACT OBJECTIVE

The level of a determinant to be achieved through the processes and activities of an intervention strategy. Impact objectives are generally intermediate in term (2 to 5 years) and must be measurable and realistic.

INCIDENCE

A measure of the disease or injury in the population, generally the number of new cases occurring during a specified time period.

INCIDENT COMMAND SYSTEM (ICS)

The model for command, control, and coordination of a response to an emergency providing the means to coordinate the efforts of multiple agencies and organizations.

INDICATOR

A measure of health status or a health outcome.

INFANT MORTALITY RATE

The number of live-born infants who die before their first birthday per 1,000 live births, often broken into two components, neonatal mortality (deaths before 28 days per 1,000 live births) and postneonatal mortality (deaths from 28 days through the rest of the first year of life per 1,000 live births).

INFECTIOUS DISEASE

A disease caused by the entrance into the body of organisms (such as bacteria, protozoans, fungi, or viruses) that then grow and multiply there, often used synonymously with communicable disease.

INFRASTRUCTURE

The systems, competencies, relationships, and resources that enable performance of public health's core functions and essential services in every community. Categories include human, organizational, informational, and fiscal resources.

INPUTS

Sometimes referred to as capacities, human resources, fiscal and physical resources, information resources, and system organizational resources necessary to carry out the core functions of public health.

INTERVENTION

A generic term used in public health to describe a program or policy designed to have an impact on a health problem. For example, a mandatory seat belt law is an intervention designed to reduce the incidence of automobile-related fatalities. Five categories of health interventions are (1) health promotion, (2) specific protection, (3) early case finding and prompt treatment, (4) disability limitation, and (5) rehabilitation.

LEADING CAUSES OF DEATH

Those diagnostic classifications of disease that are most frequently responsible for deaths, such as the top 10 causes of death.

LEADING HEALTH INDICATORS

A panel of health-related measures that reflect the major public health concerns in the United States. They were selected to track progress toward achievement of Healthy People 2010 goals and objectives. They address 10 public health concerns: physical activity, overweight and obesity, tobacco use, substance abuse, responsible sexual behavior, mental health, injury and violence, environmental quality, immunizations, and access to health care.

LIFE EXPECTANCY

The number of additional years of life expected at a specified point in time, such as at birth or at age 45 or 65 years.

LOCAL HEALTH DEPARTMENT (LHD)

Synonymous with the term local public health agency (LPHA); functionally, a local (county, multicounty, municipal, town, other) health agency, operated by local government, often with oversight and direction from a local board of health, that carries out public health's core functions throughout a defined geographic area. It is sometimes defined as an agency serving less than an entire state that carries some responsibility for health and has at least one full-time employee and a specific budget.

LOCAL HEALTH JURISDICTION (LHJ)

A unit of local government (county, multicounty, municipal, town, other), often with oversight and direction from a local board of health, with an identifiable local health department that carries out public health's core functions throughout a defined geographic area.

LOCAL PUBLIC HEALTH AUTHORITY

The agency charged with responsibility for meeting the health needs of the community. Usually this is the policy/governing body and its administrative arm, the local health department. The authority may rest with the policy/governing body, may be a city/county/regional authority, or may consist of a legislative mandate from the state. Some local public health authorities have independence from all other governmental entities, whereas others do not.

LOCAL PUBLIC HEALTH SYSTEM

The collection of public and private organizations having a stake in and contributing to public health at the local level. It involves far more than the local health department.

MANAGED CARE

A system of administrative controls intended to reduce costs through managing the utilization of services. Managed care can also mean an integrated system of health insurance, financing, and service delivery that focuses on the appropriate and cost-effective use of health services delivered through defined networks of providers and with allocation of financial risk.

MEASURE

An indicator of health status or a health outcome, used synonymously with indicator in this text.

MEDICAID

A federally aided and state-operated and administered program that provides basic medical services to eligible low-income populations; established through amendments as Title XIX of the Social Security Act in 1965. It does not cover all of the poor, however, but only persons who meet specified eligibility criteria. Subject to broad federal guidelines, states determine the benefits covered, program eligibility, rates of payment for providers, and methods of administering the program.

MEDICAL RESERVE CORPS

Locally based teams of health professionals and other personnel who provide surge capacity for emergencies.

MEDICARE

A national health insurance program for older persons established through amendments to the Social Security Act in 1965 that were included in Title XVIII of that act.

MENTAL HEALTH

Mental health is sometimes thought of as simply the absence of a mental illness but is actually much broader. Mental health is a state of successful mental functioning, resulting in productive activities, fulfilling relationships, and the ability to adapt to change and cope with adversity. Mental health is indispensable to personal well-being, family and interpersonal relationships, and one's contribution to society.

META-ANALYSIS

A systematic, quantitative method for combining information from multiple studies to derive the most meaningful answer to a specific question. Assessment of different methods or outcome measures can increase power and account for bias and other effects.

MIDLEVEL PRACTITIONERS

Nonphysician healthcare providers, such as nurse practitioners and physician assistants.

MISSION

For public health, ensuring conditions in which people can be healthy.

MITIGATION

Measures taken to reduce the harmful effects of a disaster or emergency by attempting to limit the impact on human health and economic infrastructure.

MOBILIZING FOR ACTION THROUGH PLANNING AND PARTNERSHIPS (MAPP)

A voluntary process for organizational and community self-assessment, planned improvements, and continuing evaluation and reassessment. MAPP is the second generation of such tools, following the Assessment Protocol for Excellence in Public Health (APEXPH), which appeared in the early 1990s. The MAPP process focuses on community-wide public health practice, including a health department's role in its community and the community's actual and perceived problems. It provides for a community health-improvement process to assess health needs, sets priorities, develops policy, and ensures that health needs are met.

MORBIDITY

A measure of disease incidence or prevalence in a given population, location, or other grouping of interest.

MORTALITY

Expresses the number of deaths in a population within a prescribed time. Mortality rates may be expressed as crude death rates (total deaths in relation to total population during a year) or as death rates specific for diseases and sometimes for age, gender, or other attributes (e.g., the number of deaths from cancer in white males in relation to the white male population during a given year).

NATIONAL HEALTH EXPENDITURES

The amount spent for all health services and supplies and health-related research and construction activities in the United States during the calendar year.

NATIONAL HEALTH SECURITY STRATEGY

An ongoing assessment and enhancement of public health and medical capabilities for emergency preparedness and response to all forms of threats and events with health impacts.

OBJECTIVES

Targets for achievement through interventions. Objectives are time limited and measurable in all cases. Various levels of objectives for an intervention include outcome, impact, and process objectives.

OPERATIONAL DEFINITION OF A FUNCTIONAL LOCAL HEALTH DEPARTMENT

A set of standards based on the essential public health services framework that describe the responsibilities that everyone can expect their local health department to fulfill regardless of where they live.

OUTCOME OBJECTIVE

The level to which a health problem is to be reduced as a result of an intervention. Outcome objectives are often long-term (2 to 5 years) and are measurable and realistic.

OUTCOMES

Sometimes referred to as results of the health system. These are indicators of health status, risk reduction, and quality-of-life enhancement. Outcomes are long-term objectives that define optimal, measurable future levels of health status; maximum acceptable levels of disease, injury, or dysfunction; or prevalence of risk factors.

OUTPUTS

Health programs and services intended to prevent death, disease, and disability and to promote quality of life.

PERSONAL HEALTH SERVICES

Diagnosis and treatment of disease or provision of clinical preventive services to individuals or families in order to improve individual health status.

POLICE POWER

A basic power of government that allows for restriction of individual rights to protect the safety and interests of the entire population.

POLICY DEVELOPMENT

One of the three core functions of public health. Policy development involves serving the public interest by leading in developing comprehensive public health policy and promoting the use of the scientific knowledge base in decision making.

POPULATION-BASED PUBLIC HEALTH SERVICES

Interventions aimed at disease prevention and health promotion that affect an entire population and extend beyond medical treatment by targeting underlying risks, such as tobacco, drug, and alcohol use; diet and sedentary lifestyles; and environmental factors.

POPULATION HEALTH

The physical, mental, and social well-being of defined groups of individuals and the differences or disparities in health between and among population groups.

POSTPONEMENT

A form of prevention in which the time of onset of a disease or injury is delayed to reduce the prevalence of a condition in the population.

PREPAREDNESS

All measures and policies taken before an event occurs that allow for prevention, mitigation, and readiness.

PREVALENCE

A measure of the burden of disease or injury in a population, generally the number of cases of a disease or injury at a particular point in time or during a specified time period. Prevalence is affected by both the incidence and the duration of disease in a population.

PREVENTED FRACTION

The proportion of an adverse health outcome that has been eliminated as a result of a prevention strategy.

PREVENTION

Anticipatory action taken to prevent the occurrence of an event or to minimize its effects after it has occurred. Prevention aims to minimize the occurrence of disease or its consequences. It includes actions that reduce susceptibility or exposure to health threats (primary prevention), detect and treat disease in early stages (secondary prevention), and alleviate the effects of disease and injury (tertiary prevention). Examples of prevention include immunizations, emergency response to epidemics, health education, modification of risk-prone behavior and physical hazards, safety training, workplace hazard elimination, and industrial process change.

PREVENTIVE STRATEGIES

Frameworks for categorizing prevention programs, based on how the prevention technology is delivered—provider to patient (clinical preventive services), individual responsibility (behavioral prevention), or alteration in an individual's surroundings (environmental prevention)—or on the stage of the natural history of a disease or injury (primary, secondary, and tertiary).

PRIMARY MEDICAL CARE

Clinical preventive services, first-contact treatment services, and ongoing care for commonly encountered medical conditions. Basic or general health care focuses on the point at which a patient ideally seeks assistance from the medical care system. Primary care is considered comprehensive when the primary provider takes responsibility for the overall coordination of the care of the patient's health problems, whether these are medical, behavioral, or social. The appropriate use of consultants and community resources is an important part of effective primary health care. Such care is generally provided by physicians but can also be provided by other personnel, such as nurse practitioners or physician assistants.

PRIMARY PREVENTION

Prevention strategies that seek to prevent the occurrence of disease or injury, generally through reducing exposure or risk factor levels. These strategies can reduce or eliminate causative risk factors (risk reduction).

PROCESS MEASURES

Steps in a program logically required for the program to be successful.

PROCESS OBJECTIVE

The level to which a contributing factor is to be reduced as a result of successfully carrying out a program's activities.

PUBLIC HEALTH

Activities that society undertakes to ensure the conditions in which people can be healthy. These include organized community efforts to prevent, identify, and counter threats to the health of the public.

PUBLIC HEALTH AGENCY

A unit of government (federal, state, local, or regional) charged with preserving, protecting, and promoting the health of the population through ensuring delivery of essential public health services.

PUBLIC HEALTH IN AMERICA

A document developed by the Core Functions Project that characterizes the vision, mission, outcome aspirations, and essential services of public health. See also essential public health services and Table 1-5.

PUBLIC HEALTH ORGANIZATION

A nongovernmental entity (not-for-profit agency, association, corporation, etc.) participating in activities designed to improve the health status of a community or population.

PUBLIC HEALTH PRACTICE

The development and application of preventive strategies and interventions to promote and protect the health of populations.

PUBLIC HEALTH PRACTICE GUIDELINES

Systematically developed statements that assist public health practitioner decisions about interventions at the community level.

PUBLIC HEALTH PRACTICES

Those organizational practices or processes that are necessary and sufficient to ensure that the core functions of public health are being carried out effectively. Ten public health practices have been identified: (1) assess the health needs of the community, (2) investigate the occurrence of health risks and hazards in the community, (3) analyze identified health needs for their determinants and contributing factors, (4) advocate and build support for public health, (5) establish priorities from among identified health needs, (6) develop comprehensive policies and plans for priority health needs, (7) manage resources efficiently, (8) ensure that priority health needs are addressed in the community, (9) evaluate the effects of programs and services, and (10) inform and educate the public.

PUBLIC HEALTH PROCESSES

Those collective practices or processes that are necessary and sufficient to ensure that the core functions and essential services of public health are being carried out effectively, including the key processes that identify and address health problems and their causative factors and the interventions intended to prevent death, disease, and disability and to promote quality of life.

PUBLIC HEALTH SERVICE

U.S. Public Health Service, as reorganized in 1996. It now includes the Office of Public Health and Science (which is headed by the Assistant Secretary for Health and includes the Office of the Surgeon General), eight operating agencies (Health Resources and Services Administration, Indian Health Service, Centers for Disease Control and Prevention, National Institutes of Health, Food and Drug Administration, Substance Abuse and Mental Health Services Administration, Agency for Toxic Substances and Disease Registry, and Agency for Healthcare Research and Quality), and the Regional Health Administrators for the 10 federal regions of the country.

PUBLIC HEALTH SYSTEM

That part of the larger health system that seeks to ensure conditions in which people can be healthy by carrying out public health's three core functions. The system can be further described by its inputs, practices, outputs, and outcomes.

PUBLIC HEALTH WORKER

An individual who is contributing to at least one essential public health service with greater than 50% of his or her time and effort, whether employed by, staff to, or contracting with employers or agencies, full or part time.

PUBLIC HEALTH WORKFORCE

The public health workforce includes individuals

- Employed by an organization engaged in an organized effort to promote, protect, and preserve the health of a defined population group. The group may be public or private, and the effort may be secondary or subsidiary to the principal objectives of the organization.
- Performing work made up of one or more specific public health services or activities.
- Occupying positions that conventionally require at least 1 year of postsecondary specialized public health training and that are (or can be) assigned a professional occupational title.

QUALITY-ADJUSTED LIFE YEARS (QALYS)

A measure of health status that assigns to each period of time a weight, ranging from 0 to 1, corresponding to the health-related quality of life during that period. These are then summed across time periods to calculate QALYs. For each period, a weight of 1 corresponds to optimal health, and a weight of 0 corresponds to a health state equivalent to death.

QUALITY OF CARE

The degree to which health services for individuals increase the likelihood of desired health outcomes and are consistent with established professional standards and judgments of value to the consumer. Quality also may be seen as the degree to which actions taken or not taken maximize the probability of beneficial health outcomes and minimize risk and other undesired outcomes, given the existing state of medical science and art.

RAPID NEEDS ASSESSMENT

A variety of epidemiologic, statistical, anthropological techniques designed to provide information about an affected community's needs after a disaster or other public health emergency.

RATE

A mathematical expression for the relationship between the numerator (number of deaths, diseases, disabilities, services, etc.) and denominator (population at risk), together with specification of time. Rates make possible a comparison of the number of events between populations and at different times. Rates may be crude, specific, or adjusted.

RECOVERY

Actions of responders, government, and victims that help return an affected community to normal by stimulating community cohesiveness and governmental involvement. The recovery period falls between the onset of an emergency and the reconstruction period.

REHABILITATION

An intervention strategy that seeks to return individuals to the maximum level of functioning possible.

RESPONSE

The phase in a disaster or public health emergency when relief, recovery, and rehabilitation occur.

RISK

The probability that exposure to a hazard will lead to a negative consequence.

RISK ASSESSMENT

A determination of the likelihood of adverse health effects to a population after exposure to a hazard.

RISK FACTOR

A behavior or condition that, on the basis of scientific evidence or theory, is thought to influence susceptibility to a specific health problem.

RISK RATIO/RELATIVE RISK

The ratio of the risk or likelihood of the occurrence of specific health outcomes or events in one group to that of another. Risk ratios provide a measure of the relative difference in risk between the two groups. Relative risk is an example of a risk ratio in which the incidence of disease in the exposed group is divided by the incidence of disease in an unexposed group.

SCREENING

The use of technology and procedures to differentiate those individuals with signs or symptoms of disease from those less likely to have the disease. If necessary, further diagnosis and, if indicated, early intervention and treatment can then be provided.

SECONDARY MEDICAL CARE

Specialized attention and ongoing management for common and less frequently encountered medical conditions, including support services for people with special challenges caused by chronic or long-term conditions. Services provided by medical specialists who generally do not have their first contact with patients (e.g., cardiologists, urologists, and dermatologists). In the United States, however, there has been a trend toward self-referral by patients for these services, rather than referral by primary care providers.

SECONDARY PREVENTION

Prevention strategies that seek to identify and control disease processes in their early stages before signs and symptoms develop (screening and treatment).

SOCIAL MARKETING

A program planning process that applies commercial marketing concepts and techniques in order to promote voluntary behavioral change. Social marketing facilitates the acceptance, rejection modification, abandonment, or maintenance of specific behaviors by specific groups often called target audiences.

SPAN OF HEALTHY LIFE

A measure of health status that combines life expectancy with self-reported health status and functional disabilities to calculate the number of years in which an individual is likely to function normally.

SPECIFIC RATE

Rates vary greatly by race, gender, and age. A rate can be made specific for gender, age, race, cause of death, or a combination of these.

STATE CHILD HEALTH INSURANCE PROGRAM (SCHIP)

Title XXI of the Social Security Act, jointly financed by the federal and state governments and administered by the states. Within broad federal guidelines, each state determines the design of its program, eligibility groups, benefit packages, payment levels for coverage, and administrative and operating procedures. SCHIP provides a capped amount of funds to states on a matching basis based on state expenditures under approved plans.

STATE HEALTH AGENCY

The unit of state government that has leading responsibility for identifying and meeting the health needs of the state's citizens. State health agencies can be free-standing or units of multipurpose health and human service agencies.

STRATEGIC NATIONAL STOCKPILE

Formerly known as the National Pharmaceutical Stockpile, a collection of pharmaceuticals, medical supplies, and equipment that can be immediately deployed to meet state and local needs during a public health emergency.

STRATEGIC PLANNING

A disciplined process aimed at producing fundamental decisions and actions that will shape and guide what an organization is, what it does, and why it does what it does. The process of assessing a changing environment to create a vision of the future; determining how the organization fits into the anticipated environment, based on its mission, strengths, and weaknesses and then setting in motion a plan of action to position the organization.

SURVEILLANCE

Systematic monitoring of the health status of a population through collection, analysis, and interpretation of health data in order to plan, implement, and evaluate public health programs, including determining the need for public health action.

SYNDROMIC SURVEILLANCE

The collection and analysis of statistical data on health trends, such as symptoms reported by people seeking care in emergency rooms or other healthcare settings, or even sales of flu medications, to detect disease outbreaks earlier than would otherwise be possible through conventional surveillance efforts.

TERTIARY MEDICAL CARE

Subspecialty referral care requiring highly specialized personnel and facilities. Services provided by highly specialized providers (e.g., neurologists, neurosurgeons, thoracic surgeons, and intensive care units). Such services frequently require highly sophisticated equipment and support facilities. The development of these services has largely been a function of diagnostic and therapeutic advances attained through basic and clinical biomedical research.

TERTIARY PREVENTION

Prevention strategies that prevent disability by restoring individuals to their optimal level of functioning after a disease or injury is established and damage is done.

TRIAGE

The selection and categorization of victims of a disaster or other public health emergency as to their need for medical treatment according to the degree of severity of illness or injury, as well as the availability of medical and transport facilities.

VULNERABILITY

The susceptibility of a population to a specific type of event, generally associated with the degree of possible or potential loss from a risk that results from a hazard at a given intensity. Vulnerability can be influenced by demographics, the age and resilience of the environment, technology, and social differentiation and diversity, as well as regional and global economics and politics.

WAIVER

States must obtain waivers of current federal Medicaid law provisions from the Centers for Medicare & Medicaid Services to enroll their Medicaid population in managed care plans or to deviate otherwise from law.

WEAPONS OF MASS DESTRUCTION

Any device, material, or substance used in a manner, in a quantity or type, or under circumstances evidencing intent to cause death or serious injury to persons or significant damage of property.

YEARS OF POTENTIAL LIFE LOST (YPLL)

A measure of the impact of disease or injury in a population that calculates years of life lost before a specific age (often age 65 or 75 years). This approach places additional value on deaths that occur at earlier ages.

Index

Note: Italicized page locators indicate figures; tables are noted with a *t*.

F

Fairness Doctrine (1968), 99, 100
Fall prevention, 417
Family planning, 24*t*, 151–152, 194
Family structure, U.S. healthcare system, 127, 129
Farr, William, 5, 65
Fat intake, 214
FDA. *See* Food and Drug Administration
Federal Bureau of Investigation, 431
Federal Coal Mine Health and Safety Act, 210, 211
Federal Emergency Management Agency, emergency preparedness and response, 437
Federal emergency medical assets, 440–441
Federal Food, Drug, and Cosmetic Act, 438
Federal government, 167
  funding for national expenditures on health, 123
  influence of, in health system, 161–162
  as largest purchaser of health-related services, 176
  public health activity and, 124
  role in public health, 345–346
  total national health expenditures, *177*
Federal grants-in-aid, 179
Federal health agencies, 171–176, 178–180
  emergency preparedness and response by, 434, 436–438
  health-related prevention and, 111*t*
Federal health departments, surveillance activities of, 328
Federal Highway Administration, 414
Federal Insecticide, Fungicide, and Rodenticide Act, 186, 187*t*
Federalism, 139
Federal Mine Safety and Health Act, 186, 187*t*
Federal public health activities, in United States, 6–7
Federal public health activity spending
  as percent of total federal health spending, U.S., 1960–2008, *195*
  as percent of total public health activity spending, U.S., 1960–2008, *196*
  in U.S., 1980–2008, *196*
Federal Security Agency, 176, 346
Federal surveys of health status, 322
Federal Venereal Diseases Control Act (1938), 345
FEMA. *See* Federal Emergency Management Agency
Fertility control, 151–152
Firearms control, 506
Firearms-related deaths and injuries, 76, *418*
Fire Fighter Fatality Investigation and Prevention Program, 212
First responders, emergency preparedness and roles of, 444
Fiscal resources, 330–336
  estimated total essential public health services expenditures by funding category, *336*

  federal, state, local funds supporting essential public health services, Florida, 2005–2006, *335*
  population-based public health activities, 333–336
Fitness campaigns, 387
Florida
  federal, state, local, and other funds supporting essential public health services in, 2005–2006, *335*
  public health performance standards in, 249
Fluoridation of drinking water, 24*t*, 316, 344, 371, 481–482
  dental caries reduction and, 476, *476*, 477
  older population and, 478
Folic acid, 153, 357
Food
  bioterrorist attack on, 470–475
  safety, 24*t*, 38, 353–365
    education, LHD jurisdictions and, 375, *375*
    emergency preparedness and, 436
    local health departments and, 194
    nutrition, 356–358
    public health achievements in 20th century, 353–354
    21st century challenges, 491
Food, Drug, and Cosmetic Act, 186, 187*t*
Food and Drug Administration, 174–175*t*, 264, 346, 356
  emergency preparedness and response by, 436
Food Quality Protection Act, 355
Formula grants, 179
Framingham Heart Study, 51, 323, 342, 357
Frequency, measures of, 380
Full-time equivalent (FTE) employees, 288
  of federal, state, and local government health agencies, 1994–2008, U.S., 288*t*
  growth prospects for, 299
  for state and local health agencies per 10,000 population, 1998–2008, U.S., *289*
Funding
  for bioterrorism preparedness, 511
  of epidemiologists, 300
  for essential public health services, 337*t*
  of health programs, 176–177
  national expenditures on health and, 123, *123*
  for public health and battle over priorities, 507–508
  for Public Health Training Centers, 308
Future of Public Health, The (IOM), 8–10, 237, 503, 504, 505, 506, 508
Future of Public's Health in the 21st Century, The (IOM), 503, 505, 506

G

Gastric cancer, age-adjusted mortality rates for, 55
GDP. *See* Gross domestic product